THE PETRINE REVOLUTION IN RUSSIAN CULTURE

P. Quent inuenit et fecit 1724

The Petrine Revolution
in Russian Culture

JAMES CRACRAFT

THE BELKNAP PRESS OF HARVARD UNIVERSITY PRESS

Cambridge, Massachusetts, and London, England

2004

Frontispiece: Allegory of Peter I, portrayed in contemporary European regal dress, endowing a grateful Russia—woman in traditional Russian costume—with instruments and symbols of the new culture. St. Petersburg is shown in the background, with a modern warship in the harbor and a man and woman in traditional dress greeting others in European garb. Engraving by F. Ottens, Amsterdam, 1725.

Library of Congress Cataloging-in-Publication Data

Cracraft, James.
  The Petrine revolution in Russian culture / James Cracraft.
    p. cm.
  Includes bibliographical references and index.
  ISBN 0-674-01316-6 (alk. paper)
    1. Russia—History—Peter I, 1672–1725.   2. Peter I, Emperor of Russia, 1689–1725.   I. Title.
DK133.C74 2004
947′.05—dc22   2004040581

For
N. L. R. C.

CONTENTS

FIGURES

x

PREFACE

This book examines the core verbal aspect of the Petrine revolution in Russia: "Petrine" referring to Peter I "the Great," tsar and first emperor (lived 1672–1725), and "revolution" to encapsulate the radical changes in culture engineered by his regime. Two previous books, *The Petrine Revolution in Russian Architecture* (Chicago, 1988) and *The Petrine Revolution in Russian Imagery* (Chicago, 1997), documented such changes in Russian visual culture, leaving the present volume to concentrate on language and the project as a whole. The volume recounts in detail the verbal transmission to Russia under Peter of contemporary European naval, military, bureaucratic-legal, scientific, and literary practices, values, and norms, thereby documenting the crucial first stage in the constitution of a modern Russian verbal culture, one that necessarily included a standardized written language. Throughout the discussion an effort is made to situate the subject in its wider European as well as in its local settings. Related historiographical problems are also considered at appropriate points, as are some of the wider implications of my findings. The volume's concluding chapter attempts both to sum up the Petrine revolution in Russian culture and to delimit its reach. I thus hope to help resolve the overriding question of how medieval Muscovy became modern Russia and a dominant yet distinctive presence in Europe and the world. I also hope that this book, like my companion studies of architecture and imagery, may contribute something of value to the burgeoning exchanges among scholars taking interdisciplinary and comparative if not global approaches to their work.

In the course of researching and writing this book I incurred many debts: to the John Simon Guggenheim Memorial Foundation in New York and the Davis Center for Russian Studies at Harvard University, for essential financial support and access to Harvard's marvelous libraries; to librarians at Harvard and at the Library of Congress in Washington, D.C., the New York Public Library, the Russian State Library in Moscow, and the Library of the Russian Academy of Sciences, St. Petersburg, for their expert assistance; to the Humanities Institute, the Office of the Chancellor, and the Trustees of the University of Illinois at Chicago for the grant of release time from teaching and of funds to support my research; and to Leonid T. Trofimov, Benn E. Williams, and Karl E. Wood, doctoral candidates in history at UIC, who very ably and cheerfully helped discharge some very tedious tasks. Among scholarly consultants, Edward L. Keenan offered pointed advice at a critical juncture and Michael S. Flier most helpfully reviewed two key chapters. My editor at Harvard University Press, Kathleen McDermott, provided invaluable support at a crucial time while securing anonymous (to me) expert appraisals of the submitted manuscript that proved useful in making final revisions. Acknowledgment of my debt to her and to the others mentioned can scarcely repay them. Perhaps also needless to say, I remain solely responsible for the book's contents.

NOTE ON DATES

AND TRANSLITERATION

This volume employs a simplified version of the standard Library of Congress system for transliterating Russian words. Terminal hard signs, common in pre-1918 Russian, are normally dropped; various Cyrillic forms of the letter *i* (И, Й, ī, i, ï, v) are not distinguished, nor are the letters Э and Ѣ (both rendered, along with E and Ë, as *e*); and ө, like ф, is transliterated by *f.* This practice admittedly does not meet the more exacting standards of language specialists, and can be justified only by reference to the broader historical purposes of my project and the correspondingly broader readership at which the volume is aimed. Dates are given in accordance with the Julian or Old Style calendar followed in Russia from Peter's time until February 1918; it lagged behind the Gregorian or New Style calendar (by eleven days in the eighteenth century, twelve in the nineteenth, thirteen in the twentieth) introduced by Pope Gregory XIII in 1582, which thereafter was gradually adopted throughout the rest of Europe and eventually the world.

THE PETRINE REVOLUTION IN RUSSIAN CULTURE

I

INTRODUCTION

Historiography

We begin with a brief review of the historiography of Peter the Great, which has been the subject over the years of extended critical inquiry.[1] Our purpose here is only to sample, by way of setting the scene, the most important general works in Russian, to which the major works in other languages, with respect again to our concerns, have little or nothing to add.[2] Numerous specialized monographs dealing with particular aspects of what I have termed the Petrine revolution in Russian culture have appeared, to be sure, and will be cited where appropriate in this and the succeeding chapters. But no comprehensive, fully documented cultural history of the Petrine period has yet been published in any language. Indeed that has been the goal of my project.

The several weighty volumes on the Petrine era compiled by S. M. Solov'ev, who has been called "probably the greatest Russian historian of all time," are an appropriate place to start.[3] Solov'ev seems to have coined the term "Petrine revolution [*petrovskii perevorot,* sometimes *revoliutsiia*]," although, unlike most earlier Russian historians, he did not consider Peter's reign a sharp break in Russian history, whose "organic" unfolding "from the earliest times" to the later seventeenth century occupied the first twelve volumes (original edition) of his famous *History.* Russia, in his view, was ripe for the Petrine revolution. Solov'ev's laborious archival researches along with the "organic historicism" imbibed from his reading of Hegel, Herder, Vico, Guizot, Michelet, and Ranke had convinced him that the reforms or "transformations [*preobrazovaniia*]" of Muscovite state and society undertaken by Peter were both necessary and unavoidable. Russia had thereby been wrested at last from her medieval "clannishness," "emotionality," and eastward drift and decisively oriented westward, to take, or retake, her place in Europe and so gain entry into the new or modern age *(novaia epokha)*. Russia before Peter had become grievously ill, and "severe sickness requires severe medicine." Funds had to be raised to defend the country against superior foes; foreigners had to be hired to teach the necessary skills; Russians had to be aroused from their slumbers and made to learn geometry, navigation, military science, mining, good manners, moral responsibility, and basic civic virtues. It was Peter's "genius" to perceive as much and to act on it: to grasp that it was "his duty to raise his weak, poor, virtually unknown nation from its sad state by means of civilization," the civilization of "the West." In short,

> The Russian people were thereby trained in a hard school of reform! But the terrible labors and deprivations were not in vain. A vast program was laid out for years to come—laid out not on paper but on the earth itself, which would yield its riches to the Russian who through science had earned the full right to rule her. It was inscribed on the sea, where a Russian fleet appeared; on the rivers, now linked by canals; on the state, with its new institutions and ordinances; and on the people, through education, which broadened their mental horizons and enriched their stores of knowledge by exposure to the West and to the new world created within Russia herself.

The achievement was nothing short of heroic, Solov'ev went on to assert, and by no means Peter's alone: "Never has a people accomplished as much as the Russian people accomplished in the first quarter of the eighteenth century"; the Petrine revolution was "our revolution."[4] Nor was it yet over and done with, for Russia still labored to fulfill the great "program of the reform era"— a reference, it has been reasonably suggested, to the enormous challenges facing Russia in Solov'ev's own time.[5]

Thus a modernizing revolution particularly in Russia's political forms and European standing propelled the country forward in the Petrine era, in Solov'ev's overall, generally positive estimation. Yet compelling as his vision proved to be for succeeding generations of Russian historians,[6] his own distinguished pupil and successor in the chair of Russian history at Moscow University, V. O. Kliuchevskii (1841–1911), felt obliged to demur.[7] Like his mentor, Kliuchevskii delved first into early or "old" *(drevniaia)* Russian history, and labored mightily in neglected manuscript collections to illuminate it. Unlike Solov'ev, however, he spent much less time in state archives working on political and diplomatic questions than he did in ecclesiastical repositories pursuing social, economic, and cultural themes. Additionally, Kliuchevskii was much less influenced by Hegelian idealism and recent European historiography than by the work of earlier Russian historians—especially Solov'ev himself—and the writings of contemporary Russian literary figures. The latter predilection no doubt helped impart to his historical work an imaginative or literary quality as against Solov'ev's more discursive, philosophical tone. Both were thoroughly nationalist in outlook, to be sure, in the spirit of the age. But Kliuchevskii was also something of a Slavophile and Russian populist in the mood of the ideological movement that emerged in the 1860s, a sentiment which strongly flavored his history, whereas Solov'ev, who had become a convinced "Westerner" *(zapadnik)* in the 1840s, retained an apolitical Ranke-like loyalty to, and focus on, the state. Most important here: in contrast with Solov'ev's hearty embrace of the "Petrine revolution," Kliuchevskii's assessment of the reign, rooted in a kind of cultural or nationalist nostalgia, was patently ambivalent.

The fullest expression of Kliuchevskii's views on Peter is found in Part 4 of his famous *Course of Russian History,* which comprises sixteen lectures that he first gave at Moscow University in the 1880s and later edited and partly rewrote before their publication in 1910. Eleven of these lectures, or chapters, discuss the person and policies of Peter, the remaining five "the fate of Peter the Great's reform *[reforma]*" from his death in 1725 to the accession of Catherine II in 1762.[8] Here Peter appears as the *velikii khoziain,* as the typically tightfisted, autocratic "big boss-landlord" of old Muscovy, except that, unlike his predecessors on the throne, he was not a "stay-at-home boss with soft hands *[khoziain-siden', beloruchka]*" but a "worker-boss, self-taught, a tsar-of-all-trades *[khoziain-chernorabochii, samouchka, tsar'-masterovoi]*." This startlingly new incarnation of the "Most Pious Tsar and Autocrat" of Muscovite tradition was the product, in Kliuchevskii's account, of several factors: of Peter's irregular upbringing, which began with his father's death when he was only four; of his peculiar personal enthusiasms, especially for elaborate military games and for sailing and shipbuilding; of his intensely peripatetic mode of living and ruling; of his basic "mental makeup." In Kliuchevskii's exacting depiction, Peter was "one of those simple, straightforward people *[odin iz tekh prostykh liudei]* who can be read at a glance," a characteristic that imbued his actions with a certain blunt impulsiveness. Kliuchevskii went on to suggest that as a soldier and seaman Peter was more the quartermaster and shipwright than the active commander and strategist; that he was, in consequence of his perpetual travels, virtually a "guest in his own house"; and that he re-

3

mained, throughout his reign, "instinctively arbitrary," a "ruler without rules *[pravitel' bez pravil]*." Indeed, if Peter was a "kind man by nature," no doubt "honest and sincere" in his personal dealings, "fair," even "benevolent" in outlook, and devoted to his subjects' well-being, he was at the same time "boorish," even cruel, as tsar. Irreverent to the point of blasphemy, given to fits of rage, respectful of nobody—"not even himself," he was "more a doer than a thinker" and forever the "big boss-landlord" of old-Russian lore. It was a finely detailed portrait that Kliuchevskii painted, somber, even haunting: the picture, in sum, of a compulsive, misguided, harsh, yet well-meaning tyrant whose glimpse of a better life for his people died with him.[9]

Kliuchevskii's explanation of Peter's reform program has proved equally compelling, focusing as it does on that prolonged military and diplomatic struggle known to contemporary Russians as the "Swedish War" but in Europe as the Great Northern War, a convention that Kliuchevskii (and virtually all later historians) followed. The war, he says,

> decreed the order of the reforms, determined their tempo and the very methods of reform. Reforming measures followed one another in the sequence called forth by the needs of the war. The latter dictated in the first instance reform of the country's military forces. . . . The military reform was the first of Peter's reformative acts, the most protracted and the most burdensome, both for himself and for the people. . . . The Northern War and its alarums, its early defeats and later victories, defined Peter's way of life, determined the direction and the tempo of the reforms. . . . His tireless labors in this regard, continuing for nearly three decades, formed and confirmed his outlook and feelings, his tastes and habits. . . . Peter became the reformer unconsciously, so to speak, even unwillingly; the war led him on and to the end of his life pulled him toward reform.[10]

Yet in thus emphasizing the military motive of the Petrine reforms, and their essentially military and related fiscal nature, Kliuchevskii was less than lucid on their longer-term consequences. He found the question of the overall significance in Russian history of the Petrine period both complex and deeply troubling, he confessed, but one that had to be answered: "Peter's reform *[reforma Petra]* is the central point of our history," at once the "sum of the past and the source of the future." Indeed the "question of the significance of the Petrine reform is in large degree the question of the development of our historical consciousness," so often and so intensively had it been debated by Russians since the first emperor's own time.[11]

Kliuchevskii readily conceded that Peter's military victories won for Russia the status of a recognized European power, a status best symbolized in the new imperial capital, St. Petersburg, which by 1725 had become the "diplomatic capital of the European East." These victories and Russia's new importance in the world had been made possible, Kliuchevskii further admitted, by Peter's military and associated administrative and tax reforms, by his creation of a navy and the founding of technical schools, by his expansion of Russia's foreign trade, and by a new burst of industrial development. But the whole enterprise had been enormously costly, even ruinous, for the Russian economy, as the detailed researches of one of his students, P. N. Miliukov, seemed to confirm.[12] Moreover it had been carried out against enormous opposition, in a mighty struggle with "popular apathy and indolence, a rapacious bureaucracy and a boorish landowning gentry, in a struggle with prejudice and fear, with the ignorant reproofs of the clergy." And so "the reform, modest and limited in its original design, directed to a restructuring of the armed forces and a broadening of the state's financial resources, gradually turned into a stubborn internal struggle, stirring up the stagnant mold of Russian life and agitating all classes of society. Initiated and led by the supreme power, by the customary leader and director of the nation, it took on the character and methods of a forced upheaval *[perevorot]*, of a kind of revolution *[revoliutsiia]*." It was a revolution, Kliuchevskii explained, echoing but then qualifying Solov'ev's use of the term, not by reason of its aims or results, which neither envisaged nor produced fundamental economic or social change, but because of its coercive methods and the "impact it had on the minds and nerves of contemporaries," inflicting a great "shock" on society that was the "unforeseen consequence of the reform but not its intended aim." In sum,

> Peter's reform was a struggle of despotism with the people, with their lethargy. He hoped by his terrible power to stimulate initiative in an enslaved society, and through a slave-owning nobility to establish European science and public education in Russia as the indispensable conditions of social development; he wished that the slave, while remaining a slave, should act consciously and freely. The combination of despotism and freedom, of enlightenment and slavery—this political squaring of the circle, this riddle, delivered to us from the time of Peter, is still unresolved.

Here in this last remark the portentous events of Kliuchevskii's own final years are clearly reflected, the years of the Revolution of 1905–1907 in Russia and its uncertain, quasi-constitutional outcome: here, and in the Chekhovian mood of his famous concluding simile, where he asked his audience to reconcile themselves with the legacy of the self-sacrificing despot as one "reconciles oneself with a violent spring storm, which, though uprooting the ancient trees, freshens the air, and by its downpour assists the growth of a new crop."[13]

I will take exception as we proceed and the evidence warrants with Kliuchevskii's portrayal of Peter, with his explanation of the nature and development of what he reluctantly calls the Petrine revolution, and with his overall assessment of the Petrine project. Indeed that is the burden of my previous two volumes, which portray Peter as anything but a "simple, straightforward person who can be read at a glance" while documenting a revolution in building and the more purely visual arts that was as much consensual as coercive, that cannot be explained solely by reference to the Northern War, and that resulted in the wholesale Europeanization of Russian architecture and imagery. Similarly, Peter's church reform, the most revolutionary component of his transformation of Russia's central government, facilitated in various critical ways his wider program of political and cultural modernization, a point that we'll explore later in this volume. Meanwhile the masterly treatments of the Petrine era by Solov'ev and Kliuchevskii remain foundational: a kind of epic backdrop, so to speak, for the drama to come.

Kliuchevskii's well-known student P. N. Miliukov (1859–1943), a leading liberal politician of the late Empire as well as an influential historian, a convinced "Westerner" if ever there was one and a fervent advocate of constitutionalism for Russia, was even less positive than his teacher about Russia's first emperor.[14] From his early (and still authoritative) research on financial aspects of Peter's reign, Miliukov concluded that "the political growth of the state had got ahead again of its economic development," the clearest such proof being his calculation that the tax burden on ordinary Russians had tripled in Peter's time while the total population had declined by "at least 20 percent." In short, Peter had attained for Russia a prominent place on the European stage "at the cost of ruining the country."[15] Miliukov's stunning figures would be successfully challenged, on the basis of further archival research, by later historians.[16] Elsewhere he took a broader view of "the Petrine reform," most notably in the much-augmented last or "jubilee" edition of his immensely popular multivolume *Studies in the History of Russian Culture*, which was first published in the 1890s.[17] By "culture" Miliukov meant mainly religion, formal education, and the fine arts, whose "organic" development in

Russia he outlined, in a consciously positivist or "sociological" fashion, from the late seventeenth century down into early Soviet times. He offered "secularization," conformably with what had happened in "the West," as the dominant aspect of this overall development while giving remarkably short shrift, in passing, to its Petrine phase.[18] But then a whole subsequent chapter of his *Studies* is devoted to "Peter's elemental reform" in its various political, economic, and social as well as its cultural aspects. Though obviously indebted to Kliuchevskii's lectures, Miliukov is much harsher here in his characterization of the alleged arbitrariness, brutality, and fortuitous nature of the reform, even while recognizing its "historical necessity."[19] This was ambivalence carried to a new level, along with deliberate denigration. Later, in exile from Soviet Russia, Miliukov moved closer to Solov'ev's position, casting Peter's later reign in a more positive light and Peter himself as "the founder of the Russian intelligentsia" and "the first Russian revolutionary"[20]—considerable praise from someone who had been a member in his day of the Russian intelligentsia and a liberal revolutionary. Still, the ironies implicit in this prominent Russian Westerner's frequently harsh, deeply ambivalent critique of Russia's first great Westernizer cannot pass unnoticed. And mindful of his famously visceral hatred of the last two Russian emperors and of what had become of the Imperial system founded by Peter—at once autocratic and bureaucratic, arbitrary and clumsy, obstructionist rather than enlightened—it is easy to imagine that the sources of Miliukov's critique were other than purely historical.

A more benign view of Peter's reign was taken by another distinguished pupil of Kliuchevskii, his successor in the chair of Russian history at Moscow (1910) and a leading Petrine specialist, M. M. Bogoslovskii (1867–1929).[21] Bogoslovskii's early immersion in the administrative records of the period had convinced him that in spite of its lack of a clear overall plan and its obvious short-term failures, Peter's bureaucratic revolution (as we will call it) was both rational in character and noble in purpose; that it partook, however selectively, of the general European program of "enlightened absolutism" and so was to be assessed in comparative as well as purely Russian terms; and that it revealed, in its very failures, serious shortcomings in Russian society itself (salutary lessons, again, for Russians at the beginning of the twentieth century).[22] In Bogoslovskii's detailed presentation, Peter's "noble aims in regard to enlightenment, philanthropy, and moral perfection—all of which were to be promoted by the *oblast'* [provincial government] reform of 1719—proved to be impractical, surging ahead of their time, a time when Russia still had to concentrate on the prior task of attaining its natural boundaries":[23] the latter a reference to Peter's conquest of the eastern Baltic littoral, an achievement Bogoslovskii considered essential for the "transformation of Russia into a European state" dedicated to "the common good," which was Peter's ultimate goal.[24] Bogoslovskii's relatively benign view of Peter's reign apparently also derived from his growing preoccupation with Peter himself, which culminated in five posthumously published volumes devoted to the first emperor's early life and reign (to 1701).[25] The original aim of this vast biographical project, Bogoslovskii tells us in the preface to his first volume, was to provide a more detailed description of Peter's activity than had hitherto been available—indeed, a day-by-day account—so as to correct the factual deficiencies and interpretive faults of the enormous historical literature devoted to him, the faults a matter of hasty, unsupported generalizations made "under the influence of general philosophical systems."[26] Bogoslovskii's objective—to compile a minutely documented, "critically verified depiction of so complex a historical fact as the life of Peter the Great" and thereby to answer all questions about it—was never realized; in a letter to a colleague of May 1918 he acknowledged as much while expressing the hope that somebody else would finish the job.[27] But working on the project for the last fifteen or more years of his life had brought home to him, he emphasized, the complexities of Peter's situation, of his reform program, and of Peter himself. And it did render him thoroughly skeptical of "philosophical" generalizations about these complexities, whether they were rooted in Solov'ev's idealism (or organic historicism), Kliuchevskii's patriotic populism, or Miliukov's doctrinaire liberalism—not to mention the Marxist orthodoxy that was descending on Russian historical scholarship in Bogoslovskii's last years.

Yet no more than his predecessors did Bogoslovskii abandon the fundamental statist and nationalist preconceptions animating pre-Revolutionary Russian historical scholarship on Peter. Whatever one thought of the great tsar-reformer, whatever credit or blame was to be assigned to him, whatever the costs of his wars and building projects, whatever the long-term effects of his many reforms, whatever correction they now stood in need of, the immensity of Peter's service to the cause of Russian grandeur, his establishment of Russia as a great European power, was neither doubted nor challenged as such, not by serious historians.[28] And so it was to remain, after an initial period of calculated denigration or neglect on putatively Marxist grounds, in Soviet Russia. Beginning about 1940 numerous specialized works on aspects of the Petrine period were published along with one large-scale, jointly authored, comprehensive survey of the period as a whole.[29] Indeed this survey, entitled *Studies in the History of the U.S.S.R, Period of Feudalism: Russia in the First Quarter of the 18th Century: The Transformations of Peter I* (1954), contains a lengthy final chapter on culture that was the most substantial such work yet published.[30] The chapter discusses the "social-political thought" of Peter's time, formal education in various venues, science and industrial technology, literature and theater, and the visual arts including architecture. But judged as a whole, the chapter usefully summarizes rather than adds to the accumulated knowledge on its subjects while minimizing both the radical character of the Petrine "transformations" and Peter's personal role in carrying them out. The historical significance of the period is seen to lie rather in its "preparation for the further ascent of Russian culture in the eighteenth and nineteenth centuries" and in the "psychic" boost it thus gave to the emergent "Russian nation."[31]

N. I. Pavlenko, an editor of this volume and a joint author of the chapter in question, gave full voice in the volume's conclusion to what Riasanovsky calls the "complex bipolar image" of the Petrine period typical of Soviet historical scholarship. In this view, "the first quarter of the eighteenth century witnessed accelerated development of the economy and a strengthening of the economic and political independence of our Motherland. It was a struggle with backwardness in economic life, military affairs, the state apparatus, and culture. At the same time, the organic class nature of these achievements must be borne in mind—they strengthened the rule of the nobility and the yoke of serfdom; these successes came at a great price." Again, if "Russia's role in international affairs had grown immeasurably" during Peter's reign, his reforms "did not liquidate Russia's backwardness, for they took place within the narrow confines of the feudal-serf structure and in the end were directed toward strengthening it." Russian popular culture, in Pavlenko's summation, continued in the Petrine period its fundamental work of creating modern Russian national culture even as "signs of new, historically more progressive phenomena" appeared. "Literature and art were being freed from the narrow constraints of an ecclesiastical worldview and put on a realistic basis," Pavlenko averred, as Peter's reforms had "led to the creation of a series of general and special educational institutions, to the development of technical knowledge, [and to] the creation of the Academy of Sciences; the theater arose and both secular painting and architecture underwent a new flowering, as did literature and journalism." Yet "these progressive phenomena bore a heavy price for the people," it was to be emphasized—the price of continued, if not intensified, socioeconomic backwardness.[32] Pavlenko thus revived Kliuchevskii's populist ambivalence about the Petrine achievement though now in a quasi-Marxist guise. The disjunction under Peter between popular and elite culture, however "progressive" the latter might have been, was of an "organic class nature"; Russia's continuing socioeconomic "backwardness," now also a matter of Marxist prescription, was assumed; and the concurrent strengthening of the Russian state and its international position, basic tenets of Marxism notwithstanding, was again to be celebrated.

Pavlenko went on to produce in later Soviet years a series of specialized studies that earned him appropriate praise as "an expert on the facts of Peter the Great's life and activities of a quality unequaled since Bogoslovskii."[33] In *post*-Soviet times he produced a single-volume history of Peter's reign that ranks as the most substantial such work published in Russian since Brückner's comparably large volume, also illustrated, of 1882.[34] Pavlenko's book refers, yet only in passing, to Russia's "Europeanization" under Peter and to changes he wrought in culture; indeed his detailed, frequently documented narrative, freed now of most Soviet ideological constraints, offers little in the way of interpretation or analysis of any kind. The chapter on Peter's Grand Embassy to Europe of 1697–1698, for instance, makes no attempt whatever to assess its historical significance. Another, on the early reforms, discusses Peter's alterations of the 1690s in "culture and mores" under the general rubric of the "beginnings of Europeanization in Russia"; but these beginnings are never pursued, unless it is in the penultimate chapter on St. Petersburg, described as the great "symbol of his reign" and "expression of the era of transformations." Here the building and beautifying of the new capital are described at some length together with Peter's efforts to make it a center of the new learning and manners—of European high or elite culture, in other words. Pavlenko's account is animated overall by a deterministic sense of the necessity and inevitability of the Petrine reforms as well as by a robust patriotism.[35] We have returned to Solov'ev, the last few Marxist "flowers" adorning Pavlenko's lengthy text notwithstanding.

The only other recent Russian work on the Petrine period of comparable scope and scholarly quality is by E. V. Anisimov, who explicitly pays his respects to both Solov'ev and Kliuchevskii. Like Pavlenko, Anisimov first devoted his energies to highly specialized study of the era, in his case, most notably, a detailed monograph on Peter's "tax reform."[36] In this contribution, after reviewing critically the work of both pre-Revolutionary and Soviet predecessors in the field, particularly Miliukov's, and drawing on fresh archival research, Anisimov provides a detailed account of Peter's introduction of the capitation, or "soul tax," in Russia, which required introducing the first general census of its male inhabitants. These actions, Anisimov found, largely succeeded in raising state revenue and in bringing a new stability and coherence to state finances. But while rejecting as ill-founded Miliukov's estimates of the population losses and increased tax burdens supposedly incurred by Peter's policies, Anisimov is if anything even more negative in his overall assessment of their results, suggesting as he does that the social regimentation they entailed "laid the basis for the introduction of a cruel police regime."[37] The suggestion is fully developed in Anisimov's subsequent history of the "Petrine reform period" as a whole.[38] In this general work, like Pavlenko in his, Anisimov pays close attention to Peter's personal role, accords major importance to European agents in the conception if not implementation of his policies, attributes crucial causative significance (strongly echoing Kliuchevskii) to the long war against Sweden, and fully accepts the radical and sweeping nature of the Petrine military, naval, and bureaucratic reforms. But Anisimov is more critical than Pavlenko of industrialization under Peter, finding that it was "feudal" in form and actually retarded the development of capitalism in Russia. At the same time, again unlike Pavlenko, Anisimov recounts at some length Peter's ecclesiastical and cultural reforms, readily granting their importance and their "Western prototypes." Perhaps most striking, in contrast to Pavlenko and almost all of his Russian predecessors Anisimov evinces little patriotic pride in Peter's diplomatic and military achievements. On the contrary, in assessing Peter's reign in Russia Anisimov is even more sensitive to its coercive aspects than were Miliukov and Kliuchevskii. The Petrine era, he concludes, witnessed no less than the "foundation of the totalitarian state" in Russia and the first mass propagation of the "cult of the strong personality"—unmistakable allusions, which in the book's preface are made explicit, to the much later regime of Stalin.[39] It seems that, like his predecessors, Anisimov was strongly influenced in his overall assessment of Peter by contemporary ideological and, in their way, patriotic concerns.

Nor does Anisimov offer here a comprehensive account of what he himself terms broadly, and suggestively, "Peter's cultural reform." It has been my contention that without such an account neither the Petrine period itself nor subsequent Russian history can be adequately represented, let alone properly understood. Hence the chapters that follow, like those of my previous volumes, will bring to the well-worked, ever controversial history of Peter's reign an approach that places culture, duly defined, at the center of analysis. Meanwhile, the great debt owed to the work of Anisimov as well as to that of his distinguished Russian colleagues and predecessors, right back to Solov'ev, must be expressly acknowledged.

Language, Culture, Modernity

We turn now to certain historiographical problems that arise, or rise again, in attempting to study what I have called the Petrine revolution in Russian culture. The most immediate of these is to define the term "cultural revolution." By it I mean, here as before, major changes in culture that were consciously intended, at least by an active minority; that happened relatively suddenly, making the post-revolutionary stage readily distinguishable from the pre-revolutionary one; that were recognized as such by contemporaries; and that produced transformations which were lasting.[40] As judged by these criteria, it might be thought, the revolutionary character of the changes undergone in the Petrine era in Russian architecture and imagery have been amply demonstrated, leaving it to the present volume to show as much with respect to verbal culture. We might also note that in the entire historiography of Russia the term has been employed only one other time: to designate certain aspects of the onset of Stalinism (1928–1931) under the rubric "cultural revolution as class war."[41] But this tentative use of the term and the subsequent criticism it incurred,[42] promising as they may be for a new interpretation of the whole Bolshevik project, shed little light on the concept of cultural revolution itself.

What I mean by asserting, here as in my previous volumes, that the Petrine revolution in Russian culture was not just European in its sources, analogues, and outcomes but also "modern" should be clarified, too, along with my more general notion of "culture." On the first point, in describing as modern this or that aspect of the Petrine revolution I am emphatically not endorsing classical modernization theory, let alone any notion of "modernity" as the terminal historical condition of all humanity. Modernization theory was invented, it may bear repeating, by the founders of "grand Western social science," who first diagnosed the state of being "modern."[43] For them, for Max Weber in particular, modernity was the cultural form of industrial capitalism, the cultural expression of their social present, the outcome of an extended process of historical change in Europe and a condition that Weber himself was wont to judge harshly on both moral and aesthetic grounds.[44] Weber's acute consciousness of inhabiting a world starkly different from any preceding epoch in human history, its newness new as never before, was shared by, among others, Marx and Durkheim, who also agreed, however differently they accounted for it, that this modern world was deeply, even fatally ambiguous in its capacity to satisfy human needs. A similar sense of pervasive newness inspired a variable "modernism" in European art, music, and literature—so many artistic responses to the perceived modernity of social life, ranging in content from triumphal celebration to agonized condemnation and in form from direct picturing to extreme stylistic innovation.[45] Related "modernist" breakthroughs occurred in mathematics, the natural sciences, and psychology (Freudian dream analysis), giving rise to a mode of conceptualization that viewed all knowledge as discrete, atomistic, and discontinuous.[46] These were among the seeds of modernization theory, which among social scientists in the United States after World War II, in the words of one of their students, blossomed into a triumphalist "theory of the true, the good, and the inevitable."[47]

13

"All history is modern history," declared the American modernist poet Wallace Stevens in *Opus Posthumous* (1957). The triumphalist theory of modernization, which was pervasive in Western social science until fairly recently, held that

> modernization is the current term for an old process—the process of social change whereby less developed societies acquire characteristics common to more developed societies. . . . We need a new name for the old process because the characteristics associated with more developed and less developed societies and the modes of communication between them have become in our day very different from what they used to be [i.e., in Marx's]. . . . In response to this need, the new term "modernization" has evolved. It enables one to speak concisely of those similarities of achievement observed in all modernized societies—whether Western, as in Europe or North America, or non-Western, as in the Soviet Union or Japan—as well as of those similarities of aspiration observed in all modernizing societies regardless of their location and traditions.

The hard core of this universalized process of modernization, in this classic formulation (1968) of American social science, was still, as it had been for Weber or Marx, economic. It was "along the continuum of economic performance that societies could most readily and unambiguously be aligned, compared, and rated." More precisely, "the growth of output per head of population" was the measure of such progress, and industrialization was the means:

> Modernization produces the societal environment in which rising output per head is effectively incorporated. For [this to happen], the heads that produce (and consume) rising output must understand and accept the new rules of the game deeply enough to improve their own productive behavior and to diffuse it throughout their society. . . . [T]his transformation in perceiving and achieving wealth-oriented behavior entails nothing less than the ultimate reshaping and resharing of all social values.[48]

To be sure, modernization thus conceived has more lately engendered rebuttal. It has been accused, for instance, of masking an ongoing capitalist agenda of "cultural imperialism" and colonial "nation building" while offering a "teleological recipe" that would "universally yield rationality, punctuality, democracy, the free market, and a higher gross national product."[49] On this account, history so conceptualized would promote a hegemonic, deterministic, essentially economic program of conformity—something no self-respecting historian could of course countenance. More basically still, from a "postmodern perspective" on modernity's supposed "second crisis" (in the 1980s, the first dating to the 1890s) the triumphalist vision of progressive prosperity is to be faulted simply for its untenable optimism, its "linear conception of positive historical development."[50] These and other voices have vigorously attacked the economic paradigm at the core of classical modernization theory, proposing instead pluralistic social or cultural models of development, or both; and again historians have been soundly warned. Yet a modest demurral might also be in order. Rather than rejecting outright *any* application of modernization theory to history in general, the Russian case in particular, we might consider whether, taken in its amplitude, it might not contain some analytically useful features.

A study of modernization in Japan jointly undertaken by Japanese and Western scholars in the 1960s, for instance, remains notable for the elaborate sets of "descriptive criteria" it elicited precisely to avoid a "Western" and capitalist economic bias.[51] The seven markers of *political* modernization first listed there include: "1. Increasing allocation of political roles in accordance with standards of achievement rather than ascription"; "2. Growing emphasis upon rational, scientific, and secular techniques of political decision-making"; "5. Broad and explicit governmental involvement in, responsibility for, and regulation of the economic and social aspects of individual and group life"; and "6. An increasing centralization of governmental functions." Judged by these criteria Petrine Russia was indisputably a polity undergoing rapid and intensive political modernization, a point made at length in Chapter 4 below, although with what degree of success it did so, as judged by some universal, say, Weberian ideal, we will not attempt to decide. Equally, while it cannot be said that major change was achieved under Peter as determined by the three remaining markers of political modernization listed here—"mass popular interest and involvement in the political system"; "predominance of functionally specific . . . political roles organized in an elaborate and professionalized bureaucracy"; and "regulatory, control, and judicial techniques based increasingly upon a predominantly impersonal system of law"—we *can* say that deliberate development in the last two arenas did take place, so that in this secondary sense, too, political modernization was afoot in Petrine Russia. Further, other historians (cited in Chap. 4) have shown that political modernization was well under way in the contemporary European states from which the Petrine regime borrowed the legal and bureaucratic practices and norms with which it sought to streamline its own governmental apparatus, thereby launching a bureaucratic revolution in Russia. In these descriptive and comparative senses, therefore, we may label Peter's Europeanization of Russian governmental practices, values, and norms—his bureaucratic revolution—a *modernizing* enterprise.

Similarly, the eight "descriptive criteria" of "intellectual modernization" elicited by the comparative Japanese-Western study can be said to apply in some measure to Petrine Russia, too. "Improvement of the means of disseminating ideas" and the creation thereby of "new interest and belief groups with national, class, or occupational orientations" (criteria 6 and 8) certainly occurred in Russia under Peter—if we accept that enormous increases in the number and kind of visual images in social circulation correspondingly improved the dissemination of new ideas (particularly those of monarchical absolutism and of Russia as a European state), creating an "imagined community" of European statist pretensions ruled by a regime making absolutist claims. Equally, it could be said that the eager adoption under Peter and his immediate successors of new heraldic forms—visual identifiers—by the newly redefined official-noble elite signified its advent in some sense as a newly conscious "interest group" or "class."[52] Moreover visual documents of the Petrine regime—for example, the countless portraits of its members executed in the new European style, the sitters, both women and men, dressed for the most part in contemporary European, not traditional Russian, clothes—surely attest to "an increase in the value placed upon the individual," at least among this core elite, and to the latter's "acceptance of the concept of social change" (criteria 2 and 3), meaning significant change in its self-awareness or self-understanding.[53] Then too, study of the Petrine revolutions in Russian architecture and imagery supplies numerous instances of "systematic accumulation of intellectually verifiable knowledge" at Peter's instigation by Russians in Russia; of his and their "growing attention to vocational, social, and intellectual training"; and thus of a "constantly widening orbit of individual involvement in intellectual communities beyond the family, village, or province to the state and to supranational [European] ideals" along with a corresponding "weakening of [traditional] religious or cultural dogmas" (criteria 1, 4, 7, 5). The number and variety of schools founded by Peter, his Academy of Sciences and, later, Academy of Fine Arts, his printing presses and their output, the foundation and rapid growth of St. Petersburg itself, all provide architectural and institutional proof, as judged by these criteria, of "intellectual modernization" in Petrine and immediately post-Petrine Russia.

At the same time, few if any of the markers of social and economic modernization adduced in the study cited above would apply to the Petrine period in Russia. We cannot point to a significant "shifting of population between town and country" or to a marked "tendency for relations between individuals to become less often characterized by unbridgeable gaps of status," and so on: in short, to dramatic increases in social mobility, to a notable "decline in the importance of social groups based on kinship," or to a great leap forward in social "individuation." We *can* make claim to an "increasing specialization of roles in the economic, political, and intellectual spheres" in Petrine Russia, and to an "explicit assignment of those roles and of social prestige on the basis of achievement." This kind of specialization, or diversification, with attendant training and rewards, this professionalization via ascription of crucial social or socioeconomic "roles," was described in my earlier volumes with respect to building and image-making in Russia in Peter's time, and much the same will be said in this book regarding the concurrent professionalization of military, naval, bureaucratic, scientific, technical, literary, and clerical roles. We might also notice, looking to the lower end of the social scale, a certain broadening or flattening that took place under Peter, as hitherto free, semifree, unfree, tax-exempt, or otherwise legally differentiated groups were amalgamated with the mass of variously bonded, tax-paying peasants who still made up the immense broad base of the Russian social pyramid. This development would constitute modernization via simplification of the social structure, pairing an increasingly cohesive official-noble elite at the top of society with an increasingly undifferentiated peasant mass at the bottom. More-over Peter did contribute something to the "urbanization" of his realm by adding, through his Baltic conquests, new towns whose inhabitants' legal privileges he confirmed; by creating his new capital city, whose permanent population of about 40,000 in 1725 was then second in size only to Moscow's; and by attempting to rebuild the remaining Russian towns in accordance with the new (contemporary European) principles of architecture and town plan-ning employed in the construction of St. Petersburg—all the while seeking to "regulate" the social status of townsfolk also in accord with contemporary Eu-ropean norms.[54] But when all is said and done, such "social modernization" or "social engineering" as occurred in Russia under Peter I fell far short of anything like a social revolution.

Similarly, we look in vain for large-scale modernization of the Russian economy in Peter's time as determined by the criteria posited in the study in question.[55] It may well be that he left behind him, in some measure, "a society increasingly oriented to the pursuit of economic opportunity, infused (espe-cially within the elite) by a spirit of innovation and growth, and increasingly rational in its choice of techniques and allocation of resources to achieve its economic goals"; in fact, one economic historian, deliberately focusing on a "newly emerging entrepreneurial group" of manufacturers in Petrine and post-Petrine Russia, has convincingly argued the point.[56] But nobody would argue that one could find in Russia at this time, to any significant extent, "in-creasing application of scientific technology, and of inanimate energy [hy-draulic, steam, and so forth], to enlarge and diversify the production of goods and services per capita"; or "a growing specialization of labor and subdivision of productive processes within and among firms, industries, occupations, and territories, and an increasing interdependence and mobility of individuals and groups within a network of widening impersonal markets"; or "an accu-mulation of capital goods in more productive forms and in growing amounts per worker, financed by a complex of financial institutions that characteristi-cally divorce the savings from the investment process in order to pool liquid resources for the growing stream of investment"; or "the spread of wage labor as the chief form of gainful employment, and commonly the separation of ownership and management." One does observe at this point a certain cap-italist bias in these "descriptive criteria of modernization," although they are conformable, even so, not just with the largely private enterprise typical of "Western" economic development but also with the more state-directed eco-nomic activity typical of Japan or Iran since the nineteenth century or of, indeed, Russia since Peter.[57]

Peter I was not guided in his economic policies by self-consciously cap-
italist models of development, of course, but by the contemporary European doctrines of "mercantilism," which he had absorbed to a remarkable degree. These advocated, in a succinct definition, "government regulation of the
economy in the interests of state power," or the comprehensive exploitation
by its ruler of a polity's human and natural resources, its trade and industry,
for the purpose of maintaining if not expanding his state's might in that
perpetual competition for advantage, those perpetual wars and diplomatic
démarches, that had come to characterize the European "state system."[58] Thus
Gerschenkron, another economic historian with extensive knowledge of Russia, begins his account of "Russian mercantilist experience" with the reign of
Peter—and not because "Peter had no predecessors" in this regard, but because the latter's "inchoate attempts rather pale into insignificance" when
compared with his. In fact, says Gerschenkron, the "very magnitude" of Peter's economic development effort, "its vigor, amplitude, and persistence," en-
dow his reign with "unique features" when viewed in a "European mirror."
For

> nowhere else in the mercantilist world do we encounter a comparable
> case of a great spurt, compressed within such a short period. Nowhere
> else was the starting point so low; nowhere else were the obstacles that
> stood in the path of development so formidable. And . . . nowhere else
> was the state to any comparable extent the demiurge of economic devel-
> opment.

But just as the uniqueness of Peter's mercantilist project lay in its sudden-
ness and magnitude, Gerschenkron goes on to say, so its undoubted achievements were vitiated (1) by the comparatively huge, monopolistic role the state
was obliged to play in Russia owing to the country's relative socioeconomic
"backwardness"; and (2) by Peter's correspondingly heavy reliance on coercion, which only strengthened the institution of serfdom, which later became
"the major block" to Russia's further industrial progress.[59] Peter's mercantilism, in short, fits uneasily into the pattern of European economic development. Nevertheless, in the words of still another economist, "Peter was the
first ruler of Russia to develop and implement a systematic and comprehensive industrial policy."[60] In sum, a kind of incipient modernization in the economic arena, as in the social, might best describe the Petrine achievement.

Modernization in Petrine Russia, as judged by all of the markers outlined
above, was political and cultural rather than social and economic, and by siz-

18

able margins. This finding suggests, at some more general level of analysis, a diversity of modernizations at work in the world, a diversity that has been obscured if not perhaps obliterated by advocates of the triumphalist economic model. Indeed when broadly informed by history, modernization appears not as a linear, lockstep, uniform progression toward some terminal, undifferentiated state of "modernity" but as, instead, a set of widely variable, and reversible, pathways or passages through identifiable stages or "spurts," cycles or syndromes, even pathologies, of social or socioeconomic evolution: pathways that will someday converge, it may be, in the universally networked if still highly variegated condition that scholars are beginning to term "globalization." "Global" will someday emerge as the latest identifiable period of human history, perhaps: a periodization that will succeed, or subsume, such traditional periodizations as that dividing European history into ancient, medieval, and modern.[61] In the meantime, however, students of European history continue to deploy these well-established divisions, as I will here, since connecting if not integrating Russia with Europe was the essence of the Petrine achievement. I might also note that a variety of distinctively *Russian* modes of economic, social, and cultural modernization, or "attempts to modernize *[popytki modernizirovat']*," have been identified by Russian as well as Western social scientists, although historians will find most of these applications of modernization theory excessively normative, again, as well as presentist.[62]

In short, "modern" for historians is a period term, signifying the breakthrough in time to certain distinctive forms of political and cultural formation. And to give the term still more specific content we might turn to the work of the late C. E. Black, a historian whose interests included Russia. Black imagined a complex, interactive, multidirectional search for a "rational explanation of physical and social phenomena" taking place in Europe from the fifteenth to the nineteenth century—thus echoing, while improving on, an older historiography that saw the key to modern history in the centuries-long emergence in the European world of a "modern mind" distinguished by its "rationalism."[63] In Black's view, not only did the epochal search in question yield an immense and variously problematic "accumulation of knowledge," most dramatically in the natural sciences, but applications of the latter in the form of technology "revolutionized" the conduct of human affairs, and with obviously ambiguous results. Our attention is drawn to the Renaissance and especially to the Scientific Revolution of the seventeenth century: "What is distinctive about the modern era is the phenomenal growth of knowledge since the Scientific Revolution and the unprecedented effort at adaption to this knowledge." Black was on well-trodden historiographical ground in identifying the Scientific Revolution as the seedbed of a modernity that leveled traditional hierarchies, dissolved established communities, corroded received morality, spurred innovation, promoted economic expansion, and displaced religious or mythic worldviews with rationalist and progressivist ones; and then in contrasting the "dynamism" and "openness" of this modern world with the "static, closed, and quiescent" nature of what were by comparison premodern or unmodern, medieval, traditional, or primitive societies. We need not embrace the whole picture sketched here to accept that drastic changes in thinking about the natural world, as demarcated by the theoretical, observational, and experimental work of the likes of Copernicus, Bacon, Descartes, Kepler, Galileo, Boyle, Newton, and Leibniz, took place in seventeenth-century Europe; that these changes in outlook diffused outward from their European bases, mainly via the publications of newly founded scientific societies, in the wake of European expansion and colonization; and that in their intellectual and even psychological reach, as well as in their practical or technological applications, they had profound and eventually global consequences.[64] We shall observe later how Tsar Peter I of Russia was caught up from an early age in the scientific and technological upheaval emanating from contemporary Europe; how he became personally acquainted with some of its leaders (Newton, probably; Leibniz for sure); how he formed major collections—the first in Russia—of scientific books, instruments, exhibits, and specimens; and how he founded an academy of sciences so that the new science could work its wonders in his country, too. In fact, it was at this time in Europe that the word "revolution" lost its traditional, astrological connotation of cyclical change in human affairs—the rise and fall of dynasties, and so on—and began to acquire, thanks precisely to the transformations in astronomy and physics wrought by Copernicus, Newton, and the others, its now standard sense of a major break with the past, the start of a new epoch, a transformative experience of lasting duration. For the propagandists of the early Enlightenment, such as Fontenelle of the Paris Academy of Sciences, the Newtonian "revolution" marked a new era in thought.[65] It was an era, Fontenelle proclaimed in his eulogy of "Peter the Great" (1725), that the recently deceased tsar-emperor had brought at last to Russia.[66]

It should be clear by now that it is *cultural* modernization that delimits my entire project and particularly, in this volume, its verbal manifestations, certain of which I will label "modern" or "early modern" the better to locate them, chronologically and qualitatively, in a European as well as a Russian context. As for "culture," I must also hasten to disclaim any intention of using this pregnant term in a normative, essentialist, or totalizing way, recognizing that in the increasing frequency and variety of its application by social scientists and historians, it too has become thoroughly problematized.[67] A Russian "culturologist" recently listed some 70 different definitions of culture advanced by "leading European and American scholars" while noting, a little wearily, that at an international academic conference in 1980 more than 250 usages of the term had surfaced and that by his count (in 1997), the total was approaching 500. He reduced the list, for the sake of his students, to 14 general types—"semiotic, symbolic, hermeneutic, ideational, functional, psychological, didactic," and so forth.[68] "Culture is simply that which is not nature," asserts a cultural geographer, conceding that the concept remains "something of a muddle" whereas "culture as a whole," proposes a sociologist critical of the "wildly vacillating role" the concept has played in her discipline, refers to "all intelligibilia, that is to any item which has the dispositional capacity of being understood by someone."[69] A two-year seminar on "cultural transmission" in early modern Europe held at an American university could not produce a "shared model of culture" to which its participants, some eight historians and numerous commentators, would subscribe.[70] In the face of such rampant specialization and disagreement, one can only cling to one's own definition or model, however friable, and hope that readers will find the results worthwhile. Much the same may be said for "cultural history," an old idea whose current employment is also the subject of intense scholarly debate.[71] The proof of the pudding still lies in the eating.

In this spirit, I might recall that "culture" in my earlier study of architecture embraced any and all building techniques and norms practiced in Russia in the Petrine period and in the years just before and after it, the resultant constructions including churches and government office buildings, warships and fortifications, palaces and townhouses, parks or formal gardens, whole streets and cities, even peasant villages; also embraced are architectural design and decorative techniques along with principles of town planning. The study was especially attentive to the *values* expressed in the old and the new architectures—the old, pre-Petrine architectures of Russia, on the one hand, and the new, classicist architectures of both post-Renaissance Europe and post-Petrine Russia, on the other; the elite's abandonment of traditional Russian architectural values and its adoption of new European ones constituted the essence, as I saw it, of the Petrine architectural revolution. Examples adduced of the older values include the *shatër,* signifying the distinctive pyramidal roof of Muscovite architecture, and *sorazmernost',* which meant building according to measurements taken from existing structures or models and differentiated as such from *proportsional'nost',* a term received under Peter to mean building in accordance with the principles of Classical Roman architecture. Similarly the terms *arkhitektor* and *arkhitektura,* denoting designers and edifices exemplifying the Classical tradition of post-Renaissance Europe, replaced under Peter the older *zodchii* and *zodchestvo,* denoting builders and buildings typical of the Muscovite tradition. Related new-architectural values were embodied in such representative Petrine terms as *reguliarnost'* (regularity), a matter of right angles and straight lines, of order and uniformity, of the rational organization of space; and *planirovka* (planning), meaning the construction of a building or ensemble of buildings, or of an entire town, according to a set *plan* (plan).

In my companion study of Petrine imagery, "culture" embraced pretty much the full range of contemporary visual expression (excluding architecture), meaning images in assorted fine-art, official, religious, and popular forms as depicted by various graphic media—painting, drawing, sewing, etching, engraving—on various surfaces (wood, plaster, cloth, metal, paper, canvas) or by sculpture in wood, stone, ivory, or bronze. Techniques again were foregrounded—the new, post-Renaissance techniques of image-making common in contemporary Europe that supplanted or supplemented traditional practices in Russia; similarly highlighted were the visual values or norms subsumed in critical terms like "naturalism" (*zhivopodobie* but eventually also, in Russian, *naturalizm*), which was juxtaposed to the static, sacralized character of traditional Russian icon painting: *zhivopis'* versus *ikonopis'.* That study was also concerned to elicit the "symbolic universe" of particular images or sets or systems of images with a view to discovering their ideological or mythological content: any meanings they might have had or messages they were intended to convey beyond their material selves—for example, that the Russian government was now a European monarchy supported by a properly armigerous noble elite, and that the ruler was an actual human being. Like its predecessor on architecture, the study also described the ways in which the new cultural forms were transmitted from Europe and then institutionalized and industrialized in Petrine and post-Petrine (Imperial) Russia. In sum, the techniques or practices, values or norms, and meanings or significances embodied or discovered in architectural monuments and images and related written documents surviving from the period, the chosen time-space, chosen after extensive library, museum, and archival reconnaissance as well as on-site inspection of physical remains: these all constituted so many distinct architectural or visual cultures, variously labeled as such mainly by the application of conventional chronological but also stylistic criteria (medieval, Baroque, Muscovite, Petrine, modern). They all constituted so many "webs of significance," in the familiar formula, although I strove to remain mindful of the "continual political valence and mobility of all cultural forms."[72]

And so I shall in the present work, with appropriate adjustments to accommodate its verbal emphasis. The focus, in classic Saussurian terms, will be not so much on *langue,* or the abstract system underlying a language, as on *parole,* or instances of the language in actual use. At the same time, unlike Saussure and most linguists since his day, my approach is necessarily historical rather than synoptic (diachronic rather than synchronic), and concerned far more with the meaning of the words we study than with their formal properties.[73] Equally, unlike most sociolinguists and discourse analysts, I will be dealing not with speech—"speech acts," the "flux of talk," quite ephemeral in historical perspective—but with written language, which is indeed generally considered more overtly structured and organized than speech and hence more readily susceptible of analysis.[74] Some theoretical sustenance has been found in Hallidayan systemic-functional linguistics, with its attention to both text and context and their interrelations, there viewed as profound and constitutive: language constitutes context as well as being simultaneously constituted by it.[75] Nor will I neglect the nexus between power and knowledge: the nexus, in the main, between state power as represented by the regime of Peter I in Russia and knowledge as expressed in, and constituted by, language. Institutionalized knowledges—institutionalized in newly translated texts printed at newly established government presses for use in newly founded state agencies—will regularly appear in the chapters that follow. And throughout the book I will strive to maintain, in the face of proliferating language theories,[76] a consistently historical "framework of coherence."[77]

More specifically, the task of successive chapters of this book is to set the scenes or contexts within which certain texts were produced, texts in and by means of which the Petrine regime evidently purposed to instate its military, naval, governmental, scientific, literary, educational, and, finally, linguistic agendas: agendas that the historiography designates "reforms" but which together constituted, as I shall argue, a cultural revolution. Revolutionary contexts, it will be shown, bred revolutionary texts; just as the latter helped interrelatedly to make a cultural revolution. All of the texts in question—the *Military Statute* of 1716, the *Naval Statute* of 1720, the *Ecclesiastical Regulation* of 1721, the *Project* of 1724 enacting the St. Petersburg Academy of Sciences, the numerous translated textbooks and treatises, the orations, dictionaries, grammars, and so on—are treated in the following chapters each as a semantic whole but also as a web of individual terms and words each with a semantic career of its own, usually of centuries' duration (from Peter's time to the present). The chapters are followed by two appendixes, the first a compendium of contemporary Russian printed texts, some original, most translated or adapted from other languages, the second a glossary of neologisms extracted by us and other scholars from these and other Petrine texts. Like the galleries of plates provided in the preceding volumes on Petrine architecture and imagery, these appendixes are designed to supplement the evidence presented earlier in the book—to demonstrate, in more concentrated fashion, the nature and scope of verbal Europeanization in Petrine Russia.

Much of this volume thus concentrates on the lexicon, on the new military, naval, political, scientific, educational, and other specialized vocabularies borrowed from various contemporary European languages and incorporated under Peter into the language of his regime. Indeed the volume of these borrowings, as well as their semantic range, alone offer compelling evidence of a cultural revolution. More particularly, we shall see that in lexical as in other respects modern standard Russian dates not from the beginning of the nineteenth century, as the philological and literary keepers of the language's history have generally maintained, but from the first quarter of the eighteenth. Major linguistic change thus moves to the fore in our study of the Petrine revolution in Russian culture.

Russian before Peter

In my volume on imagery, when discussing the cultural conditions of pre-Petrine Russia, it was noted that two written languages existed side by side: Church Slavonic, at once archaic, alien, and cumbersome, which was regarded as the only literary language, and the official tongue (*delovoi* or *prikaznyi iazyk*) of government and business, which was much closer to the vernacular; and that neither language—the one moribund, the other undeveloped, a "subliterary medium"—could have accommodated the literary practices of post-Renaissance Europe and served as a unifying "language of power."[78] For the purposes of that earlier discussion, which was designed to highlight the obstacles in Russia to a revolution in imagery following the European Renaissance model, the statement can stand as is. But for our present purposes it requires both expansion and refinement. We thus enter, with all due caution, a markedly contentious as well as intensively cultivated field.

Church Slavonic (Russian *tserkovnoslavianskii iazyk*), to begin, was created in the early Middle Ages to expedite the Christianization by Greek Orthodox (Byzantine) missionaries of Slavic-speaking peoples living in Moravia and

Pannonia, and was subsequently adapted to the same end in Macedonia, Bulgaria, Serbia, Dalmatia, Bohemia, Romania, and the lands of the eastern Slavs known as *Rus'* (later Ukraine, Belorussia, and Russia). As such it was *ab initio* a sacred language, the linguistic instrument of religious propagation, solemn, indeed scriptural, in both subject and style: it was used to translate, almost always from Byzantine Greek, the Bible, liturgical services, canon law and monastic statutes, saints' lives, religious chronicles, and the writings—especially homilies—of certain church fathers. Only a very restricted range of secular literature similarly made the passage: "the Hamartolos and Synkel chronicles, Flavius's *Jewish Wars,* Xoiroboskos's treatise on tropes (incomprehensible in [the Slavonic] translation), an imaginative but uninformative *Journey to India,* and a few tales of Middle Eastern or Indian origin," specifies one authority, emphasizing that none of the great literary monuments of Classical Greek—"no Homer, no Plato, no Aristotle"—were transmitted.[79] Even so, as another student points out, Church Slavonic is the first Slavic literary language known to history and the only Slavic "supranational medium" ever devised.[80]

It also bears emphasis that the language called Church Slavonic was never as such a spoken tongue and was virtually always the property of learned clerical elites (among some of whom, notably members of the higher Orthodox church schools of the seventeenth and eighteenth centuries, it was used in oral disputation and perhaps also in conversation). To be sure, it was based almost certainly on a Slavic dialect spoken in ninth-century Macedonia (the city of Thessalonika, home of its creators) and for the first century or two of its existence, specialists seem equally agreed, it was more or less readily intelligible among the southern and eastern Slavs (western Slavs—notably the later Czechs and Poles—were soon absorbed in varying degrees by the Latin culture of the Roman Catholic church, and largely abandoned its use); it also occasionally served medieval Slavic rulers as an official or administrative language. Equally noteworthy is the fact that the received corpus of Church Slavonic translations from Greek, very occasionally from Latin, copied and recopied by Slavic scribes, was augmented over the years by original works written by Slavic authors in one of the received genres, including homilies by local religious leaders, lives of local saints, new liturgical canons and offices, religious hymns, pateriks (collections of tales from the lives of monks and hermits), new editions-translations of Greek patristic writings, polemical and apologetic treatises, and local chronicles which, whether appended to a translated Byzantine original or compiled separately, seem intended to advance local ecclesiastical and political agendas; they are also replete, as in the Novgorod annals, with mundane local details as well as regional dialect features. Similarly original are the medieval military tales echoing the Slavonic translation of Flavius's *Jewish Wars* but located now in Slavic and especially eastern Slavic settings, although the authenticity of one of the latter, the so-called *Igor Tale (Slovo o polku Igoreve)*, remains a subject of serious scholarly dispute.[81] The chronicles produced in medieval Kiev, Novgorod, and elsewhere in the eastern Slavic lands have been judged overall the "most impressive" of the original literature written in Church Slavonic, "not least because they range across a variety of subject matter and styles."[82] Still, this modest accumulation of secular or semi-secular chronicles, tales, and other writings does not alter the fact that the corpus of Church Slavonic literature, handed down from generation to generation and from place to place, remained overwhelmingly, and narrowly, religious in content as well as solemn, even stilted, in style—a "learned and largely conservative literature," according to still another authority, "a good portion [of which] is actually a literature of translation."[83]

Two alphabets with associated orthographies were invented to inscribe the original sounds of Church Slavonic: one, later called Cyrillic (after its putative inventor, the ninth-century Greek missionary Constantine the Philosopher, in religion the monk, later saint, Cyril) and consisting of some forty-five letters (several in multiple forms), rapidly predominated, while the other, the somewhat earlier and more ornate Glagolitic, which most scholars think Cyril actually invented, survived the Middle Ages only in western Croatia. Cyrillic (Russian *kirillitsa*) was written at first in an uncial *(ustav)* style based on contemporary Greek majuscules supplemented by various letters symbolizing Slavic sounds, and is characterized by carefully drawn upright letters of equal size (except for initials: Fig. 1) with few ligatures or contractions. Texts often appeared without word spacing, punctuation was minimal and not fully systematized, and the placement of supralineal diacritics, to indicate, for example, the numerical values of letters, similarly followed Byzantine Greek practice.[84] Gradually this relative simplicity gave way to a less formal, semi-uncial *(poluustav)* script whose letters were slightly inclined and often curved as well as thinner and vertically elongated, and were written with frequent ligatures and various superscriptions along with more contractions and abbreviations, all evidently intended to ensure proper spelling and pronunciation as well as to ease the labor of scribes.[85] At the same time, this ever more esoteric script, on which the first Slavic typefaces were based (Appendix I, no. 1), would have worked to heighten Church Slavonic's elitist, expert aspect—as would the strong likelihood that by the fifteenth century many of its carefully preserved grammatical forms were unknown in the ever evolving Slavic vernaculars.

Figure 1   Cyrillic uncial script, 11th–15th centuries. Artist's reconstruction.

Thereafter a movement arose among educated Orthodox Slavs living in the lands of *Rus'* dominated by the Polish-Lithuanian Commonwealth—the Ruthenian lands or Lithuanian *Rus'* (Ukraine and Belorussia)—that sought to standardize Church Slavonic after Greek and Latin models in response to the challenges posed by the locally dominant Polish-Latin Catholic culture, a movement that in turn heavily influenced the standardizing drive undertaken by church leaders in the northern and eastern lands of *Rus'* subject to the growing political hegemony of Moscow.[86] But if these essentially archaizing—or classicizing—movements of the fifteenth to seventeenth centuries helped to stabilize Church Slavonic as well as to broaden its literary range, by introducing, for example, Classical principles of rhetoric and a more ornate homiletics, they did nothing to narrow the growing linguistic gap between it and the vernaculars. Nor did they work to promote the development of secular literature as such.

At this point a comparative excursus may be helpful. That marvelous cultural florescence in early modern Italy and elsewhere in Europe known as the Renaissance was regularly evoked in my previous books as a seminal if distant influence on architecture and imagery in sixteenth- and seventeenth-century Muscovy: distant in both time and space, and subject in Russia to considerable rusticalization.[87] The Renaissance also witnessed the rise of the big "language question *[Questione della lingua]*," first in Italy and then elsewhere, including the Slavic lands, where it was, as Professor Picchio says, not so much a matter of "direct influences" but rather of "formal coincidences."[88] In Renaissance Italy, to simplify grossly, it was asked with growing urgency whether the revivified Latin of the humanists could or should be joined or even replaced as the language of high culture by the vernacular and, if so, by which vernacular, "Italy" being a country of strong regional traditions and ties. For the pro-Latinists in the debate, as one of them wrote (1535) near its peak, the vernacular—*il volgare*—was to Latin "as the dregs are to wine; for the vulgar tongue is nothing but Latin debased and corrupted by time, by barbarians, and by our own neglect."[89] For others, like Pietro Bembo, himself a distinguished Latinist, the vernacular was an omnipresent reality, the official language (since early in the fifteenth century) of various Italian states, at once native and "modern"; and in his influential *Prose della volgar lingua* (1525) he argued that the Tuscan dialect of Petrarch, Boccaccio, and other writers of the Trecento (Dante would soon be so canonized) could serve as the basis of a written language comparable in dignity and luster to Latin itself, which he characterized as foreign and remote. But for this to happen the vernacular had to be codified, as both Latin and Greek had been, an effort that engendered numerous imitative attempts in the fifteenth and sixteenth centuries to provide an Italian grammar that would "remedy the deficiency of order and regularity which the Latinists repeatedly criticized" and establish the "legitimacy of the vernacular against the traditional taint of bastardy."[90] The invention of printing, which did so much to disseminate Renaissance imagery throughout Italy and the rest of Europe, eventually reaching Russia,[91] also had a potent impact on the language question: works of all kinds printed in the vernacular as well as in Latin now could achieve a breadth of diffusion that simply had not been possible in the scribal age, and in a more or less exactly duplicated form. Most notable perhaps in this connection was the publication by the Accademia della Crusca, founded in Florence in 1583, of its great *Vocabolario* or dictionary of Italian, which was first printed in Venice in 1612 and again in 1623; a third time, updated, in three volumes, in Florence in 1691; and a fourth time, again in Florence, now in six volumes, between 1729 and 1738. The impact of the *Vocabolario degli Accademici della Crusca,* it has been suggested, "was profound even outside Italy. It became the archetype of all modern language dictionaries."[92]

The Renaissance solution to the language question in Italy was partial at best: standard Italian fully emerged only with political unification in the nineteenth century and the spread of television in the twentieth. Meanwhile the question itself had passed to France, where a similarly diglossic situation had prevailed since early medieval times, with "Latin as the grammatical, written fixed *high* language and the vernacular as a variable, 'fun' *low* language" bearing "features associated with orality even when written down."[93] French was first proposed as a possible rival and successor to Latin in the kingdom of France in the sixteenth century, when the first French grammars, dictionaries, and usage guides, modeled to some extent on Italian as well as Latin and Greek works, were compiled and printed and French—"[le] langaige maternel françois et non aultrement," in the words of the key royal ordinance (1539)—became the official language of the realm; its diffusion was also abetted by the spread of the Protestant Reformation, with its emphasis on the use of the vernacular in religious discourse (the first French Bible was published in 1535, Calvin's *Institution chrétienne* in 1541). The process whereby the dialect of the Paris region became standard French was largely completed in the seventeenth century, the century of Molière, Racine, and Corneille, with the Paris-based monarchy playing a decisive role, particularly by founding the Académie Française (1635), whose mission it was to promote the purification and unification of the official tongue in tandem with the regime's promotion of the king's glory and power. Here again the pattern had been set in Italy; like the Florentine Accademia della Crusca, the Parisian Académie Française was especially concerned to delimit the realm of lexis, and between 1680 and 1694 it published dictionaries that enshrined the literary vocabulary of the day complete with technical terms, archaisms, colloquialisms, and even some dialect words.[94] Broadly the same process can be traced in contemporary Spain, where the first grammar and the first dictionary of Spanish (*Castellón*) were published in 1492. Spanish thus began to be standardized as an instrument of political consolidation, the Golden Age of Spanish literature ensued, and the Royal Spanish Academy was eventually founded (at Madrid in 1713).[95]

We digress to the early modern language question in western Europe simply to glimpse obvious precedents or parallels for what sooner or later took place on east Slavic territory, particularly Ukraine and Russia (Russia as a kind of France, perhaps, to Ukraine's version of Spain or Italy). But here, as mentioned above, the challenge was initially interpreted as one of revivifying Church Slavonic on the model of the revivified Latin or Greek of the Renaissance—Latin being the more pressing case in Polish Ukraine, to be sure, as it was also the language of the revived, Counter-Reformation Roman Catholic church. Church Slavonic was first standardized, it has been said, by exemplification: by the "ceaseless reiteration of a body of exemplary texts."[96] But standardization of the more formally codified kind began, as it had in western Europe, with the advent of printing, which reached the lands of *Rus'* in the sixteenth century. The most important books to appear in this connection were the Slavonic grammar *(Hrammatika slovenska)* and dictionary *(Leksis)* complied by Lavrentij Zyzanij and printed at Vilnius in 1596, Pamba Berynda's *Leksikón slavenrósskij* printed at Kiev in 1627 and again at Kuciejna (Belorussia) in 1653, and, most important of all, Meletij Smotryckyj's *Hrammatika Slavénska právilnoe Síntagma* first printed at Jev'je (near Vilnius) in 1619, which was reprinted in an abridged edition at Krem'janec' (Volhynia) in 1638 and at Moscow in 1648: I follow a Ukrainian or Belorussian transliteration of names and titles here, which has the merit of emphasizing their Ruthenian origins.[97] These books will surface again in Chapter 6. Now we might only note that such early attempts to standardize Church Slavonic, influenced as they were by various humanist models and theories, sought to fit its grammar into a Greek or Latin mold, rather than an earlier Slavonic one, and that the ensuing artificiality rendered these books difficult to use by writers of even the loftiest would-be style.[98] For Muscovite scribes and printers and their employers, moreover, these books required editing on phonetic and orthographic as well as lexical grounds. Thus also the *bukvari* (primers) printed in Muscovy in the seventeenth century, which evince an effort to eliminate the Ruthenianisms found in their originals or models not so much as foreign elements, perhaps, but as so many inadmissible deviations from standard Church Slavonic. For these typically "medieval" primers were religious as well as linguistic in content, their simple spelling and grammatical exercises followed by the most important prayers, the Creed, catechetical exercises, and the like; and only a Church Slavonic written or printed with literal precision, it seems, was acceptable in Muscovite church circles as the medium of sacred texts.[99]

Some Slavists would urge, as Schenker, for one, puts it, that "the importance of Church Slavonic in the cultural development of Orthodox Slavdom cannot be overstated. It served all the domains of the intellectual life of the Orthodox Slavs from the end of the Old Church Slavonic period [ca. 1100] until the modern era [from ca. 1700], when its secular functions began to be taken over by national literary languages. During the period of its preeminence Church Slavonic was the only supranational literary idiom of Orthodox Slavdom, playing a role comparable to that of Latin in the Roman West."[100] But scholars adopting a more strictly comparative perspective would observe that the Latin invoked here was a far more dynamic and capacious literary medium than Church Slavonic ever became, and that the emergence of national literary languages occurred much earlier in the Latin West, including Bohemia and Poland,[101] than it did in the Slavonic East. These facts certainly problematize, comparatively speaking, Church Slavonic's long preeminence in the lands of Orthodox Slavdom, however much its literature may be valued on its own, "medieval" terms.[102] In fact, its persistently and narrowly religious textual content as well as its more or less artificial and imitative linguistic form may well have "served to retard rather than encourage the development of verbal culture."[103] The modern literary languages of the Orthodox Slavs, in another formulation, "were formed by a process of *emancipation* from the influence of Church Slavonic."[104] Here, rather, is the analogy to be drawn between Latin and Church Slavonic, here in their respective positions in the "emancipatory" process through which their subordinate vernaculars had to pass.

In Muscovite Russia, where by the mid-sixteenth century, alone among the lands of Orthodox Slavdom, an independent state of international importance had arisen, the reign of Church Slavonic was further complicated by the fact that the everyday business of this state was conducted not in it but in a language known to scholars as *prikaznyi* (from *prikaz*, or government department) *iazyk* (tongue), in English usually "chancery language" and in Russian sometimes also *delovoi* or *bytovoi iazyk* (business or everyday language). The origins and earlier history of this second written language of pre-Petrine Russia are also a matter of scholarly dispute, as is the question of its relationship to the vernacular. Generally it is thought to have descended from legal-judicial norms orally codified in preliterate times and first recorded in *Rus'* as early as the eleventh century;[105] but such norms are fairly described as "terse, formulaic, paratactic, and certainly not identical with the spoken language" of the day[106]—although, it should quickly be added, these very features indicate its closeness to, and are evidence of, a primarily *oral* cultural matrix.[107] It is then posited that the growing hegemony of the principality and then tsardom of Moscow over northern and eastern *Rus'* gradually imposed the Muscovite variant of these norms on this ever expanding territory, with the result that by the mid-sixteenth century a quasi-standard administrative language had emerged there, one that incorporated a limited number of Slavonic terms, was written in a Cyrillic script—a shifting mix of semi-uncial and a newer cursive—that had also come from the Ruthenian lands, and was readily accessible to literate Russians living anywhere in the tsar's dominions (Figs. 2, 3; Appendix I, no. 2). But Muscovite chancery Russian soon became "fixed, even rigid, in its bureaucratic formulas," it has also been observed, so that by the end of the sixteenth century there were two established forms of written Russian—it and the Russian variant (recension or redaction) of Church Slavonic (sometimes called Russo-Slavonic)—both "vying not only with the still-evolving vernacular but also with each other." By the end of the seven-

Figure 2   Russian letter-shapes, 15th–18th centuries. Artist's reconstruction.

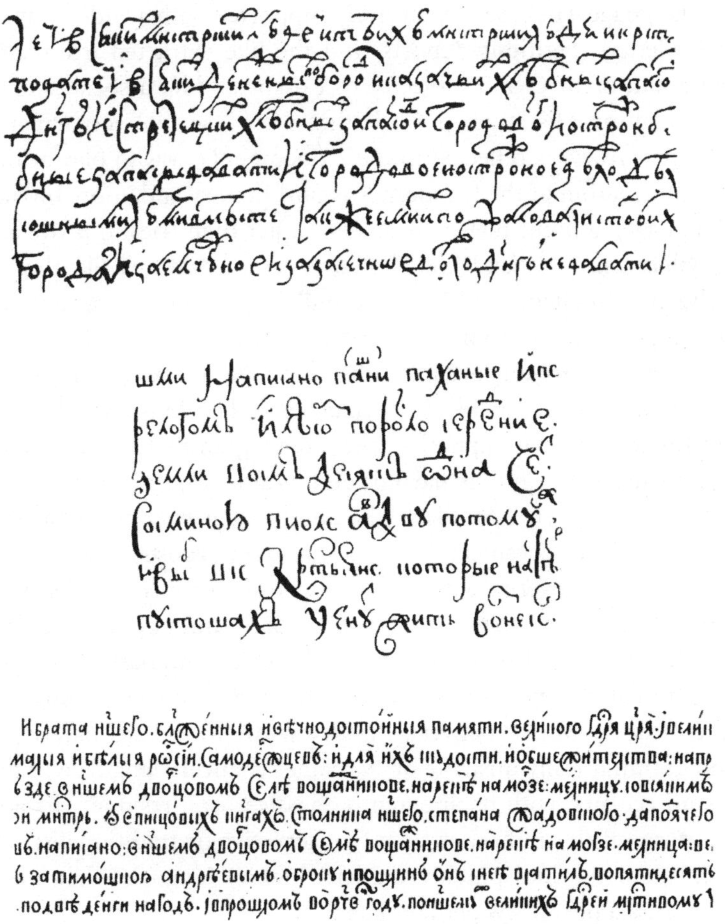

Figure 3   Examples of Muscovite chancery script dating from (top to bottom) 1627, 1675, and 1686.

teenth century, in this widely accepted view, the situation of written Russian was thus "close to chaotic," only to be resolved, as it happened—or to be put irreversibly on the road to resolution—by the decisive action of Peter I.[108]

Recent investigations particularly of late Muscovite chancery Russian offer a more detailed, less alarming picture of the situation. On the one hand, the late S. I. Kotkov took the lead in arguing that by the seventeenth century a fully formed Moscow-based *koiné* was in general use across the territory of the Muscovite tsardom and that this fact can be demonstrated by close study, with special attention to morphology and phonetics, of documents written in chancery language. His case is extensively supported with a wide array of contemporary letters, petitions, reports, and the like extracted from surviving Muscovite state archives and subjected by Kotkov and his associates to intense linguistic scrutiny. His larger point is that the Muscovite vernacular of the seventeenth century, as reflected in these documents, was to play a "defining role in the formation of the [modern Russian] literary and, more broadly, national language," a point that he proposes rather than tries to prove and one that we will certainly revisit.[109] But Kotkov's demonstrations, like those of the other scholars just cited, would seem to nullify the view that modern literary Russian simply evolved from, or represents a Russification of, Church Slavonic.[110] They are also concordant with more recent research into the sociolinguistic as well as grammatical peculiarities of late Muscovite chancery or business Russian, which emphasizes the latter's grammatical affinities if not interdependence with Church Slavonic and its at least proto-literary, or semi-standardized, character.[111] Similarly the abundant *azbuki* or alphabet books that survive from the seventeenth century, whose purpose it was to teach elementary writing to government clerks and whose exercises manifest a "blend" of Church Slavonic, officialese, foreign loanwords, and popular speech.[112] On the other hand, none of this newer research, which emphasizes morphology and phonetics at the expense of syntax and the lexicon, has yet established a clear line of development between the frequently formulaic, barely punctuated, and grammatically unstable or "variable" chancery language of the later seventeenth century, with its apparently massive "oral residue" (its additive, redundant, agonistic, and other such "conservative or traditionalist" characteristics),[113] and the indisputably modern literary language that was being written in Russia only a few decades later.

Indeed, a broad view of all available evidence reveals a highly dynamic rather than stagnant linguistic situation in late Muscovite Russia—a veritable "polyglossia," as it has been termed by a recent student,[114] supplanting the Church Slavonic–vernacular "diglossia" that has been said to characterize earlier Muscovite language history.[115] Works in the canonical genres but also in new styles of poetry and drama were being written in high or standard Church Slavonic by a small circle of clergy, many of them Ruthenian in background,[116] while elsewhere educated lay people as well as clerics, mostly native Muscovites, were polemicizing with religious opponents, composing official reports, adapting foreign tales for their amusement, or exchanging love letters and poems in a low or "hybrid" Slavonic permeated by vernacular forms as well as by assorted Ruthenianisms, Polonisms, Latinisms, and loanwords from further afield.[117] In the Moscow chanceries, meantime, business proceeded in chancery Russian, in which both Slavonic and foreign elements also found expression (Appendix I, no. 3),[118] while in the back streets of the capital and across the Muscovite lands any number of dialects were to be heard: indeed, dialectical variation in Russian, though never great by English, German, or Italian standards, seems to have peaked at about this time.[119] In sum, it is difficult to resist the overall depiction recently offered by one specialist: that, "in effect, the verbal culture of late seventeenth century Russia had not yet freed itself of the stultifying norms of an outlived and unassimilated Slavonic, nor had it yet found a newer and more natural norm in the chancery language or in the vernacular, or in any combination of these two elements with Slavonic and Western European. One might say that Russians of that time had more linguistic material than they could cope with, and no sense of how this material might be blended and systematized."[120] A point of crisis had been reached, in other words, rather as it had in those other arenas of late Muscovite culture—architecture and imagery—studied in my previous volumes; a crisis that was similarly precipitated by Muscovy's swelling commercial and cultural contacts with Europe and by the tsardom's ever growing political power.

Peter's cultural revolution, we shall see, did not fully resolve the linguistic "chaos" or crisis which he had inherited and which, indeed, his own recorded utterances and written remains plainly exemplify. But before moving on it may be useful to examine a single monument of the unfolding crisis, a monument that nicely embodies several of the larger historical themes under consideration here: Heinrich Wilhelm Ludolf's *Grammatica Russica* of 1696, a work by a German scholar, published in England, that nevertheless stands as the first grammar of the Russian language ever printed—"Russian," as it insisted, not Slavonic.[121]

Ludolf was born in Erfurt in 1655 and educated at the local *Ratsgymnasium* and then at the University of Jena, but he resided most of his adult life, as it happened, in London. A scholar of broad linguistic and related religious (Pietist) interests, he was attracted to Russia and Russian as an opportunity for pursuing those interests. The year and a half that he sojourned there—from January 1693 to June 1694—are concisely described by Simmons:

> He seems to have spent much of his time at Moscow, where he lived in the German *sloboda* [suburban settlement inhabited by the several thousand "Germans"—northern or western Europeans—in Muscovite service or doing business in Russia]. But he moved freely in Russian society and was personally known to the Tsar [Peter] . . . and to the Patriarch and other influential figures such as Prince Boris Golitsyn [a current fa-

vorite of Peter], to whom he later dedicated his Grammar. He took a great interest in the religious life both of the German community in Moscow and of the Russians themselves, but he evidently gave his linguistic curiosity full rein. He was a considerable linguist before his arrival in Russia and already knew something of its language, for Russian words occur in . . . [a] diary-fragment before the date of his arrival there; but much of his time must have been spent studying it. As a result of his stay his previous intellectual interest in languages was powerfully reinforced; for he became convinced that a knowledge of the vernacular was essential for those evangelical and ecumenical activities to which he was to devote the remainder of his life.[122]

Simmons locates Ludolf socially and culturally in the fairly numerous company of scholars and clergymen living in contemporary North Germany, Holland, and England whose outlook combined "an intellectual interest in languages with piety, a reverence for the Bible, and a desire to spread knowledge of the [biblical] Word and to see the [separate Christian] Churches reconciled"[123]: a company that included several other figures with important connections to our larger story, notably Nicolaas Witsen, the sometime burgomaster of Amsterdam, and the philosopher Leibniz, with both of whom Ludolf made contact. For these earnest men of learning Russia was, like Armenia or Ethiopia, a vaguely "oriental" country of Christian heritage whose past, mores, and language merited close study not only for the light they could shed on universal human history and particularly on the origins and spread of Christianity but also for the help they could provide in promoting religious reform in those countries as well as better understanding among Christians at large. In fact, Simmons presents evidence that it was Witsen, with his extensive commercial as well as scholarly interests in Russia and wide experience of traveling there, who encouraged Ludolf to compile and publish a Russian grammar: "Hee [Ludolf] has been for some time at Moscow, and is now at Amsterdam, entertained there by Mynheere Witsen with great respect, who adviseth him to publish the elements of the Russic language, which he judges him capable to do well," reported an interested third party to a correspondent at Oxford in October 1694; and shortly thereafter Ludolf himself wrote to the same correspondent, a delegate (trustee) of the Oxford University Press, that "Mylord Witsen took it very kindly to be remembered by you, and I have as good as promised unto him, to prepare for the press a short Russish grammar, with a Vocabulary, and the most common idiotisms."[124]

In September 1695, having traveled from Moscow via Stockholm and Amsterdam, Ludolf reached London and in due course proceeded to Oxford, there to superintend the printing of his grammar book. By this time the press had at last acquired a full set of Cyrillic types (Fig. 4), which had been cut in Amsterdam on Ludolf's recommendation by a German craftsman from a foundry in Frankfurt "famed for its oriental fonts."[125] Printing was completed in May 1696, in an edition of 300. By March 1697 Ludolf himself was back in

Caput I.
De Literis, Pronunciatione &
Orthographia

Nom.	figura	numerus	valor
Az	Д ᴀ	1	a
Buki	Б б	2	b
Vædi	В в		v conſonans
Glagol	Г г	3	g
Dobro	Д д	4	d
Ieſt	Є є	5	e
Schiviet	Ж ж		g Gallorum ante e & i
Zelo	Ѕ ѕ	6	Z Gallor. & Anglor.
Zemla	З з	7	
Iſche	Н н	8	i
I	І ї	10	
Kako	К к	20	k
Liudi	Л л	30	l
Miſlæt	М м	40	m
Naſch	Н н	50	n
On	О о	70	o
Pocoi	П п	80	p
Rtzi	Р р	100	r
Slovo	С с	200	ſ
Twerda	Т т	300	t
Ik	У у	400	u
Phert	Ф ф	500	ph.
Cheer	Х х	600	ch. Germanorum
Ot	Ѡ ѡ	800	o longum
Tſi	Ц ц	900	ts.
Tſcherf	Ч ч	90	tſch. ch. Angl. ſive C Ital. ante e & i.
Scha	Ш ш		ſch. ſive ch. Gall. & ſh Anglorum.
Schtſcha	Щ щ		ſchtſch.
Ier	Ъ ъ		non effertur in pronunciatione
Ieri	Ы ы		ui
Ieer	Ь ь		i breviſſimum
Iat	Ѣ ѣ		ie dipthongus
Ius	Ю ю		iu
Iæt	Я ᴀ		ia dipthong.
Kſi	Ѯ ѯ	60	x
Pſi	Ѱ ѱ	700	Ps
Thita	Ѳ ѳ	9	f
Iſchitze	Ѵ ѵ		pronunciatur i. Ot

Millenarios ſequenti modo ſcribunt ҂а 1000.

҂в 2000. Annus præſens ҂аχҽѕ. 1696. Ruſſis

eſt à condito mundo ҂зсд. 7204. qui

menſe Septembri præteriti anni incepit.

Figure 4 Cyrillic letters, with their names, numerical values, and a pronunciation guide in Latin letters, as printed in Ludolf's *Grammatica Russica* (Oxford, 1696).

Amsterdam, where people were preparing for the imminent arrival of Tsar Peter's Grand Embassy, during whose visit Ludolf may well have personally presented a digest of his book to the tsar: its special dedication in Russian, absent in the regular edition, is dated 1696 and signed "His Most Illustrious Tsarist Majesty's most humble servant, Andrushka Villiemka Ludolf," wording that attests to a familiarity both personal and linguistic.[126] Ludolf spent the following winter in Halle with August Hermann Francke, the Pietist leader, who had already taught himself some Russian using a copy of the *Grammar*. Francke was a founder of the University of Halle, where in 1702 he established a Collegium Orientale Theologicum that was to include a center for Slavic studies, a labor in which Ludolf assisted. But by now Ludolf's own focus had shifted to the Near East, a region to which he journeyed—to Smyrna, Constantinople, Jerusalem, Cairo, and Alexandria—in March 1698. He returned to London in December 1700 "strengthened," as Simmons says, "in his belief in Reunion [of the Christian churches] and in the necessity for evangelical and missionary endeavour in the Near East," a cause to which he devoted the rest of his public life. He died in 1712.[127]

While it is clear both textually and contextually that Ludolf intended his *Grammar* mainly to facilitate evangelical work in Russia, it is equally clear that for various of his patrons and collaborators more purely philological and straightforward commercial motives were uppermost ("would be a useful Booke to our Russian merchants [British merchants in Russia]," its chief Oxford sponsor had argued).[128] Nor was Ludolf himself indifferent to the rising commercial and political importance of Russia, as is indicated by the preface to his *Grammar* and by its appended essay on the natural products of the country. Such an awareness only added to the urgency of making available to those who shared his concerns the "most important points of the Russian language *[paecipua fundamenta Russicae linguae]*," as he subtitled his book. That language, he then explained in his preface and later exampled in his text, was to be distinguished from the "lingua Slavonica," which was the language of learned ecclesiastical works and religious verse written by erudites like "Simon Polotski" (Appendix I, nos. 5, 6), the Ruthenian divine active in Moscow court circles from 1663 to 1680 whose contributions to the concurrent Muscovite debate on sacred imagery are discussed elsewhere.[129] Ludolf knew that a learned disquisition could not proceed in Moscow without recourse to Church Slavonic, but it was the actual spoken language or "vulgar dialect" of Russia that he wished to describe, the language in which, as he also reported in his preface, that "corpus of Russian law" known as the "uloschenie" (*Ulozhenie* of 1649) had been printed (Appendix I, no. 4). The grammar proper of his book, also written in Latin and occupying some 36 of its 112 octavo pages, offers a "concise but reliable description of colloquial Russian at the end of the seventeenth century," in Professor Unbegaun's judgment, and is followed by an equally long section of colloquial phrases, mostly in dialog form, accompanied by Latin and German translations: "Its value for the history of spoken Russian," Unbegaun adds, "can hardly be overestimated."[130] In addition, Ludolf's book contains a short list of Russian words for cardinal numbers and a much longer list of Russian names for natural phenomena—sky, sun, moon, the seasons and months of the year, days of the week, stones, metals, herbs, birds, animals, and so on—with their Latin and German equivalents, various of which terms are then discussed in the appended essay, again in Latin, on the natural products of the country. All in all, Unbegaun concludes, Ludolf's *Grammar,* whatever its linguistic shortcomings (dwelled on by some Russian scholars), is the work of a "foreigner who succeeded in acquiring a remarkably thorough knowledge of Russian"—an assessment confirmed by his surviving letters in Russian[131]—and who was "surprisingly well informed about the complex and peculiar linguistic situation in Russia in his day."[132] At the same time, as Unbegaun elsewhere observes, while "Ludolf's grammar was referred to with approval in a number of Western books, mostly German, at the beginning of the eighteenth century," the edition was small, and the book "quickly became rare; it was soon almost forgotten and did little to inspire or influence subsequent Russian grammars."[133]

Ludolf's *Grammatica Russica* of 1696, rediscovered and republished in the twentieth century, has been found more or less useful by students of Russian language. But for cultural historians its interest surely also lies in the ways in which it embodies precisely "the complex and peculiar linguistic situation in Russia in his day." It bears witness to the economic, political, and religious as well as linguistic pressures that were being brought to bear in this "complex" or, as we would say, critical situation, just as it offers detailed proof of the vernacular's robust readiness to be properly codified at last, or standardized, by contemporary European standards. Nor was Ludolf's the only such effort undertaken in the seventeenth century by foreigners who had spent time in Russia and were eager for pressing practical reasons to make Russian accessible to their compatriots. The manuscript grammars left by two such men—the English physician Mark Ridley and the German merchant Tönnis Fenne—have lately been published in scholarly editions, and there are indications that several more were compiled[134]—testimony again to the readiness of Russian to be properly described, or codified, and to the urgent necessity of doing so. The point was not lost on Tsar Peter and his collaborators as they pushed forward with their program of partial and then wholesale Europeanization in Russia.

THE NAUTICAL TURN

The creation by Peter I of a Russian navy, a singular achievement by any applicable yardstick, alone occasioned a huge lexical invasion of "Russian," meaning the literary language whose emergence in the earlier eighteenth century is the underlying theme of this volume. More than 150 Petrine loanwords including derivations are listed in Appendix II under the heading Nautical Terms. Excluded from the list are the many more such terms that were borrowed during the Petrine era only to be dropped from use in later years owing to successive innovations in navigation and ship design and to the momentous transition, about the middle of the nineteenth century, from sail to steam. Thus omitted, for example, are the several hundred words imported under Peter mainly from Dutch and English to name the parts of a fully rigged sailing ship and the similarly transient vocabulary, borrowed mostly from Italian, of the galley fleet.[1] Also omitted from the list, as noted there, are numerous highly technical terms—various naval ranks and ratings, specialized navigational terminology, the names for numerous other ship parts, and the like—that remain in the lexicon but are scarcely known even to well-educated Russian speakers. The few exceptions to these rules include words which, while not current in Russian, can still be found in historical or literary works: for example, *gol* (= hull, from the English and/or Dutch *hol*); *kvarterdek* (= quarterdeck, from the English); *paketbot* (= packetboat, from the English and/or Dutch *pakketboot*, German *Paketboot*); and *takelazh* (= rigging, from Dutch *takelage*). The list also includes some technical terms that even amateur Russian sailors could reasonably be expected to know or easily understand: for instance, *bizan'* (= mizzen, mizzensail, from Dutch *bezaan* and/or German *Besan*); *bousprit* (= bowsprit, from the English and/or Dutch *boegspriet*); *kil'* (= keel, from the English and/or German or Dutch *kiel*); or *lavirovat'* (= to tack, from Dutch *laveeren* or German *lavieren*). Indeed these along with all the other words in the Nautical section of the list, all of them still current in Russian and all definitely attested to the Petrine era, provide ready evidence of the verbal scope, the lexical and attendant semantic impact, of Russia's nautical turn under Peter.

41

In this chapter we will consider in succession the historical contexts, some of the main texts, and the initial stages in the institutionalization of this great turn the better to grasp its impact on Russian culture, especially verbal culture. Discussion of the more purely linguistic aspects of the story will be left to Chapter 6.

Russia in Maritime Europe

The military and diplomatic or "strategic" importance of Peter's creation of the Russian navy has long been recognized, the more so as naval power in general, and Russian then Soviet naval might in particular, became matters of intense scholarly interest both in Russia and abroad.[2] So has the navy's economic cost to Peter's subjects, sometimes judged excessive,[3] and his deep personal investment in the project. In elucidating these points historians have published detailed narratives of the navy's foundation and early operations as well as extensive documentation.[4] This large body of scholarly work will not be systematically surveyed here, let alone replicated, even selectively; nor will I attempt to define either the navy's cost effectiveness at any time or its strategic worth. But it may be useful to reconsider Peter's personal involvement in the navy's creation, to summarize its early career, and to connect both developments with the relevant international context. The last of these tasks has been rather neglected especially by Russian historians, and we will turn to it first.

By the late seventeenth century, when Peter came to power in Moscow, a vibrant, centuries-old maritime culture flourished in the Mediterranean, Atlantic, North Sea, and Baltic ports of Europe, where as many as 400,000 mariners, fishermen, and ordinary sailors lived and plied their skills. Technical exchange among these communities in navigational matters, shipbuilding, and related aspects of commerce and administration had gradually promoted a convergence of nautical terminology, mercantile practice, and maritime law as well as the establishment by concerned governments of such typical institutions as admiralties and arsenals. A common hydrography and cartography along with common standards of naval architecture and the mathematics necessary for all of these exercises had also proliferated in maritime Europe, as had, however unevenly, the vessels and instruments of oceanic navigation, the fruits of maritime commerce, and the trophies of overseas empire. Bearers of the maritime culture of early modern Europe possessed their own lingua franca—in the North Sea–Baltic region it was mainly Dutch—and their own distinctive ethos, one of both "solidarity and independence," in the words of a leading student, that was at once religious and reckless.[5] But while Tsar Peter of Russia imbibed this culture at an early age, including a working knowledge of Dutch, it was still wholly alien to almost all of his countrymen.

A brief look at the history of the English navy may help focus our view, since it was to England, arguably the leading maritime power of his day, even more than to Holland, the other maritime giant, that Peter would turn for help in creating his own fleet. In the account of one authority, it was in the reign of Queen Elizabeth that English navigators caught up with their Continental rivals and "began to teach their neighbours." Indeed,

> In spite of the slow and unplanned nature of most of the specific changes which took place during the sixteenth century, the contrast between the navy of 1485 and that of 1603 was dramatic. At the beginning of Henry VII's reign [1485] we are still in the world of Chaucer's shipman [hero of one of *The Canterbury Tales,* ca. 1387]; by the time of Elizabeth's death [1603] a "blue water" strategy is already in place, and the pattern of fighting tactics has been set for the next 150 years. A single clerk on a part time basis has been replaced by a whole department of state, and the vast "increase of governance" so typical of Tudor England can be illustrated to perfection by this development. . . . [Moreover] sailing a great ship was [now] a highly technical operation, and navigating it across the ocean even more so. Gone were the rule-of-thumb methods, the lead line [testing depth], and the portolan. The navigator of 1600 needed charts, tables of declination, tide tables, and instruments such as the backstaff and the boxed compass. He was at the very least literate and numerate, and probably a man of some education. The sea had always been a way of life [for many Englishmen]; by 1600 it was rapidly becoming a profession, and service on the royal ships occupied a respected place in that profession. It is often said that the Tudors made England a modern state. That is only true with certain qualifications, but they created a modern navy out of the [medieval] office of the king's ships.[6]

And by the term "modern navy," this and other authorities explain, we are to understand a permanent, state-owned, gun-armed, sea-going fleet comprised mainly of sailing (rather than oar-powered) vessels. Such fleets, with their infrastructure of dockyards and storehouses, their mechanisms of recruitment, training, and supply, had become part of leading European states' institutional framework and major instruments of their power.[7] This was exactly what Peter I would create, with the aid of seasoned English specialists, in Russia.

The decade of the interregnum in England (1649–1660) has been identified as the next major phase in the English navy's history, as it was then that some 216 vessels were added to its force of about 50 warships, an unprecedented expansion. This huge buildup, motivated by the Commonwealth's need to defend itself against assorted royalists both at home and abroad and by its trade wars with the Dutch, was achieved only in part by the timeworn policy of hiring merchant ships for state service. Far more important was the massive shipbuilding program that the Commonwealth undertook, which produced warships that were not only well-armed by contemporary standards but also more maneuverable, versatile, and cost-effective than their royal predecessors. The outcome was a navy that none of England's rivals could match—not France, whose navy had dwindled to 20 vessels by 1661, nor Spain, nor even the Dutch Republic. "The lasting achievement of the interregnum's navy," another specialist rather grandly summarizes, "was to reawaken the spirit of the late Elizabethan age and reassert England's maritime destiny."[8]

Following the interregnum the restored king, Charles II (1660–1685), and his brother and successor, James II (1685–1688), eagerly embraced the policy of English naval supremacy over any enemy or likely combination of enemies. So did William III, the Dutch prince of Orange who was elected to the English throne in 1689 and with whom, as we shall see shortly, Tsar Peter dealt extensively during his Grand Embassy to Europe of 1697–1698. The Royal Navy in the reign of William's successor, Queen Anne (1702–1714), with whom Peter also treated, was comprised at different times of between 185 and 213 warships manned by a total of 40,000 to 50,000 sailors and marines. The warships ranged from the 1,700-ton to 2,100-ton "first-rates" armed with 90 to 100 guns, at the top end, to assorted sloops, bomb vessels, yachts, and other supporting craft at the bottom: about half of the total, on average, were warships of the first four rates, mounting 50 or more guns and considered fit to serve in the line of battle (ships of the line, the battle fleet). At this juncture only the navy of the kingdom of France, waxing and waning with the fortunes of Louis XIV, comprised a comparable number of ships.[9] But then the War of the Spanish Succession (1701–1713), arraying England and Holland against France, exhausted King Louis's naval resources (as it did those of the Dutch Republic); and England's naval superiority among the European powers, established by 1692, remained intact. Particularly was this so in the Baltic, where the Royal Navy was stronger than all other navies combined.[10]

Of course, England's rise as a naval power cannot be separated from English maritime history more generally—or that from the country's relatively favorable geographical situation and sufficiency of good harbors. In this larger view, the gradual expansion of trade within the country in the later Middle Ages as well as across the North Sea to Dutch and Flemish ports bred a "tough, truculent, highly individualistic," and increasingly numerous community of seafaring folk who perpetually navigated their cogs and barges and small sailing boats around the long indented coasts of their homeland and over the sea to the Netherlands or, following the herring shoals, across the other sea to Iceland. They thus gradually "learned to find their position in mist or darkness by taking note of the varying sound of the sea on cliffs, rocks, sands, and beaches, and by keeping careful watch for such adventitious aids to navigation as passing seabirds, seals, fishes, seaweed, and the colour and run of the seas. They learned to work the tides, to take advantage of short cuts, and to know the signs of the weather."[11] This burgeoning maritime culture of seafarers, merchants, and allied craftsmen, so the argument runs, as much as the push of moneyed and political interests in London, accounts for the rise of the Royal Navy; when the Tudors or Cromwell or Queen Anne needed warships equipped with able seamen to protect their realm and its overseas trade or to prey on the shipping of rivals, this rich, long-standing, ever growing maritime community was there for them to draw on.

By 1601 half a dozen overseas trading corporations had been formed in London of which the first was the Muscovy Company, whose 201 member merchants received a royal charter in 1555 and went on to open, and at first to dominate, the trade between western Europe and Russia via the northern White Sea route, a trade that came to be based at Archangel (founded for that purpose in 1584).[12] Together with the Royal Navy these trading companies gave an enormous boost to the construction of ever more efficient ocean-going vessels until, as Peter would discover personally in 1697 and 1698, English ship design and shipbuilding methods were considered the best—or among the best—in Europe.[13] The indigenous supply of naval stores could not keep pace with all of this growth, however, and by the later sixteenth century, though hulls continued to be built of English oak, wood for masts and spars, hemp for cordage, and pitch and tar for waterproofing and preservation had to be imported from the eastern Baltic lands and particularly Russia, later also

North America. These commodities were the stock-in-trade of the Muscovy Company, whose restrictive practices, along with major political setbacks and vigorous Dutch competition, eventually led a concerned English government, ever in need of more naval stores and prompted by Peter's recent visit, to pass an Act of Parliament designed "to enlarge the Trade to Russia" (March 25, 1699). Well into the eighteenth century Dutch merchants and Dutch ships continued to dominate the Baltic trade, as they had since about 1600; but an expansive new era in the history of Anglo-Russian commerce, one culminating by the middle of the century in a British commercial hegemony in Russia, had begun.[14]

English mariners were not among the inventors of the new nautical science that developed in this first great age of European overseas expansion (1400–1715), an age characterized more by commercial penetration supported by naval force, both state and private, than by extensive settlement and overt political control.[15] As late as the 1570s there was nothing in England comparable to the School for Navigators established by Prince Henry in Portugal early in the fifteenth century or the similar institution set up in Spain, at Seville, a century or so later. Indeed the Spanish-born Sebastian Cabot (1477?–1558), a graduate of the Seville school who in 1548 was induced to transfer his allegiance to the English crown, did as much as anyone to implant the new science in England, where he busied himself until his death instructing navigators, drawing up charts, and making navigational instruments. One of his pupils was Richard Chancellor, who in 1553, in a perilous voyage at sea, discovered the northern route to Russia—which in turn led to the establishment of the Muscovy Company and regular Anglo-Russian trade relations.[16] The next big boost to the development of scientific navigation in England came with the reign of Charles II, himself an avid mariner who established the Royal (scientific) Society of London in 1662, the Royal (astronomical) Observatory at Greenwich in 1675—both of which Tsar Peter would visit in 1698—and, most important for our story, the Royal Mathematical School at Christ's Hospital, also London, in 1673, this last mainly for the purpose of meeting the ever growing need for mathematically trained navigators. In 1698 two students of this school were appointed by Peter to teach in the school of mathematics and navigation that he would shortly found, on English advice, in Moscow.[17]

It is an ever remarkable fact, surely, that Tsar Peter himself was the first Russian we know of to master the new nautical science and the first, or one of the first, to learn how to build a full-scale sailing ship. These seem to have been moreover his proudest personal achievements. An important testimonial in both respects is his account of the "beginnings of this marine business" in Russia contained in his draft preface to the *Naval Statute (Ustav morskoi)* of 1720, which is the principal text to be studied in the next section of this chapter. In this document we read, deciphered from Peter's characteristic scribble,[18] how his late father, Tsar Aleksei (died 1676), had taken great care to protect and enlarge his royal patrimony "especially in military matters," and this "not only on land, but on the sea (which was such a strange thing among us, that we'd hardly heard about it)." Peter then cites the siege of Riga under his father and the "construction of two ships at Dedinov on the Caspian Sea": the former alludes to the unsuccessful campaign of 1656 to recover Narva and adjacent Baltic coastland lost to Sweden in 1581, which involved transporting troops over water and the capture of a Swedish boat; the latter, to the ill-fated effort from 1667 to 1669 to build, at the royal estate of Dedinovo on the Oka River (near where it joins the Moskva), a flotilla of warships for service on the Volga-Caspian trade route, an effort that was directed by specially recruited Dutch craftsmen and abandoned when the first vessels were destroyed or dispersed by brigands at Astrakhan at the end of their maiden voyage.[19] Professing resignation to the "will of the High Ruler" in these unfortunate outcomes, Peter also saw in them, he says, "in a strange way," the "beginnings, as from seeds, of the present marine business." He goes on to explain that when, under his father,

> it was intended to navigate *[delat' korableplavanie]* on the Caspian Sea, then from Holland was brought Captain David Butler *[kapitan Davyd Butler]* with a company of master craftsmen and seamen *[c kompanieiu masterovykh i matrozov]*, who having built a ship *[korabl']* named the Eagle and a yacht or galliot *[i iakhtu ili galiot]*, flowed off to Astrakhan. But at that time [Stenka] Razin had risen in revolt [1670–71] and, as the enemy of every good thing, he destroyed them [the ships], killed the captain, while the others left for Persia, and thence to the India Company *[Indeiskuiu kompaniiu:* presumably the Dutch East India Company]. But two of them, the surgeon *[lekar']* Ivan Tormont [Jan Termund] and the ship carpenter and gunner *[konstapel':* cf. Dutch *konstabel]* Kasters Brant [Carsten Brandt], after pacification of the revolt, returned to Moscow, and the surgeon joined doctor Simon Zomer *[doktoru Simonu Zomeru]*, while Karshten Brant fed himself by carpentry work, right up to our times.

So the Dutchman Carsten Brandt, according to Peter, was the living link for him with his father's ill-fated attempt to create a Russian navy and indeed was a critical early player, as Peter will further relate, in his own, successful effort to do so.

Phase two, as it were, of Peter's naval story began in 1687, when he was a boy of fifteen but already nominally tsar or rather co-tsar with his elder half-brother, Ivan (Ivan V: their joint monarchy lasted from 1682 until Ivan's death in 1696). As Peter tells it, again in the same document:

> Before the dispatch of Prince Iakov Dolgorukov to France [Russian em-
> bassy of 1687], amid other conversations the aforesaid Pr. Ia. said that he
> had an instrument *[instrument]* by which could be taken distances or ex-
> tents *[distantsii ili razstoianiia]*, [though] not having got to the place. I
> very much wanted to see it; but he told me that they [somebody] had
> stolen it from him. And when he left for France, then I ordered him to
> buy among other things this instrument, and when he returned from
> France [May 1688] and brought [it], then I, receiving it, did not know
> how to use it. (These instruments were an *astroliabiia* and a *kokor* or
> *gotoval'nia* [= case/instrument case; cf. Dutch *koker*] with compasses
> *[tsirkuliami]* and other things). But then [I] showed it to doctor Zakhar
> fon-der-Gulst [Zachary van der Gulst[20]], does he not know? Who said,
> that he does not know; but will seek somebody who does know; which I
> with great zeal ordered him to do, and the doctor soon found a Hol-
> lander named Frants, surnamed Timmerman, to whom I showed the
> aforementioned instruments, who, having seen them, said these words,
> that Prince Iakov had spoken of them, and that he [Frants] knew how to
> use them; wherefore I applied myself with zeal to learning geometry and
> fortification *[geometrii i fortofikatsii]*. And so this Frants, in this way,
> came to court, to be incessantly in our company.

This brings Peter to phase three of his story:

> And some time later [in 1688], we happened to be in Izmailovo [royal es-
> tate near Moscow] at the flax yard, and strolling by the warehouses
> where lay the remains of the house of ancestor *[ded]* Nikita Ivanovich
> Romanov [a first cousin of Peter's grandfather, Tsar Michael; died 1634],
> among which I found a foreign boat *[sudno]*, and [I] asked the afore-
> said Frants, what kind of boat is that? He said, an English boat *[bot
> Angliiskii]*. I asked: where do they use it? He said, on ships for riding [in]
> and hauling [back and forth]. I again asked: what advantage *[preimush-
> chestvo]* does it have over our boats (since [I] saw its form and strength

[were] better than ours)? He told me, that it goes by sails not only with the wind, but against the wind; which speech threw me into great surprise and even disbelief. Then I again asked him: is there somebody who could repair it and show how this is done? He said that there was. Then I with great joy hearing this, ordered [him] to find him. And the aforesaid Frants sought out the Hollander Karshten Brant.

After briefly reidentifying Carsten Brandt, Peter then tells how the old salt

repaired this *bot* and made a mast *[masht]* and sails, and on the Iauza [river, near Peter's suburban Moscow retreat of Preobrazhenskoe] tacked about *[laviroval]* before me, which especially surprised me and was very pleasing. Then, when I often exercised *[upotreblial]* thus with him, and the boat did not always come about well, but inclined more toward the bank, I asked: why this? He said, the water [river] is narrow. Then I moved it [the boat] to Prosianoi pond, but found little advantage *[avantazhu]* there, while hourly [Peter's] zealousness grew. Therefore I began to inquire, where more water [is]; they told me Lake Pereslavskoe (as much bigger), whereto I [went] as to the Trinity monastery, as promised to mother; but once there I entreated her, to let a yard and boats *[sudy]* be made. And so the aforesaid Brant made two small frigates *[fregata]* and three yachts *[iakhty]*, and there I satisfied my zeal for several years.

Thus Peter's own account of his boyhood introduction to sailing and shipbuilding under the tutelage of two Dutch masters, adventures that sowed the seeds, as he said, of the navy he would found in later years.

We know from immediately contemporary sources, including his own surviving notebooks and letters to his mother, that between 1688 and 1692 Peter proceeded from this seemingly chance initiation into nautical matters to the construction, outfitting, and exercising on Lake Pereiaslavskoe (now Pleshcheevo) of a veritable "toy fleet" composed of the two small frigates and three yachts Brandt had built with Peter's help, some sort of warship he had built on his own, and sundry smaller craft built on his orders at Preobrazhenskoe and Moscow and hauled overland to his new shipyard near the old town of Pereiaslavl, located by the lake of the same name about 135 kilometers northeast of Moscow. His letters to his mother convey news of these activities together with requests that rope and other supplies be sent to him from the Artillery Chancery there in Moscow; his notebooks record mathematical exercises including one in which he works with an astrolabe to calculate in "minutes [*minuty*]" and "degrees [*gradusof*]" the "declination [*deklinatsiiu*]" of the sun.[21] Brandt died in June 1692 but Peter, ever "zealous" in the "marine business," returned to Pereiaslavl in July to help Timmerman fit out the completed fleet, which on August 18, 1692, set sail across the lake under the command of "Admiral [*admiral*]" Prince F. Iu. Romodanovskii and General Patrick Gordon, trusted intimates and sometime tutor-guardians of the young tsar, with Peter himself aboard the mock warship of another favorite, François "Frants" Lefort.[22] Yet Peter—returning to his draft preface to the *Naval Statute*—found in due course that Lake Pereiaslavskoe as well as another venue, Lake Kubenskoe, were too small for his waxing nautical ambitions:

> therefore was formed my intention to see the sea directly, about which [I] began to entreat my mother, that she would permit me; who though in her usual maternal love often forbade this dangerous path, but then, seeing my great desire and unchanging zeal, reluctantly permitted. And so in the year [1693] I was at the City [Archangel] and from the City [we] went out to sea as far as Ponoi with the English and Dutch merchant ships and a Dutch convoy [*konvoem*], which was commanded [*komandoval*] by captain Golgolsen; and we were on my yacht, named the *St. Peter*.

The "we" in this expedition consisted of a large suite of high-ranking nobles and attendants, including the Dutch physician-diplomat Dr. Van der Gulst mentioned by Peter, a Russian chaplain with eight cantors, forty royal musketeers (*strel'tsy*), numerous government officials, and two favorite dwarfs, all of whom had accompanied their young tsar northward from Moscow, leaving on July 4, 1693, thence overland and by river to Vologda, Ustiug Velikii, Kholmogorii, and on up to Archangel, where they arrived on July 30. The annual summer visitation of the Dutch and English merchant fleets was about to end; in fact, their ships weighed anchor on August 4, and as they sailed off Peter tagged along in his newly built yacht as far as the mouth of the river Ponoi, a distance of some 300 versts (about 320 kilometers), where he beheld the "Northern Sea" (Arctic Ocean). He arrived back in Archangel on August 10 and on August 14, as again later that month and twice in September, he wrote to his anxious mother, who was pressing him to come home, assuring her that all was well and that he would return to Moscow as soon as possible.[23] We catch a glimpse in this correspondence of how "strange" indeed was the young tsar's growing nautical enthusiasm "among us," in his own domestic setting, let alone elsewhere in Muscovite society. Undeterred, Peter immediately made plans to sail from Archangel into the Arctic Ocean, for which purpose his *St. Peter* and two new ships were to form a squadron: the first to be built by Dutch shipwrights at Archangel under the overall direction of the region's new governor, F. M. Apraksin ("Min Her Guverneur Archangel," as Peter would address him, writing in Latin letters),[24] the second to be purchased in Amsterdam by Moscow's chief friend there, burgomaster Nicolaas Witsen (sponsor, as we saw in Chapter 1, of Ludolf's *Grammatica Russica*). General Gordon was appointed "rear-admiral" (*shautbeinakht*—straight from the Dutch) of the squadron[25] and in May 1694 Peter returned to Archangel with an even larger suite (some 300 men) to oversee completion of the *St. Paul,* as the new vessel was christened, and to await the ship purchased in Holland, which on arrival in July turned out to be the forty-four–gun frigate *Holy Prophecy* captained by Jan Flam. Soon the squadron set sail for a three-week cruise into the Arctic Ocean, Peter himself serving on board the *Holy Prophecy* as a subordinate "skipper" (*schiper,* in Latin letters).[26] He had begun signing himself, in notes to his intimates, as "Piter," the Dutch form of his name, sometimes preceded by *Bombardir* or *Kapitein* if not *Schiper,* always in Latin letters.[27]

At this point in Peter's draft preface to the *Naval Statute* the writing shifts to another hand and voice, presumably those of his frequent legislative collaborator and favorite publicist of the time, Bishop Feofan Prokopovich, whose own literary efforts on a naval theme will be studied in the next section of this chapter. But interjections again in Peter's hand, as indicated below (phrases italicized), recur:

They were gladdened by such fine sailing [at Archangel], though our Lord [Peter] was not content. *Therefore my/his [svoiu] whole thought was turned to building a navy [flot], and when because of the Tatar insults Azov was besieged and then fortunately taken* [in 1696], in his unchanging desire he did not suffer to think about this for long, but soon set to work. A convenient place for shipbuilding was found on the Voronezh River, below the town of that name, skilled craftsmen were summoned from England and Holland, and in 1696 a new thing was begun in Russia: the building at great expense of ships, galleys *[galer],* and other craft. And in order for this to be permanently established in Russia, he resolved to introduce this art to his people, and therefore sent a large number of well-born persons to Holland and other dominions to study [naval] architecture [*arkhitektury*] and navigation. And what is more wondrous, as if the Monarch [*Monarkh:* Peter] were ashamed to lag behind his subjects in this art, he himself undertook a march [*marsh:* journey] to Holland, and in Amsterdam, *at the East India wharf* [*Ost"indskoi verfi*], having given himself over with other of his volunteers [*volonterami*] to the study of ship architecture, in a short time he was accomplished in it *as far as suits a good carpenter to know,* and by his own labors and craftsmanship he built and launched a new ship.

51

We thus have in this passage Peter's version or recollection of two critical stages in the actual creation of the Russian navy: the building of a war fleet at Voronezh for descent down the Don River to support his second siege of the fortified Ottoman town of Azov (Turkish *Azak,* 1696), and Peter's own subsequent *stage* as an apprentice shipwright in Holland (1697).

The earlier of these episodes involved Peter's first serious ventures in military as well as naval architecture—fortification as well as shipbuilding—and has been described as such elsewhere.[28] Here I might add that as a result of his shipbuilding frenzy both before and after his second and successful siege of Azov, thousands of workers were conscripted, some 200 vessels were launched, bases for them were established at Azov and nearby Taganrog, and an elaborate administrative and financial support system was created, including an Admiralty Court (*Admiralteiskii dvor*) or yard at Voronezh headed by an official, A. P. Protas'ev, with the grand new title of *Admiralteits* (Dutch for "admiralty," here appropriated to mean something like "civil admiral").[29] Sawmills were built, special tools—*instrumenty*—were ordered from Europe, and dozens of Italian, English, and Dutch shipwrights were imported. And everything was done under Peter's direct supervision if not with his personal participation: one student calculates that between 1696 and 1709 (plus one last visit in 1722, in preparation for his Persian campaign) Peter spent a total of more than a year—more than 400 days—in the yards in and around Voronezh.[30] It was also mentioned in my previous book that owing to the inevitable shortage of skilled local labor, inefficient management (the first head of the Admiralty Court, Protas'ev, had to be cashiered), disputes among the foreign masters, and other factors, most of the first warships produced at the Voronezh yards proved more or less unseaworthy—but that a Dutch visitor to Voronezh in 1703, Cornelis de Bruyn, was impressed nonetheless by the extent of its "conveniences for shipbuilding" and by the "great store house" there "full of all sorts of naval stores"; Bruyn counted no fewer than 244 ships—the bulk of them brigantines (galleys with two masts and sail)—in the water, in dry dock, or under construction. Meanwhile, again as noted earlier (and as Peter noted above), in 1697 some 122 "well-born" Russians were sent abroad to study navigation and shipbuilding, more than half of them to Venice, the rest to England and Holland.[31]

The second of the critical episodes recounted by Peter in the draft preface to his *Naval Statute,* his apprenticeship in shipbuilding in Holland, took place in the course of his famous Grand Embassy to Europe of 1697–98, which has also been discussed at length.[32] Briefly to recapitulate, the approximately eighteen months that the young tsar and his suite of about 250 Russian nobles, attendants, and support staff spent in Europe during this Grand Embassy— traveling, working, living, and entertaining themselves in North Germany, Poland, and Austria but particularly in Holland and England—proved to be a crucial experience both for Peter personally and for Russia's future: proved to be a major factor, as I have argued, in the program of intensive Europeanization that would dominate the rest of his long reign. Especially was this so with respect to Russia's nautical turn under Peter, which would include the foundation of Russia's new port and capital, St. Petersburg, as well as his creation of the navy. In the course of the Grand Embassy Peter and dozens of his closest associates stopped for a total of nearly ten months in and around northern Europe's two leading centers of shipbuilding and trade, Amsterdam and London, where they hired hundreds of shipwrights and seamen for service in Russia (including Cornelius Cruys, to be the "co-creator" and first vice admiral of the Russian navy)[33] and purchased tons of naval stores and equipment for shipment back home; indeed, Peter's written instructions to the Grand Embassy make it clear that such hiring and purchasing were virtually its main purpose.[34] In Amsterdam and London, working alongside various of his subjects, Peter also completed his training as a certified shipbuilder.[35] As he goes on to tell it, again in his own hand, in the draft preface to his *Naval Statute,* while working at the East India wharf in Amsterdam he

> asked the boss [*bas:* cf. Dutch *bass*] of this wharf Jan Pol to teach him [Peter] ship preportions [*preportsii*], which he showed him over four days; but since in Holland nothing in this craft is done by geometric [*geometricheskim*] means, but only by some sort of principles [*printsipii*], as well as by longstanding practice [*praktika*], as the aforementioned boss said, and that he didn't know how to show all this on a chart, then he [Peter] became very disgusted, that he had undertaken such a long journey for this, but not achieved the desired end. And several days later H. M. [*E. V.* = *Ego Velichestvo*/His Majesty, Peter himself] hap-

pened to be in company at the suburban house of the merchant Jan Tesing,[36] where he sat most unhappily, for the aforesaid reason; but when amid the conversations was asked, why so sad? then he explained the reason. In this company was an Englishman, who, on hearing it, said that with us in England this *arkhitektura* [naval architecture] was as advanced as the others [military and civil], and that it could be learned in a short time. This speech very much gladdened H. M., wherefore he promptly went to England and there over four months completed this science, and on his return [to Russia] brought with him two shipwrights Ian Den [John Deane] and Osip Nai [Joseph Nye].

This brings us back to England, which especially in the longer term proved to be the most important link for the nascent maritime Russia. By the 1730s England would be Russia's leading trading partner, as we shall see shortly; and it was in England in 1698, as mentioned above, that Peter also hired the first teachers for the navigation school he founded in Moscow, which was the predecessor of the Naval Academy he subsequently established in St. Petersburg. Under one name or another the latter long remained the principal source of officers for the Russian navy, the home of a long line of resident British instructors, and a perdurant site of Russian anglophilia.[37]

We might well regard Peter himself as the first Russian seaman ever to visit England, as Professor Cross suggests, going on to characterize the tsar-mariner's stay of several months (January–April 1698) as a confirmation of his "high opinion of Britain's pre-eminence in both the building and the commanding of ships." As described by Cross on the basis of contemporary British sources, Peter himself was "constantly on the water, sailing with spirit, if not always with success, the small yacht *Dove* that had been made available for his personal use." He went to Portsmouth to watch a mock sea battle specially arranged for him and to Deptford, near London, for a demonstration of firing by a new bomb vessel. The visiting tsar, supposedly moving about incognito, was also frequently to be found in the Royal Dockyard at Deptford, learning to build ships. "And of course," notes Cross, "he drank deeply with numerous sea captains and particularly with his boon companion, Admiral the Marquis of Carmarthen, before reluctantly sailing away on the *Royal Transport,* King William's gift of a state-of-the-art yacht." The yacht had been designed by Carmarthen himself for speedily transporting goods, messengers, and high-ranking persons, including the king himself, over to Holland and back, and was considered by knowledgeable contemporaries the best ship of its kind in the English fleet: a handsome gift indeed.[38]

Captain John Perry, a naval engineer hired by Peter in 1698 on Carmarthen's recommendation, went on to work in Russia until 1712; he reports in his memoirs of his service there how Peter "often declared to his Lords, when he has been a little merry, that he thinks it a much happier Life to be an Admiral in England, than Czar in Russia." Perry further reports that in his personal observation (at Voronezh) Peter had become "a great Master in Shipbuilding, and takes his Chief Delight in it, [and] often says, that if he had not come to England he had certainly been a Bungler . . . at that Art"; Perry's observation may be compared to that of a relatively disinterested Italian witness at Voronezh in the summer of 1699, who recorded that "every morning His Majesty went to work on a ship which he had designed and prepared in every detail under the direction of an Englishman with whom he had studied."[39] There is, similarly, the dispatch from Moscow of June 6, 1705, by the first British ambassador to Russia (1704–1712), Charles Whitworth: "I have had the honour to acquaint you how great a lover the Czar is of shipping," he reminded his superior in London, adding that

> he is a very good master himself, and has built a ship . . . which by all reports is as good as any in his fleet. On this account he makes many voyages to Voronesch and stays there a good part of the winter, often working himself and generally conversing with the master builders; He has taken a particular fancy to the english way of building, as much cleaner and lighter than the dutch, and therefore the greater part of the hollanders have been dismissed his service; and he has such a passion for this art, that I am oblidged to assure you, nothing can touch him so nearly, as the refusing leave for the shipwrights he desires may come hither, or recalling those, who are now in his service.

And there is the testimony, finally, of one of Peter's longtime Russian associates, the craftsman (expert turner) Andrei Nartov, who in his memoirs of the tsar recounts Peter's great love of naval service born of his experiences in England, and exclaims: "I know for sure, since I heard it from the monarch's lips, that he said this: 'If I were not tsar, I would want to be a Great-British admiral.'"[40] We surely touch here on something very basic in Peter's character. Nor can we miss the prominent naval motive of the first important portrait ever painted of him, that done by Sir Godfrey Kneller in London early in 1698, which was long a favorite of Peter himself and was frequently reproduced both in Russia and abroad.[41]

Cross found it difficult to establish with any certainty how many people Peter took into Russian naval service while he was in England, citing estimates from "a few dozen" to "as many as five hundred." His own research identified some twenty-one shipbuilders and assistants in addition to the John Deane and Joseph Nye named above by Peter, some sixty naval officers (three of whom became admirals), and two naval engineers (Perry and an Edward Lane, who directed critical canal and harbor construction). Initially the shipwrights served at Voronezh until, following Peter's defeat by Ottoman forces at the battle by the Pruth in 1711, most of the Azov fleet had to be surrendered or scuttled and the supporting yards closed, whereupon Peter turned his full attention to the St. Petersburg region and the buildup of his Baltic fleet. Three British shipwrights were responsible for some twenty of the fifty-four ships of the line built there between 1708 and 1725.[42] Meanwhile, for manning as well as for building his navy Peter continued to recruit Italian (for the galley fleet) and Dutch personnel along with British. The Italian witness—a singer—quoted above had come to Russia from Venice with a large party of sailors, ships' carpenters, galley captains, pilots, and other experts hired in 1698, while in Holland that year, also acting on Peter's orders, his new vice admiral, Cornelius Cruys, had hired 528 men to go to Russia with him—400 or so sailors, the rest officers and medics.[43] Most of the latter were Dutch, the rest Dutch-speaking Scandinavians (like Cruys himself). It should be noted that owing to the rapid growth of state navies in Europe at this time, seamen were in relatively short supply, so that the hiring of foreigners was a standard recourse everywhere, especially in France and the Netherlands. Between the 1650s and the 1720s, for instance, from 40 to 60 percent of the crews on Dutch ships were not Dutch—mainly Danes, Norwegians, and Germans—as well as up to 30 percent of the officers.[44]

The Anglo-Russian naval connection established by Peter also brought numerous Russian mariners to England to complete their training in schools and in the yards and ships of the Royal Navy. Cross estimates that a total of about 150 Russians spent time in England during Peter's reign (at least 180 in Holland as well), the bulk of them so engaged.[45] The broader Anglo-Russian maritime link was also promoted by the rapid growth of the seaborne Anglo-Russian trade that followed Peter's visit and the reorganization in 1699 of the Muscovy, now Russia Company in London, which in 1723 transferred its Russian offices and residences from Archangel and Moscow to St. Petersburg. Exported from Russia were the basic staples of the Baltic trade—grain, timber, hemp, flax, pitch, tar, bar iron—as well as whale oil, potash, wax, tallow, and caviar, while imported from Britain were such manufactured and luxury goods as textiles, spices, paper, sugar, buttons, eyeglasses, tools, utensils and instruments of various kinds, glass, clothes, and so on. The trade was carried almost entirely in British ships, to be sure, necessitating a large resident British colony in St. Petersburg, although it always produced a huge specie deficit in Russia's favor; Britain's primacy in Russian foreign trade from the 1730s until the end of the century has been amply demonstrated by Kahan. Kahan has also demonstrated that from Peter's time until the end of the eighteenth century, following the conquest of the Baltic littoral with the ports of Reval (Revel), Riga, Pernau, and Vyborg and the foundation of St. Petersburg, Russia's overall foreign trade increased in real terms approximately fifteenfold; moreover that St. Petersburg quickly became both "the largest Russian port and the most significant center" of this burgeoning international, mostly seaborne exchange.[46] The resultant addition to the Russian lexicon of dozens of new commercial terms, indexed in Appendix II, will be considered in Chapter 6.

It has been calculated that some 1,260 seagoing vessels were built in Russian yards between 1688 and 1725 for fleets launched successively on the White Sea, the Sea of Azov, the Baltic, and the Caspian (supporting Peter's Persian campaign of 1722–1723).[47] By almost any measure—logistical, administrative, financial, educational, personal—this must count as an outstanding achievement of his reign. Naval support proved decisive in the successful siege of Azov in 1696 and in the eventual defeat of Sweden in the long Northern War, which included not only the celebrated victory off Hangö Head in 1714 but also the little noticed repulse of a Swedish attack on Archangel in 1701[48] and the diplomatically crucial destruction of a Swedish squadron off Grengham Island in 1720. In 1700, at the beginning of the Northern War, the majority of seamen in the infant Russian navy were foreign; in 1721, at the war's end, it was manned by some 7,215 native-born sailors.[49] The Baltic fleet in particular, the largest of the fleets and long thereafter the most important component of the Russian navy, provided vital security for St. Petersburg in its immensely important role as Russia's "window on Europe." According to a British officer who had served in it for eight long years, the Baltic fleet in 1724 comprised twenty-nine seaworthy warships of thirty-six to ninety guns, a total that gave Russia naval supremacy over Sweden (twenty-four such warships) and Denmark (twenty-five).[50] Never generous in his praise, indeed frequently critical of Russian efforts to build up the fleet, this officer still had to allow that "few if any ships in the world are able to wrong the Russian, especially those built at St. Petersburg, if well manned, in the qualification of excellent sailing; and they are incomparably provided with masts, sails, anchors, cables, and cordage, all the proper product of Russia."[51]

This brings to an end our survey of the international and domestic settings of the "Petrine naval revolution," as it has been called, quite appropriately.[52] I hope to have thus clarified the motives, methods, and initial outcomes of this revolution that lay at the heart, it should now be apparent, of the entire Petrine project. A brief account of the revolution's institutionalization—administrative and educational but also mythological—forms the last section of this chapter. Now, ever mindful of the basic purpose of this volume, we will focus on some of the principal texts of Russia's nautical turn under Peter in an effort to pinpoint and assess its impact on Russian verbal culture: "texts" rather than "documents" or "monuments" (*pamiatniki*), I say, so as to emphasize their contingent and culturally constructed as well as their verbal character.

The *Naval Statute* of 1720

The single most important Russian text codifying the great nautical turn under Peter I—more narrowly, the Petrine naval revolution—is the *Naval Statute (Ustav morskoi)*[53] first published at St. Petersburg in 1720. Its history offers further indications of Peter's motives and methods in launching the great turn, to be sure, but now we will pay special attention to its more purely verbal aspect.

Admiral Veselago, in what remains the foremost scholarly work on the creation of the Russian navy, sought a precedent in earlier Russian history for Peter's codification of his creation, finding it in a document redundantly entitled *Artykul'nyia stat'i*, which in its original Dutch form was brought in 1668 to the Ambassadorial Office or Chancery (*Posol'skii prikaz*) in Moscow by Captain David Butler: this is the same Butler, a Dutchman of English descent, referred to by Peter in his draft preface to the *Statute*, when recalling his father's ill-fated attempt to create with Dutch help a flotilla to secure the valuable Volga-Caspian trade route. The thirty-four "articles" in question, outlining the duties of a ship's captain in both war and peace, were translated into Russian and then, following the destruction of the Caspian flotilla (1670), were "forgotten to this day [1875]," as Veselago says, making them a precedent for Peter's naval legislation, where they are never mentioned, only in a rather abstract sense.[54] Peter's codification began in fact with a set of fifteen articles (*stat'i*) specifying navigational directions and signals together with battle instructions prepared for the galley fleet on its descent to Azov in 1696, their standard European character evident in the punishments prescribed for various forms of dereliction of duty, ranging from money fines to death by execution.[55] Obviously an expedient, these articles were superceded by a statute of some sixty-three regulations drawn up on the basis of Dutch and Danish models by the newly appointed vice admiral, Cornelius Cruys, in 1698. Here too duties and punishments were laid down for everybody serving on board ship, the latter including fines for missing daily prayers as well as a wide array of other sanctions drawn from the traditions of maritime Europe and previously unknown in Russian, or Muscovite, legislation.[56] The Cruys statute was far from complete and in subsequent years had to be supplemented by various measures issued by Cruys himself or by the head of the Admiralty Chancery (F. M. Apraksin, later A. V. Kikin). In April 1710 an "Instruction with military articles for the Russian navy *[Instruktsiia i artikuly voennye rossiiskomu flotu]*" was printed; it consisted of Cruys's sixty-three regulations of 1698 (never before printed) now more fully defined and with their penalties strengthened.[57] But these too, as the navy grew and new questions arose, had to be supplemented by various royal decrees regulating, for example, formal naval "salutes *[o saliutakh]*" at sea (April 1714) or the "maintenance of discipline *[distsipliny]* on board ship" (February 1715).[58] A comprehensive naval or admiralty code, one commensurate with Peter's by now vaulting naval ambitions and booming shipbuilding program, was plainly needed. Compilation of such a code was also to be expected, it might be thought, given Peter's developing "mania for written rules and regulations," a mania, Hughes proposes, that "perhaps reached its height in naval matters."[59]

Enter Konon Nikitich Zotov, a Russian who in 1707, while in England to study navigation, had actually volunteered, to Peter's grateful astonishment, to go to sea for naval training ("to serve here on ships for practice *[sluzhit' zdes' na korabliakh dlia praktiki]*").[60] He went on to study in France and to learn French, and in September 1714 was commissioned by Peter to translate the *Ordonnance* of Louis XIV regulating his "armées navales et arsenaux de marine" published at Paris in 1689, the first such regulation in history.[61] This Zotov promptly proceeded to do, his correspondence with Peter indicates, evidently completing a draft translation of the *Ordonannce* within two months.[62] In November 1715 it was printed in an edition of twenty-seven copies at St. Petersburg, literally translated as the *Ustav o voiskakh morskikh, i o ikh arsenalakh* and containing Russian versions of the original *Ordonannce* and related legislation of Louis XIV together with a glossary explaining various technical terms: the same or other terms are also explained in brackets in the text, in glosses in the margins, or at the end of an article in smaller type.[63] Russian translations of the roughly equivalent documents from Holland and Denmark appeared at this time, too: that of the Dutch statute, issued by William of Orange, was printed at Moscow in January 1714 in an edition of 107, followed by editions of unknown size later in 1714 and again in 1716; that of the Danish ordinance, issued by Frederick IV, was printed in August 1715 (20 copies), in April 1716 (49 copies), and again in July 1718 (300 copies).[64] Meanwhile in January 1715 Peter ordered Zotov to go to France in person: "Go to the sea ports [porty morskie], especially where their main fleet [flot] is," there to observe as closely as possible "everything that pertains to the fleet at sea and in port, find books, also what's not in books, but done by custom"; and all this, too, was to be translated as far as possible into the "Slavonic language in our style [na slovenskoi iazyk nashim shtilem]," the latter a typical Petrine injunction, as we'll have further occasion to see, to write in a plain Russian prose. Here Peter also instructed Zotov to sort his findings into two categories: "one about the admiralty [admiraliteistve], the other about the fleet"; and under the former, to record what he discovered "about workers in the arsenal [arsenale] and their duties, about all the materiel [o matrialakh vsiakikh], about the artillery and [ships'] proportions [artilerii i preportsii], and the rigging [takalazhu], everything"; and similarly, about the "whole establishment of the fleet [ves anshtalt o flote], when it goes out, about grades, commands [komandakh], ranks [rangakh], duties, exercises [ekzertsii], rules in court and fines [shtrofakh]—everything that pertains to both of these, whatever it's called, describe it all."[65] Not long after this Peter informed his roving ambassador in Europe, Prince B. I. Kurakin, that "we are now gathering military marine rules and admiralty *anshtalt* from all the [European] dominions, whatever fleets they have, and already the Danish and French and Dutch are translated. We need the English, take the trouble to send [it] quickly";[66] this amid a flurry of such orders to Kurakin and others in pursuit of Peter's ambition to reorganize his entire governmental structure along contemporary European lines (Chap. 4).

In June 1715 Kurakin advised Peter from London that a senior English naval officer, George Paddon, was willing to enter Russian service as rear admiral of the Baltic fleet, a post Peter had been looking to fill. He and Paddon finally met in Holland in the spring of 1717, when Peter was again on an extended European tour. Civil Admiral Apraksin in St. Petersburg was soon told that the English officer seemed to be a "good man, of little talk and much experience, knows Dutch [like Peter himself] and not too old," and a contract was signed.[67] Paddon joined the Baltic fleet at Reval in May 1717 and put it through maneuvers until autumn, when he ordered it to sail to its base at Kronshlot (founded 1703, renamed Kronstadt in 1723) for the winter. It was at this point apparently that Peter assigned him charge of drawing up the desired naval code, his admiration for England in all things maritime having long since been formed.[68] Indeed Paddon's arrival in Russia was part of that "invasion of English naval officers"[69] documented earlier by Cross and to which Admiral Veselago attributes the concurrent drive to codify (*ukazoniat'*: legalize) all aspects of Peter's naval program.[70]

At any event, in October 1717 Peter directed Apraksin to assign "to Rear Admiral Paddon *[shautbeinakhtu Paddanu]* . . . Russian officers *[ofitserof]* who know English," so as to assist him in translating the "whole complete *anshtalt*, both of the fleet and of the English magazines *[magazeinof].*" Here Peter also indicated that the equivalent Dutch documents had been assigned to Vice Admiral Cruys for translation and the Danish to Prince Michael (M.) Golitsyn (another veteran of naval training abroad); that the translation of more French sources was under way; and that he was now planning to found a "school for naval cadets *[shkola gardemarinof]*"—an institution we'll consider in the last section of this chapter. Also to be found among Apraksin's Admiralty papers dating to late 1717 are Swedish ordinances relating to naval and navigational matters together with their Russian translations, these including the statute and personnel register of the Swedish Admiralty College (in German), and the original Dutch and a Russian translation of the statute of the Admiralty College in Amsterdam—where Cruys had been a senior official when hired by Peter in 1698—along with drafts relating to various aspects of the proposed Russian admiralty college. The latter include a draft "Instruction to our equipage masters, commanders managing naval artillery and under-equipage masters living at the magazines on the wharves *[Instrukstiia nashim ekipazhmeisteram, kamendoram vedaiushchim morskuiu artilleriiu i unter"-ekipazhmeisteram, obretaiushchimsia pri magazeinakh v verfakh],*" and a draft "Instruction to the counselors of the [proposed] Admiralty College *[sovetnikam Admiralteistv-kollegii]*" compiled by Cruys.[71]

Admiral Paddon died suddenly in January 1719, but not before leaving his mark on the codification process. Thus in April 1718 we find Peter instructing his collaborators to

make two books: in the first, when the fleet is ready, what pertains to the people [crew], artillery, ammunition *[amunitsii]* and so on, according to the ranks of each rank *[po rangam kazhdago rangu]* on a ship; also an instruction, so the officers and others know their duties, also an Article of War *[Artikul Voinskii].* In the second, how to maintain the fleet in the harbor *[v gavane]* and at the wharves with the higher and lower workers and their duties, also the magazines and so on. Extract these [items]

from the English, French, Danish, Swedish, and Dutch statutes and bring
them together on each matter, beginning with the English, that is, in
both books, when the first point [punkt] of the English [statute] is
brought up on some matter, then bring up the same points from all the
aforesaid statutes . . . then another English point and the same from the
others; and so do it all. But where in the others there are none like the
English, leave empty places; and where in the others there is, and in the
English not, then leave an empty [place] in the English.[72]

61

This and other documents of the same period[73] demonstrate not only the intensive labor expended by Peter and his collaborators in drafting a naval code
in 1718–19 but also the priority given on his orders to English models or precedents. It might be noted in passing that Admiral Paddon's son, George
Paddon, Jr., was commissioned a lieutenant in the Russian navy in 1720, subsequently commanded a number of ships in the Baltic fleet, and died a captain-commodore at Kronshtadt in 1747—another instance of the ongoing
English connection.

I adduce these details of the history of the *Naval Statute* of 1720 and of
the closely related *Admiralty Regulation* of 1722 (*Reglament o upravlenii Admiralteistva i verfi*, or *Regulation on the Administration of the Admiralty and
Wharves*) in order to stress the comprehensive care Peter took—and his hand
is everywhere in the documents—to codify or regularize, to legitimize, his
many naval or more broadly marine innovations going back to the 1680s.
Here we see him and a close band of collaborators, Russian and foreign—
F. M. Apraksin, Admiral Cruys, K. N. Zotov, Kurakin, Paddon, M. M.
Golitsyn, among others—working with an array of admiralty and naval documents specially gathered from the four corners of the Baltic to produce
equivalent legislation for the fast-growing Russian fleet and its supporting administration and shipyards. We notice as well the accumulation in Russian of
an ever growing vocabulary of appropriated terms signifying all the new nautical objects, titles, procedures, and forms. The process culminated initially in
the promulgation of Peter's decree of January 13, 1720, announcing the forth-
coming *Statute* "selected out of five marine regulations, to which a fair part
was added as needed, and all done and completed through our own labor";
and here again he provided another stark revelation of motive: "this business
[maintenance of a navy] is perforce necessary for a state (as in the saying, any
potentate [potentent] who has only land forces has but one arm, but he who
has a navy, has both arms)," an assertion that would be amplified in the preface to the *Statute* itself.[74] This decree was followed by the first printing of the

Statute at the St. Petersburg Press *(Tipografiia)* on April 13, 1720: *Kniga ustav morskoi, o vsem chto kasaetsia dobromu upravleniiu, v bytnosti flota na more (The Book of the Naval Statute, on all that relates to the good management of the fleet, while being at sea).*[75] The *Regulation* governing the new Admiralty College and its staff, workers, and subordinate offices was first printed, also at the St. Petersburg Press, some two years later, on April 5, 1722.[76] It will be dealt with in Chapter 4, the better to see its place in what I describe there as Peter's bureaucratic revolution, although his memo to Cruys of January 18, 1720, urging him to get on with the job of compiling it,[77] may be registered here.

The *Ustav morskoi,* as first printed in April 1720 (pressrun unknown), is a large book of some 450 quarto pages comprising (1) a "Preface to the Benevolent Reader" (nine pages); (2) Peter's decree of January 13, 1720, announcing its publication; (3) a one-page "Regulation done by ratings *[rangam]* of ships, how many of which ranks *[chinov]* of people should be on a ship of each rate," from captain *(kapitan)* on down; (4) the *Statute* proper, in five books subdivided into parts and chapters (162 pages); (5) a long section (pages 163–392) of "Templates *[Forma tabeli]*" for entering by month the incoming, outgoing, and remaining supplies on board ship both current and in reserve under the care of secretaries *(sekretarskikh)*, gunners *(konstapelskikh:* cf. Dutch *konstabel)*, commissars *(komisarskikh)*, clergy, medics, skippers *(shkhiporskikh)*, helmsmen/naviagtors *(shtiurmanskikh)*, and others; (6) another set of forms for records to be kept "by the captain or whomever will command *[budet' komandovat']* the ship, as also the secretaries and commissars" (pages 394–402); (7) a section of "signals *[signaly]*" to be displayed when weighing or dropping anchor, in the event of a storm, and so on, with a concluding note to "galley commanders *[komandiram galernym]*" (pages 403–432); and (8) a "Register *[Reestr]*" or table of contents for the whole of the *Statute,* by chapter and "articles *[artikulam]*." A second edition of the *Statute* was printed at St. Petersburg on June 28, 1720, with minor variants, intended or not; and a third, printed in parallel columns in Russian and Dutch—the second language of the Baltic fleet as well as the lingua franca of the Baltic world—on October 12, 1720, in a pressrun of 600.[78] On November 5, 1720, again at St. Petersburg, a much shorter *Extract from the Naval Statute* was printed (pressrun again not known) pertaining to the duties, conduct, and discipline of "underofficers *[unter-ofitserof]*" and seamen, which extract, the reverse of the title-page states, the "captain must order read to all persons who take ship, as the *Statute* prescribes. But those duties that pertain not to many, but to one or several persons, such as the skipper *[shkipor]*, carpenter, and such others, these duties the captain is obliged to write down and, certified by his own hand, to give to each." Another copy of the *Extract* contains an additional ten-page list of "rewards" taken from the full *Statute,* these "so that everybody serving in the fleet should know, and be assured of, what service will be rewarded."[79]

But this was far from the end of it. Subsequent editions of the *Naval Statute* appeared in 1722 (somewhat revised and expanded), 1723, 1724 (in Russian and Dutch, edition of 146), 1746 (Russian and Dutch), 1763, 1771 (Russian and Dutch), 1778, 1780, 1785 (in Russian and Dutch as well as Russian-only editions), 1791, and 1795.[80] In 1797 it was temporarily superceded by a statute issued by Emperor Paul; published again in 1804 with Paul's statute as a supplement, it was finally displaced by the *Morskoi ustav* of 1853, which would guide the navy in the new age of steam.[81] The "classic" edition of Peter's *Naval Statute* among all these is the sixth, printed in Russian and Dutch at the St. Petersburg Press in 1724, which incorporates the revisions and expansions of the fourth (1722) edition and which is replicated in turn in the Russian and Dutch or Russian-only editions of 1746, 1763, 1771, and 1785, as well as in the Moscow 1993 facsimile edition of the St. Petersburg 1763 edition; it is also the text (Russian only) included in the *Complete Collection of the Laws of the Russian Empire* published in 1830.[82] Our further discussion of the *Statute* is based on copies of the 1746 (Russian and Dutch) and 1763 (Russian only) editions, the former at the Library of the Academy of Sciences in St. Petersburg, the latter in the 1993 facsimile edition. Close comparison of the Russian text of the two editions revealed no significant differences, so page and other references will be to the more accessible 1763/1993 facsimile edition,[83] excerpts from which are reproduced in Appendix I (no. 32).

We begin with the *Statute*'s frontispiece, which was discussed in my volume on imagery in connection with the career of its main executor, the Dutch graphic artist Pieter Picart (also Pickaerdt or Pikart), who worked as a book illustrator in Russia—in Moscow and then St. Petersburg—from 1702 until his death in 1737.[84] Picart was a major figure in Peter's graphic revolution; the frontispiece was designed by C. B. Rastrelli, the sculptor and architect brought from Paris to St. Petersburg on Peter's invitation in 1716 (and father of the hugely famous architect B. F. Rastrelli); and in etching Rastrelli's design Picart was assisted very probably by his ablest Russian pupil, Aleksei Zubov— all details that suggest the importance Peter assigned to the *Naval Statute*. The central panel of the frontispiece depicts a boy clutching the rudder of a small sailboat while guided by a winged figure of Time, the sailboat propelled on the open sea by a brisk wind and overseen by a symbolic image of Providence—a triangle with Hebrew inscription emitting bright rays—as two fully rigged sailing ships appear on the distant horizon. Assorted nautical and military symbols from the standard European repertory surround this central panel along with representations of the tsar's two-headed eagle, and below it are inscribed six lines of verse. It has been suggested reasonably enough that the verse was written by Peter himself, since a sheet was found among his papers on which these lines are written in his own hand[85] (of course, he could simply have copied the lines; and, if he did compose them, he might well have received poetic advice from the learned Feofan Prokopovich, to whom we turn shortly). In any case, the message of the verse is a typically austere Petrine meditation on the work of Divine Providence, whose will, however unexpected, is revealed to us in time and executed only by his grace, "Since his thoughts and ways are as distant from us / As the earth is from the heavens." Taken in conjunction with the image just described, the verse thus proposes that Peter had been enacting, from his boyhood essays in sailing to the publication of this magisterial *Naval Statute,* a divinely ordained mission to create the Russian navy. A similar sense of mission informs Peter's draft preface to the *Statute,* which was extensively quoted above. Nor can we forget that the top-rate warship that he personally designed and built at Voronezh in 1699–1700, also as mentioned above, was named by him the *Predestination (Predestinatsiia).*

Peter's draft preface to the *Naval Statute* was incorporated in the printed version, which is more than twice the draft's length and was the work, it is generally agreed, on both circumstantial and stylistic grounds, of Feofan Prokopovich, Peter's closest collaborator in ecclesiastical affairs and his leading publicist. Prokopovich not only embedded Peter's draft in flowery expansions and outright additions but also edited the tsar on stylistic, grammatical, factual, and diplomatic, or tactful, grounds. For instance, Peter's opening sentence (which I omitted earlier) reads: "Though everyone knows about the Russian monarchy *[monarkhii Rossiiskoi]* and its beginnings, and that before [our] ancestor Prince Vladimir we have no true history *[pravdivoi istorii]*; still, leaving that to the historians *[istorikam]*, we turn to the matter at hand." This brief remark Prokopovich expands into several paragraphs praising Peter for having at last provided Russia with a navy while assuring the gentle reader that in ancient times, well before Prince Vladimir ruled (late tenth century), Russia under Prince Rurik did have a fine fleet "on the Pontus Euxinus *[na ponte evksine]* or Black Sea"; but it was "difficult to find out about it because foreign historians *[istoriki]* did not write with diligent curiosity about our people and we ourselves not only had no historians but also no writing." Prokopovich repairs to the old chronicles both Slavic and Western to fill in the gaps, only to admit that in Prince Igor's attack on Constantinople (ca. 941) as recorded therein the "ancient Russian fleet *[flot]* was not such as we speak of here, not of great ships composed but of little boats, and won no spoils for the State, nor left any glory to succeeding ages, but rather [the memory of] a crude and ill-considered boldness and audacity." And so, alluding to Peter's remark about one- and two-armed potentates in his decree (cited above) announcing the *Statute,* Prokopovich observes that "our Russia then had only one arm." He continues: "What was to be done about this? A good occasion *[okaziia]* arose for the reception of ship architecture *[arkhitektury korabel'noi]* and instruction in navigation *[navigatsii]*" when the Russian people were christianized under Prince Vladimir (ca. 988); but that prince, saint though he was, instructed the people in theology, not in policy (*v politike:* in politics); and while leading Russia from the darkness of unbelief into knowledge of the truth, to his eternal praise, he weakened the Russian monarchy by dividing his realm among his twelve sons.[86] It is only at this point, three pages into the preface, that Prokopovich returns to Peter's draft. Still, given the close attention Peter paid to his *Naval Statute* both before and after its publication, he must not have objected to Prokopovich's editing, and the result is a fine example of the still rather churchly rhetoric employed on state occasions by his regime's leading apologist.

In his draft preface Peter had moved quickly from Russia's supposed division after Vladimir's reign and later reunion under Ivan IV (1547–1584) to the reign of his own father, Tsar Aleksei (1645–1676). But in the printed version Prokopovich, again, is more expansive as well as didactic:

> We recall all this to thee most gentle reader in testimony of how long the Russian State, its boundaries not lying near a single sea, was unable for the causes mentioned either to trade with or build a single fleet. And this was well known by foreign peoples, who when they observed Russia torn asunder and impotent, feared not naval attacks from her. But when they saw a single mighty power in the reign of Ioann Vasil'evich [Ivan IV], they declared their fear by the prohibition issued at the Lubek congress, whereby none among them could go into our land to teach ship matters and sea navigation *[dela korabel'nago i morskago plavaniia].*

This was an adroit reference to the long Livonian War (1558–1583) waged by the Muscovite tsardom under Ivan IV against a shifting coalition of enemies to the west, including the city-state of Lübeck, for expanded access to the Baltic. The war had ended badly for Russia, which had been obliged to cede terri-

65

tory to Sweden, whose pursuit from about 1563 of a Baltic dominion had frustrated Russian ambitions in the area until Peter's naval victories, won after heroic efforts against great odds, had secured for Russia a Baltic coastline.

Prokopovich catches up with Peter's draft preface to the *Naval Statute* (still in its first paragraph) on page five of the printed version, when the subject is the failed attempt by Peter's father to create a Volga-Caspian flotilla, about which Peter himself had been characteristically terse, attributing the failure to the "incomprehensible judgments of the High Ruler" while seeing in it the "beginning, as from seeds, of the present marine business." Prokopovich expands these few lines into three paragraphs, and refines in passing Peter's blunt prose: for example, his "when [it was] intended to do shipsailing on the Caspian Sea" becomes the more elegant "when he [Tsar Aleksei] conceived the intention to make ships and navigate on the Caspian Sea [*kogda namereno delat' korableplavanie na Kaspiiskom more* becomes *kogda vospriial on namerenie delat' korabli i navigatsiiu na Kaspiiskom more*]." Prokopovich then invites the reader to see in the subsequent destruction of Aleksei's flotilla by brigands and the murder or dispersal of its crew the handiwork of God,

> as in the erection of the first temple of the Lord in Jerusalem. David with great ardor intended to erect this Church, but God denied this to him and left it to his son, Solomon. So, with us, the inscrutable counsel of God did not permit fulfillment of the intention to begin shipbuilding under Tsar Aleksei, but rather his son HIS MAJESTY PETER the FIRST was fated to be the AUTHOR [AVTOROM] of this business.

Introducing Peter's account of his boyhood discovery of the "English boat" at Izmailovo, Prokopovich exclaims:

> We come now to the essential felicity of our story and mark, reader, how by a strange way and divine supervision this matter was begun and brought to complete success. Our currently reigning and Most-Merciful Monarch, at the beginning of his reign, still in his early years, showing a great soul and how worthy he was to be Sovereign, as proof also of his natural attraction to praiseworthy matters and inflexible passion for both art and action, conceived the intention to begin this great business of a sea fleet [*flota morskago*] not from observing wondrous arsenals [*arsenalov*] and fleets, but from a matter so small that nobody would have expected it, as follows.

And so to Peter's story of his induction into the "marine business," from his discovery of the boat at Izmailovo to his return from England with the shipwrights Deane and Nye, a story now told entirely in the third person—"His Majesty" did this, "His Majesty" did that—and with regular interventions from his editor: "With us hitherto the ship business was so strange, that we had scarcely heard of it"; "Then did the seed of Tsar Aleksei Mikhailovich spring to life"; "Then did His Mother of eternal memory, the Most August Russian Tsaritsa, passionately solicitous of the Filial health . . ."; and "Thus the *botik* [boat discovered at Izmailovo] served him not only as a childhood pastime, but became the cause of his building a navy, as we now see with wonder."[87]

67

In the concluding paragraphs of the preface to the *Naval Statute* Prokopovich dwells on Peter's success in creating a navy with supporting shipyards, and finally gets to the *Statute* itself:

> And since a sea fleet for success in its campaigns and actions requires a Regulation *[Reglament]*, or statute *[ustav]*, without which both winds and pilots *[kormchii]* are in vain, therefore the most wise MONARCH applied his labor to this matter, and either from his own judgment, or from foreign regulations, gathered the best rules *[reguly]* in this book [the *Statute*]. And so he has breathed as it were a living soul into his material creation [the navy], whence we see with God's help fine deeds on the whole Baltic Sea, where he has carried off many enemy ships, captured a Swedish Rear Admiral *[Shautbeinakhta]* with unwonted good fortune together with his Squadron *[Eshkvadroiu]*, and conquered the Grand Principality of Finland. . . . See now, benevolent reader, what mercy the compassionate God has shown us, and how wondrous for us his Providence has been.[88]

It is also notable that Prokopovich's language, here as throughout the preface, mixes Slavonicisms (*kormchii* for "pilots," not the new *lotsmany; vsue* = in vain; *premudreishii* = most-wise; *ovo . . . ovo* = either . . . or; *aki by* = as if; *Zri* = See, Behold) with various neologisms (*flot, Reglament, Monarkh, reguly* [from Latin *regula*]; *Shautbeinakht, Eshkvadra*) and plain Russian prose, however rhetorical, as yet, his syntax remains.

Indeed the Russo-Slavonic or, at other times, Slavonic-Russian character of the preface to the *Naval Statute* of 1720 is typical, in its varying degrees of hybridity, of the learned discourse of the Petrine period, as we shall repeatedly see. Thus Prokopovich's closely related "Sermon in Praise of the Russian Fleet and of the Victory Obtained by the Russian Galleys over the Swedish Ships on July 27" (*Slovo pokhvalnoe o flote rossiiskom, i o pobede galerami rossiiskimi nad korabliami shvedskimi Iulia kz [27] dnia, poluchennoi*), which he preached in Peter's presence in St. Petersburg on September 8, 1720.[89] The victory in question, referred to earlier in this chapter, was that of the Russian galley fleet under M. M. Golitsyn over a Swedish squadron off Grengham in the Åland Islands on July 27, 1720, which resulted in the capture of four Swedish frigates and helped compel the Swedish government to negotiate an end to the long Northern War. The triumphal themes elaborated by Prokopovich in the sermon are basically those already adduced, with Peter's help, in their preface to the *Naval Statute*, which the sermon at one point cites. The victory, here joyfully recounted, proved yet again the vital importance to Russia of having a full naval establishment; the latter had been achieved, to the world's astonishment, under Peter's brilliant direction, wherefore the "little boat [*botik*]" discovered by him at Izmailovo truly was "to the navy what the seed is to the tree"; indeed, "from this seed grew a great, wondrous, winged, armored forest of trees [*drevesa*, another Slavonicism]"—all as had been divinely ordained. The sermon also alludes to Classical Roman poets, quotes from the Bible, cites incidents from both ancient and more recent history (the Roman Marc Antony's victory over the "Germans," the English Queen Elizabeth's victory over the Spanish), and again makes free with new nautical terms as well as other (in context) neologisms: *galera, fregaty, ammunitsia, reglament, arkhitektura, peregrinatsiia, istorik, istoriia, diktatory, navigatsiia, okean, kommunikatsiia, monarkh, monarkhiia, fabula, traktament, konfuziia, piraty* ("that is, sea robbers [*morskie razboiniki*]"), *moneta, elementy, fort[r]ets, providentsia, aktsiia,* and, above all, *flot* and *viktoriia*—the last even though the Russian (and common Slavic) *pobeda* is used in the sermon's title and often, in noun, adjective, or verb form, in its text (*viktoriia*, we might note here, is one of the many Petrine neologisms that did not become standard Russian).[90] Again, the combination of mainly Latin-derived neologisms, stock Slavonicisms, and plain Russian is typical of Petrine learned discourse and may be contrasted in these respects with learned texts dating to twenty or thirty years before, with their much higher proportion of Slavonic terms, fewer such loanwords, and smaller component of plain Russian (cf. Appendix I, no. 6; also no. 14). Even so, for later generations of Russian readers—later than, say, the mid-eighteenth century—this sermon of Prokopovich as published then, in 1720, would have *looked* archaic, printed as it was in traditional

Cyrillic type complete with superscripts, contractions, extra—or "old"—letters, and Slavonic (rather than Arabic or Roman) numerals.

By contrast, the *Naval Statute* of 1720 was printed in Peter's new civil type, whose simplified, Latinized fonts replicated a simplified, Latinized alphabet that was very close to what would become the modern Russian standard—a point to be developed in Chapter 6. Equally, to move from Prokopovich's preface to the text of the *Statute* itself is to move from the religiously learned, more or less Slavonic discourse of the later seventeenth century Ruthenian-Muscovite elite to the technical, thoroughly secular, and self-consciously Russian discourse of the later Petrine era, a discourse heavily indebted, as such, to various verbal cultures of contemporary western and northern Europe. The contrast is striking—and is clear right from the opening lines of the *Statute,* where it is explained that

69

> the word *flot* is French. By this word is understood many aquatic vessels going together, or standing, both military and merchant. A military fleet, if *[ashche]* many ships, is divided into three main or general Squadrons *[general'nyia Eshkvadry]*; the first the *Kordebataliia* [main fleet; cf. French *corps de bataille*], the second the *Avangard,* the third the *Arirgard,* and these again *[paki]* are divided, each into three special divisions *[partikuliarnye divizii],* as follows. The *Kordebataliia* of the white flag *[flaga],* the *Avangard* of the white flag, the *Arirgard* of the white flag [etc., each squadron comprised again of a division "of the blue flag" and then "of the red flag"]. But if *[ezheli]* there is a smaller number of ships, then the Squadron is smaller.[91]

Three conjunctions here—*ashche, paki, ezheli*—are Slavonic but the bulk of the paragraph explains technical neologisms in a plain Russian style. Likewise the rest of this introductory section of the *Statute,* as for example: "The commanders *[komandiry]* in the fleet are the following. *General Admiral. Admiral* of the blue *Flag. Admiral* of the red *Flag. Vitse Admiral.* Rear Admiral [*Shautbeinakht,* from Dutch *Schout-bij-nacht*]. Captains-Commodore *[Kapitany komandory],*" whose positions in the fleet are then specified, as in "the General Admiral is over the whole fleet and particularly the *Kordebataliia,*" an admiral or vice admiral commands the *Avangard,* a rear admiral commands the *Arirgard,* and so on.[92]

And on. Each of the *Statute's* five books, subdivided into chapters subdivided into articles *(artikuly),* specifies the duties and responsibilities of both senior and junior naval officers, with the longest of the chapters by far devoted, not surprisingly, to those of ships' captains (ninety-five articles). Interspersed with these are chapters on flags, pennants *(vympely)*, and lamps, and the various signals *(signaly)* and formal salutes *(saliuty)* to be made with them; on the maintenance of "good order on ships" and the proper distribution of provisions *(proviant)*; on the rewards to be won for exceptional services rendered, such as capturing or burning an enemy ship, and the penalties to be incurred for specified transgressions; and on pay scales and the division of spoils or booty, all laid out in a straightforward, orderly fashion. To these chapters is appended an almost equally long section of templates or model forms *(Forma tabeli)* on which ships' officers were to record execution of their duties on a daily or monthly basis, lists of signals to accompany movements of anchor and sails, and more forms to be used by the appropriate officers to keep track of provisions and supplies. A "Register [*Reestr,* or Index] to the Articles of the Naval Statute," chapter by chapter, with the appropriate page numbers, comes last, providing a comprehensive and ready guide for the busy seaman. The *Statute* also pauses periodically to provide an "explanation *[tolkovanie]*" of this or that article or term.

The scope and detail of the *Naval Statute* of 1720 surely rank it with those of the contemporary maritime powers on which it freely drew, as Peter had clearly intended. As an operational code, moreover, it appears to have stood the test of time, remaining the basic charter of the Imperial Russian navy until advances in technology rendered it partly and then, by the middle of the nineteenth century, wholly obsolete. But our focus here is primarily on the *Statute* as a major text in the Petrine revolution in Russian verbal culture. And in this perspective its longevity alone surely attests to the durability and "modernity" of its prose, as intelligible to Admiral Veselago in 1875 as to the authors of the commemorative *Three Centuries of the Russian Navy* published for general readers in 1993, all of whom replicate its technical language without pause or explanation:[93] *flot, eskadra, flag, vympel, avangard, ar'ergard, admiral, gospital', ekipazh, komandovat', signal, komplektovat', ofitser, artilleriia, flagman, shtat, admiralteistvo, interes (gosudartsva), rang, komandir, abordazh, distsiplina, shtab, kommisar, galera, proviziia, tablitsa, forma, artikul,* and *sistema* are among the Petrine nautical and other neologisms freely employed by them. Indeed it is the huge lexical influx that the text of the *Naval Statute* represents that is most striking now: the appearance within it of hundreds of terms for which no words in Church Slavonic or chancery or business Russian existed before Peter's time—or came readily, to say the least, to his or his collaborators' minds. In short, the numerous words of nautical or more narrowly naval significance listed in Appendix II, most of which occur in the *Statute,* attest to the enduring impact of this influx, just as the excerpts from its text reproduced in Appendix I (no. 32) illustrate, better than could any translation, the modernity of its prose.

We might close this discussion, and reinforce its basic points, by highlighting a selection of new terms that, like *shautbeinakht* or *kordebataliia,* are *not* included in Appendix II as too technical, subsequently obsolete, or enduringly foreign; and then sample the *Statute's* more purely pedagogical passages, especially its recurring "explanations." Here, with their probable foreign source or sources, are some of those now largely or wholly forgotten neologisms whose appearance in the *Naval Statute* of 1720 and subsequent editions also bears witness to the verbal impact—however short-term, or highly technical—of the Petrine naval revolution:

anshef komanduiushchii = commander-in-chief, commanding officer, adapted from French *commander* = to command plus *en chef*

konduit, as in *dobryi konduit* = (good) conduct, from French *conduite*

trinket = foremast (galley), from Italian *trinchetto*[94]

andrivel' = buntline (galley), from Italian *andrivela*[95]

markitanskii = sutling, victualing (adjective), from Dutch *marketentser* = sutler, victualer and/or German *Marketender* = sutler

reid, as in *na reide* = ride, road/roadstead, place of anchorage, from English *ride*

ekipirovanie = fitting out, equipping, from German *equipieren*

gals = tack (of a sail), from Dutch *hals*

sanzhirovat' = to change, from German *changieren*[96]

kleiding = covering (for cable, rope), from German *Kleidung*[97]

galafdek = halfdeck, from Dutch *halfdek;*[98] also *fordek* = foredeck, from Dutch *voordek* and/or English *foredeck;* and *operdek* = upperdeck, from Dutch *opperdek* and/or English *upperdeck*

koler = color, as of a flag or pennant, from English *color* and/or Dutch *kleur* and/or French *couleur*

flagshtok = flagstaff, from Dutch *vlagstok;* also *ankar-shtok* = anchor stock, from Dutch *ankerstok*

giuis = jack, jack-flag, from Dutch *geus*

mars, as in *v marse* = top, at/on the top, from Dutch *mars*

formars = foretop, from Dutch *voormars*

mat = mate, from Dutch *maat/mat*[99]

gazardovat' = to hazard, as in a captain is "not to hazard his ship in a great wind," from Dutch *hazard* and/or French *hasard, hasarder*

kornet = broad pennant (galley), from Italian *cornetta*[100]

vant/a = shroud, net, rigging, from Dutch *want*

eksekutsiia = execution, death penalty, from Dutch *executie* (Latin *exsecutio*)

pretekst = pretext, from English *pretext*

rain/a = yard, from Dutch *ra* and/or German *Rahe*

triuim/intriuim = hold (of a ship), from Dutch *in/te ruim*

gal'iun = ship's head (toilet), from Italian *galleone*[101]

boteler/botoler/butelir = butler, from Dutch/English *butler*

sarvaer = surveyor, from English *surveyor*

kupor = cooper, from English *cooper* and/or Dutch *kuiper*

fordevint = before the wind, from Dutch *voor de wint*

luf = get to windward of, from Dutch *loef*

lufvards = to windward, from Dutch *loefwaarts*

leivart/leivards = leeward, from English *leeward* and/or Dutch *lijwaarts*

zeil' = sail, from Dutch *zeil*

marzeil'/marsel' = topsail, from Dutch *marszeil*

and so forth, through the names of the many sails of a contemporary ship of the line; those of the varied naval stores, including medicines, to be brought on board for provisioning and repairs; the names of the maneuvers to be enacted in various situations at sea, in port or harbor, or at anchorage; those of the numerous signals to be displayed by flag or lantern; and those of all the members of the *ekipazh,* or crew: a veritable catalog of the greater Baltic naval terminology of the time, now available entirely in Russian—in Russian letters at least, often in Russian phonetic adaptations as well. Most of the words just listed were, to repeat, sooner or later dropped from use as foreign, redundant, or obsolete (for example, *rain/a, sarvaer, kleiding, gazardovat'*) or in favor of a Russian (or Slavonic) word or calque (*parus* for "sail", *predlog* for "pretext," *podvetrenyi* for "leeward"), while others were retained in some, usually narrow technical sense (*trium* = hold of a ship; *vanty* = shrouds; *trinket* = galley foremast; *gal'iun* = ship's head). Still, it should be stressed that a very large number of the new nautical terms did permanently enter Russian, a large sample of which is available in Appendix II.

As for the many explicitly explanatory passages of Peter's *Naval Statute,* we might consider a few of them to show how, in this way too, the naval culture of the contemporary Baltic world was transferred to Russia. Thirty-eight of these "Explanations *[Tolkovaniia]*" are implanted in the body of the *Statute,* as in Article 90 of the chapter pertaining to the duties of a ship's captain.[102] This article provides that in the event of a battle at sea the captain must not only "courageously" attack the enemy himself but must also, by both word and gesture, inspire his men "to the utmost degree" and never surrender his ship under pain of "loss of life and honor." The "explanation" of these provisions appears then in smaller type: "If nonetheless the following urgencies arise, then after signature by the council *[konsilium]* of all senior and junior officers *[vsekh ober i under ofitserof],* for the safety of the men, the ship can be given up: 1. If a hole be such that the pumps *[pumpy]* cannot cope; 2. If the powder and munitions *[ammunitsiia]* have run out . . . ; 3. If in both of these urgencies there are no shallows nearby, where the ship might escape by running aground." Standard naval procedures of the time, incorporating essential concepts, values, and techniques that had developed over the centuries in maritime Europe, were now being legislated for captains of the Russian navy. Similarly most of the other "explanations" printed in the *Statute,* most of which refer to articles of the lengthy Book Five "on penalties *[o shtrafakh],*" where they spell out in greater detail than do the articles themselves who is to be punished for what.[103] For example, the "safeguard *[salvogvardiia]*" attached to certain persons and things that must not be violated under pain of death consists, it is explained, either of one or more soldiers or marines *(mariny)* or simply of a piece of paper specifying that such and such is under the sovereign's protection; later it is stipulated that the prohibition against armed attack on a senior officer is to be considered absolute, meaning with no exceptions, as variously specified in its attached "explanation"; or again, whoever intentionally disobeyed an order or incited others to do so, "under whatever *pretekst,*" was to be executed—the term "pretext *[pretekst, to est' prichina]*" defined as not fulfilling one's duty because "pay was not received, or there were shortages in the provisions, and such like; these causes cannot excuse [a seaman], who must carry out all his current duties and complain in his free time." Another such "explanation" elaborates on the prohibition against sounding the alarm on board ship after dark, on pain of loss of life if near an enemy and banishment to the galleys if not; others, on the need severely to penalize murder, desertion, rape of a woman (the degrees thereof spelled out in detail but in every case to be punished by death or banishment to the galleys), abandoning one's post in battle, concealing a prisoner or vital information, communicating with the enemy, or unintentional killing. Such lesser infractions as losing one's uniform or weapon, complaining publicly on board ship about one's wages, brawling (as distinct from fighting in self-defense) or "heartily abusing another with words," committing libel in writing or print (*paskvil'*, defined at length), are more or less fully explained as well. These "explanations," we cannot help noticing, frequently go beyond strictly naval matters and seek to inculcate certain broader values, legal and especially moral, of the contemporary European world.

The moralizing tendency on display here is evident in fact throughout the *Naval Statute* of 1720, as in the chapter (Book Three, Chapter Nine) on chaplains and their duties aboard ship, which consisted "above all" in maintaining "a good Christian life, as an example to all," and *not* in performing the Orthodox rituals, which are scarcely mentioned. Indeed, all "officers and others who serve in His Majesty's fleet shall love one another truly, as a Christian must, without [regard to] differences, whether they be of religion or nationality [*very ili naroda*]."[104] Another directive reads: "Since the root of all evil is cupidity, therefore every commanding officer must guard himself against avarice and not only that, but severely restrain others from this [evil] and specifically provide against it. For many State interests are lost through this evil."[105] Captains were not only to keep a daily journal [*zhurnal*] of the ship's movements (a full-page form is provided) but also to see that all subordinate officers did so with respect to their particular duties, as in the case of the helmsman or navigator *(shtiurman)*, whose recorded celestial *observatsii* the captain was regularly to inspect along with the condition of all his "instruments used in Navigation [*instrumenty sluzhashchie k Navigatsii*]."[106]

Nor could officers or seamen reading the *Naval Statute,* or having it read to them, ever forget that they were in His Majesty's service. Article 1 of Chapter One of Book One states, for the former's edification, that "whether Admiral or other high or low officers, [all] must protect with all care and zeal the interest [*interess*] of their Sovereign and State, wherever they may be found with the command [*komandoiu*] entrusted to them, in any circumstances." Later the *Statute* declares, for the instruction of all aboard, that the greatest of all transgressions is to speak or plot evil "against the person of His Majesty." The ensuing "explanation" affirms that the latter "is an absolute monarch [*samovlastnyi monarkh*], who need answer to no one on earth about his affairs, but has the power and authority as a Christian sovereign to rule his dominions and lands by his own will and good judgment."[107] Indeed this new definition of the Russian monarch's power, as we shall have ample occasion to note, encapsulates what was at once the theoretical basis and the basic justification of the whole Petrine program.

Other Nautical Texts

Various other texts encoding Russia's nautical turn under Peter I were published at the time, among them a handbook on sailing first printed in August
1724 at the St. Petersburg Press and written by the same Konon Zotov who   75
helped draft the *Naval Statute* of 1720. A favorite of Peter since he volunteered
for training at sea in 1707, as mentioned earlier, Zotov was one of the first pupils at the new Moscow navigation school when in 1704 he was sent for further study to England and France, returning to Russia in 1712. In 1713 he was
commissioned a lieutenant in the Baltic fleet and in 1714 dispatched to Pernau
to bring home a newly purchased warship. Later that year, as also mentioned
earlier, he translated on Peter's orders the French naval ordinance of 1689, and
in January 1715, now a lieutenant-captain, he was sent to France to serve as Peter's unofficial agent in naval matters. There he appears to have involved himself in commercial and high political affairs as well, for which he was rebuked
and restricted to his original assignment, which now included supervision of
Russian marine trainees in France. On returning once more to Russia, in 1719,
he was promoted to third captain and given his own command, saw action in
the Baltic, for which he was made a second captain, and then, while working
on the *Naval Statute,* was sent to Copenhagen to gather naval intelligence. In
1721 he was named *kontroler* of the new Admiralty College, whose *Regulation*
he also helped to draft, and in 1726 he was again given command of his own
warship—one of the largest in the Baltic. He later rejoined the Admiralty College, where he served, ultimately as *general-ekipazhmeister* with the rank of
rear admiral, until his death in 1742. It was, all told, an exemplary naval career,
one of the very first, for a Russian, in history; and we shall forgo for reasons of
space details of the political intrigues in which he became enmeshed or later
assessments, based on his letters, of his character.[108]

Zotov's principal written work, excluding translations and collaborative
editions, is entitled *A Conversation between an Admiral and a Captain about
Command, or A Complete Instruction on How to Handle a Ship in All Sorts
of Circumstances (Razgovar' u admirala s kapitanom o komande, ili Polnoe
uchenie kako upravliat' karablem vo vsiakiia raznyia sluchai).*[109] The book,
forty quarto pages in length with several engraved illustrations, begins
with the author's preface "to the good reader" in which he explains, perhaps
with tongue in cheek, that he published his little book—*knizhitsa*—not as a
learned work but only to gain the thanks and "kind Approbation *[Appro-
batsii]*" of "those sons of the nobility who fervently desire to learn how to

handle a ship in all possible circumstances": Peter's difficulty in recruiting or retaining naval officers from just this class was longstanding, as Zotov surely knew.[110] He goes on to say that the publication of a handbook like his had long been needed for aspiring officers so that a ship should be run "firmly and without confusion *[bez konfuzii]*," a captain should be "not angered but pleased by them [aspiring officers] and recommend *[rekomendat']* them as prepared," and "none among them [should] fear examination *[eksaminatsii]*." In these ways, Zotov assured his readers, his manual would guide young men in the naval service in all that they needed to know in order "always to be ready to serve the fatherland." The preface is signed "Captain Konon Zotov."

The text of the manual itself opens by stating that in handling a ship there are "eight main circumstances and [corresponding] rules"; these are duly presented in numerical order together with a "supplementary clarification of the eighth rule" (text pages 1 to 18). This section is followed by an "Explanation of the preceding rules" presented under thirty-five headings (pages 19 to 40). Both sections proceed in question-and-answer format, with the admiral asking the questions *(admiralskii vopros)* and the captain replying *(kapitanskii otvet)*. Here is the first of the admiral's eight, really nine, main questions: "Mr. Captain *[Gospodin Kapitan]*, tell me if you please, what after what should properly be commanded *[komandovat']* when it is necessary to weigh anchor in good weather and go before the wind *[fordavint]*." The captain's reply outlines nine steps in the requested procedure, beginning: "1. Sailors *[matrozy]* listen quietly to the command *[komand]*. Helmsman *[Shtiurman]* set the helm *[rur]* straight and then right to the big rope [*kanat,* an old word of Greek origin, here probably the anchor sheet], so it stands [ready] to pull into the ship. Sailors turn the rope on the capstan [*kabeliaring*[111] *na shpil'*]. Put the spindles *[vinbomeny]*[112] into the capstan. Remove the stoppers *[shtopory]*[113] behind the bitts *[bitengov]*.[114] Secure the stoppers on the anchor sheet in front of the bitts. Remove the anchor sheet from the bitts. Secure the anchor sheet to the capstan rope. Turn the capstan. Stop turning the capstan. Remove the service *[sarving]*.[115] Turn the capstan again." Alongside this first step of the "complete command," in the right margin reserved for "short commands," we read: "Helmsman stand by the helm and direct the crew to engage the capstan and anchor sheet and when ready to pull up the anchor." The captain then outlines the second step in the requested procedure followed by the third, and on through the ninth step, displaying as he proceeds his firm command of the commands, so to speak, as well as a good grasp of the technical vocabulary involved, for example: "Loosen the port-side braces *[bak bort brasy]*[116] and a few of the foresail and fore-topsail ties *[gitovy foka i formarselia]*;[117] let loose the starboard *[stiurbort]*[118] foresail and fore-topsail bowline *[bulin magar-man]*[119]"; or, still later: "sailors down with the main-topsail *[grot"mars]*,"[120] "unbind the mainsail *[grot seil']*,"[121] and "let down fully the ropes of the big rail *[gordiny grot reilia]*."[122] Then again, to the sixth "admiral's question"— "When you don't want to lose much land by turning into the wind, then how does this need to be done [?]"—the captain answers smartly: "Then I execute the turn that the English call *faksgalin*,[123] that is I order [the crew] suddenly to turn the foresails against the wind with their windward braces, and to tighten as much as possible the leeward fore-topsail bowline, and to take the rear sails in hand so that they flap (and to gather up the mizzen *[bizan']* if it be un-furled), and to pull the helm hard against the wind; then you will see that your ship has turned like a man on his heel." Or again, to the admiral's eighth question—"What rule do you have for which sails are needed when, and which to add or reduce regarding the various strengths of the wind [?]"—the captain's response is ever ready: "In moderate wind go *fordivint* under the topsails *[pod marseiliami]* and add more sails as needed and slacken the fore-sail *[fok]*; and if still more is needed add the spritsail *[blindeseil]*,[124] if still more, the upper *[boven]*[125] spritsail, the fore top-gallant and the great top-gal-lant *[for* and *grot bramseil']*,[126] then the jib *[kliufok]*,[127] and all the other fore and aft sails; and if the wind be stronger. . . ." Finally, having secured some further explanation (the admiral's ninth question) of a point in the captain's reply to question eight, the admiral says: "Mr. Captain, I am most grateful for your complete clarification of this difficulty," and the section ends.

77

The rest of Captain Zotov's handbook (pages 19 to 40) provides additional explanations of the eight, or nine, "rules" laid out in the first section that we've just sampled—these explanations in response to other questions that arise in commanding a ship of the Imperial Russian navy. Once more the ad-miral poses the questions and the captain replies. Thus the admiral's first "supplementary" question: "I am grateful to you Mr. Captain for allowing me to ask in addition to everything, tell me, please, all the signs by which it is possible to know a good ship from a bad, how to discover this [while] at an-chor," elicits from the captain assurances that he is "vigilantly most ready to serve your excellency in this he deigns to ask of my limited knowledge" and then his reply, which offers nine such signs *(primety)*. The second of these signs, for example, occurs "when a ship by the swiftness of its passage shakes at the rear, which means that its proportion in construction is good *[proport-siia ego v stroenii est' dobraiu]*"; the fifth, that "a narrow rudder *[rur]* is better for a ship's movement if the ship feels [responds to] it, for a wide rudder will hold back much water when it is turned to one side; but if the ship has a full hind part, such that the water cannot come over the rudder quickly and strongly, then a wide rudder is wanted"; the seventh, that "a ship that can lie still under little or no sail, and can stand quietly at anchor, is called a healthy ship." And so the section proceeds, through the remaining thirty-four "supplementary" questions and answers, to the end of the book, the format a courteous exchange between two knowledgeable seamen.

Indeed we are impressed, for a start, by the dialogue's courtesies, which do not reflect the earlier, highly familiar and quite servile Muscovite usages but have a more elegantly formal, contemporary French ring, reminding us that Zotov had spent several years training in France and was fairly fluent in French. His straightforward syntax and the general spareness of his prose might also reflect French models, mindful again of his considerable work as a translator from French. Yet the text of his *Conversation between an Admiral and a Captain* remains most interesting to us now for the degree to which it embodies its author's assimilation of new nautical concepts, values, and techniques and his corresponding mastery of the terminology—new words only recently appropriated, old words put to new uses—in which to express them. (See Appendix I, no. 33, for an extract from Zotov's handbook.) No longer was it simply a matter of confronting a foreign text in a new field for the purpose of somehow translating it into the mother tongue, challenging as that was. Based on his own twenty years of nautical experience in France, England, Russia, and the Baltic, Zotov himself was now teaching interested compatriots the new art of sailing and how to handle a major warship. This rather amazing *cultural* transformation—in this case, from a monolingual Muscovite landlubber into a seasoned, multilingual Russian naval officer—is something that we observe repeatedly in the history of the Petrine revolution.

Zotov's was hardly the only work on marine matters printed during Peter's reign, of course. From Peter's introduction of the civil type in 1708 until his death in 1725 at least eighty titles were published in Russia on nautical or naval subjects, these including editions and reeditions, often based on translations from Dutch, French, English, or Swedish originals, of handbooks on signals (some twenty-five titles);[128] lists of ships and accounts of the fleet in action;[129] regulations and translated textbooks for students of the new naval schools;[130] officially sanctioned prayers to be recited in the navy, along with regulations for its chaplains;[131] legislation regulating maritime trade;[132] the edited translations of Dutch and Danish naval statutes referred to earlier; and printed editions of Peter's legislation on naval matters.[133] This total does not include Zotov's translation of the French naval ordinance of 1689 or the successive editions of Peter's *Naval Statute* that we have already considered. Nor does it include the earliest known Petrine (and Russian) efforts in the nautical field, namely the illustrated textbook on navigation translated into "Slavonic-Russian" from the Dutch and published in Cyrillic types at Amsterdam in 1701 by a resident Belorussian, I. F. Kopievskii, and the illustrated "List of the Fleet of the British kingdom [*Rospis' flota korolev'stva Britaniiskogo*]" printed from an engraved plate, presumably in Moscow, in 1702.[134] The former, like other works produced by Kopievskii in Amsterdam about this time (see Chapter 6), appears to have had little impact in Russia (it is not known how many copies were printed or how many arrived);[135] but its text, like the captions in the "List," clearly registers the early struggle by Peter and his people to capture in words these particular aspects of the maritime culture of contemporary Europe. Yet distinct from any and all of these, Zotov's handbook is an entirely original work, the first practical handbook for naval officers written in Russian by a Russian and printed in Russia. And like the *Naval Statute* itself, only somewhat more personally so, it attests to the assimilation in Russian of a whole new lexical and semantic field.

Zotov's handbook, which was reprinted as late as 1816, is a guide to the art of handling a major sailing ship, not a textbook on the science of navigation. For that, Russian naval officers and students continued to rely on translations of Dutch, Swedish, English, or French originals or on the classroom teaching of the likes of Henry Farquharson, the longtime professor at Peter's Naval Academy whom he had hired in England in 1698; several of his textbooks in Russian on the basic mathematics involved, we shall see shortly, were printed between 1703 and 1739. A prominent example of the straight translation is the manual on navigating the Baltic taken directly from a Swedish original and first printed at St. Petersburg in 1721 in an edition of 300; in testimony to its usefulness, it was reprinted in 1739, 1756, 1777, and 1785 (meanwhile the Swedish edition, first published at Stockholm in 1677, was reprinted in 1748, 1760, and 1786).[136] As might be expected by now, this manual's numerous technical terms are fluently integrated in rigorously straightforward Russian prose, with sailing directions from place to place *(kursy)* stated simply and clearly and related to points on the compass—ONO, NV, and so on, given in Latin letters (= *Ost-Nord-Ost, Nord-Vest,* etc.)—and to the positions of the sun: "If the morning sun rises in the ONO, and sets in the NV, then the compass *[kompass]* points East *[Ost]*." We need not read more. Led by Emperor Peter, Russians were now navigating the open Baltic Sea with the aid of manuals in their own language.

The textual culmination as it were of Petrine navigational developments is the splendid *Complete Compilation on Navigation/Polnoe sobranie o navigatsii* by Captain, later Admiral Semen (I.) Mordvinov, which was first published at St. Petersburg in four "parts" or volumes by the Naval Academy Press in 1748 (the first three parts) and 1753 (the fourth part).[137] Mordvinov (1701–1777) was another of Peter's naval fledglings, perhaps the finest of them all, a graduate of his Naval Academy sent by him to train in France (1717–1722) who then rose from midshipman (michman) in the Baltic fleet to the highest administrative and command ranks of the Imperial Russian navy.[138] This is not the place to canvass Mordvinov's volumes, replete with diagrams and tables, compass cards and marine charts, in an effort to demonstrate his mastery of his subject in all its contemporary mathematical and astronomical complexity. Suffice it to suggest that Mordvinov's *Compilation*, written entirely in Russian, surely ranks in quality with any comparable work produced anywhere in Europe by its time. The modern science of navigation was now incontestably a Russian science as well, an achievement that is reflected in the incorporation of its technical vocabulary into what was now standard Russian.

Institutionalization

The Baltic fleet was the chief component of the new Russian navy at the time of Peter I's death and it thus represented the principal means whereby his naval revolution was institutionalized, or made permanent, in Russia. The academy founded by Peter to train naval officers was another such means, as was the admiralty created by him to administer and supply the navy. We proceed accordingly to the early history of these other two Petrine institutions before concluding the chapter with an account of the concurrent institutionalization of the navy's creation myth in the shrine of the *botik Petra Velikogo*, or "little boat of Peter the Great." In each case we shall pay particular attention, as usual, to the verbal aspects of the proceedings.

In England in 1698 Peter was given detailed advice on "establishing after the English manner such a Navy in Muscovy as his Majesty shall think most fitt for his Service" by Peregrine Osborne, Marquess of Carmarthen, one of the two British admirals appointed to attend him while in England. The quotation is from a manuscript draft of Carmarthen's five "proposalls" in this vein preserved at the British Library,[139] the fifth of which stipulates "That a Small number of young men be obteyned who have been bred in Christchurch Hospitall and have gone Schoolmasters to Sea for the well educating and instructing of all young Seamen in the Art of Navigation." Carmarthen's four other proposals related to the recruitment of English shipbuilders, officers, and seamen for service in "Muscovy," where together with the schoolmasters they would in due course "make his Imperiall Majesty's subjects (who shall be appointed to the work) perfect in their professions." It has been rather playfully proposed that for this and his many other services to Peter in England Carmarthen deserves the title "godfather of the Russian Fleet";[140] in any case, the importance of the English connection in Peter's creation of the Russian navy is emphasized and particularly in his foundation of Russia's first navigation school. In May 1698 "two mathematical boys" of the Royal Mathematical School of Christ's Hospital, London, which had begun operation in 1673 under the supervision of Carmarthen's father, were given leave to enter Russian service, namely Stephen Gwynn, age fifteen, and Richard Grice, age seventeen; and Carmarthen, it seems likely, also recommended Henry Farquharson, then Liddel Mathematical Tutor at Marischal College in Aberdeen, to teach in the proposed Russian school. Farquharson, about twenty-five years old, came down from Scotland to meet Peter and was promptly hired at an annual salary of 100 rubles plus living allowance and promised a bonus of £50 sterling for every student who should successfully complete his course. He and the two boys then left for Russia, where they arrived, at Archangel, in August 1699.[141]

Henry Farquharson proved to be one of the key figures of the Petrine cultural revolution as a whole, at once teacher and translator, model and goad, although his contributions in this respect have tended to be minimized if not ignored by Russian historians. After the usual delays, which provoked him, Gwynn, and Grice to petition Peter directly, reminding him of their existence,[142] they were expressly commissioned in August 1701 to start teaching mathematics and navigation in an old linen mill in Kadashi, the weavers' district across the Moscow River from the Kremlin. This they soon found unsuitable and so were moved to specially readied premises in the newly built Sretenskaia or Sukharev Tower located on Moscow's outermost ramparts, at the point where the main road down from Archangel—still the main road from Europe—entered the city; there also, given its unimpeded view of the horizon, an astronomical observatory was established under Peter's close associate Iakov Brius (James Bruce), a Russian-born Scot who looms large in later chapters of this volume.[143] Their school, soon known as the Moscow School of Mathematics and Navigation (*Shkola matematicheskikh i navigatskikh nauk:* literally, School of Mathematical and Navigational Sciences), enrolled a mix of volunteers and draftees mainly from the noble and lower service classes who early included both Konon Zotov and S. G. Malygin, the latter also author of a handbook on seamanship. Its curriculum, not surprisingly, was closely modeled on that of the Royal Mathematical School in

London, with students proceeding as best they could through courses in arithmetic, geometry, trigonometry, navigation, navigational astronomy, and geography: the preliminary courses for those who needed them in basic literacy and Arabic numbers (the so-called *russkaia shkola* and the *tsifernaia shkola*) were taught by L. F. Magnitskii, a graduate of the Moscow Slavonic-Greek-Latin academy founded in the 1680s under church jurisdiction and himself one of Farquharson's first students; all the other courses were taught by Farquharson himself assisted by Gwynn and the unfortunate Grice (he was killed by robbers in a Moscow street in 1709). Securing adequate funding for the school and its students as well as the promised salaries of its teachers was, as always in Petrine Russia, a constant source of grievance. But somehow the needed slates and pencils, rulers, charts, backstaffs, quadrants, and other instruments were obtained from abroad and funding was found to send top students for further training to Holland or England or to British ships stationed in the Baltic; after 1712 they also trained in the fast-growing Russian Baltic fleet. Others were drafted into the army or civil service, given the acute shortage of even minimally educated personnel, became astronomers (a few) or surveyors (geodesists), or were appointed to teach in one of the dozens of "admiralty" or "cipher schools" that were sooner or later set up in various Russian towns. At one of these affiliated schools, in Voronezh, ninety students were enrolled already in July 1703.[144]

Among the proudest achievements of the Moscow School of Mathematics and Navigation in its early years was the printing in 1703, mostly in traditional Cyrillic types, of the *Arifmetika,* a compilation by Magnitskii and others of translated foreign sources which included sections on algebra, plane and solid geometry, and celestial navigation as well as exercises in simple arithmetic.[145] It has the honor of being the first mathematical textbook printed in Russia and, with at least 2,400 copies finding their way into students' hands, it made mathematics, in the judgment of one specialist, "the first systematic body of scientific knowledge to acquire a place in Russian culture."[146] We will revive this claim in Chapter 5. On a somewhat more mundane level the *Arifmetika* of 1703 has also been rated "a landmark in Russian printing and technical publishing," its "fairly baroque Church-Slavonicised Russian," enhanced by the Cyrillic types, notwithstanding: in other words, "by the Russian standards of the time, a fine piece of fairly elaborate two-colour printing with many illustrations [which] shows some ingenuity in presentation, explanatory notes, and in adapting examples to the Russian scene"—adaptations that included printing some Arabic numerals along with the customary Slavonic numerals as well as various Latin words in Roman type (see Appendix I, no. 11).[147]

Meanwhile the school itself is "usually considered," as a leading Soviet specialist carefully put it, the "first secular Russian educational institution . . . of a technical kind,"[148] one of several such technical schools founded by Peter and distant forerunners of what one day would be world-class institutes of technology.

By the end of 1715 the Moscow School had taught some 1,200 students to one level of competence or another, 305 of them from the service nobility high and low, the rest clergy or sons of clergy, lower-level bureaucrats, military men, townsfolk, and even free peasants. That same year Peter decided to move the upper courses of the school to his new capital, St. Petersburg, there to form the core of a Naval Academy *(Morskaia akademiia)* for which the lower courses left in Moscow would become a feeder.[149] Magnitskii was left in charge of the Moscow School while Farquharson and Gwynn became the first professors of the Naval Academy, whose first class consisted of 349 youths, a sizable proportion of whom came, again, from the nobility (by 1722 its total complement had risen to 406). The academy's first director was the Baron Saint-Hilaire, a veteran of the French naval schools founded at Toulon, Brest, and Rochfort by Louis XIV, who had proposed founding a similar institution in Russia. Saint-Hilaire broadened the St. Petersburg academy's curriculum to include, in addition to the requisite mathematics and navigation, courses in gunnery, fortification, foreign languages (French, Latin, German), fencing, and dancing. He also established an elite corps of cadets, or *gardemariny,* at the academy, many of whose members, like S. I. Mordvinov, were sent to France or Venice to complete their training, others to Reval or ports nearer by. Farquharson, ever the scholar rather than the politician, resisted Saint-Hilaire's attempts to subordinate him to the new regime and appealed directly to Peter;[150] their quarrel led to the Frenchman's dismissal in 1717, but not before he had imparted to the academy's curriculum, manners, and terminology a certain elitist and French flavor. *Gardemariny* soon designated all students at the academy, which early on impressed a usually discriminating German resident, F. C. Weber, as home to "the Flower of the Russian Nobility, who [are] instructed [therein] in all the Sciences belonging to Navigation; besides which, they are taught Languages, Fencing, and other bodily Exercises by the ablest Professors and Masters, and are kept under strict Discipline."[151]

Farquharson now assumed control of the academy's curriculum, leaving discipline and administrative matters to a series of well-placed political appointees favored by Peter because of their European education or naval experience (they included A. A. Matveev, who figures prominently in my second volume;[152] G. G. Skorniakov-Pisarev, who had studied mathematics and engineering in Berlin and compiled a manual on statistics and mechanics, the first book published by the academy's press;[153] and Captain A. L. Naryshkin and his brother, I. L. Naryshkin, maternal cousins of the tsar). The division of labor seems to have suited all concerned, especially as Farquharson had been viewed by Peter virtually from his arrival in Russia as something of a national asset, the educational brains, as it were, of his grand naval project and his personal science advisor. Captain John Perry, the naval engineer who spent fourteen years (1698–1712) in Russian service, writing in about 1715, recalls how Peter asked Farquharson to teach him astronomy,

> and particularly has order'd him to calculate all the Eclipses how they will appear, that happen to be visible in his Countrey, which he has always done with very great Satisfaction to the Czar. His Majesty has order'd very good telescopes to be brought into his Countrey, as well as other useful instruments and Books, for which the said Fergharson [Farquharson] makes his Demand. . . . And wherever his Majesty is, or intends to be, whether in Poland, at Petersburgh, at Veronize [Voronezh], or at Azoph [Azov], he always appoints an Order to be writ to the said Fergharson, to send him a Draught and Account how the Eclipses, particularly those of the Sun, will happen in such Place where he is, or intends to be at the Time.[154]

In the course of his forty-year residence in Russia, Farquharson trained hundreds of native *navigatory* along with countless mathematics teachers, astronomers, and geodesists: my preceding volume records how, late in 1720, some thirty young students of the Naval Academy taught *geodeziia* by Farquharson were dispatched at Peter's command to the provinces to conduct detailed land surveys, an important phase of yet another grand Petrine project, that of mapping all of Russia for the first time.[155] More to the point here, Farquharson's work as a translator and editor of teaching materials was little short of prodigious, and documents his knowledge of Russian as well as English, German, Dutch, French, and Latin. Much of his legacy in this respect remained in manuscript and was eventually lost. But the list of his printed works includes, in addition to the *Arifmetika* of 1703, whose compilation by Magnitskii and others he doubtless supervised, a handbook translated from Latin with the assistance of Gwynn and Magnitskii, and edited by Bruce, of logarithmic and trigonometric tables *(Tablitsy sinusov, tangensov, i seksanov i logarifma sinusov i tangensov . . .),* which was also published at Moscow in 1703 in traditional Cyrillic type and was, after the *Arifmetika,* the "second technical book to be printed in Russia"; it was printed again in 1716, this time in the new civil type.[156] Farquharson's publications also include a Russian edition of a Latin edition *(Elementa geometriae)* of Euclid's geometry *(Evklidovy elementy . . .)* printed at the Naval Academy Press in the civil type in 1719 and 1739,[157] excerpts from which are reproduced in Appendix I (no. 39); an updated Russian edition of a Dutch 1697 handbook of solar declination tables printed at Moscow in the civil type in 1723 and translated with the help, again, of Magnitskii *(Tablitsy, gorizontal'nyia severnyia i iuzhnyia shiroty voskhozhdeniia solntsa so iz"iavleniem);*[158] and a little book on the use of sectors in solving mathematical problems *(Knizhitsa o sochinenii i opisanie sektora . . . v reshenii raznykh matematicheskikh problem)* printed at the Naval Academy Press in 1739.[159] Several other technical publications of the time carried commentaries by Farquharson or were also supervised by him, including an *Atlas of the Caspian Sea (Atlas Kaspiiskago moria)* compiled by his former student F. I. Soimonov and printed at St. Petersburg in 1731;[160] a navigation manual, *Sokrashchennaia navigatsiia po kartie de-rediuksion* (St. Petersburg, 1733), prepared by S. G. Malygin, a former student both of the Moscow School and of the Naval Academy who rose to be captain-commodore in charge of the Admiralty Office in Kazan, where he died in 1764;[161] and a handbook for navigators *(Ekstrakt shturmanskago iskusstva iz nauk prinadlezhashchikh k moreplavaniiu sochinennyi,* St. Petersburg, Naval Academy Press, 1739) compiled from foreign sources by, again, F. I. Soimonov.[162] Moreover a manuscript navigation manual in Russian found at the British Library and dated to 1703 has been convincingly attributed to Farquharson: "very typical," Ryan says, of English manuals of the period, it abounds in technical terms of European origin, is written in vernacular Russian, employs European (Arabic) rather than Slavonic numerals throughout, and uses both decimal fractions with a decimal point and Latin letters to denote geometrical positions—all features that distinguish this manuscript from Russian manuscript and printed books written up to this time.[163] Ryan emphasizes that European numerals, thanks crucially to Farquharson, were only now beginning to supercede in Russian writings the older Greek-style Slavonic alphabetic numerals, which were incompatible with modern mathematics but remained in use in most books— all but the few technical ones—printed in traditional Cyrillic types right through Peter's reign.

In fact, under Farquharson's leadership the St. Petersburg Naval Academy became for a time the center of scientific work in Russia,[164] until overtaken in this respect by Peter's Academy of Sciences, which opened for business in 1725 (Chapter 5). In 1737 the Imperial government promoted him to the rank of brigadier with emoluments "because through him the teaching of mathematics *[matematika]* was introduced in Russia and nearly every Russian subject [serving] in the fleet *[flot]*, from the highest to the lowest, was instructed in the navigational *[navigatskikh]* sciences": the commendation was affirmed more than a century and a half later by the author of the Farquharson entry in the standard Russian biographical dictionary.[165] He is similarly represented by a fellow Briton in Russian service, Dr. John Cook, who recalled taking tea with him at the St. Petersburg Admiralty in 1737:

> One day Mr Farcharson Professor of Astronomy came from the [Naval] Academy to drink tea with me, but, although all the younger officers had studied under him, and particularly the gentlemen at that time on guard, whom he well knew, he could not gain admittance till the commander gave orders. Indeed the Captain ran to the gate, and conducted his old regent with great deference to my house. When seated, the good old professor told him, that he was glad to have lived so long as to see many gentlemen in the fleet, formerly his pupils, of distinguished learning, who could prescribe laws to him. Compliments on both sides were not wanting.[166]

It seems fitting that Farquharson should have been remembered in Russia as a great teacher, and that on his death in 1739 about half of his library of some 600 volumes should have gone to his beloved Naval Academy (the other half to his personal heir). But here we remember him mainly for the enormous contribution he made to naturalizing in Russian the new science of navigation and related mathematical and astronomical terminology, a verbal achievement that alone might justify Cross's proportionately large claim that he was "arguably the most able and influential person Peter had brought into his service."[167]

In 1752 Empress Elizabeth, Peter's daughter, amalgamated the Naval Academy with the Moscow School and a naval artillery school also founded by Peter to form the Naval Cadet Corps *(Morskoi kadetskii korpus)*, which name the institution retained, except for the years 1867 to 1891 (when it was known as the Naval School), until 1917. Through all these years and their corresponding changes or adaptations in curriculum and discipline, the institution remained what it had been since it sprang from the mind of its founder: the principal training site for officers of the Imperial Russian navy.[168] It also long remained the stronghold of English in Russia. Two of its teachers, Mikhail Permskii (1741–1770) and Prokhor Zhdanov (died 1802), published the first English grammars in Russia (1766, 1772) and the first English-Russian dictionaries (1772, 1784); that of 1784, entitled *A New Dictionary English and Russian/Novyi slovar' angliiskoi i rossiiskoi,* was a work of 750 pages listing some 30,000 words and dedicated to Zhdanov's students at the Naval Cadet Corps.[169]

Peter's Naval Academy and its affiliates were administratively subordinate to the Admiralty, which comes next in this brief history of the institutionalization of Russia's great nautical turn. As mentioned much earlier in this chapter, the term was first applied—in the form *admiralteits*—to the official appointed in 1696 to supervise shipbuilding in and around Voronezh, on the river Don, where the galley fleet deployed earlier that year in the second and successful siege of Azov, at the mouth of the Don, had been constructed. The appointment of A. P. Protas'ev, the official in question, as *admiralteits* or civil admiral[170] with specific responsibility for building an *admiralteiskii dvor* (shipyard) at Vononezh is formalized in an *Intruktsiia* to him issued by Peter on December 28, 1696;[171] thus had begun the vast enterprise of building a permanent battle fleet of some seventy ships for the purposes of securing Azov and contiguous coastlines and of venturing out on the Black Sea itself. Two years later (decree of December 11, 1698),[172] Peter's traditional bureaucratic arrangements to that end having been overwhelmed, a Chancery of Naval Affairs (*Prikaz voinskikh morskikh del,* or Chancery of Military Marine Affairs) was created at Moscow—the first such office in Russian history—under another senior official, F. A. Golovin, who was soon named *admiral* and given charge of the hundreds of officers and seamen hired in Europe to direct and man the new navy. This act in effect separated the administration of the navy as such from that of its construction and supply, a "rationalizing" process that was completed with Protas'ev's sacking for gross peculation in November 1699 and the subsequent consolidation of his responsibilities (February 1700) in a new Admiralty Chancery (*Admiralteiskii prikaz* or *Prikaz admiralteiskikh del*) also located in Moscow and ruled by another of the tsar's closest senior officials, F. M. Apraksin, who now assumed the title of *admiralteits.*[173] That same year the fifty-two private shipbuilding "companies" (*kompaniia,* also *kompanstvo,* most often *kumpanstvo*) that had been organized on Peter's orders in 1696 from among the estate holders and merchants of the country were abolished, and shipbuilding along the Don became a state monopoly under Apraksin's (ultimately Peter's) overall direction.[174]

The joint regime of the Chancery of Naval Affairs, responsible for personnel, and the Admiralty Chancery, responsible for shipbuilding and supply, remained in effect until overtaken by events. These included the establishment in St. Petersburg in 1707 of a parallel Admiralty Chancellery (*Admiralteiskaia kantseliariia*) to manage the shipyards that had been springing up in the Baltic region since 1702—it was also run by Apraksin, who soon became the first *general admiral* of the fleet—and, in 1712, of a Naval Chancellery (*Voinskaia morskaia kantseliariia* or *Kantseliariia voinskago morskago flota*) to supervise the personnel of the budding Baltic fleet.

The Russian defeat by Turkish forces at the battle by the Pruth in 1711 entailed the destruction in 1712 of the Azov fleet and the closing of its supporting yards—whereupon, as mentioned earlier, Peter's naval energies were invested almost exclusively in the Baltic fleet in pursuit of the war against Sweden. The Admiralty Chancery in Moscow, having thus lost its main reason for being (the Azov fleet), was transformed—as the Moscow Admiralty Office (*Moskovskaia admiralteiskaia kontora*)—into a branch of the St. Petersburg Admiralty Chancellery, which it remained until abolished in 1806. Meanwhile the admiralty yard founded in St. Petersburg contemporaneously with the city became known, with the strategic shift to the Baltic and the new capital's growing prominence, as the Main Admiralty (*Glavnoe admiralteistvo*) or simply—to add more gin to our tonic—as the Admiralty. From 1709 its primary responsibility had been to provide ships of the line for the Baltic fleet, for which scaffolds and slips were constructed along with rope or rigging sheds; mast, sail, and caulking shops; barracks for naval personnel; and huts for workers, these soon followed by an Admiralty church and houses for its leading officials, starting with General Admiral Apraksin. It was also decided early on that the St. Petersburg Admiralty should be fortified with ramparts, guns, ditches, and the rest so as to serve as one of the city's main defenses. The result was that by 1718 the Admiralty complex, centering on its shipyard, constituted one of the five main administrative districts into which St. Petersburg was divided, a city within a city and easily the dominant institution, apart from the Baltic fleet itself, of the entire Russian naval establishment. With its thousands of workers and staff (between 1712 and 1721 an estimated 50,000 to 60,000 workers passed through its yard), its outlying forests and sawmills, copperworks, ironworks, and linen manufactories (for sailcloth), it had become the single largest industrial enterprise in Russia as well—in fact, the "largest industrial complex in eighteenth-century Russia."[175]

Late in 1717, as Peter began to apply the collegial principle to his central government, he announced that an "Admiralty College [*Admiraliteiskaia kolegiia*]" under General Admiral Apraksin was to be among the nine (later eleven, then twelve) new administrative organs or "colleges" to be founded shortly.[176] The new Admiralty College was, like the other colleges, to be given its own governing statute or "regulation" *(reglament),* which in its case was finally published at the St. Petersburg Press in April 1722.[177] Details of the founding of the Admiralty College and of its *Regulation* will be found in Chapter 4, in our discussion of the larger bureaucratic revolution of which it was a part. Now we might note that from 1718 on the Admiralty College, technically a board of senior naval officials, assumed control of all existing naval forces and related offices with their ships and dependent shipyards, shops, schools, hospitals, churches, harbors, fortifications, residences, and industrial enterprises, whether located in St. Petersburg—the Main Admiralty, the Kronshlot/Kronshtadt naval base, the Naval Academy—or anywhere else (Moscow, Archangel, Kazan, Narva, Riga, Reval) in what was officially termed from October 1721 the Russian Empire. The Admiralty College became responsible, in brief, for all aspects of the Imperial Russian navy's administration and economic life. And so it remained until 1802, when in connection with the central governmental reorganization of that year it was transformed into the Ministry of the Navy, an institution that continues in one form or another, perpetuating the Petrine legacy, to this day.[178]

89

The nautical component of the Petrine legacy was also institutionalized, in a quite different form, in the shrine of the *botik*—the "little boat" discovered by the youthful Peter at the royal estate of Izmailovo near Moscow in 1688. The boat apparently was built in the 1640s in England or, if not there, in Russia by Dutch craftsmen following an "English-type" design;[179] it measures seven meters in length by two in width, is single masted and shallow drafted, and is steered by a tiller attached to a large rudder attached to the sternpost: a type common in maritime Europe since late medieval times. Following his inaugural sailing lessons in the boat on waters near Moscow, Peter had it stored for safekeeping in the Kremlin (1701), evincing even then a special regard for it. Years later we find reference to the *botik* in both his draft and the printed version of the preface to the *Naval Statute,* as we saw in the preceding sections of this chapter. In the printed version of the preface, indeed, Peter's editor, Feofan Prokopovich, declared that "the *botik* thus served him [Peter] not only as a childhood pastime, but became the cause of his building a navy, as we now see with wonder"—a theme that is capsulized, also as discussed above, in the frontispiece to the *Naval Statute,* where the *botik* figures prominently. Prokopovich again evoked the *botik* in his "Sermon in Praise of the Russian Fleet" preached before Peter and entourage in September 1720, again as noted above, where he asserted that it was "to the navy what the seed is to the tree," and more: "from this seed grew a great, wondrous, winged, armored forest of trees." He then went on to exclaim: "O *botik,* worthy to be gilded! Some have looked diligently for the planks of Noah's ark in the mountains of Ararat; my advice would be to guard this *botik* and to treasure it as an unforgettable memorial unto the last generation."[180] The advice proved most welcome.

In Moscow early in 1722 Peter ordered the *botik* put on display in front of the Kremlin's Dormition cathedral—the most sacred space in the Muscovite tsardom—in celebration of the recent Peace of Nystadt (Nystad) ending at last the Russo-Swedish or Great Northern War. In honor of this event he also commissioned an engraving by Ivan Zubov, one of the first Russians trained in this art, which shows the *botik* on a plinth with an inscription proclaiming that it was now being exhibited to the public because it "could truthfully be said that this blessed peace is its fruit."[181] Peter then ordered the *botik* transported to the Alexander-Nevskii monastery in St. Petersburg, which he had founded in 1721 to commemorate the medieval warrior-saint and his victory, on the nearby Neva, over invading German and Swedish forces—thus recalling Peter's own victory over Sweden. From there on May 30, 1723, his birthday, Peter sailed the *botik* down the Neva in a convoy of yachts, barges, and other sailboats to the Main Admiralty, where it received artillery salutes from ships of the Baltic fleet and from the Peter-Paul fortress. The occasion is described in several contemporary sources including a report to his king by the French ambassador, Campredon, who felt compelled to attend: "Sire, In giving Your Majesty an account of the various institutions that the Czar has established to maintain and augment his power, I have had the honor to relate that he has given his most attentive care to that of his navy"; and there was no better proof of this fact, Campredon suggested here, than Peter's lavish celebration of this "très petite chaloupe" as "l'auteur de sa flotte." Campredon took the occasion, as he also told the king, to congratulate Peter "on the great and beautiful family which the little sloop *[botik]* had produced."[182] In August 1723 a grand regatta of the Baltic fleet was organized at Kronshtadt and this time Peter, crossing over to the base from St. Petersburg in his *botik* accompanied by a flotilla of more than a hundred other vessels, steered her between the massed ships of the line, all with flags flying, to take their salute, a rolling fusillade from a thousand guns and a sight, said one eyewitness, that was nothing less than "enchanting."[183] The *botik* was then installed in the Peter-Paul fortress on a plinth inscribed, "From the amusement of the child came the triumph of the man." On August 30, 1724, the third anniversary of the Peace of Nystadt, the *botik* joined the ceremonies at the Alexander-Nevskii monastery marking the deposition of the saint's relics in the monastery's church of the Annunciation, that "architectural jewel" designed by the first architect of St. Petersburg, Dominico Trezzini.[184] Peter ordered that every year thereafter on August 30 the *botik* be rowed or sailed upriver to the monastery to commemorate these events.[185]

Thus was solidified the legend of the "grandad *[dedushka]* of the Russian navy," as Peter himself had dubbed the now carefully preserved *botik*. Succeeding Russian monarchs, claiming his mantle, pressed the *botik* into service on various state occasions—for example, the wedding in 1745 of Grand Duke Peter (grandson of Peter I) and Grand Duchess Catherine (the future Catherine II), at the conclusion of which the *botik* appeared in a regatta along the Neva escorted by the reigning Empress Elizabeth (Peter I's daughter) dressed in a naval uniform.[186] Early in her own reign—in the 1760s— Catherine II had a pavilion built next to the church in the Peter-Paul fortress to house the "grandad of the Russian navy," where it gradually became a major tourist attraction, as witness the detailed account of the shrine, complete with its legend, provided in 1793 by the curator of Petrine memorabilia in St. Petersburg, Osip Beliaev.[187] Similarly, in a guidebook to the city published in 1846 the author pauses in his tour of the Peter-Paul fortress to comment on the "famous Grandfather of the Russian navy"; in his words, "The *botik* is precious because it inspired in Peter the wish to found a navy, and was the favorite boat of the young Tsar, in which fearlessly he first sailed. . . . To commemorate the transfer of the boat here, Peter the Great established an annual holiday on August 30; then, accompanied by all the boats found in the city, it is taken from the fortress to the Alexander-Nevskii monastery and there, after public prayers, put on display."[188] More impressively still perhaps, in conjunction with the celebrations of the bicentenary of Peter I's birth in 1872 the *botik* was brought back to Moscow in a cortege led by the reigning emperor's brother, where it was greeted by a 101-gun salute and the plaudits of an excited public and then put on display in the great Moscow fair of that year. There Russians saw it, a recent student suggests, as a symbol of the navy that had "elevated Russia to Great Power status"; in the words of a contemporary Russian educator, "The little boat at the head of a gigantic navy—that is the best manifestation of Peter's work and of the advice he gave us in our struggle for success."[189] During the early Soviet era, to be sure, the shrine of the *botik* was downgraded along with most memorials of the Imperial period, as attested by the absence of any reference to it in the standard two-volume guidebook to Leningrad published in 1933.[190] But with the outbreak of World War II and the partial, patriotic rehabilitation of "Peter the Great," conqueror of "Germans" and founder of the Russian—now Soviet—navy, his *botik* resurfaced, and was prominently installed in the newly created Central Naval Museum housed in a distinguished older building, the former St. Petersburg Bourse *(Birzha)* or Stock Exchange. It was there to inspire Russians during the tercentenary of Peter's birth, in 1972,[191] and remains so to this day.

Indeed the story of the "grandad of the Russian navy" embalmed in the *botik* is easily grasped, and moralized. In 1997 the *botik* left Russia for the first time and traveled to New York, to become the main attraction of an exhibition on St. Petersburg mounted at the World Financial Center, where a reporter for the *New York Times* was fascinated by the comments of visiting or resident Russians, both intellectuals and more ordinary folk. "It mesmerizes me," said one; "Without this boat," said another, "St. Petersburg wouldn't exist"; "I touched the wood and it was kind of an electric feeling," said a third; "This was always the least official of our official symbols, something for which we could sincerely express our patriotic feelings." Or again, from a Russian whose business involved frequent trips between Russia and the United States: "The boat symbolizes Peter the Great's attempt to break through Russia's backwardness and isolation and reach out to the West. Peter represents the promise that was never [as yet] fulfilled."[192]

The Russian navy in its successive incarnations, its bases and harbor facilities, its schools, hospitals, and administrative offices, its history, traditions, and language, demonstrates incontestably the permanence of the Petrine naval revolution.[193] But so too does Russia's intimate if often quite problematic involvement since Peter I in the larger European world, an involvement for which the wider maritime links forged by him were essential. We thus return, in the end, to the vexed question of costs versus benefits arising from Peter's creation of the Russian navy, a question that was evaded early in this chapter. There (note 3) we simply sampled a range of presumably well considered opinion on the matter—from P. N. Miliukov's harsh dismissal of the entire project as a waste of "countless lives and endless resources" to E. V. Anisimov's guarded comparison of the Petrine navy with the Soviet space program to Admiral Gorshkov's embrace of Peter as the founder of a force that was plainly necessary to the realization of Russia's destiny as a great power. Hughes surely is right to reject the first view as anachronistically extreme and to find merit in Anisimov's comparison (and, by implication, in Gorshkov's position): "Both projects," she writes, referring to the Petrine navy and the Soviet space program, "were as much for prestige as for practicality. Both generated a host of symbols above and beyond their immediate function, conveying the clear message that Russia was a major contender on the international stage. . . . Both attracted criticism for wasting public funds. . . .

92

But it is no more credible to imagine that Peter might have renounced his navy in order to build more schools or improve the nutrition of peasants than that the Soviet leaders of the 1950s to 1970s would abandon the 'space race' in order to concentrate on public welfare."[194] I must, all considered, agree. Yet in estimating Peter's achievement in this respect one should also bear in mind the contemporary international political and naval situation in which he actually worked and then recall, with all due emphasis, the role that his navy sooner or later played in Russia's acquisition of a European, and "modern," identity.

On the first point, the antiquity and vibrancy of Europe's maritime culture when Peter came to power should not lead us to suppose that in creating a navy he was simply trying to "catch up" with coevally antique and vibrant naval developments among his rivals or models—Sweden, Denmark, Holland, England, and France. The creation of permanent, state-owned, seagoing fleets of purpose-built, heavily armed, large-scale sailing warships complete with their elaborate infrastructures was a quite *recent* development in Europe and one that Peter joined, as had his rivals and models before him, at its current stage (how else?). Naval historians have demonstrated, in other words, that in the later seventeenth century a whole new period had begun in European naval history, a period marked by the emergence of great sailing warships deployed in mighty battle fleets, at one end, and by the battle of Trafalgar, in 1815, at the other—"the last great battle of the sailing-ship era."[195] More, the deployment in ever larger numbers by European states of the sailing battleship proved to be an enormously expensive enterprise as well as a technically and socially demanding one. During the seventeenth century the European states located along the Atlantic seaboard and particularly around the North Sea, on either side of the English Channel, and in the Baltic region became ensnared in successive naval races; between 1661 and 1683, for instance, in pursuit of its wars against Spain, Holland, and the Habsburg emperor, France created the largest navy in Europe and put in place the structure of ports, arsenals, and supply policies needed to support it; but the whole venture was allowed to lapse until the outbreak again of war (the so-called Nine Years War of 1688 to 1697, France against England and Holland), when the French government built "a second generation of even stronger warships."[196] We should also notice that these great battleships interacted in the various theaters with a variety of smaller craft—smaller sailing warships and oar-powered galleys—some of which were manned by pirates or privateers, and that in these situations the battleships did not invariably prevail. Both are factors to remember when considering the Baltic and its shallow coastal waters, where the

Swedish government in Peter's time promoted privateers against the Russian commerce and where the deployment of Russia's new galley fleet proved spectacularly successful in the age-old pursuit of a permanent Baltic coastline. We must judge Peter's naval program, at least initially, on its own terms.

94

The case of France well illustrates, as M. S. Anderson, prolific historian of the period, points out, the fact that naval development in Europe during the decades in question, even more than the buildup of armies, was "likely to be interrupted by sharp fluctuations and declines."[197] This was the result, I might add, of a government's perception, hardly omniscient, of the relative costs versus benefits involved in maintaining its armed forces, especially when at peace; and for navies built entirely of wood, to mention only one factor in play, the problems of both securing and preserving adequate supplies of appropriate timber were simply enormous.[198] Yet Anderson is exceptionally critical among all others of Peter's naval program, and this in spite of the "very useful role" his Baltic fleet admittedly played in winning the Northern War and in establishing Russia as "a decisively greater naval power than either Sweden or Denmark." Anderson finds it "very questionable whether Russia got good value for most of this money [invested in the navy]," and we pay heed to his objections because they echo, or are echoed by, numerous other critics. "The purely [?] personal character, and indeed the wastefulness [how measured?], of this Russian naval power was [were] marked," Anderson asserts; the latter "had no real roots in the country and was always unpopular with the ordinary Russian [with whom? how do we know? and where was naval power ever truly popular?]." The Russian navy, Anderson asserts further, "never threw off its reliance on foreign expertise"—although "never" is a very long time and reliance on foreign expertise was common in the naval buildups of various states at various times, for example in seventeenth-century Sweden, where, as the leading Swedish naval historian tells us, maritime traditions were so weak that when the kings wished to deploy a navy they had to build one from scratch; moreover, "this state navy was usually short of highly skilled manpower on all levels" and "only towards the end of this period [ca. 1650] was this partially remedied through a substantial influx of Dutch naval officers, a part of the large-scale immigration of foreigners with special skills which accompanied Sweden's rise as a great power."[199] Seemingly untroubled by any such comparison, Anderson concludes his critique by declaring that the nascent Russian navy "depended entirely on the personal ambition of Peter, to whom it was a kind of gigantic toy. . . . The result of all this was that as soon as Peter died the fleet entered a long period of neglect. Under his successors its strength and efficiency fell sharply; and from this decline it did not recover for the next four decades"—this last shot fired even though only a few pages earlier Anderson has stated without a similar hint of derision that "from the early 1690s onwards . . . a real recovery in France's naval strength did not come until the 1730s," also a period of four decades.[200]

As a matter of fact, in the Baltic the emergence of Russia as a naval force equal to Sweden or Denmark changed the balance of power for good.[201] At no point after Peter's death in 1725 did his successors cede Baltic naval supremacy to either state. Russian ships assisted in the successful siege of Danzig in 1734 and played a crucial part in the victorious war against Sweden, seeking a comeback, of 1741 to 1743. Russian and Swedish naval forces operated jointly and to good effect against Prussia in the Seven Years War (1756–1763). In 1770 a Russian squadron dispatched to the Mediterranean destroyed the main Turkish naval force at Chesme, a victory that helped secure for Russia a Black Sea coast and eventually the whole of Crimea. When after 1772 the Swedish king Gustav III launched an ambitious new naval buildup, Russia under Catherine II countered with one of its own, and in an intermittent contest lasting nearly twenty years she succeeded in defending Russia's vital Baltic interests and in maintaining its regional naval supremacy. The leading specialists make it clear that (1) Russia's supremacy in the eastern Baltic after 1721, never lost, was a product as much of the erosion of Danish and Swedish naval strength in a long series of fruitless wars as it was of Russia's very timely naval buildup; that (2) repeated Swedish attempts during the Northern War to blockade Baltic commerce brought Russia tacit British and Dutch support, both countries being ever more dependent on their Baltic imports; that (3) Russia's emergence as a Baltic naval power largely restored the equilibrium, in favor of the free flow of trade, that had characterized the region until the outbreak, in 1563, of the first of those Danish-Swedish wars for Baltic dominance; and that (4) after 1721, as Jan Glete puts it, "the Russian battle fleet was essentially a defensive force in the Baltic; its main task was to defend the Gulf of Finland with St. Petersburg and the Baltic coast [including the ports of Vyborg, Riga, and Reval] from attacks and blockades from other Baltic fleets as well as from fleets sent from western Europe." The Russian navy's deliberately "defensive character," adds Glete, "became clear in 1789 when it did not use its considerable quantitative superiority over the Swedish battle fleet for offensive operations." More pointedly still, in Glete's words, throughout the eighteenth century and on into the nineteenth "the Russian battle fleet was used with a type of caution well suited to its basic capabilities and its important task of defending the new and exposed capital of St. Petersburg."[202]

We are back to St. Petersburg and to all that this "window on Europe" rapidly came to stand for.[203] I invoke now not so much St. Petersburg the imperial capital and military base as St. Petersburg the seaport and commercial center, the great channel, as remarked in the book just cited, "through which countless Europeans, bearing their values and their ways, poured into Russia, working transformations in the culture unimaginable in an earlier age." This is St. Petersburg the home of the Russian navy, indispensable to its preservation; the home of the Admiralty complex, the largest industrial site in eighteenth-century Russia; and the home of the Naval Academy, where the science of navigation with related mathematics and astronomy were naturalized in Russian, fine French manners were first taught, and direct access to the English language was assured via publication of the first English grammars and English-Russian dictionaries. Here generations of Russians would learn the noble art of sailing on the high seas, eventually to be employed for commercial as well as naval purposes and even purely for pleasure. The very layout and architecture of St. Petersburg, thanks to Peter and his Imperial successors, especially Catherine II and Alexander I, insisted that Russia was Europe. So, to this day, does its Russified Dutch-German name.[204]

It seems fitting, all told, that the first major monument to the pre-Soviet past erected in post-Soviet Moscow should have been a gigantic sculpture—fifteen stories high—of "Peter the Great"; and that even there, in Russia's ancient, landlocked capital, it should depict him, standing tall at the helm of a tall ship mounted on a huge pedestal studded with nautical motives, as the founder of the Russian navy.[205]

3

MILITARY MODERNIZATION

Historians working in the later twentieth century determined that in the sixteenth and seventeenth centuries one or more military revolutions took place in Europe. These revolutions are linked to innovations in weapons technology and related tactics and strategy, to enormous increases in the size of armies and navies, and to the ensuing bureaucratization by warring states of their armed forces. More particularly, the advent of guns—the "gunpowder revolution"—and particularly of ever more lethal, highly mobile siege artillery, the appearance correspondingly of ever more elaborate fortifications, the deployment of increasing numbers of professional pike- and then gun-armed infantry, and the emergence of large standing armies and navies complete with sophisticated infrastructures: all of these developments are seen as constituting, taken together, the initial "modernization" of military power in Europe. This initial phase of military modernization, during which Peter I proceeded with a similar modernization of Russia's armed forces, came to an end, it is generally agreed, about the middle of the nineteenth century, when the advent of steam-powered navies, rifled artillery (putting an end to large-scale fortification), and the heavy industrialization of war ushered in a new era in the military history of Europe—indeed, of the world.[1]

The arrival of modern fortifications in Russia, piecemeal in the seventeenth century, wholesale under Peter, has been treated as an important stage in the Petrine revolution in Russian architecture.[2] The preceding chapter of this book was devoted to Peter's creation of a Russian navy. In this chapter we shall review briefly, in its international and local settings, his modernization of the army together with any precedents it may have had in Muscovite times. Then we will consider the principal texts embodying Peter's military program, keeping an eye, as always in this book, on the program's linguistic impact.

Military Revolutions: Europe to Russia

From a strictly military viewpoint, the years between 1650 or so and 1850 may be considered a distinct period in European history for three reasons: (1) the middle of the seventeenth century saw the "first formation of regular land forces and the appearance of permanent professional armies"; (2) during this period "the primary weapons of all armies—the flint-lock musket and the smooth-bore muzzle loading ordnance—remained in service in much the same form"; and (3) from the middle of the seventeenth century, as never before, artillery—cannon, howitzers, and mortars—"played a significant part in battles."[3] The period also witnessed the decline of the cavalry in European warfare from its previously dominant role to a secondary one and its reorganization into light cavalry (dragoons), employed for reconnaissance and skirmishing, and heavy, used for shock action on the battlefield, both types armed with swords, lances, and pistols or carbines (short muskets or rifles; but rifles were not generally used in war until the later eighteenth century). Early in the period the long pike was eliminated as the infantry's main weapon in favor of the musket, to which a bayonet was later fixed; and armies, made up mainly of infantry, had grown in size from the 15,000 or 20,000 men deployed on a campaign at the beginning of the sixteenth century to the well over 100,000 troops fielded by Spain, France, Sweden, and the Holy Roman (Austrian Habsburg) Empire at various points during the Thirty Years War (1618–1648) to the total of 310,000 effectives available to Louis XIV in 1710.[4] The period was further marked, it deserves emphasis, by increasingly elaborate fortifications thrown up around towns or strong points or along defensive lines to withstand the ever more powerful and accurate siege artillery.[5] These interlocking military developments contributed fundamentally to the outbreak of a virtual epidemic of warfare in sixteenth- and seventeenth-century Europe: an age of prolonged, expensive, and difficult sieges punctuated by pitched battles between infantry units—massed in huge blocks, then lines—supported by cavalry charges and artillery duels, these in addition to the naval battles at sea mentioned in the previous chapter that were conducted sometimes in conjunction with battles on land, sometimes not. It was overall "a remarkably bellicose age," in the words of one student, who reckons that between 1480 and 1700 "England was involved in 29 wars, France in 34, Spain in 36 and the Empire in 25"; or again, that "in the century after 1610

Sweden and the Austrian Habsburgs were at war for two years in every three, Spain for three years in every four."[6]

What caused all these wars? The logic of military innovation as just mentioned surely was one factor—the "use them or lose them" syndrome—but there were others. Religious zeal, dynastic ambition, and commercial rivalry (the rise of capitalism and the competitive quest for resources, then markets) are among the major causes of war in early modern Europe that historians have identified, along with ethnic, civic, and class pride, fear, simple greed, and inexplicable perversity. The ubiquity and frequency of war made it seem normal or natural to people,[7] while the concentration of power in the hands of absolutist monarchs and military elites (aristocracies, emerging professional officer corps) made it all the more likely to happen. "Dynastic aggrandizement above all fueled wars in the early-modern period," concludes the specialist who found it a remarkably bellicose age: the phenomenon understood primarily as territorial aggrandizement or "the propensity to acquire territories contiguous to the ruler's own" perhaps for their economic potential but mainly for their strategic value, so as "to round off boundaries and to render frontiers more secure" or to protect and strengthen lines of communication.[8] The analysis may seem at first simplistic. "Dynastic aggrandizement" does not explain the Anglo-Dutch commercial wars of the later seventeenth century or wholly account for the Thirty Years War. But it does account crucially for the wars of Louis XIV and of the Habsburg monarchies of Spain and the Empire as well as for those in the contemporary Baltic region between the kings of Denmark and Sweden. And it does largely explain the outbreak and persistence of the Great Northern War (1700–1721) between mainly Russia under Peter I and Sweden under Charles XII.

The policies of Charles XII have been studied by historians ranging from Voltaire to R. M. Hatton and Michael Roberts in addition to numerous Swedish specialists. Hatton, deploring the fact that Voltaire's "brilliant portrait" of a "warrior-king whose very virtues made him incapable of being the wise leader of his nation" became "etched indelibly in the European historical consciousness," has perhaps probed Charles's motives most deeply. Yet for all the complexity of the character she presents, with his interests "in law reform, in the practice of toleration, in the care for the arts and sciences, in the application of scientific knowledge to mining and manufacture, in the promotion of trade," Hatton's picture too is one of an absolute monarch animated by considerations of dynastic aggrandizement. He was a ruler who "may have toyed" with the role of protector of Protestantism in north Germany but was basically "influenced both by family temperament," meaning "an aptitude for

war," and "by Sweden's geographical position and political problems," meaning the problems of maintaining if not enhancing Sweden's Baltic empire, an
empire inherited by Charles from his predecessors of the Vasa dynasty.[9] That
such considerations motivated the entire "Swedish imperial experience" from
its onset in about 1560 until it was brought to an end by Russia's ultimate victory in the Northern War is also the view advanced by Roberts and other concerned historians.[10] Indeed one of them has characterized Sweden's intervention under King Gustav II Adolf (Gustavus Adolphus) in the Thirty Years War
not as an act on behalf of the Protestant cause (as pious legend would have it)
but as a "defensive strategy to forestall the establishment of a Habsburg naval
presence in the Baltic" and one that "soon turned into a policy of predatory
expansion." Even Charles XII's father, the relatively pacific Charles XI (ruled
1672–1697), dedicated his reign to upholding his kingdom's status, won by
Gustav II Adolf, as a major European state, although "cold analysis would
suggest that Sweden's pretensions to a place among the leading powers were
unrealistic." But to have asked Charles to do otherwise, on this view, "is to
misunderstand the vicious power game that constituted international relations in the seventeenth century. The participants could not choose to detach
themselves from it"; if Charles "had given the least sign that he accepted that
Sweden no longer had the will or the capacity to sustain her position, relative
to the other powers, the predators would have fallen on her and dismembered
her, as they had planned to do in 1675, and partially succeeded in doing
through the great Northern War after 1700." As for Charles XII, his reign "was
to demonstrate in a spectacular and brutal fashion the inbuilt fault in the system [of hereditary absolute monarchy], its vulnerability to the hazards of the
genetic lottery."[11]

Historians of the reign in Russia of Peter I, Charles XII's main antagonist,
have invariably stressed that war was its salient feature, too, as we saw in
Chapter 1; and given the international situation into which Peter stepped on
inheriting his throne and in which he then had to rule, we should not be at
all surprised. Visual evidence of Peter's dynastic consciousness—his keen
sense of being the son of Tsar Aleksei and grandson of Tsar Michael, the first
two rulers of the Romanov dynasty (the word itself, *dinastiia,* entered Russian in Peter's time)—is readily available,[12] and he frequently referred in writing to events particularly of his father's reign when explaining or justifying
his own policies. One such reference occurs in his preface to the *Naval Statute* of 1720 (Chap. 2), another in his preface to the *Military Statute* of 1716 (see
below). Indeed recovery of lands that were his by right of inheritance is
the dominant theme of Peter's elaborate public justification of what was by

far the most extended and costly of his military efforts, the long war with Sweden: the justification, entitled *Razsuzhdenie kakie zakonnye prichiny Ego tsarskoe velichestvo Petr Pervyi . . . k nachatiiu voiny protiv Korolia Karola 12, Shvedskogo 1700 godu imel* (*A Discourse Concerning the Just Reasons Which his Czarish Majesty, Peter I . . . had for beginning the War against the King of Sweden, Charles XII, Anno 1700,* in the contemporary English translation), written for the most part in 1716 and first published in St. Petersburg the following year, will be examined in the next chapter, in connection with the assimilation in Russian of contemporary European political terminology and associated legal, political, and diplomatic norms. In this as in his other public pronouncements justifying military action, to be sure, Peter would add, as occasion demanded, patriotic or religious claims.[13] But there can be no doubt that for him as for most of his allies and enemies—the Habsburg and Ottoman emperors, the kings of Poland, Denmark, and Prussia as well as of Sweden—"dynastic aggrandizement" was the main motor of war. Nor can it be doubted that Peter had any real choice in the matter. His enemies—the Ottoman Empire, the kingdoms of Poland and Sweden—were the enemies of his royal Muscovite predecessors reaching back a century and a half; although, as compared with most of their wars, his were generally successful—that against Sweden, spectacularly so.

Whatever their cause, in prosecuting his wars Peter early discovered the necessity of re-forming in accordance with contemporary European standards the entirety of his armed forces: of fully implanting in Russia the military revolutions that had already transformed the armed forces of the leading states of Europe, which at this time certainly included the kingdom of Sweden. Creating a navy was one major step in the process, as we have seen (Chap. 2), in the strikingly bold and determined taking of which Peter had little or no local precedent. Such was not the case, or not to the same extent, with regard to the army he inherited on assuming power—meaning the land forces in place or on call in about 1690, a motley combination of old and new, and their alternately cumbrous or weak administrative and armaments infrastructures. It also bears emphasis that by the time of his active reign the youthful Peter had already acquired an exceptional degree of firsthand military experience—exceptional for a Russian prince—mainly via the elaborate war games he enthusiastically mounted in and around Moscow under the direction of seasoned European officers in Muscovite service, war games that continued into the 1690s and culminated in his first Azov campaign (1695). Both points—the comparatively incomplete state of pre-Petrine Russian military reform (compared with contemporary European armies and with what came later in Russia itself), and the unusual extent of Peter's own youthful military experience—have been amply discussed in the literature, and we will concentrate here on the nature and scope of Peter's contribution to the modernization of the Russian army.[14]

Among the important advances along contemporary European lines that took place in seventeenth-century Russia, according to one student of Muscovite military history, were a considerable expansion in the size of armies—up to 100,000 men or more for a given campaign—and the creation of special "foreign formation" pike- and gun-bearing infantry regiments (soldaty) together with special new units of both heavy and light cavalry (reitary and draguny). Even so, this student concedes, "the transformation to a completely 'modern army' was not finished." For one thing, "Russia did not have a special branch of the army devoted solely to artillery until the reign of Peter the Great" (nor a distinct engineering unit); moreover, "only Peter was able to build factories to equip the army with [modern] weapons of Russian make, standardized to the extent that uniform training became possible"; and "a regular provisioning service was not set up until the beginning of the eighteenth century. . . . The problem of provisioning the army was not 'solved' until Peter's time." In this account, certain "military reforms" of the early 1680s, administrative and fiscal in nature, including abolition of mestnichestvo, or the time-honored practice of making senior command appointments on the basis of social status rather than military experience, "presaged the more dramatic reforms of Peter the Great"; yet by the 1690s Muscovy's armed forces still constituted, at best, a "semistanding, semiregular army."[15] Indeed, mustered as they still were for a single campaign and then largely dispersed, and heavily dependent on foreign officers and foreign military supplies (lead, gunpowder, weapons), Muscovy's armed forces as they stood in the later seventeenth century bear comparison with those of leading European states, including Sweden, dating to a century and more before. Nor can the poor showing of the huge Muscovite armies in the Crimean campaigns of 1687 and 1689 be blamed solely on "flawed leadership,"[16] as a more recent investigator, taking a larger view, makes clear. In the latter's overall assessment:

Seventeenth-century Muscovite Russia certainly had territorial ambitions, along with coherent strategies for their realization. What Russia did not have, however, was the military might necessary to support those strategies. Means had to be found to transcend the problems of supply and transport; manpower and training; and inadequate revenues. In short, Russia had to find the way to translate all of its resources—human, material and financial—into power. That was the problem that confronted Peter the Great. As we shall see, his unique solution was thoroughly to reinvent Russia's military system.[17]

Similarly negative is the concise conclusion to a detailed study of the "Muscovite roots" of the modern Russian army and of related questions of cost published by another leading student: "The irony was that all the expenditure did not buy much in the way of military security, since the quality of Muscovite Russia's vast armed forces did not correspond to their quantity. It would be Peter the Great's principal task to repair this basic defect."[18]

Fuller goes on to offer a somewhat confused, in part contradictory account ("quixotic" he himself calls it) of military modernization or "partial modernization" under Peter I, one that gives credit to Peter's strategic "brilliance" and "excellence" in military operations—in "fortification, mobility, and naval support"—while laying heavy emphasis on the obstacles to complete modernization posed by Russia's supposed economic, social, and political "backwardness."[19] The argument, rooted in Russian debates over Russian "backwardness" (*otstalost'*) originating in the nineteenth century and most recently advanced, with respect to Peter, by the historian E. V. Anisimov (Chap. 1), is by now a familiar one: the very success of Peter's military reforms, as fully implemented by his successors, led to "victory after victory"; but they thereby impeded, for well over a century, basic economic, social, and political reform, reform understood to mean abolition of the very institutions of "autocracy and serfdom" that had been fundamental to Russian military success. It is not an argument that we need to enter here, as it is to some extent a war over words, particularly the term "backwardness" (see again Chap. 1). Instead, let us simply register the fact that Peter's gradual solution to the strategic dilemma inherited from his predecessors was, as Fuller says, "thoroughly to reinvent Russia's military *system*" (emphasis added).

Bureaucratization is the operative term now, the "bureaucratic revolution in warfare" that is increasingly viewed by historians as a crucial component, perhaps the key component, of state building in early modern Europe. The phrase denotes the more or less extended process whereby central governments sought to monopolize the use of violence on their territories and on adjacent or even distant seas through the creation of permanent, centrally managed and supported armies and navies, forces that would in turn maintain their domestic domination, protect their territories from foreign foes, and project their power abroad. The establishment of more efficient systems of central command and control, taxation, recruitment, training, and supply necessarily followed along with more effective organization and deployment of the armed forces themselves. We touched on this subject in Chapter 2, in connection with Peter's creation of the Russian navy, where the work in particular of the Swedish historian Jan Glete was cited.[20] At the same time, in "regularizing" his land forces in response to the exigencies particularly of his war against Sweden for control of the eastern Baltic, Peter abandoned the traditional levy of noble cavalry and gradually disbanded the "semi-regular," riot-prone royal musketeers (strel'tsy), who had constituted virtually the only standing force at the disposal of his predecessors. He then created, at first ad hoc and later in a more fully rationalized and comprehensive way, dozens of new infantry and cavalry regiments, mobile artillery and engineering units, elaborate new-style fortifications (around Moscow and Kiev, at Azov, Archangel, and elsewhere, especially in the St. Petersburg area), artillery and engineering schools, and a general staff. Initially it was all done under the tutelage of foreign officers, who were to be gradually replaced by their Russian assistants or students. Annual recruiting levies were introduced as well as new taxes to pay for it all, the latter culminating in Russia's first universal head or "soul" tax collected annually from 1724. Supporting industries were built up (especially in metals, armaments, textiles, and ships), resulting in Russian economic self-sufficiency (autarky) in some sectors,[21] and the relevant bureaucracy was streamlined: from the eighteen Moscow prikazy concerned with military affairs at Peter's accession to a single College of War (from 1718) located in St. Petersburg. The college was charged with administering what had become by the time of Peter's death a standing army trained, uniformed, and equipped up to the better or best contemporary European standards and totaling as many as 130,000 men, a total that does not include an additional 75,000 to 80,000 garrison troops and perhaps 20,000 Cossack irregulars. It was an army equivalent in overall size as well as qualitatively superior to that of Russia's largest traditional rival, the Ottoman Empire.[22] It had proved capable of advanced fortification and siege operations and of joint operations with naval forces, and it had defeated in battle, not once but repeatedly, the forces of one of the pioneers of military modernization in Europe, the kingdom of Sweden. The significance of this achievement was not of course lost on contemporary observers, for example, the recently arrived French ambassador to Russia (and former ambassador to Sweden), Campredon, who in 1723 reported to his king that Peter had succeeded in forming "good land and sea officers, excellent soldiers, an army of more than 100,000 regular troops [together with] a fleet of more than 60 vessels," and that in conquering the eastern Baltic with these forces he had "rendered his territory the most extensive in Europe and made himself the most powerful Prince of the north. . . . Russia, hitherto hardly known by name, is today the object of attention of most of the powers of Europe, who seek her friendship, or fear to oppose her."[23]

The story of Peter's successful modernization of Russia's land forces has frequently been told, too, and with general accord as to its overall causes and outcomes including its social impact, notably a renewed regimentation of the nobility in service to the state and some upward mobility—as army officers— for those of lower estate.[24] The only notable disagreement arises as already indicated around the question of costs versus benefits—on which I might only suggest that, as with the navy, Peter and the Russian army have tended to be judged without adequate attention being paid either to basic geopolitical realities or to comparable rulers, states, and armies. I will briefly invoke these realities and the relevant history of comparable states in the following chapter, when discussing Peter's bureaucratization of the Russian armed forces in the context of his wider bureaucratic revolution. Now we turn to the single most important piece of legislation embodying the Petrine military program, the *Military Statute* of 1716.

The *Military Statute* of 1716

Like the *Naval Statute* of 1720, the *Military Statute* of 1716 was at once the culmination of a codifying process reaching back to the early years of Peter I's reign and the formal, legal basis of all subsequent operations and reforms. It also had, or was thought to have, again like the *Naval Statute,* a more distant precedent. In the brief preface to the *Military Statute,* drafted, once more, by Peter himself, he states that "it is known to all how our father of blessed and eternal memory in the year 1647 began to use a regular army [*reguliarnoe voisko*], and a military statute [*ustav voinskoi*] was issued."[25] Peter obviously referred to the creation under Tsar Aleksei of new infantry "regiments of foreign formation," as they were called, and to the *Uchen'e i khitrost' ratnago stroeniia pekhotnykh liudei* (*The Doctrine and Craft of the Military Organization of Foot Soldiers*), which was translated in 1647 at the Ambassadorial Office in Moscow from a German book first published in 1615 and then printed in 1649, complete with thirty-six illustrations that had been separately printed in Holland (retaining their Dutch captions) and were inserted in the Russian books before they were bound.[26] As its Russian title indicates (*Kriegs-kunst zu Fuss* in the original German), this was a detailed manual of the new-style infantry tactics and drill with musket and pike preceded by a disquisition on warfare drawn from Classical, biblical, and German sources, hardly a "statute" or full set of military regulations; and it is not thought to have had much influence on Muscovite military practice, as Beskrovnyi, the military historian, puts it, if only because of its "complexity"[27]—a reference apparently to its hybrid, Slavonic-Russian language and mix of Slavonic and Arabic numerals as well as to its detailed contents (see Appendix I, nos. 2, 3). Nor is it referred to again in Peter's *Military Statute*—or in any other document of his reign. Nothing daunted, some scholars have adduced a still earlier putative precedent, a work called *Ustav ratnykh, pushechnykh i drugykh del, kasaiushchikhsia do voinskoi nauki . . . v 1607 i 1621 godekh vybran iz inostrannykh voennykh knig (Statute of the military, artillery and other matters relating to the military science* [or *art*] *. . . selected in the years 1607 and 1621 from foreign military books),* the title under which it was printed by the War College at St. Petersburg in 1781 from a manuscript found in a Moscow government office in 1775.[28] As its title indicates, this is a compendium in Russian translation of various European writings on war—most notably, it has been established, the *Kriegsbuch* of Leonhardt Fronsperger first published at Frankfurt am Main in 1566.[29] Compiled sometime during the period indicated by a certain Anisim Mikhailov(ich) Radishevskii, a Moscow printer from Ukraine (Volynia) who probably worked from a Polish text, the *Ustav ratnykh, pushechnykh i drugikh del* of 1607–1621 is not likely to have had any influence whatever on Muscovite military practice, if only because it was never printed and few manuscript copies appear to have been made.[30]

The *Uchen'e i khitrost'* of 1647–1649 is, however, frequently cited by language scholars as evidence of the assimilation in Russian of a sizable number of modern—or early modern—military terms. Such terms include, as I can attest from my own survey of the text, the basic *soldat* (here usually *saldat*) = foot soldier, from German *Soldat*/French *soldat;* the military titles *kapitan* = captain, from German *Kapitän*/French *capitaine,* and *serzhant* = sergeant, from German *Sergeant*/French *sergent,* among others; not only *mushket* = musket, thoroughly attested to earlier times, but also *mushketir/mushketër* = musketeer, from the German/French equivalent; *regiment* (here *regement*) = regiment, from German/French *regiment,* later dropped in favor of the older, and also continuously used, *polk;* both *reitar* = heavy cavalryman (cf. German *Reiter/Ritter,* Polish *rajtar/rejtar*) and *dragun* = light cavalryman (ultimately from French *dragon*), both also attested in earlier texts; *rota,* meaning a squad or company of soldiers (cf. German *Rotte*); *sherenga* = rank or row of soldiers, file or column, from Polish *szereg;* and *pekhota* = infantry, from Polish *piechota* perhaps via Ukrainian *pikhota,* which would subsequently coexist

with the Petrine loanword *infanteriia*.[31] But most of these terms, as the authorities just cited indicate, seem to have been applied in Russian only to
foreign military units or to the regiments of "foreign formation" periodically raised for service in the Muscovite army, which were officered and sometimes also manned by European mercenaries. One may wonder, accordingly,
whether their appearance in this evidently little used manual marks their assimilation or "fixture" in Russian (see introductory remarks to Appendix II).
At the same time, the *Uchen'e* of 1647–1649 does offer important linguistic evidence of the creeping Europeanization of Muscovite military culture well before Peter I assumed command.

Under Peter, to be sure, the trickle of military neologisms entering Russian
swelled to a flood, as the *Military Statute* of 1716 abundantly demonstrates.
The process is already evident in the numerous Petrine precedents of this major monument of the reign, the first of them known as the *Veide Statute
(Ustav Veide)* after the Russian officer of German heritage, Major A. A. Veide
(Weyde), who compiled it.[32] It too is misnamed *ustav,* as it was drafted by
Veide in 1698 in the form of a report to Peter on what he had recently seen of
military interest during a tour of Europe that included a lengthy stay in Vienna. Veide wished to assure Peter that he had spared no effort to discover on
his tour "everything which pertains to good military instruction" and "to describe [it all] in the present little book with extreme diligence." Accordingly,
he found that infantrymen "can serve variously, namely: as *mukhetër, grena-
dir,* and also *pikinir [pikinër =* pikeman]"; that a "*rota pekhotnaia* [infantry
unit] is a unit of 100 to 120 men among the Imperialists [armies of the Austrian Habsburg empire], but among the French not more than 60 to 70 men";
that a "battalion *[batal'on]* comprises from 3–4 or 5 *roty* [companies], and is
usually a half or third part of a *polk* [regiment]"; and that a "brigade *[bri-
gada]*" in some "armies *[armii]*," the Dutch and French but not the Imperial-
ist, had from two to five regiments—the brigade formation being "a very necessary thing, as experience in all countries shows." Veide also found that
"among the Imperialists a colonel [*polkovnik,* from *polk,* both Russian words]
has full power, such that in his *polk* in an open military council he can order a *soldat* to be hung"; and that the "regimental quartermaster *[polkovoi
kvartirmeister]* does not have as much business [to do] in the Prussian land as
[he does] in other lands." In his observation, Veide adds, European armies
"usually have 2, 3 and 4 *serzhanty* per *rota.*"

Furthermore, on the critical question of the *sherenga* or infantry's line of
battle, Veide reported that the practice varied in the different lands, although
the four-rank line "seems best, since I can sooner and oftener fire and not

fall into confusion," and a line six ranks deep made for a "stronger *front and flanka*." His emphasis on the *sherenga* qualifies his report as the first complete explanation in Russian of the new battle formation for infantry: in lines—troops of the line—rather than squares (or other relatively dense units).[33] Veide further reported that pikemen had now been replaced almost everywhere in Europe by infantry bearing "flintlock muskets with bayonets [*fuzei s baginetami*], so as to have more firing."[34] Flintlocks had been in use for some time in Russia, primarily in the regiments of foreign formation, but many if not most were still imported—a situation that was virtually eliminated under Peter; and concerted use of the bayonet, on which Veide, once again, was the first to expand in Russian, seems to have been another Petrine tactical innovation.[35] Indeed Veide's report appears to have been taken very seriously by his superiors on all of these points, as it no doubt was in its repeated insistence on the necessity of "assiduous training" in "all the military arts." Veide had personally witnessed Prince Eugene of Savoy's great victory over the Turks at Zenta on September 11, 1697, where a well-trained Hungarian army of 40,000 (as he reports it) defeated a Turkish force of more than twice its size, with losses of 1,500 men on the Hungarian side to 25,000 on the Turkish. Strict discipline in the ranks, Veide had learned from the experience, coupled with a single chain of command, from the "*generalissimus* or *polnyi voevoda*" on down (the latter a traditional Russian term for supreme commander), was a "new and most valuable idea."

As he launched his wholesale expansion and reorganization of the Russian army—thirty new regiments were called up in 1699—Peter and his senior officers no doubt paid close heed to what the trusted Major Veide had to say in his little book. Moreover, the *Ustav Veide* was one of the sources used by General A. M. Golovin, head of Peter's own Preobrazhenskii regiment (in which Veide also served) and the official in charge of military training, when compiling in 1699 a manual of infantry exercises that was known first as the *Stroevoe polozhenie* (roughly, *The Combat Situation*) and then, augmented with new material, including Dutch models sent to him by Peter from Holland, as the *Kratkoe obyknovennoe uchenie . . . v stroenii peshkikh polkov* (*A Short Standard Instruction . . . for the Organization of Foot Regiments*). This little manual—scarcely more than a pamphlet—was printed at Moscow in 1699 (see Appendix I, no. 7), twice in the fall of 1700, and again in 1702 and 1704;[36] and it too provides grist for the linguist's mill, including such technical loanwords as *patron* (cartridge), *shompal* (ramrod), and *zalp* (salvo, volley) as well *baginet* (bayonet), again, and *sherenga* (rank or row). A manuscript prototype also shows, like so many other military documents of the reign, direct interventions in Peter's own hand.[37]

Epifanov, specialist on the genesis of the *Military Statute* of 1716, considers that these little manuals on infantry training and tactics compiled between 1698 and 1700 soon bore fruit, citing in support the testimony of Charles Whitworth, the seasoned English ambassador to Russia. In March 1705 Whitworth sent to London a long report on Peter's army, saying in part: "The foot are generally very well exercised, and the officers tell me, they cannot enough admire, what application the common soldiers use till they have learned their duty"—although Whitworth did observe shortages still of uniforms, firearms, and "able officers." His main informant was Field Marshal Ogilvy, one of Peter's top commanders, as in this passage of the report: "The artillery is at present extremely well served; and general Ogilvy tells me, that he never saw any nation go better to work with their cannons and mortars, than the russians did last year at Narva" (a town taken from Swedish control in August 1704, avenging the Russian defeat there of 1700).[38] In short, Peter's military revolution was being enacted both verbally and in the field, and by means of intensive training in accordance with contemporary European standards conveyed both orally and in writing as well as by actual combat experience. The young tsar and his collaborators were proceeding to modernize their army, or to complete its modernization, in a very deliberate way.

Further evidence of this dual process—that of modernizing the Russian army in practice and that of codifying the stages thereof in writing—is found in the various additional or supplementary directives issued by Peter and his leading commanders over the years leading up to the publication of the *Military Statute,* years that witnessed decisive Russian victories over Swedish and allied forces at Lesnaia (September 1708) and Poltava (June 1709) in addition to the Russian capture of the fortified Baltic towns of Vyborg, Riga, Pernau, Kexholm, and Reval (1710). There is, for example, Peter's list of resolutions *(rezoliutsii)* issued in February 1702 to points *(punkty)* submitted by General B. P. Sheremetev, which constitute a set of directives bristling with the new military terminology—as do his "resolutions" sent to the *Prikaz Artillerii* (Artillery Office or Chancery) in Moscow in February 1705 and those responding to a report from General Admiral Apraksin (a leading figure of the previous chapter) in November 1707.[39] General Alexander Menshikov's "Instruction for a Military Campaign" *(Instruktsiia vo vremia voinskago pokhoda),* issued in June 1704, was an early Petrine statement of the drastic punishments to be meted out for infractions of military discipline—not more drastic than was common in Europe at the time, to be sure, but new for a Russian force in their specificity and severity.[40] Here Menshikov exhorted his troops, "whether cavalry or foot, to behave and act with God's help like honorable and good soldiers should, as in the example[s] and punishment[s] of [specified in] the 43 articles of the military article *[43 stat'i artikula voinskago]*." The last referred to the so-called *Ulozhenie* or "Code" of B. P. Sheremetev, apparently the first, if still quite rudimentary code of military discipline ever drawn up in Russian.[41] It was not printed at the time (not until very much later, in a history of military justice) and its shortcomings compelled Field Marshal Ogilvy among others to press for a fuller code—a *novoi artikul,* in Peter's words, responding to an inquiry from General Repnin, to replace the "old" one.[42] Repnin was also told that funds must be allocated for new uniforms *(mundiry),* that more provisions were to be acquired by the appropriate *komissary* and cartridges *(patrony)* and pouches *(liadunki)* obtained, and that various individual officers—from corporal *(kapral)* to field marshal *(fel'tmarshal)*—were to be promoted, demoted, or reassigned.[43]

Peter's "Points to Battalion Commanders" *(Punkty komandiram batalionov)* of March 6, 1706, have been described as at once the "first military directive to be based entirely on current battlefield and training practices" and the tactical inspiration of the subsequent Russian victories at Lesnaia and Poltava.[44] Directed to the "gentlemen officers *[gospodam ofitserom]*" indicated, who were to observe its injunctions as "honorable men liable to answer before the Lord God and a military court," it covers matters of basic order and discipline, and includes the usual modicum of new military terminology— *proviant, furazh, ledunka* (i.e., *liadunka*), and so on. A note in Peter's hand indicates that copies of his directive were to be given to the local governor *(Gubernator)* and three named officers.[45] Shortly thereafter he drafted a longer *Uchrezhdenie k boiu,* or "Directive on Battle," which states that in the old days soldiers did not undergo the *ekzertsitsii* that were now standard for the *rekrut* before going into battle, exercises that included training in line tactics *(linei)* and in securing the *flanki,* in "seconding *[sikundirovanie]* one another" so that the line may be held "without confusion *[bez komfuznstvo],*" and in firing "properly and not hastily." All captains and subordinate officers were to maintain their position in the line of battle so that they could properly command *(komandavali)* their units and "not look to the major in everything and themselves do nothing." Every battalion commander *(batalion komanduiusshchii)* was to stand at the head of his battalion and order the first salvo *(zalb/zalp)* at the right moment, to array his forces in rows *(sherengi)* "from end to end of his battalion," and to see that all the staff officers *(shtap-*

afitsery) were in position on their horses. Detailed instructions followed on how "firing in time of battle is to take place." These made it clear that officers were to train their men in one of two *maniry:* the first was "by ranks or rows *[sherengami],* like this: the first row is never to fire without need, but to fix bayonets *[baginety]* and hold their arms like pikemen . . . [while] the other rows are to fire in turn from the shoulder, and officers strictly to watch that one loads while the other fires." Officers were also to take up their positions in a certain way: "the captain in the midst of the unit, the second lieutenant *[potparutchik]* on the right side, the *fendrikh*[46] (but if there is none, the sergeant) on the left, by the cavalry; all are to stand with their row, not behind it, the better to see and give orders; and the second lieutenant looks down the entire line *[linei]* of his unit, each corporal, down his—so as to convey the officers' orders." The second "manner of firing," then, was "by platoon *[plutongami],*[47] which is better and not liable to confusion *[konfuzii],* and so it's better to train this way: the soldiers are to stand four men in a row, with the corporals at the left side and the officers at the right of each platoon . . . and then [order their men to] fire by platoons, row after row, from the shoulder and not hastily, strictly observing that the fourth platoon not fire while the first is still retiring. . . . And junior officers *[under-ofitsery]* are to know how to command *[komandovat']* like the senior officers *[obor-ofitsery],*" in case they had to replace them. Meanwhile generals *(generaly)* were to have overall command of the forces, to maintain discipline, and to administer military justice. Signed "Piter" and dated March 10, 1708, the "Directive on Battle" was initially to be distributed to "the Field Marshal, Generals Repnin and Alart, and Major General *[general-maeor]* fon-Berdin."[48] Epifanov points out that the "manner of firing" recommended by Peter in this directive, "by platoons," had only recently been introduced into the French and other European armies.[49]

Such de facto precedents of the *Military Statute* of 1716 could be multiplied. Certain "Rules of Combat *[Pravila srazheniia]*" to be imparted "before a battle *[pri batalii],*" probably drawn up in July 1708 after an ignominious Russian defeat by a smaller Swedish force, "reveal in almost every paragraph the painful lessons" of that defeat, as one military historian comments.[50] Or there is Peter's directive to the cavalry earlier that year ordering it "to attack *[attakovat']* not in columns, as was formerly done, but in lines"; for it was "not right that our cavalry *[nasha kavaleriia]* should drive deep behind the enemy, but rather, having shattered him while formed in squadrons *[shkvadrony],* should await orders from their commanders *[komandirov]*" and then, in pursuit, separate into "small detachments *[detashamenty]*."[51] A report to his Senate dating to early 1712 shows Peter absorbing the lessons of his defeat by a huge Ottoman army at the battle by the river Pruth, in Moldavia, in July 1711, a defeat that had exposed serious logistical shortcomings on the Russian side; here Peter also refers to monetary penalties for officers whose soldiers deserted while under their command, a measure adopted, like others that he reports, in a "council of war *[v kansili]*."[52] Later that year General Sheremetev wrote to Peter from Kiev asking how he should prepare for a possible Turkish attack, "defensively or offensively *[defensivo ili ofensivo]*," to which Peter replied, in detail, that "at this juncture *[koniuktur]*" a defensive posture was best.[53] Or there are Peter's very detailed instructions of early 1713 on how to maintain battle readiness addressed to the commanders of an allied army in northern Germany (troops from Denmark, Prussia, and Saxony as well as from Russia), instructions that verbally exhibit his thorough immersion in contemporary European military culture.[54]

Two important precedents of the *Military Statute* of 1716 were the manuals of military justice printed at St. Petersburg in 1714 and 1715. The first was entitled *Instruktsii i artikuly voennye (Military Instructions and Articles)* and consisted of previously issued directives, "codes," "instructions," and so on; but the second, entitled *Artikul voinskii kupno s protsesom nadlezhashchii sudiashchim (The Military Article, to which is joined the appropriate judicial procedure)*, was laid out in 209 individual articles, many with an attached "explanation," followed by a *Brief Depiction of Trial Procedure (Kratkoe izobrazhenie protsesov ili Sudebnykh tiazheb)* that had been drawn from Imperial (Austrian) and Saxon models and first printed in 1712. Both manuals were the work of a German expert—Ernst Friedrich Crompein (Krompen)—in Russian pay who was supervised, as always, by Peter himself, and large portions of both would be incorporated in the *Military Statute* of 1716.[55] Numerous other books or booklets on military subjects were also printed at the new (1712) St. Petersburg Press before the *Statute's* appearance—as many as sixteen separate items (counting subsequent editions, twenty-three).[56] One of these was a *Kniga o eksertsitsii tseremoniakh i dolzhnostiakh voinskim liudem nadlezhashchikh (A Book of Ceremonial and Official-Duty Exercises Appropriate to Military Persons)* published in an edition of 1,050 in April 1715: it contained a "Part One: On Exercises (or lessons) *[O eksertsitsii (ili uchenii)]*," which was a reworked version of the *Kratkoe obyknovennoe uchenie* originally compiled in 1699–1700 by A. M. Golovin and printed in 1700, 1702 (the edition used here), and 1704; a Part Two, "On Preparations for the March *[k marshu]*"; and a Part Three, on the duties of the regiment from the soldier to the colonel—all followed by an index *(Reestr)* of the whole.[57] This manual, about 100 printed pages in length, was incorporated in its entirety in the *Military Statute* of 1716.

So much for the numerous tactical instructions, articles of war, disciplinary codes, and military directives and manuals issued and often printed by Peter's government during the nearly twenty years that elapsed before publication of the *Military Statute* of 1716. I have labored to show that all of them may be viewed as forerunners of the *Statute* or as contributors, however minor, to its contents. But more, when considered chronologically, as a series of explicitly dated texts, they also clearly mark the phased assimilation in Russian of an increasingly large vocabulary of more or less technical military terms borrowed from the standard European repertory—most often from German, or from German via Polish, but also from French, or from French via German. To turn this simple point around: linguistically as well as juridically the *Military Statute* of 1716 represents the culmination of a process that had been under way for decades, not simply a one-time Russian translation or edition of some foreign model or models. Moreover, if the *Statute* did not initiate the Petrine military revolution, it also did not bring it to completion; rather, it codified that revolution at a crucial stage. This position is somewhat at variance with that of the leading military historian of the era, Beskrovnyi, who characterizes the *Statute* as the "sum *[itog]* of the reformative activity of Peter I" in this arena[58]—a position that seems to ignore important military developments of the remaining eight years of Peter's reign, including, above all, the incorporation of the new military establishment in the massively reorganized central state bureaucracy (Chap. 4). Nor should the *Statute* be seen only as a military document. From our point of view it is also, indeed is primarily, an important text in the history of Peter's ever intensifying cultural revolution, a revolution that would not fully unfold until well into the eighteenth century.

The *Military Statute* proper, the *Kniga ustav voinskii . . . (The Book of the Military Statute . . .)*, was first published, at the St. Petersburg Press, on July 19, 1716, in a pressrun of 662 known copies (216 leather bound). It was published again on May 15, 1717, this time with a German text *(Kriegs-Reglement . . .)* on facing pages, in an edition of 300. It was republished in December 1717, May 1718, October 1719, and June 1721—all in Russian only.[59] After Peter's death it was published again in 1737 (with German text), 1742, 1748 (with German text), and 1755;[60] at least twice in the later eighteenth century as well as in 1804 and 1826;[61] and, finally, in 1830, in the *Complete Collection of Laws of the Russian Empire*, once again with the German text.[62] These data alone are evidence of the durability of this Petrine legislative monument, published and republished as operative law for more than a century. I might also note that the recurrent publication of the German text of the *Statute* evinces the continued service of German-speaking soldiers in the Imperial Russian army—both officers and men—and the persistence into the nineteenth century of German as the second official language of the Russian Empire.

What became the complete edition of the *Military Statute*—and there is considerable confusion on this point in the secondary literature—was first published at the St. Petersburg Press on October 29, 1719; my further discussion of the document—like Beskrovnyi's—is based on a copy of this edition.[63] Its full title runs as follows: *Kniga ustav voinskii, o dolzhnosti generalov, felt marshalov, i vsego Generaliteta, i protchikh chinov, kotorye pri voiske nadlezhat byt', i o inykh voinskikh delakh, i povedeniiakh, chto kazhdomu chinit' dolzhno. Kupno pri sem Artikul voinskii, i s protsesom nadlezhashchim k sudiashchym, i Eksertsitsieiu o tseremoniiakh i dolzhnostiakh voinskim liudem nadlezhashchikh (The Book of the Military Statute, on the duties of generals, field marshals, and the entire body of general officers, and of the other ranks proper to an army, and on the other military matters and procedures that are to be done by each. To which is joined the Military Article with appropriate judicial procedure, and the Exercises both ceremonial and official appropriate to military persons).* The complete edition of Peter's *Military Statute* thus consists of three separate books or parts bound together but separately paginated: the first, the *Statute* proper *(Ustav voinskii),* as first published in 1716, in sixty-nine chapters preceded by Peter's preface and followed by two content indexes, one by chapters, the other by "points *[punkty]*" within chapters; the second, the 209 mainly one-paragraph *Artikuly voinskie,* many accompanied by an "explanation *[tolkovanie]*" set in smaller type, followed by the fifteen chapters of the *Kratkoe izobrazhenie protsesov, ili sudebnykh tiazheb,* both as printed together in the manual of 1715 and both fully indexed; and the third, the three-part manual on ceremonial and other military exercises first printed in April 1715 (also mentioned above), here also fully indexed. All told this complete edition of the *Military Statute* occupies some 230 quarto pages, with the text of the *Statute* proper filling roughly half of them (101 pages plus 6 more of index).

Unlike the *Naval Statute* of 1720, which was to some extent modeled on it, the *Military Statute* of 1716 has been the subject of some scholarly study, including Korotkikh's critical analysis of its judicial significance, assessments of its military import by Beskrovnyi and Duffy, and Epifanov's investigation of its genesis and "basic ideas."[64] Korotkikh's analysis, which finds the *Statute's* judicial sections at once "progressive" and "regressive," is perhaps a little naive, in that military justice alone is at issue; moreover it is precisely in this area, as we shall see shortly, that it owed most to foreign models. At the same time, Korotkikh rather confusingly assesses the wider judicial significance of the *Statute* as a "most important monument of Russian law, having determined the development of our legislation over the succeeding century and a half": he probably refers to the fact that the inquisitorial procedure laid down in the appropriate section of the *Statute* remained the norm for all Russian courts until the Judicial Reform of 1864.[65] Meanwhile much of Epifanov's investigation of the *Statute*'s genesis revolves around the question of the extent to which it was, or was not, indebted to foreign and particularly German and Swedish sources—in other words, was or was not an indigenous Russian product; and in arguing for its Russian originality he no doubt exaggerates Peter's personal, authorial role in putting it together: "Peter I was not only the compiler or editor [*sostavitelem ili sobiratelem*], but the actual creator and author of the basic *Statute* of 1716," he asserts. It certainly is true that, as with virtually all the major legislation of his reign, Peter's hand is everywhere in the drafts of the *Military Statute* and related documents, editing or "correcting" a line or point here, adding a personal or explanatory note there, urging the project on. Yet the basic work of compiling the *Statute* was done, as Epifanov and others have shown (and my own investigations have confirmed), by an assortment of collaborators and assistants, Russian and foreign, including the already named Major Veide, Generals Menshikov and Golovin, and Ernst Friedrich Crompein; and their sources included, apart from those already mentioned, a special collection of translated French, English, Danish, and Swedish documents on judicial procedure as well as a copy, also carefully translated, of the *Kriegs-Articckel* of Charles XI of Sweden.[66] The latter date to 1683 and have been described, "all 145 of them," as "draconian" in their severity and enforceable "to the letter. . . . [They] were clear that obedience to superiors was unconditional at all levels and any refusal of orders was punishable by death, as was any cowardice in battle and serious moral offenses, including all instances of rape."[67] In short, the *Voinskie artikuly Sveiskago Karolia XI (Military Articles of the Swedish [King] Charles XI)*, as they were called in the Russian translation, exerted a major influence on the drafting of the corresponding sections of Peter's *Military Statute,* a fact that was demonstrated long ago by a Russian historian of military law.[68]

The language itself of the *Military Statute* is of course heavily indebted to foreign sources and practices, particularly German and Swedish—a point that Epifanov concedes, if only very generally. But before documenting the point we might briefly consider the *Statute*'s more purely military import, with due reference to the views of Duffy and other military specialists, the better to put its language in context. We might also recall Peter's overall motive in publishing the *Statute,* indeed in launching his entire military program. It was, as expressed in his brief preface to the document, to complete his father's business of creating a "regular army *[reguliarnoe voisko]*" so that Russia could avoid the shameful defeats suffered between Tsar Aleksei's death (1676) and Peter's own initial reforms, a period "when we were unable to withstand not only regular nations, but even barbarians *[ne tochiiu s reguliarnymi narody, no i s Varvarami]*." Peter thus refers to the "still fresh memory" of losses to the Turks in the Chigirin war of 1677–1678 followed by the unsuccessful Crimean campaigns of the 1680s, his own equally unsuccessful first Azov campaign of 1695, and his decisive defeat by the Swedes at Narva in 1700. "But when we reorganized the army, with external [divine] help," he continues, "then what great progress *[kakie velikiia progressy]* we made, and over such a glorious and regular nation [Sweden]; and as anyone can judge, this was the outcome of nothing other than good order." This *Book of the Military Statute* was compiled, Peter concludes, "so that every rank should know his duty, and be bound by his calling, and never plead ignorance" thereof.[69]

In Duffy's summary, the *Military Statute* shows how Peter, "following the western European practice, recognised no permanent subdivisions between the mass of the army as a whole and the multitude of the individual component regiments." A division *(diviziia)* was "a military formation," quoting the *Statute* itself, "in which several brigades *[bregad]* come together under the direction of a single *general,*" while a brigade in turn comprised two, three, or more regiments commanded by a *bregadir.*[70] For Peter, again in Duffy's words, "divisions and brigades were *ad hoc* groupings, and (in the case of divisions) existed in peacetime purely for administrative convenience." A second, "much more original" aspect of Petrine military practice reflected in the *Statute,* Duffy continues, is "the kind of self-sufficient mobile formation which he [Peter] used to smash [Swedish General] Lowenhaupt at Lesnaia in 1708." Such a force, quoting once again the *Statute* itself, was to be

detached *[otdetashovano (ili otdeleno)]* to lie at the disposal of the general, whether to cut the enemy off, deprive them of a pass *[pasu]*, act in their rear, or fall on their territory and make a diversion *[diverziiu]*. Such a formation *[Takie korpusy]* is called a flying corps *[korvolant;* cf. French *corps volant]*, and it consists of between six and seven thousand men. A force so constituted can act without encumbrance in every direction, and send back reliable information of the enemy's doings. For these purposes we employ not only the cavalry *[kovalerii]*, but also the infantry *[infanteria]*, armed with light guns, according to the circumstances of time and place.[71]

Duffy observes that a flying corps on the Petrine model captured Berlin in 1760, and that "these distinctive formations have reappeared in Russian strategy over the centuries" since.[72] Another such distinctively Petrine feature of the *Military Statute*, still according to Duffy, was the army's strict subordination to its supreme commander and the latter's to the monarch combined with an emphasis on the importance of councils of war. The generalissimo or field marshal, in other words, was also held strictly accountable to his own subordinate generals assembled in council: "Every important and weighty matter," quoting the *Statute*, "and every enterprise, is always to be decided with the council of generals *[konsiliia generalov]*, and never at his own pleasure."[73] Diplomats and other senior officials might join councils of war when the deliberations turned on wider matters, and Peter himself sometimes submitted his projects to such a council for its consideration. Duffy comments: "Hence Russian councils of war assumed a more important role than the councils in foreign armies, where they were a favorite resort of weak commanders. The Petrine version was designed partly to curb independently minded generals . . . and partly as a means of educating the monarch and the senior officers." It was also designed, Beskrovnyi adds, to counter a certain distrust, based on experience, of foreign officers in supreme command.[74]

As for the rest of the *Book of the Military Statute*, it is clear to Duffy that while "a prime objective" was "to ensure that holders of every rank were aware of their exact duties," its advice on the deployment of an army for battle was sensibly concise. As the *Statute* itself put it, all depended on the prudence, skill, and courage of the *komanduiushchii general;* it was up to him to consider the lay of the land and the enemy's positions, and to dispose his forces accordingly.[75] Duffy observes that the "stipulated tactics were of the linear kind, and borrowed straight from the Western practice," a point that Beskrovnyi disputes, though without explanation: "the *Statute* of 1716," he asserts, "affirmed linear tactics *[lineinuiu taktiku]*, but as distinct from Western European military theory and practice did not go so far as to become a mere copy of the Prussian type."[76] Lastly, Duffy remarks that "all ranks were to be kept up to the mark by [the *Statute's*] ferocious and comprehensive articles of war," all 209 of them, which were indebted, as he notes, to contemporary Austrian, Prussian, Danish, and Swedish as well as older Muscovite practice (Beskrovnyi acknowledges no foreign sources here whatever, only Petrine precedents).[77] It has also been suggested, by another Russian student, that the *Statute*'s emphasis on military engineering had a major influence on the development in Russia of a distinguished school of this branch of military science.[78] We will pursue this point presently.

Let us turn now to language, starting with that of the *Statute* proper, which constitutes as mentioned above the first, eponymous part of the complete *Book of the Military Statute* first published in October 1719, as well as roughly half of its total text. Its sixty-eight chapter headings alone are indicative both linguistically and substantively of the military revolution, or revolutions, that the *Statute* strove to codify. Thus: "Chapter One, "On the Volunteers *[O volunterakh]*"; Chapter Two, "Of the Officers that belong to the artillery *[Chto k artilerii prinalezhit ofitserov]*"; Three, "On the Engineers *[O inzhenerakh]*"; Four, "On the Reserve Corps *[O korpuse reservy]*"; Five, "On the Brigade *[O brigade]*"; Six, "On the Flying Corps *[O korvolante]*"; Seven, "On the Division *[O divizii]*"; Eight, "On the Army and the ranks of the general staff *[O armei i o chinakh generalnogo shtapu]*"; and so on. The next thirty-five chapters of the *Statute* (Chapters Nine through Forty-Four) specify the privileges and duties of general officers, from the supreme commander or "Generalissimo *[Generalissimus]*" and the "General Field Marshal *[General felt marshal]*" down to the "Brigadier *[Brigadir]*" and on through the "Paymaster General *[General kriks tsal meister]*"[79] and the general in charge of the wagons (*General vagen meister*)[80] to the general commanding the military police (*General gevaldiger, ili rumor meister*)[81] and the "Staff Provost General *[Shtap general profos]*," or general in charge of all prisoners. Interspersed among these chapters are others prescribing the duties of other senior officers: the "Chief Field Chaplain *[Ober polevoi sviashchennik]*," the "Field Doctor *[Polevoi doktor]*," and the "Field Courier *[Polevoi kurier]*." The *Statute*'s remaining twenty-four chapters (Forty-Five through Sixty-Eight) cover everything from the billeting of troops (*kantonir*[82] *kvartirakh*) in various situations including "winter quarters *[vinter kvartirakh]*" to the punishments to be administered for "quarreling," procedures for convening military courts, the duties of "orderlies [*ordinantsy*; cf. German *Ordonnanz*], and the distribution of food rations (*ratsiony*). The *Military Statute* of 1716 is saturated, in short, with neologisms, usually of German origin, many of which were not permanently fixed in Russian. Yet for the long life of the *Statute* (or until the ranks and functions in question became obsolete), even these terms presumably remained intelligible to the literate Russian serviceman (and his auditors) owing to the verbal contextualization, often including an explicit definition or equivalent Russian term, provided in the *Statute*.

Indeed these explicit definitions or Russian equivalents occur as regularly in the *Military Statute* as they do in the *Naval Statute* of 1720: as they do in virtually all important Petrine legislation, as we shall see. Epifanov emphasizes this feature of the *Military Statute* when praising its "soldierly, popular, clear and understandable, 'folksy' language," this "despite the appearance of foreign words, which in most cases are clarified."[83] He quotes two examples from the *Statute* of such clarifications—"'*korvolant,* that is, a light corps *[korvolant, sirech' legkii korpus]*'" and "'*ober-ofitser,* or senior head man *[ober-ofitser, ili starshii nachal'nyi chelovek]*'"—and it might be helpful to add a few more. In Chapter One "volunteers *[voluntery]*" are described as "young persons, well-off or poor, who intend to abide in military service" or as, a little later in the chapter, "voluntary persons *[volnye liudi]*," *vol'nye* of course from *volia,* an old Slavonic and Russian word meaning "wish, will, volition, agreement, freedom."[84] The artillery in Chapter Two is said "to constitute as it were a separate corps *[korpus]*" and to comprise "all the arms and instruments needed in battle, namely: howitzers *[gaubitsy],* mortars *[mortiry]* with the necessary stands, big and small grenades *[grenaty]*," and so on. Chapter Two also contains a long list of officers subordinate to the general in charge (*General felt"tseikh meister* = Master of the Ordnance);[85] surely a bewildering array of titles to the Russian recruit, more familiar equivalents are sometimes therefore offered: *ober* (German *ober*) is explained by *vyshnyi,* for example, *gauptman* (cf. German *Hauptmann*) by *glava,* and *bruken meister* (cf. German *Brükenmeister* = master bridge builder) by *mostovoi master'.* Chapter Three, "On Engineers," states: "*Inzhenery* are to be attached to the army, ordinarily their station is with the artillery, and they march *[marshiruiut]* with them. They are to be ranked according to their skill, and paid according to their merits"; it was already explained, in Chapter Two of the *Statute,* that they accompanied the artillery with their axes, hammers, and shovels in order to help emplace the guns and mount siege operations; and later, in Chapter Three, in the section "On the Chief Engineer," it is stressed that "engineers are most necessary in the attack *[pri atake]* or the defense of some site," for which reason it was essential that they understood the basics of fortification (*fortifikatsiia*). Detailed instruction follows: "When some site is to be besieged, then they [engineers] are carefully to inspect it with the senior generals and sketch as much as possible, and then submit their opinion as to where it is best and most convenient to attack *[atakovat']*. When the attack is decided upon, they must direct the workers to begin making trenches, approaches, and fascines *[transhei, aproshi,*[86] *fashiny]*," which the chief engineer was "to ensure were sufficiently wide and deep or heaped high with earth, and when ready, to report as much *[reportovat']* to his general." Earlier were quoted the *Statute*'s definitions of a *korvolant* and a *diviziia* among the many such verbal aids to the assimilation in Russian of hundreds of mostly borrowed terms, terms denoting the ranks and functions of what by now (1716) was rapidly becoming a modern Russian army.

120

The longest single chapter of Peter's *Military Statute* proper, Chapter Ten, explains the role of the "General Field Marshal, or the [commander] in chief *[General felt marshal, ili ansheft]*."[87] He was

> the commanding chief general in the army *[komanduiushchii glavnyi general v voiske]*. To his order and direction *[order i povelenie]* all in the army must submit, since the whole army *[armeia]* and its present purpose are entrusted to him by his sovereign. His rank is such that he must be not only a person of great skill and courage, but of good conduct (that is, of complete propriety) *[dobrogo konduvita (sirech' vsiakiia godnosti)]*, which qualities *[kvalitety (ili kachestva)]* should be linked with beneficent and honorable righteousness. For his courage strikes fear in the enemy, his skill moves people to rely firmly on him, and victory *[viktoriia]* and prosperity are thus much to be hoped for. His good conducts *[dobrye konduvity]* incite obedience and strongly augment his authority (or his power) *[avtoritet (ili vlast' ego)]* with the civility that all should render him. His sagacious conduct and anxious solicitude sustain the whole army, and bring good fortune in battle.[88]

Thus advocated here, as so often in the *Military Statute*, is the new ethos of service that Peter and his collaborators sought to inculcate in officers of the new Russian army along with the new military practices and corresponding terminology. In fact, the emotional or moral appeal manifested here, like its analog in the *Naval Statute*, readily mixes with the practical, for example in this further explication of the commanding general's duties:

> If something important arises, it is proper to give orders in writing, not in speech, and so equally to receive reports *[reporty]* about such matters in writing, whether on the cavalry or on the infantry and artillery *[kako Kavalerie, tako i Infanterie i Artilerie]*. For nothing important can be done against his will, nobody can act without a special Order from his commander *[Ordir ot nego komandira]*. For the commanding high general can be compared to the human soul in the body, in that without the soul it cannot move, and so with the army. . . . If a siege is intended, then

he is to order the place surrounded and watched. He himself must also inspect the place, observing how and where the lines of circumvallation and contravallation *[linei tsirkumvalantsii, i kontravalantsii]*[89] should be made; also, which side is not the strongest, where the attack *[atak]* is best made. . . . If it is necessary to do battle with the enemy, he should first secure a convenient high place and then issue the order of battle *[order debatali;* cf. French *ordre de bataille]* for the whole army, cavalry, infantry, and artillery, with all due advice. He is to order the baggage train moved to a safe place. He is to instruct all the regiments to uphold themselves in the present battle bravely and courageously, and to inspect the perimeter, and the lay of the land, and to order as needed redoubts and trenches *[reduty i tranzhamenty;* cf. French *tranchement]* dug around, and sentries posted, and the reserves *[rezervy]* readied, and to supervise everything with farseeing diligence, as is proper for a wise commanding general.

121

And if the army were idled for a time, the chief general was "frequently to inspect" his troops and encourage the regiments to train constantly so as to maintain combat readiness. "At his order the entire encampment *[lager, ili stan]* is to be set up properly, kept clean, and, by instructions *[po instruktsiia (poriadkam)]* given once, everyone is to do his duty." The commanding general was to remember that on him rested "all responsibility for the army's well-being," for which reason he was to report *(reportovat')* to his sovereign regularly as well as to his council of war—"if possible once a week, at least twice a month." On campaign and in battle he was always to be visible, "always on horseback." Nor was he, again, to neglect to consult his subordinate generals: "It is never proper to undertake grave and important matters, and any initiative, at his own pleasure, without the council of generals *[bez konsili generalov]*," who were to ratify his decisions with a show of hands, even when the enemy was nigh, whatever the occasion might be; in any and all circumstances an "oral council *[slovesnoi konsilium]* is to be held, even sitting on horseback."[90]

Chapter Ten of the *Military Statute* then turns to the judicial responsibilities of the field marshal, or commanding general, and provides among other things that "when some wrong is done by a court, he is to judge these judges"; but if he neglects his duty in this respect, "then he himself will be as worthy of punishment as the guilty." Like admirals in the navy (as we saw in Chapter 2), army commanders were to fortify themselves against cupidity or avarice (*sreboliubie* or *likhoimstvo*), "the root of all evil," and, "equal to it," sycophancy *(pokhlebstvo)*, which constantly threatened to bring them down; "for nothing so leads people into evil as a weak command *[slabaia komanda]*, like children left to their own wishes without fear of punishment, who usually fall into harm." Next came directions on how to billet the army *(na kvartiry razpolozhit')*, which was to be handled by the quartermaster-general *(general kvartirmeister)* and the head of the commissariat *(kamisariat)*—officers whose responsibilities are the subject of subsequent chapters (Twenty, Twenty-Seven) of the *Statute*. The field marshal was to see to this matter as well as to the provisioning of the troops, that "neither soldiers nor officers forget their duties," and that a rendezvous point—*Randevu plats*[91] *(ili sbornoe mesto)*—was designated for each company, battalion, regiment, and division of his army. Chapter Ten concludes:

> Whether on the march or in quarters *[v prokhodiashchikh marshakh ili na kvartirakh]*, in allied, neutral *[neitralnoi]*, or enemy lands, it is forbidden under pain of death to commit any outrage against, or exact any contribution *[kontributsiia]* or other [indemnity] from, the inhabitants, whatever one's rank, unless so ordered. So also no structure is to be broken or otherwise damaged, without a written order; for which the Field Marshal will give answer, if the army is not maintained in good order. And not only give answer, but be held equal in guilt with the perpetrators of the outrage, if he does not punish them according to their guilt. For an army that feeds itself by pillage, and houses itself by destruction of property, brings ruin on itself and harm to the whole state.[92]

In such ways did Peter also use the *Military Statute* of 1716 to instruct his officers in the rules of war recently worked out in Europe: to maintain or to establish, in other words, his state's monopoly of violence perpetrated on its own territory or, by its armies, on that of other states.

The remaining chapters of the *Statute* proper cover such matters as the field pharmacy *(polevoi apteka)*, its staff *(doktory i lekari)*, and the field hospital *(lazaret ili shpital)* (Chapters Thirty-Three, Thirty-Four). Similarly dealt with are the field post office *(polevaia pochta)* and its postmaster *(pocht meister)*, who was to keep horses ready for the dispatch of couriers *(kurierov)*, "because the army has much correspondence *[korrespondentsiia]* to dispatch" (Chapter Thirty-Five); rest camp, or *refreshir* [cf. French *rafrâichir*] *kvartiry*, defined as the moment "when the whole army, or several regiments, having labored much, repair for a time to quarters for rest, or subsistence, under a roof" (Forty-Six); courts martial (Fifty); the routines of the watch *(vakhta)*

(Fifty-Nine) and of "Reveille or Wake-up calls and Taps *[O reveliiakh ili pobudkakh i taptakh]*"[93] (Sixty); the times and days for prayers and religious services, the former to be said by "all, both officers and soldiers, in camp and on sentry duty, everywhere," and the latter to be held on Sundays and holidays by the army priests for every regiment (Sixty-Four); the rules of sentry duty, including the exchange of password and watchword *(parol' i lozung)*, these in a detailed chapter (Sixty-Five) on how officers were to make "the rounds *[O rundakh]*;"[94] and so forth, down to Chapter Sixty-Eight, the last, "On [food] portions and rations *[O portsionakh i ratsionakh]*," which were to be allotted by rank.

123

Chapter Fifty of the *Statute* proper, as just mentioned, deals with courts martial, outlining in this connection five general points. The third of these describes how, in cases where the death sentence was imposed, the execution *(eksekutsiia)* was to be carried out "publicly *[publichno]*, before the regiment, under the direction of its major or adjutant *[po prikazu maeorskomu, ili ad"iutantskomu]*."[95] The numerous infractions of discipline liable to court martial are the subject of the ensuing and second main part of the complete *Book of the Military Statute,* whose compilation Peter himself closely supervised and which consists of the 209 Articles of War *(Artikuly voinskie)* with intermittent "explanations *[tolkovaniia]*" grouped in twenty-four chapters, the whole occupying some fifty pages of text.[96] The listed infractions run the gamut from offenses against religion (blasphemy, black magic, vain swearing, disrespect for clergy, coming drunk to services), which consume the first seventeen articles, to failing to maintain one's uniform or arms in proper condition, secretly corresponding with the enemy, inciting mutiny and mayhem, indulging in abusive speech, neglecting sentry duty, partaking in a duel *(duel')*, and committing murder, "the sin of Sodomy," rape, and lechery; the specified penalties for these and other offenses range from monetary fines payable to the field hospital to confinement for various periods, various forms of corporal punishment, and death by decapitation. It should be noted, however, that many of these articles are concerned with proper military conduct in various situations, with tactics and procedures, and only secondarily if at all with alleged transgressions and their punishment. Peter's Articles of War, still less the *Book of the Military Statute* as a whole, are not simply a penal code, as some students seem to have thought,[97] although the penal element, not surprisingly, is certainly prominent. Mindful of our primary interest in the verbal aspect of the Petrine military revolution, we might consider some of these 209 articles in more detail.

Article 113 of the chapter "On the Taking of towns, fortresses, booty, and prisoners" prescribes how "standards *[shtandarty]*" were to be surrendered, while Article 102 of the chapter "On Storms or assaults *[O shturmakh ili pristupakh]*" specifies who was to man the "earthworks, batteries, and redoubts *[shantsy, batarii, reduty]*." Articles 117 to 123 outline the proper procedures for "handing over a fortress, capitulation *[kapituliatsiia]*," and reaching "accords *[akordy]* with the enemy." Officers of all ranks are warned not to compel their soldiers to perform "difficult or heavy work," with or without pay, for "their private *[partikuliarnoi]* service and benefit" under pain of "deprivation of honor, rank, and property" (Art. 54). Every soldier is enjoined "diligently to see that his uniform *[mundir]* is intact and his gun always clean," while any soldier who "wilfully despoils or breaks his gun, pickaxe, pike, sword, or anything else from the stores"—or who lost, sold, or pawned his gun or uniform—was of course liable to chastisement; "for arms," the accompanying "explanation" reads, "are the most important members and tools of the soldier, by which he vanquishes the enemy. And whoever does not take care of his gun gives a poor sign of his soldiery *[soldatstvo]*, and . . . therefore merits harsh punishment" (Arts. 56, 58, 59). Neglect of guard duty *(karaul)*, by officers or men, is excoriated at length (Arts. 36–49); "For *karaul*," it is explained, "is the vital organ *[zhivot]* of fort and camp, and not only the general, but the whole army places their trust in time of sleep in the sentries *[na karaulnykh]*. Karaul is the most important service a soldier can render in time of war."[98] Again, "Neither officers nor other ranks are to presume to write about military matters, the army, or fortresses, nor to correspond with others about this *[nizhe o tom s drugami korrespondovat']*, under pain of loss of rank, honor, or, in a substantive matter, one's life" (Art. 128). Murder *(O smertnom ubiistve)* is the subject of one whole chapter (Arts. 154–164) and considerable effort was expended in defining it—eleven sorts of wounds are to be considered mortal—and in distinguishing it from an act of self-defense; similar pains were taken in defining suicide and in settling the question, given such factors as "memory loss, sickness, and melancholia *[melenkholiia]*," of whether the deceased should be buried honorably or in disgrace or, in the case of a soldier who fails in the attempt, dishonorably discharged or put to death. The sixteen articles (133–148) of the chapter "On Inciting riot and mayhem" prohibit any unauthorized gathering of troops, even for purposes that were "not evil," such as drawing up a petition; dueling in particular, whether with pistols *(pistolety)* or swords, and serving in a duel as a second *(sekundant ili posredstvennik)* were heartily condemned.[99] Deserters *(dezertiry)*, along with those who were absent without or beyond their leave *(sverkh otpusku)*, were also, to be sure, liable to severe punishment (arts. 94–100).

Indeed anxiety about desertion, treason, mutiny, and mayhem is a dominant theme of the Petrine Articles of War—and little wonder, given their recurrence not only in the Russian armies of the time but in armies throughout contemporary Europe, as the professionalization and bureaucratization of war as well as its frequency spread and intensified.[100] Anyone found guilty of daring to correspond secretly *(taino korrespondovat')* with the enemy was to be considered a "rogue and traitor *[shelm i izmennik]*" and not only "deprived of honor, goods, and life" but also "quartered"; equally guilty was anyone who knew about such correspondence *(o takovom korrespondentsii)* and did not report it (Art. 124). Similarly anyone, whether officer or ordinary soldier, who revealed to the enemy a password or watchword *(parol' ili lozung)*, or gave "any such treasonable signs, by gunfire, song, outcry, fire, and the like," was to be so punished (Art. 125). Spies *(shpiony)* were to be treated in like manner, as was anyone who distributed "enemy patents and manifestos *[patenty i manifesty]*" (Arts. 129, 130). The severity of the punishments seems to have matched the anxiety of the legislator, whether Peter I of Russia or Charles XI of Sweden (author, as mentioned earlier, of Peter's main legislative model here). Thus also the notorious punishment called *shpitsruten* (running the gauntlet), which was to be imposed for interfering with comrades on guard duty (Arts. 45–47), for instance, or for "wilfully despoiling" one's soldierly "tools" (Art. 58). Although this practice, like the term itself, was recently borrowed from abroad, there is evidence that in Russia it came to be "regularly applied as a means of enforcing discipline, and was prescribed for quite insubstantial offences"; in fact this "horrifyingly brutal penalty," in Professor Keep's view, came to typify the subsequent Russian military penal system. Keep grants that Peter's *Military Statute* was "based in its essentials on current Western legislation and practice," and finds some further mitigation in the fact that it "was introduced at a time when the regular army was still in a formative phase . . . : soldiers still needed to be intimidated into giving their superiors the automatic and unthinking obedience characteristic of eighteenth-century armies." He also suggests that beating in any case was quite compatible with the "paternalistic principle" animating Petrine military legislation, which at other times might incline officers to treat their subordinates gently or patiently, "as if they were children." Nevertheless, Keep argues, imposing *shpitsruten*, among other "barbarous penalties," for "numerous 'major' offences" was one among "many major deficiencies in the system of military law which Peter established."[101] But it should be remembered, at the same time, that Peter borrowed not only the "essentials" of his military law from Europe but also much of its detail, as the language of both the *Statute* itself and the Articles of War amply demonstrates; and that by his own account Keep perhaps confuses later Russian military practices, for which others were responsible, with Petrine ones.[102]

126

Article 20 with its accompanying "explanation" is perhaps the best known of the Petrine Articles of War, and here again the question of its proximate source is significant. The article reads: "Whoever offends against the person of His Majesty by abusive words, scorns his actions and purposes, and treats of same in an unseemly manner, is to be deprived of life by decapitation," and the explanation that immediately follows states: "For His Majesty is an absolute monarch [*samovlastnyi Monarkh*] who need answer to no one on earth about his affairs, but has the power and authority as a Christian Sovereign to rule his dominions and lands by his own will and good judgment"; it is also stated that this article applies not only to Peter himself, but also to his wife and "the heirs of his State."[103] Both the article and its explanation are virtually identical with those found in the corresponding parts of the *Naval Statute* of 1720, as cited in Chapter 2 (p. 74 above), where the explanation was described as encapsulating the theoretical basis, and basic justification, of the whole Petrine program. Yet it also deserves notice that such formulations were common in the ordinances of royal absolutism promulgated in early modern Europe and particularly in neighboring Sweden, that "glorious and regular nation" as Peter called it in his preface to the *Military Statute*. Indeed contemporary Swedish notions of absolute "Christian monarchy," particularly as expounded by Charles XI (1672–1697),[104] suggest compelling precedents for these Petrine formulations, unprecedented as they were in Russia itself. Further, it is highly likely that they were inserted in the first draft of Peter's Articles of War (from which they were later copied into the *Naval Statute*) by the Saxon jurist Ernst Friedrich Crompein (Krompen in Russian), who in drafting the articles for Peter appears to have drawn on, among other sources, Charles XI's *Kriegs-Artickels* of 1683. Peterson has pointed out that Crompein certainly possessed "detailed knowledge of Swedish law" and that in drafting the Petrine articles he most probably made "extensive use of Swedish military legal procedure."[105] More proximately still, the "explanation" of absolute monarchy asserted in Article 20 of Peter's Articles of War and again in his *Naval Statute* is taken directly from a Russian translation of the Swedish *Land Law* (first printed in 1608) as revised, to accommodate the claims of royal absolutism, in the 1680s and 1690s.[106] The revisions were made to the first section or "title" of the *Land Law* (*Shvetskogo gosudarstva Zemskoe Ulozhenie*, in its Russian translation), the so-called Royal Chapter, which states (translating from the Russian edition) that "the King is fully sovereign and absolute *[edinoderzhavneishii i samoderzhavneishii]* in the state over all living beings and their properties, he is obliged to answer to no one on earth about his affairs, but by his own will, as a Christian king, has complete power and authority to rule his state."[107] It is curious, to say the least, that this clear Swedish precedent for the first verbalizations of Russian absolutism had not been cited before by scholars.

Following the Articles of War in Peter's *Book of the Military Statute,* and continuously paginated (55–78) with them, is the *Kratkoe izobrazhenie protsesov, ili sudebnykh tiazheb (Brief Depiction of Trial Procedure)* that was first printed in 1712 and that was also drafted by Ernst Crompein under the tsar's direct supervision. Its pedagogical tenor is apparent from the outset:

A court *[sud]* is always made up of a certain number of honorable persons who have been given authority and power in the administration of justice *[pravosudie]* by the supreme governor. These solemnly charged persons conduct their lawsuits *[tiazhebnye dela]* accordingly, and by [applying] the laws to them are able to obtain decisions from them. In our view, justice may be most conveniently administered in the following way: (1) In a civil court, which in times of both peace and war is solemnly established in every state, various disputes and quarrels which have arisen between subjects of various ranks are submitted to this judicial authority. (2) In a military court, in which only disputes that have arisen between officers, soldiers, and other persons attached to the army are investigated, and upon discovery decided; and it is our intention to explain the latter now at greater length.

And so the authors (Ernst Crompein and Peter I) do:

A military court, or court martial *[voinskii sud, ili kriksrekht],*[108] is similarly divided into a general court martial *[v generalnoi kriksrekht]* and a regimental court martial. In a general court martial the following causes are adjudicated: (1) the accusation *[vina]* of offense against Majesty [the ruler; cf. French *lèse-majesté*], or state matters *[gosudarstvennye dela];*[109] (2) faults *[progresheniia]* arising from the whole, or half, of the regiment, battalion *[batalion]*, squadron *[shkvadron]* or company. (3) When complaints relating to the honor and life of eminent and high officers *[ofitserov]* are brought. (4) Also, if the field marshal *[felt'marshal]* or another high officer is to be deprived of honor and life. And to the regimental court martial *[k polkovomu kriksrekhtu]* belong causes that arise between junior officers *[under ofitserami]* and the other ranks. Or when a transgression is committed between them and others. . . . (5) The judicial authority of said courts martial *[kriksrekhtov]* does not extend further than to officers, soldiers, and other people attached to the army, among whom are considered officers' servants, victualers, and others, except for women and babes. (6) It was customary that 13 persons were always appointed to sit on courts martial. Also, that on a general court martial the field marshal or his deputy sat as president *[prezidentom]*, and on a regimental court martial, the colonel or lieutenant-colonel. But since various military needs do not always permit having the full number of officers in judicial cases, because cases often arise that are impossible to conclude quickly, therefore it is now permitted in many places to seat only 7 persons on courts martial. And if the ruling Sovereign is present with the army, then he is to preside *[preziduet]* at a general court martial.

Thus were transmitted from Sweden to Russia the practices and norms of contemporary European military justice. The *Brief Depiction of Judicial Procedure* proceeds in its remaining chapters to explicate the calling of witnesses, the issuing of safe-conducts *(O salve Kondukte)*,[110] the role of the lawyers *(advokaty)*, the taking of written and oral testimony, and sentencing, the latter to include the procedure for appealing a sentence. The close substantive correspondence at several points between these procedures and those outlined in the relevant parts of the *Kriegs-Artikels* of Charles XI has also been documented by Peterson, who suggests that the inquisitorial process which both prescribe was "designed to tighten up and maintain strict discipline in the army."[111] Peter's codification of military justice in Russia—in Russian—can be seen, in short, as an integral part of his larger program of military modernization.

Lastly, the complete edition of the *Book of the Military Statute* contains, separately paginated (36 pages) and indexed, the *Book of Ceremonial and Official-Duty Exercises appropriate to military persons* first printed at St. Petersburg in 1715. The brief preface to this book, or rather booklet, explains that it

comprises three parts, as follow: at the beginning, on the customary training, and on what to inspect the infantry *[infanteriia]* for, and in what manner to behave ceremoniously on the march *[tseremonialno v marshu]*, in rendering compliments *[komplementov]* to the generals *[generalitetu]*. [Then,] On entering and departing from garrison and field quarters *[garnizonnikh i polevykh kvartir]*, and how to command *[kako komandu]*, and to maintain good order in other ways *[v protchikh manerakh]*. Following this, on the titles and duties of the regimental ranks, from the soldier even to the colonel, all written with the briefest explanation.

129

This passage is sufficient to convey both the Europeanized vocabulary and the mundane content of the booklet as a whole, and we will leave the *Military Statute* at that. A page from its first complete edition is reproduced in Appendix I (no. 28).

Textbooks and Schools

Peter's reorganization and expansion of the Russian army began in earnest in November 1697, with the call-up of twenty-seven new regiments of foot soldiers, two of dragoons, and a special unit for Novgorod, the old Russian city near the western frontier of his realm. The ensuing muster combined innovation along current European lines with established Muscovite practice. Not only, as usual, were peasants and other dependents—bondsmen, domestics, laborers—conscripted from the estates of their lords in proportion to the latter's holdings as measured in dependent households (one peasant or other conscript per so many peasant or other households), exempting only court peasants and those living in the state-controlled "black-earth" regions, but, in addition, a special effort was made to enlist suitable sons of the service nobility, of Cossacks and *strel'tsy* (the semi-regular royal musketeers), and of freemen working as hired hands in the towns along the Volga. Moreover, all of these men, conscripts and "volunteers" alike, soon to be known as "recruits *[rekruty]*," were to be inducted not for a season or a particular campaign, as tradition would have dictated, but for more or less permanent service in one of the new regiments. The first of many such recruiting drives under Peter, this one yielded by the summer of 1700 a total of some 11,000 conscripts and 22,300 volunteers, who were then grouped into regiments of 800 to 1,300 men each. Colonels were appointed to command these regiments—they were all foreign veterans of Russian service, most, to judge by their names, of German heritage—and the regiments were then assembled into three "divisions *[divizii]*" headed respectively by Generals A. M. Golovin, A. A. Veide, and A. I.

Repnin—all three, as we know, trusted officers of Peter's own Preobrazhenskii regiment, from whose ranks many subordinate officers of the new army were also drawn.[112]

The Preobrazhenskii regiment and its compeer, the Semenovskii, had been founded by Peter in 1692. Both were outgrowths of the increasingly elaborate war games that the young tsar had staged in and around Moscow between 1683 and 1694 and were made up initially of assorted playmates, courtiers, servants, and veteran soldiers, including foreign mercenaries. Their exercises at the suburban royal estates of Preobrazhenkoe and Semenovskoe (hence their names) were directed by officers and men of the only full-time, new-style units functioning in Russia at the time, the Moscow First and Second Select Regiments *(vybornye polki)*, whose origins went back to 1642 and whose men were permanently quartered in their own district *(sloboda)* of the capital. In 1690, when they were summoned to Preobrazhenskoe for maneuvers with the tsar's "play soldiers," the Moscow regiments were commanded by the Genevan François "Frants Iakovlevich" Lefort and the considerably more senior Scots Patrick "Petr Ivanovich" Gordon, the first of whom became Peter's boon companion (also the "admiral" of his initial naval exercises, as recounted in Chapter 2) and the second, his closest military advisor (both men died in 1699, to Peter's utter, well-documented dismay). The war games culminated in the so-called Kozhukhovskii campaign of 1694, when a new-style miniature "citadel *[sitadel/tsitadel']*" Peter had constructed near the royal village of Kolomenskoe was besieged by half of his combined forces—the Preobrazhenskii, Semenovskii, and two Moscow Select regiments—and defended by the other half. General Gordon later wrote that the siege, which entailed a number of casualties, was "looked upon as a preludium of some important business in hand." That "business," in which Gordon played a prominent part and Peter and his "play regiments" were first tested in battle, proved to be the Russian sieges of Azov in 1695 and 1696, the first a near disaster, the second a stunning success.[113]

Indeed the Preobrazhenskii and Semenovskii regiments, soon to be designated the sovereign's personal "guards" or "life-guards" *(gvardii* or *leibgvardii)*, along with the two Moscow regiments—soon renamed, after their commanders, the Lefortovskii and Butyrskii—formed the core of Peter's new army. In 1694 the two future guards regiments were formally subdivided into companies and then, in 1698, into battalions, the structure that was soon imposed on all regiments of the new army and subsequently codified in the *Military Statute* of 1716. Peter himself, as well as the majority of his senior commanders, served in the ranks of these regiments, an experience he would later make mandatory for noblemen and officers' sons (including his own son) who aspired to be officers themselves.[114] In 1694, again, a special artillery company—*bombardirskaia rota*—was formed within the Preobrazhenskii regiment and in 1698 an artillery school was set up at the regiment's headquarters: both the first of their kind in Russia. The school was headed by *Kapitan ot bombardir* Skorniakov-Pisarev, who was later to teach at the St. Petersburg Naval Academy (Chap. 2), its teachers were veteran officers of the regiment, and its curriculum embraced courses in applied mathematics, fortification, and artillery. The regiment also sponsored an elementary school for illiterate soldiers, where it taught basic letters, numbers, and *bombardiskie dela*.[115]

And so it went. The first "regular" cavalry regiments were formed in 1701, the year that a fully fledged artillery regiment was also founded complete with a company of engineers. But Peter's ambition to create a thoroughly modern or "regular" army required that he initiate training of a kind and to a degree that were largely unknown in Russia, particularly for officers and particularly in the technical branches. In fact, such training had only recently taken root in Europe itself, where it had barely kept pace with the interlocked developments in artillery, fortification, and siegecraft that together had transformed the nature of war. An assortment of noble riding and fencing academies, officer cadet corps, and professional military schools, often short-lived, had risen in the later sixteenth and the seventeenth centuries to meet the need for specialized training—and so to erode, as J. R. Hale puts it, "the notion of the well-born individual's right to command on the basis of birth and a familiarity with horse and sword."[116] Courses in mathematics and fortification were also taught at the Jesuit and Protestant colleges founded all over post-Reformation Europe. But among military men themselves practical experience was still prized, including the *Kavalierstour,* or trip abroad, during which the young nobleman or officer candidate sought not only to broaden his mind by acquaintance with other lands and foreign languages but also to acquire military knowledge if not actual combat experience in the army of some famous commander.[117] Peter readily adopted this convention, too, as witness Major Veide's *Kavalierstour* of Europe in 1697 recounted earlier in this chapter and especially his service under Prince Eugene of Savoy; in fact, the more purely military aspects of Peter's own Grand Embassy to Europe of 1697–1698, which included close inspection of fortifications and frequent artillery displays, may be considered such a tour. Still, the mathematics essential for mastering modern fortification and siegecraft and for successfully deploying the latest artillery could not be learned, or best learned, by passive observation or simply on the job. Like the military monarchs of Europe before him (and the Venetian and Dutch republicans), Tsar Peter of Russia would discover that institutionalized military education was essential to fulfilling his program of military modernization.

His problem in this regard was acute. Not only were there no military schools whatever in Russia before Peter took charge, but, as he complained to the head of the church, Patriarch Adrian, early in October 1700, there was little formal education of any kind, adding that what did exist relied heavily on foreign tutors who did not speak Russian properly—"kotoryia slavenskago nashego iazyka ne znaiut pravo govoriti"—and did not share their Orthodox faith.[118] Peter's institutionalization of naval education was discussed in Chapter 2 and hardly less important, he had come to see, was the launching of some such project for the army, particularly its technical branches. More than 3,400 senior and junior officers were needed to staff the new army regiments mustered in 1699–1700, for a start, and the available supply of at least minimally qualified foreigners, some 300 men, could barely begin to fill the bill. Nor could the newly founded school at Preobrazhenskoe train sufficiently all 2,000 of the Moscow court nobility selected from a special muster for officers held in the spring of 1700.[119]

Peter's solution to the problem was to redouble efforts to recruit officers abroad—his famous Manifesto, in German, of April 1702 promising religious freedom to all interested parties was one such measure[120]—and until late in his reign nearly all of the most senior ranks of the Russian army and many of the junior were occupied by foreigners (hence the German edition, as we have seen, of the *Military Statute* of 1716).[121] He also founded more schools. The *Pushkarskaia shkola* opened in Moscow in 1699 was renamed the *Artilleriiskaia shkola* and put on a firmer financial footing in January 1701, when it took in 250 students, roughly the number it would maintain in the years to come; its curriculum, typically divided into elementary and higher levels, included numbers and letters, geometry, trigonometry, and drafting, and its faculty included at least one German. Two other artillery schools were opened under Peter: one in Moscow, in 1712, headed by the German commander of his first artillery regiment, the other in St. Petersburg in 1721. Meanwhile a *Shkola inzheneraia* was founded in Moscow in 1709 whose complement of students was set at 150 and one of whose teachers was a Swedish prisoner of war. This school continued to operate until 1723, when it was transferred to St. Petersburg and merged with the army engineering school established there in 1719 under the direction of a Frenchman. What records there are indicate that the latter school's curriculum concentrated on mathematics and fortification, and that its student body ranged from 68 boys in 1719 to 176 (with the influx from Moscow) in 1723. As with the best of his naval cadets, some of Peter's engineering and artillery students were eventually sent abroad to complete their training: in one such case, in his words, "30 good & young officers from captain to lieutenant, regardless of family *[familiia]* or wealth, with a good heart and dedication to service," were sent to France in 1712. Nor should we neglect to mention the elementary garrison schools for soldiers' children founded by him in tandem with the Admiralty schools mentioned in Chapter 2, although, unlike the latter, these survived him: some fifty garrison schools existed at the time of Peter's death and the system remained intact long thereafter.[122]

The artillery and engineering schools founded by Peter in St. Petersburg also continued to function long after his death, and in 1731 were joined by a military academy for noblemen with a broader curriculum of arts and sciences, the *Shliakhetskii kadetskii korpus*. This Noble Cadet Corps, its name redolent of cognate institutions in Europe, had been established on the initiative of one of his generals, P. I. Iaguzhinskii, and was housed in the vacated palace of another, the recently disgraced A. D. Menshikov; over the next thirty years some 2,058 noble cadets passed through its portals, some 1,200 of whom became officers.[123] In these several ways the institutionalization of military education in Russia, as in Europe generally, proceeded apace. More to the point now, the Petrine military schools engendered a series of translated textbooks that gave their Russian students direct access to the vocabularies of contemporary European military culture. These textbooks also contributed importantly to the modernization of Russian military and, more broadly, verbal culture.

Eleven such translated works on artillery or fortification were printed during Peter's reign, four in multiple editions (leaving aside for now the discussion, initiated in Chapter 2 and continued in Chapter 5, of purely mathematical textbooks). The first is a didactic account of the successful siege of Azov in 1696 written in German by Peter's Austrian master of siegecraft at the time, Baron Ernst Friedrich von Borgsdorf. Translated into Russian and dedicated to Peter, the book purports to offer lessons drawn from the Azov siege in the form of twelve principal rules of siegecraft. It was first printed in Moscow at the end of 1708 on fifty-five quarto pages complete with etching-engravings of the attack, defense, and profile of the Azov fortress by P. Picart, the most prolific of Peter's imported graphic artists. It was reprinted in either large or small format three times in 1709 (see Appendix I, no. 15) and twice in 1710, as much to trumpet the memory of this victory over the Turks, it would seem, as to inculcate the basic rules of siegecraft in Russian engineering students.[124] A related effort was the translation from German of a handbook by a leading representative of the contemporary "German school" of fortification, Georg Rimpler;[125] entitled *On Rimpler's Method of Building a Fortress (Rimplerova manira o stroenii kreposti)*, it was also first printed in Moscow at the end of 1708, on fifty-eight quarto pages with illustrations apparently reengraved from those in the original German edition. The manuscript translation from which the Rimpler book was printed shows numerous corrections mainly in Peter's hand. Nor was he satisfied with its first edition. Peter complained to the official in charge of the Moscow press that the appearance of his advance copies of both this and the Borgsdorf book was "very bad, [the letters] not clean and thick, very hard to read." He also protested that the plates *(v kuporshtikherse)*,[126] especially in the Rimpler, were of poor quality and badly placed, and in both books should be printed "like big figures *[figury]*," that is, in folio.[127] Like the Borgsdorf, accordingly, the Rimpler was promptly reprinted in "several dozen" large-format (folio) copies and then, as Peter had also ordered, in "several hundred" small (quarto) copies.[128]

Four other works on the art and science of modern fortification were printed in Peter's time, facilitating the transfer of contemporary European military architecture to Russia.[129] They included a translation "into the Russian language *[na Rossiiskii iazik]*" by Ivan Zotov, brother of Konon (the naval officer and translator from French active in Chapter 2) and himself fluent in French,[130] of the Paris 1683 edition of François Blondel's *Nouvelle manière de fortifier les places (Novaia manera, ukrepleniiu gorodov)*, with Peter himself the editor of the section on Blondel's "practice" *(Praktika gospodina Blondelia, o sochinenii fortifikatsii po ego novoi manere)*; this book was published at Moscow in March 1711.[131] Then there was the translation (by A. G. Golovkin) of L. C. Sturm's *Architectura militaris hypotetica et eclectica (Arkhitektura voinskaia gipoteticheskaia i eklekticheskaia)*, which had been published in German at Nuremberg in 1702, the Russian edition a volume of some 240 octavo pages and fifty-five illustrations with a text consisting of eighty-one dialogues in which a teacher acquaints his pupil with the methods of some thirty-nine European experts on fortification, all as adumbrated in its full Russian title: . . . *To est, vernoe nastavlenie kak raznymi nemetskimi, frantsuskimi, galanskimi, i italianskimi manerami. S dobrym pribytkom, tak v reguliarnoi, kak v irreguliarnoi fortifikatsii polzovatisia vozmozhno. Iz sedmidesiat i bolee raznykh manir, kotorye ot lutchikh nyneshnykh Inzhenerov vybranny, ot chasti zhe samim avtorom izdany. V razgovore s nekotoroiu vysokoiu Osoboiu iz"iavleno (Military Architecture Hypothetical and Eclectic. That is, trusty instruction by various German, French, Dutch, and Italian methods, which can be utilized to good advantage whether in regular or in irregular fortification; selected and published from seventy and more various methods of the best current Engineers, including the author himself, and presented in conversation with a certain distinguished Person).* This book was printed at Moscow in March 1709, its illustrations etched or engraved by Johann van Blicklant, another of the Dutch graphic artists brought to Russia by Peter's master printmaker, Adriaan Schoonebeck.[132] Sturm, we might note, was a leader of the German school of fortification, whereas Blondel was an engineer who had distinguished himself under Louis XIV of France: Tsar Peter and his advsiors had chosen well. Next came their translation of a famous Dutch work on the "new fortification," which we shall consider in a moment, and last but not least a Russian edition of the *Manière de fortifier* by Vauban himself, master of them all, printed at the St. Petersburg Press in February 1724 in an edition of 510.[133] This Russian Vauban is a solid tome of some 300 quarto pages with twenty-five illustrations copied by Russian graphic artists (one identified on the plate as "Semen Matfiev") from those in the French original published at Amsterdam in 1689, their work some additional proof that Peter's revolution in graphic art had taken hold.[134] But the work is notable here for the painstaking effort by its translator, Vasilii Suvorov, to provide both Russian explanations for each item in the original's list of French technical terms *and* a separate list of the same terms now in their Russian equivalents; the latter usually take the form of literal calques or simple Russifications of the French, since Russian words evidently did not yet exist for most of these terms. A typical "fledgling" of the Petrine nest, Suvorov had attended Peter's military schools and gone on to study in France. He rose in time to become a full general—*general-anshef*—in the Imperial Russian army, a senator, and the father of another professional soldier, the legendary Generalissimo A. V. Suvorov.[135]

The Dutch work in question is Menno van Coehoorn, *Nieuwe Vestingbouw op een natte of lage horizont (The New Fortification on wet or low land),* the second edition of which, published at Leeuwarden in 1702, served as the basis of the Moscow edition of 1709. Baron Coehoorn (sometimes Koehorn) along with Vauban and the Swedish master Erik Dahlberg comprised "the trio of great late seventeenth-century engineers [who] were at pains to institutionalize fortress warfare by setting up self-regenerating corps of expert practitioners,"[136] and Peter had gone to great trouble to acquire a copy of his work and to have it properly translated into Russian. The result was a substantial volume of 178 large-format pages entitled *Novoe krepostnoe stroenie na mokrom ili nizkom gorizont . . . gospodina barona fon Kugorna,* which was printed at Moscow in November 1709 and again, in smaller format, in September 1710—

135

each time in a relatively huge run of 1,000 copies.[137] The Russian edition was prepared under the supervision of James Bruce (Iakov Brius), Peter's close collaborator in cultural revolution, and translated by Michael Shafirov, brother of Peter Shafirov, another major figure of the Petrine regime who will be more fully identified in Chapter 4; their association with this project confirms its importance in Peter's eyes, as does the fact that the volume is illustrated with fourteen engravings by Peter's favorite graphic artist, Pieter Picart. My further comments are based on a copy of the 1709 edition of this work.[138]

But first, a brief digression, the better to contextualize the work. "New" or "modern" fortifications appeared in Europe following a revolution that began in fifteenth-century Italy, as the historians cited at the beginning of this chapter and again just above (note 136) make clear. Responding to the growing range and power of siege artillery, which rendered existing defenses obsolete, towers were gradually reduced to wall-top level; the walls themselves were made lower and thicker or set in wide, deep ditches from which only their upper parts projected; and triangular or arrowhead "bastions" were pushed out from the walls to permit defending artillery to sweep all approaches to the fort, which was now preferably pentagonal in plan rather than square or rectangular (or irregular). The guiding principle was one of horizontal rather than vertical defense, with the bastion instead of the tower playing the key role: the batteries of up to four cannon emplaced in each of the two flanks connecting the bastion's angular head with the wall behind it—the curtain—protected both the curtain itself and the slanting faces of the neighboring bastions. An entire city could be ringed with bastions of the new type to provide a defensive system with no blind spots. Then, the space beyond the ditch surrounding the bastioned enceinte or city wall might be invested with a long sloping glacis, tamped earth ramparts, lunettes and ravelins: with various outworks designed to protect additional artillery emplacements and to provide a clear, progressively longer, and more sweeping field of fire. Vauban—Sébastien le Prestre de Vauban (1633–1707)—was indeed the leading figure here, having built or rebuilt several hundred strongholds for Louis XIV and furnished his realm with a cordon of powerful fortresses. He was in addition a master of the siege, his success in this field owed mainly to his famous system of parallels, whereby he advanced his troops and siege artillery in a series of carefully calculated and methodically executed movements under the protection of earthworks and trenches dug parallel to the defensive lines, until both troops and breaching batteries were securely established at the counterscarp or outer edge of the ditch surrounding the fortress under siege. As a designer of fortifications, Vauban's response to the greater firepower of siege artillery was to expand the ditch to 100 meters or more and fill it with enormous out-works, also built of brick, which dwarfed the bastions and assumed the chief burden of withstanding an assault. Following Vauban, military architects and engineers especially in northern Europe—on the northern and northeastern frontiers of France—outdid one another in the invention of new and ever more complicated outworks. "Hornworks" and "crownworks" as well as the basic ravelins and lunettes, "redans" and "demi-lunes," "tenailles" and "double tenailles" sprouted around towns and fortresses in an ever greater profusion and near fantastical complexity. Sprawling fortification belts, many hundreds of meters wide, became a prominent feature of the eighteenth-century European landscape.

Baron Coehoorn, author of the work under review, was an advocate of what he calls there "the most current or French manner" of fortification; but as befit a patriotic Dutchman, he was also an authority on building fortifications on wetlands. Both qualifications impressed Tsar Peter, conqueror of the eastern Baltic, and hence the publication, we can readily surmise, of no fewer than 2,000 copies of the Russian edition of Coehoorn's *The New Fortification on wet and low land*. Here is a sample of the new military and other technical words and phrases that appear, now in Russian, in the book's preface and first few chapters (after which severe repetition naturally sets in). They are listed roughly in the order in which they first occur, and retain their Russian case endings, verb forms, and other grammatical features—concrete evidence, here as in the other texts we are considering, of their Russification:

po nyneshnemu maniru krepost' pokryvaniem flankov, da by protivnym
    bateriam
pred shpitsami glavneishikh bastionov
18 (30, 40, etc.) *gradusov*
ataka/otakovat'
flank/flanki/flankovat
kontrasharp = counterscarp, "the slope or retaining wall on the outer side
    of the ditch,"[139] from French *contrescarpe*
perpendikuliarno
oni svoimi slabymi ravelinami zaboroniti ne mogut
kavard/kuvord/en = cover, covered way, from Dutch *cowerten*/French
    couvert
defens lineiu/lineia defensii = line of defense, "an imaginary line extending
    from the salient of a bastion along a face and thence to the curtain or
    flank of an adjacent bastion"

vo vsei evrope

v svoei arkhitekture

na dvukh poligonakh = polygon/s or, here, ordnance yards, from German *Polygon*/French *polygone*

kommandovat', ego kommanduiushchikh ofitserov

fosebrei/fosebreiov = false-bray/s, "a low outer rampart, usually built of earth," from French *fausse-braie/s*

orelion/oreliony ili plecha = orillon/s, "a projecting shoulder of the bastion, which partially screens a retired flank from fire," from French *oreillon* = ear, handle

menshim frontom streliat' bylo vozmozhno, v fronte, s bolshim frontom

pervo prolom ili bresh', nashi breshi, breshnye strelby

profil/profil' = profile, here "a cross-section of fortification," as in *nashi profili iavstvenno izobrazili*

fas/fasy, v glavnykh fasakh = face/s, "outer sides of a work which converge to form a salient angle," from French *face* = face, front

kortin/na = curtain (wall), from Dutch *gordijn*/French *courtine*/Italian *cortina*

obyknovennaia manira est' pred kortinoiu raveliny stroit'

fortetsa, glavneishaia krepost' fortetsy = fort, fortress, from Italian *fortezza*

gornverk/i, gorn i kronverk/ov = hornworks and crownworks, the former "an outwork composed of two branches at the sides and a small bastioned front at the head," the latter "a kind of hornwork," from German *Hornwerk* and *Kronwerk*[140]

brustver, 2 brustvera but also, elsewhere in text, *borstver/do borstvera/ugly bortsverov*

mina, dva prigotovlennykh min, and *iskat' ikh kontraminy naiti i razorit'*

v malykh lozhamentakh = lodgment, quarters, from French *logement*

bolverk, ikh bolverkov, v vyskoi fasy glavnogo bolverka

edin velikii inzhener frantsuskii skazal

v takuiu konfuziiu

fortifikatsiia/fortifikovat', fortifikovannye grady

ataka na nyneishnuiu maniru fortifikatsii, i pervo na ikh kontresharpy

berm/berma, na ikh bermy = berm/s, "a space left between the edge of a ditch (or trench) and the foot of the slope of the rampart (or parapet)," from Dutch *berm*/French/German *Berme*

ponton, pontony zakryty byli

kontragardiia = counterguard, "a detached bastion, standing in front of a bastion of the enceinte," from French *contregarde*

iz inoi materii

u malago tsitadela = citadel, "a compact, independent and very strong work of four or five sides. It is usually sited next to a town enceinte"

ot onoi esplanada = esplanade, "the open space left between a citadel and the buildings of a town," from French *esplanade*

do 16 sot futov = feet, from Dutch *f/voet*

dotserung/doserung = escarpment, from German *Dossierung*[141]

glasii/glasis = glacis, "the open slope descending from the crest of the covered way to the open country," from French *glacis*

bonet = bonnet, "a triangular work placed in front of the salient angle of a ravelin," from French *bonnette*

redan/redany/redanov = redan/s, "a V-shaped work, open to the rear," from French *redan*

abshnit/abshnity/abshnitov = sector/s, from German *Abschnitt*[142]

banket = banquette, "an infantry fire-step, built behind the parapet of a rampart, a covered way, or a trench," from French *banquette*

palisad/riad polisadov, i ponezhe polisady vozle ili na borstvere esplanady stoiat'

kaponier/kopanier = caponier, "a covered communication, usually in the form of a trench with raised sides, running from the enceinte to a detached work," or "a powerful casemated work, projecting perpendicularly across a ditch for the purpose of delivering flank fire," from French *caponnière*

galeriia = gallery, "the largest kind of mine tunnel," from Italian *galleria*

neskolko malykh retra(n)shamentov ili shantsov = retrenchment/s, "an interior defence," from French *retranchement*

gorizont, as in *po vysote gorizont smotria, stroenie fortetsii na mokrom gorizonte, iz pod gorizonta, postanovliaemmy gorizont 4 futa vyshe obyknovennoi letnei vody*

As in the verbal samples extracted from naval or nautical texts in Chapter 2, we have in this selection of military terms taken from the Petrine edition of Coehoorn's *The New Fortification* so much hard evidence of the entry into Russian of a whole new technical vocabulary. Many of the terms (those listed in Appendix II) made the passage permanently, as far as we can tell. Other terms found here—*kontrasharp, fas, fosbrei, retranshement, berma, orelion, glasis, redan, kaponir, esplanada,* and so on—lasted as long in Russian as their referents remained militarily current, which might have been several decades or more or even a century or two (as highly specialized terms that are for the most part now wholly obsolete as well, they are not listed in Appendix II).[143] Still other terms in this Petrine text—*abshnit, do(t)serung, defens, poligon, kortina, fortetsa, kuvrefasy, furnier, fut*—were never accepted in Russian or not for long, presumably because they were plainly redundant of existing Russian words (*fortetsa* of *krepost'*) or could be readily calqued (*poligon* as *mnogougol'nik,* except in the very specialized sense of "ordnance yard").[144] To be sure, the process of assimilation—or initial assimilation—encoded here was not always smooth, as witness the orthographic inconsistencies and the sometimes awkward grammatical constructions in the selections from the Coehoorn/Kugorn presented above. Both of these features of the text, like the occasional Slavonicims to be encountered in it (*ponezhe,* the infinitive verb ending *-ti*), can be attributed as much to the still unsettled state of literary Russian as to any shortcomings of the translator. Yet when all is said and done the Kugorn translation of 1709–1710 remains an important document of the verbal impact of the Petrine revolution, the most telling evidence in this regard being the many new technical terms embedded in its text along with others of a more general import (*Evropa, arkhitektura, gorizont, perpendikuliarno, materiia*) that permanently entered the Russian language. And much the same can be said for the Moscow 1711 edition of Blondel's *Nouvelle manière de fortifier,* with its steady flow of lexemes adapted from French—for example, *manera fortifikatsii, flank, fas (dlia oboronu fasov), ugol bastionov/ litso bastiona, poligon, korpus, kurtina (perpendikuliarnyia kurtiny), oriliony (bez orilionov), baterei, kontreskarp, profil tenalii,* and so forth. Extracts from both books are reproduced in Appendix I (nos. 16, 19).

Before concluding this chapter on military modernization under Peter we might also look briefly at the works on artillery printed in his time. There were four. The first was a folio of engraved plates illustrating with captions *The Throwing of Bombs and Firing of Cannon (O metanii bombov is strelianii pushek);* it seems to have been copied from an unknown source by unidentified artists working at the Armory Chamber in Moscow, where it was published in 1708.[145] The second was a translation from German of a lengthy illustrated treatise on the "newest principles and practice of artillery," printed in large format at Moscow in September 1709 and again in July 1710.[146] The third was a solid textbook by T. N. Brinck, captain of artillery, translated from the Dutch—perhaps by Andrei Vinius, who was bilingual in Dutch and Russian and a longtime Petrine collaborator[147]—and first published at The Hague in 1689; its Russian edition was printed at Moscow in March 1710 (Fig. 5).[148] And the fourth, a wide-ranging work titled *Uchenie i praktika artilerii (The Doc-*

Figure 5   Title page of *Opisanie Artilerii Chrez Timofea Brinku Artileriiskago Dela Kapitana (A Description of Artillery, by Timothy Brinck, Captain of Artillery)*, printed at Moscow, 1710.

trine and Practice of Artillery), was translated from the German of "Saxon artillery lieutenant J. S. Buchner," illustrated by Picart, and printed at Moscow in August 1711.[149] The second of these works, which was translated from a German original by "artillery captain Ernst Braun" published at Danzig in 1687 and titled, in Latin, *Novissima fundamentum et praxis artilleriae*, is worth dwelling on: it, and seemingly it alone among the four works, was given a substantial pressrun (1,000 copies) and it, and seemingly it alone, went into a second edition. Indeed both facts suggest the special importance attached to this work both by Peter himself and by General James Bruce, his chief of artillery, who personally edited it; so does the fact that it was richly illustrated by Henryk de Witte, another Dutch master recently recruited to work in Russia.[150] Of further interest is the handwritten note found in a copy of the second edition now at the Russian National Library in St. Petersburg: "This book of artillery *[kniga artilleriia]* the student of artillery science *[artilleeriiskoi nauki]* Fedor Evseev[ich] Pushchin bought in Moscow on May 20, 1719, for 1 ruble 6 *altyn* 4 *den'gi* or 121 kopecks"[151]—an inscription notable, as one might have said in Petrine circles, for its *punktual'nost'*.

New military terms to be found in this Russian version of Braun's *The Newest Principles and Practice of Artillery*[152] include, apart from those already adduced, *kontrabatareia* as well as *batareia, kanon* and *kanonir* as well as *gaubitsa, kalibr, mortir/martir/a, raketa, bomb/a*, and *shvermer;*[153] also, *petard/a* along with *petardir*,[154] *kartaun*,[155] and *shturmovalnoe oruzhie* meaning "assault weapon" or "siege gun." Among the transient curiosities located in this text are *shpilraum* (German *Spielraum* = room to move in) and *trompet* (French *trompette* and here meaning a gun barrel), neither of which is to be found in a Russian dictionary, and *dalekost'* (extension of *dalëkii/daleko* = distant, far, afar), presumably a calque of *distantsiia*. Also noteworthy are such Petrine technical neologisms of broader application as *kvadrant, masshtab, metall, shlak*, and *tsentner*.[156] Some of these terms did not survive very long in Russian, presumably because they were plainly redundant of well-established words (e.g., *kanon* of *pushka*) or because they more or less rapidly became, with their referents, obsolete *(kartaun, petardir, shvermer)*; while others, as just noted, remained mere curiosities. Still, a large portion of the technical neologisms studding this text permanently entered Russian (see Appendix II), in part no doubt because of their appearance in this authoritative, much replicated text. Equally arresting is the large proportion of technical terms (*pushkar'* = gunner, as well as *pushka; granata* = grenade, shell; *pishchal'* = harquebus, small cannon; *selitra* = saltpeter, *porokh* = gunpowder, *stvol* = barrel, *mushket* = musket) that were already more or less fixed in Russian and so, presumably, were not thought to need any explanation here. These terms provide verbal evidence, in short, of corresponding advances already made in this branch of military affairs in Muscovite times. They thus constitute a timely reminder that in modernizing his army Peter did not have to start, as with his navy, virtually from scratch.

4

BUREAUCRATIC REVOLUTION

At several places in the preceding chapters the term "bureaucratic revolution" was applied to the wholesale reorganization of the central administration of his state undertaken by Peter I. The occurrence of such a revolution was posited in Chapter 1 and then briefly described in support of my contention that when judged by the criteria of political modernization adduced there, Petrine Russia was indisputably a polity undergoing rapid and intensive modernization. In Chapter 2 the new offices created to administer the new navy were dealt with, as was, at some length, the *Naval Statute* of 1720, leaving discussion of the related *Admiralty Regulation* of 1722 to the present chapter: the *Regulation,* as noted there, was intended to govern the shore-based administration of the navy while the *Statute* was designed to regulate naval operations at sea. In Chapter 3 the reorganization or suppression of existing offices as well as the creation of new ones to administer the newly reorganized, expanded, and now standing army were mentioned, again leaving to this chapter detailed discussion of the bureaucratization of the Russian armed forces as distinct from the tactical, disciplinary, logistical, and other such matters covered in the *Military Statute* of 1716. Issues connected with the relocation from Moscow to St. Petersburg of the central administrative and command structures of the new army and navy have also been raised, particularly in Chapter 2, which ended by emphasizing the new capital's symbolic as well as actual importance in subsequent Russian and European history.

This chapter focuses on the cultural significance of Peter's bureaucratic revolution as manifested in the new administrative, legal, and diplomatic terminology—the language of political modernization, as it might be called—that was employed in carrying it out. But some clarification of my own crucial terms may be in order, particularly "modern" as distinct from other kinds of states (later, the Petrine as distinct from the Muscovite state) and "bureaucratic revolution." Such clarification is offered in the first two sections of the chapter, after which I revive the language question in a selection of representative texts taken from this third major arena of intensive Petrine reform.

Advent of the Modern European State

It is not much of an exaggeration to say that the disciplines of both political science and modern history have been largely devoted to studying the emergence, subsequent course, nature, and interrelations of modern states. Even when confining ourselves to the emergence of the *early* modern state in Europe we tap an immense literature, some small part of which was cited in the two preceding chapters. But for our purposes now the single most valuable work in that literature is the collaborative volume edited by Tilly, which jointly and severally offers the well-considered views of eight specialists on the process of state-building in Europe from about 1500 to about 1800.[1] Conceptual points made in this sizable volume will be supplemented here by information and perspectives gleaned from several more recent publications, also cited earlier: all this by way of providing a brief general account of the advent of the modern state in Europe as the backdrop to an assessment of Peter's reorganization of the Russian polity.

Tilly and his collaborators, he reports, agreed with relative ease on the nature of the political entity, the "sovereign state," that became dominant in Europe after 1500: "(1) it controlled a well-defined, continuous territory; (2) it was relatively centralized; (3) it was differentiated from other organizations [on the same territory]; (4) it reinforced its claims through a tendency to acquire a monopoly over the concentrated means of physical coercion within its territory." Such a political entity was to be distinguished then and thereafter from preexisting or concurrent, loosely controlled political federations or empires, theocratic or utopian commonwealths, commercial networks or leagues, and especially from the city-states and feudal structures that had dominated Europe politically for the several centuries before 1500. "Stateness" in this sense was and is to be measured by "formal autonomy, differentiation from non-governmental organizations, centralization, and internal coordination," and a "modern state," in turn, was and is "an organization employing specialized personnel which controls a consolidated territory and is recognized as autonomous and integral by the agents of other states." In other words, Tilly and his collaborators agreed that "an organization which controls the population occupying a defined territory is a state *in so far as* (1) it is differentiated from other organizations operating on the same territory [like churches, businesses, or armies, kinship, business, or professional associations, underground or criminal bodies, etc.]; (2) it is autonomous; (3) it is centralized; and (4) its divisions [departments] are formally coordinated with one another."[2] We will see shortly that, judged by these criteria, the Muscovite tsardom as it stood about 1690 had achieved at best a low or early level of modern statehood but that, more important, its "stateness" would come to be seen by its new ruler, Peter I, as seriously deficient in comparison with that of certain European powers, particularly the kingdom of Sweden.

It is of course one thing to define, as Tilly and his collaborators make clear, the general characteristics of the modern state, quite another to discover exactly how and why it arose. Nor need that be attempted here. Now it is enough to emphasize, following Tilly, that "war made the state, and the state made war." In early modern Europe, as he says,

> the building of an effective military machine imposed a heavy burden on the population involved: taxes, conscription, requisitions, and more. The very act of building it—when it worked—produced arrangements which could deliver resources to the government for other purposes. (Thus almost all the major European taxes began as "extraordinary levies" earmarked for particular wars, and became routine sources of government revenue.) It produced the means of enforcing the government's will over stiff resistance: the army. It tended, indeed, to promote territorial consolidation, centralization, differentiation of the instruments of government, and monopolization of the means of coercion, all the fundamental state-making processes. War made the state, and the state made war.

Their reciprocity was indeed crucial:

> The formation of standing armies provided the largest single incentive to extraction [of resources from subject populations] and the largest single means of state coercion over the long run of European state-making. Recurrently we find a chain of causation running from (1) change or expansion in land armies to (2) new efforts to extract resources from the subject population to (3) the development of new bureaucracies and administrative innovations to (4) resistance from the subject population to (5) durable increases in the bulk or extractiveness of the state. . . . Preparation for war has been the great state-building activity.

At the international level, moreover, "wars and war settlements" were the "greatest shapers of the European state system as a whole." Beginning with the Peace of Westphalia ending the Thirty Years War (1648), the major modern war settlements "produced incomparably greater alignments of the identities, relations, and relative strengths of European states than any long periods of incremental change between them. . . . War shaped, and reshaped, the European state system."[3] And this was the system that Russia under Peter I, its statehood markedly enhanced, would struggle to join.

Since Tilly wrote, research in early modern European sources propelled by the "new military history" (studying the wider ramifications of war) has substantiated his "reflections" though with certain revisions, inevitably, and some fine-tuning.[4] Yet even as the newer work has demonstrated that the effects of warfare on the growth of the early modern state "were both more complex, and more variable, than Tilly and others have shown,"[5] one is struck by the affirmation of Tilly's reflections that the more recent investigators provide. In the words of one: "The principal catalyst" for the "significant increase in administrative activity" throughout the early modern period in Europe "was the new scale and increased frequency of warfare." In those of another: "Where it occurred, bureaucratic growth and the expansion of military effort tended to proceed in tandem and to be self-reinforcing." And both offer cases in point: "In Denmark, for example, a more efficient bureaucracy emerged after the mid-decades of the seventeenth century, divided into specialist departments, and capable of undertaking the major task of compiling a Land Register in 1688 on the basis of which recruitment and tax yields could be evaluated, all of which permitted an extension of Danish military effort." Again: "The interdependence of the military and administrative reconstruction carried out in Brandenburg-Prussia by the Great Elector [Frederick William, reigned 1640–1688] is even more striking. . . . By 1688 [he] had an elaborate network of officials established in all of his dominions to supervise the extraction of taxes, which went to maintain a permanent force of soldiers, who were used when necessary to enforce the payment of taxes." Or again: "From the middle decades of the seventeenth century onwards the trend amongst many states in Europe was towards the development of bigger and more specialized bureaucracies, capable of mobilizing the demographic and fiscal resources of the state with an unprecedented efficiency"—and for the fundamental purpose of waging war; "we have noted something of this process in relation to Denmark, Sweden, Brandenburg-Prussia, and France. . . . In Austria, too. . . . In Piedmont-Savoy. . . . In England as well, war was the great catalyst of administrative innovation from the late seventeenth century onwards. Military and fiscal departments burgeoned." If "Europe" still comprised a "plurality of states" throughout the early modern period, by the last decades of the seventeenth century it was increasingly dominated by "a handful of great powers possessing the resources to enable them to wage war on a large scale."[6]

Unfortunately for my project, little of this new history has yet reached Russia, where it could certainly help put in perspective the military, fiscal, and related policies of Peter I, which have been treated by most historians, Russian and foreign, as virtually unique in their time if not indeed uniquely malignant. Re-embedding Peter in his wider European world is one main task of the project, to be sure, and the next section of this chapter will offer concrete verbal evidence, drawn from Petrine documents, of the deliberate transfer to Russia of the Europe-wide "bureaucratic revolution in warfare" that is the key development under review. In the meantime, it deserves mention that the phrase itself belongs to Jan Glete, the Swedish historian whose fundamental work on the rise in Europe of the modern navy was cited in Chapter 2.

Drawing on his own extensive research as well as on the thinking of others, Glete contends that "the great change in warfare" between about 1500 and 1700 was the growing ability of European states "to enforce a *monopoly* on the use of violence and on the control of armed force. It was the states, usually monarchies, which [thus] grew in armed strength and the losers were independent-minded feudal nobles and trading cities." Further, the "enforcement of a state monopoly on violence and the establishment of permanent state-controlled armed forces which effectively asserted that monopoly," a process that served in turn a crucial "state-building" function, was based not only on "technical innovations (gunpowder, guns, gun-carrying warships)," which together constituted a "technical revolution" in warfare, but on "organizational change" as well: on the "rise of military and administrative bureaucracies." Glete is thus led to call this second and decisive phase in the establishment of a state monopoly on armed force a "bureaucratic revolution," a term he then explains:

> It is not used because civilian bureaucrats became important in the armed forces, although that was undeniably the case. It is used because the attitudes and behavior of the military and civilian elites in these forces gradually came to conform with the "ideal type" of a modern bureaucrat in the Weberian sense of the term. Officers in bureaucratic armed forces feel a basic loyalty towards the state and the political aims pursued by the government of the state. . . . [They] are professionals and pass through some kind of formal career where each level has a well-de-

fined amount of authority over soldiers and other officers. Promotion along this career path is supposed to be based on merit or seniority, not on social status. War operations as well as peacetime activities are planned and prepared in an orderly way, with a substantial amount of paperwork in communication and decision-making. . . . Skills and professional capabilities . . . are transferred from older to younger members within the organization, not through the traditional master-apprentice relationship, which normally confers decisive advantages in the promotion procedure on sons and other close relatives.

Weber's "ideal" bureaucracy, I might interject, was conceived by him as an integral part of a modern or "rational-legal"—as distinct from either a "traditional" or a "transitional"—political system. The crucial characteristics of bureaucracy, in this view, include the assignment of specialized, highly differentiated roles to its members; their recruitment on the basis of educational achievement, usually measured by examination, rather than ascription on the basis of birth or social rank; their placement, transfer, and promotion according to universalistic, not merely local or particularistic, criteria; their self-identification as administrators who are salaried professionals and view their work as a career; and their practice of decision making within a rational and readily understood context of hierarchy, responsibility, and discipline.[7]

Weber himself did not suppose that functioning bureaucracies always conformed in every respect to his "ideal type"; nor does Glete make any such supposition regarding the "bureaucratic revolution" in early modern European warfare that he is at pains to document. As he readily admits,

The ideal type of bureaucratic armed force existed nowhere [in Europe] after the "bureaucratic revolution" in warfare of the 17th century. In the 18th century it was still much easier for members of the aristocracy to reach higher levels of command, various kinds of patronage were common, and officers' commissions were often for sale. . . . But the formal chain of command was undoubtedly there, the loyalty of the armed forces to the state was seldom in doubt, and the standardization of tactics, equipment and regulations was practically complete. . . . Most importantly, the *permanent character* of the armed forces was no longer in doubt. They were institutions of the European states as firmly founded as the states themselves. The officers' corps had become powerful parts of the establishment in the states they served, which of course increased their loyalty to these states. This was a tremendous change compared to the situation in 1550 or even 1600, when the idea of standing armies and navies was still highly controversial and far from universally adopted.

Glete goes on to recount in great detail the establishment of permanent navies in early modern Europe, thus supplementing the similarly detailed work done by others on early modern European armies.[8] He also supplements important earlier work on the rise of the modern bureaucratic state in Europe perceived as a social as well as a political process, as in Rosenberg's classic study of the professional class of bureaucrats that emerged in Prussia under the aegis of an absolute monarchy.[9]

We have glimpsed these processes at work in Russia, in Peter I's creation of a Russian navy (Chap. 2) and his modernization of the Russian army (Chap. 3). Both undertakings, as we saw, were closely modeled on European practices, doctrines, and norms, and so became part of the larger "bureaucratic revolution in warfare" taking place throughout contemporary Europe. And both projects led Peter directly, once again following European precedent, to his wholesale reorganization of the Russian state.

The Petrine State

The state that Tsar Peter Alekseevich inherited has been represented by historians as at once monarchical, dynastic, patrimonial, and theocratic in form. This very mix of still active political ingredients, each the legacy of earlier or more recent developments, militates against classifying such a state as modern according to the criteria outlined above. In particular, the still strongly patrimonial and theocratic aspects of the late Muscovite state must give us pause in this regard, the one signifying that the ruler was regarded as the residual owner by hereditary right of the entire country—his patrimony—and all its resources, both human and material; the other, that he was simultaneously a kind of high priest, custodian of the one Orthodox church to which all Russian Christians at least notionally belonged and whose "mysteries" or sacraments, administered by a priestly caste, alone gave them access to the kingdom of heaven. The Muscovite tsardom, in this typically "traditional" belief, was God's kingdom on earth and the tsar, His earthly viceroy. "The sovereign was at the center of a theocratic vision of government," as one student puts it, or again, in the words of another: "The image of a Russian Orthodox community served a unifying function in Muscovy and in significant measure determined the outlines of Muscovite political culture."[10] Ceremonial depictions of Peter's father, Tsar Aleksei, and of his elder half-brother, Tsar Fedor (ruled 1676–1682), show them arrayed in sacerdotal dress: these are sacred images or icons rather than secular portraits of the kind that became prominent in post-Renaissance Europe and then under Peter in Russia, and presumably were venerated as such.[11]

The central power of the Muscovite state that Peter inherited was vested in the tsar-father, his family, and his court, the latter composed of several hundred grandees (magnates, or boyars) and senior noble servitors all living with their families and numerous dependents in and around the citadel (kremlin) of Moscow when the men were not serving as governors in the provinces, leading the army on campaign, conducting embassies abroad, trading in Archangel or Astrakhan, or running ironworks in the Tula region or saltworks in the Urals. This establishment was paralleled by the much smaller court of the Moscow patriarch, the senior bishop of the Russian Orthodox church, whose constant ceremonial presence, pretensions to cosovereignty, and network of subordinate bishoprics and monasteries evoked the aura of theocracy. Apart from the hodgepodge of semi-feudal, semi-regular armed forces described in Chapter 3, the tsar's power was exercised in and through a royal council (boiarskaia duma) and a welter of some eighty or more central offices (dvory, prikazy) whose overlapping, at times duplicative functions varied enormously in territorial as well as administrative or judicial scope:[12] they were not, in any case, the clearly demarcated, formally coordinated governmental departments called for by theorists of the modern state. The officials and staffs of these offices, semi-professional at best (by modern educational and other standards), together with their sparsely distributed provincial counterparts, attempted to govern in some rudimentary fashion—to extract resources from—a vast realm of subordinate tsardoms and principalities that in turn were composed mainly of landed estates controlled by court, ecclesiastical, and local gentry servitors and worked by peasant families, the latter living under krepostnoe pravo, or the law of bonded servitude (serfdom). The prevalence of serfdom alone, the basic socioeconomic condition of the great majority of the tsar's subjects, has been taken by historians as a major marker of Muscovy's "medieval" or premodern character. So has its comparatively paltry urban network, which in the later seventeenth century, with respect now to population aggregates and the level of its administrative and commercial development, resembled China's in the late fourteenth century or those of Japan, France, England, Italy, Germany, or the Netherlands in the late fifteenth and early sixteenth centuries.[13] Still, it is not society or the economy that concerns us here but the nature of the Muscovite state.

The highly personal as well as patrimonial features of late Muscovite gover-

152

nance have frequently been noticed by historians, but so too has its highly centralized, pervasive, even "hypertrophic" character.[14] By contemporary European standards, in other words, we seem to have something of an anomaly here: a decidedly medieval society and economy dominated by a semimodern, protomodern, or early-modern state (and in that comparative sense "hypertrophic" is perhaps an accurate descriptor). The best known contemporary account of the late Muscovite polity, for all its more or less obvious limitations, was written in 1666–1667 in Stockholm by the renegade *pod'iachii* (undersecretary) Grigorii Kotoshikhin, a seasoned insider—nearly twenty years' service (1645–1664) in the Ambassadorial Office *(Posol'skii prikaz)*—whose relatively sophisticated language, a chancery Russian laced with Slavonicisms and Polish and other loanwords, was cited in Chapter 1. His treatise, intended as an intelligence report or memorandum for the Stockholm government, for which it was twice translated into Swedish (in 1669 and 1682), is divided into thirteen chapters subdivided into 235 paragraphs or articles *(stat'i)*, to give some idea of its length.[15] The first five chapters concern the tsar's family (Aleksei Mikhailovich, Peter's father), his court, and official Muscovite relations with other states; Chapter VI deals with the tsar's household administration; Chapter VII (the longest), with the central government offices; Chapters VIII and IX, with provincial administration and the military levies; and Chapters X and XII, with the "trading people" and the "tsar's trade"; meanwhile, Chapter XI looks briefly at the peasantry, classified by owner (tsar's court, the patriarch, boyars, monasteries, noble servitors, and so on), and Chapter XIII relates to the "life"—marital and religious customs, housing and domestic arrangements—of the boyars, other courtiers, and "other ranks of people." A further breakdown of Kotoshikhin's report is not needed here. For our purposes it fully confirms or substantiates, both implicitly and explicitly, the strongly patriarchal, patrimonial, and ostensibly religious character of Muscovite society described by historians as well as the highly centralized, ritualistic, protocol-bound but also highly personalized, sacrosanct, and ramshackle constitution of the Muscovite polity. Kotoshikhin simultaneously conveys a certain vagueness about the extent of the tsar's power. He explains to his Swedish readers that after the time of Ivan IV (died 1584) the tsar was "elected *[obiranyi]*" to the tsardom, whereupon he swore not to punish people without cause and to take counsel "in all matters" with the boyars and other senior courtiers *(dumnye liudi)*, and "without their knowledge *[vedomosti]* to act in nothing either secretly or openly." But on *his* election (in 1645) the present tsar, Aleksei Mikhailovich, did not execute such a promise nor was he asked to, because he was considered "very peaceable *[tikhim]*";

thus he is styled *samoderzhets,* or autocrat, "and his state he rules as he will *[i gsdrstvo svoe pravit po svoei voli],* and he makes war and peace with whom he wishes."[16] More, in "all other great and small matters of his state" this tsar "does as he wishes by his own intention. With the boyars and other senior courtiers he consults little about that which he has decided to do; nevertheless whoever of the boyars and courtiers and simple folk wishes to plea, he consults and takes counsel with them about any matter." Such conduct was in contrast to Tsar Aleksei's "father of blessed memory Tsar Michael Fedorovich," who, "though styled autocrat, was able to do nothing without the counsel of the boyars."[17] Some of Kotoshikhin's comments here can be explained by the course of events to which he alludes: the old Muscovite ruling dynasty died out with the death of Ivan IV's childless son Tsar Fedor in 1598, whereupon several usurpers succeeded one another on the throne until in 1613 an "Assembly of the Land" chose as tsar Michael Romanov, who was dominated by his father, the Patriarch Filaret, who until his death in 1633 actually ruled while his son reigned (the high point, perhaps, of Muscovite theocracy; Tsar Michael, ever weak, died in 1645). But Kotoshikhin's depiction of Tsar Aleksei in action, along with the details he provides of current Muscovite government procedure, tend to confirm what historians have otherwise documented: that there was little if any formal or institutional restraint on the Muscovite ruler's power. There was by the same token little formal or institutional *definition* of the state that this *tsar'* or king ruled, as his God-given possession, like a big father and high priest. And it has recently been shown that popular representations of royal or state power in Muscovy were remarkably similar, in their amorphous, sacralized character, to those of the ruling elite.[18]

We might consider in this connection the main legal monument produced by this state, the so-called *Ulozhenie* promulgated by Tsar Aleksei in 1649, which is as difficult to characterize, in modern terms, as the state itself (see Appendix I, no. 4). Consisting of twenty-five chapters subdivided into 968 paragraphs or articles, it is certainly the "weightiest" such document of Muscovite provenance as well as the "first attempt to regulate by statute the activities of the whole community in so far as such activities affected the interests of the state."[19] It is at first sight a kind of juridical code in that much of its content explicates "judicial process" or *sud* (court, trial, litigation),[20] the term covering both proper trial procedure itself and its application to various persons and cases. *Sud* in both senses is explicitly the topic of the longest chapter by far of the *Ulozhenie* of 1649 (Chapter 10, 287 articles) and, mainly in the applied sense, of several other chapters as well: for example, Chapter 11, on peasants, whereby they are in effect legally enserfed; Chapter 12, on the patriarch's dependents, which guarantees special status for church people; and Chapter 20, on bondsmen or slaves (*Sud o kholopakh*, in 119 articles), a category embracing perhaps 5 percent of the tsar's people but the subject, the numerous provisions of this chapter suggest, of endless litigation. Judicial matters—the definition of crimes and prescription of punishments—are also dealt with in Chapter 21, on cases of robbery and theft (104 articles); in Chapter 22, on offenses that either merit or do not merit the death penalty; in Chapter 2, on treason and offenses against the tsar's honor; in Chapter 1, on the punishment of persons who disrupt church services or blaspheme against "the Lord God and our Savior Jesus Christ, or against the Lady Most Pure Who gave birth to Him, our Beloved Virgin Mary Mother of God, or against the Holy Cross, or against His Holy Saints"; and in Chapters 3, 4, 5, and 25, which prohibit, respectively, misconduct on the tsar's properties (down to fishing without permission in his lakes or ponds), forging royal charters or patents, counterfeiting or debasing coins or defrauding buyers of works in gold or silver, and running illicit (untaxed) taverns. Still other chapters govern the taking of oaths, the payment of official fees, and the administration of "tolls, ferry fees, and bridge fees." The *Ulozhenie* of 1649 is in these many and varied respects both a civil code, regulating property matters and private disputes in great detail, and a criminal code. But as Lewitter reminds us, "it also embodies in statutory form the obligations and restrictions imposed by the state on all subjects and the privileges granted to some."[21] It prescribes, in short, the taxpaying, residential, rental, and service obligations imposed on ordinary townsfolk and peasants along with the proprietorial privileges granted to the landholding elite in return for military service, above all the privilege of having its peasants bound in perpetuity to the land.

At once a civil code, a criminal code, and a digest of statutory law, its hundreds of major and minor provisions invoking a complex network of overlapping central and local jurisdictions, the *Ulozhenie* of 1649 is not a rationalized, regularized, Roman-inspired legal compilation of the sort being published in contemporary Europe and that later would be thought typical of "modern juridical thought."[22] Nor would the informality of its procedures or the nature and severity of its penalties qualify it as such, the latter being a mix of execution by various means, flogging and other forms of physical torture, forced bondage, imprisonment, and monetary compensation payments. Nor would, again, its preoccupation with slander and other affronts to one's honor—not just the tsar's, but that of everyone from the patriarch, bishops, and boyars on down to clerks, cantors, and nuns (dishonor is the subject of seventy-two articles in Chapter 10, sixty-two of them relating to clergy). Nor would the reli-

154

gious cast of much of the *Ulozhenie* be considered typically modern by historians, or the privileged position it grants to churchmen. Nor would, indeed, its language, a prime example of that premodern or subliterary chancery Russian mixed with Church Slavonic—formulaic, barely punctuated, grammatically unstable—that was also used by Kotoshikhin and was discussed in Chapter 1. Last but not least, the *Ulozhenie* of 1649, it is somewhat astonishing to think, was initially inscribed on scrolls.[23]

On the other hand, the *Ulozhenie* does represent a well-nigh heroic effort by officials and clerks of Tsar Aleksei's government to bring some order into the mass of existing Muscovite legislation and litigation with the help of Slavonic versions of Byzantine canon law and the Lithuanian Statute of 1588; and it does seem to have been compiled with some input from selected representatives of the middle as well as upper ranks of society, who were summoned for that purpose to an Assembly of the Land meeting in Moscow in the fall of 1648. More to the point now, the *Ulozhenie* offers abundant testimony to the highly centralized character of political power in Muscovy, at least notionally. The document makes it clear that it was compiled, read out to the Assembly, printed, and then distributed "to all the chanceries and *goroda* [fortified settlements]" by decree of Tsar Aleksei, whose "own sovereign and great royal land business" it dealt with. The *Ulozhenie* makes it clear that defending *his* honor was paramount and that it was *his* justice that was to be "meted out to all people of the Muscovite state, from the biggest to the smallest"; even the patriarch, or rather his dependents, were subject to his authority—although the issue of secular versus ecclesiastical jurisdiction over clergy was to remain in dispute until finally resolved, as we shall see, by Peter I. The *Ulozhenie* also clearly assumes that the "Lord Tsar and Autocrat *[Samoderzhets]* of all Russia" was directly or indirectly the ultimate owner of the whole land (the sole possessor, as we would say, of eminent domain). Indeed figures from 1678 show that he owned outright some 10 percent of all taxpaying households (belonging to peasants, mostly, and some townsfolk) while another 11 percent of taxpayers held their allotments directly from him (no intermediary lord); also, that nearly two-thirds of remaining households lived on lands held by noble servitors obliged to render military service at his call, leaving some 14 percent of the total attached to ecclesiastical establishments (a status they retained, under increasing state pressure, until the secularization of all church lands carried out in the 1760s).[24] The taxes paid by all of these mostly peasant households went to support the tsar and his state, or *gosudarstvo*, as did, additionally, the various feudatory dues in cash, labor, or kind extracted from the tsar's own lands—as did, of course, the customs and other fees and imposts spelled out in the *Ulozhenie*. Even so, the constitution of this state, its lineaments or salient features, its origins or legal basis, its justification for being: this the *Ulozhenie* did not define, or even attempt to. It was an omission that Tsar Peter would move decisively to repair.

156   Peter also moved decisively to make the state he inherited function more efficiently: to make it perform better at extracting resources from its subjects. For Muscovy, as Kollmann says, was in fact "a minimally governed society in most ways," its state "far more similar to medieval European states than to its European contemporaries." The Muscovite state, to quote Lewitter once more, "had neither a ministry of finance nor a ministry of war, nor indeed any other department of state in the modern sense of the term." The centralization of administrative power in Moscow, as he points out,

> was not matched by a corresponding degree of coordination. A *prikaz* [literally, a command or order][25] was essentially a commission—permanent or temporary—appointed by the tsar to exercise authority on his behalf in discharging tasks as varied as the dispensation of justice to certain categories of the population, the collection of particular taxes and dues, the supervision of public works, the organization of various corps of the army, control over the tenure of landed estates together with adjudication of disputes arising therefrom, and the retrieval of runaway peasants. Not only the four main judicial *(sudnye) prikazy*, but most other *prikazy* too, exercised judicial as well as executive—including fiscal—authority over those sections of the population to which its functions appertained. Even the *prikaz* in charge of foreign affairs, the *Posol'skii,* [also] exercised jurisdiction over foreign merchants in Russia and was responsible for the administration of certain recently annexed territories such as the Ukraine and the region of Smolensk.

Lewitter notes that this "combination of centralism with the lack of distinction between the process of law and administrative procedure made for interminable and notorious delays in the dispensation of justice and these in turn opened the door to bribery and corruption"—features of Muscovite administration regularly denounced by foreign visitors and the object of sustained criticism by at least two conscientious Russian subjects in petitions to Tsar Peter: Elder *(starets)* Avraamii of the Andreevskii monastery outside Moscow and Ivan Pososhkov, the peasant entrepreneur and self-taught economist whose critique of the system achieved some modest posthumous fame. Lewitter (like other historians) further observes how "a similar lack of unity and coherence can be seen in the regional administration of the tsar's dominions" as we enter Peter's reign—a factor that allowed for considerable gentry autonomy in local affairs.[26] To make matters worse, in the absence of a succession law, a dynastic feud broke out in the 1680s between the relatives and supporters of the late Tsar Aleksei's two wives, a feud that became embroiled in bloody revolts by units of the royal musketeers and was exacerbated by the failure of the Crimean campaigns of 1687 and 1689. A prolonged crisis had set in at the very center of this highly centralized yet blatantly ramshackle Muscovite state.[27]

Peter's solution to the dynastic crisis, and to the perceived shortcomings more generally of the political system that he inherited in stages (death of his elder half-brother, Tsar Fedor, in 1682; deposition of his half-sister, the regent Sofia, in 1689; death of his other half-brother and co-tsar, Ivan V, in 1694; death of his mother, Tsaritsa Natalia, in 1696), was to lay down a succession law and to launch what I have been calling a bureaucratic revolution. It was to bring to Russian government the bureaucratic revolution of seventeenth-century Europe particularly as it was implemented in Prussia, certain other German states, and Sweden. This story too has been told in detail, and we need only consider its salient points before focusing on the principal texts that transmitted the revolution to Russia.

The salient features of Peter's bureaucratic revolution include, apart from his decree of February 1722 regulating the succession to the throne (by appointment of the incumbent), the establishment, with his military and naval statutes serving as models, of a comprehensive system of state-service ranking based on seniority and merit (achievement) rather than kinship or custom (ascription), all as provided by his famous Table of Ranks of January 1722, among many related measures.[28] They also include his design of a new state administrative apparatus consisting, at the center, of newly amalgamated and functionally defined executive agencies (the Colleges *[Kollegii]* of War, Foreign Affairs, Justice *[Iustits]*, Commerce *[Kommerts]*, Admiralty *[Admiralteiskaia]*, and so on) coordinated and controlled by a Senate *(Senat)* and a regime of procurators *(prokurory)*, their members all appointed by the monarch; and the transfer of this newly rationalized and greatly expanded central administration (between 1715 and 1721 its staff more than doubled) of the newly named (1721) All-Russian Empire *(Imperiia)* to the newly created capital, St. Petersburg, where it was to be housed in buildings specially constructed for the purpose in the new architectural style, a variation of the northern European Baroque.[29] Still more, Peter's bureaucratic revolution encompassed the Russian Orthodox church, whose traditional leader, the Moscow patriarchate, was replaced by a committee of the monarch's clerical appointees which was dubbed the Holy Synod *(Sinod)*, was assisted by a Senate-like staff under its own chief procurator *(ober-prokuror)*, and was also headquartered in St. Petersburg. "Secularization" in this quite specific sense of the term, meaning significant institutional and legal enlargement of the state's wealth and authority at the expense of those of the church, and the political subordination of the latter to the former, has long been regarded as one of the "major transformative processes of modernization."[30]

Other notable instances of Peter's bureaucratic revolution are his foundation of the tax-supported St. Petersburg Academy of Sciences (Chap. 5), whose duties included training officials for state service and conducting state-sponsored research (this in addition to his naval and military schools for the training of officers and civil servants, as discussed in Chaps. 2 and 3); his unprecedented extension of central-government control over the economic and social life of the country, especially by means of new taxes—especially the universal head tax, initially administered by the army—and a web of financial inspectors *(fiskaly)*; and, to justify it all, his adoption of a newly secular, national-imperialist ideology of monarchical absolutism that was given expression in a series of texts printed on newly founded presses in the new "civil" type (several such texts will be studied shortly) as well as in a huge array of new visual forms, including printed and painted official portraits, medals, coins, maps, seals, flags, and coats of arms.[31] I could also mention, among major initiatives to reform (re-form) his state, Peter's efforts to establish a comprehensive new judicial code based on current European models that would supplant his father's *Ulozhenie* of 1649.[32] True, those efforts failed (as did analogous attempts under successive monarchs until the reign of Nicholas I, more than a century later). But neither that failure (a draft code was completed but never promulgated) nor the related failure to separate judicial process from administration, nor the variously limited or incomplete outcomes of his other reformative efforts, particularly in the field of urban and local government, can erase the fact that the modern Russian state, in its bureaucratic, military, legal, and ideological essence, dates to Peter I.[33]

What kind of state was the Petrine state? A "well-ordered police state" of the type emerging in contemporary Germany is the most meditated descriptor so far devised, although its author seems somewhat reluctant to apply it to Petrine Russia; nevertheless, Raeff concludes, by "energetically and systematically" adopting the "concepts and practices of the well-ordered police state" *(reguliarnoe politseiskoe gosudarstvo,* in Russian) the Petrine governmental structure gradually if unevenly attained a "coherence of form that provided a framework for all of Peter's other innovative enterprises as well as the institutional basis of the imperial regime throughout the remainder of its existence [to 1917]."[34] A "modernized service state" has also been proposed, meaning one still characterized by a "universal regime of services and exactions" but marked now by "the transition from personal to bureaucratic rule"—the former associated, in the minds of both contemporary reformers and later students, with arbitrariness and corruption, the latter with honesty and rationality; but "taken as a whole," the proponent of this view concludes, "the Petrine system of domestic administration in its final, albeit unfinished, form comes closer to the modern police state or a military dictatorship than to the early eighteenth-century ideal of the *Polizeystaat*."[35] An "absolute monarchy"—secular, dynastic, militarist, bureaucratic, juristic, and personal—of the type emerging (or emergent) in contemporary France, Prussia, or Sweden and arguably as successful, in its time and place, as these others were in theirs, might seem a more apposite, and neutral, term.[36] Yet however technically defined, the Russian polity as Peter left it in 1725 was indisputably an early modern European state according to the criteria outlined above by Tilly and others. In the terms eventually deployed by the Petrine regime itself, "Russia" was now much more than the Orthodox community and royal patrimony of old centered in Moscow. It was a European-style "empire" of all its Christian subjects headquartered in St. Petersburg, a state that even the "monarch" himself, though legally absolute in his power, was morally bound to serve for the "common good." And so it would remain for some two hundred years.

159

The *General Regulation* of 1720

The single most important document encoding Peter's bureaucratic revolution was the *Generalnyi reglament ili ustav. Po kotoromu gosudarstvennye kollegii, takozh i vse onykh prinalezhashchikh k nim kantseliarei, i kantor sluzhiteli, ne tokmo vo vneshnikh, i vnutrennikh uchrezhdeniiakh, no i vo otpravlenii svoego china, poddanneishe postypat' imeiut (The General Regulation or Statute. To which the governing colleges, as well as all servitors of chancelleries and bureaus belonging to them, not only in [their] external and internal determinations, but in the performance of their office, are to be subject)*, which was first printed at St. Petersburg on February 27, 1720, and, sometime later that year, in a separate German edition.[37] It was printed again in Moscow at the Synodal Press in March 1725 in an edition of 550; in St. Petersburg under the auspices of the Academy of Sciences in 1735 and 1750 and at the Naval Academy Press in 1746; in St. Petersburg once more at the presses of both the Senate and the

Academy of Sciences, in 1765; and thereafter, in either Moscow or St. Petersburg, in eleven more known editions until that of 1800, apparently the last.[38] An excerpt from the *General'nyi reglament* consisting of a somewhat revised version of Chapter 50 of its fifty-six chapters, this one dealing with "the rewards for good conduct and, contrary to this, if someone offends against [his] duty, the penalties *[o shtrafe]*," was also published several times in St. Petersburg, at the Senate Press, in 1724.[39] These bare facts of the publishing history of Peter's *General Regulation* themselves suggest that there was both time and occasion for its new bureaucratic terminology, even the new ethos of service it more generally represented, to be assimilated by successive generations of Russian officials, at least some of whom, inscriptions in surviving copies indicate, owned it personally.[40] The suggestion is bolstered by the fact that the *Regulation* was intended, as its title plainly states, to govern all of the activities, procedural and substantive, of the new administrative colleges founded by Peter I.

As early as 1715, a note to the Senate dated March 23 of that year indicates, Peter had decided to institute a regime of such colleges or boards in Russia.[41] But his growing dissatisfaction with the perceived shortcomings of the administrative apparatus that he had inherited, particularly in taxation and recruitment, went back to the earliest years of his active reign—to 1696, in fact, and his initial attempts to create a navy (Chap. 2). His core problem, the persistent inability of his government to extract from his realm the volume and quality of resources needed to achieve his interrelated domestic and international aims, was far from resolved by the series of largely ad hoc administrative reforms undertaken in subsequent years, often in the heat of one military campaign or the wake of another. Such measures included the creation of new central offices, the abolition or consolidation of old ones, the establishment of his personal *kabinet* (1704) and of the *Senat* (1711), and the division of his realm into eight great substates or *gubernii* (1708–1710) headed by as many governors *(gubernatory)*. In the meantime proposals that the solution to this core problem lay in adopting the collegial system of government practiced to one degree or another in England, France, Denmark, much of Germany, Sweden, and the Austrian Habsburg lands went back almost as far—to 1698, quite possibly, when in England a certain Dr. Francis Lee presented a paper to the visiting tsar on "the right framing of his Government" by means of "seven Committees or Colleges."[42] In subsequent years there was talk within Peter's government of founding a college of mines to promote the extraction of ores "as in European states" and a college of commerce *(kolegium dlia torgovago)* for the improvement of trade, the latter to include among its members "one or two foreigners" with appropriate expertise because, in Peter's words, "their trade is incomparably better than ours."[43] In September 1715 Peter ordered that information be gathered in Copenhagen on the colleges established there: "how many [there were] and how many persons in each College *[v Kolegii kazhdoi]*, their duties, salaries, ranks *[rangi]* and everything else, from the big to the small." In December of that year his resident in Vienna was directed to seek out Slavic speakers who were knowledgeable about the Imperial colleges and might be willing to help establish similar organs in St. Petersburg; at roughly the same time, he requested one of his generals residing in Sweden—as a prisoner of war awaiting exchange—to get hold of "law books and any definitions of office, the ranks and duties of all the Colleges, also the land requisitions and rules, in a word, the whole establishment *[ves anshtalt]* of the Swedish state, from the peasant and soldier *[ot muzhika i ot soldata]* even to the Senate *[do Senata]*."[44] In August 1715 General Veide had written to Peter from Reval asking what compensation to offer local jurists—"learned persons skilled in law"—whom he had been ordered to recruit for service "in the [prospective Russian] Colleges"; and in January 1716 Peter decreed that thirty or forty young Russian clerks should be sent to Königsberg "for study of the German language, the better to be [to serve] in a *Kalegium*" (Veide had pointed out that jurists recruited in Livonia, Swedes or Baltic Germans "unskilled in the Russian language," would all need translators).[45]

Two lengthy memorandums to Peter vaunting the advantages of collegial government, also dating roughly to this time, have been found among his papers.[46] The first is attributed to Leibniz, the famous philosopher, with whom Peter had personally met in 1711, 1712, and 1716;[47] it urges, in rather orotund Russian prose, faithful no doubt to its putative German original, that like the absolute monarchs *(samovlastnye monarkhi)* of Europe the tsar could bring good order *(dobroe poriadok)* to his realm by instituting good colleges *(dobrye Kolegii)*, which should include those of war, finance, police, justice, commerce *(Voinskii Kolegium, Finantsii Kolegium, Politsei, Iustits, Komertsii)*. The memorandum reflects in essence contemporary German "cameralist" ideals of rational administration by an absolutist *Polizeistaat*, a state whose policies redounded not just to its monarch's well-being but also to that of its subjects.[48] The second memo proposed that the tsar institute "7 colleges in his state and capital city *[7 Kolegii v gosudarstvo svoe i v stolitsu]*" each to be headed by one of the (nine) senators, who should thus divide the government among them with "great benefit to [the tsar's] high interest *[vysokomu interesu]* and less burden to [his] faithful subjects": this provision alone, Peterson points out, reveals how closely the central administrative structure recommended here resembled that of the Swedish royal government. Peterson goes on to demonstrate that the author of this second memorandum was Heinrich Fick, a German from Hamburg who had once served in the Swedish administration and had entered Russian service, it is not clear how, by late 1714. Fick's memo, Peterson suggests, was the source both of Peter's note to the Senate of March 23, 1715, initiating his collegial reform and of his related decision to send Fick back to Sweden to gather intelligence on the Swedish governmental system, a mission that Fick conscientiously carried out for most of 1716, returning to St. Petersburg with hundreds of written documents and a rich store of oral testimony. Early in 1717 he was sent by Peter to Germany to recruit personnel for the prospective Russian colleges, from which he returned that autumn eager to begin creating a Russian collegial system. Indeed Heinrich Fick proved to be a key figure in the history of Peter's bureaucratic revolution and so, like other foreign experts who labored to implement the Petrine program, was amply if not always punctually rewarded for his services by the grant of lucrative contracts, titles, and, in his case, an estate in Estonia, where his collected papers were later found.[49]

The collegial project was sufficiently advanced by December 1717 for Peter to announce the establishment of nine such offices—the Colleges (*Kollegii*) of Foreign Affairs (*Inostrannykh del*), War (*Voinskaia*), Admiralty (*Admiral-teiskaia*), Justice (*Iustits*), Commerce (*Kommerts*), Revenue (*Kamer*), Auditing (*Revizion*), Budget (*Shtats-Kontor*), and Mines and Manufactures (*Berg-i Manufaktur*)—each to consist of a president (*prezident*), vice president (*vitse-prezident*), four councillors (*sovetniki*), and four assessors (*assesory*) assisted by a secretary (*sekretar*), notary (*notarii*), actuary (*akturaii*), registrar (*registrator*), copyist (*shreiber;* cf. German *Schreiber*), translator (*perevodchik*), and clerks (*pod'iachie*), several of which officials were supposed to be foreigners. Peter then named their presidents and, in six cases, their vice presidents, who were to set up the colleges "in the new year [1718]" but not to "interfere with things" until 1719 (a date later deferred to 1720), when "they shall begin to govern."[50] The presidents were all seasoned veterans of the Petrine regime and, in most instances, also members of old noble clans; the vice presidents, Swedes recruited for Russian service or Russian-born "foreigners" like General Veide and P. P. Shafirov. In a memo to the Senate from this time Peter ordered that members of a college were not to be relatives of its president or "his own creatures [*kreotury*]" but worthy persons chosen by ballot (*balatirom*) from among two or three nominees.[51] Similarly, in a public announcement of December 1718 he explained that for the sake of better government he was creating "Colleges, that is, assemblies of many persons in place of the *prikazy*, in which the presidents or presiding officers *[prezidenty ili predsedateli]* do not have such power, as did the old judges *[sud'i* = heads of *prikazy]*, to do as they wish. In Colleges the president can do nothing without the agreement of his colleagues *[tavaryshef].*" Here too Peter announced that the further advantages of the collegial system would be apparent when their governing statutes—*reglamenty*—were published.[52] The latter, he had instructed the Senate in April 1718, were to be drafted following Swedish models except where these were "not convenient *[neudobny]* or not compatible with the situation of this state *[ili s setuatseieiu sego gosudarstva neskhodny]*," in which case the drafters were to use their own judgment; meanwhile questions were to be directed to Herr Fick, now "back from Sweden," and the colleges were to submit their draft regulations to the Senate "one after another," where disputed matters would be resolved and a report prepared for Peter's personal review.[53]

163

Work also began promptly on the document that would lay out a uniform code of bureaucratic norms for the whole new administrative system. In fact, the relevant archive in St. Petersburg contains no fewer than twelve successive manuscript editions of the *General'nyi reglament*, the first of which was completed in December 1718 and marked "Translation. First *[Perevod. Pervoi]*," and the last of which was edited by Peter himself between January 21 and February 10, 1720.[54] The appearance of the word "Translation" on the last leaf of the first draft of the *Regulation* has been taken to mean that it was compiled by Heinrich Fick on the basis of a certain Swedish prototype, the *Cantselie Ordningh* of 1661.[55] But Peterson argues persuasively that while Fick most probably wrote this first draft, he did so not on the basis of a specific Swedish prototype, certainly not the one suggested (since it relates to one Swedish college only, and anyway bears no textual similarity with its supposed Russian counterpart), but on the basis of his own written compilation, in German, of Swedish administrative law and practice: the oath of office provided in Chapter 1 of the *General'nyi reglament*, for instance, was taken directly from an oath devised by Charles XI as found in royal instructions issued to Swedish provincial governors in 1687.[56] In any event, there can be no doubt that the compilers of Peter's basic administrative code, following his direct orders and working under his close supervision, drew heavily on Swedish precedent as mediated, in German, by Fick and three Swedish officials appointed vice presidents of the new Russian colleges (two were recruited in Livonia, after the Russian conquest, the other was a former prisoner of war); perhaps Admiral Cornelius Cruys (Chap. 2), the first vice president of the Admiralty College, also lent a hand.[57] Their deliberations, in German and then Russian, were doubtless assisted or facilitated by Generals James Bruce (ever active in Peter's projects and the first president of the College of Mines and Manufactures) and Adam Veide (first vice president of the War College and a former prisoner of war in Sweden), not to mention the tsar himself, and by various staffers. The completed *General'nyi reglament* was printed on February 27, 1720, and signed by Peter the next day, whereupon, as recounted above, numerous additional copies were printed for distribution to all concerned.

The care, indeed the rationality shown by Peter and his collaborators in drafting this major legislative monument of the reign reminds us of their preparation of the *Military Statute* of 1716 and of the *Naval Statute* of 1720; so does the radical nature, in the Russian context, of the document itself. Both points are amply borne out by a close reading of the *General'nyi reglament*.[58] Its fifty-six chapters, as its title promises, cover everything from the legislative *prerogativy* of the colleges, subject only to the monarch and, in part, the Senate, to the days and hours appointed for their meetings; from the procedures for promptly registering decrees of the sovereign and Senate to guidelines for promptly ordering the business that came before them (e.g., "first public *[publichnye]* state matters, pertaining to His Majesty's interest *[interesu]*," were to be considered, "then private *[privatnye]* affairs"); from the methods for reaching decisions *(rezoliutsii)*—by majority vote of members present, the president to break a tie, after everyone had freely expressed his view, the results to be recorded by the notary *(notarius)* in the day's protocol *(protokol)*—to the rules for dividing up responsibilities among the members, it being emphasized that the president had only a general supervisory or managing function *(general'nuiu i verkhovnyiu direktsiiu, ili upravlenie)*, not an exclusive or comprehensive authority. The new Russian bureaucrats or would-be bureaucrats could also readily find in the *General Regulation* the procedures for filling vacancies *(vakantsii)* in a college or its staff, the former by vote of the Senate among several nominees (as Peter had earlier decreed), the latter by appointment of the president and other members of the college concerned after considering, again, "several worthy persons" for each position. The proper use of seals in official correspondence *(koreshpondentsiia)* is also spelled out in the *Regulation,* as are the rules for how such correspondence was to be conducted. So are the proper conduct of the president's office *(kamor)* and the form of the compliments he was to receive (*O komplementakh presidentov:* other members were to rise only on his arrival and departure, though always to render him appropriate *respekt*), and the proper furnishing of a college's audience chambers *(kamory audientsii)* for the reception of petitioners. Presidents and vice presidents were charged with full responsibility for the conduct of their college's staff—the *sekretar', notarius, perevodchik, aktuarius, registrator, kantseliaristy, kopeisty*—all of whose duties are also spelled out in detail. The duties of the college translator—*perevodchik*—are notable, too: he was, on receipt of a document, to see that it was translated "from the foreign language into Russian *[na russkoi]* clearly and distinctly, so that the right sense *[sens]* and opinion of the original is conveyed *[soglasno bylo]* in the translation"; and "it will be sufficient if in each College there is one translator very skilled in the Russian *[rossiiskom]* and German languages, except for the College of Foreign Affairs, which will require more translators skilled in other languages." The ongoing necessity of working with German models and with German-speaking advisors and of getting it right in Russian, the crucial bureaucratic importance of accurate translation, were thus underlined.

165

And so on. Penalties for derelictions of duty, usually monetary fines *(shtrafy)*, are specified throughout the *General Regulation* as well as in a separate chapter (Chapter 50), which, as noted above, was separately printed in 1724 and which provides *shel'movanie*, or various forms of public dishonor, including execution, for serious infractions of the rules. The organization of the colleges' archives *(arkhivy)*, chancelleries *(kantselarii)*, and subordinate bureaus *(kantory)*, the last usually to be located in Moscow and the provinces, is laid down in detail, as are the responsibilities of the special inspectors *(fiskaly)* to be attached to each college under the overall supervision of an inspector general *(generalnyi fiskal)* attached to the Senate. So are the duties of the college watchmen and guards *(O vakhmistrakh i kollegiinykh storozhakh)*. Rules are prescribed even for the expenditure of petty cash *(melkie roskhody)* on candles, sealing wax, and firewood for a college's use. And all of these topics are clearly listed by chapter in an appended Register *(Reestr)*, or index, of the *Regulation*'s contents.

Also helpfully appended is a glossary or "Explanation of the foreign locutions *[rechei]* that [are] in this *reglament.*" Only three of the thirty-three terms listed here in parallel columns with their nearest Russian equivalents were not themselves assimilated in Russian: *aksidentsii, privatnye,* and *eksekutsiia,* the last to mean, here, not capital punishment but "fulfillment/acting as ordered *[ispolnenie po ukazu]*." The remaining thirty terms—permanent additions to Russian and as such listed in Appendix II—include, in the order (and spelling) found in the glossary: *prerogativy, interes, approbuetsia, publichnye, rezony, rezoliutsiia, kriminal'noe, publikatsii, direktsiia, v partikuliarnykh, v spetsialnykh, balatirovat', report, ordinarnykh, korrespondentsiia, o komplementakh, respekt* (appears twice), *kvitantsiuiu, kontseptov, instruktsiia, diplomy, patenty, memorialy, formuliary, dokument, akuratno, rekommendatsiia, khar-*

166

aktera, and *traktovany* (from *traktat/traktovat'*). Nor was the assimilation of these terms in Russian a narrowly lexical event only; in many cases, here as elsewhere in this study, a semantic or conceptual alteration took place as well, as a comparison of such terms with their would-be Russian equivalents in the glossary clearly indicates. For example: *prerogativy* is a more technical or legalistic term than *preimushchestva,* meaning advantages or privileges more generally, the Russian equivalent given; *interes* is something more than, or more abstract than, *pribytok i pol'za; vsenarodnye,* which later also came to mean "international," is offered as the Russian equivalent of *publichnye,* from which it was doubtless calqued; *ballatirovat',* to vote by ballot, is other or more than just *izbirat',* to choose, *diplomy* than *zhalovannyia gramoty, formuliary* than *obraztsy, akuratno* than *ispravno,* and so on. Still, the effort by the compilers of the *General Regulation* to make the new terminology intelligible to Russian readers of the day is striking, even when it required several words to do so, as in *rekommendatsiia,* explained as *proshenie ob odnom k drugu.* At the same time, the oddities or uncertainties, or perils, of translation are in evidence here, too, as in the definition *vina podlezhashchaia smerti* (fault or guilt deserving death) for *kriminal'noe.* And some of the new terms listed in this official glossary were little more than additions to the lexicon that bore, at best, depending on context, special connotations (here, highly official connotations): for example, *rezony* for *razsuzhdeniia,* or *rezoliutsiia* instead of *reshenie.*

In their brief preamble to the *General'nyi reglament* Tsar Peter and his collaborators offered this rationale for the new collegial regime—in essence, for their bureaucratic revolution:

Whereas H[is]. Ts[arist]. M[ajesty]. our most merciful lord, on the example of other Christian [= European] realms, has been pleased to conceive the most merciful intention, for the sake of the orderly administration of his state affairs and correct determination and calculation of his revenues and the improvement of beneficial justice and police *[iustitsii i politsii]* (that is, in dispensing justice and citizenship *[sudnoi i grazhdanstve]*), and also so far as possible for the preservation of his faithful subjects and the maintenance of his sea and land forces in good condition, and also commerce *[komertsei],* the arts and manufacture *[manifaktur]* and the good management of his sea and land duties [taxes], and for the increase and increment of his ore-extracting plants and other state needs: pursuant to these appropriate requirements, to found State Colleges *[Kollegii],* which are then named. Peterson, steeped in the probable Swedish prototypes of Peter's collegial project, finds that this passage exhibits "a clear touch of [the] cameralist thinking" that animated them.[59] It is also clear that whatever their sources may have intended or provided, the drafters of the *General Regulation,* including the tsar himself, were deliberately expanding the scope of Russian government. Now it was to include the preservation if not improvement of its subjects' economic and social welfare, this to be achieved by the establishment of more orderly administration particularly in revenue collecting and the dispensing of justice. The articulation of such a goal and related administrative norms certainly constituted a radical departure from the well-nigh exclusively patrimonial and theocratic as well as static political values of Muscovite government as verbalized, most prominently, in the *Ulozhenie* of 1649. The *Regulation*'s repeated insistence on administration by qualified personnel should also be noticed in this connection, qualified by reason of education and "good conduct" rather than birth or good connections, as in its Chapter 34, "Concerning young people for training in the chancelleries," which again, Peterson reports, was directly modeled on a Swedish ordinance.[60] However poorly the *General Regulation* of 1720 may have been understood and implemented at first—and there is plenty of evidence that this was so at both the central and local levels[61]—the vocabulary of political power had been greatly and, as it proved, permanently augmented in Russia. Thus also was inaugurated, arguably, a corresponding shift in political values together with a professionalization of administrative practice: a shift, in sum, from medieval or traditional ways of doing government business to what have been defined as rational or modern ones.

167

Regulations and Justifications

Individual governing statutes or "regulations" or, sometimes, "instructions *[instruktsii]*" were drafted for the new administrative colleges in the remaining years of Peter's reign (he died in January 1725) and most of them were printed then or later—thus promoting, in Ong's terms, the "interiorizing" of their prescribed practices and norms by successive generations of Russian officials.[62] We will look at three of these texts now in our continuing effort to track the Petrine revolution in Russian verbal culture: the *Regulation* of the Revenue *(Kamer)* College, that of the Admiralty College, and that of the Ecclesiastical College founded in 1721, which was promptly renamed the Holy Synod. These texts have been selected both for their immediate historical importance, to be explained presently, and for their longevity as basic legal components of the Imperial Russian governmental system. Next we will examine with the same purpose in mind two extended justifications produced by the Petrine regime, the one in support of its long war against Sweden, the other in defense of political absolutism. Both were printed in thousands of copies and both significantly altered Russian political theory—Russian political consciousness, indeed.

The primary purpose of Peter's *Kamer-Kollegiia* was to supervise the collection and disposition of all the tsar's revenues from taxes, fees, imposts, customs, and duties—more of which had been imposed under Tsar Peter than ever before in Russia. As such, the Revenue College initially was assigned the second largest staff of the new colleges (twenty-six foreigners and sixty-one Russians, second only to the ninety-seven persons—fifteen foreigners, eighty-two Russians—appointed to the Justice College) as well as the broadest range of responsibilities. It was also closely modeled on its Swedish counterpart, the *Kammarkollegium* in Stockholm. In fact, its governing statute or *reglement,* Peterson once again argues persuasively, "constitutes a summary of the operational procedures" of its Swedish model "written by a person who had observed that college at close hand," namely Heinrich Fick.[63] The *Regulation of His Tsarist Majesty's Revenue College (Reglement [Ustav] E. Ts. V. Kamor-Kollegii),* in other words, was not a straight translation of a Swedish original (as once was thought) but a more or less adroit adaptation in Russian of the relevant Swedish ordinances and practices as conveyed to his Russian collaborators—preeminently Peter himself—by the ever industrious Herr Fick, who was then appointed a member (councillor) of the college. And this *Regulation,* too, the archival remains indicate, went through successive drafts—at least four—before being approved by Peter on December 11, 1719.[64] It was first printed, in Moscow under Senate auspices, in 1731. It was reprinted in either Moscow or St. Petersburg in 1748, 1750, 1765, and the 1770s,[65] thus remaining in force until the Revenue College itself, whose staff had grown to 249, was reformed out of existence as such under Catherine II in 1785.[66] The intervening period of sixty-five years was time enough, it might be thought, for its cameralist norms of royal revenue administration to be absorbed by the Imperial Russian bureaucracy.

Here are some of the new terms to be found in the *Regulation* of the Revenue College which, our research has shown (Appendix II), permanently entered Russian (leaving aside most of those already adduced in our previous discussions): *o situatsii (sostoianii); k onomu natsei i provintsei; o iustitskom shtate . . . o shtate akademei, shkol, goshpitalei . . . o arkhitekturnom shtate; ot E. V. aprobannoi shtapovoi . . . shtatskoi knigi; so onykh kopiiu; reguliarno*

uchinit'; O reguliarnom opredelenii vsekh prikhodov; o toi materii; publikovat';
po drugim potrebnym rezonom; po preportsii; komertsii; manifaktury; do
morskikh komertsei kasaiutsia; s direktorom; vse takie kommunikatsii
(snosheniia); v Kamor-Kollegii protokolom (zapiskoiu) zachat'; velikaia summa
roskhodu; o korrespondentsyi Kamor-Kollegii s gubernatorami; kamisar, 169
kamisarov; aprobatsiia; O kontraktakh; s kem kakiia kontrakty uchinit/
zakliuchennye kantrakty; nikakim otkupam ili monopoliiam ne byt'; generalnye
i partikuliarnye (spetsyal'nye) sshchety; ekstrakty; transport; monetnoe delo;
vysokogo sorta; o inspektore Kamer-arkhiva; proviant; aktsiznoi kantore;
aktsiznye dela; and so on. Many of these terms, not surprisingly, given the
breadth of the Revenue College's responsibilities, have more than a narrowly
fiscal or administrative significance. And this is not to count neologisms
found in the college's *Regulation* that did not, as far as we can tell, survive very
long in Russian, for example, *kamerir* and *podkamerir, shreiber, distrikht,*
rent"meister, proviant"meister, and other such official names, mostly Germanic in origin. Nor need we consider here the many more elaborate phrases
in this text that register the translation into Russian of standard cameralist organizational and accounting procedures, as exemplified by this definition, in
Chapter 2, of the Revenue College's essential mission: "This College has the
ultimate supervision and management of the tax and non-tax revenues of His
Tsarist Majesty and of his entire realm, which now obtain or henceforth shall
be instituted and fixed, whatever they might be called." Here certainly were
formulated, now in Russian, that rational delineation of a crucial state function and its concentration in a specific state office called for by students of
modern bureaucracy.[67]

In contrast to the Revenue College and others, the Admiralty College was
relatively slow to organize, owing at least in part to Herr Fick's inability to
provide more than a "very meager" description of the corresponding institution in Sweden.[68] Even so, given the scale of the existing naval and support
operations for which it assumed responsibility, it rapidly became the largest
of the colleges in number of personnel, with a total complement, by mid-
1720, of 176; and after 1722, together with the colleges of War and Foreign Affairs, it assumed a position in the Imperial bureaucracy that was, unlike the
other colleges, independent of the Senate and directly subordinate to the
ruler. This development, which remained in effect long after Peter's death,[69]
should not surprise us, given the military and related diplomatic motives im-
pelling the bureaucratic revolution throughout contemporary Europe highlighted early in this chapter (and in Chaps. 2 and 3). The Petrine and subsequent Imperial Russian state, it perhaps needs to be emphasized, was

decidedly not in its wider European setting an exceptionally bellicose or martial state or one preoccupied, to some extraordinary degree, with maintaining its status as a European power.

General Admiral Apraksin was appointed the first president of the Admiralty College and Vice Admiral Cruys, also known to us from Chapter 2, its first vice president. Cruys was, interestingly, the only foreigner among its senior administrative personnel—a fact that doubtless reflects the relative success of Peter's Russification of the new navy by the time of his collegial reform.[70] A veteran of the Admiralty in Amsterdam, Cruys had been put in charge of drafting the regulation-statute for Peter's Admiralty College, as we saw earlier, and it drew accordingly as much on Dutch as on Swedish models, if not more so. It also drew on the extensive Russian legislation already enacted, most notably the *Naval Statute* of 1720, and was closely supervised in its preparation by Peter himself; in fact, he seems personally to have drafted sizable portions of it.[71] The resulting *Reglament o upravlenii Admiralteistva i verfi i o dolzhnost'iakh Kolegii Admiralteiskoi (Regulation on the administration of the Admiralty and the wharves and on the duties of the Admiralty College)*, promulgated in 1722, was at once the most detailed and the most original of the Petrine collegial statutes (excepting only the *Ecclesiastical Regulation,* a special case, as we shall see)—surely a tribute, again, to the central importance of the navy in the Petrine scheme of things (excerpts reproduced in Appendix I, no. 29).

The *Admiralty Regulation,* as I will term it, was first printed at the St. Petersburg Press on April 5, 1722, in a run of 600 copies, at least some of which contained a Dutch version of the text—Dutch being the second language of the Petrine navy, indeed of Peter himself.[72] It was reprinted at Moscow in March 1724 and again at St. Petersburg in November of that year.[73] Subsequent editions appeared in St. Petersburg in 1740, 1753, 1778, 1780, 1786, and 1795,[74] making it, excepting again the *Ecclesiastical Regulation,* the most frequently reprinted of the Petrine collegial statutes as well as the most detailed and original in content. The Admiralty College itself endured as such until the year 1828, when its administrative functions were appropriated by the new naval ministry, after which it survived as an advisory council on ship construction, naval personnel, and naval finance until 1917.[75] But Admiral Vselago, writing a century and a half after its initial publication, felt that its *Regulation* still captured in print the ethos and service ideals of the Imperial Russian navy: a sentiment that spoke well, to say the least, for the document's enduring intelligibility.[76]

Peter's *Admiralty Regulation* is divided into fifty-two chapters, thirty-three of which are subdivided in turn into a total of 476 numbered *artikuly,* all specifying the duties of the college members themselves, the officials of their chancellery, and those of the many clerks, craftsmen, and workers assigned to their subordinate offices *(kontory);* eleven such offices were herewith established along functional lines in St. Petersburg (for provisions, uniforms, ship construction, munitions, salaries, and so on) and one, representing the college as a whole, in Moscow. Two supplementary "determinations *[opredeleniia]*" specified by title and number the personnel to be assigned to each of these administrative units, starting with the staff—the chancellery—of the college itself. These sections are followed by a series of templates or model forms *(formy)* for use by the appropriate officials in keeping track of personnel, funds, provisions, "and other things," and these are followed at last by an index *(Reestr)* to the *Regulation* as a whole organized by chapter, article, and page number.

The longest chapter of the *Admiralty Regulation* (112 articles) outlines the duties of the Admiralty College itself, which was to have (article 1) "supreme direction *[direktsiiu]* of the personnel, buildings, and other matters belonging to the Admiralty, by whatever name, in the entire Russian State. And [it] must in loyalty and zeal conduct [itself] as is written in the first chapter of the first book of the Naval Statute under the duties of the commanding officer *[Ansheft komanduiushchago],* under [pain of] the same punishments and penalties *[shtrafami]*." The college was to consist of no fewer than seven senior or retired flag officers and captains-commodore *(flag ofitserov i kapitanov komandorov)* of whom the incumbent "General Admiral or first Admiral" was to be the president *(Prezident),* the naval officer ranking second to him the vice president *(Vitse Prezident),* unless he was holding a distant command *(komandu),* while the others were to be councilors *(sovetniki)* and the titles and ranks of the staff of its chancellery *(Kantseliarii)* were to accord "with [those of] the other Colleges" (article 2). The Admiralty College was to meet to transact its business as specified in the *General Regulation* (article 3). The president was to inspect the wharves, schools, hospitals, and other places where Admiralty personnel worked on a weekly basis "if time allows," but certainly every two weeks, to see that all was done according to the *Admiralty Regulation* and nothing was in need of correction; meanwhile the fleet stationed at Kronshlot was to be inspected monthly, but certainly every six weeks, and that at Reval once a year (article 4). Thus the *Regulation* proceeds, down through the relentlessly defined duties of the college members and their subordinate officials—*Prokuror, kontrolor, General Kriks-Komisar, Obor proviant meister, Tsalmeister, Tseikhmeister,* the *Direktor* of the wharves—to those of the Admiralty's chief *botsman,* the *komisar* in charge of the ropery, the *obor sarvaer,* the *komisar* of forests, its shipwrights and other craftsmen, its inspectors *(fiskaly)* and provost *(profos),* and so forth. One whole section of the *Regulation*—chapters forty-seven to fifty-two—constitutes a distinct *Reglament gospitalakh (Hospital Statute)* concerned with defining the duties of the attendant *komissarov, doktorov,* and other staffers. It has been studied in connection with the birth of modern medicine in Petrine Russia, a topic to be discussed in the following chapter.

Unsurprisingly, much of the new terminology employed in the *Admiralty Regulation* of 1722, as these samples will have indicated, repeats that found in the *Military Statute* of 1716, the *General Regulation* of 1720, and especially the *Naval Statute* of 1720, and so need not be highlighted here. Much of the rest is excessively technical for our purposes—Russified forms of Germanized borrowings from Swedish or Dutch administrative nomenclature, again as the examples above will have indicated—and sooner or later became obsolete. Still, a large number of the new naval and administrative terms found in these documents endured in Russian and so are indexed, to repeat, in the Nautical and Official sections of Appendix II.

Considerably more interesting from a substantive point of view is the *Ecclesiastical Regulation (Dukhovnyi reglament)* of 1721, the last of the statutes prescribing Peter's bureaucratic revolution that we will review and the only one to have been subjected to intensive scholarly analysis.[77] Remaining in force until 1917, it was also the most durable of the Petrine administrative "regulations," which it actually resembles only in overall form and, in part, intent. It was in effect the governing charter of the Russian Orthodox church throughout the Imperial period, and was drafted by Feofan Prokopovich, Peter's favorite cleric (Chap. 2), who imbued it with a literary quality that further distinguishes it from its regulatory counterparts. Moreover, the *Ecclesiastical Regulation* and closely related documents contain some of the clearest available statements of Petrine political ideology, another point of major interest here, as is the fact that the church reform that they ordained would constitute, all considered, Peter's single greatest administrative break with the Muscovite past.

Captivated by the collegial principle of government, Peter publicly indicated his intention of founding an "Ecclesiastical College" to manage clerical affairs—in effect, to abolish the venerable Moscow patriarchate and take administrative control of the church—in November and December 1718.[78] Prokopovich completed his draft of the regulation intended to implement Peter's decision by the beginning of 1720. The tsar went over the draft on February 11, annotating or amending it at various points, and the revised draft was then read by a group of senators and senior clergy assembled for the purpose in St. Petersburg on February 23 and 24; on February 25, they and Peter signed two copies of the final version. One copy was sent in the care of a trusted colonel to Moscow and the provinces to collect the signatures of the rest of the senior clergy, some eighty-seven in all, which mission was completed by early January 1721. On January 25, 1721, a Manifesto *(Manifest)* announcing the establishment of the Ecclesiastical College, also drafted by Prokopovich and amended by Peter, was promulgated. The new college was to consist, much like the other colleges, of a president, two vice presidents, four councillors, and four assessors *(assessory)*, although in this case all were to be clerics appointed by the monarch; and all were to take essentially the same oath of loyalty, based on that in the *General Regulation* (based in turn on a Swedish prototype), that was required, on taking office, of all senators, members of other colleges, and provincial governors. The *Regulation* together with a Supplement, the Manifesto, and the oath were first printed at the St. Petersburg Press, in the new civil type, on September 16, 1721.[79]

173

A second edition of the *Ecclesiastical Regulation* and the first to be printed, at Moscow, in traditional Cyrillic types (the civil-Cyrillic typographical divergence under Peter is discussed in Chap. 6), appeared on February 23, 1722.[80] But it did so without the original Supplement *(Pribavlenie)*, also drafted by Prokopovich, on the duties of the parish and monastic clergy, which are anticipated but not dealt with as such in the *Regulation* proper. It transpires that the Supplement had somehow not been inspected and approved by Peter himself before being printed in September 1721, which oversight was rectified in the winter of 1721–22. The revised Supplement was then printed at the Moscow Press on June 14, 1722, and bound with the second edition of the *Regulation*—that printed, but not published, on February 23.[81] A third edition of the *Ecclesiastical Regulation,* complete with the revised Supplement and an index *(Reestr)* to the whole, was printed at both St. Petersburg and Moscow, once more in traditional Cyrillic types, on January 18, 1723, and again at Moscow on August 21.[82] It was officially reprinted numerous times thereafter: we know of editions that appeared, usually in Moscow and usually in Cyrillic types, in 1738, 1749, 1761, 1765, 1776 (two issues), 1779, 1794, 1802, 1818, 1820, 1823, 1830,[83] 1856, 1861, 1869, 1879, 1883, 1897, and 1904.[84] This count omits editions published in other languages—German, of course (St. Petersburg, 1721; Danzig, 1724, 1725; Riga and Leipzig, 1769, 1771, 1772), English (London, 1729), French (Paris, 1745), Latin (St. Petersburg, 1785), and so on—as well as scholarly editions.[85]

Peter's interpolations as preserved in the drafts of the *Ecclesiastical Regulation* and related documents offer explicit evidence of his intentions in reorganizing the administration of the church. The Manifesto of January 25, 1721, for example, proclaimed the establishment of an "Ecclesiastical College [*Dukhovnuiu Kollegiiu*], that is, an ecclesiastical conciliar administration [*dukhovnoe sobornoe pravitelstvo*] which in accordance with the following regulation [*reglament*] is to manage all the ecclesiastical affairs in the All-Russian church"; but at this point in its draft Peter inserted the line, "because this is too much trouble for a single person [the former patriarchs] whose authority is not hereditary." Later, at the end of the document, Peter wrote: "On taking office all members of this college must make an oath or promise on the Holy Gospels according to the form [*po forme*] hereto affixed." To the draft of this oath—it was, as mentioned, basically the oath of office now required of all senior officials as printed in the *General Regulation*—Prokopovich then added the sentence: "I acknowledge on oath that the Supreme Judge [*Krainii Sud'ia*] of this Ecclesiastical College is the Monarch [*Monarkh*] of All Russia himself, our Most Gracious Sovereign."[86] These three textual emendations—two by Peter himself, one by his chief clerical collaborator—amount to a straightforward assertion of the principle of hereditary monarchical absolutism as applied now to church governance, their obvious purpose being to institutionalize the monarch's authority over the church by means of the Ecclesiastical College. The monarch also claimed in these same documents the right to initiate, again by means of the new college, a major reform of the church. This right is expressly proclaimed in the opening sentences of the Manifesto:

Among the many responsibilities of the authority divinely bestowed on us for the improvement [*o ispravlenii*] of the All-Russian people and the other dominions subject to us, is watching over the ecclesiastical order [*dukhovnyi chin*]; and seeing in it much disorder [*nestroeniia*] and great poverty [*skudost'*] in its affairs, we would in conscience not vainly fear to seem ungrateful to the Most High if, having received from him such timely assistance in improving both the military and the civil orders, we neglect improving the ecclesiastical order: lest, when the Impartial Judge asks us to account for the trust conferred by him on us, we will have none to give [*ne budem bezotvetni*]. Therefore on the example of the pious kings in both the Old and the New Testaments, having assumed responsibility for improving the ecclesiastical order, and seeing no better means to this [end] than conciliar administration, we establish an Ecclesiastical College.[87]

And such is the underlying argument or theme of the *Ecclesiastical Regulation* itself.

175

The *Regulation* is divided into three main parts dealing successively with Peter's reasons for founding the Ecclesiastical College, the matters that were now subject to its jurisdiction (touching bishops, church schools, preachers, laypeople), and the duties of the college itself. The Supplement, as mentioned, spells out the corresponding duties of the parish and monastic clergy. Most of Peter's thirty-five or so emendations to these texts in effect affirmed the importance of proper religious and especially moral instruction for both clergy and laypeople as well as the necessity of maintaining tight clerical discipline, including the prompt removal from office of incompetent bishops. In other words, the picture painted in these documents by their clerical authors—mainly Prokopovich—is of a church and especially a clergy badly in need not of a doctrinal or liturgical reformation but of a moral and spiritual rebirth, a picture that Peter then highlighted by placing marks in the margin indicating his emphatic agreement with this or that point.[88] But Peter's single most substantive amendment to these texts arose from his reaction to a provision of the Supplement requiring a candidate for priestly ordination "publicly [*publichno*] to curse all schismatic groups by name" and more, to swear on oath that he would not conceal any such persons discovered in his parish but report them in writing to his bishop; here Peter noted that the candidate must also swear loyalty to the sovereign and report "any opposition" he might discover, even when hearing confession. Accordingly, the final, published version of the Supplement contains the infamous injunction obliging priests to report to the appropriate government offices anything they might hear in confession about "an unfulfilled but still intended criminal act, especially [one] of treason or rebellion against the Sovereign or the State, or an evil design against the honor or health of the Sovereign and the family of His Majesty," supposing such intention or design was confessed "not as a sin but rather to be confirmed in [it] by the assent or the silence of the confessor."[89] This injunction plainly violated the canon law then supposedly in force in Russia, which prohibited priests from divulging anything heard in confession; and so Prokopovich, the presumed author of the injunction, went to considerable trouble to defend it in both religious and political terms here in the Supplement as well as in a major "Announcement to the Entire Ecclesiastical Order [clergy] of the Russian State" issued on May 17, 1722, by the Holy Synod (the name adopted by the Ecclesiastical College, with Peter's permission, at its formal opening on February 14, 1721). This story has been told elsewhere, as part of the whole "curious history of the Supplement to the *Ecclesiastical Regulation*."[90] What is of interest now is the evidence thus provided of the lengths to which Peter was prepared to go in establishing absolute monarchy in Russia and of the typically bureaucratic means by which he went about it.

Indeed the Russian Orthodox church in which Peter himself was raised, with its tens of thousands of clergy and its hundreds of thousands of lay dependents, its pervasive rituals, laws, and traditions, its antiquity and prestige, its countless church buildings, shrines, and hostels, was not just another government office to be summarily closed, renamed, amalgamated, or otherwise "regulated" in conformity with the principles of German or Swedish cameralism.[91] Swedish-Lutheran models of church governance in particular, notably the *Kirchenordnung* of 1686, could have had only limited influence here, the allegations of later Russian critics notwithstanding.[92] Prokopovich naturally understood this point well, and the *Ecclesiastical Regulation,* as its opening sentence states, contains accordingly both a "description of and a justification *[rassuzhdenie]* for an Ecclesiastical College," the latter concentrated in the first of the document's three main parts, which was read over in draft by Peter but not significantly altered by him before approving it. A remarkably original fusion of Russian Orthodox church tradition and the new political thinking thus emerged.[93]

"What is an Ecclesiastical College *[Dukhovnoe Kollegium]*," Part One of the *Ecclesiastical Regulation* asks, "and what are the weighty reasons for such an administration *[pravleniia]*?"

An administrative College *[Kollegium Pravitel'skoe]* is nothing but an administrative assembly *[sobranie]*, whence certain appropriate matters are subject to management not by a single person but by the many suitable [persons] appointed thereto by the supreme authority. A temporary College *[Kollegium edinovremennoe]* is one thing, but a permanent *[vsegdashnee]* is another. It is temporary when the suitable persons are gathered together at one time to resolve some one or more urgent matters. Such are church synods *[sinody]*, extraordinary civil inquisitions, tribunals *[tribunaly]* and councils. A college is permanent when some sufficient number of men is appointed to manage certain specified matters that arise often or always in a country *[v otchestve]*. Such was the church Sinedrion [Sanhedrin] in the Old-Testament church in Jerusalem, the civil court of the Areopagites in Athens and other administrative assemblies in the same city called Dikasteria, and the like in many other states both ancient and present [nyneshnikh]. Such are the various Colleges [Kollegii], varied according to state matters and needs, the Most Potent All-Russian Tsar, the most-wise Peter the First, established for the benefit of the fatherland and of his realm in the year 1718. And as a Christian Sovereign, guardian [bliustitel'] of orthodoxy [pravoveriia] and all good discipline in the Holy Church, and having seen ecclesiastical shortcomings [nuzhdy] and been desirous of their better management, he has been pleased to establish an Ecclesiastical College, which would diligently and unceasingly see to the benefit of the church, and that all is done properly [po chinu], and there be no disorders. For such is the wish of the Apostle, or rather the benevolent will of God himself.[94]

Moreover:

Lest anyone imagine that this [kind of] administration is not suitable, and that it would be better if the ecclesiastical affairs of the whole society [vsego obshchestva] were ruled by a single person, as the affairs of particular regions, or dioceses, are ruled by bishops, weighty reasons are here put forth to show that this permanent conciliar administration [sie pravlenie sobornoe vsegdashnee], like a permanent Synod or Sanhedrin, is the most perfect, and better than one-person administration, especially in a Monarchial state [v gosudarstve Monarsheskom], as is our Russian [state].

There follow, as promised, nine such "weighty reasons" or arguments in favor of collegial rather than patriarchal (bureaucratic rather than traditional) church governance, to wit:

1. In the first place, the truth [istinna] is more certainly discovered by a conciliar body than by a single person. . . . 2. And so far as there is certain knowledge, there is greater power to act in deciding matters, since more [people] are inclined to credit and obey a conciliar decision [prigovor sobornyi] than a single person's edict [ukaz]. The authority of Monarchs is autocratic [Monarkhov vlast' est' samoderzhavnaia], which God himself commands be obeyed in good conscience; yet they have their councillors, not only the better to discover the truth, but in order that disobedient persons should not allege that this or that Monarch

rules by force or caprice rather than by justice and truth. How much more so in church administration, where the government is not monarchical *[monarsheskoe]* and the governor rules but does not domineer over the clergy.[95]

Reasons 3, 4, 5, and 6 proceed in the same vein to argue the practical and moral superiority of collegial versus "mono-personal" rule at any level of society or the state below that of the monarchy itself. Reasons 7, 8, and 9 then focus more directly on the immediate question of church governance in Russia, where the office of patriarch had been vacant for more than twenty years—in fact, since the death of its last incumbent, Patriarch Adrian, in October 1700 and Peter's ensuing refusal to permit the customary election of a successor. Thus reason 7 urges that

the fatherland need not fear from a conciliar administration the sedition and disorders that proceed from the personal rule of a single churchman *[ot edinago sobstvennago pravitelia dukhovnago]*. For the simple folk do not understand how different ecclesiastical authority is from the autocratic, but dazzled by the great honor and glory of the supreme pastor *[pastyria]*, they think that such a ruler is a second sovereign, equal in power to the autocrat or even bigger than he, and that the ecclesiastical order is another and better state. Thus the people are used to reasoning among themselves . . . so that in some matters they look not so much to their autocrat as to the supreme pastor. And when they hear of some dispute between them, they blindly and stupidly take sides with the ecclesiastical rather than the secular ruler.

This cut to the heart of the matter, since, as Prokopovich goes on to say, with Peter looking over his shoulder,

in a conciliar ecclesiastical administration there is no room for such evil. For here to the president *[prezydent]* himself [belongs] neither the great glory which dazzles the people, nor excessive luster and notoriety; there can be no lofty opinion of him; nor can flatterers exalt him with inordinate praises, since what good is done by such an administration cannot be ascribed to the president alone. . . . And when the people see that this conciliar administration is established by Monarchical decree and Senatorial decision, they will remain meek, and put away any hope of receiving help in their rebellions from the ecclesiastical order.

Similarly, reason 8:

Church and State will benefit still further from such a conciliar administration in that not only each of its members, but the president himself
is liable to the judgment of his brothers, that is of the College itself, in
case of notable transgression. It is not done like this where a single absolute [samovlastnyi] Pastor rules. For he does not wish to be judged by his
subordinate bishops; and if he should be compelled to this, then the
simple folk, ignorant of judicial process and liable to reason blindly,
would be suspicious of such a trial and subject it to abuse. Hence it
would be necessary to summon a general church council to try such a
ruler, with great trouble for the whole fatherland, and not inconsiderable
expense. And at the present time (when the eastern patriarchs live under
the Turkish yoke, and the Turks are more than ever wary of our state) it
would seem impossible.

Reason 9, finally, suggests that

such a conciliar administration will be a kind of school of ecclesiastical
governance. For from the exchange of the many and various reason-
ings, counsels, and sound arguments required by current business each
of the members can conveniently learn ecclesiastical policy [dukhovnoi
politiki], and by daily practice learn how best to manage the house of
God. Hence the most suitable members [kollegov] will deserve to advance to the episcopal rank. And thus in Russia with God's help rudeness
[grubost'] will soon disappear from the ecclesiastical order and all the
best may be expected.

Taken as a whole, then, Part One of the *Ecclesiastical Regulation* of 1721
comprises the official rationale of Peter's church reform, which amounted in
essence to the abolition of the Moscow or "All-Russian" patriarchate and the
establishment, in its place, of an Ecclesiastical College (soon renamed the
Holy Synod). Part One of the *Regulation* registered, otherwise put, the ideological aspect of the typically modern policy of secularization that was implemented by Peter during the latter part of his reign with some quite limited
precedents dating back to the reign of his father.[96] This ideology, which would
be further developed by Prokopovich and others in writings soon to come, asserted that even the government of the church was to be legally and institu-
tionally subordinate to the "absolute monarch" now ruling in Russia, whose

180

authority in this respect was limited only by his Christian conscience. The immediate effect of this assertion was disclosed in the numerous provisions of Parts Two and Three of the *Regulation* as well as in its Supplement, whereby the monarch empowered the new Ecclesiastical College both to administer the routine business of the church, here defined in detail, and to "improve" it in conformity with the kind of moral and spiritual ideals, supported by biblical and canonical references, that were regularly invoked throughout post-Reformation Europe. On the one hand, clergy were to become agents of the absolute state to which they, too, now took a mandatory oath of loyalty: apart from reporting suspicious political utterances heard in confession they were to register the vital statistics of the population, to read out government decrees to their congregations in church, to administer loyalty oaths to their parishioners, and, in the case of monks, to take care of retired soldiers. On the other hand, the clergy of the reformed Russian church were to be better educated than before, and therefore better behaved in their role as pastors, teachers, and performers of the sacred rites. The *Ecclesiastical Regulation* of 1721, in short, served as a primary text articulating the Russian variant of the general European ideology of what came to be called enlightened absolutism.

Meanwhile the language itself of the *Ecclesiastical Regulation,* mindful of the overall purpose of this volume, is not distinguished by the kind of novelty encountered in Peter's other major legislative acts. Partly, of course, this relative linguistic conservatism is a matter simply of the subject—church and religion—of this *Regulation;* in the sociological calculus of modernity, as Max Weber put it, "the sacred is the uniquely unalterable."[97] Even as they radically reformed traditional Russian Orthodox church governance, Peter and his clerical collaborators obviously sought to project an aura of religious continuity and canonical legitimacy; hence also the urgency with which the first eleven members of the new Ecclesiastical College, all clerics, petitioned Peter at their first official meeting to change its name to the more dignified and churchly "Most Holy Synod," a request he promptly granted.[98] The more conservative, Slavonicized language of the *Ecclesiastical Regulation* may also be attributed to its principal author, Feofan Prokopovich, all of whose printed works (mainly sermons) in "Russian" retain strongly marked traces of his formative Baroque Ukrainian-Slavonic verbal culture (born in Kiev in 1681 and educated at the academy there, in Poland, and in Rome, he settled in Russia—St. Petersburg—only in 1716). It is a trait his writing shares, though certainly to a lesser degree, with that of many of the learned divines of the day in St. Petersburg and Moscow, so many of them Ukrainians like himself—a subject broached in Chapter 1 and pursued in Chapter 5. The audience at which this

Regulation was principally aimed, the clergy and especially the higher or educated clergy, similarly accounts for its learned pretensions particularly in
church history and theology, its frequent canonical and biblical references,
and its Slavonicized prose. And the fact that almost all editions of the *Ecclesi-*
astical Regulation were to be printed in the traditional Cyrillic rather than the
new civil type would not have encouraged the kind of verbal streamlining
characteristic of comparable Petrine legislation (see Appendix I, no. 30). The
language itself of the *Dukhovnyi reglament,* in sum, is not very interesting to
us, our eyes fixed firmly on the future. It is rather the conceptual novelties
which this language conveyed that we find remarkable: its justification, now
in the ecclesiastical arena, of bureaucratization in the service of monarchical
absolutism. And this feature links it with the two major political tracts produced by the Petrine regime, which we will consider next.

The first of these tracts is entitled *Pravda voli monarshei vo opredelenii*
naslednika derzhavy svoei (*The Right* [the legal/moral right, the legitimacy] *of*
the Monarch's Will in Designating the Heir/Successor to His Power/Realm), and
was first published at Moscow, in civil and then Cyrillic types, late in 1722, the
former in an exceptionally large edition of 1,200.[99] It was written, at least in
part, by Feofan Prokopovich,[100] who in August 1722 advised Peter in Astrakhan, where he had stopped on his Persian campaign, that the tract was ready
for his "approval *[approbatsii]*."[101] This Peter granted on his return to Moscow
in December 1722, and there is some evidence that over the next few years
some 600 copies of the civil edition were in fact sold or distributed *gratis.*[102] A
second edition of *Pravda voli monarshei* was printed in the civil type at Moscow in July 1726 and at St. Petersburg in August, both times in several issues and for an astonishing total of 19,531 copies—of which some 5,000 had
been distributed before the booklet was officially withdrawn from circulation in 1727.[103] A German edition—*Das Recht der Monarchen, in willkühriger*
Bestellung der Reichs-folge—was printed at Berlin in 1724 by the official publisher to the Prussian king and the Society of Sciences (the future Berlin
Academy of Sciences),[104] and Russian editions were published by Novikov at
the Moscow University Press in 1784 and by Tumanskii at St. Petersburg in
1788, the latter in a multivolume collection of materials relating to Peter's
reign.[105] Still later Russian editions were published at Moscow in 1826, at St.
Petersburg in the official collection of laws *(PSZ)* in 1830,[106] and in England in
a scholarly edition in 1996.[107]

The fact that the 1726 edition of *Pravda voli monarshei* was officially withdrawn from circulation in 1727 gives some hint of its controversial nature at the time. The controversy grew from post-Petrine disputes over application of the succession law he had promulgated in 1722, whereby the reigning monarch was empowered to designate as successor whomever he pleased and, "having once designated him, to set him aside should he observe that he is in any way unfit."[108] The *Pravda* offers an extended justification of the law (which was finally abrogated in 1797 in favor of hereditary male succession by primogeniture) and, more broadly, of absolute monarchy as such, a feature that is more interesting here than is its actual language, which is rather like that of the *Ecclesiastical Regulation:* a Slavonic Russian sprinkled with Latin and other loanwords, some of them Petrine favorites and destined to endure in Russian, others not. Such neologisms include, for the record: *slavno publikovanyi, aki prezervativa, na konferentsii, ustava sego avtor, s krepkimi rezonami, monasherskaia korona, svoi tol' vysokoi familii, sovet iskusnykh ministrov, slavnaia tsarei titla, evropeiskie narody, chiny i tseremonii, antetsessor, eksempli, o knizhnoi tipografii, o arkhitekture,* and so on. Many of these words proved to be permanent additions to the Russian lexicon, and are indexed as such in Appendix II.

The main body of the *Pravda* consists of sixteen numbered "Reasons or Arguments *[Rezony ili dovody]*" in support of absolute monarchy and Peter's succession law, some of them subdivided into numbered paragraphs or points, these followed by forty-seven "Examples or Instances *[Eksempli ili primery]*" drawn from both "human history *[ot istorii chelovecheskikh]*" and the "history of Holy Scripture *[ot istorii sviashchennago pisaniia]*" to illustrate or affirm the arguments advanced; a few prefatory passages and a kind of afterword complete the text.[109] The first nine of the sixteen *rezony* outline the "authority of all parents generally," the last seven, the "authority of sovereign parents *[roditelei gosudarei]*"; six of the *eksempli* are taken from Scripture, the remaining forty-one from "human history" as recorded by assorted authors, the earliest of them writing at the time of Cyrus, king of Persia, as cited by Grotius in his *On the Law of War and Peace (Grotsius, o pravde mira i voiny),* the most recent in the reign of Great Prince Ivan III of Moscow (fifteenth century). But the relatively small number of biblical examples should not obscure the "preponderant weight," as Lentin says, that the *Pravda* gives to scriptural authority. Indeed the work as a whole contains by his count more quotations from the Bible than from any other source, and several of these passages are further bolstered by extended quotations from the Greek and Latin fathers of the early Christian church.[110]

In other words, the new doctrine of absolute monarchy was defended in the *Pravda* first and foremost by reference to a set of religious texts long revered in both Christian East and West, a fact that in itself is not unexpected, given the work's origins in the Holy Synod under Archbishop Feofan Prokopovich, the Synod's leading member. But these *rezony* and their supporting *eksempli* had not been deployed before in Russia, in a language that was more or less readily accessible to literate Russians and in defense of monarchical absolutism. More, the *Pravda* also deployed arguments drawn from the natural-law theorists—here called "political philosophers *[filosofov politicheskikh]*"—of early modern Europe, most notably, as just mentioned, Hugo Grotius. In the discussion of parental authority, for example, we read: "Hugo Grotius, the famous teacher of law, in his most-wise consideration of the legality of peace and war *[Gugon Grotii, slavnyi zakonouchitel', v premudrom svoem rassuzhdenii o pravde mira i voiny]*, in the second book under numbers five and seven, shows from ancient authors *[avtorov]* that among many peoples . . . parents had the authority, if needed, to sell their children; and especially among the Romans, parents had the authority to put their sons to death for cause, as Grotius also shows us, in the same place."[111] Or again, when discussing "sovereign parents" the *Pravda* invites its Russian readers to "approach still closer to the royal throne, and to ask, what signifies the glorious royal title *[tsarei titla]*, majesty *[velichestvo]*, or, as other European peoples say from Latin, *maestat* or *maestet [ili, iakozhe prochi evropeiskie narody s latinska naritsaiut, maestat ili maestet]*." An explanation quickly follows:

This vocable simply means, in grammatical usage *[v upotreblenii grammaticheskom]*, any kind of precedence of one thing over another. . . . But we are considering *majesty* here not in this spacious sense, but only in that of political philosophy . . . ; wherefore in general, among all the peoples whether Slavic or other, this vocable *maestet* or *velichestvo* is used for the very highest precedent honor, and is given to the supreme authority alone, and signifies not only their transcendent dignity, than which, after God's, there is none greater in the world, but also [their] supreme lawgiving, executive, and judicial authority, undeniable and itself not subject to any laws whatsoever. Thus the most distinguished law teachers describe *majesty*, among whom Hugo Grotius says as follows: *The highest authority (called majesty) is that whose actions are not subject to another authority, such that they could be annulled by the will of another; and when I say another, I exclude him who has such supreme authority: for him it is possible to change his will. (Hugo, On the Legality of War and Peace, book 1, chapter 3, number 7).*[112]

Moreover:

> It must be understood, that when the teachers of law say that the highest
> authority, called *majesty,* is not subject to any other authority, they speak
> only about human authority; it is subject to divine authority, and to the
> laws of God, whether those written in human hearts or in the Ten Com-
> mandments. . . . But in being subject to divine law, it is liable for trans-
> gression thereof only to God, not to human judgment. . . . We know this,
> first, from natural reason *[ot estestvennago razuma]:* since this authority
> is called, and is, the supreme, highest, and ultimate, how can it be subject
> to human laws? If it were subject, it would not be supreme. And when
> sovereigns themselves do what civil statutes command, they do so by
> will, not by need: so that by their example they inspire subjects to willing
> observance of the law, or they affirm that the laws are good and bene-
> ficial. We also know this from Holy Scripture.[113]

At this point in the text numerous quotations from Scripture and the early
church fathers are adduced, all leading ineluctably to the conclusion that an
autocratic (or absolute) monarch "is fully empowered and free *[ves'ma volen i
svoboden est']*" to designate his own successor.

Also noteworthy in *Pravda voli monarshei* are the distinctions drawn between natural, divine, and civil laws *(estestvennye, bozhestvennye, grazhdanskie zakony)* and between canon or church and civil law *(kanon est' pravilo
tserkovnoe, zakon zhe ustav grazhdanskii).* Similarly its abstract use of the term
"the crown *[korona]*" to mean royal authority or power in general; its extended disquisition, replete with historical examples, on hereditary versus
elective monarchy *(monarkhia naslednaia* versus *izbiratel'naia);* its lengthy
quotations from the *Novellae* of Justinian *(ustav Iustiniana . . . mezhdo
Novellami ego)* and from Cicero's oration *Pro Roscio Amerino (Tsitseron v slove
za Rostsia amerina);* and its guarded explication of the supposed contractual
origins between people and ruler of all forms of government *(pravitel'stvo).*
All of this somehow leads, to be sure, to a recitation of the "duties of subject
people" to their sovereign, most particularly in a hereditary absolute monarchy such as that now ruling in Russia. The *Pravda's* argumentation, while not
always logically consistent, and certainly not original in its European setting,
thus exhibits in many of its passages as well as in its overall thrust a distinctly
modern, or early modern, outlook. Lentin fairly compares it to Bossuet's *La
Politique tirée des propres paroles de l'Ecriture Sainte* (1709), written for Louis

184

XIV, and especially to *The True Law of Free Monarchies* (1598) attributed to King James I of England.[114]

Lastly, we might observe the geographical as well as intellectual expansion of horizons that the text of the *Pravda voli monarshei* of 1722 represents. The reference, quoted above, to the Russians as among "other European peoples" was not customary but novel, the word "Europe" itself in Russian—*Evropa*—being a neologism fixed in the written language by means of this and other Petrine texts. Elsewhere the *Pravda* similarly refers to the wider European world, as in this passage:

> Innumerable so to speak are the books composed by many authors on civil statutes and laws, and nowhere in them is any doubt raised as to whether a parent can deprive a son of his inheritance: and so the whole civilized world *[ves' chestnyi mir]* is our witness to this. And should someone doubt that there are so many teachers and lawmakers, then one can show him even here in Russia, and especially in royal St. Petersburg, up to three hundred, and more, law books in which are discussed the causes and circumstances of disinheriting unworthy sons; and what more [might be found] should we enter the famous and great libraries all over Europe? *[to chto, est'li by nam vniknuti v slavnye i velikie po Evrope knigokhranitel'nitsy?].*"[115]

And there are, as well, the many illustrative examples adduced in the *Pravda* from European history to support its central contentions. Locating Russia in Europe, here verbally, at other times by means of imagery or architecture, was the salient feature, it bears repeating, of the entire Petrine project.

The other major political tract produced by Peter's regime is the *Razsuzhdenie kakie zakonnye prichiny ego tsarskoe velichestvo Petr Pervyi Tsar' i povelitel' vserossiiskii i protchaia, i protchaia, i protchaia: k nachatiiu voiny protiv Korolia Karola 12 Shvedskogo [v] 1700 godu imel . . .*, which was translated at the time as *A Discourse Concerning the Just [Legal] Reasons Which his Czarish Majesty, Peter I, Czar and Emperor of all the Russias [Tsar and All-Russian ruler], &c. had for beginning the War against the King of Sweden, Charles XII, Anno 1700 . . .* and was first printed, at St. Petersburg, in 1717. A second edition was printed at Moscow in 1719 and a German edition was published abroad, probably with official Russian backing, between 1718 and 1721 (from which the English translation, first published in 1723, was then taken). The book was printed again at St. Petersburg in 1722 in several issues for a total

185

run of 20,000 copies, an enormous number for the time and rivaled among Petrine publications only by the *Pravda*. Although there are indications that some 16,000 of these copies remained unsold as late as 1756 despite the government's ongoing promotional efforts, the fact that approximately 4,000 copies had been distributed, whether sold or given away, surely is evidence of the book's relatively wide reach for the time; so are the owners' inscriptions, mainly of merchants, officials, and military officers, found in the numerous surviving copies.[116] Publication of the book abroad as well as the repeated printings and size of the 1722 Russian edition clearly demonstrate Peter's eagerness to disseminate the book's message as widely as possible: the message, in a nutshell, that Russia's long war with Sweden was both necessary and just. But we are mainly interested in the linguistic significance of this verbal monument of the Petrine era.

The *Razsuzhdenie* opens with a lengthy Dedication—*Dedikatsiia*—to Peter's infant son, Peter Petrovich, signed by the author "P. Sh." (for Peter Shafirov). After a short Introduction, the bulk of the book itself comprises three numbered sections or "articles *[artikuly]*," the first explaining the "old and new legal reasons *[o drevnikh i novykh zakonnykh prichinakh]*" why Peter had gone to war, the second, why the war had continued so long (it was Sweden's fault), and the third, how it had been conducted on the tsar's side with moderation "following the practice of all polite/politic Christian peoples [*po obychaiu vsekh politichnikh khristianskikh narodov;* "the Custom of all civilized and Christian nations," in the contemporary English translation]." A section titled "Conclusion to the Reader" is followed by an appendix of documents in support of the Russian cause taken from Russian official repositories and reproduced here "word for word in the old style *[ot slova do slova po staromu shtiliu]*": the first of these documents is a copy of the Russo-Swedish peace treaty *(kopiia s traktatu peremirnogo)* of 1564, the last, a copy of the Universal *(s universalu)* issued by the Swedish king on December 3, 1700, declaring war on Russia.[117] The book as a whole has been called the "first Russian work on an international political theme where the author's position is substantiated by historical documents."[118] Yet the *Razsuzhdenie,* historically speaking, is a good deal more than that, too. It articulated for the first time, and in *Russian,* Russian acceptance of the norms of international law as understood in contemporary Europe and Russia's corresponding bid for membership in the European state system.

Peter Shafirov (1669–1739), the *Razsuzhdenie*'s author, was among the most literate stars in the Petrine firmament and uniquely well qualified to write it. His father was a Polish-Ukrainian Jew from the Smolensk area who migrated to Moscow following the Russian takeover of eastern Ukraine (1667) and there was baptized, became a translator at the Ambassadorial Office, pursued commercial interests on the side, and did well enough to be granted, about 1680, noble status. Son Peter was thus brought up in Moscow, where, following his father's example, he engaged in trade and studied languages both at home and with resident foreigners, becoming adept at Latin, Polish, German, French, and Dutch; he later added Italian to his repertory. Such skills were in high demand in Moscow at the time, and by 1691 he too was working as a translator at the Ambassadorial Office while accepting personal commissions from members of the Muscovite elite, including the young Tsar Peter, eager to read European publications on a broadening range of subjects. His ensuing diplomatic career placed him at nearly every crucial juncture of the Northern War. He was a member of Peter's Grand Embassy to Europe (Germany, Holland, England, Austria) of 1697–98, during which, while passing through Riga, the tsar allegedly suffered an insult from the local Swedish authorities that subsequently became, according to the *Razsuzhdenie,* a major casus belli. In 1699 he took part in the negotiations among representatives of Denmark, Poland-Saxony, and Russia preliminary to their joint declaration of war against Sweden, and in 1701 in those between Tsar Peter himself and Augustus II of Poland-Saxony cementing their alliance. In 1703 he became personal secretary to F. A. Golovin, the Muscovite grandee in charge of the Ambassadorial Office who had assumed the new title of chancellor *(kantsler),* or de facto minister of foreign affairs; on Golovin's death in 1706 and replacement by another grandee, G. I. Golovkin, Shafirov became vice chancellor, a title *(vitse-kantsler)* he formally assumed in 1709 after working diligently behind the scenes to pave the way for the Russian victory over Sweden at Poltava. In 1709, following the victory, he was created a baron of the Holy Roman Empire and appointed to distinguished knightly orders by the kings of Poland and Prussia; in 1710 he was created *baron* in Russia by Peter. He also received for his efforts large landed estates (300 peasant households in one case, two large villages in another).[119]

In the post-Poltava years, as Russia under Peter became steadily more involved in European affairs, Shafirov's diplomatic activity grew apace. High points included negotiating the marriages of Peter's nieces Anna (the future empress) and Catherine with, respectively, the dukes of Courland (1710) and Mecklenburg (1716). In 1717 he accompanied the tsar and Chancellor Golovkin to Paris and Amsterdam, where the conclusion of a Franco-Prussian-Russian trade and political agreement (August 1717) formally recognized Russia's role as a European power. He spent much of the period from 1711 to

1713 under house arrest in Constantinople as hostage to Russian commitments made after the defeat by Turkish forces at the battle by the Pruth, until a peace treaty was finally concluded. On his return to St. Petersburg he received still more material rewards and in 1717 was named vice president of the new College of Foreign Affairs. In 1719 he was appointed a cavalier of Peter's highly exclusive Order of St. Andrew the First-Called, and in 1722 he became a senator. Shafirov's allegedly lavish lifestyle, taste for intrigue, and subsequent rather checkered career (seemingly unavoidable for anyone deeply involved in Petrine politics) have been recounted in salacious detail.[120] We will focus instead on the author of the *Razsuzhdenie,* the bulk of which Shafirov wrote in 1716 on commission from the tsar. Peter considered that the war with Sweden was essentially over—he had secured his main objective, a Baltic coast for Russia—and that it was now a matter of bringing pressure on Charles XII to accept what was and to make peace. He was also eager, the Conclusion of the *Razsuzhdenie* makes clear, to assure his own restive subjects as well as the European powers that prolongation of the war was the Swedish king's fault.

Shafirov's biography embodies the transition in Russian officialdom from the closed world of the Muscovite Ambassadorial Office, with its monopoly on foreign news and information dutifully translated, as best it could be, into an awkward chancery Russian, to the grand world of European diplomacy, whose practices and norms could now be articulated in a Russian comparable in this respect with German, Dutch, English, Spanish, Italian, and even French. In his introduction to the *Razsuzhdenie* Shafirov refers to himself as a "loyal Russian patriot (son of the Fatherland) *[vernoi patriot (Otechestva syn) iz Rossiiskogo naroda]*" moved to defend his sovereign, Tsar Peter, against the calumnies heaped on him by Swedish propaganda. The text that follows has been described by its editor, an authority on the subject, as "a legal-historical brief . . . written by an individual well versed in the theory and practice of early eighteenth-century international law and diplomacy."[121] This individual, I would stress, was also a Russian writing in Russian (*na Rossiiskom iazyke,* as he would say), just as his book was the first of its kind ever produced in Russia.

Seven major areas of international law treated in the *Razsuzhdenie* demonstrate Shafirov's command of the field. These are, as identified by Professor Butler: the sources of international law (the "customs and maxims of the law of nations," specific international agreements); the historical "continuity of the realm," and therefore of its territorial rights and claims; the law of embassies; the law of treaties; the resort to third-party mediation of disputes; and the law of war, the last subdivided into nine main aspects, including the "doctrine of the just war," the formalities of declaring war, the status of the diplomatic agents of belligerents when war breaks out and of subjects resident on enemy territory, breaches of armistices and capitulations, the status of prisoners of war, and the use of reprisals.[122] It is an impressive curriculum, to be sure, as even the reader not much conversant in international law could surmise on reading Shafirov's densely argued book. But our main concern now is to discover how its language represented a major lexical and perforce semantic expansion of Russian while promoting, as we shall see in passing, some further "regularization" of its grammar and style.

From its very first page the text of the *Razsuzhdenie* is fairly studded with neologisms of a governmental, naval, or military significance as well as with others that are specifically legal or diplomatic in nature. We have sampled the former in previous chapters, perhaps to a surfeit; here some of the more specialized borrowings to be found in this text might be highlighted, along with some terms of a more general import. These include, confining the selection to words that we know permanently entered Russian and are therefore listed in Appendix II: *agent, akord, akt, ambitsiia, arest/arestovat', assessor, afront, garantiia, gistoriia, deklaratsiia, imperiia, interes, kantsler, kantseliarist, kapituliatsiia, komisar, komissiia, kommunikatsiia, komplement, kongress, konditsiia, kontributsiia, konferentsiia, konfiskatsiia, kontsept, kon"iunktura, korona, korrespondentsiia, kurioznyi, kur'er, manifest, materiia, ministr, natural'nyi, neitral'nyi, original'nyi, parol', patent, patriot, plakat, politika/ politicheskii/politichnyi, pretenziia/pretendovat', provintsiia, protektsiia, protest/ protestovat', protokol, ratifikatsiia, reguliarnyi, rezident/rezidentsiia, revoliutsiia, rezoliutsiia, represalii, svita, sekvestr, subsidiia, traktat/traktovaniia/traktovat', faktor, familiia, flag, kharakter,* and *tseremoniia.* Also appearing in the *Razsuzhdenie* of 1717 are such likely calques as *vsenarodnoe pravo* (public or international law), *grazhdanskoe pravo* (civil law), *estestvennoe* (also *natural'noe) pravo* (natural law), *dobrye nravy* (good manners), *dolzhnost'* (office), *oboronitelnoi soiuz* (defensive alliance), and *udovol'stvo* (satisfaction; though *satisfaktsiia* also frequently appears). Short phrases in which the above or other neologisms are used include: *v svite/iz svoei svity, v svoiu possesiiu, deklaratsiia voiny, dobrye offitsii, pod belym flagom, pod tem pretekstom, iz arestu svobodit', iskat' satisfaktsii/dostatochniiu satisfaktsiiu, na parol' ne osvobozhden, ot onogo akreditovannomu komisaru, Tsarskaia Familiia/Familiia Rossiiskikh Tsarei, logicheskimi argumentami dokazyvat', v gistoriiakh prezhnikh vekov, Evropeiskie politizovannyia Gosudarstva, agent kommertsii, dva originalnye kontsepta, po negotsiatsii dogovorilis', pod komandoiu, pod ego protektsieiu, s takoiu konditsieiu/na takovykh zhe konditsiiakh, traktovali o mire, o posleduiushchikh revoliutsiakh, protiv voinskikh i politicheskikh obychaev,* and so on. In each case, Russian readers will readily see, the Russian writer's command of contemporary European political language is manifest.

190   The semantic expansion or refinement of Russian obvious even in such short phrases is all the more evident, of course, in many of the longer expressions and in whole sentences found in Shafirov's *Razsuzhdenie,* for example: *pod oblast' i protektsiiu korony Rossiiskoi; s konditsiiami zelo poleznymi; chrez kotoruiu kommunikatsiiu Rossiiskogo Gosudarstva s drugimi Evropeiskimi; i po obyknovennym khristiianskikh narodov regulam postupano, i zakliuchit' s nim protiv korolia oboronitelnoi soiuz; po obychaiu natury chelovecheskoi; tako v drugikh Evropeiskikh Gosudarstvakh razsuzhdali i pisali; po prisloviiu Latinskomu, Pod zvonom oruzhiia prava grazhdanskie molchat;* or . . . *prezhde sego krome Rossiiskogo iazyka knig chitaniia i pisma nikto iz Rossiiskogo naroda ne umel . . . no nyne vidim i samogo Ego Velichestvo nemetskim iazykom glagoliushchago, i neskolko tysiashchei podannykh Ego Rossiiskogo naroda, muzheska i zhenska polu, iskusnykh raznykh Evropeiskikh iazykov, iakozhe Latinskogo, Grecheskogo, Frantsuzskogo, Nemetskogo, Italianskogo, Aglinskogo, i Galanskogo, i takogo pri tom obkhozhdeniia chto nepostydno mogut ravniatisia so vsemi drugimi Evropeiskimi narody.* Indeed the last sentences or sentence fragments just quoted,[123] which translate ". . . before this except for the Russian language none of the Russian people knew how to read and write . . . but now we see even His Majesty himself speaking German, and several thousand of His subjects of the Russian nation, male and female, skilled in various European languages, such as Latin, Greek, French, German, Italian, English, and Dutch, and of such conduct moreover that they can be shamelessly compared with all other European peoples": these verbalizations sum up much of what Shafirov had to say of substance in the *Razsuzhdenie* as a whole. Whatever had been Russia's position in the world before the reign of Peter, he was urging, it was now, thanks to Peter's "regularization" of the army, his creation of a navy, his victories over Sweden, his introduction of the arts and sciences, and his reform of the Russian government, indisputably a *European* power and, as such, deserved equal treatment by the other European powers. Nor could readers miss Shafirov's firm reiteration of the underlying doctrine of absolute monarchy, as in this rather stylish formulation: *Velikie potentaty na sem svete nikogo krome vyshago sudii Boga nad soboiu ne imeiut:* "Great potentates in this world have over them none but the supreme judgment of God."[124] This doctrine, new to Russia, ultimately justified everything that Peter had done.

Indeed the fluency with which the *Razsuzhdenie* of 1717 integrates its dozens of new terms and associated concepts in a distinctly Russian prose, one comparatively little touched by Slavonic usages, is remarkable. This aspect, too, of the document can be sampled directly in Appendix I (no. 23). But three further examples might be considered here, as they would seem to reflect the deliberate adoption by Peter's vice chancellor of a contemporary European high or polite or fine style. The first example refers to the Grand Embassy of 1697–1698, *v kotoroi Ego Tsarskoe Velichstvo sam izvolil mezh drugimi kavalerami iako volentir byt', i vse ikh postupki i obrashchenii observovat':* "in which His Tsarist Majesty himself was pleased to be among the other cavaliers as a volunteer, and to observe all their steps and turns." Later, Shafirov declines to go into further detail on some legal point for the sake of brevity: *Ia pri sem radi kratkosti ne khoshchu eshche podrobno upominat'.* And he concludes his book with this flourish: *I tako sie ob'iavia, proshu blagosklonnyi chitateliu, priniat' sie razsuzhdenie ot malogo talanta moego sochinennoe priiatno, i verit', chto khotia onoe ne vysokim i uchenym slogom sochineno, no samoiu istinnoiu s osnovaniem predstavleno, i iz vernykh aktov sobrano: i sim chiniu semu okonchanie:* "And thus declaring, I beg the benevolent reader to receive kindly this justification composed by my small talent, and to believe that, although it is not composed in a high and learned style, the truth itself has been presented with good grounds, and gathered from genuine documents; and so to end this proceeding." We might view the very style of these and comparable sentences in Shafirov's book as evidence of a kind of mental or moral Europeanization taking place within at least a segment of the contemporary Russian elite, a community perhaps numbering, in Shafirov's own count, "several thousand . . . both male and female, skilled in various European languages . . . and of such conduct moreover that they can be shamelessly compared with all other European peoples."[125]

This was the same official-noble elite who implemented in their personal lives the Petrine revolutions in Russian architecture and imagery, flaunting their new coats of arms, building their town and country houses in the new European style, and filling them with equally new *portrety* of themselves and their families dressed entirely in contemporary European fashion *(moda).*[126] It was for this same core elite, no doubt, that successive editions of a manual entitled *Priklady, kako pishutsia komplimenty raznye na nemetskom iazyke to est', pisaniia ot potentatov k potentatam Pozdravitelnye i sozhaletelnye, i inye; Takozhde mezhdu srodnikov i priiatelei (Models of how various compliments are written in German, that is, Congratulatory, commiserative and other writings from potentates to potentates; As also between relatives and friends)* were printed at Moscow and then St. Petersburg in 1708 (two issues), 1712, and

1725.[127] Translated *na rossiiskii iazyk* by Michael Shafirov, brother of Peter, from a German original published at Leipzig in 1696, the manual contains 130 letters and replies, models of politeness all, for various social occasions (extract reproduced in Appendix I, no. 34). These run the gamut from proper forms of royal and princely correspondence, mainly on family matters, to letters of *rekomendatsia* to be "presented to a notable person" in seeking his favor; from a letter of New Year's greetings to a "good friend" *(Pozdravitelnoe pisanie Pri nachatii novago leta k dobromu priiateliu),*[128] to one from an admirer congratulating a woman on her saint's day, to another from a student thanking his father for sending him money via a bill of exchange *(veksel').* Always the formal *vy* or "you" (second person plural) is used, not the familiar Muscovite *ty* or "thou"; and the standard European courtesies abound: "My lady" *(Moia gospozha),* "Your devoted servant" *(Vash prilezhnyi sluga);* "Your excellency" *(Vashe prevoskhoditelstvo),* "[Your] Obedient servant" *(Obiazanno poslushnym slugoiu);* "Most esteemed friend" *(Vysokopochtennyi priiatel'),* "[Your] Devoted friend" *(Prilezhnyi priiatel');* "Most esteemed father," "Your obedient son"; and so forth. In their official correspondence with their European counterparts as well as in their internal communications, Peter and his government had steadily abandoned the relatively cumbersome, indeed slavish Muscovite forms of address in favor of the polite European styles made customary by the practices preeminently of the court of Louis XIV of France.[129] Now, by means of this manual, its formulas no doubt fortified in practice by the dramatically increased Russian-European social intercourse of the time, such courtesies were being diffused among the larger official-noble elite.[130] A "spreading Reformation of Manners," as it was termed about 1720 by a German diplomatic veteran of "eleven Years Conversation with the Natives,"[131] played its part, too, in the Petrine revolution—a fact to which we were alerted by various passages in the Petrine legislation governing the behaviors of naval and military officers and even of bureaucrats studied earlier in this and the previous two chapters. We shall return to this somewhat elusive subject in Chapter 5.

5

SCIENCE AND LITERATURE

The two large terms in this chapter's title were understood in the learned European world of Peter's time rather differently than they are today. "Science" denoted any body of properly constituted knowledge—knowledge conducive to basic principles or necessary universal truths—while "literature" referred to the arts of elegant discourse, preeminently poetry and oratory (or eloquence). By the end of the seventeenth century the most important of the sciences among the more dynamic thinkers of Europe, their patrons and followers, was not theology as in the long-reigning Scholastic scheme or metaphysics as in the underlying Aristotelean tradition, both still entrenched in the universities, but "natural philosophy." The latter inquired into what sorts of things existed in nature while its younger sibling, "natural history," studied the causal structure of the natural world. Practitioners of these natural sciences, gathered in formal or informal societies and academies and corresponding among themselves by letter and learned journal (Latin still the main language), were generally designated natural philosophers or natural historians or, depending on their special interests, mathematicians, astronomers, physicists, zoologists, botanists, and so on: this subject was broached in Chapter 1, under the rubric of a seminal "scientific revolution" in seventeenth-century Europe and the advent of cultural modernity. Meanwhile European literature or "fine letters" *(belles lettres)*, rooted in the "classics" of ancient Greece and Rome as revived or reassessed in the Renaissance, was increasingly political or secular in its subjects and settings, rather than sacred or ecclesiastical, and vernacular in its language (Italian, Spanish, French, or English rather than Latin, or Latin alone). This subject too was broached earlier, in the last section of Chapter 1.

The comprehensive, state-sponsored society or academy of sciences became the institutional hub of these somewhat convergent developments and particularly as modeled on the academy launched in Paris in 1666. The founding by Peter I of an analogous institution in Russia will occupy the last section of this chapter. But here I might note, still justifying the linkage of these two supposedly disparate bodies of culture, that as originally planned the Paris academy was to consist of sections for *belles lettres* (grammar, eloquence, poetry), history (general history, geography, chronology), philosophy (anatomy, botany, chemistry, experimental physics), and mathematics (algebra, astronomy, geometry); and that the cognate institution in St. Petersburg was similarly to concern itself with three "classes" of science: "all the mathematical sciences and those that depend on them," particularly astronomy, geography, geodesy, and navigation; "all the parts of Physics," including theoretical and experimental physics, anatomy, chemistry, and botany; and the "humanities, history and law," these to include "eloquence, the study of antiquities, history ancient and modern, natural and public law, together with politics and ethics."[1] I find some further justification for this approach in the fact that the same linkage was made by Pekarskii, the learned compiler of the first detailed and still valuable catalog of Petrine contributions to Russian high culture, his splendid two-volume *Nauka i literatura v Rossii pri Petre Velikom (Science and Literature in Russia under Peter the Great)* published at Moscow in 1862.

It is not my purpose here to describe and document these contributions or to offer comprehensive narratives of the Petrine achievement in the later quite discrete fields of science and literature. This also has been done, if not always perhaps with the kinds of sophistication currently expected of historians.[2] Rather is it the task of this chapter to demonstrate, on the basis of selected scientific and literary texts of the period, the Petrine impact in these respects on Russian verbal culture—and so to connect with the rest of this book. In his account of the rise of science in Russia Vucinich observes in passing, as he embarks on the career of Henry Farquharson (a hero of Chapter 2), that foreign specialists active in the Petrine period "added to the Russian language hundreds of new terms, by means of which Russia could begin to achieve intellectual rapport with the West."[3] That is the point I wish to take up now, expand on, document, and thus prove.

To some extent, with respect to science, this has already been done, too. I refer to the sections on navigation and fortification found elsewhere in this volume (Chaps. 2, 3) and to the corresponding sections—Nautical Terms, Military Terms—of Appendix II, with its citations of specialized works by

Avery, Bond, Rozen, Ryan, and Whittall among others, works that register the naturalization in Russian during the Petrine era of hundreds of European scientific and technical terms. I also refer to the scientific entries in the fourth section of Appendix II, which lists Other Technical Terms (other than nautical, military, or official) appropriated from various European languages during these years, and particularly to the two monographs cited there by L. L. Kutina on "the formation of the language of Russian science" in the first decades of the eighteenth century and on, more specifically, the "terminologies of mathematics, astronomy, geography, and physics": her very headings—*matematika, astronomiia, geografiia, fizika*—are Petrine neologisms, certainly in any modern sense of these terms. Readers will find in this fourth section of Appendix II numerous scientific as well as literary entries, and there is no need to repeat all of these terms here. In this chapter we will focus instead on selected scientific and literary texts in an effort to illustrate and contextualize the transmission to Petrine Russia and into Russian of contemporary European scientific and literary values and practices. We will then turn to the institutionalization of these cultural acquisitions in Peter's Academy of Sciences, always with an eye to the process's linguistic import.

A word on science in pre-Petrine Russia, a subject charged with nationalist and Marxian assertions during the long reign in Russia of Soviet historiography. Astronomy is a good test case, as developments in astronomy marked the initial passage from medieval to modern science in Europe itself. A British student has investigated more than a hundred printed and manuscript "scientific" texts in Church Slavonic produced mostly in Russia and the Ruthenian lands between the eleventh and the eighteenth centuries (nothing "scientific" was produced before Peter's time in the East Slavic vernaculars), most of them translations from Byzantine Greek. He found that "the level of astronomy in these texts is very basic: essentially the so-called Aristotelian System with the seven planets, including the Sun and Moon, revolving around the Earth." No Copernicus here, nor even Ptolemy: "The concept of the Zodiac is dimly perceived and zones, climes, the equator, the equinoctial, the antipodes and eclipses all receive some mention. The Ptolemaic system is not known, nor mathematical astrology, nor angular measurement. There are no astrolabes or quadrants and probably no sundials. In fact the necessary mathematical knowledge for a more sophisticated understanding of astronomy was simply absent."[4] In short, mathematics beyond simple computation using Slavonic numerals (or the abacus) and the new natural sciences were simply unknown in pre-Petrine Russia, whatever the broader cultural or economic preconditions for their subsequent development that some historians have identified.[5] Nor should this situation be at all surprising given the almost exclusively religious nature of the Byzantine inheritance in Muscovite Russia, the paucity of even elementary schools, and Muscovy's prolonged isolation, much of it self-imposed, from the main currents of European learning. The situation was only just beginning to change when young Tsar Peter came on the scene.

Geometry, Geography, History

Mathematics was the key to the practice of the new natural sciences, and Vucinich is probably right to conclude that mathematics constituted "the first systematic body of scientific knowledge to acquire a place in Russian culture."[6] His main evidence for saying so was the printing in 1703 and subsequent wide distribution of the *Arifmetika* compiled from various foreign sources by Magnitskii and others working under Farquharson at the new Moscow School of Mathematics and Navigation, a textbook that included sections on algebra, plane and solid geometry, and celestial navigation as well as exercises in simple arithmetic (Chap. 2). But the contingent nature of this event should be remembered: neither Farquharson nor his patron, Peter I, meant thereby to implant the full panoply of contemporary European science in Russia, only to facilitate the training of navigators for Peter's new navy. We should also be attentive to the fact that the *Arifmetika* was written in "a fairly baroque Church-Slavonicised Russian" (quoting Ryan again, as cited in Chapter 2), that it utilized a mix of Slavonic and European (Arabic) numerals, and that it was printed in traditional Cyrillic type: all features that tended to impede rather than promote the broader advance of European science in Russia. As noted earlier in this volume, when discussing Farquharson's printed legacy in Russia (also Chap. 2), all mathematical works subsequently published in Russia were printed in the new civil type, used European numerals exclusively, and were written in (usually translated into) a progressively more straightforward, everyday Russian: *thus* were the mathematical sciences implanted in Russia, as it happened, not in Church Slavonic served up in traditional Cyrillic type.

Farquharson's further contributions to the teaching of mathematics in Russia—in Moscow and then in St. Petersburg—were also mentioned in Chapter 2, where it was observed that under his academic direction the St. Petersburg Naval Academy became for a time (from 1715 to 1725 or so) the center of the new scientific work in Russia, until superceded in this respect by Peter's Academy of Sciences. During these years geodesy and astronomy as well as mathematics and navigation proper were taught by Farquharson and others at the Naval Academy, from which hundreds of young Russians went on to serve as astronomers and geodesists as well as math teachers and navigators. We concentrate now on the core subject of geometry, whose prompt mastery by Russians opened the door to most of the other new sciences and particularly those—navigation, geodesy, cartography—for which there was an urgent state demand.

The first geometry book ever printed in Russia, indeed the first book to be printed in the new civil type, was a translation of A. E. Burckhard von Pürckenstein's *Handgriffe des Zirkels und Lineals oder Ausserwählter Anfang zu denen mathematischen Wissenschaften* published at Augsburg in 1690. The first Russian edition of this manual, which appeared in Moscow in March 1708, bore the title *Geometria slavenski zemlemerie Izdadesia novotipografskim tisneniem poveleniem . . . tsaria . . . Petra Aleksievich (Geometry, in Slavonic zemlemerie,[7] published by the new-typographical means by order . . . of Tsar . . . Peter Aleksievich)*. Indeed Peter himself had edited the draft of "the Geometry book *[Geometricheskaia kniga]*" sent to him by its translator, Iakov Brius (Jacob or James Bruce); and the printing had been done at the Moscow Printing House by three masters recruited in Amsterdam under the supervision of Fedor Polikarpov assisted, as interpreter, by another Dutch recruit (see Appendix I, no. 13). Two hundred copies of this geometry book were printed and bound, though not all with the engraved illustrations of the original German edition, as the supply sent from Germany seems to have run short.[8] Nor was Peter happy with the size and placement of the illustrations, the book's large format, or the design of the type,[9] and preparations for a second edition, apparently never completed, were undertaken in the second half of 1708.[10] Even so, the printing of this first geometry book had been a signal occasion in the history of Russian print culture and one we shall return to in the following chapter.

A third edition of the geometry book—really, the second—was printed at Moscow in February 1709, somewhat redesigned as well as expanded to meet Peter's specifications and with illustrations—164 of them—reengraved in Moscow by Pieter Picart, the Dutch master who went on to become a critical figure in the development of graphic art in Russia (Fig. 6).[11] This edition was titled, closer to the German original, *Priemy tsirkulia i lineiki, ili Izbranneishee nachalo v matematicheskikh iskustvakh (Uses of the Compass and Ruler, or an Introduction to the mathematical skills)*, the title under which it was reprinted, at St. Petersburg, in June 1725.[12] My further remarks are based on copies (at GBL and LC) of this edition.

198

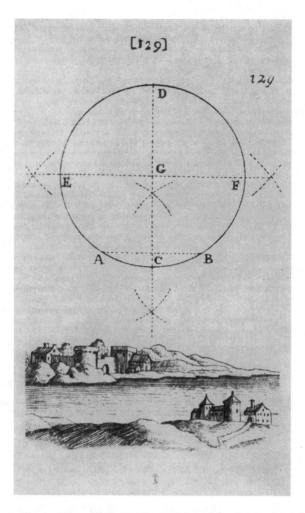

Figure 6   Illustration in *Priemy tsirkulia i lineiki (Uses of the Compass and Ruler)* printed at Moscow, 1709. The Rhinelandish vignette is obviously unchanged from the German original.

But first, a note on Iakov Villimonovich (or Vilimovich) Brius—Jacob or James Bruce, grandson of James Bruce and son of William Bruce, Scottish soldiers of fortune who attained high rank in the Muscovite army; the latter, as colonel of a "new-style" regiment, died in battle in 1695 during Peter's first Azov campaign. Son Jacob or James was born and died in Russia (1670–1735) and rose even higher in the tsar's service, which he entered at the age of sixteen when he joined Peter's "play regiment" at Preobrazhenskoe. Thereafter he served in every major campaign of Peter's Turkish and Swedish wars, achieving the rank of major-general, became commander of the tsar's artillery and director of fortress construction, and was rewarded for his gallantry at Poltava with the Order of St. Andrew the First-Called. He also carried out important diplomatic assignments—in fact, he headed the Russian delegation in the negotiations at Nystadt that ended the Northern War, for which he was made a count. But it was his role as a principal agent of Peter's cultural revolution that most interests us here. Bruce was a member of the Grand Embassy to Europe of 1697–1698 (he seems to have learned Latin and German and some Dutch in addition to Russian and English) and was one of sixteen companions Peter took to England, where he investigated the new minting practices and bought mathematical instruments and books on navigation and shipbuilding; when the tsar returned to Holland, he stayed behind to study mathematics and astronomy. In England he met the astronomers Flamsteed and Halley as well as the great Isaac Newton, who was then warden of the Royal Mint in London. On returning to Moscow, Bruce took over Peter's ambitious new minting operations[13] and established an astronomical *observatoriia*, Russia's first, in the Sukharev Tower, also the home of Farquharson's School of Mathematics and Navigation (Chap. 2), of which Bruce became a patron. Amid his many official responsibilities he also became a patron of the new publishing in Russia, a cause in which he actively participated as editor of translated works on fortification and artillery (Chap. 3), as compiler of the first Dutch-Russian dictionary (Chap. 6) and of a series of almanacs long known in Russia as the *Briusov kalendari,* as a collaborator in Peter's vast cartographic enterprise,[14] and as author, editor, or translator of works on mathematics and astronomy including the geometry textbook now under review. He was also one of the authors of the famous Petrine book of etiquette, the *Iunosti chestnoe zertsalo (The Honorable Mirror of Youth),* to which we shall also return. In 1717, owing to his technical and administrative competence, he was appointed the first president of the College of Mines and Manufactures, having played an important part in designing Peter's entire collegial reform (Chap. 4). At last, in March 1725, he assumed direction of Peter's elaborate state funeral, after which he retired from the Imperial service (as it now was) first to a house near the Sukharev Tower in Moscow, then to a fine old suburban estate. There, at Glinka *(usad'ba Glinkyi),* which has lately been restored in his honor, he devoted himself to his spectacular collections of mostly scientific books and manuscripts in various languages; astronomical devices and instruments; sculptures, drawings, paintings, and engravings; minerals, maps, coins, and medals; and numerous "curiosities *[kur'ëzy],*"

199

or objects of ethnographic and botanical interest. Contemporaries called Glinka the "Moscow chamber of curiosities" (*podmoskovskaia kunstkamera*, or science and natural history museum), and on Bruce's death a large portion of his collection did go to the Kunstkamera founded by Peter in St. Petersburg, the rest to the library of Peter's Academy of Sciences (BAN). His bookplate *(ekslibris)*, possibly the first to be used in Russia, is still to be found in books preserved at the academy's library and at those of Moscow and Helsinki universities, where they were deposited in the nineteenth century.[15]

Bruce's geometry book consists of sections or chapters titled "On Geometry in General *[O Geometrii vo obshche]*," "On the Utility of the Art of Measuring *[O polze vo mere khudozhestve]*," and "On the Rudiments of the Art of Measuring *[O nachatii mery khodozhestva]*," together with an "Explanation of certain words that are customarily used in the mathematical arts *[pri matematicheskikh iskusstvakh]*." The latter include such basic terms as *punkt, lineia, linei parallelny, lineia diagonalis, linea tsirkuliaris, lineia periferia, perpendikuliar, tsirkumferentsia tsirkulia, angulus (ugol), diametr, ploskaia superfitsia, ellipticheskaia figura, bazis/ko baze, parallelogramm, triangulum (triugolnik), izostseles, mnogostoronnyia figury (ili poligony), irregulares, pentagonum (ili reguliarnoi piatugolnik), korpus, kubus, sfera ili globus, sferoid, konus, tsilinder (krugloi stolp ili val), piramid, lineia parabolika, lineia giperbolicheskaia, gipotenuza,* and so on. Exercises on the use of ruler and compass follow this basic glossary and then six chapters or "books" of *problemy,* after which comes an index in alphabetical order *(Reestr azbuchnym chinom)* of the contents as a whole. A list of the figures to be found in the book is also provided, by title or caption and page number (*"Izobrazhenie figur raznykh geometricheskikh, kak kotoraia nazyvaetsia"*/"Representation of various geometrical figures, as such are called").

Most of the geometrical terms to be found in Bruce's textbook permanently entered Russian while others, not listed in Appendix II, remained foreign, overtaken sooner or later by semantic or literal calques or by already existing Russian terms, some of which were used when explaining the new terms. Thus, to take the examples just cited, *piatugolnik* soon overtook *pentagonum; treugolnik (triugolnik),* even here, appears far more often than *triangulum,* as does *ugol* rather than *angulus; poligon* did not supercede *mnogougolnik* but rather the opposite; *okruzhnost'* and *poverkhnost'* sooner or later replaced *tsirkumferentsiia* and *superfitsiia;* and *krug* and its adjective, *kruglyi,* were not displaced by *tsirkul'* (here = circle) and *tsirkuliaris* but rather were used, for a while, interchangeably with them. The linguistic process at work here, like that in the main texts looked at in the preceding chapters, is apparent from the book's outset, as Bruce adapted its contents (as best he could) to the Russian reader: "*GEOMETRIA est' slovo Grecheskoe, na ruskom zhe iazyke, est' onoe zemlemerie, i khudozhestvo polia izmeriati. I imeet mezhdu iskusstvami matematicheskimi Pervenstvo. . . . Geometria est' suguba. Pervaia . . . nazyvaiutsia na Latinskom iazyke geometria theoretika. Drugaia . . . geometria praktika.*" ("Geometry is a Greek word, in Russian it is *zemlemerie* [literally, land-measuring, originally calqued no doubt from the Greek], or the art of measuring a field. And among the mathematical arts it has Preeminence. . . . Geometry is twofold. The first . . . is called in Latin theoretical geometry. The other . . . practical geometry."). This process of selective adaptation, as we might call it, combining Russian (or Slavonic) with Russified foreign words, is also exemplified in the book's thirty-nine "problems," as in these I pluck from the sequence:

201

> 10. *Problema, kakoi danoi treugolnik v parallelogramm obratit', kotoroi by imel edin ugol i stranu ravnu danoi strane i uglu* [Problem, how to convert a given triangle into a parallelogram that would have an angle and one side equal to the given side and angle].
>
> 11. *Problema, danoi treugolnik obratit' vo rektangulum, ili vo priamougolnoi parallelogramm* [Problem, to convert the given triangle into a rectangle, or a right-angled parallelogram].
>
> 12. *Problema, danoi treugolnik prevratit' vo kvadrat, to est', ravnostoronnoi chetvertougolnik* [Problem, to covert the given triangle into a square, that is, an equal-sided four-angled thing].

The book concludes, like so many Petrine texts, with concrete applications of the science or theory being taught. In this case, Peter himself is thought to have added to the original set of problems in the Bruce geometry the three concerning sundials *(solnechnye chasy)* that are found in later editions, namely: "How to make a horizontal [level] sundial *[Kak delat' na gorizontalnom meste solnechnyia chasy]*"; "How to make a south-facing sundial *[litsem k Ziuidu]*"; and "How to make a sundial facing east or west on a perpendicular side or wall *[na Ost i na Vest, na boku ili stene perpendikuliarnoi]*." Sundials, it seems, were first made in Russia and used by Russians under Peter's direct supervision.[16]

The process of cultural transmission via linguistic adaptation evident in this geometry book—a process consisting, more exactly, of transliteration with morphological or phonetic adjustment combined with semantic or literal calquing and resort to existing Russian (or Slavonic) terms—is also evident in another such manual produced under Peter and printed at St. Petersburg in 1714 (see Appendix I, no. 22): "produced," I say, because it is not known whether it is an original Russian work or a translation or, as is very likely, some combination of the two.[17] It comprises four chapters subdivided into sixty-eight *problemy*, each of which is presented, often with an illustration, in three parts. Chapter One, for example, is devoted to "*Tregenometriia ploskaia, iazhe nadlezhit ko mereniiu, kak dalekostei, tak i vysot vsiakikh tel* [Plane Trigonometry, as pertains to measuring, both the length and the height of every body]"; and its "Problem One" considers "lines and angles," beginning with this:

> *V treogol'nik nazyvaiutsia linei, nizhnaia v literakh DR, Sinus, perpendikuliarnaia v literakh RS, Tangens, presekaiushchaia obe onyia linei, v literakh DS, Sekans, iakozhe iavno ob'iavleny v posleduiushchem chertezhe, pri numere L* [In a triangle the lines are called: the lower one in [marked by] the letters DR, the Sine; the perpendicular one marked by the letters RS, the Tangent; and the one connecting both these lines, marked by the letters DS, the Secant, as is clearly explained in the following drawing numbered L].

which statement is followed by the *Predlog* (Proposition):

> *Da budut naprimer vedomyia ugly, pri litere R, na 90 gradusekh, pri litere D, na 60 gradusekh* [Let there be for example the known angles, marked by the letter R, of 90 degrees, and that by D, of 60 degrees].

and then by the solution *(Pravilo iskaniia):*

> *Gradusy onykh uglov 60 i 90 slozhit', i budet 150, i onuiu 150 vychest' iz 180 gradusov (ponezhe vsiakoi treugolnik sostoit vo 180 gradusekh), ostanetsia 30. Na tolikh gradusekh sostoit nevedomoi ugol, sostoiashchei pri litere S, iakozhe iavno ob'iavleno v posleduiushchem iskanii i chertezhe* [Put together/Add the 60 and 90 degrees of these angles, which makes 150, and take away/subtract this 150 from 180 degrees (since every triangle consists of 180 degrees), which leaves 30. Of so many degrees consists the unknown angle, marked by the letter S, as is also clearly explained in the following demonstration and drawing].

And so forth. Repeated in countless lessons in Peter's new schools in Moscow, St. Petersburg, and elsewhere in Russia, and reprinted in these and other textbooks down through the eighteenth century,[18] exercises like these introduced not just the "terminology of mathematics" in Russian, as Vucinich earlier put it, but the comprehension of mathematics itself in Russia (wherever Russian was read)—and with lasting, eventually spectacular, results.

Bruce was also responsible for the first astronomy book printed in Russia, the *Kniga mirozreniia ili mnenie o nebesnozennykh globusakh, i ikh ukrasheniiakh (A Book of World-speculation, or an opinion [a conjecture] on the celestial globes [planets] and their qualities)*. This is a translation, evidently from a German edition, of Christian Huygens's *Kosmotheoros, sive de terris coelestibus earumque ornatu conjecturae* (The Hague, 1696), which was written by the famous Dutch natural philosopher in an attempt to popularize his views. The Russian edition was printed at St. Petersburg in 1717 and again at Moscow in 1724.[19] Bruce wrote the introduction, perhaps with Peter's collaboration, and despite his troubles with the German text, about which he complained to the tsar, he seems to have translated the book himself.[20] For various political reasons, including the machinations of a printer who much later claimed to have been religiously shocked by the book's heliocentrism, its pressrun, both times, was quite small, making it today, even in the company we've been keeping, a bibliographical rarity (one known copy in Russia of the 1717 edition, four of the 1724). We must suppose therefore that its impact on the development of modern Russian—modern scientific Russian—was slight. Kutina, the historical linguist, while praising it as a "brilliant example of popular-scientific prose" containing a wealth of new astronomical information, actually credits it with fixing in Russian very few astronomical terms. She suggests that it yielded much in this respect to the translated geographies by Varenius and Hübner that we are about to consider and especially, in popularization, to Antiokh Kantemir's translation of Fontenelle's famous *Entretiens sur la pluralité des mondes* (first published in 1686); the translation, entitled *Razgovory o mnozhestve mirov gos. Fontenella,* was published at Moscow in 1730 and again at St. Petersburg in 1740 and 1761.[21] This was Kantemir's best known work in Russia throughout the eighteenth century, while Fontenelle's original, in its countless editions and translations, is "sometimes regarded as the most successful popularization of the 'new science' ever written."[22] Seen in this light, the *Kniga mirozreniia* of 1717, which has been acclaimed as the first work printed in Russia to expound the heliocentric theory and the "first book in the Russian language to describe the Newtonian cosmology" (which Huygens had come to share),[23] was a lonely scientific pioneer of quite limited historical significance. Implanting the new astronomy in Russia and in Russian was the achievement, in fact, of Peter's Naval Academy (Chap. 2) and then of his Academy of Sciences (see below).

Geometry, explains the first of the geometry manuals discussed above, was of great use to, among others, *"geografy, ili zemel' opisateli"* ("geographers, or describers of the land"). Indeed the charter of the St. Petersburg Academy of Sciences would define geography as one of the sciences—along with navigation and astronomy—that was "dependent upon" mathematics, which was to be the first of the subjects engaged by members of the new academy and their students. Such use of the term "geography" *(geografiia),* to mean studies and activities relating mainly to cartography, navigation, geodesy, and surveying, each having close affinities with astronomy as well as mathematics, was common in Europe at the time; and it was geography in this sense, along with the word itself, that was implanted in Russia and in Russian under Peter I. This is another arena of Petrine activity that has been closely examined by historians,[24] and for our purposes here we need only observe that geography thus understood was taught in varying degrees in the military and naval schools founded by Peter and later made part of the research program, and eventually a separate department, of his Academy of Sciences. A corresponding program of geographical publication, exclusively in the new civil type, was also launched under Peter, an effort that necessarily entailed the translation of standard European geography textbooks and treatises into a usable Russian. That is the point on which we will focus.

"Russian geographical understanding prior to Peter was rudimentary," concludes a British student, his judgment at least implicitly accepted by his Russian colleagues; what geographical information was available in Muscovy before Peter's time was "largely unsystematic, episodic and, being mainly unpublished, was confined to official circles."[25] Language was of course also a factor here, as the few fragmentary seventeenth-century manuscript translations of European geographical works that have been located in Russia were written in Church Slavonic and by, in the most notable case, immigrant Ukrainian divines.[26] Indisputably the first geography book printed in Russian was the *Geografia ili kratkoe zemnago kruga opisanie (Geography, or a Brief Description of the Earthly Sphere),* which appeared in Moscow in 1710 in the new civil type (Appendix I, no. 17) and was reprinted, with corrections and additions, at St. Petersburg in 1715 and again, at both Moscow and St. Petersburg, in 1716.[27] It appears to be a considerably reworked version of a Dutch original published at Amsterdam in 1697,[28] its "author" a Russian who was conveying to Russian readers for the first time in print information about the discovery of America by "a certain Khristofor Kolumbus, an inhabitant of the Italian lands, who went to the Spanish king Ferdinand and asked him for a ship" and was followed to the "new world [*novyi svet*]" by "a certain Amerikus, from whom the country itself took its name and is called *Amerika*." This "fourth part [*chast'*]" of the world, it was further explained, "is divided from the other parts by an oceanic sea [*morem okeanom*]" and was long unknown "because of the unskilled sailing of olden times": most of what is then briefly described relates to "New Spain [*Gishpaniia Novaia*]" or the northern and eastern sections of South America and the southeastern sections of North America. In addition, the "first part" of the world, "which is called Europe [*Evropa*]," consisted of Spain, France, Italy, the Austrian Habsburg Empire (*Gosudarstvo Tsesarskoe*), the Netherlands, Denmark, Sweden, Poland, England, and the Crimea (!); the "second part, Asia [*Asiia*]," of Turkey, Persia, "the steppe peoples [*narody steppye*]," China, India, and the "Indian islands"; and the "third part, *Afrika*," of Egypt, Ethiopia, and certain "barbaric countries," or the Muslim maritime states of North Africa: all of these countries are briefly "described" in elementary political and economic terms. The book was intended, its author says, for readers who had no time to read "large books" but wished to "converse intelligently [*iskusno*] about each country." A Table (*Tablitsa*) providing the coordinates (*dolgota i shirota*) "in degrees [*po gradusam*]" of important world cities taken from the work of a certain Philip of Ferrara (*iz knigi geograficheskiia . . . Filippa Ferrariia vypisana*) is appended, and to it are added those of various Russian towns, including "the new *Piterburkh*." The labor was not in vain. It has been plausibly argued that the details of the discovery of America and other geographical information provided in this little book were steadily augmented and corrected in successive periodicals and books published in Russia until Russians reading only Russian sources could, by the end of the eighteenth century, keep abreast of geographical developments as well as other Europeans.[29]

Two much more substantial geographical works were translated and published in Peter's time: the *Geographia Generalis* of Bernhard Varenius (Amsterdam, 1650, 1664, 1671, and so on), which was printed at Moscow under the title *Geografia generalnaia* in 1718, with full acknowledgment of the original; and the *Kurtze Fragen aus der neuen und alten Geographie* (Leipzig, 1696, 1707, etc.) of Johann Hübner, or *Zemnovodnago kruga kratkoe opisanie, iz staryia i novyia geografii, Po voprosam i otvetam sobranoe* (*A Brief Description of the Amphibious Sphere, gathered from old and new geography, in questions and answers*) in its Russian edition, which was also printed at Moscow, in 1719, also with full acknowledgment of the original.[30] Both were well-known works of their time in Europe, the first a comprehensive and weighty academic tome, the second a pedagogical handbook complete with illustrations; and both popularized the new astronomy of Copernicus, Kepler, and Tycho Brahe. We might look at each of their Russian editions in turn.

The *Geografia generalnaia* of 1718 (Fig. 7; also Appendix I, no. 27) was very likely based on the 1664 Amsterdam edition of the original and was perhaps proposed for translation by James Bruce, although there is equally good reason for believing that it was Tsar Peter's own idea.[31] The book opens with a preface "to the sagacious reader" from its translator in which he apologizes for his shortcomings as such while explaining that he had proceeded anyway because "Our Most Sagacious Monarch *[Monarkh]*" had ordered that "this most difficult [learned] and wise Geography book *[mnogotrudnuiu i premudruiu knigu siiu Geografiiu]*" be translated from the original Latin "into a Russian text *[na rossiiskii tekst]* for the benefit of students and readers"; and so the "poor little ship of my understanding embarked with others [assistants] on this wide ocean *[okeane]* of translation." He also explains that while his translation was "not in the highest Slavonic language *[ne na samyi slavenskii vysokii dialekt]*" as compared with the original author's (Latin) prose *(protiv avtorova sochineniia)*, it did observe the "rules of grammar *[pravil grammaticheskikh]*"; further, that "many locutions of mundane [vernacular] origin were used so as to preserve the meaning of the language itself of the foreign original *[mnozhae grazhdanskago posredstvennago upotrebliakh narechiia, okhraniaia sens i rechi samogo originala inoiazychnago]*." Similarly, some "Greek and Latin terms *[rechiia zhe terminalnaia grecheskaia i latinskaia]*" were left untranslated "for the sake of better understanding the subject *[radi luchshago v dele znaniia]*," while other such terms were explained "in parentheses *[v parenthesi]*, that is, between the indicated signs [ ] and ( )," this done, again, the better to understand them. Examples of such explanations follow, though without the parenthetical marks, which do appear later in the text (my parentheses, as follow, contain English equivalents of the terms in question): *angul'* = *ugol* (angle); *archus* = *duga* (bow, shaft-bow, yoke, hence "arch"); *aksis* = *os'* (axle); *distantsia* = *rastoianie; differentsia* = *razlichie; Ekvator* = *uravnitel'* (equalizer); *Zona torrida* = *poias goriachii* (hot belt), *Zona frigida* = *poias khladnyi; Zona temperata* = *poias blagorastvorennyi, ili umerennyi* (healthful or moderate belt). These examples are followed by a further apology from the translator for his ignorance of the "geographical and mathematical sciences" and, with flourishes in Latin and Greek, by his

Figure 7   Title page of *Geografia generalnaia (General Geography)* printed at Moscow, 1718; engraving by Aleksei Zubov.

name and title: "Feodor *[sic]* Polikarpov, corrector *[spravshchik;* copy editor] of the [Moscow] Press *[Tipografii]*."[32]

There we have it. The sagacious Polikarpov offers in the preface to his translation of Varenius's *Geographia Generalis* an explanation or rationale not just of this particular project but of, in essence, the entire Petrine program of transferring to Russia selected aspects of the higher verbal culture of contemporary Europe. The program was fraught with difficulties, as Polikarpov emphasizes, not least because of the domestic language question; as he himself also indicates in his preface, he would have preferred to employ more "high Slavonic locutions" in his translation rather than "simple Russian speech" but Peter himself, on reviewing a draft of his work, had ordered him to do the opposite. In fact, in his preface to that draft—a carefully transcribed manuscript submitted to Peter in the fall of 1716—Polikarpov had stated forthrightly that only Slavonic and not the "common Russian dialect *[obshchenarodnym dialektom rossiiskim]*" was suitable for rendering the "elevated and beautiful" Latin of the Varenius even while conceding that, given its intended readership of "young students of science," he had sometimes used Russian so as "not to hide the *sens* from their understanding."[33] Peter's assessment of the draft, as conveyed to Polikarpov by the responsible official in Moscow, was: "quite poor. Therefore make it much better and not with high Slavonic locutions, but with the simple Russian language . . . of the Ambassadorial Office," that is, chancery Russian.[34] Polikarpov took the admonition to heart. Comparisons of his 1716 draft translation of the Varenius with the 1718 printed version show that numerous "corrections" were duly made, including the replacement of what in current Russian practice were obsolete or archaic verb forms, adverbs, nouns, pronouns, and conjunctions by "common Russian" equivalents; for example, *biashe* by *byla, vospriiasha* by *vospriali, ne vedakh* by *ne vedali, im zhe* by *kotorym, koeizhdo* by *vsiakoi, ashche* by *khotia, ucheniia* by *nauki, prishestvie* by *prikhod, ibo vemy iako* by *ponezhe vedaem, on nikago prelstiti* by *on nikago obmanul, prelshchen byst'* by *obmanut byl.* In fact, the majority of the changes were grammatical rather than lexical, and were usually made to eliminate the aorist or imperfect tenses of verbs or to substitute the Russian infinitive verb ending *-t'* for the Slavonic *-ti.*[35] But then, as if to highlight this domestic dimension of the challenge he faced, Polikarpov was by no means consistent in thus editing his translation to satisfy the tsar's order.[36]

At any rate, the printed Moscow edition of the Varenius is a volume of some 650 large-format pages and composed of three main parts or books subdivided into a total of forty chapters, the whole preceded by a detailed table of contents *(Katalog knigi seia).* Book One, comprising the first twenty-one chapters, defines geography as a "mathematical science *[uchenie mate-maticheskoe]*" that "describes the Earth" in various ways, proceeds to outline the basic geometry and trigonometry required to pursue it, explains how the Earth is measured or figured in accordance with the views of various authorities ("authors *[avtory]*"), and expounds the Earth's movements "according to the Copernicans *[po kopernikantsam]*" and its place at the center of the universe *("v tsentre vsego mira")* in relation to the other planets and stars *("po respektu planet i zvezd")*, again according to Copernicus *("mesto zemli kopernikanskoe")*. Attention then turns to the composition of the Earth *("iz kakikh korpusov [ili teles] prostykh i podobnykh krug zemnovodnyi sostoitsia")*, which is the theme of chapters on oceans and islands, on mountains, on ores and forests and plains, on hydrography *("[g]idrografiia, sirech' vody opisanie")*, on the movements (tides and currents) of the seas, on rivers and lakes and ponds, on mineral waters *(vody mineralnye)*, on the Earth's atmosphere *(atmosfera)*—here a Table of Refractions *(Tabel' refraktsei)*—and on the winds, a chapter that explains why, for instance, the air *(aer)* "is often still at the equator on the Atlantic sea between America and Africa *[chasto byvaet tishina pod ekvatorom na more atliantskom mezhdu amerikoiu i afrikoiu]*." Book Two (Chapters 22 to 30) is devoted to the Earth's climatic zones *(zony)* and their characteristics—affects or qualities *("o affektsiakh ili svoistvakh mest kruga zemnago")*—including heat, cold, sunlight, rainfall, and the systems of time employed by various peoples. Book Three (Chapters 31–40) moves to a more technical discussion of these "affects," for example, of the Earth's division into longitudes *(dolgoty)* and the ensuing methods of locating one's position on maps at sea *(na mappakh navigatskikh)* or on land *(mappy geograficheskie)* or on a globe *(na globuse)*. The science or art of navigation *("nauka pravleniia ili upravleniia karabelnago, khudozhestvo navigatsago")* is explained in the last four chapters of the volume.

As the foregoing indicates, the contents of this Russian edition of Varenius's *Geographia Generalis*—of this first substantial work on geography ever published in Russian—are wide-ranging, and abound in the technical vocabulary of the science as it had developed in Europe and particularly Holland by the later seventeenth century. This vocabulary included, in addition to the numerous geometrical and other technical terms sampled just above or earlier in this chapter (or elsewhere in this volume), the following: *obiektum, korpulentsiia, sferichnaia, meteor, trakt, promonotorium, vertilal/vertikalnyi/ vertikalno, meridian/meridiannyi, elementalna, materik, vapor, peninsula, thermometr, efir, elevatsiia, insidentsiia, refleksiia, ekvatornyi, geodeticheskii, periodichnyi, arktik/arkticheskii, antarktik/antarkticheskii, polius, klimat, arti-*

fitsialnyi, ekvinoktsialnye, ekliptika, antipody, apparentsiia, moment, istmus, konstelliatsiia, tropik, kalkuly, theorema, radius, magnitnyi, and *loksodromiia* (from loxodrome = a rhumb line) along with other, often now obsolete, terms. At the same time, the extent to which the translator could find Russian (or Slavonic) words with which to approximate or explain the new technical terms and concepts being transmitted is notable once again: translation, not simply transliteration, was taking place. Not all of the new terms deployed here by Polikarpov were permanently added to the Russian lexicon (those listed in Appendix II, as usual, were), although some of them were soon calqued, like *poluostrov* on *peninsula* and *peresheek* on *istmus,* presumably with the help of his definitions: i.e., for the former, *ostrov ne okruzhennyi vodoiu* (island not surrounded by water), and, for the latter, *mesto mezhdu mor'* (a place between the seas). Still, we can reasonably assume from our knowledge of subsequent events that the array of new geographical and related astronomical *concepts* presented by Varenius via Polikarpov in a mixture of extant Russian (or Slavonic) terms and assorted neologisms contributed fundamentally to the development of geography in Russia: to the subsequent acquisition, expansion, and diffusion in Russian of geographical knowledge about both Russia itself and the rest of the world. Some proof of the rapid success of this development is found in the minutely recorded geographical researches of that typical Petrine "fledgling," I. K. Kirilov (1695–1737), and in the equally prodigious labors of the Geography Department of the St. Petersburg Academy of Sciences, which between 1739 and 1765 published no fewer than 250 maps of many previously uncharted or vaguely charted areas of the Earth, including the first complete atlas of the Russian Empire (*Atlas Rossiiskoi,* 1745), itself widely recognized in Europe as a cartographic achievement of the first rank. *Geografiia* had become a Russian science, one fully practicable in Russian, within a few decades of the publication of the Russian Varenius.[37]

A similar claim to foundational importance may be made for the other substantial geographical work translated and published in Petrine Russia, as mentioned above, Hübner's *Kurtze Fragen . . .* or, in its Russian edition of 1719, the *Zemnovodnago kruga kratkoe opisanie . . . (A Brief Description of the Amphibious Sphere . . .).* This second large-format volume consists of a series of nineteen *landkarty* (literally, maps) or geographical disquisitions on as many countries or regions of the world, these preceded by a table of contents (*Katalog knigi seia*) and a two-page preface in dialogue form entitled "A Preparation for Geography [*Pred"ugotovlenie na geografiiu*]."[38] The first question asked here, "What is important to notice in every *landkarta?*" is followed by the response that a map's position (perspective), form, and relation to the heavens should be strictly observed, each of which points is then explained: the volume, it becomes clear, was designed as a guide to the making and more, the reading of maps, including those of the countries or regions discussed in the succeeding nineteen chapters. The first chapter is a *landkarta* "on which the globe, or the whole world, is figured *[na kotoroi globus, ili ves' svet izobrazhen]*," which serves as an introduction to the rest of the volume. Chapters 2 through 15 deal with the *landkarta* of Europe (*O landkarte Evropskoi):* what is presented, essentially, is a very basic political geography— form of government, capital city, administrative subdivisions, population, and so on—of Portugal, Spain, France, England/Scotland/Ireland, the Netherlands, Switzerland, Italy, Germany, and the "northern kingdoms and states," namely Denmark, Sweden, Poland, and Prussia with Courland. Chapter 13, remarkably (we are still on the "European map"), presents a map of Russia (*O landkarte rossiiskoi)* with St. Petersburg as the capital, replacing the tentative "Muscovy" of the original German edition, thus providing further evidence of the bold Petrine assertion via cartography and geography that "Russia" (no longer Muscovy) was to be considered an integral part of Europe.[39] Indeed, the stark Eurocentrism of this work is itself remarkable. Chapters 14 and 15 offer "maps" of Greece and the Balkans (thus completing "Europe") while the volume's last four chapters are devoted in rapid succession to Asia, Africa, America, and the "unknown lands" of the Arctic and Antarctic. Russians were importing with their *geografiia* a decidedly Eurocentric view of the world.

Our friend James Bruce oversaw publication of the Russian Hübner and at one point in its preparation he had advised Peter that this geography book would be essential reading for anybody who wished to be informed about "all the states, also their laws, customs, and neighbors, also the families of their rulers."[40] In his view, and Peter's, "history *[(g)istoriia]*" also served the same general purpose. In their world—in late seventeenth-century Europe—"history" meant representations of the political past drawn from genuine documents and was a valued instrument of policy, as witness the institution of the official historian, which went back to fifteenth-century Italy and had spread to the rest of Europe in the train of humanism. History thus understood could provide compelling justification for dynastic or other jurisdictional claims, gratifying celebration of one's nation, a proper grounding for the study of law, and important moral lessons; and it was the more potent for being factually true rather than mythical or purely philosophical or religious in nature. Peter himself formed a high regard for history in this sense—for the political utility of history—an attitude that easily spread to his entourage and one that we've already seen demonstrated in his draft preface to the *Naval Statute* of 1720, whose final version was amplified in the same historical spirit by Feofan Prokopovich, who also drew on history in his closely contemporary "Sermon in Praise of the Russian Fleet" (Chap. 2). It was probably Prokopovich, again, who loaded the regime's lengthy defense of absolute monarchy, the *Pravda voli monarshei* of 1722, with numerous historical examples and allusions, while Shafirov's defense of the war against Sweden—the *Razsuzhdenie* of 1717—was little other than an extended "legal-historical brief" (Chap. 4): a well-nigh perfect instance of the contemporary European practice of using documentary history to advance current dynastic and legal claims.

Peter's active participation in the compilation of a thoroughly documented history of his own reign for the purposes of rightly informing foreigners, instructing his successors, and edifying his subjects, a project that entailed the efforts of numerous members of his entourage and the collection of innumerable primary sources, has itself been well documented from the surviving manuscripts (none of the project was published in his lifetime; large and small fragments were published in various editions thereafter).[41] Indeed the scope of this and related historical projects and the degree of their grounding in official documents were such that recent students have dated the birth of Russian archaeography and archival science, even modern Russian historical consciousness, to the Petrine era.[42] Certainly V. N. Tatishchev, the first Russian to publish a documented history of Russia (his *Istoriia Rossiiskaia*, written in the 1730s and 1740s, first published in successive parts or books in 1768, 1769, 1773, 1774, 1784, 1848) and the first to be recognized as a historian, found his vocation as such under Peter I and with the direct encouragement both of the tsar himself and of James Bruce, for many years his administrative superior.[43] It has been proposed, quite reasonably, that Tatishchev got his first inkling of how his European contemporaries approached history on reading Samuel Pufendorf's *Einleitung zu der Historie der Vornehmsten Reiche und Staaten so itziger Zeit in Europa sich befinden (Introduction to the History of the Principal Empires and States of Contemporary Europe)*, a copy of which—the copy later found in his personal library—he might well have acquired during his time as a student (1712–1716) in Germany.[44] At one point in his *Razsuzhdenie* of 1717 Shafirov invokes certain "ancient political maxims that Pufendorf recalls in his well-known book, Introduction to History [*vedenie v gistoriiu*],"[45] evidence not only that he also knew the work in question but that he too might have had a hand in preparing its Russian edition. Later in this chapter we shall see that Prokopovich had read Pufendorf's *Historie* as well—

as had one of the first members of the St. Petersburg Academy of Sciences, and its first historian, G. F. Müller.[46]

The *Vvedenie v gistoriiu evropeiskuiu chrez Samuila Pufendorfiia* was printed at the St. Petersburg Press in 1718 (600 copies) and again, in a slightly revised version, in 1723 (300 copies).[47] It was translated into Russian *(na rossiiskom iazytse)* from a Latin edition of the work—*Introductio ad Historiam Europaeum* (Frankfurt am Main, 1704)—by Gabriel *(Gavriil)* Buzhinskii, another of those Ukrainian divines from the Kiev Academy who, like Prokopovich, had been called to serve in the Russian church and who, again like Prokopovich, had risen high in Peter's favor, serving as the first priest-monk of the Alexander-Nevskii monastery in St. Petersburg, the first chief chaplain of the fleet, and one of the first members of the Holy Synod; to the last position he then added the lucrative and prestigious headship of the famous old Trinity-Sergiev monastery near Moscow and the politically sensitive posts of protector of the Moscow Slavonic-Greek-Latin Academy and of the Moscow Press. He was, as well, one of the principal activists in Peter's church reform and a contributor, no doubt, to the *Ecclesiastical Regulation* of 1721.[48] In any event, his background doubtless accounts for the rather Baroque, Church-Slavonicized Russian of his translation of Pufendorf's *Historie* as well as for its lavish dedication to "Our Most Illustrious, most august, invincible sovereign tsar, the All-Russian monocrat and emperor *[monokratoru i imperatoru]* Peter the First, the forever triumphant conqueror and my most gracious lord."[49]

Pufendorf's work certainly was well known in contemporary Europe, having gone through at least five German editions, five Latin, and ten each in English and French within half a century or so of its initial publication (1682)[50]—these in addition to the two Russian printings and a later Russian edition, which was translated anew from the German and published by the St. Petersburg Academy of Sciences, in two volumes, in 1767 and 1777, this time in pressruns of some 2,400 copies each.[51] Written while its author was a professor of law at the University of Lund in Sweden, the work was intended as a textbook for "youth of high rank" destined for "offices of state"; it became a model, says Professor Krieger, "for the juristic adaptation of universal history to political utility."[52] Following a brief sketch of "ancient Empires, especially the Roman, from whose ruins modern empires and states have grown," the work settles down to a series of discrete political histories, annalistic in form, of various European polities of the day, the whole aiming to elucidate the "the interest" or "common good" of each against the claims of universal monarchy abroad or divisive "private" factions at home. It is not one of the great works

213

of history. "Overburdened by annalistic narrative," complains Krieger, the bulk of the work is "without inner coherence, general principle, or real linkage with the notion of 'interest' that was supposed to serve as [its] historical principle."[53] In his preface to the first Russian edition, the translator (Buzhinskii) complains further that the Latin edition at his disposal was in many places obscure and that he therefore sought to convey the sense of the original rather than translate it word for word. He was also concerned to provide Russian readers with a brief "explanation" of "certain difficult locutions employed in this book"—mostly European ethnic and geographical names but also such general terms as *monarkhiia, aristokratiia,* and *demokratiia,* for which he offered simple translations. Also noteworthy is the book's brief chapter (some 6 of a total of 558 pages) on "Russia or more commonly Muscovy *[O Rossii ili obshche Moskovii]*," whose generally negative tone— Muscovy as a "slavish nation" located on the fringes of Europe—Buzhinskii apparently tried to moderate in his translation until ordered by Peter to restore the original as a lesson to his people (the translator of the 1767–77 Russian edition let the passage stand, while noting that the Russian people were no longer as Pufendorf had described them).[54]

Still, it is not hard to see why Peter and his entourage, like so many of their European contemporaries, valued Pufendorf's *History.* It presented an entirely secular account of the emergent European system of sovereign states, each naturally possessing its own laws, traditions, and "interest" or "common good" yet subject at the same time to the mutually agreed terms of an international law that was similarly grounded in nature. Moreover Pufendorf's *History* acted no doubt as a goad to the creation of a positive and properly documented, up-to-date history of Russia itself, a project that did preoccupy, as mentioned above, Peter's last years. Pufendorf's *History,* in short, provided the larger political-historical map on which politically conscious Russians of Peter's time could position themselves. For this reason, presumably, it was used as a textbook at the St. Petersburg Naval Academy for many years, and copies of it as well as other works by the celebrated German jurist were to be found in the libraries of prominent Russians until late in the eighteenth century.[55]

Nor was it the only one of Pufendorf's works to be translated under Peter. The same fate befell his even better known *De officio hominis et civis juxta legem naturalem (On the Duties of Man and the Citizen according to Natural Law),* which was an epitome of the author's magisterial *De jure naturae et gentium (On the Law of Nature and Nations),* which together went through at least thirty-five editions in the original Latin, thirty-nine in French translation, and fourteen in English as well as "sporadic publication in German, Italian, and Russian."[56] The *De Officio* was designed by its author as a textbook for students preparing for state service, and in the *Ecclesiastical Regulation* of 1721 Prokopovich recommended it for study in his projected ecclesiastical academy; he no doubt drew on its formulations when composing the *Pravda voli monarshei* of 1722 as well as various other political writings (Chap. 4). Perhaps he told his master about it, too, for in September 1724 Peter sent a copy of "Pufendorf's book . . . on the duties of man and citizen" to the Holy Synod (of which both Prokopovich and Buzhinskii were members) with orders that it be translated in a "fine style *[khoroshim shtilem]*."[57] The ensuing *O dolzhnosti cheloveka i grazhdanina po zakonu estestvennomu* was duly printed under Synod auspices, in two "books" continuously paginated, at the St. Petersburg Press in 1726 in an edition of 600; its dedication to "Emperor Peter the Great," now deceased, was signed by Gabriel Buzhinskii.[58]

215

This Russian edition of Pufendorf's best-known work, copies of which were owned by "almost every" Imperial Russian administrator of the eighteenth century,[59] is significant for its propagation of recent European theories of natural law and the attendant duties of citizens.[60] But of greater moment now is the lengthy "Index of memorable locutions used in this book *[Reestr pamiatstvuemykh rechenii v knize sei obretaiushchikhsia]*," which contained more than a hundred technical or philosophical Latin terms employed in the text and their rough "Russian" equivalents. The list is especially interesting for the fact that the translator, presumably Buzhinskii again, could come up with such Russian (or Slavonic) equivalents for most of the Latin terms included: *deistvie chelovecheskoe* for *actio humana; um* for *intellectus; pristrastie uma* for *affectiones; pogreshenie* for *error; nevedenie* for *ignorantia; volia* for *voluntas; samovolie* for *spontaneitas; konets* for *finis; sredstviia* for *media; prilichnoe* for *decorum; strast'* for *affectus; vmenenie* for *imputatio; obiazatel'stvo* for *obligatio; spravedlivost'* for *aequitas; pravda* for *justitia; razsuzhdenie o chesti* for *opinio praestantiae; veshchi nevrednyia pol'zy* for *res innoxiae utilitatis; dolzhnost'* for *officium; obeshchanie dobrovolnoe* for *promissum gratuitum; sposoby pervonachalnyia* for *modi originarii; proizvodnyia* for *derivativi; pribytok* for *accessio; pravilnyi vladetel'* for *bonae fidei possessor; zakon estestvennyi* for *lex naturalis; zakon blagotvoreniia* for *lex beneficientiae; otritsatel'nyi* for *negativum; polozhitelnyi* for *positiva; grazhdanin* for *civis;* and so on. Only in a relatively few cases did Buzhinskii's attempt to find or invent a Russian equivalent fail and the corresponding Latin take hold in Russian instead, for example, *vid* for *forma; obshchestvo* for *respublica; pravilnyi* for *regularis; povelitelstvo sovershennoe* for *imperium absolutum; bogopochtenie ili bogochtenie* for *religio; zhelanie* for *appetitus; pravilo* for *norma; obshchii* for *universalis:* in all such cases, we now know, the Latin given here was sooner or later naturalized in Russian (as *forma, respublika, reguliarnyi, imperiia, absoliutnyi, religiia, appetit, norma, universal'nyi*), as were such other terms in Buzhinskii's list as *pacta (pakta), hypothetica (gipoteticheskii)*, and *contractus (kontrakt)*. Indeed at one point Buzhinskii himself uses a Latinism to explain the Latin: *conditiones casuales seu fortuitae*, he says, means *konditsii sluchainyia ili prikliuchaiushchyiasia*. Elsewhere in his translation he leaves the Latinism alone, to be explained in context rather than by hazarding an equivalent word or phrase, as with the term—to take one conspicuous example—*iurisprudentiia*. We are reminded that the Petrine revolution in Russian verbal culture entailed an enormous semantic as well as lexical expansion, a matter of putting old words to new uses as well as adopting new words for new things.

Other histories broadly speaking published during Peter's reign include a translation from the *latinskago iazyka na rossiiskii* of the semilegendary account of Alexander the Great by the Roman historian Quintus Curtius Rufus, which was printed in civil types at the Moscow Press in 1709, 1711 (see Appendix I, no. 20), and 1717 and at the St. Petersburg Press in 1722 and 1724.[61] Widely popular in Europe and already known in manuscript in late seventeenth-century Muscovite court circles, the *Kniga Kvinta Kurtsia o delakh sodeianykh Aleksandra velikago* was reprinted at least five more times in the eighteenth century, a record that surely attests to its popularity among "a wide spectrum" of Russian readers.[62] We might suppose that this popularity, remarkable for a nonreligious printed work of the time, was owed not only to its dramatic narratives of the hero's exotic adventures but also to the rather homely lyrical style in which it was written by the unknown translator, presumably a Muscovite court official: a style that probably drew on, whether consciously or not, the well-developed local tradition of oral "historical tales."[63] Somewhat the same may be said for the Petrine edition of a history of Troy that had been translated into Latin from ancient Greek authors in fourteenth-century Italy by one Guido de Columna and was widely popular in Europe thereafter. It too had reached Russia in the later seventeenth century, in a Ukrainian-Slavonic version,[64] and fed the same courtly taste for adventurous tales from afar. Printed at Moscow in the civil type in 1709 and 1712 and again at St. Petersburg in 1717,[65] this *History of the Ruin of Troy* seems to have been much less popular in Russia than the Alexander tale, owing in good part, it might be thought, to its still quite Slavonicized prose and rather pedantic presentation of an unfamiliar subject. But neither of these largely fictional works can be said to have promoted a specifically modern historical consciousness in Russia, although their *secular* content (or "pagan" rather than Christian) has been emphasized by later students.

One other historical text published in Petrine Russia deserves comment: the *Kniga istoriografiia pochatiia imene, slavy i razshireniia naroda slavian-skogo . . . Sobrana iz mnogikh knig Istoricheskikh chrez Gospodina Mavrourbina Arkhimandrita Raguzhskogo (History of the Beginning, Fame and Spread of the Slavonic People . . . Compiled from many History books by Master Mauro Orbini, Abbot of Ragusa)*, 1,200 copies of which were printed at the St. Petersburg Press in August 1722.[66] The book was translated from the original Italian, *Il Regno degli Slavi* (Pesaro, 1601), by Sava Vladislavić, a merchant from Ragusa (Dubrovnik) who in 1703 had taken refuge from the Turks in Russia, where he was known as Savva Raguzinskii. In Russia he remained active in commerce while performing special services for Tsar Peter, most notably as his unofficial agent in Venice (1716–1722) supervising visiting Russian students, purchasing art works, and making diplomatic representations to the Venetian government.[67] It is probable that he brought Orbini's book to Peter's attention, to whom he dedicated his translation, implying that the "most august All-Russian emperor" might see himself as "protector" of all the Slavs.[68] Peter had eagerly recruited Slavic sailors and shipbuilders from the greater Venetian maritime world (Chap. 2), to be sure, and had indulged in a kind of Christian Pan-Slavism in his anti-Ottoman propaganda over the years; but otherwise his enthusiasm for the greater Slavic cause, still in its ideological infancy, had been muted, particularly after his defeat by the Turks at the battle by the Pruth in 1711.[69] Publishing a book for the literate Russian elite vaunting the historical achievements of the Slavic peoples was, however, another matter.

Mauro Orbini was an obscure Benedictine monk who had spent his life, except for a brief period in Italy to finish his *History* and see it published, in several monasteries in the Ragusa region. There he is thought to have absorbed the indigenous Pan-Slavism, itself fueled by resentment of the Venetian hegemony and the pretensions of the local "Dalmatian Romans."[70] His *History*, marked by its "poor Italian and inept composition,"[71] drew on a welter of ancient, Byzantine, and more recent sources found in Ragusan and Italian libraries to offer a correspondingly fanciful, even incoherent account of the origins and early history of the Slavs down to the foundation of their first states. The focus is on the South Slavs, not surprisingly, and the book has served, in the abridged Russian as well as in its original Italian editions, as an important source for subsequent South Slavic historians. But one brief sec-

217

tion is devoted to the "Russian Slavs, who are now generally called Muscovites by foreigners" or, as it appears in the Russian edition: *"O Slavianekh rossiiskikh ili Moskvitianekh/Slaviane Rossiistii sut' nyne ot inozemtsov, obshche zovomy Moskvitiane"*; the section then provides a characteristically fanciful account of the "Slavs of *Rus' [Slaviane Rusi]*" from their supposed origins in Scandinavia *("s nachala vyshli iz Skandii")* to their eventual establishment of a great state stretching from the "Northern Ocean" to the Mediterranean Sea.[72] This section provoked a response from within learned Petrine circles in the form of a commentary—*Rassmotrenie seia povesti*—appended to the Russian edition and written by Feofilakt Lopatinskii, another learned Kievan divine who had become a teacher and then the rector of the Moscow Slavonic-Greek-Latin Academy. The gist of the commentary was to score the original for asserting, on the basis of "Latin" sources, papal responsibility for the conversion of the Slavs to Christianity—for the mission of Sts. Cyril and Methodius (mentioned in Chapter 1); Lopatinskii invoked in rebuttal "our Slavic historian, the Venerable Nestor of the Caves *[nash Slavenskii istorik, Prebodobnyi Nestor Pecherskii]*," that is, Nestor the medieval East Slavic chronicler and monk of the Monastery of the Caves in Kiev whose account of the conversion favored the Byzantine-Orthodox version.[73] In so doing Lopatinskii no doubt drew on the recent Russian edition of the *Sinopsis, ili kratkoe sobranie ot Razlichnykh letopistsev, o Nachale Slaviano-Rossiiskogo Naroda (A Synopsis, or Short Compendium from Various chroniclers, on the Origin of the Slavonic-Russian People/Nation)*, which had been published in the civil type at Moscow in 1714 and again at St. Petersburg in 1718[74] and itself is evidence of a budding historical consciousness among at least some Russians and Ruthenians.

The importance for us of the Russian edition of Orbini's *Il Regno degli Slavi* lies much less in its language—its translator, in fact, later apologized to the Russian authorities for being "insufficiently adept in the Russian dialect *[nedovol'nago v rossiiskom dialekte iskusiia]*"[75]—and much more in the interest it obviously provoked, both within Russia itself and abroad, in Slavic history: in the idea that the Slavs were a family of peoples united by a common ancestral language who had a history equal in dignity and antiquity to that of the Latin peoples of the West (Orbini's obvious paradigm). We know that Thomas Consett, the Anglican chaplain serving in Russia in the 1720s and a well-known figure in St. Petersburg learned society, possessed a copy of the Russian Orbini, which he had begun to translate into English;[76] and this information, taken together with the Lopatinskii commentary just referred to and the fact that more than 700 copies of the book had been sold by 1756,[77] argues again for a significant *semantic* expansion of Russian under Peter: in this case, for the establishment in Russia of the vocabulary of Pan-Slavism, which sooner or later would acquire major political valence.

We might leave the last word here to Peshtich, author of the detailed history of eighteenth-century Russian historiography cited earlier. In the Petrine period, he concludes, "historical knowledge not only was much more widely disseminated than in the seventeenth century [or at any time before in Russia], but thanks to major reforms in the socioeconomic and cultural spheres it began to play a most active role in diplomacy, military affairs, legislation, literature, church life, and so on." Peter and his collaborators, in the various ways indicated, virtually invented modern Russian historiography, says Peshtich. Yet we must not exaggerate, he also warns: "History as an independent discipline was not yet taught in the schools, and historical textbooks . . . did not yet exist."[78] True enough. In fact, this was one of the tasks taken up in the aftermath of his reign by Peter's Academy of Sciences, as we shall soon see.

Eloquence, Theology, Philosophy

The Petrine era has generally not been viewed as one of any great distinction by literary scholars, however they may have classified its poetry and prose with respect to genre or style, trend or school. When it comes to writing regarded for its aesthetic rather than its didactic or informative value, when attention turns to imaginative or creative writing of recognized artistic merit, when the subject is verbal art or *belles lettres,* literary specialists usually do not invoke the period of Peter I. Indeed it was not by general agreement either a golden age or a silver age in the history of Russian letters, nor even, be it said, a bronze age: these would all come later. Instead, the Petrine period is normally considered the last phase of a more or less prolonged "transition" from medieval to modern Russian literature: as marking, in fact, the great "break" *(perelom)* between the two. And if various of Peter's "reforms"—in elite dress codes, manners, education, entertainment, and the like—were "responsible for the appearance of a modern, secular culture in Russia," as one student writes, his "own generation continued to live off the out-of-date products and tastes of the previous age. . . . The first quarter of the eighteenth century produced little or nothing that was new in literature."[79]

Nor did the literature produced in Russia during the rest of the eighteenth century reach the highest standards of what had come to be considered literature—*literatura*—by educated Russians, thanks in considerable measure to the Petrine revolution. In an exceptionally concise digest of the received scholarship, another specialist observes that "to a great extent the history of Russian literature in the eighteenth century is the history of literary trends [Classicism, Sentimentalism, Romanticism, and subsets thereof] imported successively from western Europe." To be sure, Professor Drage adds, the characteristic genres of "the literature of Russia's medieval age"—chronicles, sermons, saints' lives, and so on, predominantly religious in content and written in Church Slavonic mostly by clerics—continued to be practiced in remoter areas until well into the nineteenth century, and literature typical of "Russo-Ukrainian scholasticism"—sermons, syllabic verse, school drama, exercises in rhetoric and poetics, all inspired by Polish Baroque or Classical Latin models and composed in a classicized (archaicized) Church Slavonic mostly, again, by clerics—continued to be practiced in Russian ecclesiastical academies and seminaries until the later eighteenth century. But Russia's first modern writers as such—Antiokh Kantemir (1709–1744), Vasilii Tradiakovskii (1703–1769), Mikhailo Lomonosov (1711–1765), Alexander Sumarokov (1718–1777)—all "taught with only episodic deviations that the future of Russian literature lay in discarding its past and in following the development of the more advanced literatures of western Europe." This meant, Drage continues, that there were three main tasks to perform:

> *First was that of translation* [emphasis added] from the languages of western Europe into Russian. Initiated by Peter I, it was carried on right through the century by such writers as Kantemir, Trediakovskii, Novikov [N. I., 1744–1818], and [Nicholas] Karamzin [1766–1826]. Early in the century the works chosen for translation were mostly scientific and technical: from the 1740s literary works began to predominate. *Second was the task of working out a body of literary theory* which should include poetry, prose, and drama. Here the purpose was to provide the theoretical framework for a new Russian literature on west European lines, and it was met primarily by the three founders of modern Russian literature, Trediakovskii, Lomonosov, and Sumarokov. *The third task was to create the new literature itself* in all the genres familiar in west European literature. This was largely the work of the three last named writers together with [Gavrila] Derzhavin [1743–1816] and Karamzin[80]

—only the very last of whom, it will be noticed, achieved anything like an international literary reputation.

Thus in the standard account of the beginnings or "emergence" of modern

Russian literature, the Petrine era inaugurated, or greatly expanded, the crucial work of translation from western European literary languages (still to include Latin) even as it nurtured, in a rapidly Europeanizing cultural environment, Russia's first writers. The latter were personal beneficiaries both directly and indirectly of Petrine educational and other initiatives, certainly, and we have sampled in this and the preceding chapters the nature and extent of the Petrine translation program. But that program was more extensive with respect to literature as well as more varied than is usually realized, particularly in the realm of drama, where translated plays produced by short-lived court, school, and public theaters set up by and under Peter laid the basis for the later flourishing in Russia of theater in the modern sense ("scripted drama staged by paid performers in specific arenas for a paying audience").[81] Still, when all is said and done the literary significance of the era cannot be fully or properly estimated without directly addressing the language question. As we have repeatedly seen, finding an appropriate Russian into which to translate foreign works became under Peter, given the urgency and scope of his program, a correspondingly urgent matter; and so the "elaboration of a new, modern, secular Russian literary language," in another authoritative statement, quickly became "one of the great tasks of Russian literature in the eighteenth century." As Professor Segel says further, "standards and canons had to be established. To be more exact, a modern Russian literary language had to be created, and the task of eighteenth-century Russian literary theory was to create this language."[82]

The process by which a modern Russian literary language was both theorized and exemplified in the middle decades of the eighteenth century in works by, most prominently, Trediakovskii, Lomonosov, and Sumarokov is not one that needs to be gone over here. Rather will I emphasize, and in some measure demonstrate, the fundamental importance to the process of the Petrine contribution, which took two basic forms. The first was finally and fully to implant the European print revolution in Russia, which proved to be a necessary condition, in Russia as in Europe, for the establishment of both a modern national literary language and a modern national literature. And the second was to promote the adoption in Russian of huge new technical, scientific, administrative-legal, and, yes, literary vocabularies while insisting that all translations and indeed almost anything else that was to be published should be written in a simple or plain *(prostoi)* Russian: a language readily comprehensible to the naval and military students and officers, government officials, merchants who dealt with foreigners, artists, craftsmen, and others who together constituted the activist elite of the Petrine revolution, very few of whom had received the essentially religious formation in Church Slavonic with a smattering of Latin and Greek that had passed for higher education in Russia. It was a class that included Peter himself, whose own tutelage in this higher learning, owing to the recurrent dynastic crises of his childhood and youth, had been considerably less than complete. Both aspects of the Petrine contribution to the creation of modern Russian will be investigated in the following chapter, readers having already imbibed, to be sure, much food for thought in its predecessors.

Meanwhile we should note that an exception to literary scholars' generally deprecatory view of the literary production of the Petrine era has been made for "oratorical prose" and particularly for the efforts in this genre of Feofan Prokopovich (1681–1736), another old friend (Chaps. 2, 4). Public or panegyrical orations on political themes composed in a tradition of eloquence stretching back from Moscow and St. Petersburg through Kiev and the Roman Catholic colleges of greater Poland to Renaissance Italy are at issue now, and a dozen or so of those given by Prokopovich on various state occasions, all published at the time, are considered the best representatives of the tradition dating from the Petrine period.[83] Its other leading practitioners of the era—Stefan Iavorskii, Dimitrii Rostovskii, Joseph Turuboiskii (see Appendix I, no. 14), Feofilakt Lopatinskii, and Gabriel Buzhinskii—were all, like Prokopovich, graduates of the Kiev Academy, where the tradition had flourished since the earlier seventeenth century. Two Kievan scholars, Epifanii Slavinetskii and Simeon Polotskii, had brought the tradition to Moscow in the time of Peter's father, Tsar Aleksei; Polotskii also introduced Polish-derived syllabic versification to Moscow (Appendix I, no. 6), which reigned until the introduction, again mainly by Trediakovskii and Lomonosov, of the syllabo-tonic system, which was considered more suitable to the natural rhythm of Russian.[84] And Kantemir, Lomonosov, even Sumarokov among the leading lights of eighteenth-century Russian letters are known to have composed orations in this essentially seventeenth-century, Russo-Ukrainian, scholastic or Baroque (school Baroque) oratorical mode (Sumarokov as a kind of pastiche).[85]

In Prokopovich's hands, or mouth, the tradition produced orations (*slova*, in the plural, or sometimes *rechi*: "sermons" or "speeches") remarkable for their relatively faithful adherence to Classical forms, attention to secular topics, and unusual clarity and directness of style, features that imparted to his utterances, to cite Segel again, "a strong, forceful, masculine character that sets them apart from the more typically Baroque efforts" of his colleagues.[86] An edition of Prokopovich's collected sermons and speeches, both printed and still in manuscript, was published in three volumes at St. Petersburg between 1760 and 1765,[87] testimony surely to the esteem in which they were still held. Both Lomonosov and Sumarokov considered him virtually their only Russian predecessor in the art of official eloquence, as good a public orator for his time as any in Europe, although his "style," admittedly, was not "pure": "*On ritor iz chisla vo vsei Evrope glavnykh,*" as Sumarokov put it, "*khot' v chistom sloge on i chasto pogreshal*"—a reference to the frequent Slavonicisms and Ukrainianisms (or Polonisms) characteristic of Prokopovich's diction.[88] Even so, in his dictionary of Russian writers of 1772, the first of its kind, Novikov ranked Prokopovich "the first of our finest writers *[pervym iz nailuchshikh nashikh pisatelei]*" largely on the basis, once again, of his best orations.[89] But then that is, in the end, the main point: "The oratorical prose of Feofan Prokopovich proved a rich and valuable source for the writers of Russian classicism"[90]—for the creators, in other words, of modern Russian literature. Considered purely as a *literary* figure, in short, Prokopovich is the exception to literary scholars' generally deprecatory view of the literature of the Petrine era that rather proves the rule.

At the same time, to have been a recognized pioneer or predecessor of a great literary tradition is no mean achievement, especially if it was in conjunction with being the chief publicist in his time of the broader Petrine cause. In the last decade of Peter's reign, and for a decade thereafter, hardly a state occasion of any importance passed in St. Petersburg or Moscow without a speech, prominently featured, by Feofan Prokopovich. As the author or principal author of the *Ecclesiastical Regulation* of 1721, the *Pravda voli monarshei* of 1722, a famous account of Peter's death (Appendix I, no. 36),[91] and some twenty-three contemporaneously published state orations, he proved to be the most articulate and consistent promoter in Petrine Russia of what came to be called enlightened absolutism *(prosveshchennyi absoliutizm)*.[92] And it was in this capacity that he made his most lasting impact on Russian verbal culture, not as a poet, school dramatist, or literary theorist, in all of which roles he also tried his hand, also with very mixed results.[93]

In Chapter 2 we considered Prokopovich's sermon of 1720 in praise of Peter's creation of the navy. Before leaving this most distinguished orator of his time in Russia, we might look at another of his published speeches the better to illustrate, or affirm, his place in our story. Prokopovich's "Sermon of Praise on the Poltava Battle *[Slovo pokhvalnoe o batalii Poltavskoi]*" was given on June 27, 1717—the eighth anniversary of the famous Russian victory over Sweden—in the Trinity cathedral in St. Petersburg and was printed on July 28, also at St. Petersburg.[94] Like all but one of his contemporaneously published orations, it was printed in the traditional Cyrillic type complete with Slavonic rather than Arabic numerals, letters that had been dropped from the new civil alphabet, sundry scribal marks, and other features that would soon lend it an ecclesiastical and obsolescent character (see excerpts reproduced in Appendix I, no. 24).[95] This fact aside, and disregarding the typical Slavonicisms and Ukrainianisms such as would later be scored by Lomonosov and Sumarokov, the unusual vigor and straightforwardness of this speech are impressive, especially in contrast to the Baroque orations of Prokopovich's contemporaries (or even, be it said, to Lomonosov's). The subject is victory, or the "memory of the most glorious Poltava victory *[pamiat' preslavnyia* Poltavskiia viktorii]*," which is attributed much less to divine intervention than to the wisdom and courage of Tsar Peter and his lieutenants *(vel'mozhi,* voenachal'nitsy,* i voini rossiistii*)* and was to be seen by every good Russian *(vsiak syn rossiiskii)* as a victory for all of Russia, one in which Russia was "reborn, powerful, and fully come of age *[V sem edinom ouvidish rossiiu otrozhdennuiu,* vozmogshuiu,* i sovershenno vozrastushuiu*]*."[96] The Swedish king Charles XII is referred to throughout as the *supostat** (adversary, foe, even "satan"), as in "the ferocity and power of the foe *[liutost'* i silu supostatskuiu*]*," and Sweden itself is described as a land and people "glorious in arms, this Sweden, feared in all of Europe, this Gothic nation, frightful name, this Gothic nation [which] has fought nine years with Russia *[Shvetsiia oruzhiem slavnaia, se shvetsiia vsei Evrope strashnaia, Gofskii narod, imia ouzhasnoe, narod gofskii s rossieiu devat' let boretsia]*." Russia's martial spirit *(bran'*)* had been aroused by righteous anger in the face of insult and injury, but Sweden's, by envy born of overweening pride and contempt for Russian weakness—this followed by an extended reference to St. Basil the Great's sermon against envy. Indeed before Peter's reign Russia still had "no military regulation, no engineering art, no architecture of either sort [presumably military or civil], no navy, no force upon the sea *[ne byla eshche regula voinskaia, ne byli iskusstva inzhenerskii, ne byli oboego china arkhitektury, ne byl flot, ne byla sila na more]*," whence her neighbors were led to belittle her, however mistakenly, as may be read in the history of Samuel Pufendorf.

The reference to Pufendorf along with Prokopovich's rehearsal of the incident at Riga in 1697, when the Swedish commandant allegedly insulted the visiting Tsar Peter, recalls of course Shafirov's *Razsuzhdenie* or *Discourse* on the legal-historical reasons for Russia's pursuit of the war against Sweden (Chap. 4), a treatise that was first published at this very time (mid-1717), when the Russo-Swedish or Great Northern War had entered a phase of intense international diplomacy in search of a negotiated peace. Again the political timeliness of his "sermons," and Prokopovich's role as an adroit and well-informed defender of official Russian policy, is underlined. Equally clear, here as in his other orations, is his role as an early and passionate propagator of the Petrine myth—Peter as the heroic creator, by means of his many innovations, of a new Russia. We also notice, as before, his advocacy of a kind of Russian state nationalism, here especially evident in his interpretation of the Poltava victory as a "wresting" of Ukraine or "Little Russia," Prokopovich's homeland, from the "Polish yoke"; as a well-deserved rout for his "treason" of the Ukrainian Hetman Mazepa (who had sided with the Swedes), and a welcome "return to the mighty fortress of her [Little Russia's] hereditary monarchs." For "every lawfully ruling monarch [Zakonno Tsarstvuiushchii Monarkh vsiak] has his power from the Lord and his strength from on High," Prokopovich admonished his audience, citing chapter 13 of St. Paul's Epistle to the Romans[97]; and historians of Russia, he proudly asserted, would someday record that "not on a single European ruler was there to be seen as precious a crown as [that] on the Russian monarch [Pishut istoriki, kotoryi rossiiskoe Gosudarstvo opisuiut, chto ni na edinom evropiiskom gosudare ne videti* est' tak dragotsennoi korony, kak na Monarkhe rossiistem*]." Prokopovich reached for comparisons to Alexander the Great and other heroes of ancient Greece and Rome, as well as to supposed biblical parallels (for example, Mazepa as "a second Judas"); his praise of Peter, somewhat sparing by contemporary Baroque standards, was still fulsome. And Poltava was hailed not only as a splendid victory in its own right but also as the "mother of many other victories [Poltavskaia bo* pobeda mnogikh innykh pobed mati* est']," meaning, as the speaker pronounced the name of each province and city that had been captured, the gradual Russian conquest of the eastern Baltic region between 1709 and 1717. "O Russians!" Prokopovich at length exclaimed: "At Poltava was sown all that the Lord has been pleased to let us reap since [O rossiane!* pod Poltavoiu seiano bylo vse sie, chto posle blagovoli* nam Gospod' pozhati*]." It was strong stuff, no doubt about it: a strong message forcefully delivered; but delivered in a language and in a style that pointed back, as literature, to the East Slavic–Church Slavonic past as much as it looked forward to the Russian future. Owing to the very success of modern Russian literary culture, it would transpire, Prokopovich would come to be seen as only one of its forerunners.

The formal disciplines of philosophy and theology, as they had been practiced in Europe since medieval times, were also brought to Russia by Kievan divines in the later seventeenth century and institutionalized, most notably, at the Slavonic-Greek-Latin Academy in Moscow. Founded by immigrant Greek scholars in about 1685 under the jurisdiction of the patriarch of Moscow, the school was decisively oriented in the direction of Kievan scholasticism with Peter's appointment in 1700 of Stefan Iavorskii, following the death of Patriarch Adrian, as acting head of the Russian church. Iavorskii, in the view of Grecophile Muscovite traditionalists, was yet another "Latinizer" of the type that had been favored by the tsarist court for the past thirty or forty years. A native Ukrainian and graduate of the Kiev Academy, he had completed his studies at several of the Jesuit colleges in greater Poland, whence he had returned *Artium liberalium et philosophiae magister, consummatus theologus.* In Kiev again, he had become professor, successively, of rhetoric and oratory at the academy and then of philosophy and theology: the latter subjects had only recently been introduced at Kiev, and were modeled on the corresponding courses taught at the Jesuit and other Catholic colleges located all over Europe. By this time not only Iavorskii himself but also most of his colleagues at Kiev had completed their studies at some such college located in Poland-Lithuania or even further afield, in Prague, Olomouc, Paris, or Rome—in Rome at the Jesuit-run Greek College of St. Athanasius, Prokopovich's alma mater. Thus the language of instruction at Kiev, particularly in the higher forms, was Latin, while the philosophy was based on Aristotle and considered preliminary to theology. Theology constituted the summit of the curriculum and in Iavorskii's time (and long thereafter) it comprised a four-year course based on the teachings of the great medieval schoolmen—Aquinas, Albertus Magnus, Duns Scotus—as updated to account for the disputes of the Reformation by the Jesuit divines Robert Bellarmine, Francisco Suárez, Tirso González, and especially Tomasz Młodzianowski, whose *Praelectiones Philosophicae* and *Praelectiones Theologicae,* published at Cracow and elsewhere in the 1670s and 1680s, seem to have been a major influence at Kiev in the earlier eighteenth century. This was the academic orientation that Iavorskii brought to Moscow and then imposed on the Moscow Academy when, by Peter's order, late in 1700, it came under his jurisdiction. With Peter's blessing he promptly appointed several Kievan scholars to be teachers at Moscow, three of whom—Feofilakt Lopatinskii, Joseph Turuboiskii, and Gabriel Buzhinskii—we have already met in their ensuing roles as preachers and translators.[98]

The philosophy and theology transplanted from Kiev to Moscow in the earlier years of Peter's reign, in other words, were of a Baroque Scholastic piece with the poetry, oratory, and drama that came with them, and shared much the same fate. Alien flowers in an inhospitable environment—inhospitable for religious, nationalist (or religio-nationalist), and linguistic reasons—

Kievan or "Russo-Ukrainian" scholasticism never really took root on Russian territory, no more in philosophy or theology than in poetry or drama. Kievan learning forever remained "Latinist," even "papist," in conservative Muscovite, indeed Orthodox, eyes, particularly when it came to theology. As the most distinguished historian to date of Russian theology has put it, at Kiev

> an academic tradition was formed, a school grew up, but a spiritual and creative movement did not arise. What came forth was an imitative and provincial scholasticism, precisely a "theology of the school," *theologia scholastica*. This did signify a certain step forward in religious-cultural consciousness. At the same time, however, theology was torn from its living roots. An unhealthy and dangerous split developed between thought and experience. The outlook of the Kievans was broad enough, the link with Europe was quite lively, and news of the latest movements and strivings in the West came readily to Kiev. Still, there was something foredoomed in all this activity. It was a pseudomorphosis of religious consciousness, a pseudomorphosis of Orthodox thought.

Yet in thus condemning "Kievan learning" from an essentially Orthodox religious perspective, Florovskii did not deny its "undoubted significance from the cultural-historical standpoint."[99] And that is what interests us. Another student of the Kievan academic program and of its legacy for Russian intellectual development readily concedes its formalistic, imitative, elaborately rhetorical character—to the point where "the Orthodoxy of Kievan writings could be questioned"—while insisting that it nevertheless "forged a clear and disciplined way of thinking. It obliged one to define and to justify. It did not reject outright everything that came from the West nor did it assume in the face of Western science an attitude of fright and disdain. It encouraged Orthodox theologians to use to their own advantage all that Western thought could do better. This constituted, in fine, the birth of the academic mind *[la naissance de l'esprit académique]*."[100] And on this account, indeed, we can in some measure credit the "birth of the academic mind" in Russia to Peter I.

On this account, the breakthrough to formal, systematic, abstract thinking that indoctrination in Kievan scholasticism represented for several generations of students at the Moscow academy can be attributed to Peter's vigorous promotion of Kievan scholars, admittedly for his own larger political purposes. He also backed, however fitfully, the spread of Kievan learning to the analogous academy founded in stages in St. Petersburg and to the twenty-six diocesan colleges or seminaries established by 1750 elsewhere in the Russian

Empire, all as projected by Feofan Prokopovich in the *Ecclesiastical Regulation* of 1721. Equally important in the short run was Peter's ready reliance on the linguistic, rhetorical, and academic expertise of the Kievan scholars in implementing his program of rapid and intensive Europeanization. In these several ways, and whatever the other freight that came in the Kievan train, the spread in Russia and in Russian of habits of "clear and disciplined thinking" and of related technical vocabularies—literary, scientific, philosophical, theological—was greatly facilitated. In the early 1720s and 1730s Trediakovskii and then Lomonosov studied at the Moscow academy, to name two luminaries of subsequent literary and, in Lomonosov's case, scientific fame, and Gregorii Teplov (1717–1779), author of the first Russian textbook on philosophy (published by the St. Petersburg Academy of Sciences in 1751), spent his formative years in Prokopovich's school in St. Petersburg, a precursor of the St. Petersburg Ecclesiastical Academy.[101] But these developments lay mainly in the future bequeathed to Russia by Peter. In his own time the innovative emphasis fell much more heavily on what might be called practical or civic philosophy and on moral theology.

Three such works vie for our attention. The first, the Russian edition of Pufendorf's *On the Duties of Man and the Citizen,* translated (probably) by Gabriel Buzhinskii, was discussed earlier in this chapter, where its contribution to the creation of a Russian philosophical lexicon was emphasized. The second is a manual of etiquette entitled *The Honorable Mirror of Youth, or a guide to social conduct gathered from various authors (Iunosti chestnoe zertsalo ili pokazanie k zhiteiskomu obkhozhdeniiu. Sobrannoe ot raznykh Avtorov),* which was first published at St. Petersburg in February 1717 and again in July of that year (see Appendix I, no. 25). It was reprinted at St. Petersburg in July 1719 and then at Moscow in November 1723 and still later, at one place or the other, in 1740, 1742, 1745, and 1767. Buzhinskii has been identified as its chief compiler but with significant help, apparently, from James Bruce and from a resident German scholar, poet, and translator named Johann Werner Paus;[102] certainly the text itself of the manual—more or less Slavonicized, more or less coherent—suggests the work of several translators variously familiar with literary Slavonic and written or spoken Russian. In any case, the manual is a small-format book of eighty-eight pages consecutively numbered (Arabic numerals) and printed with exceptional clarity in the civil type; and its first section consists of sixty-three numbered paragraphs laying down as many rules of social conduct for youths aspiring to be proper noblemen, "true courtiers," and fine "cavaliers."[103] This is followed by a brief section on "How a young person should behave when in conversation with others *[Kako mladyi otrok dolzhen postupat', kogda onyi v besede s drugimi sidit]*"; by a somewhat longer section prescribing how young people—in context, still mainly young men— are to behave "among strangers *[mezhdu chuzhdymi]*"; and then by three sections (pages 47–88) devoted to proper female behavior, the first entitled "The Crown of maidenly honor and virtue *[Devicheskoi chesti, i dobrodetelei* 229 *venets]*," the second, "Maidenly chastity," and the third, "Maidenly meekness." Roughly the first half of the manual thus provides guidance to aspiring young Russian gentlemen, the second half, to aspiring young Russian ladies; and the differences between the two in both tone and text, perhaps not surprisingly, are striking.

The opening section of the *Mirror* begins with the time-worn admonition that "First and most important of all, children should hold father and mother in great honor," an admonition that is explained at length and becomes indeed a recurrent theme of the remaining sixty-two rules of etiquette; for example:

3. It is not proper *[ne nadlezhit]* to interrupt the speech of parents, nor to cut [it] short, nor to fall into speech with others of their age, but to wait while they speak. Do not repeat something often; do not lean on the table, a bench, or anything else, like a village lad *[derevenskomu muzhiku]* lolling in the sun, but stand straight.

Or:

6. When parents or others ask something or call, then respond or answer them at once, as soon as their voice is heard. And then say: What does my lord father *[gosudar' batiushka]* wish, or my lady mother *[gosudaronia matushka]*, or what does my lord command me; and [answer] not, okay, what, whatever, but: As you say, whatever you wish. Nor boldly reply: Yes, okay, and then suddenly say in refusal, No; but say: So be it, my lord; I hear you, sir; I understand, sir, and will do as you, sir, have commanded. And do not say it with a grin, as if despising them; and. . . .

Or:

8. With clergy children should speak in an orderly, serious, courteous, polite way, and say nothing foolish, but ask about spiritual things and other clerical matters.

Or later:

> 45. In church one's eyes and heart are turned firmly to God, and not to the female sex, for the house of God is a house of prayer and not a den of lechery . . .!

Numerous other of these rules for aspiring young Russian gentlemen similarly proscribe gossiping, lying, drunkenness, lechery, boasting, stinginess, disparaging others, tomfoolery, "and other such crude conduct *[i podobnyia takiia grubyia deistviia]*" while offering advice on how to behave before servants—(13) "for not vainly is it said, as the abbot does so do the monks *[kakov igumen takova i bratiia]*—and on how to deal with any "rebel or plotter" discovered among them—(52) "he should be sent away as quickly as possible, for from one black sheep the whole flock can suffer . . . as the saying has it: in the beggar's pride the devil takes his comfort *[v nishcheskoi gordosti imeet diavol svoiu utekhu]*." Or again (27): "Young persons should always speak foreign languages among themselves, so as to become accustomed to them; and especially when something secret is to be talked about, so that the servants cannot understand," which is followed by another of the homely sayings that are sprinkled throughout these rules, this one, not uniquely, of somewhat obscure relevance: "for every merchant, praising his wares, sells as much as possible *[ibo kazhdyi kupets tovar svoi pokhvaliaia prodaet kak mozhet]*."

In fact, here as elsewhere in these rules of good gentlemanly conduct it is strongly implied that speaking foreign languages, far from an odd or derisive ability, was a most desirable accomplishment:

> 30. Young persons who have returned from foreign lands and learned languages at great expense should struggle not to forget them, but rather study them to perfection, by reading beneficial books and conversing with others, and should sometimes write and compose something in them *[chto-libo v nikh pisat' i komponovat']*.

Moreover,

> 31. Those who have not been in foreign countries, but rather have come to court from school or other such place, should humble and restrain themselves before the others, wishing to learn from them, and should not look down on them . . . and strut about proudly, as if having no in-

terest in the matter; for such proud behavior will rouse the detestation of others and cause the company *[kompanii]* to disdain and flee it.

And more,

18. The young nobleman *[shliakhtich', ili dvorianin]* should complete his education *[v eksertsitsii (v obushenii)]* especially in languages, horseman- ship, dancing, and swordsmanship, and be able to converse well, and in eloquence and book learning to comport himself with such ease as to be a true courtier *[s takim dosugi, priamym pridvornym chelovekom byt']*.

The "true courtier" is another facet of the new identity being offered here to members of the Russian elite, as again in this rule:

19. The true courtier is audacious, brave, and not shy, though he speaks to his sovereign with great deference. He can present his business him- self, and speak out, and not rely on others. For wherever such is to be found, there is one faithful as to oneself. Whoever behaves bashfully about the court, leaves it with empty hands. For when someone serves his sovereign faithfully, to him properly goes the faithful and expected reward.

Or in this:

20. The clever courtier does not reveal his intention and will, so as not to warn another who might wish for the same.

Lest this conduct seemed excessively self-interested, the aspiring Russian gen- tleman was also to know that he should always behave honorably and virtu- ously, "for [15] it is not his glorious *familia* nor lofty clan that elevates him to nobility *[v shliakhetstvo]*,[104] but honorable and praiseworthy deeds"; indeed, "a truly honorable cavalier *[kavaler]* must be modest *[smiren]*, affable, cour- teous" (16), must scorn "excess luxury" and live within his means (40, 41), and must keep his word (43) lest he be said to "promise like a lord but keep his word like a peasant *[obeshchat' to dvorianski, a slovo derzhat' to krest'ianski]*."

The two succeeding sections of the *Mirror* (pages 40–46) offer brief essays on good manners and especially good table manners, the first and briefer of the two rather more blunt in its advice ("don't rush like a pig . . . avoid drunkenness, drink and eat only as much as you need"), the second rather nicer ("Where two are speaking secretly between themselves, do not approach, for eavesdropping is a shameless rudeness *[Gde dvoe taino mezhdu soboiu govoriat, tam ne pristupai, ibo podslushivanie est' bezstydnoe nevezhestvo]*").

Then follow the sections of the manual—its other half—offering advice to young women, and both tone and text, as noted above, change abruptly. The "Crown of maidenly honor and virtue" consists by its own count of "the following twenty virtues, namely: An inclination for, and love of, God's word and divine service, true knowledge of God, fear of God, appealing to God, gratitude, confessing the faith, deference to parents, industriousness, decency, affability, charity, bodily cleanliness, modesty, abstinence, chastity, thrift, generosity, truthfulness, and reserve." These twenty "maidenly virtues" are then explained in as many numbered paragraphs, with various scriptural citations, and followed by separate essays titled "Maidenly chastity" and "Maidenly meekness." The essays fairly bristle with affirmative references to the Bible, the church fathers (both Eastern and Western), various Classical authors and figures, a "great poet of the present time," Martin Luther, "a certain Spanish writer," and "Emperor Frederick III"—although those to the Bible, both Old Testament and New, predominate. It was as if aspiring Russian gentlewomen were to be authoritatively quoted into submission and proper maidenly behavior. "Among all the virtues that adorn the honorable lady, or maiden *[chestnuiu damu, ili devitsu]*, and are required of them," begins the second essay, "meekness is the most basic and important," and was to be understood thus: "It is not enough to wear simple dress and bow the head and appear meek in outward behavior and say sweet things, not nearly enough; for the human heart must know, love, and fear God, wherefore one must recognize one's own weaknesses, frailties, and imperfections, and humble oneself before God and care for one's neighbor more than oneself."

We cannot of course know to what extent the standards of gentlemanly and maidenly behavior prescribed in the Petrine *Mirror* ever took hold among the Russian social elite—although readers of Russian literature of the later eighteenth and earlier nineteenth centuries will recognize in various characters their fictional embodiments. Memoirs of the period similarly suggest successful efforts to conform.[105] There is also some anecdotal evidence, mainly in the comments of contemporary European visitors, that while progress in this respect was at first slow, fitful, or merely superficial, it was remarkable nonetheless,[106] much as anthropologically sensitive observers of a later time would surely expect. There is in addition considerable visual evidence of the Europeanization of elite Russian manners beginning with Peter.[107] In any event, it remains a fact that the *Mirror* was the first such manual of behavior ever published in Russia and that its four Petrine editions totaled 2,478 copies, of which 1,859 appear to have been sold at or near the time.[108] Its compilers drew on such standard European works as Erasmus's *De civilitate morum puerilium* of 1530 and the *Miroir de la jeunesse pour former à bonnes moeurs et civilité de vie* published in France in 1539, along with contemporary German handbooks like the *Spiegel für der Bildung* and *Der Goldne Spiegel;*[109] but frequently the language itself of the *Mirror* as well as its sprinkling of pithy sayings suggest considerable adaptation by the translators. Nor should we be surprised to discover that Tsar Peter, yet again, contributed personally to its preparation. Its maxims certainly accord well with the highly political and worldly yet moralistic values that we know he often espoused, especially those of personal discipline and submission to authority, which even religion was to serve. In any case, our chief concern here, as always, is with the provable or probable verbal effects of this particular text: with its place in the Petrine revolution in Russian verbal culture.

We notice at once, in this connection, that relatively few new words appear in the *Iunosti chestnoe zertsalo* of 1717. In addition to those listed in Appendix II, we find only *kamor/kamer, v tseremoniiakh, banket, sup, v komedii (na podobie durakov v), shtraf, v artikulakh (ili chlenakh nasheia pravoslavnyia very/*in the articles or parts of our Orthodox faith), and *istoriia,* as in *iako istoria svidetlestvuet o nekoei miloserdoi dshcheri* (as history testifies about a certain loving daughter). It is as if most of the words deployed were already there in the lexicon, in familiar Slavonic terms or common Russian speech, or could be readily calqued; for example, among words cited above, *molchalivost'* for "reserve" or "taciturnity," which did not survive, and *privetlivost',* which became standard Russian for affability, cordiality. This left the translators with the still tricky task of making mostly familiar words express new concepts or new connotations, namely those of the prevailing European code of courtly etiquette. The vocabulary of the *Mirror,* in short, was much less novel than the social practices and values that its language encoded. Nor should we assume that the ostensibly devout and submissive role advocated for noble maidens in the *Mirror* is evidence of a strong Muscovite residue in the text.[110] These sections of the manual, as much or more than those directed at young men, read like straight translations of their German or French originals complete with various neologisms and a host of references—to the Latin church fathers (Sts. Augustine, Jerome) or to Martin Luther—that were unlikely to be adduced by a Muscovite traditionalist. The ambivalences and inequities, by today's standards, embedded in the *Mirror's* advice to young Russian women compared with that to young men, the reserved and pious modes of behavior espoused for them, were pan-European in nature rather than simply Muscovite and grounded, almost always, in the Bible.[111]

Indeed that was the point of the whole exercise. The *Mirror* obviously was intended to help bring elite Russian manners into conformity with those prevailing at the courts and other social centers of Europe; to make "true courtiers" and "cavaliers" of Russian diplomats, officers, and politicians in their dealings with their European counterparts and "honorable ladies" of their wives, lest by their conduct they should "rouse the detestation" of their European hosts or colleagues or visitors and cause the latter to "disdain and flee" them. This was not, in view of the contemporary European testimonials already alluded to, a vain apprehension: even Russians who had "by their Politeness and good Behaviour gained the Affection and Esteem" of their German acquaintances, observed one such witness in about 1720, were still likely on occasion "to throw off foreign Manners, and conform with the old Way," a way characterized as "so rude and unpolished, and at the same time so refractory to all Culture," as to defy belief.[112] By the same token, the language of the *Mirror* had to be intelligible to those for whom it was intended, who were not clergymen or seminarians but career-minded young noblemen and students in the Petrine military and naval schools and their female compeers. Thus the clear civil type in which the *Mirror* was printed, the Arabic numerals used throughout, the generous sprinkling (especially in its first sixty-three rules) of familiar sayings, the relatively few Slavonic words or forms employed, and the generally straightforward prose. Such readers no doubt found useful the simple abecedarium *(azbuka)* or primer *(bukvar')* appended to some copies of the *Mirror* (it was also sold separately),[113] with its listing of the "old and new" letters of the alphabet in juxtaposed traditional Cyrillic and current civil types, its syllabic exercises (civil type only), its parallel columns of Slavonic, Arabic, and Roman numerals, and its sequence of "Moral teachings *[Nravoucheniia]*" allegedly "from Holy Scripture," also printed in the civil type. The last are arranged in alphabetical order by initial letter of their first word, three "teachings" for each letter of the alphabet. Some of these teachings obviously derive from Scripture—"Love the Lord thy God with thy whole heart, thy whole spirit, and thy whole mind"—others less obviously so ("To curse father or mother means death," "Priests read, elders bless," "The sky is high, the land wide, but the heart of the tsar is hidden"); but either way, these moralisms, unlike the rest of the *Mirror,* are couched in a more or less heavily Slavonicized Russian, perhaps inevitably so, given the still prevalent notion that Church Slavonic was the only language fit for religious texts. Yet with or without the appended primer the *Iunosti chestnoe zertsalo* of 1717, along with the epistolary *Komplimenty* first published in 1708 (Chap. 4), were the first manuals of their kind to be published in Russia and were thus the creators, it would seem, of a whole new semantic field in Russian, that of good manners *(manery)* or etiquette *(etiket)*.[114]

235

The last of the moral guidebooks under review here comes with a recommendation from V. N. Tatishchev, the Petrine "fledgling" who became an important Imperial administrator as well as the first Russian historian, as noted earlier, to be recognized as such. In his *Instruktsiia* of 1736 to teachers of the newly founded Ural factory schools, Tatishchev stipulated that two textbooks be given to the students as soon as they had learned their letters: the *Zertsalo* or *Mirror* of 1717 and a certain "little book *[knizhitsa]* composed by the most reverend Feofan Prokopovich," from which two texts the students would "learn conjointly God's law and honorable conduct."[115] The "little book" in question was the religious primer or catechism first published in 1720 pursuant to a provision of the *Ecclesiastical Regulation* and written, as Tatishchev stated, by Prokopovich, the *Regulation*'s principal author (Chap. 4). It was entitled *A Primer for the Instruction of Youth, with letters and syllables, as also a Brief Explanation of the Ten Commandments, the Lord's Prayer, the Creed, and the Nine Beatitudes (Pervoe uchenie otrokom. V nemzhe bukvy i slogi. Takzhe: Kratkoe tolkovanie zakonnago desiatosloviia, Molitvy Gospodni, i deviati blazhenstv)* and was printed in the traditional Cyrillic type at the Alexander-Nevskii monastery press in St. Petersburg on March 1, 1720, as well as numerous times thereafter (twelve times in the remaining five years of Peter's reign, for a total of approximately 16,000 copies). In 1722 the Holy Synod ordered that in accordance with a stipulation of the *Ecclesiastical Regulation,* copies of the *Primer* were to be sent to all the dioceses, where they were to be used in the local schools and studied—indeed "memorized"—by all the clergy. Early in 1723, in a further endorsement, the Synod resolved that passages from the *Primer* were to be read in all the churches of Russia during the seven weeks of the Great Lent preceding Easter so that "parishioners preparing for confession and communion may, on hearing the commandments of God and their explanations, examine their consciences, and be better disposed to true repentance."[116]

Prokopovich was well aware of the fact, as he stated in the *Regulation*, that various catechisms were already in print, including the *Homologia* or *Orthodox Confession (Pravoslavnoe ispovedanie very)* usually attributed to Peter Mogila (Mohyla), the founder of the Kiev Academy and sometime metropolitan (bishop) of Kiev, which was first published at Kiev in 1640 and repeatedly thereafter in the Eastern Orthodox world in either abridged or complete editions including those at Moscow in 1649, 1696, and 1707 and at St. Petersburg in 1717 and 1722; indeed its appearance has been taken to mark the beginning of modern Orthodox dogmatic theology.[117] But most of these catechisms, Prokopovich stated further, were "written in Greek and are intelligible only in that language; their Slavonic translations have become obscure and are understood with difficulty even by an educated person, while for an ordinary ignorant person they are completely incomprehensible." Moreover they "contain many sublime theological mysteries and refer to many things . . . which no ignorant person would know how to employ to his own benefit." The *Orthodox Confession* in particular was "long, and cannot readily be memorized by ordinary people; moreover it is not written in the vernacular and therefore is not readily comprehensible to them." Prokopovich's complaints were echoed by Thomas Consett, the learned Anglican divine serving the British community in St. Petersburg at the time, who remarked in the preface to his compilation of documents on Peter's reign and church reform that the *Orthodox Confession* was an "excellent summary of the Christian religion" but was of little use to "simple and ignorant folk" because it was "wrote in a sublime stile in the Slavonian tongue," which was why "not only the vulgar have very little knowledge of the doctrines of the Christian religion, but even many of their priests."[118] Pressing linguistic and pedagogical reasons seemingly compelled Prokopovich to recommend, and then to compose, the *Primer for the Instruction of Youth.*

The preface to the *Primer,* which is addressed to "pious parents, teachers, guardians, and all others who exercise paternal authority over children," contains a concise statement of what could be taken as the rationale behind the larger Petrine project of moral or social renewal in Russia:

> The whole moral life of man depends, pious Christians, on the education received in childhood; as the child is, so the grownup shall be. If sound schooling and the fear of God (which is the beginning of wisdom) are inculcated in youth, it may be hoped that in maturity a person will be good; equally, if in youth he is defiant and unrestrained, there can be little hope that he will lead another and better life; for such rarely happens. And we have seen this to be true not only with regard to individual persons, but with regard to whole nations. Where a people abide in goodness, there, it is to be noted, the children receive good instruction; and where there is much quarreling, animosity, duplicity, thievery, violence, and other forms of immorality, it cannot be doubted that there the children do not receive good instruction. Childhood is as it were the

root whence both good and evil grow throughout the whole of life. The reason for which is this: because of the sin of our first parents, we are inclined from birth to evil. . . . Thus what good can be expected where there is no good instruction for children?

237

Proceeding from these sentiments, Prokopovich described how such education was lacking in Russia:

> There are many conscientious and apparently good people among us who, not knowing the power and law of God *[zakon bozhii]*, do not know many of their sins, and remain without fear. They know, for example, the commandment: "Honor thy father and thy mother"; but how many know the force of this commandment, who is to be understood by the name of father, and what is commanded by the word "honor" . . . ? And the same may be said about the other commandments. How can such people teach children? And what of the many others who remain in such darkness and ignorance that they have not heard of the law of God, and place all piety in external rites and physical exercises, never thinking that the foundation of true piety lies in believing in God the Savior and in observing his law in fear and charity.

Prokopovich echoed here the criticisms of Russian religious practice leveled by many European observers, especially Protestants from England, Holland, or Germany like the Reverend Consett,[119] criticisms that Tsar Peter himself had come to share, perhaps with Prokopovich's help.[120] Therefore, Prokopovich continued,

> since many among us who exercise paternal authority themselves know little of the law of God, there has arisen a need for a little book explaining the Ten Commandments given by God. For although a few such books already exist in Russia, they are written in the high Slavonic dialect and not in the Russian tongue. And our youth have not been instructed by these books, wherefore until now they have been deprived of the education appropriate to them.

And so,

> having perceived such a need in his people, and having being grieved at heart by the impiety of his subjects, the All-Russian Monarch . . . began diligently to consider how to establish in Russia an efficacious and indis-

pensable rule for the instruction of youth. And God inspired him with this most wise counsel: to command that a little book clearly explaining the law of God [i.e., the Ten Commandments], the Creed [literally, the *simvol very*, or symbol of the faith], the Lord's Prayer, and the nine beatitudes should be written and printed together with a primer *[bukvar']*, so that in learning their letters children may learn not psalms and prayers [as in the traditional *bukvar'*] but these explanations; and having been thus instructed in the faith and the law of God, they could [then] read with profit the psalms and prayers. And in accordance with His Majesty's command this little book has been written and printed.

Following a section of literal and syllabic exercises the text of the *Primer* itself contains, as promised, a lengthy exposition of the Ten Commandments in dialogue form, a phrase-by-phrase devotional commentary on the Lord's Prayer and another on each article of the Nicene Creed, and a brief essay on the Beatitudes, the last a pious exhortation to lead a Christian life of humility, submissiveness, righteousness, and purity. From a strictly historical perspective the religious or theological doctrines advanced in the *Primer* do not seem incompatible with contemporary Orthodox teaching as embodied in, say, the *Orthodox Confession* referred to above; but in the political-ideological conflicts that waxed and waned in Russia in ensuing years, critics would charge that they reflected "foreign" or "heretical" or "Protestant" notions particularly on the question of original sin. Prokopovich was not induced by these attacks to modify the *Primer* in any way, however; and it was repeatedly reprinted without alteration throughout the eighteenth and early nineteenth centuries, making it, in the view of a Soviet student of primary education in Russia, a "book of extraordinary importance in the history of Russian pedagogy."[121]

As for the language of the *Primer,* it is more Slavonic than Russian, admittedly—a kind of "plain Slavonic *[prostoi slavianskii iazyk]*," one expert calls it.[122] It was also printed, every time, in the traditional Cyrillic rather than the new civil type. Yet the comparative clarity and directness of the *Primer's* style as well as the insistent moralism of its contents were unprecedented among catechisms or primers hitherto available in Russia, and it proved remarkably durable in its stated purpose of providing religiously couched moral instruction for the ordinary parish clergy and, through them, the broad mass of the tsar's subjects. In this respect it resembles Luther's short catechism, which may well have inspired it.[123] Nor was the resemblance simply one of style. Lutheranism in the German lands was nothing if not famous for its respect for civil authority, and a similar spirit pervades the *Primer,* particularly its lengthy exposition of the Ten Commandments and particularly that of the commandment to honor father and mother, the supposedly inadequate understanding of which Prokopovich had highlighted in his preface. Thus "Question: What is ordained by God in [this] commandment?" evokes the response:

> To honor all those who are as fathers and mothers to us. But it is not only parents who are referred to here, but others who exercise paternal authority over us.
> Question: Who are such persons?
> Answer: The first order of such persons are the supreme authorities instituted by God to rule the people, of whom the highest authority is the Tsar. It is the duty of kings to protect their subjects and to seek what is best for them, whether in religious matters or in the things of this world; and therefore they must watch over all the ecclesiastical, military, and civil authorities subject to them and conscientiously see that they discharge their respective duties. This is, under God, the highest paternal dignity; and subjects, like good sons, must honor the Tsar.

The second order of persons enjoying divinely sanctioned paternal authority, the *Primer* goes on to explain, were the "ecclesiastical pastors, senators, judges, and all other civil and military authorities subordinate to the Tsar." Then followed parents—"thought first in the natural order, the first two orders have responsibility for the common good, and therefore greater dignity"—and other older relatives, teachers, lords, and masters, to all of whom children or students or servants owed love, honor, obedience, and loyalty. Guidance in the performance of these duties was provided—for example, "Aged persons enjoy paternal authority, but civil authority takes precedence over age; for a young king is a father to his aged subjects." Again:

> Question: What is to be done when one paternal authority commands one thing and another forbids it?
> Answer: When neither of them has authority over the other, you must look not to the persons who command, but to what is commanded. For instance: if your master commands you to do something with regard to the service you owe him, and your father forbids it, obey your master and not your father. But if one authority is superior to the other, obey the superior: thus if your master or father commands you to do something that is forbidden by the civil authorities, obey neither your father

nor your master. And if the civil authorities order you to do something that the Tsar forbids, obey the Tsar.

240

The distinctly Petrine cast of Prokopovich's doctrine of parental authority is unmistakable. It presented, in traditional paternalist and biblical dress, the new Petrine ideology of monarchical absolutism in perpetual service to the common good, such service understood to comprise the defense of the realm against external and internal enemies, the dispensation of justice, and the protection of religion, whose function it was to inculcate a strict morality of upright living in loyalty and obedience to the monarch and his subordinates. This was essentially the same civic morality expounded at more or less greater length, in more or less elaborate prose, and with more or less frequent resort to both religious and secular authorities, including Grotius and Pufendorf, in the relevant parts of the *Ecclesiastical Regulation* of 1721 and the *Pravda voli monarshei* of 1722 (Chap. 4). The excellence of monarchical absolutism is also a recurrent theme, indeed the dominant theme, of the public orations given by Prokopovich and others in the later years of Peter's reign, just as it reverberates in numerous legislative acts of the time. Whether the message was clearly perceived, let alone internalized, by the clerical readers of the *Primer* of 1720 and their parochial audiences we cannot know. But for the next century and more Prokopovich's *Primer* remained the basic textbook of religious instruction in Russia—ongoing testimony, in its way, to the Petrine impact on Russian moral culture.

The Academy

The genesis of the St. Petersburg Academy of Sciences, in which so many of Peter I's cultural acquisitions were institutionalized, can be traced to his visit to the Royal Society in London in 1698 and to his subsequent contacts, particularly through James Bruce, with what was then generally considered the most distinguished of the new scientific societies in Europe. Isaac Newton (whom Peter may well have met; Bruce certainly did) was the society's long-time president and it was to Newton, in that capacity, that the St. Petersburg Academy of Sciences addressed its first formal communication, in Latin, on October 11, 1726.[124] But the idea of founding such an institution in Russia certainly had other sources, too, most notably Peter's correspondence from 1697 and personal meetings (in 1711, 1712, and 1716) with G. W. Leibniz, the father of the Berlin Society—later Academy—of Sciences (1700). Leibniz, it is thought, was the author of a lengthy memorandum submitted to Peter sometime before their last meeting that proposed a wide range of measures to improve his government, including the foundation of a "college of sciences."[125] Also significant in this regard were Peter's visit to the Paris Academy of Sciences in 1717, which elected him an honorary member, and his subsequent contacts with that venerable prototype of institutionalized science.[126] Meanwhile a series of initially uncoordinated but related practical steps—most notably Peter's gradual buildup, from early in his reign, of a scientific library and a collection of scientific specimens and instruments, and his ever-expanding cartographic and related geographical endeavors—pointed to the necessity of creating some such central institution both to house and administer it all and to plan for the future (not to mention establishing parity, in this respect too, with the "other" European realms). It was only, quite literally, a question of time—of time free from the exigencies of a major war and from the distractions of Peter's many other projects, like his restructuring of the Russian state and the building of St. Petersburg. In 1718, on one of the many governmental reform proposals submitted to him by the assiduous Heinrich Fick (Chap. 4), Peter noted: "create an Academy [sdelat' Akademiiu]." It would be done.[127]

One other tributary to the project of a Russian academy of sciences should be emphasized: Peter's multifarious activities as "the Father of Russian medicine."[128] The epithet refers, of course, to typically modern or scientific medicine, not traditional or folk medicine, which was widely practiced in Russia long before, during, and well after the reign of Peter—to this day, indeed. As Alexander points out, Peter was the first (in fact, the only) Russian ruler to learn the rudiments of modern medicine and surgery, to observe medical procedures firsthand (not just those performed on himself), and to frequent medical institutions both at home—all but one of which he created—and abroad. In Holland in 1697–98, for instance, he visited hospitals, botanical gardens, and insane asylums, attended medical lectures at the University of Leiden—where Herman Boerhaave (1668–1738) pioneered the new, clinically oriented surgery based on the study of anatomy through dissection of corpses—and visited Dr. Fredrik Ruysch's famous anatomical museum in Amsterdam. The latter so delighted him that on his return visit to Holland in 1717 Peter bought Ruysch's anatomical collections and had them shipped to St. Petersburg, where remnants are still on view in his Kunstkamera; also in 1717, it was reported, he "did not repent lying all night in his pleasure barge against Boerhaave's house, in order to have two hours conversation with him on various points of learning the next morning before college time."[129] Some fifty surgeons were recruited for the nascent Russian navy in Holland alone in 1698, and on Peter's orders a Dutch physician, Dr. Nicolaas Bidloo, was hired to build a hospital and surgical school in Moscow (it opened in 1707), the first institution of its kind in Russia. The school drew for its students on the Moscow Slavonic-Greek-Latin Academy, who supposedly knew enough Latin—a recourse Peter had urged in an interview with the dying Patriarch Adrian in October 1700, when he declared, still under the influence of his European travels, that the academy should produce graduates knowledgeable in such socially beneficial subjects as architecture and "the physician's art *[doktorskoe vrachevskoe iskustvo]*."[130] By 1723 Bidloo's school had trained at least 73 Russian medical personnel—some 800 by the end of the century—and had promoted the founding of two *gospitali* in St. Petersburg (1715, 1717) as well as one each in Reval (1715), Kronshtadt (1716–17), and Kazan (1722) and later also in Tavrov (near Voronezh, 1724), Astrakhan (1725), and Arkhangel'sk (1733; Bidloo died in 1735). One of the new hospitals in St. Petersburg and that at Kronshtadt were under Admiralty auspices and soon added their own surgical schools, all as provided in the "Hospital Statute *[Reglament o gospitalakh]*" contained in the *Admiralty Regulation* of 1722 (Chap. 4). This section of the *Regulation* together with its other provisions of medical import, all showing considerable indebtedness to the French naval ordinance of 1689 that had also influenced Peter's *Naval Statute* (Chap. 2), have been separately studied for their influence on the development of a modern medical service in Russia; the study notes, for example, that a general regulation of 1735 governing all hospitals in Russia drew heavily, and often explicitly, on the corresponding parts of the *Admiralty Regulation* of 1722.[131] Meanwhile army medical services had been regularized in the *Military Statute* of 1716 (Chap. 3), which provided that surgeons were to be assigned to every regiment supported by paramedics *(fel'dshery)* and portable pharmacies *(pokhodnye apteki)*.

The only medical institution, broadly understood, that predated Peter's reign in Russia was the *Aptekarskii prikaz* or Apothecary Office in Moscow, whose origins went back to the sixteenth century. It was staffed by foreign medical specialists—physicians, surgeons, and chemists *(alkhemisty)*—assisted, after 1653, by Russians; but it remained an office of the tsar's household, whose members and various dependents, except in time of war, it served almost exclusively.[132] After 1653, to be sure, the Apothecary Office did bring at least some Russians—the sons of royal musketeers and lower palace functionaries who served in it as assistants—into personal contact with contemporary European medical science; and it did provide a living for a succession of European medics in the tsar's service, in both respects setting precedents that Peter unhesitatingly followed. Not only did he charter eight apothecary shops in Moscow to serve the public, commission Dr. Bidloo's hospital and school, greatly expand the medical services available to his military forces, and support the studies (at Padua, Paris, and Leiden) of the first certified Russian medical doctor (Peter Postnikov), but two of his personal physicians were to play critical roles in the founding of his Academy of Sciences.[133]

The first of these, the Scottish Dr. Peter Erskine (usually Areskin in the Russian documents), an Oxford-trained member of the Royal Society, entered Russian service in 1704, was appointed head of the Apothecary Office in 1707, and in 1713 became *leib-medik* to the tsar. In this position he also supervised medical education and the hiring of foreign medical personnel, oversaw the founding (1714) of the Apothecary Chancellery (alternately, Medical Chancellery *[Meditsinskaia kantseliariia]*) in St. Petersburg, of which he then became head, and took charge of Peter's burgeoning library and scientific collections, which were moved to the new capital in 1714 and lodged in his newly built Summer Palace. Also in 1714 one Johann Daniel Schumacher arrived from Germany, a graduate with honors of Strassburg University, to become Erskine's assistant with special responsibility for organizing the tsar's library and *kabinet* of scientific "curiosities." In fact, the lodging of Peter's books and scientific collections in the Summer Palace in 1714 under Erskine's overall supervision and Schumacher's direct control has been taken to mark the founding of the academy's library and associated *kunstkamera*.[134] Erskine died in 1718, having willed all his "curiosities, medals, and other instruments *[kurioznyia veshchi, i medali, i vse drugiia instrumenty]*" to Peter, and was succeeded as the tsar's personal physician and senior medical official *(arkhiatr')* by Lavrentii Bliumentrost (Laurentius Blumentrost). The latter was born in Moscow in 1692 to a physician of the same name who treated the Russian royals from 1668 until his death in 1705. The younger Blumentrost was a graduate of Pastor Glück's short-lived Lutheran school in Moscow's German Settlement and had studied under Boerhaave at Leiden before taking up Erskine's posts. He went on to become the first president of the St. Petersburg Academy of Sciences, for whose actual establishment, at last, he was to a considerable extent responsible.[135]

Before his death in December 1716 Leibniz had urged Peter to seek further advice in his scientific and educational endeavors from the celebrated Christian Wolff, professor of mathematics and natural philosophy at Halle University and later at Marburg. At Peter's behest Blumentrost duly corresponded with Wolff, and in 1719 he was dispatched to Germany with an invitation to Wolff to come to Russia to help found an academy of sciences together with a subordinate university and *gimnaziia*. Wolff declined the invitation and recommended that the tsar begin instead by establishing a university and several lower schools that eventually could supply the kind of educated personnel needed to staff an academy. His recommendation was earnestly pondered by Peter and his advisors, ensuing documents in the case make clear, but in the end rejected. In February 1721 Blumentrost sent Schumacher to Europe with a broad commission to buy books and scientific instruments and objects of interest and to recruit scholars who might assist in the "creation of a society of sciences like those in Paris, London, Berlin and other cities [dlia sochineniia sotsieteta nauk, podobno kak v Parizhe, Londone, Berline i prochikh mestakh]." The quotation is from the lengthy, detailed report that Schumacher submitted to Emperor Peter after his return to St. Petersburg in 1722 and according to which, writing in a lightly Slavonicized Russian loaded with scientific and other neologisms, he had amply fulfilled his kommissiia. He had visited academies, museums, libraries, and cabinets of curiosities both public and private (kabinety kak publichnye tak i privatnye) in France, Germany, Holland, and England, had brought back numerous scientific objects, instruments, prints, drawings, and books (some 541 volumes), had recruited two prospective academicians in Paris, and had consulted with Professors Wolff, Ruysch, and seemingly everybody else who was anybody at all in the northern European learned world.[136] Schumacher's haul was duly deposited in the "Kikin Chambers" in St. Petersburg, a sizable mansion that had been confiscated from its owner (A. V. Kikin, an official accused of treason) in 1718 and to which Peter's collections, bursting the walls of his Summer Palace, had been moved in 1719 pending completion of their permanent quarters.[137] Also in February 1721 Peter had written to the Paris Academy of Sciences expressing his delight at being elected a member and advising it that he was instructing Blumentrost "to communicate to you from time to time about anything that's new in our states and lands and worthy of the Academy's consideration," in return for which "we will be very pleased if you will maintain a korrespondentsiiu with him [Blumentrost] and from time to time communicate any new discoveries [dekuverty] made by the Academy."[138]

So by 1718 if not earlier the creation of a Russian academy of sciences was definitely only a question of time. The impression is strengthened on perusal of the numerous other documents that have been preserved relating to the academy's foundation, the most important of which is a Project (Proekt) drawn up by Blumentrost on Peter's instructions sometime late in 1723 and submitted to him in the presence of the Senate, meeting in the Winter Palace in St. Petersburg, on January 22, 1724. The Project is fluently written in a Russian that is larded, again, with loanwords. It consists of twenty-nine unnumbered sections, most a paragraph long, several subdivided into several numbered points; and at thirteen different places on the original manuscript Peter added a comment or made a correction. No single text better documents the verbal transmission to Petrine Russia of contemporary European scientific culture in the organizational sense, hence we should consider its provisions with care.[139]

The *Project* opens with the statement, "For the dissemination of the arts and sciences *[khudozhestv i nauk]* two kinds of institution [literally, building: *zdanie]* are customarily needed: the first kind is called a *universitet,* the second—an *Akademiia,* or *sotsietet* of arts and sciences." The two terms are then defined in the first section of the document:

> A *universitet* is an assemblage *[sobranie]* of learned people who teach young people the high sciences like theology and jurisprudence (skill in law), medicine, and philosophy *[theologiia i iurisprudentsii (prav iskusstvu), meditsiny, filozofii],* that is, to the level these [sciences] have now reached. But an Academy is an assemblage of learned and skilled people who not only know these sciences in that form, and to that degree *[v tom graduse],* in which they are now found, but through new inventions *[inventy (izdaniia)]* strive to perfect and augment [them]; and they have no responsibility *[popecheniia]* for teaching others.

Furthermore (section two):

> Although an Academy comprises the same sciences and the same members as a university, nevertheless in other states these two institutions have no connection between them, as there are numerous learned people from whom various assemblages can be formed; so that an Academy, which strives only to bring the arts and sciences to the best condition by study through speculation and investigation *[ucheniem v spekuliatsiiakh (rozmyshleniiakh) i roziskaniiakh],* whence both the professors in universities and the students *[kak profesory v universitetakh, tak i studenty]* derive benefit, is not distracted and the university is not deflected by clever investigations and speculations from teaching, and the young people are thus neglected.

Blumentrost's *Project* then suggests that

> Since now in Russia an institution for promoting the arts and sciences is to be founded, it would be impossible to do so after the example of other states; rather should the situation of this state be looked at regarding both those teaching and those to be taught, and an institution founded

which would not only redound to the glory of this state for increasing the sciences at the present time, but through teaching and disseminating them would benefit the people in future.

246   Moreover,

> Both of these intentions would not be fulfilled by establishing only an Academy of sciences, for although the arts and sciences would be cultivated and disseminated by it, they would not take root in the people—and still less by establishing only a university: for when one considers that there are as yet no regular schools, gymnasiums and seminaries [gimnaziev i seminariev], in which young people could learn the basics and then apprehend to their advantage the higher levels of science, then it is impossible in such a situation that a university could do any good.

And so "needed here most of all" was an institution comprised of "highly learned men" who would "1. Cultivate and perfect the sciences, but in such a way as to, 2. Publicly [publichno] teach young people (if there are those who will profit from it) and thereby, 3. Some of those taught by them could teach [other] young people the first rudiments (fundamentals) [pervym rudimentam (osnovatel'stvam)] of all the sciences." In this way "one institution at little cost could do as great a benefit [in Russia] as is done by three different institutions in other states." For such an institution, Blumentrost goes on to say, would

> 1. Be like a proper Academy, since it would have a sufficiency of members working to perfect the arts and sciences; 2. When these members lecture publicly on these arts and sciences, it will be similar to a university, and produce a like return; 3. When certain young people have been taught by an academician who will have been appointed to the charge and sufficiently remunerated by His Imperial Majesty, and learned the science and passed the test [probu iskusstva], they will teach [other] young people the first fundamentals; and so the institution will also be of such benefit as one specially founded to do this, or a gymnazium.

On the other hand,

> Since this institution is to be an Academy like that found in Paris (except for this difference and avantazh, that this Academy is also to do what is

appropriate to a university or college *[universitetu ili kollegii]*), therefore I hope that this institution would most conveniently be called an Academy. And the sciences which would be taught in this Academy could be freely divided into three classes *[v tri klasa]:* the 1st class would comprise all the mathematical sciences *[nauki matematicheskie]* and those that depend on them; the 2nd—all the parts of physics *[fiziki];* the 3rd—the humanities, history and law *[gumaniora, gistoriia i prava].*

We thus see in these opening seven sections of Blumentrost's *Project* for a Russian academy of sciences how he, his master, Emperor Peter, and his close assistant, Schumacher, had taken into account the objection of Christian Wolff and others that founding an academy before there existed appropriate supporting schools was premature: their new academy, in addition to its research program, would assume the pedagogical functions of both a university and a gymnasium, and thereby advance the greater cause of both creating and disseminating useful knowledge to the greater glory of the Russian state and the benefit of the Russian people. Succeeding sections of the document specify what would be taught in the three classes, namely *arifmetika, algebra, geometriia, astronomiia, geografiia, navigatsiia,* and *mekhanika* in the first class; *fizika teoreticheskaia i eksperimental'naia, anatomiia, khimiia,* and *botanika* in the second; and, in the third, *elokventsiia i studium antikvitatis . . . gistoriia drevnaia i nyneshnaia,* and *pravo natury i publichnoe, kupno s politikoiu i etikoiu (nravoucheniem)* ("eloquence and antiquities . . . history ancient and modern, together with politics and ethics"). Eleven *person* were to do the teaching, four each in the first and second classes, three in the third; and it would be "most beneficial," finances permitting, if the students could live together in a dormitory *(v obshchem zhitel'stve).* In addition, a *sekretar'* should be appointed to keep the academy's *protokol* and look after its other business, including what it published *(publikuet)* and, together with its librarian *(bibliotekar'),* its *korrespondentsiia.* As for the academicians—*akademiki*—themselves, nine "duties" are listed: (1) all were to conduct research, and report their findings to the secretary; (2) every academician was to "read the good authors in his science who are published in other states" and compile extracts—*ekstrakty*—from them, which the academy at appointed times would publish with "other findings and proceedings"; (3) all were to assemble weekly "for several hours" for an exchange of views and to hear news of their individual *eksperimenty,* for this was after all "a society of persons who for the cultivation of science are to aid one another"; (4) all "discoveries *[dekuverty (izobretenii)]*" were to be submitted (to the academy as a whole) for "approbation *[aprobatsiiu]*" according to three (really two) criteria: "was it really a discovery, is the benefit great or small, and was it known before or not"; (5) "If His Imperial Majesty requires that an academician investigate some matter within his science, then he is obliged to do it with all diligence and to report on it at the appropriate time (though there are many matters which, seeming small, will require a long time to investigate)"; (6) "Every academician is obliged to prepare a system or course *[sistem ili kurs]* in his science for the benefit of the young people studying, and then they will be printed in Latin at Imperial expense; and since the Russian people will benefit greatly when these books are printed in the Russian language *[na rossiiskom iazike]*," a translator was to be assigned to each class as well as to the academy's secretary; (7) three public assemblies *(publichnye assamblei)* were to be held each year, as was done in other countries, at which an academician would speak on his science and salute the academy's "protector *[protektor (zashchitelia)]*," namely Emperor Peter and his successors; (8) the academy was to open a library and natural history museum *(biblioteka i naturalnykh veshchei kamora)*, lest its members lack anything needed to pursue their science; and (9) the academy was also to have draftsmen and engravers on its staff to illustrate its publications. The *Project*, in sum, offered a short course in the academic organization of "royal science" as it had been worked out over the preceding decades in similar institutions in Europe, particularly in Paris and Berlin, and would subsequently be implemented in the royal academies or societies founded elsewhere in France (Dijon, 1740; Toulouse, 1746), Germany (Munich, 1730; Göttingen, 1750; Erfurt, 1754), and Italy (Bologna, 1712; Turin, 1760; Verona, 1780), and in Edinburgh (1731), Dublin (1739), Stockholm (1741), Copenhagen (1743), and Lisbon (1790), among other places.[140]

But the distinctiveness of the new Russian academy, already apparent in the *Project*'s stipulations regarding the classes to be taught under its aegis, was especially apparent in its related provisions for a university. The latter was to consist of four *fakul'teti*, namely of theology, jurisprudence, medicine, and philosophy—although the first was to be the exclusive responsibility of the Holy Synod and nothing more was said about it here. As for the other three, under the *iuridicheskii fakul'tet* the appropriate academician would teach such "practical sciences as politics, ethics, and natural law *[nauki praktiki, iako politiku, etiku i pravo natury]*"; under the *meditsinskoi*, anatomy, chemistry, and botany; under the *filozofskoi*, *logika*, *metafiziki*, and *matematika general'naia* along with general and experimental physics, astronomy, and mechanics, as well as eloquence, antiquities, and history. The academicians concerned would be obliged to give weekly hour-long public lectures in their science, as was done in other universities *("akademiki obiazany budut v svoei nauki ezhednevno odin chas publichnye lektsii imet', kak v protchikh universitetakh")*. The *Project* thus sought to recapitulate centuries of European university experience, and with the obvious result that scholars who became members of the new Russian academy would be unusually busy. As if recognizing the weight of this point, the *Project* further provided that one or two outstanding students would be assigned to each academician and given a stipend to assist him in teaching—which students, in turn, would go on to instruct others in the basics of the science (that is, to teach in the academy's gymnasium). At this point—his only substantive amendment to the text— Peter noted: "Two more people should be added, who are of Slavic nationality *[iz slovenskogo naroda]*, the better to teach Russians and to write [translate] these sciences exactly." Here was another explicit reminder, again from Peter himself, of the crucial importance of translation to the whole enterprise.

249

Blumentrost's *Project* concludes with a polite request that His Imperial Majesty grant the necessary "privilege *[privilegiiu]*" to inaugurate the academy. Peter wrote "granted *[pozvoliaetsia]*" at this point on the original document and then assigned to the academy's support the sum of 24,912 rubles, which was to be taken from the customs and licence fees collected at four Baltic towns. He also stipulated that the academy should have a *direktor* with two assistants and a *kamisar* of finances. The deed was done. Six days later, on January 28, 1724, the Senate issued a decree announcing the academy's foundation and affirming Peter's assignment of support, although the *Project* itself was not published. In fact, the academy came to life and carried out its work for more than twenty years before it formally received an Imperial charter or *Reglament* from Empress Elizabeth, Peter's daughter, on July 24, 1747. This is a lengthy, detailed document in Russian covering the academy's various operations and departments whose very language constitutes impressive evidence of the institution's rapid maturation: the charter takes as its point of departure "the *proekt* personally signed and approved by Emperor Peter the Great."[141] In the intervening years the *Project* had likewise been invoked in official documents as the de facto founding charter of the fledgling academy.[142]

A special "Academy office *[Akademicheskii kontor]*" was promptly set up to handle the relevant correspondence, and with Peter's full backing, and Schumacher's eager help, Blumentrost moved energetically in the winter and spring of 1724 to flesh out their creation.[143] An announcement of the academy's founding was published in the April 1724 issue of the *Neue Zeitungen von gelehrten Sachen,* an influential journal edited at Leipzig by J. B. Mencke, a distinguished historian and member of the royal societies of Berlin and London who submitted nine or ten names for positions in the St. Petersburg academy's humanities class. The groundwork was laid in the new Russian capital for a permanent academy building (it would be ready in 1726; the construction of a building to house Peter's library and *kunstkamera* had begun in 1718), and a renewed invitation to join the academy, along with a request for nominees, was sent to Christian Wolff, now at Marburg University. Wolff again declined the invitation for himself but recommended several of his best students; he shortly became the academy's first honorary member. The scholars initially recruited by Schumacher in Paris in 1721, the astronomer Joseph Delisle and the zoologist and surgeon J. G. Duvernois, were contacted by Peter's ambassador in Paris and agreed to come. During the winter of 1725 four new professor-academicians and two student-teachers settled in St. Petersburg and by the end of the year sixteen European scholars—all highly qualified, some even distinguished, most still quite young, their interests typical of the science of the times—had taken up their appointments. Besides Delisle and his younger brother Louis, also an astronomer, and Duvernois, they included the Bernoulli brothers Daniel and Nicolaus, both mathematicians from a famous Swiss family of scholars, the latter to specialize now in mechanics; G. S. Bayer, a Classical historian and the founder of the study of antiquities (in effect, of archaeology) in Russia;[144] Jakob Hermann, a mathematician and original member of the Berlin Society of Sciences and sometime professor at the Universities of Bologna and Padua, whose early arrival heralded the academy's subsequent distinction in mathematics; and various other specialists in moral and natural philosophy (two in physics, one in chemistry and medicine), history, eloquence, and law. Informal meetings of the new academy were held in St. Petersburg in the summer of 1725 and its first formal gathering took place in November. In the meantime, of course, Emperor Peter, the founder, had died (January 28, 1725). But there was no turning back; it became academy lore that "Peter, falling sick some time after the foundation of the Academy, in his last moments earnestly requested the Empress Catherine, who was to succeed him, to put the finishing hand to the work."[145] Indeed Catherine soon ratified the *Project* of 1724 and formally nominated Blumentrost to be the academy's first president, to the general satisfaction, it seems, of the assembled members. Schumacher was confirmed as its first secretary as well as its first librarian, positions he continued to occupy, consolidating the academy's administrative structure, assiduously guarding its interests, ever the adroit bureaucrat, until his retirement in 1759 (Blumentrost remained president until 1733).[146]

The St. Petersburg Academy of Sciences moved into its grand new premises, a typically Petrine palatial structure on Vasilevskii Island, in 1726, and later that year the *Neue Zeitungen von gelehrten Sachen* in Leipzig published enthusiastic accounts of its facilities, privileges, and potential "for the growth of science" by G. S. Bayer and G. B. Bülfinger, another of its first members.[147] In 1727 the academy's membership and supporting staff totaled eighty-four, including seventeen professor-academicians, nineteen students and apprentices of various kinds, two teachers, six translators, a "master of astronomical instruments," three library assistants, seven printers and seven engravers, two painters (illustrators), ten clerks, and ten servants, all in receipt of a total of 24,626 rubles in annual salaries:[148] the number of its personnel, it might be noted, was nearly as large as the largest of the new central government colleges (compare the staff of eighty-seven for the Revenue College, ninety-seven for the College of Justice, mentioned in Chapter 4), while its annual salary budget was roughly equivalent to that of a regiment of guards. In 1728 the academy's library, now numbering over 12,000 volumes, and its *kunstkamera,* both based on Emperor Peter's collections but already significantly augmented by purchase and other bequests, moved into the splendid new building designed for them on a site adjacent to the academy's main building, where it stands to this day, still known informally, indeed affectionately, as the Kunstkamera. On successive floors of the building's central tower were located the anatomy theater, a huge globe—the "Gottorp globe"—acquired by Peter from the duke of Holstein in 1713, and Delisle's astronomical observatory, now reputedly one of the finest in Europe;[149] a botanical garden, physics and chemistry laboratories, and an "Instruments' Chamber *[Instrumental'naia palata]*" or separate department for making scientific instruments, were established in the 1730s and 1740s. The academy's press, its capacities enormously enhanced by the arrival from Holland early in 1727 of two new printing presses and sets of both Russian and Latin types (soon German-Gothic, Georgian, and Arabic types would be added), began printing a monthly almanac—*Kalendar'*—in Russian later that year and an annual journal, the *Commentarii,* in Latin, in 1728. At the same time, the Kunstkamera's already substantial collections of minerals, instruments, anatomical and botanical specimens, *monstry,* and other *kur'ëzy* were greatly augmented by the many natural and ethnographic items collected on official scientific expeditions to Siberia, particularly those led by Daniel Messerschmidt (1720–1727) and Vitus Bering (1725–1730), both of which had been commissioned by Peter I.[150]

251

We rehearse these details of the academy's initial history only to emphasize the seriousness of the whole project and the European measure of its origins, connections, pretensions, and, soon enough, contributions to knowledge. The first volume of its journal contained papers on theoretical mathematics presented at the academy between September 1725 and December 1726 by Jakob Hermann, Nicolaus Bernoulli, Christian Goldbach, and Christian Wolff (that by Goldbach and another by Johann Bernoulli, father of Nicolaus and Daniel and professor at Basel, discussed the integration of differential equations, a topic at the forefront of the field); by Hermann again and the Delisle brothers on astronomy, the former theoretical in nature, with extended reference to Kepler, the latter reporting their current *observationes astronomicae;* by Duvernois on zoology, J. C. Buxbaum on botany, Bülfinger on certain problems in physics, and Daniel Bernoulli on mechanics (a "new theory" of muscle power); by a corresponding Italian scholar on anatomy, and by Bayer on the history of the ancient Scythians, among others. The papers frequently cited the research of colleagues working in St. Petersburg or elsewhere in Europe, and the volume as a whole was very handsomely printed—at the academy's press—and handsomely illustrated, with numerous tables and graphs and mathematical, anatomical, botanical, and other figures.[151] Fourteen volumes of the journal were published by the academy, in Latin, between 1727 and 1751, when it was renamed *Novi Commentarii Academiae Scientiarum Imperialis Petropolitanae* and continued publication (twenty substantial volumes), still in Latin, until 1775, when it was succeeded by one and then another series published in Latin but increasingly also in French, later German, until 1862, from which date the academy's annual *Zapiski* and other publications appeared mainly or exclusively in Russian. But from the beginning, digests of the academy's work and proceedings as well as related and other titles were regularly published in Russian—although at first, as viewed by one later student, pointing to the purely scientific publications, "with bewildering results, owing to the limited Russian scientific vocabulary and the scientific ineptness of the translators."[152]

This brings us back to the language question in connection with the earlier history of the St. Petersburg Academy of Sciences, a question that is often fudged by Russian scholars and raised critically by their foreign counterparts, also thinking in nationalist categories.[153] Of course Latin was the language of the academy's formal proceedings and related publications in its first decades, as it was of learned societies and academies throughout contemporary Europe. Latin was the one language in which all of the early St. Petersburg academicians could communicate about their scientific work both among themselves and with their colleagues abroad; Latin was the language to learn, therefore, by their aspiring Russian students; and Latin, accordingly, was reaffirmed as the language of science by the academy's charter of 1747, which stipulated that "Latin or Russian *[na latynskom ili rossiiskom]*" or "Latin translated into Russian *[latynskii iazyk chrez ruskoi]*," and "never German or French," must be used by the academy on all occasions and that its "students therefore must be skilled in Latin."[154] The St. Petersburg Academy of Sciences was from its inception a European rather than narrowly Russian institution, in short, and quite deliberately, indeed necessarily so, given the educational and other circumstances in Russia in which its founders worked, and given Emperor Peter's ambition, never repudiated by his successors, to have an academy that would rank with the best in Europe. Equally, the early academicians, in light of what's just been said, had to be recruited in Europe and particularly in neighboring Germany, that land of poets and philosophers and home at the time to more than thirty universities; and naturally these learned recruits, once in St. Petersburg, were not greatly concerned with promoting the development of scientific Russian. That would come later, with the advancement of native Russians to the academy's professional ranks.

Dozens of Russian youths were trained in the St. Petersburg Academy of Sciences' gymnasium and university in those first years, and by 1733, less than a decade after its establishment, one of these students, V. E. Adodurov (or Adadurov), had been appointed *ad"iunkt* in mathematics; he was also an accomplished translator from German, taught Russian to the future Empress Catherine II, in 1762 was appointed by her curator of the recently founded Moscow University (which he remained until his death in 1780), and in 1778 was named an honorary academician.[155] Adodurov was followed at the academy by G. N. Teplov (adjunct in botany, 1742; academician from 1747), M. V. Lomonosov (adjunct in physics, 1742; professor of chemistry from 1745), V. K. Trediakovskii (professor of eloquence, 1745), and S. T. Krasheninnikov (adjunct in natural history, 1745; professor of botany and natural history from 1750); and they in turn were followed, from the 1750s until the end of the eighteenth century, by the appointments of another twenty-four Russians (along with sixty foreigners) to professional positions *(ad"iunkt, professor, akademik)* in the academy.[156] Among the first of the Russians so appointed, one, Krasheninnikov, died at the age of forty-two, within five years of assuming his professorship, but Teplov went on to write the first philosophy textbook in Russian (published by the academy's press in 1751) and both

Lomonosov and Trediakovskii, also as noted earlier in this chapter, made important contributions to the creation of modern Russian literature and the standardization of modern literary Russian.

This is not the place to pursue the subsequent history of the St. Petersburg Academy of Sciences, its ups and downs, successes and failures, its direct links with the foundation of Russia's first two fully fledged universities (those of Moscow and St. Petersburg),[157] its contributions, indeed, to science and to the dissemination of science in Russia. We might only observe that from a Petrine perspective its creation was an end as well as a beginning, the natural culmination of developments reaching back to the earliest years of Peter's reign, to the tentative beginnings of the Russian navy and to his Grand Embassy to Europe. The ensuing importation of unprecedented numbers of European technical experts and the incessant translation of technical and scientific manuals and treatises, all to enable Peter's soaring political and scientific or technical ambitions, whether for himself (his dynasty) or for his country (people, state): all this enormously expanded the Russian technical and scientific lexicon, as I have tried to show in this and the preceding chapters and in the appropriate parts of the two appendixes. After 1725 the St. Petersburg Academy of Sciences was the chief agency advancing this process notwithstanding its resort to Latin—indeed, to a great extent because of it, given Latin's continuing role throughout Europe as the premier language of science.[158] Through its research, teaching, and publication the academy became the institutional heart of the onrushing effort to naturalize in Russian the concepts and terms, the very vocabulary, of early modern European science. "In these varied ways," as one student observes of eighteenth-century European academies generally, "a tiny minority of European citizens had access to the teaching of science."[159] But in the case before us, writes the leading American student of the St. Petersburg academy's history, "scientific thought spilled over the Academy's rigid confines" during the later eighteenth century "to wash a vast area of Russian culture." In this considered view,

> The social effect of science in eighteenth-century Russia cannot be over-emphasized. It destroyed once and for all the intellectual supremacy of the Church, which fed on outmoded Scholasticism and sacrosanct superstitions; and it became the rallying point for a frontal attack on ignorance. Science gave strength to the emergent national consciousness of the Russian people; the results of historical and geographical research and of the scientific expeditions were reflected in a broader and more widely distributed literature. As teachers, writing and translating books,

the scientists also led the struggle to raise the educational level of the Russian people. Slowly and painstakingly, they made the Russian language a vehicle of scientific communication.[160]

The assessment is a shade positivistic, even grandiose. But it is also essentially true, no doubt, especially with respect to making the Russian language into a "vehicle of scientific communication," which was the key to the rest of the program.

6

THE LANGUAGE QUESTION

The "language question" has been raised intermittently throughout this volume, beginning with Chapter 1. There we saw how the *Questione della lingua*, as classically formulated in Renaissance Italy, challenged the literary supremacy of the revivified Latin of the humanists, insisting that it could or should be joined or even replaced as the language of high culture by the vernacular. The Renaissance solution to the language question in Italy, a country of strong regional ties and traditions, was partial at best: foundations were laid but the structure was not completed; standard Italian fully emerged only with political unification in the nineteenth century. But meanwhile the question itself had passed to France, as we also saw, where a similarly diglossic situation had prevailed since early medieval times, with Latin serving as the fixed, grammatical, written language of the learned world while the variable, irregular, uncodified vernacular was written and spoken by the rest of society. The process whereby the dialect of the Paris region became standard French was largely completed in the seventeenth century, with the Paris-based monarchy playing a decisive role. Analogous developments sooner or later took place everywhere Latin had once enjoyed preeminence, including the West Slavic lands of the Czechs and Poles. In the somewhat comparably diglossic East-Slavic world, however, in Ukraine, Belorussia, and Russia, the language question initially was interpreted by scholars as one of revivifying Church Slavonic on the model of the revivified Latin or Greek of the Renaissance: the vernaculars did not come into it. This newly classicized (or archaicized) Slavonic could serve as the language of high culture so long as the church controlled education and dominated the communications media (scribal or print) and the state was either supportive of the situation or indifferent to the question.

In Muscovite Russia, as Chapter 1 made clear (also Chapter 4), the state's attitude was generally supportive of Church Slavonic's cultural pretensions even as the tsardom conducted its own business in chancery Russian, which was not exactly the Muscovite vernacular, to be sure, but certainly not Church Slavonic either. That attitude changed drastically with the accession to power of Peter I, and the language question in Russia soon assumed a form roughly parallel to that it had taken in western Europe: should "Russian," the language of government and business and more ordinary life, join or even replace Church Slavonic as the language of high culture, and if so, how was this to be done? The question became increasingly urgent in Chapters 2 through 5, as we considered successive Petrine efforts to translate and publish in "plain Russian" a wide range of technical, scientific, historical, and pedagogical works.

In Chapter 5 I proposed that the Petrine contribution to the resolution of the language question in Russia—to the standardization of written Russian—took two basic forms, the one physical, as it were, or mechanical, the other linguistic. The first was finally and fully to implant the European print revolution in Russia, which proved to be a necessary condition, in Russia as in Europe generally, for the establishment of both a national literary language and a modern national literature. And the second was to promote by any and all means the adoption of huge new vocabularies of variously specialized terms while simultaneously insisting that all translations and indeed almost anything else that was to be officially published should be written in a "simple" or "plain" (prostoi) Russian. What this program meant in practice, as we have seen, was a language at once enriched by the addition of countless new words and pruned of obsolete or archaic Slavonicisms as well as arcane bureaucratic formulas, a language that was thus more useful, and more readily comprehensible, to the naval and military officers, technical teachers and students, diplomats and bureaucrats, merchants, builders, craftsmen, artists, and others who made up the Petrine reading public (publika). In this chapter we will consider in some detail both aspects of this Petrine contribution to the resolution of the language question. We will then look at the linguistic situation in Russia in the wake of Peter's death.

The Print Revolution in Russia

The advent of book printing by means of movable cast-metal type and the ensuing communications revolution in Europe have been recounted in detail by historians. The feat was first achieved in certain German towns in the mid-

258

dle of the fifteenth century, and by the end of the century print shops with their presses and specialized craftsmen were established all over Europe— mainly in towns in Italy north of Rome, in Switzerland, in other German towns along the Rhine and the Danube, and in the Netherlands but also in such cities as Prague, Cracow, and Lübeck in the east and Lyon, Barcelona, Paris, London, and Oxford in the west. These were university towns, important ecclesiastical sees, and major commercial centers, all containing political, social, and economic elements that stimulated the necessary demand. The majority of the first titles printed—the so-called incunabula of these first fifty years (ca. 1450–1500)—were religious in content: editions of the Bible, devotional works, service books, and lives of saints. But textbooks of grammar and rhetoric were also printed, as were works by Classical authors, almanacs, chronicles, and popular fables. Heinrich Quentell's print shop in Cologne, started about 1475, had produced more than 200 titles by 1500, a total that was not unusual; Anton Koberger of Nuremberg published 237 titles between 1471 and 1500, while some twenty shops in Augsburg were printing hundreds of titles *annually* by the end of the sixteenth century. The 236 towns in Europe where print shops had been established by 1500 together are thought to have printed from 10,000 to 15,000 texts in 30,000 to 35,000 editions, amounting to something like 15 million to 20 million books. Such figures give quantitative weight to the concept of a "print revolution." But more, the shift from script to print, with its capacity for nearly endless production of closely duplicated texts, the latter frequently illustrated by woodcuts or by metal-plate etchings or engravings, occasioned a "communications revolution" that underpinned every major intellectual or cultural movement in early modern Europe, from the Renaissance and the Reformation to the Scientific Revolution. Or so it has been forcefully argued. It has even been argued that the print revolution, in combination with the promotional and distributive capabilities of commercial capitalism, produced the stabilized, unifying "print-languages" and "languages of power" that generated in turn the phenomenon of national consciousness, which then contributed crucially to the making of the modern nation-state. The modern literary languages of Europe, in short, were an outcome in large measure of the print revolution.[1]

Two additional factors fostering the print revolution in Europe were the availability of cheap paper and the existence of an established alphabet (the Latin) whose autonomous letters were formed from a small number of pieces (the lack of such a simple, established alphabet hampered the development of printing in China, where movable type had long been known; the Chinese also invented paper). The Renaissance emphasis on proportion and symmetry and related calligraphic reforms helped to ensure that by 1500 or so Italian Roman and cursive ("italic") letters had become standard in printing in Europe; the elaborate "Gothic" lettering of Gutenberg and other printers survived to some degree only in Germany. It was in Italy, too, that paper made from linen rags was produced cheaply and in growing quantities from the mid-fourteenth century, a development which itself presupposed the spreading use of linen in European households, the proximity of abundant clear water, and certain breakthroughs in milling.[2] A third factor that should also be mentioned was the thriving scribal culture in these university, ecclesiastical, and commercial towns of Europe *before* 1450: the expanding production, going back a century and more, to meet the ever growing demand for *handwritten* editions of religious, Classical, and other works. In fact, the first printed books were closely modeled on the contemporary manuscript book or codex, which had replaced the manuscript scroll; and the same would prove true, eventually, in Russia.[3]

259

Indeed, these observations on the print revolution in Europe all point to economic and cultural factors the comparative absence of which worked to inhibit the rapid and effective development of printing in Russia. Printing itself, the mechanical production of printed sheets by means of screw-press and movable metal type, arrived there only in the 1550s and between then and the 1690s fewer than 500 titles had appeared, nearly all of them devotional in content and nearly all produced at a single shop in Moscow, the *Pechatnyi dvor* or Printing House controlled by the Moscow patriarch.[4] The few secular exceptions to this rule include the *Ulozhenie* or law code of 1649 discussed in Chapter 4; the manual, translated from German, entitled *The Doctrine and Craft of the Military Organization of Foot Soldiers,* also printed at Moscow in 1649 and cited in Chapter 3 (excerpts from both books are reproduced in Appendix I, nos. 2–4); and Smotritskii's Slavonic grammar printed at the Moscow Printing House in 1648, which was mentioned in Chapter 1. Moreover most of Moscow's pre-Petrine print production, all but 16 of the nearly 500 titles, took place after 1620, the initial effort to establish both printing presses and paper mills in Muscovy having collapsed by the 1570s for lack of sufficient official support in the face of intense local hostility. To put the point another way, by 1600 or so only about 100 books had been printed in the entire East Slavic world—Muscovy, Ukraine, Belorussia—compared with 25,000 titles in Paris alone, 45,000 in Germany, and 10,000 in England. And throughout the seventeenth century Russians had to import all of their paper for printing from western Europe, which was an expensive proposition given the distances such paper had to travel—typically, from France overland and by sea to Archangel and thence down to Moscow—as well as the rudimentary state of the Russian market.[5]

Paper mills were permanently established in Russia only under Peter—in part a response, as can be readily imagined, to the huge increase in printing that occurred during his reign. By 1719 the consumption of paper in Russia had risen from the 4,000 to 8,000 reams imported annually in the later seventeenth century to some 50,000 reams or more a year, only about 10 percent of which were imported; the rest of the paper was produced by the five mills founded in Russia between 1708 and 1718 with the help of Dutch, German, and Swedish craftsmen. Peter was properly proud of this achievement: a note in his hand written in 1723 on a sheet of paper with the watermark of the St. Petersburg wind paper mill reads, "This paper was made here at the mill, and as much can be made [here/in Russia] as needed, so do not just order [it] from France."[6] At the same time, he founded new print shops or *tipografii* as he called them, so that, by the end of his reign, in addition to the Moscow Printing House or Press (*Tipografiia,* as it was usually called after 1710), four shops were functioning in St. Petersburg: the St. Petersburg Press (1711), the Senate Press (1719, with a branch in Moscow), the Alexander-Nevskii Monastery Press (1719), and the Naval Academy Press (1721).[7] The combined output of these presses, or the total number of publications—books, booklets, pamphlets, single sheets—that were printed in Russia between 1700 and Peter's death in January 1725, in pressruns of anywhere from a few dozen to a few thousand or more copies (the average edition was 300 to 600), has been put at 1,312 (308 religious in content, the rest secular).[8] This total is considerably more than twice the number of titles (almost all of them religious) published during the entire previous century and a half of printing in Russia, although it was, as yet, a very modest achievement by contemporary European standards.

Implanting the European print revolution in Russia was also furthered by Peter's foundation of the medical, naval, military, and elementary schools discussed in previous chapters and by his creation of the Academy of Sciences, which soon (1727) set up its own press; all of these institutions worked to promote literacy and some expansion, however modest at first, of the reading public. It was also facilitated, at a still broader level, by Peter's promotion of trade especially with Europe and by his expansion of Russia's urban network, particularly by the creation of St. Petersburg and the conquest of several Baltic cities. We can point in addition to his curtailing of the church's role in printing (implicit in the huge expansion of the state's) while greatly broadening its educational mission, and to his reform and expansion both of the armed forces and of the state itself, also as discussed in previous chapters. All of these actions inevitably stimulated the demand for print—for printed textbooks, scientific treatises and technical manuals, government regulations, catechisms and service books—although it is impossible to quantify this demand with any certainty on the basis of contemporary sources.[9] Finally, and back to the more technical level, there was the matter as mentioned of an established alphabet whose letters were appropriately designed for efficient printing by the new methods. It was only under Peter, again, that such an alphabet was created at last in Russia.

To simplify drastically the relevant section of Chapter 1, the so-called Cyrillic alphabet, which emerged in medieval times to inscribe the language later called Church Slavonic, consisted of some forty-odd letters, more than half of which were Greek or Greek-based, the rest invented to accommodate Slavic sounds. It was inscribed at first in an uncial *(ustav)* style characterized by carefully drawn upright letters of equal size with relatively few ligatures, superscriptions, contractions, or abbreviations (see again Fig. 1). But gradually this original simplicity gave way to a less formal, semi-uncial *(poluustav)* script whose letters were often curved as well as thinner and vertically elongated and were written with frequent ligatures, diacritics, and stress marks along with more abbreviations or contractions. The Slavonic fonts employed by printers in the East Slavic lands from the sixteenth century onward were based on this semi-uncial script, with alphabetic variations reflecting concurrent attempts to reform or revivify Church Slavonic on the model of the revivified Latin and Greek of the Renaissance (Appendix I, nos. 1, 5, 6). Such variations included the use of additional Greek letters and of letter-shapes that were clearly influenced by the Roman and italic styles that had become standard in printing in Europe, although printers in Moscow were much slower to introduce such innovations than were their counterparts in the Ruthenian lands (Ukraine and Belorussia). Meanwhile the few books published in Moscow in chancery Russian—the *Ulozhenie* of 1649 and other secular titles mentioned above—were printed in a shifting mix of semi-uncial and newer cursive *(skoropis')* characters that were based, again, on contemporary script (Appendix I, nos. 2, 3, 4; cf. Figs. 2, 3). The outcome of this concatenation of letters and styles may be viewed in the illustrated primer titled *Bukvar' slavenorossiiskikh pismen ustavnykh i skoropisnykh, Grecheskikh zhe Latinskikh i polskikh (Primer of Slavonic-Russian uncial and cursive letters, also Greek, Latin and Polish)* compiled by the monk Karion Istomin, sometime head of the Moscow Printing House, and printed there in 1694 from forty-four plates engraved by Leontii Bunin of the Moscow Armory Chamber: thirty-eight of

Figure 8 First page, illustrating the letter *A,* of the *Bukvar' (Primer)* compiled by Karion Istomin, engraved by Leontii Bunin, and printed at Moscow, 1694.

263

Figure 9   Three Cyrillic alphabets from the *Bukvar' (Primer)* compiled by Fedor Polikarpov and printed at Moscow, 1701.

the pages printed from these plates offer an alphabet of some forty-one letters (one page presents four letters, the rest, one letter per page) with each letter printed in a dozen or more different styles, these followed by captions and verses using words that begin with that letter (e.g., Fig. 8). This *Primer,* originally prepared for members of the tsar's family, was printed in a small, not to say minuscule edition;[10] and the variety and frequently elaborate form of its letters along with the archaic or alien character of some of them suggest nothing so much as perdurant alphabetic instability—something that could also be said about the alphabets of forty-five (or forty-seven) letters variously printed in a primer compiled by Fedor Polikarpov and published at Moscow in 1701 (Fig. 9).[11] All of these alphabets were obviously less than ideal for efficiently printing the kinds of books that Tsar Peter wanted to publish.

What Peter had in mind here is clearly indicated in his charter of February 1700 to Jan Tessing, a merchant of Amsterdam, granting him the right to print "for sale throughout our Russian realm" an unspecified number of "European, Asiatic and American land and marine pictures and charts, and all kinds of printed sheets and portraits, and mathematical, architectural, town-planning, military, marine, and other artistic books in the Slavonic and Latin languages together, or in Slavonic and Dutch together or separately, whence the subjects of our royal majesty shall receive much use and profit and be instructed in all the arts and specialties, and glory [shall accrue] to our royal majesty's name and to our entire Russian realm among the European monarchs." This privilege, for which Tessing had petitioned when Peter was in Holland in 1698, was to be held exclusively among European printers for a period of fifteen years but was not to extend to the printing of "church Slavonic books of the Greek rite, because church Slavonic Greek books, with the approval of the whole Orthodox authority of the Eastern church, are printed in our royal city of Moscow."[12] In other words, by the terms of this privilege Peter had decided that whereas "church books" would still be printed at the Moscow Printing House (which was still under church jurisdiction), the books, maps, charts, and picture-prints that he needed to pursue his military, naval, architectural, and other projects in Russia and to promote his realm's reputation in Europe would better be printed, for a limited time, in Amsterdam, that leading European center of printing and the book trade. Also in Amsterdam in 1698 he commissioned one Il'ia Kopievskii (Elias Kopijewitz), a longtime resident of Belorussian origin who had once lived in Moscow and later converted to Calvinism, to compile and translate, perhaps also to select, the books that Tessing would print.[13] The known fruits of their collaboration include textbooks on history, arithmetic, astronomy, military tactics, and navigation; an edition of Aesop's fables and a panegyric by Kopievskii celebrating Peter's victory over the Turks at Azov in 1696; a Latin grammar and a Latin-Russian glossary in verse *(Vokabuly stikhami latinskie i russkie)*; and two *nomenklatory* or lexicons, the first in Russian *(ruskom)*, Latin, and German, the second in Russian *(russkom)*, Latin, and Dutch—all printed at Tessing's press in Amsterdam between 1699 and 1701 (see Appendix I, nos. 8, 9).[14] In 1702 Tessing's heirs (he had died in 1701) printed a *Kalendar'* (almanac) for the Russian market, apparently without Kopievskii's help, while Kopievskii himself printed a textbook on rhetoric at his own press in Amsterdam sometime between 1700 and 1702 and a *Manual of Slavonic Russian or Muscovite grammar (Rukovedenie v grammatyku. Vo slavianorosiiskuiu ili Moskovskoiu)* at a press in Stoltzenberg, near Danzig, in 1706.[15] In such ways was Peter's commission of 1698–1700 to print non-church books for the Russian market carried out: more secular titles in the space of a few years than had been published in the entire previous history of East Slavic book printing.

265

Most of the Tessing-Kopievskii publishing output had little impact on developments in Russia, however. As Bykova makes clear, these books were for the most part awkwardly written in an odd or alien Slavonic, few copies were printed, and fewer still actually reached Russia—the result in some degree of an apparent dispute between the partners before Tessing died and Kopievskii, with little or no capital, tried to continue the business on his own. Still, as Bykova goes on to say, we must give the latter his due, working as he did alone in a foreign country while attempting to translate a wide variety of works into a language, "Slavonic-Russian," of which he had at best an uncertain grasp.[16] A revised edition of his *Aesop's Fables,* which he had translated from a Latin edition published at Amsterdam in 1672, was printed in the new civil type at Moscow in 1712 and at St. Petersburg in 1713 and again in 1717 (it was a favorite book of Tsar Peter's), thus launching Aesop's proverbially successful career in Russia; and an augmented as well as corrected edition of his thematically organized Russian-Latin-German lexicon was printed at St. Petersburg, also in civil types, in 1718 and 1720 and again in 1732.[17] Still more, the fonts used by Tessing to print non-church books for the Russian market reflect in varying degrees the Roman and italic styles characteristic of contemporary European typography (Fig. 10; Appendix I, nos. 8, 9)—a feature of the Tessing books, both contemporary and subsequent events in Russia would show, that was not missed by the tsar and his entourage.

Nor was Peter content simply to wait for books that he urgently required to be printed in Amsterdam and shipped from there to Russia, a lengthy and, with the onset of war with Sweden (October 1700), perilous procedure. In 1699 the *Kratkoe obyknovennoe uchenie . . . v stroenii peshkikh polkov (A Short Standard Instruction . . . for the Organization of Foot Regiments),* mentioned in Chapter 3, was printed at Moscow (Appendix I, no. 7) and reprinted in 1700 (twice), 1702, and 1704.[18] In 1703 the *Arifmetika* compiled by Magnitskii and others was also printed on Peter's orders at the Moscow Printing House, also as noted earlier (Chap. 2; cf. Appendix I, no. 11).[19] These were the first non-church books to be published in Moscow during Peter's reign and both were printed in traditional Cyrillic fonts (what else?) complete with superscripts including accent marks, contractions, Slavonic numerals, and so on. Moreover the texts of both books are larded with neologisms, not surprisingly given their subjects, and the language itself is a comparatively "plain" Russian, as Peter himself would call it, a feature of both books but particularly of the military manual (whose manuscript Peter had personally edited) which also is not surprising given their basic pedagogical purpose.[20] Linguistic as well as typographical traditions were being tested. Later in 1703 a manual of logarithmic tables adapted by Farquharson from a Latin original published at Amsterdam in 1681 was first printed at Moscow for the use of students at the new Moscow School of Mathematics and Navigation, again as mentioned earlier (Chap. 2).[21] Here the Slavonic numbering system had to be abandoned in favor of Arabic numerals (as it had been in the exercises printed in the *Arifmetika*) and Roman and italic types introduced to print the Latin terms used along with Greek type for the Greek words (also as done in the *Arifmetika*). In 1703 the first issues of the official *Vedomosti* also appeared in Moscow. These were printed versions of the manuscript *Kuranty* or *Vesti-kuranty* (cf. French *courant*/Dutch *krant*), or bulletins of military and political news from Europe that had long been prepared from foreign, primarily German sources by clerks, themselves often foreigners, of the Ambassadorial Office for circulation within the government.[22] Now such news, expanded to include domestic Russian, mainly court, developments, was being made available to a considerably wider readership via the *Vedomosti*, which is therefore often dubbed Russia's first printed newspaper. Issues of the *Vedomosti* appeared periodically, at times weekly, in pressruns of several hundred to several thousand copies, in Moscow and then, from 1711, in St.Petersburg as well, until 1727, when responsibility for publication was taken over by the Academy of Sciences and the *Vedomosti* took on a rather different, broader, more generally social and cultural character.[23] To be sure, the *Vedomosti* appeared at first in the Cyrillic type. But starting with the issue of February 1, 1710, its issues were printed, like the logarithmic manual just mentioned, in the newly invented civil type (Appendix I, no. 18):[24] evidence again in both cases that for "civil" purposes the traditional Cyrillic had been judged inappropriate.

We must tread carefully here, as the creation of the standard Russian alphabet, no less, is at issue. "Church books" continued to be published in these earlier years of Peter's reign as a matter of course, a fact that he affirmed in his privilege to Tessing of February 1700 when expressly excluding any such publication from the Dutchman's purview. Church books also continued to be printed exclusively in the traditional Cyrillic, rather than the new civil type. A good example is the collection of pious *Monthly Readings (Minei chet'i)* compiled by Dimitrii (or Dmitrii) Rostovskii, the Kievan divine (born Daniil Tuptalo in Ukraine) who in 1702 was appointed by Peter metropolitan (bishop) of the venerable Russian see of Rostov Velikii, and whose sermons and school dramas are usually listed among the literary monuments of the time.[25] His *Monthly Readings*, mostly saints' lives, were first printed in four volumes at the press of the Kiev Monastery of the Caves, now under the ultimate jurisdiction of the Moscow patriarchate, between 1689 and 1705. The collection proved to be very popular, and one or more of the volumes were reprinted at Kiev in 1711, 1714, 1716, and 1718 and at Moscow in 1759, 1762, 1764, 1767, 1782, 1789, and 1796 (confining the count to the eighteenth century and to Moscow and Kiev imprints).[26] The author of numerous other religious works published both during his life and posthumously (he died in 1709), Dimitrii Rostovskii was declared a saint of the Russian Orthodox church in 1757. But most interesting here is the fact that all of this popular saint's many books, like all of Feofan Prokopovich's famous sermons (Appendix I, no. 24), were printed and reprinted exclusively in traditional Cyrillic types, a fact that now worked to identify such types with publications of religious content.

267

Equally if not more striking in this connection is the spate of books on *nonreligious* subjects published in the earlier years of Peter's reign—"several dozen times" as many titles, observes one authority, as had been published in Moscow during the previous half century.[27] Printing such books at the Moscow Printing House in the available Cyrillic types was proving to be, as already noted (Chaps. 2, 3, 5), a difficult matter, as virtually all of them were translations of technical works originally published in Latin, German, or Dutch and were intended for naval and military students; they were *not* the books of religious content written in a Church Slavonic often newly translated from Greek and intended for learned clergy, their students, and flocks that normally were printed in Moscow. Fedor Polikarpov (Polikarpov-Orlov), who served from 1698 to 1731 as a corrector (copy editor) and then as director of the Moscow Printing House, later (1727) recalled how in 1702 and 1703 Tsar Peter had "wished to publish by printed means, for the instruction of youth in science, books civil, military, architectural, manufactural, and historical *[knigi grazhdanskie, voennye, arkhitekturnye, manufakturnye i istorial'nye]*, and to this fine end was pleased to design *[izobrest']* by his own untiring labor and care a new abecedarium, or alphabet *[novyi avetsadl, ili azbuku]*, which to this day is used in all civil matters."[28] In other words, by 1703 Peter had fully realized that to advance the ambitious publishing program necessitated by his aggressive military, naval, and related educational projects, he would have to establish a new alphabetic norm for printing in Russia, one not unlike that already devised in Amsterdam by Tessing expressly for printing books and other items of "civil" content (Fig. 10; Appendix I, nos. 8, 9). Meantime

268

АБВГДЕЖЅЗ

НІКЛМNꙍО

ПРСТУХЦЧ

ҘѦѢ

Figure 10   A Russian font devised in 1699 for Jan Tessing at Amsterdam to print books commissioned by Peter I.

Polikarpov himself took the stand, as in his *Primer* of 1701, that "church books" could be printed *only* in the traditional Cyrillic type because only it could reproduce Church Slavonic texts with the needed orthographic precision, down to the last diacritic: a matter not alone of the sacred character of such texts but also, we may surmise, of his own hard-won knowledge of Greek and the supposed Greek originals or prototypes of these texts. Polikarpov thereby exemplified, as one student puts it, the "post-Nikonian reform" view (post-1660s) typical of learned Russian churchmen of the day, whereby "faithfulness to Greek forms in language was the external manifestation of faithfulness to Eastern Orthodoxy in religion." This same student cites a letter of February 1709 to Polikarpov from I. A. Musin-Pushkin, the senior government official to whom he reported: "You told me that without all the letters of our old alphabet it is not possible to print church books," an opinion that Musin-Pushkin most probably conveyed to Peter himself.[29]

The story of how Peter I invented the modern Russian alphabet has long fascinated scholars, most notably Academician A. G. Shitsgal, who in several well-documented studies published since 1947 has provided the most detailed account.[30] As Shitsgal sums it up, over a period of two years (1708–1710) Peter excluded nine whole letters from the received Cyrillic alphabet and ordained that the rest were to be written and then typecast in more or less drastically simplified forms, the latter as designed by Dutch craftsmen in Amsterdam on the basis of contemporary European types *and* by Russian craftsmen working in Moscow with specimens of contemporary chancery script to hand. Shitsgal's emphasis on the Russian contribution here is notable, as credit is usually given to the Amsterdam masters working on Peter's instructions: "The whole ensemble of letters in the Petrine alphabet," he observes, "has a distinctive character and, in significant degree, an organic form. . . . This alphabet lacks elements typical of the Slavonic semi-uncial [style] that *were* adopted by the various Russian alphabets engraved and printed in Amsterdam. Creation of the civil type drew on various sources, but they were so reworked that the alphabet established by Peter may be judged one of the major achievements of Russian culture of the time."[31] True enough, no doubt. But we might briefly consider the salient evidence ourselves before consigning the Dutch masters, and the larger European influence, to a secondary role in this momentous development.

269

Peter had recourse in 1698 to Tessing and Kopievskii in Amsterdam in his quest for printed materials to support his various projects, as we observed earlier, and in 1699 he initiated for the same purpose the printing of technical books in Moscow. The output of both presses over the next few years demonstrates, in the mix of types employed, continued alphabetic and related orthographic instability (Appendix I, nos. 7–12). Not surprisingly, official correspondence of the time indicates both an awareness of the problem and a search for solutions. In a letter of July 1706, for instance, Peter instructs an agent in Amsterdam to see about ordering "100 iron matrices [*martirtsov zheleznykh*]" to be cast after models that would be sent to him and about hiring a "company of book printers [*kumpaniia drukarei*[32] *knizhnykh*]" to come to work in Moscow.[33] This missive was followed in January 1707 by a letter to the same agent, Christopher Brandt, complaining about the "very great cost" as reported by Brandt of securing the services of such a company of printers and enclosing a "new Russian alphabet [*azbuku Ruskuiu novuiu*] in three hands" against which three sets of type—three different fonts—were to be cast and then used to print, on one press, the "Our Father [prayer] or something else short." Brandt was to send the results to Russia promptly, where Peter and his associates would determine which "letters [*litery*] were the best made." Detailed instructions on casting the matrices for the new types were also enclosed, as were clarifications concerning the printers to be hired: now, "not a whole company and a big shop, but just one press [*stanok, ili pres*]" and three workers, one of whom "knows how to make letter forms [*formy na litery*], the second, how to cast the letters, the third, how to ink and print on this press; and others are not needed, as they do not know our language," for which reason "a Russian person [*odnomu cheloveku Ruskomu*]" was to supervise the work.[34] Brandt reported from Amsterdam in May 1707 that all was done as Peter had ordered and that the three Dutch masters with their letters, matrices, and punches *(stempeli),* hired for a term of three years and each obliged by their contract to train one or two Russian apprentices, were ready to go to Moscow.[35] In August 1707 he reported that the masters had duly left Amsterdam in June, again as Peter had ordered.[36] The Peter-Brandt correspondence of 1706 and 1707 thus documents the fact that Dutch craftsmen were to play a major part in the creation of the modern Russian alphabet *and* that their services in this respect were closely supervised, from the outset, by the tsar and his agents.

Other contemporary sources demonstrate that alongside this Dutch initiative Peter and his subordinates were working with Russian printers in Moscow. A petition submitted to the tsar in January 1708 by one such master, Mikhail Evfremov, indicates that in May 1707 he had made punches and matrices at the Moscow Printing House following models sent to him from Peter's current military headquarters, and that sometime afterward he had made a second set of punches and matrices in conformity with a specimen sheet printed in Amsterdam that had also been sent to him for guidance.[37] In May 1707, moreover, we find Peter telling I. A. Musin-Pushkin, the senior official in overall charge of the Moscow Press,[38] that he was sending him a second "new-style abecedarium [*azbuku novogo maniru*]"—presumably the specimen sent from Amsterdam, to follow one previously printed by Evfremov—and that Musin-Pushkin was to order that "against it are to be printed anew all abecedaria to be sold for children, since in this abecedarium the old letters are figured with the new, whence they [children] will be better able to understand the new letters and people become accustomed to them."[39] But this scarcely ended the matter. Ensuing correspondence between Peter and either Musin-Pushkin or Polikarpov show that work on the new alphabet continued through the latter half of 1707 and on into 1708, as new fonts were cast, specimen sheets were printed and sent for correction to Peter, ever on campaign, and the sheets, duly "corrected," were returned by him for printing anew.[40] By early 1708, Moscow Printing House records show, "three alphabets of newly designed Russian letters *[novoizobretennykh russkikh liter tri azbuki]*" had been selected for printing a newly translated geometry book.[41] This was the first Russian edition of Burckhard von Pürckenstein's *Handgriffe des Zirkels und Lineals,* which was first printed at Moscow in March 1708 "by the new typographical means" (as its title page says: *"izdadesia novotipografskim tisneniem"*), meaning by the three newly arrived Dutch masters working with their punches and matrices under the direction of Polikarpov assisted by an interpreter. This book, whose mathematical significance was discussed in Chapter 5, has gone down in Russian history as the first book ever printed in the new civil type (Appendix I, no. 13).[42]

271

But that was not the end of the matter, either. The technical manuals, almanacs, and political books or pamphlets subsequently printed at Moscow in civil types, various of which were also discussed in preceding chapters, continued to exhibit considerable alphabetic-orthographic instability along with certain visual or other practical shortcomings identified by Peter himself (the first edition of the geometry book just mentioned thus fell short in Peter's eyes, again as noted in Chapter 5). Such shortcomings seem to have been corrected to his satisfaction in succeeding printings: clearer typefaces were cut, more appropriate formats adopted, better illustrations provided, and so on. But a newly printed *azbuka* sent to him in 1709 elicited more precise criticism: the actual design of two letters was "very badly done," he complained, wherefore Musin-Pushkin was to order a certain "Saxon" working at one of the tsar's new mints to engrave new punches *(shtempeli).*[43] In another case, the printing in 1709 of a Russian translation of Vignola's well-known treatise on architecture, Peter was directly confronted, as never before, with the problem of rendering first in Russian and then in print a whole new technical vocabulary—in this case, the vocabulary of European Classical architecture as originally published in Italian. Both cases are variously illustrative of the obstacles to be overcome in establishing an alphabet suitable for printing in Russia works of "civil" content, and we shall look at them in turn.

The *azbuka* sent to Peter in 1709 had been in the works for several months at the Moscow Printing House, and it took several more months of labor to produce, print, and send a new version for his review. Musin-Pushkin advised him that the Saxon master in question, shown the "Amsterdam punches," had demurred, saying he was unable to do the job, but that somehow the offending letters would be corrected; and that meanwhile, on two other points the tsar had earlier raised—whether to print with or without accent marks *(s aksetami, bez aksentov),* and whether to use "old-style [Slavonic]" numerals in printed calendars—he would most assuredly get back to him.[44] The revised *azbuka* was duly submitted to the tsar later in 1709. On January 29, 1710, this *azbuka* was returned to its makers with a cover note in Peter's hand that reads: "Print historical and manufactural books with these letters. And those [letters] that are crossed out, do not use them in the aforesaid books."[45] The attached five-page printed *azbuka,* entitled *Representations of old and new printed and manuscript Slavonic characters (Izobrazhenie drevnikh i novykh pismen slavenskikh pechatnykh i rukopisnykh)* and displaying in parallel columns eight graph-shapes for each letter of the Russo-Slavonic alphabet, shows all the shapes in the first or left-most column crossed out by hand, as are various other letters in the remaining columns (Fig. 11). Thereby eliminated by Peter, in general, were the more elaborate of the "old" Cyrillic letter-shapes, leaving "new" shapes that clearly reflected contemporary European typographical norms as well as those of contemporary Russian chancery script; also thus eliminated were *all* the graph-shapes shown of three letters. Shitsgal takes Peter's order of January 29, 1710, together with its attached, corrected *azbuka* as marking the decisive step in the creation of the modern Russian alphabet; and books printed thereafter at the Moscow Press and then at the presses founded by Peter in St. Petersburg certainly exhibit an effort by all involved to follow the tsar's bidding.[46] Even so, as Bykova points out,[47] a continuous if quite subtle evolution of the civil type is detectable in the faces employed by printers in the remaining fifteen years of Peter's reign, as new presses were founded and more stocks of type acquired to meet the ever increasing demand for printed materials generated by agents of the Petrine regime.

After 1710 traditional Cyrillic types were used at presses in Russia at first mainly and then exclusively to print books of religious content, that is, lives of saints, catechisms, sermons, prayer books, church service books, Bibles and biblical extracts, church calendars, and so on—a corpus that no doubt constituted, until well into the eighteenth century, the great bulk of books printed and actually distributed in Russia.[48] The distinction between "church books" and all other kinds that had been drawn by Peter in his charter of 1700 to Jan Tessing, the former to be printed on church authority in traditional Cyrillic characters, the latter to be printed with the tsar's privilege in appropriately "civil" fonts, was thus institutionalized. The traditional Cyrillic alphabet and corresponding modes of printing became in effect the property of the Orthodox church, where they had, indeed, originated; while the civil alphabet and related types, elicited in stages from traditional Cyrillic, became with only minor changes thereafter the norm for all other printing—in short, the modern Russian standard. It was indeed a major achievement of the Petrine revolution in Russian culture.

Figure 11   Initial letters of the specimen Russian alphabet *(azbuka)* printed at the Moscow Printing House, 1709, showing "corrections"—letters to be eliminated—made (1710) by Peter I.

Another big problem to be resolved under Peter in printing works of "civil" content is exemplified, as mentioned above, by the Russian edition of a famous Italian textbook on architecture. Vignola's *Regola delli cinque ordini d'architettura,* a concise illustrated treatise first published at Rome in 1562, had enjoyed an immense popular and academic success all over Europe, having gone through scores of editions in all of the main European languages over the course of a century and a half. This success was owed to the economy

274

with which it encapsulated in drawings and words the architectural revolution inaugurated in Renaissance Italy. More particularly, it was the first book to demonstrate a simple method or "rule" for proportioning each of the five Classical orders revived in the Renaissance—the Tuscan, Doric, Ionic, Corinthian, and Composite—in all of their component parts (column, capital, entablature, and so on) and various applications (building facade, doorway, fireplace, tomb, etc.).[49] Russian editions of the Vignola, titled *Pravilo o piati chinekh arkhitektury,* were printed at Moscow in 1709, 1712, and 1722, making it the first such book to appear in Russia, where it remained the best known work on architecture for nearly a century. It thus played a critical part in the Petrine revolution in Russian building techniques and norms.[50] But it did so only after Peter and his collaborators had struggled to make it comprehensible to its intended readers—initially, the Russian students and assistants of the European and especially Italian architects recruited to build St. Petersburg.

In January 1709 Peter ordered the Vignola to be printed and sent to him for review, and in September of that year he duly advised an official in charge of the project that

> we have looked over the little architectural book *[knishku arkhitekturnuiu]* sent by you, and [find that] in certain places it is incorrect, about which we send herewith a list of notes. Following this list order architect Fantanna *[arkhitekturu Fantanne* = G. M. Fontana, one of the Italian masters recruited] to correct [the mistakes] together with some Russian who might know architecture, however little *[s kem-nibud' ruskim, kotoroi by khotia nemnogo znal arkhitekturu].* And after correcting [it], order a hundred copies to be printed, and send us five or ten as soon as possible.

The list of mistakes for correcting was attached, according to which the captions to various *figury* were misplaced and in "many places" were "unclear."[51] Fontana and his Russian assistant endeavored to revise the Vignola in compliance with the tsar's order, as the subsequent Russian editions show, while adding an Italian-Slavonic glossary of technical terms—"*Perevod Gospodina Arkhitektura Fantanna Obretaiushchikhsia vo arkhitekturnoi knige italianskikh rechenii na slovenskoe rechenie* [Translation by Mr. Fontana the Architect of Italian locutions found in [this] architectural book into Slavonic locutions]"— which was printed in parallel Italian and "Slavonic *[po slavenskii]*" columns. The glossary is remarkable for its mix of forms, to say the least. In

the Italian column straight transliterations are printed in the drastically simplified Cyrillic or "civil" type that Peter was simultaneously introducing, these
paralleled by the roughly equivalent extant terms, attempted literal or semantic calques, and, again, straight transliterations similarly printed in the Slavonic column: thus *Modeliony* in the one column is simply *Modeliony* in the
other, *Arkhitrave* becomes *Arkhidrat*, *Plinto* becomes *Plintus*, *Regula* is *Sposob
mery*, the phrase *Kolonna ili paliastr* is rendered *Stolby*, and so on. The same
sort of mix occurs in the lists of architectural terms accompanying various diagrams in the book, in the captions to its hundred or so illustrations (reengraved in Moscow by artists working under the Dutch master Pieter Picart),
and in its longer descriptive or instructional passages. These passages begin
on the first page, where it is explained that the book's purpose is

> to treat of the five orders of columns, that is, the Tuscan, Doric, Ionic,
> Corinthian, Composite, wherefore it is fitting first to show figures of
> each separately, which will [then] be discussed, even though their rule is
> still unknown [still to be explained here]. For only then are they ready
> for an explanation of the general rule. After that what is peculiar from
> one part to another will be clear. [*Traktovat' o piati ordinakh kolonov,
> to est', O toskane, Doriko, Ionika, Korinto, Kompozito. Pokazalosia za
> dostoino, da by v nachale pokazat' figury vsiakuiu osobno, o kotorykh
> traktovat' budet, khotia eshche mery ikh neizvestny. Ibo tokmo zdes' onye
> polozheny sut' dlia ob'iavleniia generalnoi reguly. A posle sobstvenno ot
> onoi chasti k drugoi ob'iastemo budet.*] (cf. Appendix I, no. 21)

Later in the book (page 10) it is explained that the five *ordiny* are divided
into "a certain number of modules [*moduli*]": in the *ordona dorika,* for example, the base under the column *(baza pod kolumnoiu)* and the surmounting
capital *(kapitel')* are each one module high and the column itself, fourteen
modules. The precise number and ratio of the modules one to the other
(Arabic numbers used throughout), the explanation continues, established
the strength, proportions *(proportsii),* and regularity *(reguliarnost')* for which
ancient Roman architecture was justly praised. And so the book proceeds
through each of the architectural orders, with its component parts and various applications, the whole exercise copiously illustrated.[52]

There can be little doubt that the detailed illustrations or *figury* provided in
the Russian editions of Vignola's tract mightily assisted the transmission from
Italy to Russia of the vocabulary and verbalized concepts of architecture in
the Renaissance tradition. At the same time, it deserves emphasizing, the very

act of translating Vignola's *verbal* building instructions and architectural descriptions facilitated the transition in Russia from Slavonic to Russian: from a heavily Slavonicized Russian or Russified Church Slavonic (Russo-Slavonic), where such discourses were virtually unknown, to a newer, simpler, more vernacular "civil" language capable of embracing this as well as the other arts and sciences of contemporary Europe and appropriately encrypted in a newer, simpler, more European-looking "civil" type. We have repeatedly observed this process at work in the preceding chapters, though without the present stress on its alphabetic and typographical aspects, which may now be seen as fundamental. One thing usually leads to another. Not only a newly steamlined, Europeanized Russian alphabet but a newly streamlined, Europeanized Russian language were among the outcomes of Peter's drive to renovate his realm—here, its architecture—along contemporary European lines. And the newness of this emergent language was most readily apparent, as we have also had ample occasion to see, in its rapidly expanding lexicon.

Lexical Proliferation

It has been said that the vocabulary of all languages undergoes continual change in accordance with the four arithmetical operations: *addition*— loanwords taken from other languages; *subtraction*—obsolescence of native words; *multiplication*—new derivations from native words or from acclimatized loanwords; and *division*—new meanings of a word via subdivision, or extension, of its semantic field.[53] In all four respects, but particularly via addition and multiplication, the lexicon of written Russian underwent enormous expansion during the roughly three-decade reign of Peter I. We cannot be definitive on this point, to be sure, since a comprehensive historical dictionary of Russian does not yet exist and more specialized research in the field, as exemplified by the scholarly works cited in Appendix II, is still fragmentary. The following section will summarize instead the lexical evidence adduced in the preceding chapters and that assembled in Appendix II with the aim of providing a fuller, more exact account of this crucial aspect of the Petrine revolution than has hitherto been available.

Linguists postulate that the common core of all the Slavic languages was formed in prehistoric times and reflects infusions from neighboring Baltic and Iranian tongues. In the early historic period—third to eighth centuries A.D.—Germanic, Latin, and Greek words were added and then, with Christianization (ninth to eleventh centuries), entire Greek or Latin religious vocabularies. In the meantime, following outward migrations from the Common Slavic homeland, distinct East, West, and South Slavic linguistic groups gradually formed (sixth to fourteenth centuries), groups that would subsequently diverge into the modern Slavic languages: in the East Slavic case, into Russian, Ukrainian, and Belorussian. Factors promoting this divergence within the East Slavic group included considerable Turkic as well as further Greek influence, the former acting mainly on the vernaculars (political, military, and commercial terms), the latter, still mostly religious in nature, on the literary language we call Church Slavonic. In addition, the East Slavic vernacular of the Novgorod region absorbed new Baltic and especially Germanic terms, mainly commercial terms, while the Church Slavonic written both there and in the Ruthenian lands (Ukraine and Belorussia) borrowed a few Latin scientific, philosophical, and literary words. Over the centuries since its introduction, in short, the *lexical* differences between Church Slavonic and the East Slavic vernaculars, initially considerable, had grown markedly—the result not only of external influences, of course, but also of internal political, economic, and social developments.[54]

In the sixteenth and especially the seventeenth century, homing in on our target, the most important external influence on the written languages of Muscovy—Russian Church Slavonic (Russo-Slavonic) and chancery Russian—was Polish. The influence was twofold. The Latin, Greek, and Polish terminology of Polish humanism that had infiltrated the Church Slavonic of Ruthenian divines (Chap. 1) was guardedly taken up by Muscovite churchmen; at the same time, hundreds of words of Polish provenance, a high proportion of them previously borrowed from Latin, German, or French, invaded the language of the Muscovite government and, to a lesser extent, of Muscovite court society. Diplomatic, administrative, military, and medicinal terms predominated in the latter case, not surprisingly, more abstract or learned terms in the former; and the prime mediators of this quickening Polish linguistic stream were Polish and Ruthenian interpreters and translators hired for service in Moscow who were bilingual in Latin and a Slavic tongue close enough to Russian to be understood. Nor was the influence purely lexical. By the end of the seventeenth century Polish had popularized the creation in Russian (or Russo-Slavonic) of verbs ending in *-ovat'* (or *-izovat'*), abstracts in *-ost'*, and abstract nouns of Latin type in *-iia* and *-tsiia* (e.g., *risovat'* = to draw, from Polish *rysować*; *spravedlivost'* = fairness, from Polish *sprawiedliwość*; and *natsiia* = nation, from Latin *natio* via Polish *nacja*).[55]

Under Peter this stream of European words irrigating Russian discourse became a veritable flood, while the channel of transmission ceased to be mainly Polish and became more broadly international. Both points deserve emphasis. According to the most authoritative work published to date on the question, some 4,500 individual foreign words entered Russian in the Petrine period (5,153 including contemporary derivations) as compared with about 1,000 items (764 words plus 232 derivations) in the preceding thirty or so years: more than a fivefold increase.[56] These totals incorporate and correct those compiled by previous scholars, as explained in the introductory remarks to Appendix II, but themselves are necessarily approximate. Even so, we can confidently assert that the sheer *volume* of loanwords entering Russian in Peter's time constituted a lexical invasion of unprecedented proportions and that continuing research in the field will only refine, not substantially alter, this conclusion. But equally, the *breadth* of linguistic borrowing during the Petrine era in Russia stands in marked contrast to the semantically much narrower and predominantly Polish channeling of the preceding period, as hundreds and then thousands of new words were added to the Russian lexicon directly from Dutch, German, English, French, Italian, Swedish, Latin, and Classical Greek (usually via Latin). And it is on this point that we shall dwell now by way of assessing the qualitative aspect of the Petrine impact on the Russian lexicon.

Neologistical proliferation under Peter plainly was driven by his regime's program of selective and then comprehensive Europeanization. For instance, what I term Russia's nautical turn under Peter—his embrace of European maritime culture and particularly his creation of a Russian navy—entailed the adoption in Russian of huge new specialized vocabularies. Some sixty-five nautical loanwords including derivations were quoted from contemporary sources in Chapter 2, most of which became permanent acquisitions in Russian as attested in the Nautical section of Appendix II, which lists 211 such terms. At the same time, several hundred more terms were borrowed from Dutch and English to name the parts of a fully rigged sailing ship and from Italian to designate those of an oar-powered galley—terms that for the most part became obsolete in the nineteenth century along with the ship types that gave rise to them and so are not listed in Appendix II. Nor does Appendix II include, as mentioned there, highly technical navigational, naval, and other nautical terms (for instance, most of the naval ranks imported by Peter), many of which are still in use (a few examples appear in Chapter 2). In short, as many as 600 nautical terms entered Russian in the Petrine era some half of which remain in specialized use, many of them gaining new applications (extending their semantic fields), as they did elsewhere in Europe, in the construction and flying of airplanes and then of spacecraft. And a good number of these enduring words, as a perusal of the Nautical section of Appendix II will indicate, remain in common Russian parlance today (*abordazh, bort, bot, verf', gavan', dok, kompas, konvoi, kurs, matros, navigatsiia, port, rul', signal, flot, ekipazh, iakhta,* and so on).

Chapter 3 sought to contextualize the wholesale adoption in Petrine Russia of contemporary European military terminology. Some 240 such words (including sample derivations), almost all of them still in use, are listed in the Military section of Appendix II and many of these, again, acquired additional meanings over the years (for example, *barrikada, blokada, brigada, volontër, gvardiia, diversiia, kvartira, komanda/komandirovka, korpus, lozung, marshrut, militsiia, ofitser, palisad, pioner, raketa, remont, shtab, shturm*). This section of Appendix II, like its predecessor, also excludes numerous Petrine neologisms that more or less rapidly became obsolete—in this case, Germanic military ranks, the names of outmoded weapons and their parts, and technical terms involved in late medieval–early modern siegecraft and fortification. Examples of such relatively fleeting loanwords are cited, in passing, in Chapter 3; so too are examples of contemporary European military terminology borrowed well before Peter's reign. Even so, several hundred military loanwords permanently entered Russian in the Petrine era primarily but by no means exclusively from German, a lexical influx that was far in excess of what had occurred earlier and one that assumed, as with the language of Peter's nautical turn, foundational importance in the modern Russian lexicon. In Peter's time, it is fair to say, the bases of modern Russian naval and military thought were laid—"thought" understood to mean the capacity for precise verbalization of all the new tactics, strategies, maneuvers, weapons, and equipment that the Petrine regime had brought into play on the battlefield or parade ground, at sea or in port.

What earlier was dubbed the "official" vocabulary adopted in Russian under Peter I, primarily again from German (or from German via Polish, Swedish via German, or Latin or French via German), was similarly huge and foundational. This was no less than the "terminology of political modernization," as I called it in Chapter 4: the administrative, legal, and diplomatic language of the modern European state as utilized in implementing Peter's bureaucratic revolution and in articulating his doctrine of absolute monarchy. Nearly 200 such terms plus another nearly 200 contemporary or later derivations are listed in the Official section of Appendix II, and the reception of about 100 of these terms is documented in Chapter 4. Nor is the Appendix exhaustive in this respect either. As stated there (with examples), a large number of generic European and especially Germanic political and administrative terms borrowed by the Petrine regime in reforming the state—typically, names for officials and their offices, terms of diplomatic, bureaucratic, and judicial protocol—more or less quickly became obsolete or simply remained foreign in Russian. That still leaves hundreds of Petrine loanwords with contemporary derivations which vastly expanded the Russian political lexicon and sooner or later reverberated, often enough, in other semantic fields. A small sampling of such terms would include *agent, advocat, administratsiia/ administrator, akt, amnistiia, arenda, arest/arestovat', arkhiv, attestat, ballotirovat', vizit/vizitnyi, garantiia, gubernator, dezhur/dezhurnyi, deklaratsiia/ deklarirovat', departament, diplom, diplomat, direktor, dokument, inspektor, institut, interes/interesnyi, kabinet, kavaler, kandidat, kommissar, kongress, konstitutsiia, konsul/konsul'stvo, kontora, kontrakt, korrespondent/korrespondentsiia, kredit, kriminal, lakei, litsenziia, magistrat, mandat, marka, medal', moneta, pakt, partizan, partiia, pasport, patent, patriot, plakat, politika/ politicheskii, politsiia, pochtamt, prezident, provokatsiia, prokuror, protest, protokol, publika/publichnyi/publichno, punkt, rang, reviziia, revoliutsiia, registrator, rezoliutsiia, raport, respublika, saluit/saliutovat', sekta, sessiia, shtat, statut, subsidiia, traktat, tribunal, flag, tseremoniia, shpion, shtraf,* and *zhurnal.* The elementary importance of many of these terms in modern political discourse, and the ramifying significance of others, could scarcely be exaggerated.

Something of a parallel case can be made for what is labeled Other Technical Terms in Appendix II—meaning other than the military, nautical, and official terms that are previously listed there. This is a bulky, somewhat amorphous lexical category, admittedly, including as it does some 780 mathematical, medical, musical, literary, art and architectural, philosophical, technological, scientific, and other technical terms (400 main words, 380 mostly contemporary derivations) borrowed from German (or German via Polish), Latin (or Latin via German or Polish or Ukrainian), Greek (or Greek via Latin), Dutch, French, Italian, English, and/or Polish (or Polish via Ukrainian). The reception of many of these terms was documented in previous chapters (especially Chapter 5) and, in the case of architecture and the other visual arts, in my two earlier volumes;[57] the Petrine adoption of Renaissance Italian architectural terminology also figured in the preceding section of this chapter. Again, it is the breadth of the borrowings that must impress as well as the modern significance of so many of them, both features indicative of the scope of the Petrine translation program and, behind that, of the regime's urgent interests and needs. We might consider just the medical terms listed in this section of Appendix II (a few are cited in Chapter 5): *anatomiia, arteriia, bandazh, vena, gonoreia, gospital', ipokhondriia, karantin, karbunkel, koliki, komplektsiia, lazaret, lantset, medik, medikament, meditsina, mikstura, muskul, okulist, operatsiia, paralich, pul's, retsept, flius, khirurg/khirurgiia,* and *shprits,* to which may be added (from the Military section of Appendix II) *invalid* and *fel'dsher.* These terms stand in sharp contrast to the predominantly herbal and folk-medicinal terms borrowed from Polish and Polish-Latin in the decades preceding Peter's reign,[58] and reflect in their turn the more typically modern or scientific practice of medicine—*meditsina*—implanted under Peter in Russia (Chap. 5). Likewise significant are the many mathematical terms listed in the same section of Appendix II, which denominate practices going well beyond simple computation: the word *matematika* itself, to start, and, indeed, *arifmetika* as well as *geometriia, algebra,* and *trigonometriia;* also *gipotenuza, diametr, diogonal'nyi, kvadrant, konus, kub, liniia, logarifm, masshatb, nol', parallel', parallelogramm, perferiia, perpendikuliar, piramida, proportsiia, radius, romb, sinus, sekant, sektor, summa, sfera, tangens, tsilindr, tsifra,* and *ellips,* among others, along with the names of such related instruments as *lineika* and *tsirkul'.* The basic vocabulary of mathematics up through trigonometry was fixed in Russian in Peter's time, in sum, as were the basic vocabularies of the new and closely related sciences of navigation, astronomy, geodesy (or cartography), fortification, and geography (discussed in Chapters 2 and 5).

Musical, literary, and philosophical loanwords listed in the section of Other Technical Terms in Appendix II stand out even more sharply, perhaps, given the obsessive technological bias usually attributed to the Petrine regime. The musical borrowings include *ariia, bas, valtorna/valtornist, garmoniia, goboi/goboist, kapella, klavesin, kontsert, melodiia,* and *muzyka* itself, as well as *opera, oratoriia, serenada, tenor, ton, fleita,* and *tsimbaly;* the literary terms, besides *literatura* itself, *avtor, aktsent, annotatsiia, aforizm, dialekt, drama, idiliia, kompozitsiia, paragraf, paskvil', poet, tragediia,* and *fabula,* together with, as usual, numerous derivations; and among philosophical terms, including those of the new natural sciences and various abstract political, ethical, or historical words, *absoliut/absoliutnyi, avtorizovat', avtoritet, akkuratnyi, analiz, antik, antipatiia, argument, aristokratiia, ateist, atmosfera, atom, balans, vakuum, general'nyi, gipoteza, deduktsiia, demokratiia, demonstratsiia, definitsiia, diktator, disput, ideia, informatsiia, istoriia, konditsiia, konspiratsiia, kontroverza, kontsept, kon"iunktura, laboratoriia, lektsiia, materiia, metamorfoza, metafizika, mekhanika, mikroskop, model', muzei, nabliudenie, natural'nyi, natsiia, novshestvo, obligatsiia, ob"ekt, optika, original, personal'nyi, printsip, proba, progress, proekt, rezon, religiia, reguliar/reguliarnyi, sistema, teoriia, tiran, universal'nyi, fenomen, fizika, funda-*

mental'nyi/fundamental'nost', khimiia, khronologiia, eksempliar, ekspeditsiia, eksperiment, ekstrakt, element, essentiia, and *effekt.* The semantic range of the hundreds of words in this broad "philosophical" category of Petrine neologisms alone offers striking testimony to the scope, perhaps unexpected, of the Petrine revolution's impact on Russia's verbal culture. And the larger section of which this category is a subset, like the subset itself, is no more exhaustive of possible entries than are the other sections of Appendix II.

Appendix II also lists, under Commercial Terms, some ninety words including derivations of financial or industrial as well as commercial import borrowed in Peter's time mainly from German and/or Dutch, many of those borrowed in turn from French. The bulk of these terms—for example, *aktsiia, bank, bankir, birzha, bukhgalter, veksel', galantereia, debet, inventar', karton, kassa, kvitantsiia, konosament, makler, manufaktura, produkt, protsent, rynok, tarif, fabrika, faktura*—remain in common use, and to them may be added the more technical, less common, but still current mining, mineralogical, and metallurgical Petrine loanwords listed previously in Appendix II under Other Technical Terms, including *bril'iant, bronza, vismut, vol'fram, gneis, karat, kvarts, kizel'gur, kobal't, kristall, latun', marganets, metall, mineral, slesar', stal', fol'ga, tsink, shakhta, shifer, shikhta, shlak, shlikh, shpur, shtanga, shtuf, shurf;* most of these words, too, were of German origin. The fixing of all these commercial and industrial words in Russian during Peter's reign reflects, of course, concurrent economic developments as well as the regime's efforts to inculcate in Russian merchants the "science of commerce *[nauka komertsii]*."[59] Similarly reflective are the loanwords listed under Other Technical Terms connected with engineering, printing, and construction, such as *abris, brandspoit, gorizont, graviura, damba, domkrat, inzhener, instrument, kazemat, kanal, karkas, klapan, klemma, kran, matritsa, mashina, mufta, pompa, ponton, tipografiia, trakt, sliuz, shrift, shtempel', fal'ts, fundament, tsement, shpunt,* and *estamp.* The reference to construction evokes in turn the new *arkhitektura* and its professional vocabulary, various instances of which are also to be found in this section of Appendix II, including *alebastr, alleia, arka, arkhitektor, arkhitrav, baza, baldkhin, balkon, baliustrada, bassein, gazon, grot, interval, kapitel', karniz, kartush, kaskad, kolonna, mezonin, obelisk, oval, oranzhereia, ornament, panel', park, piliastr, plan, plintus, proekt, p'edestal, reguliar/reguliarnyi, fasad, fligel', fontan, fronton, tsokol',* and *shtukaturit';* some of which were documented earlier in this chapter as well as in my first volume. Similarly the new terminology of the other visual arts: *graviura* and *estamp* were already mentioned in connection with printing, but also remarkable are *barel'ef, biust, galereia, gobelen, grifel', kartina, malevat'/maliar, manera, moda, pergament, portret, profil', risunok/risovat', skul'ptor/skul'ptura, statuia, stil',* and *emblema,* among others; various of these terms, too, are documented in my second volume. All of these neologisms, however categorized, plainly evince both the quality and the scope of the lexical impact of the Petrine revolution.

Nor could I neglect to highlight here other Petrine neologisms in Russian signifying the finer things of life and indicative of that "reformation of manners" evoked in Chapters 4 and 5—words that also were borrowed from German, Italian, or French. Numerous examples are found in Appendix II under Other Technical Terms as well as in its concluding, catch-all section, Other Terms. They include the names for new foods, for clothes or parts of clothes, for tableware and other utensils, for furniture and living quarters, for fruits, flowers, drinks, and entertainments: *assambleia, balet, goroskop, illuminatsiia* (also *feierverk*), *kant, karnaval, loteraia, muzyka, spirt, tants/tantsevat', teatr, traur, tiul'pan, farfor, fekhtmeister,* and *iubilei;* also, under Other Terms, *abrikos, ambroziia, anchous, apartament* (see also *kvartira,* initially a military term), *apel'sin, artishok, bagazh, bant, baul, bil'iard/y, biskvit, bul'on, butylka, vaflia, veer, galstukh, garderob, glazur', duel', zala, zontik, kamzol, kapor, kastriula, kegli, konfety, koridor, kotleta, kofe, krakhmal, krendel', krep, lampa, latskan, lenta, likër, limonad, lokon, manzheta, mebel', meniu, obshlag, paket, parik/parikmakher, persik, pokal/bokal, probka, pudra, ragu, salfetka, sarzha, sel'derei, serviz, sous, ustritsa, fartuk, figa, flër, frukt, futliar, shampanskoe (vino), shkaf, shlafrok, shokolad, shtof,* and *ekipazh.* It is astonishing to consider how basic many of these terms are to modern gastronomical, culinary, sartorial, social, and other cultural practices in Russia, and how current many of them still are in Russian.

The loanwords listed in all sections of Appendix II—main words, closely related words, and sample derivations—total about 1,700. This figure represents only about a third of the 5,153 individual foreign words, including derivations, that scholars have so far ascertained were fixed in Russian in the Petrine era. Still, Appendix II does provide a fair sampling of the proffered total and one that is deliberately limited, it might be stressed, by its bias in favor of fully naturalized words that remain current today. Indeed the semantic range of the words listed in Appendix II and reviewed here amply testifies to the lexical impact of the Petrine revolution, an impact that in several hundred cases was more or less fully contextualized, as space and available sources permitted, in the preceding chapters of this volume. And the lexical, to repeat, was only the most obvious aspect of the Petrine impact on Russian verbal culture.

Dictionaries and Grammars

Printed dictionaries and grammar books had served both to codify and to disseminate the leading vernaculars or "languages of power" in western Europe in the sixteenth and seventeenth centuries, and so to enshrine them as the literary and scholarly standard (instead of or alongside Latin) as well as the official tongue of their respective realms (Chap. 1). So it would be in Russia, via a somewhat more extended process, in the eighteenth century. The process was given an enormous push forward by the Petrine regime both directly, by encouraging the compilation and publication of such works in Russia, and indirectly, by founding the Academy of Sciences. In both cases the need for effective translations—mainly, as we have seen, from scientific or technical works in Latin, Dutch, and German—was a decisive factor.

In Chapter 1 the combined Church Slavonic grammar and dictionary compiled by Lavrentij Zyzanij and printed at Vilnius in 1596 was mentioned, as was Pamba Berynda's *Leksikón slavenrósskïj* printed at Kiev in 1627 and at Kuciejna (Kuteino, in Belorussia) in 1653, and Melitij Smotryckij's Slavonic grammar printed at Jev'je (near Vilnius) in 1619 and again, in abridged form, at Krem'janec' (in Volhynia) in 1638 (I preserve the transliterations adopted in Chapter 1 for reasons given there). In that chapter the Ruthenian origin of all of these books was emphasized as well as their more or less artificially standardized character (standardized by recourse to Latin and Greek models); and while all of them were known in Russia, only the abridged edition of Smotryckij's grammar, somewhat Russified, was printed at Moscow in 1648. This abridged edition of the Smotritskii (adopting now a Russian transliteration of his name) remained the only Slavonic grammar book available in Russia until 1721, when the complete Jev'je-Vilnius edition of 1619 was printed in the traditional Cyrillic type, with the sanction of the Holy Synod, at the Moscow Press.[60] Our friend Fedor Polikarpov, the learned Greco-Slavonicist and current director of the press, contributed a preface to this new Moscow edition of the Smotritskii grammar in which he gave three reasons for reprinting it: (1) it had become hard to find, "like a spark amid the ashes," while thanks to the labors of great Peter such textbooks were now badly needed in the schools; (2) a good knowledge of grammar, experience had shown, was essential for effective translation; and (3) such knowledge was also essential for correctly reading Holy Scripture, so as not to "sin against the faith." In preparing Smotritskii's grammar for printing, specialists have shown, Polikarpov "corrected" (Russified, but also re-Slavonicized) the text at various points on lexical, orthographic, and grammatical grounds and added a section in which he laid out in dialogue form a grammatical analysis of the standard Slavonic version of the Lord's Prayer.[61] It has also been shown that this added section was linked with Polikarpov's larger plan to compile a whole new grammar of Church Slavonic—a project that he did complete, sometime in 1725, but never published.[62] To understand the significance of these efforts let us consider his career as a whole, emblematic as it is of the dilemmas posed by the language question in Petrine Russia.

285

Polikarpov appeared earlier in this chapter as well as elsewhere in the volume in his role as a corrector and later the director of the Moscow Printing House or Press, as the author of a primer *(bukvar')* printed there in 1701, and as the translator of the *Geographia Generalis* by Bernhard Varenius, which translation was also printed, in 1718, at his press. Born in Moscow about 1670, the son, apparently, of a minor official, he was a student at the Greco-Slavonic school attached to the Moscow Printing House when, in 1685, he was transferred with a group of his peers to the new Slavonic-Greek-Latin Academy run by the recently arrived Greek monks, the brothers Ioannikiia and Sofroniia Likhudy (as they are known in Russian; Ioannikios and Sophronios Leikhoudis, in Greek). The academy was divided at the time into three levels or *shkoly:* the boys in the first or lower school studied Church Slavonic; those in the middle school, Greek grammar; and those in the upper school, rhetoric, logic, and physics in both Greek and Latin. Polikarpov's first translations—of religious works written by his teachers and done while a student at the academy—were from Greek into Slavonic; and when the Likhudy brothers left the academy in 1694, he and another student took over the basic teaching (the academy would receive a new, "Latinizing" lease of life, as mentioned in Chapter 5, when Stefan Iavorskii, the learned Kievan divine, took over its direction in 1701). Polikarpov continued to teach Greek and Slavonic at the academy until 1698, when he became first a corrector *(spravshchik)* at the Printing House and then, in 1701, its director, a post he retained until his death in 1731 except for the period from 1722 to 1726, when, willingly or not, he withdrew from the directorship and meanwhile compiled his never-published Slavonic grammar.[63]

Two aspects of Polikarpov's biography deserve highlighting: his education, more Scholastic perhaps than humanist, and with its emphasis on Greek; and his career as a press corrector, one exemplifying the Muscovite tradition, dating back to the 1660s if not earlier, that "faithfulness to Greek forms in language was the external manifestation of faithfulness to Eastern Orthodoxy in religion."[64] In other words, Polikarpov absorbed from his teachers the notion that Greek was the primary language of both religion and "wisdom,"

286

with the corollary that translation from Greek into Slavonic should strive to be as literal as possible and that all Russian church books—the great bulk of what his Moscow Press printed—should conform as closely as possible to their Greek originals or equivalents. This was the "Nikonian way," referring to the Grecocizing liturgical reforms launched in Moscow by Patriarch Nikon in the 1650s and confirmed by the Moscow church council of 1666–67. Yet Polikarpov also came to understand that languages other than Greek had value, starting with his "native *[otechestvennyi]*" Slavonic and its Russian "vernacular *[recheniia]*" offshoot; thus Hebrew was a sacred language as well, while Latin, as he also wrote, was the language preeminently of "civil and scholarly matters." Here then was the source of the tension that has been detected in Polikarpov's surviving linguistic works, namely, his *Primer* of 1701 (Appendix I, no. 10), a *Leksikon* of 1704 (to which we will turn shortly), the 1721 edition of the Smotritskii, and his own unpublished grammar: a tension between his allegiance to the principle of Greek linguistic primacy, on one side, and, on the other, his recognition of the unique value and even parity with Greek of these other languages. This tension, or "struggle" (or ambiguity), was characteristic of the writings of the Grecophile Muscovite traditionalists, mostly learned monks, often of Ruthenian origin, with whom he continued to consort. And, like most of the latter, Polikarpov upheld in the end the traditional approach to the language question in Russia, devoting his grammatical and lexical labors to the codification of Church Slavonic as Russia's one true literary language.[65]

In compiling his Slavonic grammar of 1725, we should also note, Polikarpov drew on Smotritskii's grammar of 1619, on his own reading of certain Latin and Greek models, including a Greek manual provided by the Likhudy brothers, and on a Slavonic grammar published at St. Petersburg in 1723. This was the work of one Feodor Maksimov, a teacher at the Greco-Slavonic school, also founded by the Likhudy brothers, which was attached to the episcopal palace in old Novgorod. Printed at the Alexander-Nevskii Monastery Press in traditional Cyrillic types, this manual is remarkable both for its insistence on the necessity of learning grammar in order to read, write, and speak one's language properly and for its attempt to simplify its presentation of the subject—the latter effort based on its author's conviction, as he says in his preface, that the existing Slavonic grammar (Smotritskii's) was too complicated for young minds.[66] This approach in effect recognized, with Polikarpov, the urgency of codifying Russia's literary language but also, going beyond him, of somehow streamlining the process—finding a simpler language—for the sake of reaching more users, which in practice meant employing forms and examples taken from vernacular Russian. Still, Maksimov too thus affirmed that Church Slavonic was Russia's sole literary language and that the "simple" vernacular was merely a coarsened variant of it. Maksimov, in short, like Polikarpov, "did not accept the language reform of Peter I."[67]

But we cannot leave it at that. Polikarpov worked right through Peter's reign, after all, and at one of the institutions, the Moscow Press, that was in-   287 strumental in carrying out his cultural revolution. And the tension or struggle evident in his writings is nowhere more conspicuous than in his transla-tion—from Latin, not his beloved Greek—of Varenius's *Geographia Generalis,* which was printed at the Moscow Press, in the new civil type, in 1718 (Appen-dix I, no. 27). The translation had been undertaken and then revised on Pe-ter's direct orders "for the benefit of students and [ordinary] readers," for which reason, as Polikarpov explained in his translator's preface, the "high Slavonic" words and forms that he would have preferred to use in translating such a learned work had to be abandoned in favor of "simple Russian speech." The task also required, try as Polikarpov might to find Russian or Slavonic equivalents, the adoption mainly by simple transliteration of an extensive new technical vocabulary—that of the science of geography as it had devel-oped in Europe and particularly in Holland by the later seventeenth century. Polikarpov's rather reluctant compliance with the tsar's orders here, and the published outcome of his labors (a translation of some 650 large-format pages), were discussed in Chapter 5. Now I would emphasize that the struggle observable in this case was not only linguistic in nature but also, or more broadly, cultural. It was a struggle between the claims of the late Muscovite, Grecophile Church Slavonic culture in which Polikarpov had been nurtured as against those of the secular, scientific, and more cosmopolitan European culture that Peter was vigorously promoting—here with Polikarpov's help. Polikarpov himself eventually withdrew from the struggle, and lived out his career "correcting" church books for printing at the Moscow Press in tradi-tional Cyrillic types even as he worked to codify, by the best available stan-dards, Russian Church Slavonic. He recalls in this respect the proponents of the so-called Moscow Baroque in late seventeenth-century church architec-ture or those of the "Italianate" trend in contemporary Muscovite icon paint-ing, both of whom manifestly sought to reconcile in their works what they valued in their Greco-Muscovite (or Byzanto-Russian) religious heritage with what they found attractive in the new cultural forms emanating, however circuitously, from Renaissance and Baroque Europe.[68] And like those works of late Muscovite architecture and painting, Polikarpov's philological efforts would soon be marginalized, so far as elite Russian society was concerned, by the onslaught of the Petrine revolution.

The manuals compiled by Polikarpov and Maksimov were not the only such works undertaken in Peter's time to standardize and disseminate the rules of Russo-Slavonic grammar. Among the books compiled for the Russian market by Il'ia Kopievskii (Elias Kopijewitz) on commission from the tsar, as mentioned early in this chapter, was a *Manual of Slavonic Russian or Muscovite Grammar* (*Rukovedenie v grammatyku. Vo slavianorosiiskuiu ili Moskovskuiu* or, in its Latin title, *Manductio in Grammaticam. In Sclavonico Rosseanam seu Moscoviticam*), which was printed at Stoltzenberg, near Danzig, in 1706.[69] This manual consists of (1) a glossary of 144 everyday Russian (not Church Slavonic) words printed (as throughout) in traditional Cyrillic characters followed by Latin and German translations; (2) a list of 69 Russian verbs in the first person singular, again with Latin and German translations; (3) an alphabet of forty-two letters, with their names (transliterated) and, in parallel columns, their Latin literal or phonetic equivalents; (4) a list of common abbreviations and short expressions, some transliterated, all with Latin equivalents; (5) the grammar proper; and (6) a phrase book comprising standard greetings and simple dialogues, again with Latin and German equivalents—the German printed throughout in Gothic letters. The various sections of Kopievskii's manual were found by Professor Unbegaun to be alternately "interesting," "curious," and "extremely poor"; the grammar itself, a rather hapless mix of Russian and Belorussian words with Church Slavonic paradigms, patterns, and forms "plainly lifted from Smotrickij's grammar"; and the work as a whole, not a description of Russian or "Muscovite" at all but a grammar of sorts of a "modernized Church Slavonic."[70] No wonder, as was noted early in this chapter, that it had little impact on developments in Russia. Nevertheless the philological and political motives that gave rise to Kopievskii's manual should be stressed, intended as it plainly was to standardize for Russians their written language and to help both them and certain foreigners (German speakers/Latin readers) better understand each other. In these respects it recalls Ludolf's *Grammatica Russica* published at Oxford in 1696 (Chap. 1), which was a far more successful attempt to provide a grammatical description of and an introduction to the living Russian language but which also had little impact in Russia. Nor should I neglect to mention still other, never-published yet worthy efforts in the same vein undertaken by German scholars living and working in Petrine Russia—for example, by Pastor J. E. Glück (1652–1705)[71] or, in another case, by a Russian student of Pastor Glück, one Ivan Afanas'ev, who went on to serve in Russian diplomatic missions in Vienna and then London. There, in 1725, he compiled a *Grammatika russkago i nemetskago iazykov,* which was actually a Russian grammar with the corresponding German forms given in parallel columns and which Uspenskii characterizes as the first Russian grammar ever compiled by a Russian, albeit while living abroad. Uspenskii also suggests that this grammar exhibits a typically Petrine "western-European orientation," an orientation that was crucial, we might readily agree, in the standardization of modern Russian.[72]

289

The march toward linguistic normalization under Peter was lexicographical as well as grammatical, and Polikarpov once more is a leading figure. His *Leksikon treiazychnyi, sirech' Rechenii slavenskikh, ellinogrecheskikh i latinskikh sokrovishche. Iz razlichnykh drevnikh i novykh knig sobranoe. I po slavenskomu alfavit v chin razpolozhenoe (A Trilingual Dictionary, that is, A Treasury of Slavonic, Greek, and Latin vocables, gathered from various ancient and new [modern] books, and arranged in Slavonic alphabet[ical] order)* was published at the Moscow Press in 1704, a book of some 400 pages and the first dictionary ever printed in Russia (see Appendix I, no. 12).[73] In his prefatory remarks Polikarpov asserts the dignity and antiquity of "our Slavonic language," suggesting its comparability to Greek and Latin, and then offers, as was his wont, three reasons why this book was needed: because of the international importance of Slavonic; because of the flood of foreign words invading Slavonic in "both speech and books"; and because of the undoubted importance of both Greek and Latin, the first the source-language of Russia's church books, the second, the now universal language of "civil and scholarly matters," meaning "all the arts and sciences necessary for human life" as well as "military matters." In so many words did Polikarpov recognize the gathering force in Russia of cultural Europeanization under Peter I. He also says here that his dictionary had been presented for their review to the rector of the Moscow Slavonic-Greek-Latin Academy, to Metropolitan Stefan Iavorskii (the Kievan divine who was now acting head of the Russian church and, as such, in overall charge of the academy), and to the Likhudy brothers (his former Greek teachers); archival sources indicate, as well, that several clerks at the press had assisted him in compiling it and that the heads of two of Moscow's leading monasteries had also reviewed it—all evidence, in short, of the importance attached to the project by Moscow's learned clerical elite. At the same time, the thousands of entries printed in the dictionary in Cyrillic, Greek, and Latin faces, the Slavonic headword followed by its Greek and then Latin equivalent, are notable (1) for the large number of loanwords simply transliterated into Cyrillic; (2) for the numerous ecclesiastical terms in the list and the otherwise esoteric or "medieval" character of many of the remaining entries (for instance, *Alkhimia . . . alchymia, scientia docens facere aurum*); and (3) for the occasional appearance of the "simple vernacular" equivalent after the Slavonic headword *(Az, proste glagolema, ia)*, thus acknowledging the existence of two distinct languages in Russia. The *Trilingual Dictionary* of 1704, certainly a major monument of linguistic codification in Russia, advanced the cause of Russo-Church Slavonic, in other words, not of Russian as such. And as such it served the needs of the mostly clerical users of that language, not Tsar Peter's purely secular purposes.

Those purposes did animate, as we have seen, Kopievskii's publication in Amsterdam in 1699 and 1700 of his Latin-Russian glossary and his Russian-Latin-German and Russian-Latin-Dutch dictionaries, whose "Russian," again as noted early in this chapter, was actually a quite alien Slavonic. Nor did the Petrine urge to codify a usable Russian stop there. Well after Kopievskii himself had passed from the scene, his Russian-Latin-German *nomenklator* of 1700 was republished in St. Petersburg in 1718 and again in 1720, retitled— *Vokabuly ili rechi na slavenskom, nemetskom i latinskom iazykakh*—and rewritten, its mostly quotidian entries recast in a now markedly Russified Slavonic and supplemented by a list of Russian cities, including St. Petersburg, as well as a short grammar; 800 copies in all were printed and in the new civil type.[74] In the meantime, at Peter's urging the ubiquitous James Bruce undertook to compile a Russian-Dutch dictionary. Drawing on a contemporary Dutch-English dictionary published in Amsterdam, this *Kniga leksikon ili Sobranie rechei po Alfavitu s Rossiiskogo na Gollandskii iazyk (A Lexicon book or Collection of vocables in Alphabetical order from Russian into the Dutch language)* was printed in civil types at St. Petersburg in 1717, a small volume of 270 pages with the entries listed in parallel columns—Russian to the left, Dutch to the right—in Russian alphabetical order.[75] Here were hundreds of everyday Dutch words and basic technical (especially maritime) terms for which the lexicographer (Bruce and his helpers) provided Russian equivalents, sometimes readily, at other times by means of literal or semantic calques, the latter often amounting in effect to a definition (Appendix I, no. 26). Whatever its value as a source for studying the verbal culture of the day— a question scholars have contested[76]—this Russian-Dutch dictionary of 1717 does offer proof of the Petrine effort to normalize Russian by contemporary European, here Dutch, lexical criteria. So do the various glossaries and word lists included in the grammar books that we discussed above, as do, of course, the purely lexicographical projects carried out in Peter's time that were never published.[77] The latter include a *Leksikon vokabulam novym* which Peter edited himself but which was only printed in 1910 (see Smirnov, Appendix II, Works Cited).

The Petrine campaign to standardize Russian by means of dictionaries and grammar books reached a culmination of sorts in 1731. In that year the St. Petersburg Academy of Sciences published a *Teutsch-Lateinisch-und Russisches Lexicon/Nemetsko-latinskii i ruskii Leksikon (German-Latin-Russian Dictionary)* to which were appended certain *Anfangs-Gründen der Russischen Sprache/S pervymi nachalami ruskago iazyka (Basic Principles of the Russian Language)*, the latter filling some forty-five separately numbered pages and constituting a concise grammar of Russian written in German with the Russian examples printed, of course, in the civil type (Appendix I, no. 38).[78] The German-Latin part of the dictionary—the German headwords followed by their Latin equivalents—was based on the *Lexicon Latino-Germanicum* compiled by Erich (Ehrenreich, Ericus) Weismann (Weissmann) and published at Stuttgart in 1674,[79] as the translators themselves in effect tell us in their brief preface: "Herewith Benevolent Reader we offer you the whole of Weismann's German-Latin Dictionary translated into the Russian language [*Nyne sovershenno predlagaem Vam Dobrokhotnyi Chitateliu na Ruskii iazyk perevedennyi Veismannov Nemetsko-Latinskii Leksikon*]." This dictionary had been selected, they added, because its many German words were already translated into Latin, for which they could then provide Russian equivalents—*Ruskikh slov i rechei*—having themselves only an imperfect knowledge of German. They also begged readers not to judge their effort—"the first in this language"—too harshly, citing in their defense the *Dictionaire de l'Académie Françoise*, which had been compiled, they asserted, over a period of forty years yet still contained errors. The comparison itself, one cannot help noticing, is remarkable; it is the first reference to a European vernacular dictionary to be found in a Russian lexicographical source. The translators have since been identified—I. I. Il'inskii, I. S. Gorlitskii, I. P. Saratov[80]—and one of the three, Gorlitskii, has been further named as the compiler of a short (sixty-four octavo pages) Russian-French grammar plus dictionary intended "to facilitate commerce" that was published by the Academy Press in 1730.[81] It was probably Gorlitskii who invoked the French academy's dictionary in the preface to the St. Petersburg edition of Weismann's *Lexicon*, which he and his academy colleagues had begun to compile in 1728.

As for the grammar appended to the St. Petersburg Weismann, which was similarly intended primarily for German speakers, its author has been identified as V. E. Adodurov, the first Russian to hold a professional position *(ad"iunkt)* at the St. Petersburg Academy of Sciences (Chap. 5) and another largely unsung hero of the Petrine revolution. His grammar followed the Smotritskii model (itself patterned on Latin and Greek models) in technical terminology and arrangement of material, to be sure, but eliminated at the same time many Church Slavonic forms while adducing numerous vernacular Russian examples, in both respects going even further than Ludolf's *Grammatica Russica* of 1696. In fact, Unbegaun concludes that it was Adodurov's intention "to write a grammar of Russian, not of Church Slavonic," observing that "whenever he mentions the latter, it is usually in a context of warning or censure. . . . [T]he language recommended by Adodurov may be described as the colloquial Russian of educated society of the day."[82] There is more. It turns out that Adodurov's appendix to the Weismann was indeed part of a larger grammar that he wrote, in Russian, sometime around 1730. This discovery was made by Professor Uspenskii, whose reconstruction of Adodurov's long-lost original, based on a sizable fragment preserved in manuscript, shows that Adodurov was fully aware of the difference between Russian and Church Slavonic and that he advanced an orthographic reform even more radical than that inaugurated by Peter I some twenty years before. Uspenskii thus describes Adodurov together with Trediakovskii and Tatishchev as the "first native Russianists." These three men were the leading representatives, as Uspenskii sums it up, of a period in the history of the language that was "closely linked with the Petrine alphabetic reform and in general with the ideology of the Petrine era," a period that was marked by its "radical program" of delimiting the spheres, respectively, of Church Slavonic and Russian, by its "struggle for the emancipation" of the latter from the former, and by "its orientation to the western-European linguistic situation." This "process of emancipation of the Russian literary language," Uspenskii emphasizes, "properly began with the creation [under Peter] of the new norms of Russian civil spelling."[83]

Adodurov's grammar of 1730–31 was used in turn by Lomonosov, another early *ad"iunkt* and translator at the St. Petersburg academy, when compiling his famous *Russian Grammar (Rossiiskaia grammatika)* of 1755 (Appendix I, no. 40), which again drew, for terminology and formal structure, on Smotritskii. But Lomonosov sought for a change to *integrate* Church Slavonic with educated spoken Russian in defining the literary standard (rather than to reject one in favor of the other), and mainly by assigning them different stylistic functions. The one "Russian language *[Rossiiskii iazyk]*" was unique "among all in Europe" precisely for its very capaciousness *(prostranstvom)*, he averred, and was divisible into three main *dialekty*—the Muscovite, the Northern, and the Ukrainian—among which the Muscovite, "not only for the importance of the capital city, but for its superior beauty," was "rightly preferred over the others."[84] Church Slavonic had assimilated the riches of ancient Greek, Lomonosov proposed further, here as in other of his philological works, and so a preponderance of Church Slavonic words, not ordinarily used but still understood by educated Russians, was appropriate for heroic poems, odes, and solemn orations written in a "high style." Plays, letters, eclogues, satires, and such were to be composed, on this view, in a "middle style" combining assimilated Slavonicisms with purely vernacular terms, leaving comedies, humorous epigrams, burlesques, and the like to be written in a "low style" Russian comprised mostly of vernacular words. It was a remarkably commonsensical solution to the long-standing language question in Russia and one that was impelled, as Lomonosov clearly understood, by the imperatives of the Petrine revolution: his veneration of the first emperor, hero of his boyhood, was a constant theme of his own literary efforts.[85] Lomonosov's *Rossiiskaia grammatika,* first printed at the St. Petersburg Academy Press in 1755 in the civil type (cf. Fig. 12), went through five more editions between then and 1799,[86] and is generally recognized as at once the "major achievement of Russian eighteenth-century linguistics" and the first fully systematized attempt at "the codification of the Russian literary language."[87]

The St. Petersburg edition of Weismann's *Lexicon,* with Adodurov's grammar appended to it, was printed at the Academy Press in 1731 in an edition of 2,500—a very large run for the time—and reprinted in 1782 (1,240 copies) and again in 1799. It was also enormous in size, a work of some 800 to 1,000 pages listing approximately 20,000 German headwords, that number again of Latin equivalents, and several times that number of suggested Russian equivalents.[88] Its decisive early role accordingly in standardizing the Russian lexicon has long been recognized by scholars, including various of the authorities cited in Appendix II, most notably the compilers of the seventeen-volume dictionary published by the Academy of Sciences between 1950 and 1965, which remains the most authoritative as well as the most comprehensive dictionary of the Russian language published to date.[89] The St. Petersburg edition of Weismann's *Lexicon* thus stands as an enduring tribute to the lexicographical and grammatical as well as the more general lexical impact of the Petrine revolution.

Russian after Peter

It was suggested near the end of Chapter 1 that Peter's language program, powered of course by his regime's political ambitions, did not fully resolve the linguistic "chaos" or crisis that he had inherited along with his throne and that some of his own policies initially exacerbated. For several decades after Peter's death in 1725, as we have seen, literate Russians continued to debate the expressive or pragmatic merits of Church Slavonic versus a more vernacular

глава I,

О АЗБУКѢ РОССІЙСКОЙ.

§ 84.

Россійская азбука тритцать буквъ обще употребительныхъ имѣетъ, которыхъ начертанія и имена суть слѣдующія:

а,	азъ,	К,	како,
б,	буки,	Л,	люди.
В,	вѣди,	М,	мыслѣте.
Г,	глаголь.	Н,	нашъ.
Д,	добро,	О,	онъ,
е,	есть,	П,	покой.
Ж,	живѣте,	Р,	рцы,
З,	земля,	С,	слово,
И,	иже,	Ш,	твердо.
У,	у	Ъ,	еръ,
Ф,	фертъ,	Ы,	еры,
Х,	хѣръ,	Ь,	ерь,
Ц,	цы,	Ѣ,	ять,
Ч,	червъ;	Ю,	ю,
Ш,	ша,	Я,	я,.

§ 85. I, Щ, Э. ю, хотя въ Россійскомъ письмѣ употребляются; однако въ азбуку свойственно приняты быть и на ряду чи-слиться не должны. для слѣдующихъ причинъ.

Figure 12   Lomonosov's "Russian alphabet [*Rossiiskaia azbuka*]," as printed in M. V. Lomonosov, *Rossiiskaia grammatika* (St. Petersburg, 1755). Lomonosov stipulates that "the Russian alphabet as generally used has thirty letters," which he lists, and then notes that four more letters were also used but did not properly belong in the alphabet as such, as they were variants of other letters. Subsequent standardization elevated all four letters (Й, Щ, Э, and Ё) to the alphabet proper, and eliminated one that Lomonosov included (the *iat'* = Ѣ).

Russian, to conduct literary experiments in either or both following western European, usually French, models, and to take steps to codify one or the other as the written standard for Russia. But the debate was conducted entirely on the terms laid down under Peter, which meant that it was lopsided in favor of Russian over Slavonic from the start.[90] There would be no reverting to the "polyglossia" that had characterized the linguistic situation in late Muscovite Russia, the Russia of Peter's childhood and youth, also as discussed in Chapter 1. The way forward was set.

In fact, it could be said that in the decades immediately after Peter's death Russians first fully experienced the kind of diglossia known in the Europe of the Latin dispensation since the Renaissance. Works primarily of religious content but also of a more purely literary or philosophical significance continued to be written in a high or standard Church Slavonic, while scientific and technical but also philosophical and literary works as well as most official (nonecclesiastical) publications were written in a Russian that was more or less close to contemporary educated Russian speech and whose use was coming to be viewed as a "definer of nobility."[91] The Church Slavonic in question was a direct continuation of the literary language codified in the East Slavic lands in the sixteenth and seventeenth centuries, a language only lightly touched by Russian usages and the lexical invasion of Petrine times. The new written Russian, in turn, was a continuation at base and in varying combinations of the hybrid Slavonic and chancery Russian of the late Muscovite period.[92] It was a language largely shorn of bureaucratic formalisms and the learned grammatical devices of standard Slavonic (notably, its use of simple preterites, participles as gerunds, a vocative case, and the independent dative) along with the latter's excess letters and profusion of diacritics, contractions, and other scribal conceits. In the hands of writers like Trediakovskii, Antiokh Kantemir, Tatishchev, Lomonosov, Sumarokov, and others this new literary Russian made free with the innumerable European loanwords that continued to expand the lexicon while freely adopting contemporary European literary forms (such as the ode, the epic, the novel, new forms of drama, the civilities of courtly European discourse), which practices inevitably influenced both morphology and syntax.[93] So did the burgeoning work of translating all manner of European technical, scientific, and fine literature into this new Russian, work that through the 1770s remained concentrated at the St. Petersburg Academy of Sciences, where, to quote an instruction of 1734, translators were to "strive for the perfection of the Russian language." There too the project of codifying the grammar of Russian with an eye to Latin, German, and French as well as Slavonic and Greek models continued apace, as did the academy's similarly modeled lexicographical labors.[94] Both tasks eventually were assumed by the Russian Academy *(Rossiiskaia Akademiia)* founded for this purpose in St. Petersburg (1783) by Catherine II; the new academy also assumed responsibility for the huge program of literary translations especially from English and French that she had inaugurated in 1768.[95]

The linguistic activities of the St. Petersburg Academy of Sciences and then also of the Russian Academy, perpetuating Petrine initiatives, ensured the rapid demise of Church Slavonic as the literary language of Russia and its replacement, except in liturgical and other church publications, by the new Russian. All of the leading Russian writers mentioned above were affiliated at one time or another with the Academy of Sciences, whose press was far and away the leading publisher of works of secular content in eighteenth-century Russia.[96] This number included most of the grammar books and dictionaries compiled in the decades after Peter's death, most notably Lomonosov's *Rossiiskaia grammatika* first published in 1755 and successive editions of the Russian edition of Weismann's *Lexicon* of 1731. In addition to these standard linguistic works of the eighteenth century we should note the publication in 1771 by the newly founded Moscow University Press of A. A. Barsov's *Kratkiia pravila rossiiskoi grammatiki,* which was based on the Adodurov and Lomonosov grammars and went through eight editions to 1802,[97] and the *Slovar' Akademii rossiiskoi,* which was first published in six volumes by the Russian Academy between 1789 and 1794. This dictionary, the flower of the Russian Academy's labors (a second edition was published in the years 1806 to 1822, well before the academy's demise in 1841), embodies in its way that eighteenth-century "synthesis" of Church Slavonic and Russian in a single "Slavonic-Russian *[Slavenorossiiskii]*" language that marked another major step forward in the "normalization" of modern literary Russian.[98] But its Slavonic bias is clear from the outset, perhaps a reflection of the fact that among the Russian Academy's members when it was first published clerics outnumbered secular writers and scholars by as many as two to one (the rest, including the president, Princess E. R. Dashkova, were court favorites).[99] As the preface to their *Dictionary* makes plain, the academy clung to the notion that Russian or "the language of the Russian people *[narod Rossiiskii]*" derived from the ancient Slavonic tongue (like French or Italian from Latin), although it "indisputably has changed and is changing more than Slavonic" owing to the influx of numerous scientific, artistic, commercial, industrial, military, and "civil" terms "unknown to our forbears." At the same time, in devising the criteria to guide them in compiling their *Dictionary* the Russian Academy deliberately excluded "words and locutions of the Sciences and Arts which are not in general use but known only to scholars and artists." They also excluded "all foreign words introduced without need" as well as all improper words *(blagopristoinosti protivniia)* and "all localisms *[oblastnyia slova],* except those which by their clarity, strength, and beauty can serve to enrich the language."[100] Most of the more than 43,000 words entered in this dictionary, accordingly, are "Church Slavic or Russian coined on the Church Slavic pattern," as one student has cautioned: "The spoken language and loanwords are poorly represented." Yet the Russian Academy's *Slovar'* of 1789–1794, as Stankiewicz goes on to say, was also "a theoretically arranged, normative dictionary; the first to base Russian lexicography on scientific principles."[101] And as such it is the first chronologically of the standard Russian dictionaries cited in Appendix II.

297

The "process of emancipation of the Russian literary language" from the norms of Church Slavonic, Professor Uspenskii was quoted earlier as saying, "properly begins with the creation of the new norms of Russian civil spelling," a view that another leading Russianist has in effect also taken.[102] That act was ordered, as we know, by Peter I in connection with his urgent need for appropriately printed translations of technical works originally published in Latin, German, or Dutch and was carried out, as recounted in the first section of this chapter, between 1708 and 1710. Peter's alphabetic and related typographical reform, it perhaps bears repeating, was threefold in character. The total number of letters was reduced, making the alphabet more representative of actual Russian speech (subsequent adjustments were made, on the recommendation of the St. Petersburg Academy of Sciences, in 1735, 1738, 1758, 1797, and 1918); the graph-shapes of the reduced alphabet were made more conformable to, at times identical with, the relatively simple and easily legible letters used in contemporary Europe; and the use of ligatures, abbreviations, contractions, diacritics, accents, and other supralineal marks was almost entirely, if in some cases only gradually, eliminated. Nor were the letters of this new "civil" alphabet assigned numerical values, an obvious signal that the Arabic or general European numbering system was to be used in conjunction with it. The resultant letters and numbers and related printing fonts thereby greatly facilitated, as clearly they were intended to do, the implementation of Peter's rapidly expanding publishing program. And the latter in turn entailed the full implantation in Russia of the European print revolution—itself a necessary condition, as experience all over Europe had shown (or soon would show), for the establishment of a national literary language. At the same time, by Peter's decree, evidently yielding in this to the views of respected Muscovite and Ruthenian traditionalists, the relatively elaborate traditional Cyrillic alphabet and related fonts complete with Slavonic numerals were retained in all their ornateness for the printing of all "church books," which continued to be written in Church Slavonic (as it now began to be called) and to be published under the tight supervision, after 1721, of the Holy Synod.[103] Substantially more copies of such titles, of catechisms and service books in particular, were printed and distributed in Russia in the decades after Peter's death, it seems; but in the volume and variety of titles published in the new civil rather than the traditional Cyrillic type after 1710, there was no contest. Existing inventories of eighteenth-century Russian book publication indicate that while some 1,500 titles including separate editions were printed in traditional Cyrillic types, the total number printed in civil types was about 10,000, a nearly seven-to-one preponderance.[104]

Russian translations from the major European languages continued to make up the bulk of the secular titles—the technical, scientific, literary, and philosophical works—published in the civil type in the decades after Peter's death, it is true, just as the bulk of these books continued to be published by one press, that of the St. Petersburg Academy of Sciences.[105] But right from the debut of the civil type under Peter this secular list included original works in Russian along with more or less extensively adapted translations. The former included, just in Peter's own time, all the major "regulations" of his bureaucratic revolution with the partial exception of that reforming the church (written in a still heavily Slavonicized Russian and printed in traditional Cyrillic), particularly the *General Regulation* of 1720, his *Military Statute* of 1716, and *Naval Statute* of 1720. It also included the first mathematical textbook ever printed in Russia and the first manual on statistics and mechanics, both original compilations from standard European sources; the first etiquette book, *The Honorable Mirror of Youth* of 1717; Konon Zotov's sailing manual of 1724, which was identified (Chap. 2) as the first guidebook for naval officers written in Russian by a Russian and printed in Russia; Shafirov's lengthy legal-historical defense of the Russian cause in the Northern War, the *Razsuzhdenie* of 1717, hailed as the first Russian work on international law (Chap. 4); and Prokopovich's articulation of the new Russian doctrine of absolute monarchy, the *Pravda voli monarshei* of 1722, which was printed in civil types both then and in 1726 although its language was still, given its author, as much Slavonic as Russian. All of these original Russian texts of the Petrine years, and more, were contextualized in the preceding chapters of this volume. And to them may be added the roughly 1,000 other lesser or occasional works of secular content, translations or originals, manuals, decrees, and treatises, printed in the civil type in Peter's time; not to mention the countless other secular writings—other decrees, letters, journals, book drafts, and so on—that remained in manuscript, some of which, like the historical works mentioned in Chapter 5, were printed later in the eighteenth century and went on to considerable, if sometimes quite belated, posthumous fame.

But it was not only the volume and variety of secular titles published in the new civil type under Peter that gave such a boost to the development of the new secular or "civil" Russian language against the time-honored claims of Church Slavonic. It was also, as we have had ample occasion to observe, Peter's insistence that all such translations or original works be written in a plain style, one readily accessible not only to the learned clerical elite of the day but also to the intended readership of military and naval officers and their students, diplomats, technocrats, and civil administrators, aspiring new-style courtiers both male and female, natural scientists and other purely secular scholars, artists and skilled craftsmen: the several thousand individuals we have identified as the initial Petrine *publika*. Nor could I fail to emphasize again the massive lexical influx that all of this new writing entailed, an influx for which, apparently, suitable equivalents in Russian or Church Slavonic could usually not be found. As was seen so often in the preceding chapters, simple transliteration with some phonetic-orthographic and/or morphological adaption became the rule, the resultant neologisms sometimes supplanted, following the age-old practice, by literal or semantic calques, but normally not.[106] The outcome was an enormous expansion of the *secular* Russian lexicon, an achievement that is inseparable in its impact on linguistic developments in Russia from Peter's creation of the civil type and promotion of a plain style.

This last point seems to be contested by Zhivov, a leading student of the "Petrine language reform *[petrovskaia reforma iazyka]*," who in his most comprehensive work to date on the subject at one point scores the "illegitimacy *[nepravomernost']*" of considering the "borrowings from western European languages assimilated in the Petrine era in extraordinarily large numbers" as the "basic" or "most important" aspect of the larger linguistic history of the period. But it turns out that Zhivov's apparent discounting of the lexical aspect of the Petrine reform is intended to move us from the narrowly focused linguistic approach and quantitative emphasis of the lexical historians (he mentions the works cited in Appendix II by Christiani, Smirnov, Birzhakova et al., and Otten) onto a higher, semiotic plane. In his own terms,

The wide adoption of loanwords in the Petrine era was closely connected with intensive development in the various spheres of science, economy, state and military organization, culture; and the impression forms that the lexical borrowings of the Petrine era were motivated for the most part by the borrowing of new things and concepts *[poniatii]*. This pragmatic factor unquestionably played a definite role in the process of borrowing but it was not the only one and, possibly, not the most important. The borrowings emerge as above all proof of a new cultural orientation, that is, they fulfilled in the first instance not a pragmatic but a semiotic function. . . .

—a function Zhivov later defines as the adoption of a "new system of values."[107] We might heartily agree with this conclusion, while prefering the rather more capacious, typically historical way of grounding it that has been followed here.

Under the combined weight of official pressure and literate Russian practice, the Slavonic-Russian diglossia characteristic of the linguistic situation in Russia during the decades after Peter's death steadily waned in favor of a single written standard, one eventually to be known as modern literary Russian and ranked as a major world language. Linguists generally consider that the process of "stabilizing" this language was completed early in the nineteenth century, with any dialectisms, specialized jargons, or stylistic variations appearing thereafter to be viewed as so many deviations from the standard. Canonization of a modern Russian literature proceeded concurrently, indeed symbiotically, as it had elsewhere in Europe, with the writings of the "best authors" being quarried for instructive examples by rhetoricians and literary critics as well as by the grammarians and lexicographers. And the orations of Peter's favorite cleric, Feofan Prokopovich, as noted in Chapter 5, soon came to mark the beginnings, however tentative, of the canon.[108]

To be sure, two "parallel language systems," sometimes interacting, sometimes colliding, continued to coexist in Russia until 1917, if not later, however much that fact may have been officially ignored during the Soviet era.[109] Not only did most church books continue to be written in Slavonic and printed in traditional Cyrillic types, but most Orthodox Russians—most Russians— knew some Church Slavonic from an early age. They learned their prayers in Church Slavonic and often, in its traditional Cyrillic letter-shapes, began to learn their alphabet. Throughout their lives they heard the church services spoken or sung in Church Slavonic (compare the persistence of Church Latin among the contemporary Roman Catholics of Europe and the Americas). Church Slavonic continued to be used in their prayers by the millions of "Old Believers" (or Old Ritualists) who began to separate themselves from the official Russian church in the later seventeenth century. Yet to the historian if not to the philologist these are all linguistic residues of a distant, pre-Petrine past, one that is as unlikely to be revived in Russia as is that of Latin in the West. Russians owe this solution to their language question above all to Peter the Great.

7

CONCLUSION

The Petrine Revolution in Russia

This study of the cultural revolution launched by Peter I in Russia began with architecture—setting the stage, I called it in my book on the subject. There it was shown how architecture in the European Renaissance tradition along with contemporary European practices in fortification and shipbuilding were implanted in Russia following a massive injection of European expertise and how, in consequence, the modern Russian built world came into being. It was also shown, drawing on extensive visual as well as verbal sources, how this architectural revolution went through several distinct yet interrelated stages. A crisis was precipitated in late Muscovite architecture by the haphazard encroachment on patrons and builders of the new architectural norms emanating from Europe, which had arrived chiefly via the work of immigrant Ruthenian craftsmen and the use made by native masters of the European architectural prints that happened to come their way. The crisis was unfolding even as Peter assumed power, and was accelerated by the wholesale conversion of members of the topmost Russian elite, including the young tsar himself, to building in the new style, a style that may generally be dubbed the northern European Baroque. A huge flurry of such building ensued in Russia, most notably in and around St. Petersburg, a whole new capital city built almost entirely in the new style. The architectural revolution that St. Petersburg thus embodied was then institutionalized in various ways, most conspicuously by the foundation in the new capital under Peter's daughter Empress Elizabeth, consciously following paternal initiatives, of the Imperial Academy of Fine Arts (1757). Catherine II endowed her revered predecessors' academy with a magnificent home—still standing—designed in the then current Neo-classical style (1764–1788). And through its training, publications, exhibitions, prizes, and innumerable building commissions the St. Petersburg Academy of Fine Arts fully certified Russia's place in the European architectural mainstream.[1]

Crisis, conversion, institutionalization: actions by Peter I and his associates at first exacerbated the crisis looming in late Muscovite architecture, by favoring the new over the old, and then resolved it, by institutionalizing in Russia their wholehearted conversion to contemporary European building practices and norms. These were more or less radically different from traditional Muscovite architectural ways, my first volume labored to show, the latter considered "medieval" in technique by the standards of the former and in style, "coarse and deformed to the utmost degree." This judgment was pronounced by the famous eulogist Bernard Fontenelle, in his memorial of Peter I delivered to the Paris Academy of Sciences in 1725, where he went on to declare that the recently dead tsar-emperor had "caused architecture to be born in his country."[2] This was only the most dramatic expression of an assessment that was common among Europeans familiar with the Russian scene and, more important, one that had come to be shared by Russia's core elite.

The Petrine revolution in Russian architecture was thus a top-down "revolution by decree," to be sure, but a revolution nonetheless: "a process whereby the values and techniques of contemporary European architecture were deliberately brought to Russia, there to be so firmly implanted in the first decades of the eighteenth century that they determined the subsequent course of Russian architectural history." In fact,

> ordinary domestic housing, parks and gardens, warehouses and wharves all came within the revolution's purview as did churches and palaces, official buildings of every variety, fortresses and other military structures, and ships—overwhelmingly naval ships—of every known kind. The Petrine architectural revolution was responsible for bringing to Russia everything from the idea of large-scale and detailed town planning to the art of applying plaster and alabaster modeling in the interior decoration of buildings. Scarcely any building or ensemble of buildings of any social importance would ever again be the same.

Nor was it only a matter of cities and towns, or of architecture at the upper levels of society. In due course Peter's revolution reached into the villages of the vast Russian hinterland, where succeeding Imperial regimes, pursuant to his decree of August 1722, required that houses should be built in standard sizes following new-style designs and should face forward in a straight line flush with a would-be street, thereby supplanting the semisubmerged huts and random "circular plan" of the traditional Russian settlement. Initially a matter of necessity with respect to fortification and shipbuilding (still considered coeval branches of architecture) but essentially one of taste with regard to "civil" construction, the revolution affected every aspect of the building art in Russia as well as every element of the built environment, sooner or later imbuing it with a more or less European—or modern—appearance. After Peter, in sum, every major advance in European, soon world architecture would be immediately reflected in Russia, where fully realized variants of the successive international styles—Baroque, Neoclassical, Empire, Romantic, Modernist—were promptly produced and related technical innovations readily absorbed.[3]

The Petrine revolution in Russian architecture was also, I suggested in that earlier volume, part of a wider process, at once political and economic as well as cultural, whereby the Muscovy of Peter's fathers was transformed into the Empire of his successors. The suggestion was pursued in my companion volume on concurrent developments in the other visual arts, or the Petrine revolution in Russian imagery as I called it there, "imagery" understood to include any visual representation of persons or things, pictorial or figurative (or symbolic), as painted, drawn, etched, engraved, sewn, or otherwise rendered on a flat surface or as sculpted in stone, bronze, wood, ivory, or other material. Imagery in the Renaissance tradition, characterized, I proposed, rehearsing the standard scholarship, by its three-dimensional naturalism (or realism), had flooded Europe in one form or another by the end of the seventeenth century, when Peter and dozens, then hundreds of his subjects came visiting for months, then years at a time. This newly prolific imagery, executed in what art scholars name Renaissance or Mannerist or Baroque styles and displayed in religious, civic, palatial, and domestic settings, included painted or engraved portraits and landscapes, religious and mythical representations, still lifes and genre scenes, marine, battle, and history pictures, sculpted busts, tomb effigies, equestrian and other statues in the round, newly accurate charts and maps, new-style medals and flags, coins, seals, and coats of arms. These pictures, sculptures, and official insignia ranged in size from the miniature to the monumental, were portable or permanently affixed, and were created and sold everywhere, particularly in such major European cultural centers as Rome, Venice, Paris, London, Antwerp, and Amsterdam. But by the late seventeenth century scarcely any of this enormous efflorescence of imagery had yet reached Russia, where the closely connected print revolution had barely arrived and where such images as existed, principally icons or holy pictures painted in egg tempera on wood panels in the age-old Byzantine tradition, had been sacralized to a degree unrivaled in the Christian world, thus fortifying resistance to any intrusion of the new.[4]

304

Yet intrude the new imagery certainly did, mainly by means of illustrated Bibles and individual prints published in Europe which, like the architectural representations referred to above, had made their way to Russia mainly in the baggage of Dutch, German, and English merchants. There they found a ready reception among local patrons and artists impressed by their fineness and naturalism, and demand particularly for portraits sharply rose, a demand bolstered by the portraiture seen by visiting Russian dignitaries in noble houses in neighboring Poland. A crisis of visual taste and outlook was thereby provoked that paralleled in its way the contemporaneous crisis in architecture. Indeed the two were at some points interconnected, as paintings and sculptures executed in the new "Italianate" style by foreign masters or their native epigones adorned the interiors of the palaces and churches erected in and around Moscow in the 1680s and 1690s in the transitional "Moscow Baroque" style, all to the utter dismay of Muscovite traditionalists. Meanwhile Peter and his close associates again underwent a wholesale conversion, this time to imagery in the new style, whose production and dissemination in Russia, they clearly understood, would vastly expand the ruler's capacity for advertising his policies and projecting his power. The dynamics of this conversion along with details of the transmission to Russia of the new imagery and its subsequent institutionalization and industrialization there were then recounted in my second volume, where a definition of "cultural revolution" was also offered.[5] Such a broadly serviceable formulation has not been found elsewhere in the historical literature, and so it was repeated above (Chap. 1). As readers will recall, it refers to changes in culture that were consciously intended, at least by an active minority; that happened relatively suddenly, making the postrevolutionary stage readily distinguishable from the prerevolutionary one; that were recognized as such by contemporaries; and that produced transformations which were lasting.[6] The volume concluded by asserting that in accordance with these criteria the case for the revolutionary character of Peter's rapid and intensive Europeanization of Russian imagery had been amply made.

So much for the scenery, costumes, and props left by Peter to fill the stage of the new Russia built by his architectural revolution. In this book, to complete the metaphor, we turned to the scripts to be spoken or read by the actors destined to tread that stage. And here the importance of context, indeed of what have been referred to as the constitutive relations between text and context (Chap. 1), became especially apparent, starting with Russia's nautical turn under Peter and the numerous texts, particularly the *Naval Statute* of 1720, that it generated: their translation, adaptation, or original composition in Russian, and subsequent publication, often in successive editions, steadily moved the great turn forward, movement that the texts themselves reflect (Chap. 2). Much the same can be said about the numerous texts that encoded Peter's program of military modernization (Chap. 3): production of the former impelled implementation of the latter, and vice versa. Similarly the regulations and justifications registering for all to read, historians as well as contemporaries, Peter's bureaucratic revolution (Chap. 4). In each of these chapters the reciprocal relationship between text and historical context, like that between contemporary actors and later students, was at least adumbrated, if not established. Such relationships also subsisted, and continue to subsist, between the scientific and literary texts discussed in Chapter 5 and their corresponding circles of readers and writers, if somewhat less dramatically so: an army and a navy were not being remodeled or created here nor a new apparatus of government, all of which naturally required much more vigorous state intervention in the public sphere than did adoption of current European literary norms or aspects of the new natural sciences. Yet even then the contemporary European moral, political, and diplomatic rhetoric adapted to their needs by agents of the tsar-emperor and published in theoretical and historical tracts or in orations and practical guidebooks clearly aided the production of new or recast power relations: namely, those of absolute monarchy at home and, abroad, of Russian membership in the European state system (Chaps. 4, 5). At the same time, the transactions required to invent the St. Petersburg Academy of Sciences, an extension at one level of analysis of Peter's bureaucratic revolution, document with considerable precision the verbal impact of these same procedures, an impact that the academy itself enormously augmented once it opened its doors (Chaps. 5, 6). Here again the revolutionary political context created by the sudden intervention of royal power in ever more sectors of public life engendered revolutionary texts, which promoted in turn an expanding cultural revolution that was verbal at its core even more than it was visual.

The last assertion rests on the perhaps problematic notion that language is the core of any human culture worthy of the name, with its corollary that a standardized literary language is the core of any advanced, or literate, culture. The notion is made somewhat more problematic here by the fact that if

305

we were to consider *all* Russians of Peter's time, all speakers of the Muscovite *koiné*, inhabitants of a single linguistic community, the culture thereby evoked would have to be described as an overwhelmingly illiterate, or oral, one; even elite Petrine writing retained, as we have noted, a sizable oral residue (Chaps. 1, 6). Moreover the coexistence of distinct if more or less closely related literate and nonliterate verbal cultures, not to mention major regional, class, and other variations within them, would persist in Russia well into the twentieth century[7]—longer than in western European countries or the United States, it seems, where the faster spread of literacy and the earlier establishment of national school systems would blend them that much sooner into a single national tongue. But I have refrained in this volume from letting the story balloon in this way, preferring to focus on the crucial first stage in the constitution of a modern verbal culture in Russia, one that is defined, necessarily, by its codification in a standard written language. That crucial first stage was the Petrine verbal revolution—the verbal aspect, indeed the core, of Peter's cultural revolution.

The coexistence in Imperial Russia—in Russia of the eighteenth and nineteenth centuries—of distinct if interrelated verbal cultures, literate and oral, the one as codified in a standard literary Russian, the other as spoken in a regionally and socially variable patois, was paralleled by the concurrent coexistence of elite (official-noble) and vernacular architectures and by that of elite and popular systems of imagery—with the cult art and architecture of the Russian Orthodox church and its Old Believer or dissident offshoots serving in some ways as intermediaries. Indeed the parallels, on rereading my earlier volumes, are striking, and are surely not coincidental. Those volumes independently adduced visual and verbal evidence of concurrent, at some points interconnected crises in late Muscovite architecture and image-making just as the present volume, on reviewing late Muscovite written texts and the related scholarship, has identified a contemporaneous crisis in the late Muscovite linguistic situation.[8] The evidence further demonstrates that the crisis in each instance was precipitated by the increasing encroachment on Muscovite traditions of contemporary European cultural practices and norms, these as conveyed by the various European diplomats, soldiers, clerics, artists, medics, and commercial agents active in late Muscovite Russia and by the European prints and books that happened to circulate there. Before Peter's active reign the presence of such persons in Muscovy and the circulation of such materials were strictly controlled by the tsar's government for religious as well as political reasons. Particularly in the case of imagery did the protectors of Orthodoxy abhor the infection of holy pictures by "Italianate" naturalism, while the sculpted figures of saints and angels and the crucified Christ adorning churches of the Moscow Baroque were viewed by them as nothing short of idolatry. But with Tsar Peter in power a tentative conversion to the new values evident in elite imagery and architecture from the 1680s on became, from the late 1690s, a determined effort to implant these values in Russia, an effort that progressively confined traditional practices and norms in building and im-age-making to the suddenly shrinking spheres of religion and the church—shrinking for this as well as other reasons in the universal process known as secularization (Chap. 1). Yet even here, even in the cult art and architecture of Imperial Russia, the naturalism and the classicism of the new art and archi-tecture made striking inroads. More important now, the forceful introduction and institutionalization or industrialization of the new values in building and image-making, together with Peter's creation of a navy, modernization of the army, restructuring of the government, and introduction of the new science and literature, had a massive impact on the language of Russians, an impact that is most obviously reflected in the lexical evidence surviving from the Petrine era. The main task of this volume has been to adduce, contextualize, and index large samples of this lexical and related verbal evidence by way of documenting this impact—an impact that again entailed a form of secular-ization, in this case, the literary marginalization of the traditional language of the church.

Peter's linguistic initiatives, like those in architecture and imagery, soon took on a life of their own, as this volume has also tried to show. The new knowledges needed to effect his naval, military, and bureaucratic programs were institutionalized via the translation and publication of handbooks, text-books, and treatises, by the introduction accordingly of a more suitable "civil" type and the establishment of new printing presses, by the foundation of pri-mary and specialized secondary schools, by the creation of the St. Petersburg Academy of Sciences, and by the compilation of grammars and dictionaries of the new Russian language that was thus being constructed. It was the Rus-sian spoken by the Petrine elite, or at least by its better-educated members (at least on suitable occasions), a class I defined as the decisively influential sector of the aggregated landholders, officials, clergy, merchants, and their respective families and friends who together made up the top 3 or 4 percent of the total Russian population. This innermost or core elite included the monarch and his or her family (after Peter, thanks in large measure to his succession law of 1722, women reigned in Russia for sixty-six of the remaining seventy-five years of the eighteenth century), the senior military, naval, and civil officers together with the largest landholders (often one and the same), some of the senior clergy, and the top merchants and industrial entrepreneurs: at most several thousand men and their spouses, nearly all of them resident in and around Moscow and, now, St. Petersburg. It was the members of this core elite, with their dependents and clients, who built and furnished their houses in the new style, established picture galleries, cabinets of curiosities, and libraries within them, and hired European masters or their newly trained Russian pupils to paint their portraits and tutor their children. It was these leading members of the official-noble elite who constituted the social matrix of the Petrine revolution, along with persons of lesser status, meritocrats or *arrivistes* as we might call them, often foreign-born or natives of the newly acquired Baltic provinces: persons who already possessed or were acquiring newly defined and valued skills as military or naval officers, artists or scholars, civil servants or diplomats, and were hopeful of eventual promotion into the dominant official-noble class in accordance with the Petrine Table of Ranks.[9] By the time of the first emperor's death, so far as we know, members of this Imperial elite all dressed in the new style (frequently a uniform) and read, wrote, and spoke the new Russian (with varying degrees of confidence, to be sure, and with various accents). These were the practitioners of the new military and courtly etiquettes encoded in the military and naval statutes of 1716 and 1720 and in the *Honorable Mirror of Youth* of 1717 (Chaps. 2, 3, 5). It was among these "several thousand" people "both male and female," as calculated by one of them (Peter Shafirov, in 1717), that a "spreading Reformation of Manners" was observed by a resident German diplomat in 1720, a "reformation" whose verbal impact is also recorded in the manuals of epistolary *komplimenty* published at Moscow and St. Petersburg in 1708, 1712, and 1725 (Chap. 4). Networks of such persons within and around the official-noble elite of the newly named All-Russian Empire were the initial bearers and perpetuators of the Petrine revolution in Russian culture, the creators indeed of "modern" Russian culture, or that synthesis of indigenous and more general European elements which became the Russian variant of modern European civilization.

"Europeanization" has been the most pregnant of the historiographical terms employed in all three of my volumes, more so even than "modernization," which for Russia as for much of the rest of the world has essentially meant assimilation or, more accurately, appropriation in some degree of European cultural practices and norms. Indeed I have argued in this as well as in the previous volumes that Europeanization in this quite specific sense—later Westernization, now globalization—has been the central development, or defining theme, of "modern" history; and Russia since Peter certainly provides an excellent proof case. As the largest country in the world since the seventeenth century and one of the first to undergo intensive Europeanization without losing political sovereignty, Russia has been well placed to accumulate a record that should be of major interest to the emergent school of global historians. Most interesting perhaps in this regard is the history of cultural transfer across established political and linguistic boundaries thus exemplified—the transmission of values as well as whole technologies, styles as well as beliefs and knowledges, from one quite distinct cultural matrix to another; and thus the potential of culture in explicating large-scale historical developments wherever they occur. To turn the point around, the expansion of "Europe" in modern times—commercial, military, political, demographic—bore innumerable cultural connotations, overt or residual, that were sooner or later appropriated by the growing numbers of people caught in the wake of this vast operation, a process that produced transformations in their environments, even in themselves, which proved lasting. So it was in the Russian case. The steadily more pressing commercial and political encroachment of a dynamic Europe on its relatively static Muscovite borderland precipitated the Petrine revolution in Russian culture, which then assumed a life of its own, implicating in varying degrees ever wider circles of society. Nor have periodic bouts of atavism in Russia, or attempted reversions to cultural autarky—most conspicuously that engineered by Stalin's regime in the earlier decades of the twentieth century—succeeded in reversing it. In this quite specifically cultural-historical sense, "Peter the Great" lives on.

The Persistence of Muscovy

Students of great transformative events in history sometimes seem reluctant to acknowledge the persistence of countervailing trends, the tenacity of "small" traditions in the shadow of "great" ones, the perseverence of popular or local resistance to elite impositions alongside acts of compliance or accommodation. Their vision of the forest seems to block their perception of the trees. Or so their critics sometimes contend. Yet even the most dedicated student of Peter's legacy in Russia could scarcely maintain that the Petrine "transformations [preobrazovaniia]" were total in their scope or consequences, either then or anytime later: that Muscovy, in short, was completely effaced from the cultural map of Eurasia. Indeed I have gone to considerable trouble in this and my previous volumes to show that Peter's was a top-down "revolution by decree," narrowly elitist at first and often coercive, and only gradual in its effects as it reached out and down into society. Cases in point include my discussions of persistent Old-Russian traditions in architecture and particularly wooden architecture and in icon painting and icon veneration.[10] The latter also sketched the variegated and circuitous ways in which the new imagery of the Petrine elite only gradually penetrated the figural and decorative arts and crafts of urban and peasant Russia, thereby "creating a fund of visual epithets that would fascinate artists and scholars ever after."[11] Elsewhere I surveyed the internal opposition to Peter's regime, contending that it was widespread in society and directed as much against his apparent contempt for Muscovite customs and traditions—particularly dress codes and religious rites—as it was against his increased taxation, intensified military conscription, or anything else; that it was a kind of cultural resistance, occasionally flaring into violence, to the perceived *Kulturkampf* of the regime.[12] Marc Raeff has made a similar case with respect to the popular attitudes driving the Pugachev rebellion of the 1770s,[13] the last large-scale popular disturbance in Russia until the revolutions of the early twentieth century.

In much the same way, it might be stressed, the Petrine revolution did not eliminate all vestiges of Muscovite verbal culture. Far from it. Muscovite verbal as well as visual culture possessed mechanisms of resistance as well as accommodation, these aided and abetted by the persistence over large areas of the country of "backward" socioeconomic conditions. Until well into the twentieth century the majority of Russians, living in rural isolation, working the land in largely self-sufficient village economies, were bearers of a peasant, still mainly oral culture, one that by the "modern" standards of the Europeanized official-noble elite (and of later scholars) was saturated with "traditional" patriarchal and religious values and often expressed in "archaic" or "obsolete" speech.[14] The point is too familiar to interested students, even to more casual readers, to need elaboration here. But the relatively huge size and prolonged socioeconomic stagnation of rural Russia ensured that the new vocabularies imported with the Petrine revolution only gradually became available to large numbers of ordinary Russians via military or government service and commercial, industrial, or other forms of specialized employment. Equally, the "regularized" syntax, grammar, and orthography of standard written Russian became widely used only with the institution of popular education and the spread of popular literacy, which did not take place on any quantitatively significant scale until the later nineteenth century.[15] Pronunciation, that most sensitive marker of speech, remained as variable as society itself, with distinct regional and class differences persisting well into the twentieth century.[16] But these are all, to step back once again, universal phenomena in modern history, not unique to Russia. Nor could they vitiate in any substantive way the impact of the Petrine verbal revolution. They only indicate why, by comparison with similar processes at work in smaller countries located further west, its effects took longer to be felt throughout society as a whole.

The persistence of Muscovy as a cultural force embodying political, religious, social, economic, and personal attitudes, practices, and values viewed by successive educated elites as traditional, archaic, obsolete, or primitive in nature is a feature of modern Russian history that cannot be denied by historians—no more than we could deny the persistence, until the twentieth century, of the specific Muscovite (or Old-Russian) architectural, visual, and linguistic forms referred to above (or the still more basic influence on culture of Russia's geographical location). Most glaring perhaps from a moral as well as socioeconomic standpoint was the persistence until the later nineteenth century of the Muscovite institution of serfdom, which can be seen as a cultural construct, progressively a rooted tradition, that ensnared up to half the rural population of Russia in habits of deference, servility, and petty cultivation. This was a world that in its vital and moral essentials long remained untouched by the secularizing, aggrandizing, cosmopolitan imperatives of the Petrine revolution, and testimony to its persistence is abundant.[17] Among the most striking in this regard are the remarks of a sympathetic, well-informed outsider, G. T. Robinson—his sympathy rooted in his own rural origins in the United States and his observations informed by years of research in Russian documentary sources as well as by extensive travel in the Russian countryside in the 1920s. At one point in his classic study of rural Russia between the serf emancipation of 1861 and the "agrarian revolution" of 1917 Robinson writes:

> The traveller of our own day who has journeyed across-country in Russian peasant wagons; watched the plowing, harvesting, and threshing; eaten from the common bowl, heard the peasant songs, and felt the rhythm of the peasant dances, can hardly help but think of the Russian village as a world apart; and yet times have changed, and already at the end of the nineteenth century many influences were at work to break the circle of the peasants' isolation.

These "many influences" stemmed of course from the Emancipation act of 1861 and its complex aftermath, until which time

> the village had not ceased to be the chief repository of the past: there was ample evidence that this was so, in the primitive land-system [of com-

311

munal tenure]; in the organization of the household and the commune; in the peasant folk-lore, with its occasional traces of a paganism officially abandoned nearly a thousand years ago; in the material arts, which still created many a fine thing in the old tradition.

Yet even with the advances in popular education and literacy of the decades succeeding the Emancipation and the concurrent growth of peasant land-ownership, even as "the Church, the conscript army, the school, and the press all helped to wear down the cultural isolation of the village," even while industrialization and urbanization were transforming parts of the Russian Empire, drawing some peasants away from the land and increasing the productivity, and improving the methods, of those that remained, even then

> a pre-war [pre-1914] traveller from the United States would still have been strongly impressed by what might be called the mature and complex primitiveness of Russian peasant agriculture. It was not the primitiveness of pioneering; not new and raw, but stained and weathered, and worn round by time; not the beginning of a new history so much as some late chapter of an old one. All about, in the compact village, in the intricate pattern of the fields, in the routine of the seeding and the harvest, there were the evidences of a venerable tradition.

Robinson wrote after the 1917 revolution had at last "brought in the peasants to possess the land," all of the land, but before the calamity of Soviet collectivization had descended on rural Russia, destroying forever its traditional ways.[18]

Nor did Robinson neglect to research, and to observe the remnants of, that other social component of rural Russia in the Imperial period, the noble landlords living in·their European "nests of gentility" scattered across the countryside, all summarily dispossessed by what he calls the "peasant *jacquerie*" of 1917. Indeed his book begins by depicting one such nest encountered while traveling in the south-central steppe in the fall of 1926:

> Against a horizon of rolling fields, banded black, green, and yellow with strips of fresh-plowed earth, sprouting winter grain, and fallowed stubble, there appeared a formal block of tree-tops; then, eventually, a keeper's cottage, and the wide gateway of a park. Walled here from the casual *step,* was a deliberately conventional grove, now very much bedraggled; and beyond, facing upon a broad crescent of brambles, stood

the wreck of a manor-house—one of those classical structures that speak so clearly of the wealth and the self-conscious culture of the nobility of the old regime.

Robinson was moved by the sight of "these architectural bones" to muse about the life that had been lived there, a life he will subsequently document using both visual and verbal sources:

313

> *troikas* at the door; bearded servants bowing and scraping; harpsichords and hunting feasts; the gossip of St. Petersburg and Paris; hoopskirts, silks and sabres; medaled dignitaries with powdered wigs, or the mutton-chop whiskers of a later day; daughters in French gowns, home from the Riviera; sons in the Guards' uniform of the Napoleonic Wars or the Great War—all musty and remote, buried more deeply by these last ten years than by the ten decades that went before.

Robinson later observes that "already, before the Great War and the Great Revolution, many of the nobles were (for a price) surrendering their land," a point he substantiates from official records. "Yet at the end of every road," he adds,

> one might still find a "nobleman's nest"[19]—in a house of wood or plastered brick which would almost certainly present (if it were a building of any size) at least four of those classical columns which had been since the eighteenth century so necessary a part of the stage-setting of manorial life. The house might of course be a small and tumble-down affair, not much better than a peasant's. Or it might be a modest place of a single storey with several thousand volumes in its library, and the walls of its drawing-room overcrowded with eighteenth-century portraits in wig and powder, and nineteenth-century photographs in sideburns and epaulets . . . such was the home on the small estate of the Marshall of the Nobility of a certain northern *guberniia*

—a home Robinson had learned about from "photographs and an interview." "Dogs and hunting-horses," he completes the picture, "parks and gardens, cars, carriages, and sleighs, the portrait of Catherine II in the library of the Nobles' Club, the portrait of Nicholas II in the ball-room—what else on earth can be so near, and so sidereally far away?"[20]

It has been tempting for historians working in post-Soviet Russia, some sixty or seventy years after Robinson wrote, to ascribe to the legacy of Peter not only all that is modern in Russian history in a positive or progressivist sense but also all that is somehow negative or disreputable, from the persistence of serfdom and the failures of capitalism to the catastrophe of 1917 and the whole "totalitarian" project of Stalinism.[21] Whatever else might be said, the temptation itself is a tribute to the magnitude and complexity over the longer term of the cultural revolution whose causes and initial effects I have sought to clarify and document.

314

ABBREVIATIONS

APPENDIXES

NOTES

BIBLIOGRAPHY

INDEX

ABBREVIATIONS

BAN   Biblioteka Akademii Nauk (Library of the Academy of Sciences),
                    St. Petersburg
BL   British Library, London
GBL   Gosudarstvennaia Biblioteka im. Lenina (Lenin State Library,
                    now Russian State Library), Moscow
HU   Harvard University libraries
JGO   *Jahrbücher für Geschichte Osteuropas*
L.   Leningrad
LC   Library of Congress
M.   Moscow
MERSH   *The Modern Encyclopedia of Russian and Soviet History*, ed. J. L.
                    Wieczynski et al., 58 vols. (Gulf Breeze, FL, 1976–94)
NYPL   New York Public Library (Slavic and Baltic Division)
OED   *The Oxford English Dictionary*, 13 vols. (Oxford, 1933)
Opis. I   T. A. Bykova and M. M. Gurevich, *Opisanie izdanii grazhdanskoi
                    pechati (1708–1725)* (M./L., 1955)
Opis. II   T. A. Bykova and M. M. Gurevich, *Opisanie izdanii,
                    napechatannykh kirillitsei (1689–1725)* (M./L., 1958)
Opis. III   T. A. Bykova, M. M. Gurevich, and R. I. Kozintseva, *Opisanie
                    izdanii, napechatannykh pri Petre I: svodnyi katalog. Dolpolneniia i
                    prilozheniia* (L., 1972)
PiB   *Pis'ma i bumagi imperatora Petra Velikogo*, 13 vols. (SPb./L./SPb.,
                    1887–1992)
PSZ   *Polnoe sobranie zakonov rossiiskoi imperii s 1649 goda*, 1st ser., 46
                    vols. (SPb., 1830–43)
Rbs   *Russkii bioigraficheskii slovar'*, 25 vols. (M./SPb., 1896–1918)

SIRIO	*Sbornik imperatorskago russkago istoricheskago obshchestva,* 148 vols. (SPb., 1867–1916)
SPb.	St. Petersburg
Svod. kat.-kirillovskoi	A. S. Zernova and T. N. Kameneva, *Svodnyi katalog russkoi knigi kirillovskoi pechati XVIII veka, 1701–1800* (M., 1968)
Svodnyi katalog	E. I. Katsprzhak et al., *Svodnyi katalog russkoi knigi grazhdanskoi pechati XVIII veka, 1725–1800,* 5 vols. (M., 1962–67)
TsGADA	Tsentral'nyi Gosudarstvennyi Arkhiv Drevnykh Aktov (Central State Archive of Historical Documents, now Russian State Archive of Historical Documents), Moscow
TsGIA	Tsentral'nyi Gosudarstvennyi Istoricheskii Arkhiv (Central State Historical Archive, now Russian State Historical Archive), St. Petersburg
ZAP	*Zakonadatel'nye akty Petra I,* ed. N. A. Voskresenskii (M./L., 1945)

Note: Additional abbreviations, some of which are also employed in the notes, are listed under Works Cited in Appendix II.

APPENDIX I: TEXTS

The forty contemporary texts reproduced in this appendix and arranged in chronological order of printed publication illustrate graphically several important aspects of the Petrine revolution in Russian verbal culture. The most obvious is the alphabetic and typographic switch in official printing from the traditional Cyrillic system of letters, numerals, and fonts (see Nos. 1–7) to the newly devised "civil" system (Nos. 13 and following) that rapidly displaced it in all but ecclesiastical or religious publication. A commensurate Europeanization–or modernization–of syntax and style and especially of the lexicon is also more or less apparent, as bodies of contemporary European knowledge of one kind or another were now being conveyed in an appropriately adapted "plain Russian," one shorn of rigid bureaucratic formulas and of various grammatical as well as lexical Slavonicisms. Texts exemplifying these further aspects of the Petrine revolution (especially Nos. 13, 15–19, 23, 25, 27–29, 32–35, and 37) may be contrasted in these respects with others (Nos. 1–7, again) representing pre-Petrine chancery Russian and Russo-Church Slavonic. Still other texts reproduced here (Nos. 8–12, 14, 24, 30, 31, and 36) exemplify in various ways–typographical and lexical, among others–states of transition in Petrine verbal culture from typically traditional or "medieval" forms of written expression to recognizably "new" or modern ones. These "states of transition" may be otherwise regarded as so many steps or stages in the Petrine march to standardization of modern literary Russian.

All of the texts reproduced in this appendix were referred to, and in some degree contextualized, in the preceding chapters of this book (page references follow the captions). It should be emphasized that the first criterion for their inclusion here was the current state of a given text and its suitability for rea-

sonably clear reproduction by photographic means. The second such criterion, unavoidably, was the capacity or willingness of the host institution to
make such reproductions available at an affordable cost. I am grateful to the
institutions cited in the captions below for providing photographs or mi-
crofilms of the captioned texts, and to Benn Williams for his invaluable assistance in preparing them for publication here.

NO. 1 First page of the *Apostol* (*Book of the Apostles,* or Acts plus Epistles) printed at Moscow, 1564. Typefaces reflect contemporary semi-uncial *(poluustav)* Cyrillic script. From Shitsgal, *Russkii tipograficheskii shrift* (1985), p. 17, fig. 11. (See above pp. 26, 259n4, 261)

322

Ã ГЛАВА

ДЕМЕН НАПИСАНО ПРОУРАДННКОВЪ ОДНОЙ РОТЫ ИЛИ ЗНАМЕНИ о КАКЪ
ТОН РОТѢ УРАДННКАМИ СПОДОБЛЕНОЙ И УСТРОЕНОЙ БЫТИ •

ОТИ А БЫЛЪ ВМЫСЛЬ СВОЮ ВЗАЛЪ ВСѢМЪ СВОЕМЪ ПИСАНІИ
ТОЛКО ЛИШЕ ПИСАТИ ЧТО ВСАКОМУ САЛДАТУ ОРОУЖІЕ ГОДНО
И НАДОБНО • НОДНАКО А ВНАЧАЛѢ НЕМНОГИМИ СЛОВАМИ ПОМА
НУ о КАКЪ ОДНОЙ РОТѢ ПЕХОТНОЙ ПОЛОУЧТЧЕМУ ОЗЫЧАЮ
ОУРАДННКАМИ ИСАЛДАТАМИ ОУСТРОЕНОЙ БЫТИ о НѢТ СВОЕ
ОУЧЕНІЕ ВСѢМЪ ЧТИ ЛЮБИТЕЛЬНЫМЪ ВОИНО ПРИКАЗАТИ ИПРЕ
ДАТИ • ВСАКАА РОТА ИЛИ ЗНАМА ИМѢЕТ КАПИТАНА СВОИ о ИСРѢЧЬ ГЛАВУ
ИМЕНЧ КАПИТАНА о ИСРѢЧЬ ГЛАВОУ о КОТОРОМУ ПОПРАМОМУ ЦЕСАРСКОМУ
ИЗЫКУ ЛУПМАНЪ о ИСРѢЧЬ ГОЛОВА • А ДРАНЦОУЖСКИМ ИЗЫКОМЪ
КАПЕТЪ ГОЛОВА о ИПОКАПИТТУ КАПИТАНОМ ИМЕНОУЕТСА • ИПОТОМУ
КАКЪ ГОЛОВА НАЧАЛНѢЙШЕЕ ЕСТЬ о И ВСѢМЪ ВЛАДѢЕТЪ о И ПО ГЛАВѢ
ВСѢ СОСТАВЫ ХОДАТ ИНСПРАВЛАЮТСА о ТАКОЖЕ НАДОБНО ВСѢМЪ
ИННЫМЪ ОУРАДННКОМЪ И СОСТАВОМЪ ПОПРИНКАЗУ ИВЛАДѢНІЮ ГОЛОВЫ
И КАПИТАНА ИСПРАВЛАТИ •

А ПОДЛЕ КАПИТАНА ПОРУТЧНКЪ ЕГО о ИТОГО ПОПОВЕЛѢНЫЮ КАКЪ
КАПИТАНА САМОГО ВЛИЦАХЪ НѢТЪ о СТОЛКОЖЕ СЛУШАТИ ДОВЕДЕТСА
КАКЪ И САМОГО КАПИТАНА • ИПОРАТНОМУ ОБЫЧАЮ ВРАТНОМЪ ДѢЛЕ
ДОВЕДЕТСА ПОРУТЧНКУ НАЧАЛНОЕ ВЛАДѢНІЕ о ИПОВЕЛѢНІЕ ИМѢТ ЕН
КОГДА КАПИТАНА УРОТЫ НѢТЪ ТАКЪЖЕ КАБЫ ИПРИКАПИТАНѢ •

А ПЕРВОЕ А ВОПРОШАЮ ДЛА ЧЕГО ЛЮТЕНАНТА о ИСРѢЧЬ ПОРОУТЧНКА

ı д̃

ε̃

NO. 3   Page from *Uchen'e i khitrost' ratnago stroeniia pekhotnykh liudei* (see No. 2). Text in chancery Russian laced with Slavonicisms and Western neologisms. Cyrillic semiuncial typefaces. First work of secular content printed in Russia. Slavic and Baltic Division, NYPL, Astor, Lenox, and Tilden Foundations. (See above pp. 35, 106, 259, 261).

гла́ва , а҃і

Кто́ комꙋ́ ѿда́етъ бѣглыхъ кре́стьꙗнъ , й   а҃
бо́быле́й   .

Кото́рые кре́стьꙗна й бо́были , в пи́сцо́выхъ   в҃
кни́гахъ напи́саны в бѣглыхъ .

Й́з зꙋ́кого бѣглые кре́стьꙗна й бо́были , по   г҃
сꙋ́дꙋй й по пи́сцо́вымъ кни́гамъ , бꙋ́дꙋтъ
ѿда́ны .

Оу́ кото́рыхъ во́тчинниковъ , по сꙋ́дꙋй кре́сть   ѕ҃
ꙗ́на бꙋ́дꙋтъ й кꙋ́плены во́тчинъ .

Оу́ кото́рыхъ во́тчинникꙋ й помѣ́щиковъ , ѽ   н҃
бѣглыхъ кре́стьꙗнехъ й ѽ бо́была́хъ былꙗ
сꙋ́дъ , й с зꙋ́дꙋ ѿка́зано пре́жним гдре́вы
оу́ка́зомъ , йли оу́кого ски́тꙗмъ во кре́стьꙗне
былꙗ полю́бо́внаꙗ зди́лка .

Кото́рые кре́стьꙗна за кꙋ́мъ напи́саны , в҃   д҃
пере́пи́сныхъ кни́гахъ , й по́сле то́го бежа́ли ,
йли впере́де оу́чнꙋ́тъ бѣга́ти .

Кто́ с ны́нешнꙗго оу́ло́женіꙗ оу́чнетъ кре́стьꙗ   ҃і
й бо́быле́й при́йма́ти й дер́жа́ти за собо́й .

Бꙋ́детъ за кꙋ́мъ бѣглыхъ кре́стьꙗнъ й бо́бы   а҃і
ле́й , й ѽ цо́въ й́хъ в пи́сцо́вы кни́гꙗ не на́пи
са́но , й напи́саны за кꙋ́мъ в пере́пи́сны ке́ни́гꙗ .

                                                                                    к҃г

NO. 4   Page from Chapter 11 of the *Ulozhenie* (law code) printed at Moscow, 1649. Text in chancery Russian with Slavonicisms, including Slavonic numerals. Cyrillic semi-uncial type. Second work of secular content printed in Russia. Slavic and Baltic Division, NYPL, Astor, Lenox, and Tilden Foundations. (See above pp. 35n18, 38, 153, 259, 261)

ѡ҃ Предисло́вїе к̾правосла́вному чита́телю

Є҆́же у҆́бо ви́димъ в̾ ц҃рквахъ строе́нїа на
ро́днаа и̑ ко́емꙗ́ждо и̑справле́нїе ве́щи,
чи́нъ же и҆з̾ве́щанїе, ра́ди бы́ва́емы, и̑
ча́сто приключа́ющихса, пово́лному и̑
нево́льному хоте́нїю вину̑ и҆страсте́й,
в̾наꙗ́же у҆до́бъ любовеще́ственныи и̑скорш
насло прилежа́телныи ра́зумъ ч҃ческїй
зри́тъ па́че, не́жели на̑любому́дрїе и̑сти
ннаго и̑поле́знаго сво́иственаго все́мъ
ми́ра · сего̑ у҆́бо ра́ди и̑вса́къ ви́дъ му̑
ченїа и̑гоа́зни, и҆згна́нїа́же и҆за́точе
нїа, и̑в̾за́тїа и҆ме́нен, и̑ и̑на мно́га и҆з
ѡ҆б̾ре́тенїа су́ть, да́же у҆́бо пра́вда, в̾
не́й́же бл҃гово́литъ вы́шнїй, све́тлитса:
непра́вда́же, в̾не́й́же и̑скони вра́гъ и́сꙋ̑
постатъ нашъ дїа́волъ вселиса ю҆бличи
тса и̑ и̑сче́знетъ · и̑та́ко в̾мире́, сире́чь
в̾поко́и вса̑ на́ша прево́дитъ, а́ще лю
бовъ дру́гъ к̾дру́гꙋ по ꙱бра́зу созда́вша
го на́съ сохрани́мъ · а́щели не́сице и̑ме́
тиса бу́дутъ, вса̑ на́ша ꙗ́же горе́,

а҃

326

ПРЕДИСЛОВЇЕ КЪ ЧИТАТЕЛЮ

Аго єстъ книги ст҃ыа читати ,
и полезнаа ѿнихъ собирати :
Та бо бг҃ови жити наставляютъ ,
добродѣтелемъ оудобь научаютъ .
Вся оубw книги имутъ блг҃а многа ,
точнѣ и ѿа в ползу не оубога :
Юже рукама твоима держиши ,
прочти точїю , истинну оузриши .
Дивна здѣ повѣстъ миру явленна ,
какw поживета мужа бж҃твенна .
Варлаамъ ѻц҃ъ , їwасафъ ст҃ый
цр҃вичъ и цр҃ь въ їндїи богатый .
Оудивишися каа оумышляше ,
варлаамъ старецъ , и начто дерзаше ,
їwасафу спастися желаа ,
душу сѝ ради єгw полагаа .
Почюдишися промыслу дивному ,
ѿ старца мудра изwбрѣтенному .
Какw словомъ си тщася оуловити
їwасафа , да бы вѣрну быти ,
Мрежен слово єгw наречеши ,
єгда повѣсти дивныа прочтеши :
Тѣмн бо якw сѣтми оуловиса
иноша , и рабъ хр҃ту сотвориса .

Ѝмже

NO. 6   Preface (first page) to the *Istoriia o Varlaame i Ioasafe (Tale of Barlaam and Joasaph)*, by Simeon Polotskii, printed at Moscow, 1681. Church Slavonic syllabic verse printed in traditional Cyrillic types. From Shitsgal, *Russkii tipograficheskii shrift* (1985). (See above pp. 38, 68, 222, 261)

Кра́ткое ѻбыкнове́нное ѹ҆че́нїе, съ кре́пча́йшимъ и҆ лꙋ́чшимъ ра́столкова́нїемъ, [в҆ стрⷪ҇е́нїи пѣ́шихъ полкѡвъ,] ка́къ при то́мъ постꙋпа́ти, и҆ во ѻ҆смотре́нїи и҆мѣ́ти надлежи́ господа́мъ капита́нѡмъ, и҆ про́чей нача́лны, и҆ ѻ҆ѵꙗⷤднниⷨкѡ.

Прїе́мы въ трѝ ра́зы , и҆ли тѐмпа .
а҃ : Кꙋ́ди на мꙋ́шкѣ́тъ рꙋ́кꙋ .

NO. 7   First page of the *Kratkoe obyknovennoe uchenie . . . v stroennii peshkikh polkov (A Short Standard Instruction . . . for the Organization of Foot Regiments)*, M., 1699. Russian text (with Slavonicisms and Western neologisms) printed in traditional Cyrillic type. From Opis. II, p. 63, fig. 2. (See above pp. 108, 265, 269)

328

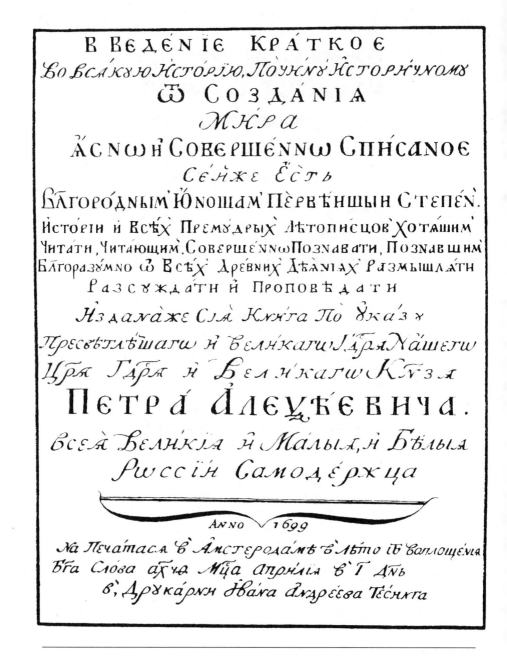

NO. 8   Title page of *Vvedenie kratkoe vo vsiakuiu istoriiu . . . (A Brief Introduction to All History . . .)*, Amsterdam, 1699. Typefaces reflect Jan Tessing's attempt to create a Russian alphabet suitable for printing secular works commissioned by Peter I. From Shitsgal, *Russkii tipograficheskii shrift* (1985), p. 28, fig. 14. (See above pp. 264, 265, 267, 269)

ӣ҃н . Э҆ссо́повы Притчи

з҃і .

Вранъ .

Вранъ недꙋ́гꙋющыꙵн гла́ше
мтри . мти не пла́чь егꙋ̀
моли́са . ѿвѣща̀ е҆мꙋ̀ мти
и҆ре́че , которыꙵн егъ помн-
лꙋетъ та̀ сне мои , чꙵего́жъ
ты мꙗ́са не кра́лъ .

Прилага́нїе .

При́тча зна́менꙋетъ , ко-
торіи въ житіи своемъ тво-
ратъ мно́гихъ врагові , тіи
во вре́мꙗ ско́рби и печа́ли ,
ни е҆ди́нагѡ не ѡ҆брѣта́ютъ
дрꙋ́га . н҃ꙁ

329

no. 9   Text page with illustration from the *Essopovy Pritchi (Aesop's Fables)* printed by Jan Tessing at Amsterdam, 1700. From *Opis. I*, appendix I, p. 287, fig. 22. (See above pp. 264, 265, 267, 269)

330

ХВАЛИ́ТИ БГА ЧЕЛОВѢ́КУ ВСЯ́КУ,
ДО́ЛГЪ ОУЧИ́ТИСѦ ПИСМЕ СЛОВЕ́СЪ ЗНА́КУ.
ОУЧЕ́НІЕМЪ БО БЛА́ГѠ РАЗУ́МѢЕТЪ,
В ЦРТВО НБНО С СТЫ́МИ ОУСПѢ́ЕТЪ.
ТѢ́МЖЕ ЮНІ́Й В ТРУДѢ́ СЕ БЫВА́ЙТЕ,
ВРЕ́МѦ И ЧАСѠ́ВЪ ВЪ ГУЛБѢ НЕ ТЕРѦ́ЙТЕ.

NO. 10   Page from Fedor Polikarpov, *Bukvar' (Primer)*, M., 1701. HU-Houghton. (See above pp. 269, 286)

ЧА́СТЬ ПЕ́РВАѦ

ѡ҆ числѣ́хъ цѣ́лыхъ .

Коли́кѡ сїѧ̀ ча́сть и҆мѣ́етъ въ себѣ̀ предѣле́нїй ;
И҆мѣ́етъ предѣле́нїй пѧ́ть .

1 .	Συναρίθμησις ,	Numeratio .	Счисле́нїе .
2 .	Συμαρισμὸς .	Additio .	Сложе́нїе .
3 .	Γ φειλμὸς .	Subtractio .	Вычита́нїе .
4 .	Πολυπλασιασμὸς .	Multiplicatio .	Оу҆множе́нїе .
5 .	Δια:ρεσις .	Divilio .	Дѣле́нїе .

ПРЕДѢЛЕ́НЇЕ ПЕ́РВОЕ .

НꙊМЕРА́ЦЇО , и҆лѝ счисле́нїе .

Что̀ є҆́сть нꙋмера́цїо ;

НꙊмЕРА́ЦЇО є҆́сть счисле́нїе є҆́же соверше́ннѡ всѧ̀ чи́сла
ре́тїю и҆меновати , ꙗ҆́же въ десѧтѝ знаменова́нїахъ ,
и҆лѝ и҆з̾ображе́нїа содержа́тсѧ и҆ и҆з̾ображаютсѧ си́це :

1 , 2 , 3 , 4 , 5 , 6 , 7 , 8 , 9 , 0 ,

и҆з̾ ни́хже де́вѧть назнаменова́телны сꙋ́ть :
послѣ́днее же 0 [є҆́же цы́фрою , и҆лѝ ничемъ
и҆менꙋ́етсѧ] є҆гда̀ оу҆́бѡ (Ѻ҆но̀) є҆ди́но стои́тъ ,
тогда̀ само̀ ѡ҆ себѣ̀ ничто́же зна́читъ . є҆гда̀
же кое́мꙋ ѻ҆́ныхъ знаменова́нїй приложе́но бꙋ́детъ ,
тогда̀ оу҆множа́етъ въ десѧтеро , ꙗ҆́коже пред-
ложе́но є҆́сть ни́же сегѡ̀ .

332

ΛΕΞΙΚΟΝ ΤΡΙΑΖΫΨΝΙΙ

ΛΕΞΙΚΟΝ ΤΡΙΓΛΩΤΤΟΝ
ἤτα
Λέξεων σλαβονικῶν, ἑλληνικῶν τε καὶ λατινικῶν
θησαυρὸς
Ἐκ διαφόρων παλαιῶν τε καὶ νέων βιβλίων
συλλεχθεὶς
καὶ κατὰ τὸ σλαβονικὸν ἀλφαβητάριον εἰς τάξιν
διατεθεὶς

DICTIONARIUM TRILINGUE
hoc est
Dictionum Slauonicarum Græcarum & Latinarum
thesaurus
Ex varys antiquis ac recentioribus libris
colletus
Et iuxta Slauonicum alphabetum in ordinem
dispositus

NO. 12   Title page of Fedor Polikarpov, *Leksikon treiazychnyi, sirech' Rechenii slavenskikh, ellinogrecheskikh i latinskikh sokrovishche . . . (A Trilingual Dictionary, that is, A Treasury of Slavonic, Greek and Latin vocables . . .)*, M., 1704. LC-Rare. (See above pp. 269, 289)

333

АЛТІТУДО ФІГУРЕ, ілі ВЫСОТА ФІГУРЫ, есть та перпендікуларная лінеа, которая ізb верхнеі острінЫ ко базе начерпітся. А

РАВНОУГОЛНАЯ фігура есть та которая всѣ углы велічествомb равны імѣеть. В

Когдя двѣ фігуры, какb едіна, такb другая между дву равныхb сторонb, а велічествомb равные углы імѣють, то назЫваются онЫя равноуголныя фігуры, ілі ФІГУРЕ ЕКВІАНГУЛЕ.

Ежелі стороны у фігуры длиною да равны суть, назЫвается оная равносторонная фігура, ілі ФІ-ГУРА ЕКВІЛАТЕРЛ.

РАВНОПОДОБНЫЯ ФІГУРЫ ілі ФІ-ГУРЕ SIMILES суть тѣ, яже імуть равныя углы, і стороны около равныхb угловb пропор-ціоналныя. EG

ПРОПОРЦІОНАЛНЫЯ же стороны хотя бу-дуть потомb едінаго велічества, ілі менши, ілі не равны между собою. HG

РАВНОСОДЕРЖЛЩІЯ, ілі ФІГУРЕ ЕКВАЛЕS суть тѣ, которыя равное содержаніе ілі арею обвемлють, хотя снЫя будуть образомb каковы хотять. HI

ПРЯМОЛІНЕІНАЯ ФІГУРА, вb другоі ПРЯМО-
Г 3 ЛІ-

NO. 13 Sample text page from *Geometria slavenski zemlemerie . . . (Geometry, in Slavonic land-measuring . . .)*, M. 1708. First book printed in the new civil type. From Shitsgal, *Grazhdanskii shrift, Reproduktsii*, no. III. (See above pp. 197, 271)

полїтіколѣпнаѧ

ÁΠΟΘÉΩΣÍΣ

достохвалньıѧ храбрості

всерѡссíйскагѡ
геркѵлеса

пресвѣтлѣишаго, і великодержавнѣишаго,
богомъ вѣнчаннаго, і богомъ укрѣпляемаго,
і богомъ прославляемаго,
великаго ГОСУДАРѦ нашего ЦАРѦ
і великаго КНѦЗѦ

ПЕТРА̀ АЛЕѯíЕВНЧА

всеѧ великíѧ, і, малыѧ і бѣлыѧ
россíи
ímПЕРАТОРА і АВТОКРАТОРА.

NO. 14   Title pages (two) and Preface (first page) of *Politikolepnaia Apotheosis dostokhvalnyia khrabrosti vserossiiskago Gerkulesa . . . nashego tsaria i velikago kniazia Petra Aleksievicha . . . po preslavnoi viktorii . . . na generalnoi batalii . . . pod Poltavoiu . . . (An Apotheosis of the propitious bravery of the All-Russian Hercules . . . our tsar and grand prince Peter Alekseevich . . . on the most glorious victory . . . at the battle . . . by Poltava . . .),* M., 1709. Oration by Joseph Turuboiskii at the Moscow Slavonic-Greek-Latin Academy commemorating the Russian victory at the battle of Poltava (June 1709). Slavic and Baltic Division, NYPL, Astor, Lenox, and Tilden Foundations. (See above pp. 68, 222)

По преславноі вікторіі надъ хімероподобными́ді́вамі ГОРДЫНЕЮ рекше НЕПРАВДОЮ і ХІЩЕНІЕМЪ СВѢІСКІМЪ.

На ГЕНЕРАЛНОІ БАТАЛІІ

Въ ны́нѣшнемъ 1709 году, въ ‿7 і 30 день, мѣсяца і́уні́а.

бывшеі подъ Полтавою, блізъ пересволочно́й, і на і́ныхъ премногіхъ Марсовыхъ случаяхъ, со подвігоположнымъ і побѣдоноснымъ православнымъ воінствомъ своїмъ, всенароднымъ радованіемъ,

В О З В Р А Щ А Ю Щ А Г О С Я.

Въ царствующіі градъ своі Москву

въ премудрыя Аѳіны [сіесть палады] веліко россіїскія Арсопагъ.

У З А К О Н Е Н Н А Я

отъ елліінославенолатінскія же Его Царскаго Пресвѣтлаго Велічества

А К А Д Е М І І   М О С К О В С К І Я

Т О Р Ж Е С Т В О В А Н А

Лѣта Господня 1709 Мі́роздані́я же 7218 мѣсяца декемврі́а въ   день,

[о]

ПРАВОСЛАВНОМУ ЧІТАТЕЛЮ.

о господѣ здравствоваті.

Лово сїе АПОѲЕОСІСЬ, вь тіптлѣ кнїжі-
цѣ сея положенное. їногда знаменаеть
ПОСВЯЩЕНІЕ, їлі между богї почтеніе. Сїе же бываше у древнїхь обіч-
нѣ убо храбрьімь славньімь ї добро-
дѣтелньімь монархамь ї монархїнямь. ї тако
первьї всѣхь Августь Іулїа кесаря. Тіверїї же
августа посвятілї, ї їньіхь между богї почлї.
їнїїже народї їньіхь разумьі геркулесса, Кастора
ї воллюкса ромулюса ї прочїїхь отвнїхже велїкая
нѣкая благодѣянїя воспрїімаху посвящаху, їчесть
божїю храмьі ї служебнїкі своя їмь постановляху.
НО АПОѲЕОСІСЬ їногда прїемлется за честь їпо-
хвалу за нѣкїа добродѣтелї людемь знаменїтьімь
даемую. Ї тако маркусь тулїї цїцеро вь 1 кнїзѣ
до аттікі вь 13 посланїї глаголеть; Vides ne con-
latum illum noſtrum, quem curio antea apotheoſi uocabat.
Сїесть. Відіші лі сеї нашь консулять [честь бѣ
у рімлянь вмѣсто царскїа чессті по Ізгнанїї Тарквіні.
ушевь царєї рімскїхь. прі двоїхь на всякої годь пре-
мѣнляемьіхь. бьівшая] егоже курїо прежде Апоѳе-
осінь

* 3

ПОБѢЖДАЮЩАЯ
крѣпостЬ
кЬ счастлівому поздравленію
Слáвноі побѣ́ды надЬ АЅОВЫМЬ
і кЬ счастлівомȢ ввѣ́ѕдȢ
вЬ москву.

ЕГО

ЦАРСКОМУ

ВЕЛІЧЕСТВУ

покóрнѣ́йше поднесено

Ѿ

ЭРІСТА ФРІДЕРІХА БАРОНА,
фонЬ боргсдорфа, Цеса́рского Велíче-
ства рíмского, настоя́ще учрежде́н-
наго нача́лного Інженéра.
ВЬ лѣ́то Госпóдне,
1696.

NO. 15   Title page and sample text page from Baron E. F. von Borgsdorf, *Pobezhdaiush-chaia krepost'/k schastlivomu pozdravleniiu/slavnoi pobedy nad Azovym . . . (Vanquishing the fortress/in happy celebration/of the glorious victory at Azov . . .)*, M., 1709. Account of the Russian siege of Azov in 1696 by Peter's master of siegecraft. From Shitsgal, *Grazhdanskii shrift, Reproduktsii*, nos. III, IV. (See above p. 133)

[8]

338

пости жіті возможно , і егда ова тѣ счі-
сленія вмѣстѣ сложішь , I тогда овря-
щется ₃,₇₀ человѣкъ салдатъ , по вышшеі
мѣрѣ сілы осадныхъ людеі : і по тому
надлежітъ намъ на овлеженіе по послѣд-
неі мѣрѣ ₃,₇₀ человѣкъ салдатъ імѣті.

ВТОРОЕ ПРАВІЛО

Въ томъ чісле ₃,₇₀ человѣкъ салдатъ
учредіть , четвертую часть коннїцы .
А імянно 89₂ человѣка , да трі четверті
пѣхоты. а імянно ₂₆,₇₈ человѣкъ.

Коннїца потревна есть поля очіщаті,
і проходіті, і которое ні будъ въ нуждѣ
оврѣтающееся мѣсто въ овоѣ выручаті,
і прївоѕъ всякіхъ запасовъ провожаті.

Пехота же потревна ко оборонѣ ста-
новіщъ , на которые нападеніе учінено
вудетъ , на всякую же 100 человѣкъ пѣхоты даютъ, по едіноі фалконетѣ , пу-
шкѣ , і того вудетъ ₂₆ фалконетовъ ,
для удержіванія непріятеля іѕдалі отъ
нападенія.

₃. ПРАВІЛО.

Лутчее время къ начінанію около крѣ-
пості устанавлїватіся есть. то доколѣ
хлѣв

NO. 15 (continued)

НОВОЕ крѣпостное

СТРОЕНІЕ

НА мокромъ їлї нїскомъ горїзонтѣ.

Котороє на трї манїры показуется во фортїфїкованїе
внутренної велїчїны.

фРАнцузского роялного штїуголнїка, въ чемъ крѣпость нынѣ-
шнїхъ сухїхъ прї мокрыхъ рвахъ оорѣтаются.

КУПНО ЖЕ

КАКО нынѣ прї морѣ, їлї рѣкахъ, крѣпостї дѣлаются,
ї кыїмъ образомъ тамо подобаетъ строїть.

Каждая манїра атакована, ї въ прїмѣрь положена, какъ въ їхъ
крѣпостяхъ на обѣ стороны, такожъ ї о проторяхъ
со француѕскою, їлї съ нынѣшнїмъ крѣпостнымъ
строенїемъ.

ГОСПОДІНА БАРОНА фонъ КУГОРНА,
генерала артїлерїї, генерала порутчїка їнфантерїї, генерала
правїтеля крѣпостного строенїя статовъ недерляндскїхъ
ї губернатора фландерского, ї крѣпостеї
прї шелдѣ рѣкѣ.

Въ левардснѣ 1702 года.

NO. 16   Title page of Baron von Kugorn (van Coehoorn), *Novoe krepostnoe stroenie na mokrom ili nizkom gorrizonte . . . (The New Fortification on wet or low land . . .)*, M., 1710. LC-Rare. (See above p. 140)

340

[96]

Здѣ живетъ началнѣишïи воевода,
иже управляетъ всѣ приналежащïя
страны америтпскïя, духовенство
ихъ имѣетъ началника архïепïскопа

Во странахъ сихъ родится,
злато, сребро, жемчюгъ, балсамъ,
краска коченинла, корень мехоаканъ,
древо сасафрасъ, сѣра горючая, и
прочая. жители странъ сихъ предъ
тѣмъ были, и нынѣ многïе супь
ïдолопоклонники, нынѣ же многïе
обратилися и вѣруютъ во хрïста.

О С Т Р А Н Ѣ
Ф Л О Р И Д Ѣ.

Флорида есть страна изрядная
и воздуха растворенна, и вся-
кими аще и странными, обаче
изрядными плодами исполнена.
такъ же и звѣря всякого много sѣло,
мѣдвѣ-

NO. 17 Page from *Geografia ili kratkoe zemnago kruga opisanie* (*Geography, or a Brief Description of the Earthly Sphere*), M., 1710. From Shitsgal, *Grazhdanskii shrift, Reproduktsii*, no. IX. (See above p. 204)

Апрѣль

В Ѣ Д О М О С Т И.

Прїсланые чрезъ почту Марта въ 30 день.

Ізъ КРАКОВА Февраля въ 11 день. Воїска генерала голца на венгерскїхъ гранїцахъ еще стоятъ, увѣдомїлїся гдѣ воевода кїевскїи съ своїми людми обрѣтается, и говорятъ что онъ съ нѣсколкїми хорунгвми къ рагоцкому пошелъ.

Ізъ ВАРШАВЫ Февраля въ 11 день. Королевское велїчество августъ прї своеи бытности воїска свои осмотрѣлъ. І всѣ въ добромъ состоянїи обрѣлъ, и чаютъ полкамъ вскорѣ подыматца.

Ísb САКСОНІІ въ варшаву прївозятъ велїкую артїлерїю, такъ же и нѣкоторые понтоны.

Въ 5 день февраля цесарскїи резїдентъ шиполь въ варшаву прїѣхалъ, и еще цесарского посланнїка графа вїлцека ждутъ, которои къ Его Царскому Велїчеству назначенъ къ Москвѣ итти,

Отъ ВІСЛЫ рѣки Февраля въ 12 день. Еще невѣдомо куды полонянїковъ изъ элбїнга повезутъ. Генералъ ностїцъ въ городѣ хрѣпкїи гварнїзонъ заложїлъ.

8   Ísb

NO. 18   First page of the *Vedomosti (News)* for April 1, 1710, M., 1710. From Shitsgal, *Grazhdanskii shrift, Reproduktsii*, no. XII. (See above p. 266)

[47]

Чрез сїе употребленїе уголъ бастїона содержитъ, четвероуголнои крѣпости 60 градусовъ, пятїуголнои 66. шестїуголнои 70 . Подобно сему и въ протчїхъ полїгонахъ прїбавляяся по малу, даже до лїнїи прямои, гдѣ онъ содержитъ 90 градусовъ.

Уголъ куртїны, четвероуголнои крѣпости 150 градусовъ , пятїуголнои 138. шестїуголнои 120 .

Подобно сему и въ другїхъ полїгонахъ ,убавляяся по малу , даже до лїнїи прямои , гдѣ содержитъ 90 градусовъ.

Уголъ умаленнои , четвероуголнои крѣпости, 15 градусовъ , пятїуголнои 21. шестїуголбнои 25. и такъ мало прїбавляяся въ другїхъ полїгонахъ, даже до лїнїи прямои , гдѣ сочиняется , из 45. градусовъ.

Уголъ фланка на лїнее оборонїтелнои , въ четвероуголнои крѣпости , 107, градусовъ , 47. мїнутъ , въ пятїуголнои 100 градусовъ , и , 41. мїнута. въ шестїуголнои , 97 . и 48 мїнутъ: Сему подобно и въ послѣдующїхъ полїгонахъ, умаляяся по малу , даже до лїнїи прямои , гдѣ бываетъ 90 градусовъ.

Уголъ фланка над куртїною , въ четвероуголнои крѣпости , 122, градуса , и 47 мїнутъ . въ пятиуголнои 123 градуса , и 11 мїнутъ. въ шестиуголнои 123 градуса , и 48 мїнутъ. такѣ же и въ протчїхъ полїгонахъ прїбавляяся по малу , даже до лїнїи прямои , гдѣ бываетъ 135 градусовъ.

И понеже

NO. 19 Sample text page from *Novaia manera, ukrepleniiu gorodov uchinennaia chrez gospodina Blondelia . . . (The New Manner of Fortifying Towns, composed by Mr. Blondel . . .)*, M., 1711. Slavic and Baltic Division, NYPL, Astor, Lenox, and Tilden Foundations. (See above p. 140)

КНІГА

КВІНТА КУРЦІА

О ДѢЛАХЪ СОДѢЯНЫХЪ

АЛЕКСАНДРА

ВЕЛИКАГО

ЦАРЯ МАКЕДОНСКАГО.

ПРЕВЕДЕНА ПОВЕЛѢНІЕМЪ

ЦАРСКАГО

ВЕЛІЧЕСТВА.

СЪ ЛАТІНСКАГО ЯЗЫКА НА РОССІИСКІИ
ЛѢТА 1709 ГО.
И напечатана въ МОСКВѢ 1711 году,
въ Дскабрѣ мѣсяцѣ.

NO. 20 Title page and sample text page from *Kniga Kvinta Kurtsia o delakh sodeianykh Aleksandra velikago tsaria makedonskago (The Book of Quintus Curtius on the noble deeds of Alexander the Great, king of Macedonia)*, M., 1711. Slavic and Baltic Division, NYPL, Astor, Lenox, and Tilden Foundations. (See above p. 216)

КНІГА ПЕРВАЯ.

шѣла отъ ударенія Алеѵандръ ухранілся. Тогда Алеѵандръ поносівъ отца своего, взялъ олімпіаду матерь съ собою, и отъіде во епірь. обаче его філіппъ. [поношающу демарату корінѳяніну сіе ихъ несогласіе] мало послѣди по многімъ прошеніямъ едва назадъ прігласілъ. Между сімъ клеопатріны дщери со Алеѵандромъ братомъ олімпіадінымъ, [котораго, изгнану бывшу арізбѣ, царя епіру учінілъ] філіппъ бракъ отправлялъ. день былъ преславенъ ради велічества двухъ царей, и дающаго дщерь, и жену поемлющаго, и не безъ игръ знаменітыхъ былъ, которыхъ на зрѣніе філіппъ, егда безъ оберегателеи между двѣма Алеѵандрами сыномъ и зятемъ, шелъ, Павсаніа славныи отъ македонянъ юноша, въ тѣсномъ мѣстѣ філіппа идущаго, таіно убілъ, и день веселію опредѣленыи, съ горкімъ рыданіемъ о смерти філіпповѣ окончілся.

Сеи отрокъ павсаніа, содомствомъ насілованъ обідно отъ атталя, которыи его пьянъ послѣди аки нечістую блудніцу похітівъ, пірующімъ подверже. о семъ павсаніа філіппу жалобу пріносілъ, которыи толь мерзостнымъ дѣломъ хотя и велми разгнѣванъ былъ, но атталу за велікую дружбу, и яко дѣла его тогда управлялъ, да бы мѣсть учініти не возмогъ. былъ такожде атталъ ради клеопатры не давно отъ царя въ супружество взятыя, бліжнімъ велми ему совокупленъ сродствомъ, и надъ полками прежде

б 2

во Асію

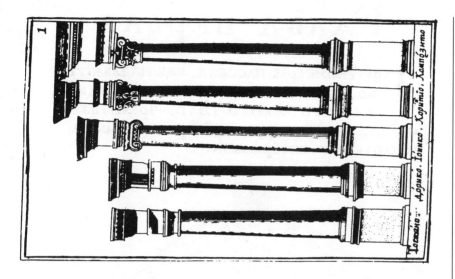

1

Тосано :. Дорико . Іонико . Коринто . Композито .

Имѣя Трактовать о пяти ордінахъ коло-
новъ, то есть, Отоскано , Дорко , Іонко,
Коринто , Композіто . показалося за достой-
но , да бы въ началѣ показать фігуры всякую особно , о которыхъ трактовать бу-
демъ, хотя еще мѣры ихъ неизвѣстны . ибо
токмо здѣсь оные положены суть для
объявленія генералной регулы . А послѣ
собственно от оной части къ другой объя-
снено будетъ.

1

NO. 21   Page 1 and figure 1 from *Pravilo o piati chinekh arkhitektury Iakova Barotsiia devignola* (*Rule of the Five Orders of Architecture* by Giacomo Barozzi da Vignola*), M., 1712. GBL. (See above p. 275)

346

ГЛАВА ПЕРВАЯ

Трегенометрія плоская, яже надлежітъ ко мѣренію, какъ далекостеи, такъ и высотъ всякіхъ тѣлъ, чрезъ нiже-объявленныи iнструментъ кратко опiсана, и чертежми изображена.

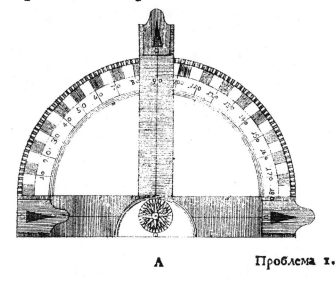

А   Проблема 1.

No. 22   Chapter One (title page) and "Problem One" from *Geometriia praktika (Practical Geometry)*, SPb., 1714. LC-Rare. (See above p. 202)

ПРОБЛЕМА ПЕРВАЯ.

о познаніи лінѣи, и угловъ.

Въ треугольникѣ называются лінѣи, нижняя въ літерахъ DP, Сінусъ, перпендікулярная въ літерахъ РС, Тангенсъ, пресѣкающая обѣ оныя лінѣи, въ літерахъ DC, Секансъ, якоже явно объявлены въ послѣдующемъ чертежѣ, при нумерѣ і мъ.

О ИСКАНІИ ЧРЕЗЪ ДВА ВѢДОМЫЯ УГЛЫ,

градусовъ третьяго угла.

ПРЕДЛОГЪ.

Да будутъ напрімѣръ вѣдомыя углы, при літерѣ Р, на 90 градусѣхъ, при літерѣ D, на 60 градусѣхъ.

ПРАВІЛО ИСКАНІЯ.

Градусы оныхъ угловъ 60, и 90 сложітъ, и будетъ 150, и оную 150 вычестъ изъ 180 градусовъ, [понеже всякои треугольнікъ состоітъ во 180 градусѣхъ,] остнется 30. На толікихъ градусѣхъ состоітъ оныи невѣдомои уголъ, состоящеи при літерѣ С, якоже явно объявлено въ послѣдующемъ исканіи и чертежѣ.

Проб: 2.

NO. 22   (continued)

РАЗСУЖДЕНІЕ

КАКІЕ ЗАКОННЫЕ ПРІЧІНЫ ЕГО ЦАРСКОЕ ВЕЛІЧЕСТВО

ПЕТРЪ ПЕРВЫИ

ЦАРЬ И ПОВЕЛІТЕЛЬ ВСЕРОССІИСКІИ

И протчая, и протчая, и протчая: къ начатію воіны протівъ Короля Карола 12, Шведского 1700 году имѣлъ, и кто изъ сіхъ обоіхъ потентатовъ, во время сеи пребывающеи воіны, болѣе умѣренности и склонности къ пріміренію показывалъ, я кто въ продолженіи онои, съ толь велікімъ разлітіемъ крови Хрістіянскои, и разореніемъ многіхъ земель віновенъ; и съ которои воюющеи страны та воіна по правіламъ Хрістіянскіхъ и політічныхъ народовъ болѣе ведена.

Все безпрістрастія фундаментално изъ древніхъ и новыхъ Актовъ и трактатовъ, такожъ и изъ запісокъ о воінскіхъ операціяхъ опісано, съ надлежащею умѣренностію и истінною. Такъ что въ потребномъ случаѣ можетъ все, а имянно: Первое орігіналными древніми, межъ Коронами россіискою, и Шведскою постановленными Трактатами, грамотами, иканцеля- ріискіми Протоколами, такожъ многое и безпрі- страстными Гісторіями, съ стороны россіискои доказано, и любопытнымъ представлено быть; съ соізволенія Его Царского Велічества всероссі- ского, собрано, и насвѣтъ издано, въ Царствующемъ САНКТЪПІТЕРБУРГѢ, Лѣта Господня 1716 года, А напечатано.

NO. 23   First page of Peter Shafirov, *Razsuzhdenie kakie zakonnye prichiny ego tsarskoe velichestvo Petr Pervyi . . . k nachatiiu voiny protiv Korolia Karola 12 Shvedskogo [v] 1700 godu imel . . . (A Discourse Concerning the Just Reasons Which his Tsarist Majesty Peter I . . . had for beginning the War against the Swedish King Charles XII in the year 1700 . . .)*, SPb., 1717. Facsimile reprint, Dobbs Ferry, NY, 1973. (See above p. 191)

СЛОВО, ПОХВА́ЛНОЕ

Ѿ БАТА́ЛІИ ПОЛТА́ВСКОЙ :

Ска́занное въ Санктъпитербу́рхъ въ Це́ркви живонача́льныѧ Тро́цы : чрезъ Ре́ктора, Чтнѣ́йшагѡ Оц҃а̀ Прокопо́вича. Іѡ́на в к҃з де́нь а҃ѱ҃з҃і.

Постоухва́лное дѣ́ло, слы́шателіе : дѣ́ло вои́стинну достоухва́лное, с ра́достію и весе́ліемъ, и с до́лжнымъ всеси́лному Бг҃у бл҃года́реніемъ, лѣ́тнꙑ твори́ти па́мѧть, пресла́вныѧ Полта́вскіѧ викто́ріи, є҆сть всеми́рныѧ рода нашегѡ сла́вы, кра́йнегѡ супоста́тъ на́шихъ посты́жде́нїѧ, и б҃жіихъ къ намъ бл҃годѣѧ́нїй неѡписа́нныхъ. А҆́ще бо и҆ не мо́жетъ не памѧтова́ти сегѡ всѧ́къ сн҃ъ рѡссі́йскїй, ꙗ́кѡ не забве́ннагѡ своегѡ бл҃гополꙋ́чіѧ : а҆́ще и҆ непрїѧ́тель забы́ти не мо́жетъ, ꙗ́кѡ ꙗ́звы своѧ́ неисцѣ́льныхъ : ѡ҆днакоже да не неблгода́рни вомни́мсѧ бы́ти, та́кѡ намъ бл҃годѣ́авшему гд҃ꙋ, достоухва́лнѣ наверша́емъ пра́зденственное сїе толи́кїѧ побѣ́ды воспомина́нїе. Бꙋ́ди намъ не в приме́ръ дре́вній, е҆́ллинскихъ и҆ ри́мскихъ, и протчи́хъ славолюбныхъ люде́й ѻ҆бꙑ́чай, кото́рые вели́кимъ иждиве́нїемъ сооружа́ли столпы̀, и҆ врата̀, и҆ ѡ҆бели́ски, и пирами́ды, и҆ и҆ннꙑе тропеи, и҆ли побѣдонѡ́сныѧ зна́менїѧ, е҆́же бы в ни́хъ, ѡ҆ста́вити не ꙋ҆мира́ющꙋю сла́вныхъ дѣ́лъ свои́хъ па́мѧть послѣ́днимъ вѣ́кѡмъ : хотѧ́ и҆ намъ таково́агѡ попече́нїѧ ничто́же возбранѧ́етъ : но и҆ вопрекѝ, чл҃вѣ́къ ѡ҆ сла́вѣ ѻ҆те́чества своегѡ нерадѧ́щїй всегда̀ ꙋ҆ мꙋ́жей мꙋ́дрыхъ

217

а҃

NO. 24   First and last pages of Feofan Prokopovich, *Slovo pokhvalnoe o batalii Poltavskoi (Sermon of Praise on the Poltava Battle)*, SPb., 1717. Printed in traditional Cyrillic type with Slavonic numerals. LC-Rare. (See above pp. 224, 267)

350

Не сꙋмнюсѧ , ꙗкω сїе проповѣдꙋетъ всѧкомꙋ
нелицемѣрнѣ православномꙋ совѣсть своѧ , паче хꙋдоꙋмїѧ
моегω , и ꙗкω въ сладость ѻнꙋю послꙋшаетъ дꙋша
благочестиваѧ . И аще такω есть , то достоино
въ празднество нынѣшнее дрꙋгъдрꙋга возбꙋждати имамы
къ ѻбщей радости , достоинω дрꙋгъ къ дрꙋгꙋ с игранїемъ
срца восклинкемъ . Радꙋитесѧ Бгꙋ помощникꙋ нашемꙋ ,
воскликните Бгꙋ ꙗкωвлю : Прїимите ѱаломъ , и
дадите тꙋмпанъ , ѱалтирь красенъ съ гꙋслꙑ .
Кто возглетъ силꙑ гдни , слꙑшанꙑ сотворитъ всѧ
хвалꙑ егω ; велїй Гдь нашъ , и велїѧ крѣпость егω ,
и разꙋма егω нѣсть числа . Десница гдня сотвои силꙋ ,
десница Гдня вознесе насъ . Ѿ гда бꙑсть се , и есть
дивно во ѻчїю нашею . Съ нами Бгъ , разꙋмѣйте ꙗзꙑцꙑ
и покарѧйтесѧ , ꙗкω съ нами Бгъ : Аще бо паки воз-
можете , и паки побѣждени бꙋдете , ꙗкω съ нами Бгъ .
Гдь силъ съ нами , застꙋпникъ нашъ Бгъ ꙗкωвль .
Благословенъ Гдь Бгъ їилевъ ,
и да рекꙋтъ вси людїе ,
бꙋди бꙋди .

Печатано въ Санктъпитербꙋрхѣ ,҂аѱѕі годꙋ ,
Мца їꙋлїа въ ки день .

NO. 24   (continued)

ЮНОСТИ

ЧЕСТНОЕ ЗЕРЦАЛО

ИЛИ

ПОКАЗАНІЕ КЪ ЖІТЕІСКОМУ ОБХОЖДЕНІЮ.

Собранное отъ разныхъ Авторовъ.

НАПЕЧАТАСЯ ПОВЕЛѢНІЕМЪ

ЦАРСКАГО ВЕЛІЧЕСТВА,

ВЪ САНКТЪПІТЕРБУРХѢ

Аѣта Господня 1717, Февраля 4 дня.

NO. 25   Title page and pages 1–3 of *Iunosti chestnoe zertsalo ili pokazanie k zhiteiskomu obkhozhdeniiu . . . (The Honorable Mirror of Youth, or A Guide to Social Conduct . . .)*, SPb., 1717. Facsimile reprint, Moscow, 1990. (See above p. 228)

ЮНОСТИ

ЧЕСТНОЕ ЗЕРЦАЛО.

или

ПОКАЗАНІЕ КЪ ЖІТЕИСКОМУ ОБХОЖДЕНІЮ.

Собранное отъ разныхъ Авторовъ.

Ъ первыхъ наипаче всего должни дѣти отца и матерь въ велікои чести содержать. И когда отъ родітелеи что имъ пріказано бываетъ, всегда шляпу въ рукахъ держать, а пред німи не вздѣвать, и возлѣ ихъ не садітіся, и прежде оныхъ не засѣдать, при ніхъ во окно всѣмъ тѣломъ не выглядовать, но все потаеннымъ образомъ А съ велікімъ

2 Зерцало

сь велікімъ почтеніемъ, не сь німи врядъ, но немного уступя позади оныхъ къ сторонѣ стоять, подобно яко пажъ нѣкоторыи или слуга. Въ домѣ нічего своімъ имянемъ не повелѣвать, но имянемъ отца или матере, отъ челядінцевъ просітелнымъ образомъ требовать, развѣ что у кого особлівыя слуги, которыя самому ему подвержены бываютъ. для того, что обычаіно служітели и челядінцы не двумъ господамъ и госпожамъ, но токмо одному господіну охотно служатъ. А о кромѣ того, часто проісходятъ ссоры и велікія между ими бываютъ отъ того мятежи въ домѣ, такъ, что сами не опознаютъ, что кому дѣлать надлежітъ.

2. Дѣти не имѣютъ безъ имянного пріказу родітелского, никого бранітъ,

бранїть, или поносїтелными словами порекать. а ежели то надобно, и оное они должни учїнїть
вѣжлїво и учтїво.

3. У родїтелеи рѣчеи перебївать
не надлежїтъ, и нїже прекословїть,
и другїхъ ихъ сверстнїковъ въ рѣчи
не впадать, но ожїдать пока они
выговорятъ. Часто одного дѣла
не повторять, на столъ, на скамью,
или на что иное, не опїратся, и
не быть подобнымъ деревенскому
мужїку, которои на солнцѣ ва-
ляется, но стоять должни прямо.

4. без спросу не говорїть, а когда
и говорїть имъ случїтся, то
должни они благопрїятно, а не
крїкомъ и нїже съ сердца, или
съ задору говорїть, не яко бы
сумозброды. но все что имъ говорїть, имѣетъ быть правда истїнная

А 2   ни

355

Карабелнои бордъ.	Boord , ſcheeps- boord. o.
Карабïнъ.	Karbyn. v.
Караванъ.	Karavane. v.
Караулъ отводнои на морѣ.	Brandwacht. v.
Кардамонъ.	Kardamom. v.
Кардïналъ.	Kardinaal. m.
Карѣта.	Koets. v.
Кармазïнъ краснои-цвѣтъ.	Karmozyn. o.
Карманъ , сумочка.	Tas ‚ Taſch. v.
Карпузъ , калпакъ , и-камïлавка.	Keuvel. v.
Картаунъ пушка.	Kartouw.. v.
Картузïанъчернецъ.	Karthúyſer. m.
Картузъ.	Kardoes. v,
Карчма.	Kroeg. v.
Карчемнои домъ ïлï блядскои домъ.	Kuf. v.

NO. 26   Page from *Kniga leksikon . . . s Rossiiskogo na Gollandskii iazyk (A Lexicon book . . . from Russian into the Dutch language)*, SPb., 1717. Slavic and Baltic Division, NYPL, Astor, Lenox, and Tilden Foundations. (See above p. 290)

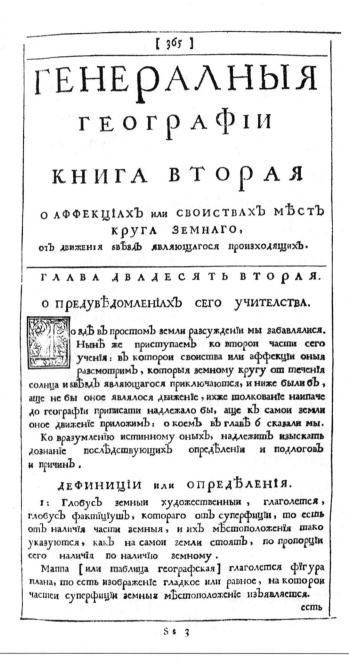

[365]

ГЕНЕРАЛНЫЯ

ГЕОГРАФІИ

КНИГА ВТОРАЯ

О АФФЕКЦІАХЪ или СВОИСТВАХЪ МѢСТЪ
КРУГА ЗЕМНАГО,
отъ движенія звѣздъ являющагося произходящихъ.

ГЛАВА ДВАДЕСЯТЬ ВТОРАЯ.

О ПРЕДУВѢДОМЛЕНІАХЪ СЕГО УЧИТЕЛСТВА.

До здѣ въ простомъ земли разсужденіи мы забавлялися. Нынѣ же приступаемъ ко второи части сего ученія: въ которои своиства или аффекціи оныя разсмотримъ, которыя земному кругу отъ печенія солнца и звѣздъ являющагося приключаются, и ниже были бъ, аще не бы оное являлося движеніе, ихже шолкованіе наипаче до географіи приписати надлежало бы, аще къ самои земли оное движеніе приложимъ: о коемъ въ главѣ 6 сказали мы.

Ко вразумленію истинному оныхъ, надлежитъ изыскать дознаніе послѣдствующихъ опредѣленіи и подлоговъ и причинъ.

ДЕФИНИЦІИ или ОПРЕДѢЛЕНІЯ.

1: Глобусъ земныи художественныи, глаголется, глобусъ фактіціушъ, котораго отъ суперфиціи, то есть отъ наличія части земныя, и ихъ мѣстоположенія тако указуются, какъ на самои земли стоятъ, по пропорціи сего наличія по наличію земному.

Маппа [или таблица географская] глаголется фигура плана, то есть изображеніе гладкое или равное, на которои части суперфиціи земныя мѣстоположеніе изъявляется.

есть

Ss 3

NO. 27   Page from the *Geografia generalnaia (General Geography)*, M., 1718. HU-Houghton. (See above pp. 206, 287)

357

ГЛАВА ПЯТАЯ.

о брігадѣ.

Брігада при воїскѣ называется, когда 2: 3: или болѣе полковъ подъ команду едіного отданы бываютъ. И тогда оныи, которыи тѣ полки командуетъ, называется брегадіръ. Таковые брігады могутъ конные и пѣшіе быть.

ГЛАВА ШЕСТАЯ.

о КОРВОЛАНТѣ.

Корволантъ [сірѣчь легкіи Корпусъ] которое лібо така уже было, или отъ велікои армеи въ нѣсколко тысячахъ нарочно отдеташовано [или отдѣлено] бываетъ, и отдается къ нѣкоторому дѣлу въ команду Генералу, лібо у непріятеля для пресѣканія или отніманія пасу, или оному въ тылъ итти, или въ его землю впасть, и чінітъ діверзію. Такіе Корпусы называются Корволантъ, которои состоитъ отъ 6, до 7 тысячь рядовыхъ, и такімъ способомъ, можетъ оное всюду поворачіватіся безъ тягости, и на непріятелскіе дѣла прімѣчать добрымъ поведеніемъ, которои сочіняется не токмо отъ ковалеріи однои, но при томъ употребляема бываетъ и інфантеріа съ легкіми пушками, смотря случаи и мѣста положенія. А егда бываютъ малыя деташаменты командрованные изъ полковъ, лібо чініти какои поіскъ, или наряжены бываютъ для Конвоя, и къ такімъ штандаріповъ, знаменъ и пушекъ не дается.

Б　　　　　ГЛАВА

NO. 28　Page from the *Kniga ustav voinskii . . . (The Book of the Military Statute . . .),* SPb., 1719. HU-Law School Library (Rare Unclassed). (See above p. 129)

ГЛАВА ПЕРВАЯ.

О ДОЛЖНОСТИ АДМІРАЛТЕІСКОИ КОЛЕГІИ.

1.

О дѵрекцїи надъ всѣми дѣлами Адмїралтеїскїми вездѣ.

Олегія Адмїралтеїская , имѣетъ верхнюю дїрекцїю, надъ людми, спросенїемъ, и протчїми дѣлами къ Адмїралтеїству надлежащїми , каковабъ званїя оные нїбыли, во всемъ Россїискомъ Государствѣ. И должна въ вѣрности и ревности такъ поступать, какъ въ морскомъ Реґламенгпѣ, въ первои главѣ, первои книги, въ должности Аншефтъ командующаго напїсано, подъ такїмъ же наказанїемъ и штрафами.

2.

О персонахъ въ Колегїи Адмїралтеїскои.

Колегія Адмїралтеїская , состоитъ изъ флаг офїцѣровъ , также и Капїтановъ Командоровъ: [ежели флагмановъ недоволное чїсло будетъ] Оные члены Колегїи, обыкновенно выбїраются изъ старыхъ или увѣчныхъ, которые мало удобны уже къ служѣ воїнскои. Здѣсь же, за новостїю, надлежїтъ и изъ тѣхъ, которые еще службу отправляютъ , развѣ которые вдаль для команды опредѣлены. А имянно: чтобъ не менше семи человѣкъ , а понуждѣ пяти. А тѣмъ у которыхъ что есть на рукахъ, въ совѣтѣ небыть, кромѣ того, когда о чьеи должности дѣло случїтся, тогда долженъ быть въ Колегїи и совѣтовать. Такожъ когда изъ такїхъ кому нужда будетъ о чемъ предлагать въ Колегїи, то имъ надлежїтъ тогда въ Колегїю прїходїть.

ИМЯНА ЧЛЕНАМЪ.

Презїдентъ Генералъ Адмїралъ, или кто первои Адмїралъ Віце Презїдентъ, кто по Генералѣ . Адмїралѣ первои рангъ имѣетъ , ежели онъ на особлївую команду вдаль куды не) будетъ посланъ.

А   Совѣтнїки

ОПРЕДѢЛЕНІЕ О ОФІЦѢРАХЪ

комісарахъ и о пріказныхъ служітеляхъ и
протчіхъ чінахъ, коликое чісло какіхъ
чіновъ укакого дѣла надлежітъ имѣть.

359

ВЪ КОЛЕГІЮ.

Оборъ секретарь	1
Секретарь	1
Нотаріусъ	1
Переводчікъ	1
Регістраторъ	1
Канцелярістовъ	3
Подканцелярістовъ	3
Копіистовъ	6
Вахмістровъ	2 } для розсылокъ
Сторожеи	6 } и топленія.

ГЕНЕРАЛУ КРІКСЪ КОМІСАРУ ПРИ АДМІРАЛТЕІСТВѢ.

Канцелярістовъ	2
Подканцелярістовъ	3
Копіистовъ	6

ВЪ ПОРТѢ.

Подканцеляріетъ	1
Копіистовъ	3

ВО ФЛОТѢ.

Подканцеляріетъ	1
Копіистовъ	3

КОНТРОЛОРУ.

Комісаръ	1 изъ пріказныхъ
Канцеляріетъ	1
Подканцеляріетъ	1
Копіистовъ	4

т   въ ревелѣ.

NO. 29 (continued)

360

РЕГЛА́МЕ́НТЪ

и҆лѝ

Оу҆ста́въ

Дꙋхо́вныѧ Колле́гїи , по
кото́ромꙋ ѻ҆́наѧ зна́ть
до́лженства своѧ̀ , и҆ всѣ́хъ
дꙋхо́выхъ чинѡ́въ , та́кожъ
и҆ мїрски́хъ ли́цъ , по е҆́лику
ѻ҆́ные оу҆правле́нїю дꙋхо́вномꙋ
подлежа́тъ , и҆ при то́мъ
въ ꙋ҆правле́нїи дѣ́лъ свои́хъ
постꙋпа́ть и҆мѣ́етъ. •

м҃зрла

NO. 30   Two pages from the *Dukhovnyi Reglament (Ecclesiastical Regulation)*, M., 1722.
Printed in traditional Cyrillic type. LC-Law Library (Rare). (See above pp. 173n81, 181)

регламентъ

а҃ . На конецъ въ таковомъ Правителствѣ Соборномъ бꙋдетъ аки нѣкаѧ школа правленїѧ дꙋховнагѡ : ибо ѿ сообщенїѧ многихъ и различны расꙋжденїй , и совѣтовъ , и доводѡвъ правилныхъ , ꙗковыхъ частые дѣла требꙋютъ , всѧкъ ѿ соꙁѣдателей ꙋдобнѡ можетъ наꙋчитисѧ дꙋховной полїтїки , и повседневны искꙋсствомъ навыкнꙋти , какъ бы лꙋчше домъ Бж҃їй ꙋправить возмоглъ , и по томꙋ самые ꙋгоднѣишїе ѿ числа колле- гѡвъ , или соꙁѣдателей ѻсобы , ꙗвѧтсѧ на степень Арх҃їереиства вос- ходить достоиныѧ . И такѡ в Рѡссїи помощїю Бж҃їею скорѡ и ѿ дꙋховнагѡ чина грꙋбость ѿпадетъ , и надѣꙗтисѧ всегѡ лꙋчшагѡ .

Втораѧ

362

КРАТКОЕ СОБРАНІЕ

ІСТОРІЧЕСКОЕ НАРОДА СЛАВЯНСКОГО, ЕГО СЛАВЫ И РАЗШІРЕНІЯ.

Ікакоже удівітелно есть, что слава народа Славянского, нынѣ не такъ ясна, какъ оноя довѣло разславітіся по Вселеннѣи. Ежели бы сси народъ, такъ достаточенъ былъ людми учсными и книжными, какъ былъ доволснъ военными и превосходітелными оружіемъ, тобъ ни едінъ другои народъ во вселеннѣи, былъ въ прімѣрѣ имени Славянскому. А что протчіе народы, которые ѕѣло были ніжше его, нынѣ велми ссбя прославляютъ, то не ради чего иного, токмо чрезъ бывшіхъ въ ихъ народѣ людеи ученыхъ.

А ИМЯННО.

Іудеіскіе дѣла опісывали; Ѳілонъ, Эезіѳъ, и Юзеѳъ, Історіки велікопочтенные, которымъ опісаніемъ прославляли дѣла Іудсіская; не оставілібъ то учініть многіе иные Історіки Греческіе велікоученые, ежеліѳъ имъ было свободно обьявлять странные дѣла, и сскрстпная исінінны, какъ пішетъ Лстанціи въ 4 книгѣ,

въ 11

NO. 31   Page from the *Kniga istoriografiia pochatiia imene, slavy i razshireniia naroda slavianskogo . . . chrez Gospodina Mavrourbina . . . (History of the Beginning, Fame and Spread of the Slavonic People . . . by Master Mauro Orbini . . .),* SPb., 1722. HU-Houghton. (See above p. 218n72)

⁘ (☼) ⁘

КНИГА ПЕРВАЯ

ГЛАВА ПЕРВАЯ.

О ГЕНЕРАЛѢ АДМИРАЛѢ.

и всякомъ Аншефъ командующемъ.

1.

всѣмъ должно хранить интерессъ государевъ
и государственной ·

АкЪ АдмиралЪ, такЪ и прочïе вышнïе и нижнïе
Офицеры, должны охранять со всякимъ тщанïемъ
и ревностïю интерессъ своего Государя и Госу-
дарства, гдѣ ни будутъ обрѣтаться со врученною
имъ командою, во всякихъ случаяхъ.

2.

о послушанïи указовъ и о почтенïи
отъ нижнихъ вышнимъ

КакЪ главное все морское войско должно быть въ послушанïи нашихъ указовъ нынѣ учиненныхъ и впредь учиняе-
мыхъ, такЪ и Генерала Адмирала, или перьваго Адмирала;
такЪ равно должны послушны быть подчиненные всякому
Аншефъ командующему. ТакожЪ въ эскадрахъ и дивизïяхъ,
по высокости чина и старшинству, во время ихъ команды.
ТакожЪ и прочïе офицеры каждаго корабля командиру онаго,
не только морскïе, но и сухопутные обрѣтающïеся на кораб-
ляхъ: а салдаты, канониры, матрозы и прочïе всякаго чина,
офицеромъ и ундеръ офицеромъ, со всякимъ почтенïемъ послушны да будутъ, не пренебрегая того ни како, подъ наказанïемъ,
что тѣ, которые во всякое время, вѣдѣнïемъ и волею противъ
такого указу поступатъ, за то казнены будутъ смертïю.

А

NO. 32   Two pages from the *Kniga ustav morskoi . . . (The Book of the Naval Statute . . .)*,
SPb., 1724. Moscow 1993 facsimile reprint of St. Petersburg 1763 edition, which replicates
St. Petersburg 1724 edition. (See above pp. 63, 71)

О ФЛОТѢ

Лотъ слово есть Французское. Симъ словомъ разумѣется множество судовъ водныхъ вмѣстѣ идущихъ, или
стоящихъ, какъ воинскихъ, такъ и купецкихъ.
Флотъ военный, аще многое число кораблей, раздѣ-
ляется въ три главныя или генеральныя Эшквадры; первая
Кордебаталіи, вторая Авангардъ, третія Ариргардъ и сіи
паки дѣляшся, каждая на три паршикулярные дивизіи, яко
слѣдуетъ.

Кордебаталіи бѣлаго Флага, Авангардъ бѣлаго Флага,
Арпргардъ бѣлаго Флага. Кордебаталіи синего Флага,
Авангардъ синего Флага, Арпргардъ синего Флага. Кордѣ-
баталіи краснаго Флага, Авангардъ краснаго Флага, Арпргардъ краснаго Флага.

Ежели же меньшее число кораблей, шо и Эшквадръ меньше.

КОМАНДИРЫ СУТЬ ВО ФЛОТѢ СЛѢДУЮЩІЕ.

Генералъ Адмиралъ.
Адмиралъ отъ синего Флага.
Адмиралъ отъ краснаго Флага.
Вице Адмиралы.
Шаутбейнахты.
Капитаны Командоры.

И ПОНЕЖЕ ИМѢЕМЪ ТРИ ФЛАГА, ТОГО РАДИ КОМАНДОВАТЬ ИМѢЮТЪ ПО СЕМУ.

Генералъ Адмиралъ всемъ Флотомъ и паршикулярно
Кордебаталіи.
ВЪ ЕГО ЭШКВАДРѢ ТРИ ПАРТИКУЛЯРНЫЕ ДИВИЗІИ.

Первая его Кордебаталіи.

Вторая Вице-Адмирала отъ бѣлаго Флага, яко его Авангардія.

Третія Шаутбейнахта отъ бѣлагожъ Флага, яко его Арир-
гардія Ежели же когда сего чина Генерала Адмирала нѣтъ,
тогда Адмиралъ отъ бѣлаго Флага сіе мѣсто имѣетъ.

Адми-

NO. 32 (continued)

РОЗГОВОРЪ УAДМIРAЛA СЪ КAПIТAНOMЪ
ИЛИ
ПОЛНОЕ УЧЕНIЕ КAКО УПРAВЛЯТЬ КAРAБЛЕМЪ ВО ВСЯКIЕ, РAЗНЫЕ СЛУЧAИ.

365

NO. 33   First contents page of Konon Zotov, *Razgovar' u admirala s kapitanom o komande . . . (A Conversation between an Admiral and a Captain about Command . . .)*, SPb., 1724. GBL. (See above p. 78)

366

РЕКОМЕНДАЦІА,
или вручителное пісаніе къ знатному человѣку.

благородныи, особліво высокопочшенныи
господінъ таїныи совѣтнікъ, высокїи
Патронъ, [или благодѣтель.]

Ваше превосходітелство да не
изволітъ за sло воспріяти,
что я дерзаю вамъ самімъ,
сіми малыми строками поклонъ
отдать, ибо ищу себя оными
вашему превосходітелству послуш-
но рекомендовать, и ваше много-
мощное заступленіе себѣ испросіть.
понеже вашего превосходітелства
іскусство и особлівая мілость ко
ученымъ людемъ, къ вашеи всегда
пребывающеи славѣ вездѣ ізвѣстна.
того ради и я онаго себѣ домогатіся
обязанъ есмь: понеже мнѣ знатныхъ

М 2 и высоко-

NO. 34 Page from *Priklady, kako pishutsia komplimenty raznye na nemetskom iazyke to est', pisaniia ot potentatov k potentatam Pozdravitelnye i sozhaletelnye, i inye; Takozhde mezhdu srodnikov i priiatelei* (Models of how various compliments are written in German, that is, Congratulatory, commiserative and other writings from potentates to potentates; As also between relatives and friends), SPb., 1725. LC-Rare. (See above p. 192)

ГЛАВА ДВАДЕСЯТЬ ШЕСТАЯ

о РЕСПЕКТѢ НАДЛЕЖАЩЕМЪ ПРЕЗІДЕНТОМЪ.

Понеже Презіденты, а во отличеніи ихъ Віцепрезіденты, вышшіе главы суть, и въ лицѣ Его Імператорскаго Величества сидятъ, ради управленія всѣхъ дѣлъ въ Коллегіяхъ, такожъ на каждаго вѣрность, прилѣжность, и поступку надзираютъ: того ради надлежитъ всѣмъ членамъ, какъ Коллегиннымъ, такъ и Канцелярнымъ учрежденному ихъ Презіденту всякое достоиное почтеніе и респектъ, и послушаніе чинить, и по указомъ ихъ въ дѣлахъ, которые Его Величества высокои службѣ и Інтересу касающца поступать. Между тѣмъ не надлежитъ Презідентамъ, данную имъ отъ Его Імператорскаго Величества власть презирать, и членовъ того Коллегіа ни чемъ не отягощать, чего они противу чину и должности своеи исполнять недолжны, толь наименшее жестокими и чувственными словами укорять, но всѣ дѣла Коллегиннымъ членамъ по благоизобрѣтенію всего Коллегіа давать, и каждаго по состоянію особы Его, и погрѣшенія наказывать. Ежели же которои членъ тяжко согрѣшитъ, и о томъ въ Коллегіи явится, или чрезъ фіскала донесено будетъ, въ такихъ преступленіяхъ, которыя надлежатъ тѣлесному наказанію, отсылать съ его дѣломъ въ Юстицъ Коллегію, а въ прочемъ кто противъ сего преступитъ, тотъ будетъ наказанъ, смотря по силѣ вины ево, денежнымъ шпрафомъ, въ своеи Коллегіи.

-А

NO. 35   Two pages from the *General'nyi reglament (General Regulation)*, M., 1725. GBL. (See above p. 164n58)

ГЛАВА ТРІДЕСЯТЬ ПЕРВАЯ

О ДОЛЖНОСТИ ПЕРЕВОДЧИКА.

Переводчика должность въ Коллегіяхъ есть, чтобъ онъ все оное что до Коллегіи касается, и ему дано будетъ изъ Іностраннаго языка на рускои явственно и ясно переводилъ· да бы сенсъ справедливъ, и мнѣніе подлиннаго писма въ переводѣ, согласно было : и доволно будетъ, когда при каждомъ коллегіи одинъ въ Россіискомъ, и Нѣмецкомъ языкахъ, весма искуснои Переводчікъ обрѣташися будетъ, кромѣ Іностранныхъ Государствъ Коллегіи, которыя болши во всякихъ языкахъ, искусныхъ Переводчиковъ требуетъ· и когда Переводчику какое дѣло для переводу, дано будетъ, то ему по должности своеи, толь скоро переводишь, какъ возможно, го состоянію дѣла, и нужды, подъ опасеніемъ штрафа, и вычешу изъ жалованья· такожде надлежитъ ему свои переводъ во свидѣтелство подписывать: сіе повиненъ онъ исполнять, подъ такимижъ штрафами и наказаніями, какъ въ должности Секретарскои написано.

NO. 35 (continued)

Ѡ см́ерти
Петра̀ вели́кагѡ
Імпера́тора Рѡссíйскагѡ .
кра́ткая по́вѣсть .

Я тщáтелнѡ и вѣ́рнѡ смéрть нáшегѡ
Монáрха изобрази́мъ , ѡ чéмъ никогдà
дово́лнѡ плáкатися не мóжемъ , сегѡ̀ ѡ́
нáсъ вели́чество мýжа трéбуетъ : и́бо таковы́хъ
людéй , котóрыхъ житíе нáмъ во удивлéнíи
бы́ло , каковà и смéрть и́мъ приключи́лась , всѧ́къ
приро́днымъ любопы́тствомъ вѣ́дать и́щемъ и
желáемъ . Понуждáетъ къ семỳ и то̀ , что̀
ѡ сéмъ не совершéнные по́вѣсти ѿ инострáнныхъ
печáтные

NO. 36   First and last page of Feofan Prokopovich, *O smerti Petra Velikago, Imperatora Rossiiskago. Kratkaia povest'* (*A Brief Account of the Death of Peter the Great, Russian Emperor*), SPb., 1726. Printed in traditional Cyrillic type. LC-Rare. (See above p. 223)

370

кругъ поставлены, и трижды всѣ выпалили
тучнымъ огнемъ. По окончанїи же погребенїа,
ѿ всегѡ паки мѣлкагѡ оружїа, такожде
изъ всѣхъ пушекъ въ крѣпости и в адмиралтей-
ствѣ вдругъ страшный трижды громъ великїй
зданъ. Но сїа и прочаа къ сей церемонїи
погребалной принадлежащаа нарочнѡ, тщателнѡ
и ѡбстоателнѡ ѿ прочїихъ ѡписана и публи-
кована суть.

И таковое то ѿ насъ было Великому
Герою, Гдрю, и Оцу нашему послѣднее послу-
женїе: которагѡ желали мы паче многолѣтнѡ
живущаго и црствующаго видѣть съ радостїю,
не погребалными почестми украшать во ѡбщей
печали и горести.

Печатано въ Санктпетербургской Тѵпографїи, ҂аѱкв года,
Августа аі дне.

NO. 36   (continued)

О ДОЛЖНОСТИ

По второму разсужденїю невѣденїе есть ВОЛНОЕ или НЕВОЛНОЕ. Волное, когда кто или самоволно, отрінувъ средствїя познанїя истінны, или должнаго непріложівъ тщанїя, погрѣшілъ. Не волное есть, когда кто не зналъ, и не возмогъ нїже долженъ былъ знати, а погрѣшілъ: и сїе паки СУГУБОЕ. Первое, когда кто тогда не зналъ, обаче вїновенъ есть, чего ради въ такомъ состоянїи обрѣтался. Второе не токмо тогда незнанїя не могъ одолѣти, но и въ вінѣ нѐ обрѣтается, для чего въ таковыи попалъ случаи.

9. Вторая сіла, которую человѣкъ паче протчіхъ жівотныхъ имѣетъ, имѣнуется САМОВОЛІЕ, которымъ, аки внутренніъмъ двіженіемъ къ творенїю человѣкъ возбуждается и избіраетъ что ему угодно: отвергаетъ же, еже

NO. 37 Page from Samuel Pufendorf, *O dolzhnosti cheloveka i grazhdanina po zakonu estestvennomu* (*On the Duties of Man and the Citizen According to Natural Law*), SPb., 1726. GBL. (See above p. 215n58)

372

Teutsch-Lateinisch-und Rußisches
LEXICON,

Samt
Denen Anfangs-Gründen
der Rußischen Sprache.
Zu allgemeinem Nutzen
Bey der Kayserl. Academie der Wissenschafften
Zum Druck befördert.

НѢМЕЦКО-ЛАТИНСКІИ И РУСКІИ

ЛЕѴИКОНЪ

купно

съ первыми началами

РУСКАГО ЯЗЫКА

къ общеи пользѣ

при ІМПЕРАТОРСКОИ АКАДЕМІИ НАУКЪ

печатію изданъ.

St. Petersburg,
Gedruckt in der Kayserl. Academie der Wissenschafften Buchdruckerey
1 7 3 1.

NO. 38   Title page of the *Teutsch-Lateinisch-und Russisches Lexicon/Nemetsko-latinskii i ruskii Leksikon . . . (A German-Latin-Russian Dictionary . . .)*, SPb., 1731. Facsimile reprint, Munich, 1982–1983. By permission of Kubon & Sagner, Munich. (See above p. 291)

ЭѴКЛІДОВЫ

ЭЛЕМЕНТЫ

ИзЪ ДВЕНАТЦАТИ НЕѲТОНОВЫХЪ КНИ

ВЫБРАННЫЯ,

И

ВЪ ОСМЬ КНИГЪ

ЧРЕЗЪ ПРОФЕССОРА МАѲЕМАТІКИ

АНДРЕЯ ФАРХВАРСОНА

СОКРАЩЕННЫЯ,

СЪ ЛАТІНСКАГО на РОССІИКІИ ЯЗЫКЪ

ХІРУРГУСОМЪ ІВАНОМЪ САТАРОВЫМЪ

ПРЕЛОЖѢННЫЯ,

НАПЕЧАТАНЫ при САНКТЪПЕТЕРБУРГѢ

въ Морскои Академіческои Тупографіи

Первымъ Тѵсненіемъ 1739 Лѣпıa·

NO. 39   Title page and page 2 of Henry Farquharson, *Evklidovy elementy . . . (Elements of Euclid . . .)*, SPb., 1739. LC-Rare. (See above p. 85)

2   Элементовъ Эвклідовыхъ

374

Д Е Ф І Н І Ц І И,

или
істолкованія
словъ.

1. Точка, есть знакъ въ велічінѣ нераздѣлны·
се есть, которои ни помышленіемъ
раздѣлітіся не можетъ.

Точка всея велічіны есть бутто начало
якоже едініца начало есть числа.

2. Лінея есть толко величина долгая. сиречь,
лішающаяся всякія шіріны. Разумѣется раждати
отъ теченія точки.

1.   3. Лінейныя предѣлы суть точки.

4. Прямая лінея есть, которая прямо лѣжітъ
между своіхъ краінⷯіхъ точекъ. Или всѣхъ есть
кратчаішая, которые межъ двема точками
вестіся могутъ.

5. Суперфиція, или поверхность есть толко
величина долгая и широкая. И для того два
размѣренія имѣетъ. Разумѣется раждати отъ
линѣинаго тѣченія.

6. Поверхности краинія суть линеи.

7. Плоскость, или поверхность плоская есть
которая

Оглавленїе.

НАСТАВЛЕНИЕ ПЕРВОЕ,
о человѣческомъ словѣ вообще.

Гмк

no. 40   Table of Contents (first of two pages) from M. V. Lomonosov, *Rossiiskaia grammatika (Russian Grammar)*, SPb., 1755. HU-Houghton. (See above p. 292)

APPENDIX II: WORDS

The list that follows consists of about 1,000 words (hereafter List) that were first "fixed" *(fiksirovannye)* in Russian during the Petrine era, as well as another 700 or so contemporary or later derivations. The List is comprehensive rather than exhaustive, since to have aimed for the latter would have required scrutinizing every scrap of written evidence from both the era itself and the preceding and subsequent periods, a task that was well beyond the capacities of the author and his assistants. The List is also selective, meaning that it does not include highly technical terms, words that remained foreign in Russian, or words that more or less rapidly became obsolete. At once comprehensive and selective, the List offers a representative sampling of the words that were permanently added to Russian in Peter's time and of those that were sooner or later derived from them. We thereby hope to demonstrate, now in convenient tabular fashion, the nature and scope of the verbal impact of the Petrine revolution in Russia.

The List draws on our own research in contemporary verbal sources as well as on that of previous scholars, most notably N. A. Smirnov's monograph of 1910 (see Works Cited). Smirnov lists in alphabetical order some 3,000 foreign words found in twenty-nine documents of the Petrine era, including a manuscript "Lexicon of new words *[Leksikon vokabulam novym]*" drawn up late in the reign partly by Peter himself which Smirnov prints as an appendix (pp. 363–382). Although subsequently criticized for including simple variants as separate words, much later derivations, and terms that had entered Russian as much as a century before Peter's time, Smirnov's "Dictionary" has remained the basic compilation of Petrine neologisms to this day. In their authoritative study of 1972, Birzhakova and her colleagues (Birzhak. under

Works Cited) verify some 2,500 of its entries while proceeding to add another 2,000 words derived from Christiani (Christ., 1906), Hüttl-Worth (H-W., 1963), and their own research—for a total of 4,504 individual foreign words (5,153 including contemporary derivations) that were fixed in Russian in the Petrine period. With these figures we may compare those adduced by Birzhakova and her colleagues for preceding and subsequent periods: 764 words plus 232 derivations (total 996) for the period roughly 1660–1690; 2,268 words plus 824 derivations (total 3,092) for the period roughly 1740–1770; and 1,694 words plus 1,191 derivations (total 2,885) for the period roughly 1770–1800 (Birzhak., pp. 171–174, especially chart on p. 172; totals computed by the author and his assistants). The figures alone indicate not only that lexical augmentation under Peter was on a hugely unprecedented scale (by a factor of five and more), but that the process thus set in motion—call it intensive lexical Europeanization—continued apace after his death.

Christiani's 1906 survey of mostly German loanwords found in seventeenth- and eighteenth-century Russian sources proved to be the first of a series of more or less specialized studies by foreign scholars, a series that includes, in addition to Hüttl-Worth's glossary of 1963, those subsequently compiled by Avery, Bond, Gardiner, Gribble, Kaiser, Koch, Leeming, Otten, Ryan, and Whittall, all of which are also identified below and regularly cited in the List. The List is similarly indebted to the variously specialized works by Russian scholars published since Smirnov and to the Russian historical and etymological dictionaries—especially Vasmer/Fasmer—that we likewise identify and cite. For guidance in eighteenth-century Russian historical lexicology we are particularly indebted to the incomparable volume by Birzhakova and her colleagues (Birzhak.), a work that includes, in addition to the glossary of eighteenth-century loanwords in Russian (pp. 101–170) intended to supplement those published by Smirnov, Christiani, and Hüttl-Worth, an index (pp. 337–408) of all such words—some 2,200—mentioned anywhere in their volume. But owing to the often repetitive nature of their glossary and index—repetitive of the other works that both they and we cite—as well as to the fact that their volume does not provide full details of their findings (presumably in anticipation of the multivolume dictionary of eighteenth-century Russian [Barkh.] compiled by this same group of specialists), "Birzhak." appears in the List only when the attribution to the Petrine period of a word's "initial fixture" in Russian (pervaia fiksatsiia) seemed to require added support.

We should perhaps make more explicit the criteria for inclusion in, or exclusion from, the List. In general, we have tried to *include* all the Petrine neologisms adduced in the preceding chapters of this volume and/or in one or more of the scholarly works just mentioned, but to *exclude* any such words that the more recent scholarship and/or our own research have determined were fixed in Russian—*Russian,* not Ukrainian or Belorussian—either before or after Peter's time (roughly 1690–1730). More particularly, and again as distinct from previously published glossaries, the List includes only words that can be said to have *permanently* entered Russian in the Petrine period as judged by their appearance with roughly the same meaning in one or more of the standard Russian dictionaries that we have also consulted, the earliest dating to the late eighteenth century (Slov. Akad., under Works Cited), the next to the mid-nineteenth (Slov. Russ.), and the most comprehensive to the midtwentieth (Slovar'). Also included are some Petrine words that subsequently became obsolete, that are labeled as such in one or more of the dictionaries consulted, but that retain enduring *historical* significance. There are exceptions to this rule of durability or "permanence," to be sure, notably many of the highly technical naval and military terms borrowed in Peter's time from German, Dutch, English, or Italian that are still in specialized use in Russian. Also excluded are the many more such terms that sooner or later became completely obsolete; most of the Petrine bureaucratic nomenclature, mostly Germanic in origin, which eventually also suffered the same fate; and Petrine loanwords that remained foreign in Russian even though some might be found, sometimes labeled as such, in later Russian dictionaries (most such words, as the same dictionaries often indicate, were sooner or later displaced in general usage by older Russian or Slavonic words with the same meaning or by newly minted Russian calques). In this connection we should note that a few Russian calques of foreign words coined in the Petrine era are included in the List but only a few, mainly because calques are harder by nature to trace than straightforward Russifications via transliteration with some phonetic-orthographic and/or morphological adaptation, which was the preferred method of assimilation at the time—a function, no doubt, of the sheer number of foreign words needing to be adopted. This typically Petrine method of assimilation stands in marked contrast to that prevailing in the later eighteenth century, when the calquing of foreign words (overwhelmingly French or German) by Russian writers, translators, and editors was practiced on a large scale—a function, no doubt, both of the growing sophistication of Russian wordsmiths and of the contemporaneous flowering of Russian national consciousness.

A cautionary note is also in order. It is in the nature of the beast under scrutiny that determination of the linguistic source of a given loanword can never be more than highly probable, just as the year of its fixture in Russian

379

can never be more than closely approximate. The first point is particularly apposite with respect to the apparent Polish origin of so many pre-Petrine and, indeed, Petrine borrowings, when the actual source may well have been a Ruthenian (Ukrainian or Belorussian) intermediary. Similarly, Polish in turn frequently "interfered," as linguists say, with the assimilation by emergent literary Russian of German, Italian, and Latin words, as did Dutch or Swedish with German, German with French, and so forth. It is frequently also possible or probable that a given loanword in Russian, especially one that was common throughout the European languages, had in effect multiple foreign sources. All of which is not to say that the linguistic source of many Petrine loanwords cannot be documented with a high degree of probability, as we have seen in numerous instances in the preceding chapters of this volume. Moreover, we are concerned here much less with establishing the exact route of a given word's arrival in Russian than with dating that event to the Petrine era.

Lastly, in matters of transliteration we continue to follow the simplified version of the Library of Congress system as described in our initial Note on Dates and Transliteration (p. xiii above).

WORKS CITED

The following scholarly works, including dictionaries, are cited in the List (abbreviations are given first):

Avan. = R. I. Avanesov, *Slovar' drevnerusskogo iazyka (XI–XIV vv.)* (M., 1988–); vols. I–IV (through -*molenie*) available at time of writing

Avery = R. Avery, "Foreign Influence on the Nautical Terminology of Russian in the Eighteenth Century," *Oxford Slavonic Papers* XIV (1981), pp. 73–92

Barkh. = S. G. Barkhudarov, N. E. Birzhakova, et al., *Slovar' russkogo iazyka XVIII veka* (L./SPb., 1984–); vols. I–XI (through -*L'nianoi*) available at time of writing

Barkh-Bog. = S. G. Barkhudarov, G. A. Bogatova, et al., *Slovar' russkogo iazyka XI–XVII vv.* (M., 1975–); vols. I–XXIII (through -*Sdymka*) available at time of writing

Birzhak. = E. A. Birzhakova, L. A. Voinova, L. L. Kutina, *Ocherki po istoricheskoi leksikologii russkogo iazyka XVIII veka: iazykovye kontakty i zaimstvovaniia* (L., 1972)

Bond = A. Bond, *German Loanwords in the Russian Language of the Petrine Period* (Bern and Frankfurt/Main, 1974)

Chernykh = P. Ia. Chernykh, *Istoriko-etimologicheskii slovar' sovremennogo russkogo iazyka,* 2 vols. (M., 1993)

Christ. = W. A. Christiani, *Über das Eindringen von Fremdwörtern in die russische Schriftsprache des 17. und 18. Jahrhunderts* (Berlin, 1906)

D'iachenko = G. D'iachenko, *Polnyi Tserkovno-slavianskii slovar'*, 2 vols. (M. 1900; re-printed M., 1993)

Fadeev = V. G. Fadeev et al., eds., *Morskoi slovar'*, 2 vols. (M., 1959)

Fasmer = M. Fasmer, *Etimologicheskii slovar' russkogo iazyka,* trans. O. N. Trubachev, ed. B. A. Larin, 4 vols. (M., 1964, 1967, 1971, 1973); Russian edition, supplemented, of Vasmer, below

Gard. = S. C. Gardiner, *German Loanwords in Russian, 1550–1690* (Oxford, 1965)

Grib. = C. E. Gribble, *A Short Dictionary of 18th-Century Russian* (Cambridge, MA, 1976)

H-W. = G. Hüttl-Worth, *Foreign Words in Russian: A Historical Sketch, 1550–1800* (Berkeley and Los Angeles, 1963: University of California Publications in Linguistics, vol. 28)

Kaiser = F. Kaiser, *Der europäische Anteil an der russischen Rechtsterminologie der petrinischen Zeit* (Berlin, 1965: Forschungen zur osteuropäischen Geschichte, vol. 10)

Koch. I = S. Kochman, *Polsko-rosyjskie kontakty językowe w zakresie słownictwa w XVII wieku* (Warsaw, 1967)

Koch. II = S. Kochman, *Polsko-rosyjskie stosunki językowe od XVI do XVIII w. Słownictwo* (Opole, 1975)

Kot. = *Grigorij Kotošixin [Kotoshikhin], O Rossii v carstvovanie Alekseja Mixajloviča: Text and Commentary,* ed. A. E. Pennington (Oxford, 1980); includes Kotoshikhin's original text based on surviving mss. (pp. 17–183) with editor's Commentary (pp. 185–400) and Index of Forms (pp. 401–758)

Kutina I = L. L. Kutina, *Formirovanie iazyka russkoi nauki: terminologiia matematiki, astronomii, geografii v pervoi treti XVIII veka* (M./L., 1964)

Kutina II = L. L. Kutina, *Formirovanie terminologii fiziki v Rossii: period predlomonosovskii: pervaia tret' XVIII veka* (M./L., 1966)

Leeming = H. Leeming, *Rola języka polskiego w rozwoju leksyki rosyjskiej do roku 1696* (Cracow, 1976)

Otten = F. Otten, *Untersuchungen zu den Fremd- und Lehnwörtern bei Peter dem Grossen* (Cologne and Vienna, 1985: Slavistische Forschungen, vol. 50)

Ox. Russ. = M. Wheeler, *The Oxford Russian-English Dictionary,* 2nd edn. (Oxford, 1984); normally cited only to confirm, after or in lieu of Smirnitskii (below), word's current English definition

Plekhov = A. M. Plekhov, *Slovar' voennykh terminov,* ed. S. G. Shapkin (M., 1988)

Preob. = A. G. Preobrazhenskii, *Etimologicheskii slovar' russkogo iazyka,* 2 vols. (M., 1910–1914; reprinted with supplement New York, 1951)

Rozen = S. Ia. Rozen, *Ocherki po istorii russkoi korabel'noi terminologii petrovskoi epokhi* (L., 1960)

Ryan = W. F. Ryan, "Navigation and the Modernisation of Petrine Russia: Teachers, Text-books, Terminology," in R. Bartlett and J. Harvey, eds., *Russia in the Age of the Enlightenment: Essays for Isabel de Madariaga* (New York, 1990), Glossary (pp. 90–95)

Sergeev I = F. P. Sergeev, *Russkaia diplomaticheskaia terminologiia XI-XVII vv.* (Kishinev, 1971)

381

Sergeev II = F. P. Sergeev, *Formirovanie russkogo diplomaticheskogo iazyka* (L'vov, 1978)

Shanskii = N. M. Shanskii, *Etimologicheskii slovar' russkogo iazyka,* vol. I- (M., 1963-); vols. I-VIII (through letter *K*) available at time of writing

Shanskii-Bob. = N. M. Shanskii and T. A. Bobrova, *Etimologicheskii slovar' russkogo iazyka* (M., 1994)

Slov. Akad. = *Slovar' Akademii rossiiskoi,* 6 vols. (SPb., 1789–1794)

Slov. Russ. = *Slovar' tserkovno-slavianskago i russkago iazyka,* 4 vols. (SPb., 1847)

Slovar' = *Slovar' sovremennogo russkogo literaturnogo iazyka,* 17 vols. (M./L., 1950–1965)

Smirnitskii = A. I. Smirnitskii, *Russko-Angliiskii slovar'* (M., 1959)

Smirnov = N. A. Smirnov, *Zapadnoe vliianie na russkii iazyk v Petrovskuiu epokhu* (SPb. 1910)

Srez. = I. I. Sreznevskii, *Materialy dlia slovaria drevnerusskogo iazyka,* 3 vols. and supplement (SPb., 1893, 1895, 1903, 1912; reprinted M., 1958, supplement bound with vol. III)

Vasmer = M. Vasmer, *Russisches etymologisches Wörterbuch,* 3 vols. (Heidelberg, 1953, 1955, 1958: cf. Russian edition = Fasmer, above)

Wade = T. Wade, *Russian Etymological Dictionary* (Bristol, U.K., 1996)

Whittall = S. Whittall, *A Study of English Nautical Loanwords in the Russian Language of the Eighteenth Century* (Frankfurt/Main and Bern, 1985)

OTHER ABBREVIATIONS USED IN THE LIST

Du.	Dutch
Eng.	English
Fr.	French
Germ.	German
Gr.	Greek
Ital.	Italian
Lat.	Latin
Pol.	Polish
Rus./Russ.	Russia/Russian
Slav.	Slavonic/Church Slavonic
Span.	Spanish
Sw.	Swedish
Ukr.	Ukrainian
acad.	academic
arch.	architecture
astron.	astronomy
cent.	century
dim.	diminutive
doc.	document
dpl.	diplomatic

eccl.	ecclesiastical
esp.	especially
estab.	established
fr.	from
interj.	interjection
jud.	judicial
litt.	literary
math.	mathematics
med.	medical
mil.	military
ms.	manuscript
mus.	music
naut.	nautical
nav.	navigation
obs.	obsolete
ref.	in reference to
trans.	translation

ORGANIZATION

The entries are grouped successively under six general headings: Military Terms, Nautical Terms, Official Terms, Other Technical Terms, Commercial Terms, and Other Terms—although there is inevitably some overlap, e.g., a "military" term that had or subsequently acquired non-military meanings; even so, there is no repetition of words from one group to another. The individual entries then proceed, in *Russian* alphabetical order, as follows: *first* the new Russian word/Petrine neologism, transliterated, in italics, with any prominent alternate or later spelling or spellings (the most recent entered last); next, its meaning briefly in English, as translated from or given by, occasionally with some modifications by us, the standard Russian and Russian-English dictionaries listed under Works Cited; then, again in italics, and in descending order of probability, its possible or likely foreign source or sources, or intermediaries—word or words in Polish, Latin, German, Dutch, French, English, etc.—followed by a full stop. The *second* component of each entry consists of abbreviated citations, in chronological order of publication, of scholarly works—including etymological and historical dictionaries—affirming the word's Petrine origins followed by reference to one or more of the later Russian dictionaries, similarly listed under Works Cited, in which the word appears with the same or similar meaning; and again a full stop. *Thirdly,* many entries offer sample contemporary or later derivations from the main word—adjectives from nouns, other noun forms (including diminutives), verbs, adverbs—once more as attested by the scholarly works including dictionaries already cited. Any supplementary data given in square brackets— suggested date of the main word's initial appearance, if not fixture, in Russian; variant spellings; the designation "obsolete" (obs.)—are taken from the work just cited. In some instances the main word is followed by one or more new words closely related to it, and evidently received as such in Russian (rather than subsequently derived from it); this is done instead of listing such words separately, and so to save space. As readers by now will know, many of the words to be found in the List also appear in the preceding chapters of this book, where their reception in Russian was in some measure contextualized.

The List was compiled by the author with the crucial assistance, most gratefully acknowledged, of Karl Wood and Leonid Trofimov.

MILITARY TERMS

abshid/abshit = resignation, retirement (milit.), fr. Germ. *Abschied.* Smirnov (27, 364); Vasmer (I, 2); Fasmer (I, 58); Shanskii (I, 23); Kaiser (204); Bond (45); Grib. (5); Barkh. (I, 11); Slov. Akad. (I, 3); Slov. Russ. (I, 2); Slovar' (I, 24); Fadeev (I, 10 [18th cent.]).

avangard(i)ia/avangard = advance guard, vanguard (also naval), fr. Pol. *awangarda*/Ital. *avanguardia*/Germ./Fr. *avantgarde.* Smirnov (28, 363); Vasmer (I, 2); Fasmer (I, 58); Shanskii (I, 23–4); Barkh. (I, 12); Chernykh (I, 23); Slov. Russ. (I, 2); Slovar' (I, 24–5); Fadeev (I, 10); Plekhov (6); Smirnitskii (32).

avansirovat' = to advance (in the field), fr. Germ. *avancieren*/Fr. *avancer.* Smirnov (28); Vasmer (I, 3); Fasmer (I, 58); Shanskii (I, 23–4); Bond (45); Barkh. (I, 12–13); Slovar' (I, 26); Smirnitskii (32). Term later acquired meaning "to advance money."
Derivations: *avans* (cf. Fr. *avance*/Germ. *Avance*), *avansovyi* (Chernykh, I, 23)

ad"iutant = aide-de-camp (later also naval), fr. Du./Germ. *Adjutant.* Christ. (32); Vasmer (I, 6); Fasmer (I, 68); Shanskii (I, 50); Bond (34); Chernykh (I, 29–30); Slov. Akad. (I, 11); Slov. Russ. (I, 4); Slovar' (I, 59–60); Fadeev (I, 23); Plekhov (11). Leeming (32) cites *otiutant/ot'iutant,* fr. Pol. *adjutant,* in dpl. docs. of 1660, 1677.

amunitsiia = ammunition, fr. Pol. *amunicja*/Fr. *amunition.* Chist. (36); Smirnov (37); Vasmer (I, 17); Fasmer (I, 74); Shanskii (I, 97); Slov. Russ. (I, 8); Slovar' (I, 121); Smirnitskii (37); Ox. Russ. (7).

armatura = armaments, army, later armature, fittings, framework, mounting, fr. Pol./Lat. *armatura.* Smirnov (45); Vasmer (I, 25); Fasmer (I, 87); Shanskii (I, 145); Grib. (8); Barkh. (I, 92–3); Slov. Russ. (I, 12); Slovar' (I, 186–7); Fadeev (I, 35); Smirnitskii (41).
Derivation: *armaturnyi*

armei/armiia = army, fr. Germ. *Armee*/Fr. *armée*/Pol. *armeja/armia*/Ukr. *armeia*. Christ. (37); Smirnov (46, 364); Preob. (I, 8); Vasmer (I, 25); Fasmer (I, 87); H-W. (60); Shanskii (I, 145); Bond (34); Barkh. (I, 93–4); Chernykh (I, 52); Slov. Akad. (I, 46); Slov. Russ. (I, 12); Slovar (I,187–8); Plekhov (15); Smirnitskii (41).
Derivation: *armeiskii*

arsenal = arsenal (also naval), armory, fr. Germ./Fr. *arsenal*. Christ. (35); Preob. (I, 8); Vasmer (I, 26); Fasmer (I, 88); Shanskii (I, 146); Barkh-Bog. (I, 48 [1699]); Barkh. (I, 95); Chernykh (I, 53); Slov. Akad. (I, 48); Slov. Russ. (I, 13); Slovar' (I, 190); Fadeev (I, 35 [obs.]); Plekhov (15); Smirnitskii (41).
Derivation: *arsenal'nyi*

artileriia/artilleriia = artillery, fr. Germ./Fr. *artillerie*/Pol. *artyleryja*. Christ. (33); Smirnov (364); Preob. (I, 8); Vasmer (I, 26); Fasmer (I, 89); Shanskii (I, 149–50); Bond (35); Barkh-Bog. (I, 49 [1698]); Barkh. (I, 97); Chernykh (I, 54); Slov. Akad. (I, 49); Slov. Russ. (I, 13); Slovar' (I, 193–4); Fadeev (I, 38); Plekhov (17–8); Smirnitskii (41).
Derivations: *artillerist, artilleriiskii*

ataka = attack, fr. Germ. *Attacke*/Pol. *atak*/Fr. *attaque*. Smirnov (49); Vasmer (I, 31); Fasmer (I, 95); Shanksii (I, 169); Barkh. (I, 109); Chernykh (I, 57); Slov. Russ. (I, 15); Slovar' (I, 213); Fadeev (I, 40); Plekhov (18); Smirnitskii (42).

atakirovat'/atakovat' = to attack, fr. Germ. *attackieren*/Pol. *atakować*. *Christ. (36); Smirnov (50); Vasmer (I, 31); Fasmer (I, 95); Bond (46); Barkh. (I, 109–10); Chernykh (I, 57); Slov. Russ. (I, 15); Slovar' (I, 213); Smirnitskii (42).*

barak = barrack (wooden), hut, fr. Germ. *Baracke*/Fr. *baraque*. Smirnov (56); Preob. (I, 16); Vasmer (I, 53); Fasmer (I, 123); Shanskii (II, 38–9); Barkh. (I, 140); Chernykh (I, 72); Wade (20); Slovar' (I, 272); Smirnitskii (46).

barikada/barrikada = barricade, fr. Fr. *barricade*. Vasmer (I, 52); Fasmer (I, 128); Shanskii (II, 48); Barkh. (I, 144); Chernykh (I, 75); Slovar' (I, 284–5); Plekhov (22); Smirnitskii (47).
Derivations: *barrikadirovat', barrikadnyi*

bastion = bastion, fr. Fr. *bastion*. Christ. (36); Smirnov (365); Vasmer (I, 60); Fasmer (I, 132); Shanskii (II, 54); Barkh-Bog. (I, 79 [1697]); Barkh. (I, 149); Otten (483); Slov. Akad. (I, 108); Slov. Russ. (I, 24); Slovar' (I, 293); Smirnitskii (48).
Derivation: *bastionnyi*

batalion/batal'on = battalion, fr. Pol. *batalion*/Germ./Fr. *bataillon*. Christ. (33); Smirnov (57); Preob. (I, 19); Vasmer (I, 61); Fasmer (I, 133); Shanskii (II, 55); Barkh-Bog (I, 79 [1697]); Grib. (10); Barkh. (I, 150); Slov. Akad. (I, 109); Slov. Russ. (I, 24); Slovar' (I, 294); Plekhov (23); Smirnitskii (48).
Derivation: *batalionnyi*

bataliia = battle, fr. Pol. *batalija*/Germ./Fr. *bataille*. Christ. (37); Smirnov (57); Vasmer (I,

61); Fasmer (I, 133); Shanskii (II, 55); Grib. (10: also *batalishche*); Barkh. (I, 150); Slov. Russ. (I, 24); Slovar' (I, 294 [obs.]); Fadeev (I, 62 [obs.]); Smirnitskii (48 [obs.]).

batarei/bateriia/batareia = battery, fr. Du. *batterij*/Germ./Fr. *batterie*. Christ. (35); Smirnov (365); Vasmer (I, 61); Fasmer (I, 134); Shanskii (II, 55); Bond (35); Barkh. (I, 150); Otten (26–9); Chernykh (I, 77–8); Slov. Russ. (I, 24); Slovar' (I, 295); Fadeev (I, 62); Plekhov (23); Smirnitskii (48).
Derivation: *batareinyi*

bereiter/bereitor = riding master, fr. Germ. *Bereiter*/Pol. *berejter*. Smirnov (59); Vasmer (I, 77); Fasmer (I, 154); Shanskii (II, 95); Bond (46); Slov. Russ. (I, 45); Slovar' (I, 396–7); Smirnitskii (54).

blokada = blockade, fr. Germ. *Blockade*, perhaps via Pol. *blokada;* also *blokirovat'* = to blockade, fr. Germ. *blokieren*. Smirnov (61, 365); Vasmer (I, 94); Fasmer (I, 176); Bond (47); Barkh. (II, 68–9); Chernykh (I, 95); Slov. Russ. (I, 62); Slovar' (I, 517); Fadeev (I, 73); Plekhov (26–7); Smirnitskii (63).
Derivations: *blokadnyi, blokirovanie, blokirovat'sia, blokirovka, blokirovochnyi*

bolverk/bol'verk = bulwark, bastion, fr. Germ. *Bollwerk*/Pol. *bolwerk*. Smirnov (62, 365); Vasmer (I, 102); Fasmer (I, 186); Shanskii (II, 159); Bond (47, 69); Barkh. (II, 96); Slov. Russ. (I, 74 *[bolverk]*); Slov. Akad. (I, 270 *[bol'verk]*). Term became obsolete in 19th cent.

bomb/bomba = bomb, fr. Germ./Du./Fr. *bombe*, perhaps via Pol./Ital. *bomba*. Christ. (35 [1688]); Smirnov (62, 365); Preob. (I, 36); Vasmer (I, 105–6); Barkh-Bog. (I, 289 [1695]); Barkh. (II, 107); Otten (33–6); Chernykh (I, 102); Slov. Akad. (I, 283); Slov. Russ. (I, 72); Slovar' (I, 569–70); Fadeev (I, 80); Plekhov (36); Smirnitskii (67).
Derivations: *bombovyi, bombit'*

bombardir = gunner, rank in artillery service (also naval), fr. Ital./Pol./Germ. *Bombardier;* also *bombardirovat'* = to bombard, fr. Germ. *bombardieren*. Smirnov (62, 365); Vasmer (I, 106); Fasmer (I, 191); Shanskii (II, 162); Bond (35); Barkh-Bog. (I, 289–90 [1696]); Barkh. (II, 107–8); Otten (37–8, 406–10, 496–9); Slov. Akad. (I, 283); Slov. Russ. (I, 75); Slovar' (I, 570); Fadeev (I, 80); Smirnitskii (67).
Derivations: *bombardirovanie, bombardirovka, bombardirovochnyi, bombardirshchik, bombardirskii*

bresh' = breech, gap, fr. Fr. *brèche*. Christ. (36); Smirnov (66, 366); Vasmer (I, 124); Fasmer (I, 213); Chernykh (I, 111); Slov. Russ. (I, 82); Slovar' (I, 627–8); Smirnitskii (70).

brigada = brigade (also naval), fr. Pol. *brygada*/Germ./Fr. *brigade*. Christ. (33); Smirnov (66); Preob. (I, 45); Vasmer (I, 122–3); Fasmer (I, 213); Shanskii (II, 196); Barkh. (II, 139); Chernykh (I, 111); Slov. Akad. (I, 337–8); Slov. Russ. (I, 82); Slovar' (I, 628–9); Fadeev (I, 88); Plekhov (38); Smirnitskii (70).
Derivation: *brigadnyi*

brigadir = brigadier, brigade-leader, fr. Pol. *brygadier*/Germ. *Brigadier*. Smirnov (366);

386

Vasmer (I, 123); Fasmer (I, 213); Shanskii (II, 162); Bond (47); Grib. (14); Barkh. (II, 139); Otten (415–7); Slov. Akad. (I, 338); Slov. Russ. (I, 82); Slovar' (I, 629 [obs.]); Smirnitskii (70 [obs.]).

brustver = breastwork, parapet, epaulement, fr. Germ. *Brustwehr.* Christ. (36); Smirnov (67); Vasmer (I,128); Fasmer (I, 221); Bond (36); Barkh. (II, 148); Slov. Russ. (I, 84); Slovar' (I, 651); Fadeev (I, 92 [obs.]); Plekhov (40); Smirnitskii (72).

valentir/volontir/volunter/volontër = volunteer, fr. Germ. *Volontär*/Eng. *volunteer.* Smirnov (75, 366); Vasmer (I, 221); Fasmer (I, 342); H-W. (64); Shanskii (III, 151); Kaiser (205); Grib. (15); Barkh. (IV, 43); Slov. Russ. (I, 155); Slovar' (II, 620–21); Smirnitskii (107).

vakhta = watch, guard (also naut.), fr. Pol. *wachta*/Germ. *Wacht/Wachta/Wache*/Du. *wagt.* Preob. (I, 68); Vasmer (I, 174); Fasmer (I, 280); Shanskii (III, 27–8); Gard. (77); Birzhak. (127–8); Bond (36); Barkh-Bog. (II, 25 [1667; cf. Kot., 419, 395]); Barkh. (II, 222); Slov. Akad. (I, 513); Slov. Russ. (I, 101–2); Slovar' (II, 64–5); Fadeev (I, 104); Plekhov (41); Smirnitskii (80).
Derivation: *vakhtennyi*

vakhter/vakhtër = watchman, later also porter, janitor, storekeeper (naut.), fr. Germ. *Wächter* Vasmer (I, 174); Fasmer (I, 280); Shanskii (III, 28); Bond (36); Barkh. (II, 222); Slov. Russ. (I, 102); Slovar' (II, 65); Fadeev (I, 105 [obs.]); Smirnitskii (80).
Derivation: *vakhterskii*

vakhtmeister/vakhmistr = cavalry sergeant, fr. Germ. *Wachtmeister*/Pol. *wachmistrz.* Smirnov (71, 366); Vasmer (I, 174); Fasmer (I, 280); Kaiser (173–4); Gard. (77); Bond (48); Barkh. (II, 222); Otten (464–5); Slov. Akad. (I, 513); Slov. Russ. (I, 101); Slovar' (II, 64 [obs.]); Smirnitskii (80 [obs.]).

vezir'/vizir/visir = sight, sighting device, fr. Germ. *Wisier.* Smirnov (72); Vasmer (I, 199); Fasmer (I, 313); Bond (36); Slovar' (II, 368); Fadeev (I, 119); Plekhov (47); Smirnitskii (93).

verbovat' = to recruit, fr. Pol. *werbować*/Germ. *werben.* Smirnov (72); Vasmer (I, 185); Fasmer (I, 284); Bond (36); Slovar' (II, 169–70); Smirnitskii (84). Vasmer/Fasmer dates term to 17th cent.
Derivation: *verbovka, verbovshchik*

garnizon = garrison, fr. Germ./Fr. *garnison.* Christ. (36); Smirnov (82, 368); Preob. (I, 119); Vasmer (I, 259–60); Fasmer (I, 394); Shanskii (IV, 32); Barkh. (V, 91–2); Slov. Akad. (II, 21); Slov. Russ. (I, 256); Slovar' (III, 41–2); Plekhov (66); Smirnitskii (148).

gaubitsa = howitzer, fr. Germ. *Haubitze.* Christ. (34); Smirnov (82, 367); Vasmer (I, 262); Fasmer (I, 397); Shanskii (IV, 38–9); Bond (36); Grib. (21; also *goubitsa,* 23); Barkh. (V, 93); Otten (275–80); Slov. Akad. (II, 25); Slov. Russ. (I, 256); Slovar' (III, 48); Fadeev (I, 163); Plekhov (66); Smirnitskii (148).
Derivation: *gaubichnyi*

gauptvakhta = guard house, guardroom, fr. Germ. *Hauptwache/Hauptwacht.* Smirnov

387

(82); Preob. (I, 120); Vasmer (I, 262); Fasmer (I, 397); Shanskii (IV, 39); Bond (36–7); Barkh. (V, 93); Slov. Russ. (I, 256); Slovar' (III, 48); Plekhov (67); Smirnitskii (148).

gvardiia = guards, fr. Pol. *gwardia*/Ital. *guardia* and/or Germ./Fr. *garde*/Eng. *guard*. Christ. (33); Smirnov (83, 367); Preob. (I, 121); Vasmer (I, 263); Fasmer (I, 398); Shanskii (IV, 41); H-W. (65); Barkh. (V, 94–5); Chernykh (I, 183); Slov. Akad. (II, 27); Slov. Russ. (I, 257); Slovar' (III, 49–51); Plekhov (67); Smirnitskii (148).
Derivations: *gvardeets* (= guardsman), *gvardeiskii*

general = general, fr. Germ. *General*. Term known earlier in Russ. (Gard., 85–7; Barkh-Bog., IV, 17; Leeming, 56–7; Kot., 449, 387; Chernykh, I, 185) but fixed in Petrine period as top military rank, both by itself and in various compounds and forms, e.g. *general-ad"iutant* fr. Germ. *Generaladjutant*; *general-leitenant* fr. Germ. *Generalleutnant*; *general-maër* fr. Germ. *Generalmajor*; *generalissimus*, fr. Germ. *Generalissimus*. Christ. (32); Smirnov (85, 367); Preob. (I, 122); Vasmer (I, 265); Fasmer (I, 401); Shanskii (IV, 50); Kaiser (319); Bond (37, 50–51); Barkh. (V, 100–01); Otten (433–7); Slov. Akad. (II, 32); Slov. Russ. (I, 258); Slovar' (III, 65–7); Fadeev (I, 164); Smirnitskii (149).

generalitet = body of general officers/senior ranks of army, fr. Germ. *Generalität*/Du. *generaliteit*. Smirnov (85); Preob. (I, 122); Vasmer (I, 265); Fasmer (I, 401); Shanskii (IV, 51); Bond (37); Barkh. (V, 101); Slovar' (III, 66); Smirnitskii (149).

grenadir/granadir/grenader = grenadier, fr. Germ/Fr. *grenadier*. Christ. (33); Smirnov (94, 367); Vasmer (I, 307); Fasmer (I, 456); Shanskii (IV, 167); Bond (51); Grib. (21); Barkh. (V, 219); Chernykh (I, 215); Slov. Russ. (I, 291, 288); Slovar' (III, 385); Smirnitskii (166).
Derivation: *grenaderskii*

dezertir = deserter, fr. Pol. *dezerter*/Lat. *desertor*/Germ. *Deserteur*/Fr. *déserteur*. Smirnov (100); Vasmer (I, 336); Fasmer (I, 494); Kaiser (229); Bond (37); Barkh. (VI, 71); Chernykh (I, 237–8); Slov. Russ. (I, 316); Slovar' (III, 648); Plekhov (83); Smirnitskii (179).
Derivations: *dezertirovat'* (cf. Germ. *desertiern*/Pol. *dezertovać*), *dezertirstvo*

desant = landing, fr. Fr. *descente*. Smirnov (102); Vasmer (I, 345); Fasmer (I, 505); Shanskii (V, 83); Birzhak. (127); Barkh. (VI, 110–11); Chernykh (I, 244–5); Slov. Russ. (I, 320); Slovar' (III, 738); Fadeev (I, 204–5); Plekhov (85–6); Smirnitskii (184).
Derivations: *desantirovanie, desantnyi*

defileia/defile = defile, marching in line; also ravine, narrow pass (through which troops must pass), fr. Germ. *Defilee*/Fr. *défilé*; also *defilirovat'* = to march past, fr. Germ. *defilieren*/Fr. *défiler*. Smirnov (104, 368); Vasmer (I, 348); Fasmer (I, 509); Shanskii (V, 94–5); Bond (51); Barkh. (VI, 119–20); Slov. Russ. (I, 322); Slovar' (III, 755–6); Plekhov (86); Smirnitskii (185).

diverziia/diversiia = diversion, later also subversion, sabotage, fr. Pol. *dywersia*/Germ./Fr. *diversion*. Christ. (37); Smirnov (104, 368); Vasmer (I, 350); Fasmer (I, 513); Bond (51); Barkh. (VI, 126); Slov. Russ. (I, 322); Slovar' (III, 777); Plekhov (87); Smirnitskii (186).

divizion/diviziia = division (milit.and naval), fr. Pol. *dywizia*/Du. *divisie*/Germ./Fr. *division.* Smirnov (104, 368); Preob. (I, 184); Vasmer (I, 351); Fasmer (I, 513); Shanskii (V, 115); Barkh. (VI, 126–7); Otten (573); Chernykh (I, 251–2); Slov. Russ. (I, 322); Slovar' (III, 779); Fadeev (I, 208–9); Plekhov (87–8); Smirnitskii (186).

dispozitsa/dispozitsiia = disposition, deployment (also naut.), fr. Pol. *dyspozycja*/Lat. *dispositio*/Germ./Fr. *disposition.* Grib. (26); Barkh. (VI, 138); Slovar' (III, 808); Fadeev (I, 211); Plekhov (89); Smirnitskii (188).

389

eger' = rifleman, hunter, chasseur, fr. Germ. *Jäger.* Preob. (I, 211); Vasmer (I, 390); Fasmer (II, 7); Shanskii (V, 245); Kaiser (162 *[egermeister]*); Bond (37); Barkh. (VII, 59); Chernykh (I, 280–1); Slov. Akad. (II, 935); Slov. Russ. (I, 388); Slovar' (III, 1226–7); Smirnitskii (208). Derivation: *egerskii*

efreitor = lance-corporal, fr. Germ. *Gefreiter.* Smirnov (114); Preob. (I, 218); Vasmer (I, 406); Fasmer (II, 29–30); Shanskii (V, 267); Bond (37–8); Barkh. (VII, 86); Chernykh (I, 288); Wade (56); Slov. Akad. (II, 1025–6); Slov. Russ. (I, 396 *[efreiter]*); Slovar' (III, 1286); Smirnitskii (211).

zalfa/zalv/zalp = salvo, volley of fire, fr. Germ./Du./Fr. *salve.* Christ. (35); Smirnov (115, 368); Preob. (I, 241); Vasmer (I, 440); Fasmer (II, 76–7); Shanskii (VI, 44); Bond (38);Grib. (31: also *zalf, zalb*); Barkh. (VIII, 19); Chernykh (I, 316); Wade (62); Slov. Russ. (II, 32); Slovar' (IV, 626); Fadeev (I, 237); Plekhov (100); Smirnitskii (237).

invalid = invalid, disabled (soldier), fr. Germ./Fr. *invalide.* Vasmer (I, 481); Fasmer (II, 130); H-W. (73); Shanskii (VII, 66); Grib. (35); Chernykh (I, 345); Slov. Russ. (II, 132); Slovar' (V, 325); Smirnitskii (272). Deivations: *invalidnost', invalidnyi*

intendant = commissary officer, quartermaster (also naut.), fr. Germ./Fr. *intendant.* Smirnov (121); Vasmer (I, 485); Fasmer (II, 135); Shanskii (VII, 94–5); Slovar' (V, 390); Fadeev (I, 263); Plekhov (117); Smirnitskii (274).

infanteriia = infantry, fr. Pol./Span. *infanteria*/Germ./Fr. *infanterie.* Christ. (33); Smirnov (123, 370); Vasmer (I, 485); Fasmer (II, 136); Kaiser (194); Bond (52); Grib. (35); Barkh. (IX, 107); Slov. Russ. (II, 134); Slovar' (V, 415 [obs.]); Ox. Russ. (258 [obs.]).

kavaleriia = cavalry, also chivalric order, fr. Pol. *kawaleria*/Germ. *Kavallerie*/Fr. *cavallerie.* Christ. (27, 33); Smirnov (125, 370); Vasmer (I, 497); Fasmer (II, 152); Shanskii (VIII, 9); Kaiser (214); Bond (38); Barkh-Bog. (VII, 10 [1699]); Grib. (36); Barkh. (IX, 189); Slov. Russ. (II, 150); Slovar' (V, 633–4); Smirnitskii (283). Leeming (67) cites *kovaleriia* in undated ms. Derivation: *kavaleriiskii*

kadet = cadet (also naval), fr. Germ. *Kadett.* Smirnov (125, 370); Vasmer (I, 500); Fasmer

(II, 156); Shanskii (VIII, 12); Kaiser (250); Wade (77); Slov. Akad. (II, 354); Slov. Russ. (II, 151); Slovar' (V, 643); Fadeev (I, 272); Smirnitskii (283).

Derivation: *kadetskii*

kazarma = barracks, fr. Pol. *kazarma*/Germ. *Kasarme*. Christ. (36); Smirnov (126, 370); Preob. (I, 282); Vasmer (I, 503); Fasmer (II, 159); Shanskii (VIII, 17); Kaiser (235); Barkh. (IX, 193); Chernykh (I, 368); Wade (78); Slov. Akad. (III, 389); Slov. Russ. (II, 151); Slovar' (V, 656–7); Plekhov (122); Smirnitskii (283).

kalibr = caliber, bore, gauge, fr. Pol./Germ./Du. *kaliber*/Fr. *calibre*. Christ. (35); Smirnov (126); Vasmer (I, 508); Fasmer (II, 166); Shanskii (VIII, 26); Barkh-Bog. (VII, 35 [1699]); Barkh. (IX, 213); Otten (441–4); Slov. Akad. (III, 399 *[kaliber]*); Slov. Russ. (II, 154 [*kaliber,* also *kalibir*]); Slovar' (V, 708–9); Fadeev (I, 274); Plekhov (123); Smirnitskii (285).

kamandor/komandor/kamendor/komandir = commander, also commodore (naval), fr. Germ. *Kommandeur*/Fr. *commandeur*/Eng. *commander*. Smirnov (147, 370–1); Vasmer (I, 606–7); Fasmer (II, 300–1); Shanskii (VIII, 222–4); Kaiser (129); Bond (39); Barkh-Bog. (VII, 262 [1698]); Otten (85–7); Slov. Russ. (II, 194); Slovar' (V, 1216–18, 1220–1); Fadeev (I, 305, 306–7); Plekhov (130); Smirnitskii (303).

Derivations: *komandirovat'* (= to commission, send on mission; cf. Germ. *kommandieren*), *komandirovka* (= mission, commission, business)

kampaniia = campaign, also voyage, cruise (naval), fr. Pol. *kampania*/Germ. *Kampagne*/ Du. *kampanje*/Fr. *campagne*. Christ. (37); Vasmer (I, 515); Fasmer (II, 175); Shanskii (VIII, 39–40); Barkh. (IX, 228); Wade (79); Slov. Russ. (II, 158); Slovar' (V, 736–7); Fadeev (I, 275–6); Plekhov (123); Smirnitskii (286). Barkh-Bog. (VII, 268 [2]) cites *kampaneia* in 1631. Term later took on more general, non-mil. meaning as well.

kanoner/kanonir = gunner (also naval), fr. Germ./Du. *kanonier*. Smirnov (130); Vasmer (I, 519); Fasmer (II, 181); Shanskii (VII, 47); Birzhak. (119–20); Bond (53); Barkh-Bog. (VII, 56–7 [1712]); Grib. (37); Slov. Akad. (III, 427); Slov. Russ. (II, 159); Slovar' (V, 756–7 [to 1917]); Fadeev (I, 277 [obs.]); Ox. Russ. (272). Related word *kanon* = cannon, fr. Germ. *Kannon/e*/ Du. *kanon,* did not survive the Petrine era (cf. Birzhak., 119).

karabiner = car(a)bineer, fr. Pol./Germ. *Karabinier*/Fr. *carabinier*. Shanskii (VIII, 61); Barkh-Bog. (VII, 70 [18th cent.]); Barkh. (IX, 250–1); Slov. Akad. (III, 438); Slov. Russ. (II, 162); Slovar' (V, 796); Smirnitskii (288). Related term *karabin* spelled variously = car(a)bine, fr. Pol./Germ. *Karabin*/Fr. *carabine,* borrowed earlier (Vasmer, I, 525; Fasmer, II, 190; Shanskii, VIII, 60; Barkh-Bog., VII, 70; Gard., 116; Leeming, 64).

kartecha/kartech' = shrapnel, shot, fr. Pol. *kartecz*/Germ. *Kartätsche*. Christ. (34); Smirnov (135, 372); Vasmer (I, 536); Fasmer (II, 204); Shanskii (VIII, 76–7); Bond (38); Barkh. (IX, 264–5); Slov. Akad. (III, 455); Slov. Russ. (II, 164); Slovar' (V, 833); Fadeev (I, 282); Plekhov (124–5); Smirnitskii (289).

kvartira = quarters, billet, lodging, later also (rented) flat, apartment, fr. Pol. *kwatera*/ Germ. *Quartier*/Du. *kwartier*. Christ. (16, 36); Smirnov (139, 368); Vasmer (I, 546); Fasmer

(II, 217); Kaiser (200); Shanskii (VIII, 112); Bond (38–9); Grib. (39); Barkh. (X, 25–6); Chernykh (I, 391); Wade (86); Slov. Akad. (III, 493–4); Slov. Russ. (II, 169); Slovar' (V, 907–8); Smirnitskii (292). Both Gard. (121) and Leeming (74) cite *kvatera* in 1677 dpl. report fr. Poland (cf. Barkh-Bog., VII, 103).

Derivations: *kvartirka, kvartirnyi, kvartirovat'*

kvartirmistr/kvartirmeister = quartermaster (also naval), fr. Pol. *kwatermistrz*/Du. *kwarteirmeester*/Germ. *Quartiermeister*. Christ. (32); Smirnov (139–40, 372); Vasmer (I, 546); Fasmer (II, 217–8); Gard. (121–2 [1632]); Kaiser (201); Bond (49); Grib. (39); Barkh. (X, 26); Otten (447–9); Slov. Akad. (III, 494); Slov. Russ. (II, 169); Slovar' (V, 908–9); Fadeev (I, 289); Smirnitskii (292). Barkh-Bog. (VII, 103) cites precedent of 1670.

kirasa/kirasir = cuirass/cuirassier, fr. Germ. *Kürass*/Fr. *cuirass*/Germ. *Kürassier*/Fr. *cuirassier*. Smirnov (142); Preob. (I, 309); Vasmer (I, 560); Fasmer (II, 236–7); Shanskii (VIII, 135); Barkh-Bog. (VII, 133 [1715]); Barkh. (X, 39); Slov. Akad. (III, 535); Slov. Russ. (II, 173); Slovar' (V, 960–1); Smirnitskii (294).

komand/komanda = order, command, also detachment, party, crew (naut.), team, fr. Pol. *komenda*/Du. *commando*/Germ. *Kommando*/Fr. *commande*. Christ. (35); Smirnov (146–7); Preob. (I, 341); Vasmer (I, 606); Fasmer (II, 300); Shanskii (VIII, 222); Kaiser (129); Barkh. (X, 113–14); Chernykh (I, 415–6); Slov. Akad. (III, 759); Slovar' (V, 1214–16); Fadeev (I, 305–6); Plekhov (130); Smirnitskii (303).

Derivations: *komandovat', komanduiushchii*

komendant = commandant (of fortress), fr. Pol. *komendant*/Germ. *Kommandant*. Christ. (36); Smirnov (148, 366 *[vits- komendant]*, 371); Vasmer (I, 607); Fasmer (II, 302); Shanskii (VIII, 228); Kaiser (129); Bond (39); Barkh. (X, 117); Slov. Akad. (III, 762); Slov. Russ. (II, 194); Slovar' (V, 1230); Plekhov (132); Smirnitskii (303). Gard. (131–2) finds precedents dating to 1656, but "only of foreign holders of this office" (cf. Leeming, 68; Chernykh, I, 417).

Derivations: *komendantskii, komendantstvo*

kornet = cornet (rank), fr. Pol./Germ./Du. *kornet*/Fr. *cornette*. Christ. (33); Smirnov (162); Vasmer (I, 628); Shanskii (VIII, 320); Grib. (42); Slov. Akad. (III, 833); Slov. Russ. (II, 205); Slovar' (V, 1441); Smirnitskii (311). Barkh-Bog. (VII, 328), Fasmer (II, 330), Leeming (71) cite precedents in 17th-cent. dpl. docs.

korpus = corps, later also building housing the corps; also body, ship's hull, collection of texts, fr. Germ. *Korps*/Lat. *corpus*. Smirnov (163, 371); Preob. (I, 362); Vasmer (I, 634); Fasmer (II, 337); H-W. (80); Bond (39); Slov. Akad. (III, 843); Slov. Russ. (II, 207); Slovar' (V, 1467–9); Fadeev (I, 323); Plekhov (140); Smirnitskii (312). Barkh-Bog. (VII, 344) cites two 17th-cent. precedents.

kronverk = a kind of fortification, fr. Germ. *Kronwerk*. Smirnov (168); Bond (54); Barkh. (XI, 33); Slov. Russ. (II, 225); Slovar' (V, 1699).

kurtina = curtain (wall between bastions of fort), later also row of trees along garden, then parterre, flower-bed; fr. Fr. *courtine.* Smirnov (171); Vasmer (I, 702); Fasmer (II, 429); Barkh. (XI, 88); Slov. Russ. (II, 238); Slovar' (V, 1879–80); Smirnitskii (326); Ox. Russ. (314).

lager' = fortified encampment, camp, fr. Germ. *Lager.* Christ. (37); Smirnov (173, 373); Preob. (I, 427); Vasmer (II, 3); Fasmer (II, 445); Bond (39); Grib. (45 *[lagar]*); Barkh. (XI, 103); Chernykh (I, 462–3); Shanskii-Bob. (162); Wade (104); Slov. Akad. (III, 1126); Slov. Russ. (II, 242); Slovar' (VI, 19–20); Plekhov (145); Smirnitskii (327).
Derivation: *lagernyi*

lafet = gun carriage, fr. Germ. *Lafette.* Smirnov (175); Preob. (I, 438); Vasmer (II, 19); Fasmer (II, 467); Bond (40); Barkh. (XI, 127); Chernykh (I, 469); Shanskii-Bob. (164); Slov. Akad. (III, 1144); Slov. Russ. (II, 246); Slovar' (VI, 84); Fadeev (I, 347); Plekhov (146); Smirnitskii (329).

legeon/legion = legion, fr. Germ. *Legion;* also *legioner* = legionary, fr. Germ. *Legionär.* Smirnov (175, 373); Vasmer (II, 24); Fasmer (II, 473); Bond (55); Barkh. (XI, 132); Slov. Russ. (II, 247); Slovar' (VI, 102–3); Smirnitskii (329). Barkh-Bog. (VIII, 188), following Vasmer/ Fasmer, cites *legion/legeon* in Old-Russ./Slav. texts; also D'iachenko (I, 280), Slav. fr. Lat., no date.

leib-gvardiia = life-guards, monarch's personal guard, household troops, fr. Germ. *Leibgarde.* Smirnov (176, 373); Vasmer (II, 27); Fasmer (II, 479); Bond (55); Barkh. (XI, 145– 6); Slov. Russ. (II, 250); Slovar' (VI, 140–1); Smirnitskii (319).

leitenant = lieutenant (also naval), fr. Germ. *Leut(e)nant/*Pol. *lejtnant,* replacing earlier *liutenant.* Christ. (33); Smirnov (177, 373); Vasmer (II, 27); Fasmer (II, 477); Bond (40); Barkh. (XI, 147); Otten (449–51); Chernykh (I, 474); Shanskii-Bob. (165); Slov. Russ. (II, 250); Slovar' (VI, 142); Fadeev (I, 353); Smirnitskii (333).

lozung = password, watchword, later also slogan, catchword, fr. Germ. *Losung.* Christ. (36); Smirnov (181, 373); Vasmer (II, 54); Fasmer (II, 513); Bond (40); Shanskii-Bob. (170); Barkh. (XI, 221–2); Wade (111); Slov. Russ. (II, 262); Slovar' (VI, 335); Smirnitskii (338).

liadunka = kind of cartridge, cartridge pouch, fr. Germ. *Ladung/*Pol. *ładunek.* Christ. (34); Preob. (I, 497); Vasmer (II, 82); Bond (40); Slov. Russ. (II, 278); Slovar' (VI, 457–8); Fadeev (I, 365–6 [obs.]); Ox. Russ. (331). Barkh-Bog. (VIII, 350) and Fasmer (II, 550) cite 17th-cent. precedents.

magazein/magazin = magazine, supply store (also naut.), fr. Du. *magazijn/*Eng. *magazine/* Germ. *Magazin.* Christ. (41); Smirnov (183, 374); Preob. (I, 500); Vasmer (II, 85); Fasmer (II, 555); Bond (40); Barkh-Bog. (IX, 5 [1698]); Otten (308–17); Chernykh (I, 500–1); Shanskii-Bob. (175); Slov. Akad. (IV, 2); Slov. Russ. (II, 278); Slovar' (VI, 465–7); Fadeev (I, 367 [obs.]); Plekhov (151); Smirnitskii (342).

marsh = march, fr. Germ. *Marsch/*Fr. *marche,* perhaps via Pol. *marsz;* also *marshirovat'* = to march, fr. Germ. *marschieren/*Fr. *marcher.* Christ. (37); Smirnov (189, 374); Preob. (I,

512); Vasmer (II, 101); Fasmer (II, 576); Bond (40–1); Shanskii-Bob. (180); Slov. Russ. (II, 288); Slovar' (VI, 648–50, 652); Plekhov (152–3); Smirnitskii (347).

marshal = marshal, fr. Germ. *Marschall*. Smirnov (189, 374); Vasmer (II, 101); Fasmer (II, 576); Fasmer (II, 576); Kaiser (160); Bond (41); Shanskii-Bob. (180); Slov. Russ. (II, 288); Slovar' (VI, 650); Fadeev (I, 375); Smirnitskii (374). Barkh-Bog. (IX, 32) cites term in 1633 *kuranty*. See also *felt-marshal* below.

393

Derivations: *marshal'skii, marshal'stvo*

marshrut = route, itinerary, fr. Germ. *Marschroute*. Smirnov (189); Vasmer (I, 101); Fasmer (II, 576); Bond (41); Chernykh (I, 512); Shanskii-Bob. (180); Slov. Russ. (II, 288); Slovar' (VI, 653); Fadeev (I, 375); Plekhov (153); Smirnitskii (347).
Derivation: *marshrutnyi*

militsiia = militia, volunteer force, fr. Pol. *milicja*/Lat. *militia*/Germ. *Militie/Miliz*. Vasmer (I, 134); Fasmer (II, 621); Chernykh (I, 531); Shanskii-Bob. (186); Slov. Russ. (II, 303); Slovar' (VI, 984–5); Smirnitskii (357).

min/mina = mine (mil.), fr. Du. *mijn*/Germ. *Mine*/Fr. *mine*. Smirnov (196); Preob. (I, 536); Vasmer (II, 135); Fasmer (II, 622); Otten (136–40); Chernykh (I, 532); Slov. Russ. (II, 304); Slovar' (VI, 1005–6); Fadeev (I, 392–3); Plekhov (159); Smirnitskii (358).

mortir/martir/mortira = mortar, fr. Du. *mortier*/Fr. *mortier*. Christ. (34); Smirnov (200, 374); Preob. (I, 558); Vasmer (II, 161); Fasmer (II, 658); Barkh-Bog. (IX, 269); Otten (142–9); Slov. Akad. (IV, 258); Slov. Russ. (II, 324); Slovar' (VI, 1277–8); Fadeev (I, 406); Plekhov (166); Smirnitskii (367).
Derivations: *mortirka* (dim.), *mortirnyi*

mundir = (dress) uniform, fr. Germ. *Montierung/Mundierung/Montur*/Fr. *monture*. Christ. (37); Smirnov (200, 374); Preob. (I, 568); Vasmer (II, 173); Fasmer (III, 9–10); Bond (41); Chernykh (I, 548); Slov. Russ. (II, 331); Slovar' (VI, 1363–4); Plekhov (167); Smirnitskii (369).
Derivations: *mundirnyi, obmundirovanie*

mustrovat'/mushtrovat' = to muster, train, drill, fr. Pol. *musztrować*/Germ. *mustern*/Eng. *muster;* also *mushtra* = military training, drill, fr. Pol. *musztra*/Germ. *Musterung*. Smirnov (201); Preob. (I, 573); Vasmer (II, 182); Fasmer (III, 21); Bond (41); Slov. Russ. (II, 334); Slovar' (VI, 1407); Plekhov (168); Smirnitskii (370).
Derivations: *mushtrovanie, mushtrovat'sia, mushtrovka*

ordir/order = order, command, also order/good order (to maintain in state of); fr. Pol./Germ./Eng. *order*. Slovar' (VIII, 1014); Fadeev (II, 28); Plekhov (188); Smirnitskii (466).
Derivations: *ordernyi, orderovat'* (obs.; cf. Birzhak., 112–13)

ofitser = officer (also naval), fr. Pol. *oficer*/Germ. *Offizier*/Swed. *officer*. Christ. (33); Smirnov (215, 375); Preob. (I, 671); Vasmer (II, 293); Fasmer (III, 174); Bond (41); Barkh-Bog. (XIV, 80); Grib. (16); Chernykh (I, 611); Shanskii-Bob. (220); Wade (146); Slov. Akad.

(IV, 669); Slov. Russ. (III, 143); Slovar' (VIII, 1731); Fadeev (II, 40); Plekhov (196); Smirnitskii (491).
Derivations: *ofitserskii, ofitserstvo*

394

palisad = palisade, stockade, later also paling, fence, fr. Fr. *palissade*/Germ. *Palisade*. Smirnov (216); Preob. (II, 8–9); Vasmer (II, 306); Fasmer (III, 192); Chernykh (I, 617); Shanskii-Bob. (222); Slov. Akad. (IV, 701); Slov. Russ. (III, 156); Slovar' (IX, 60–1); Smirnitskii (495).
Derivations: *palisadnik* (dim.), *palisadnyi*

parat/parad = parade, review, fr. Pol. *parat*/Fr. *parade*, replacing earlier *parada* fr. Pol. *parada* (Barkh-Bog., XIV, 150). Smirnov (217); Vasmer (II, 313–4); Fasmer (III, 203); Grib. (62); Chernykh (II, 4–5); Shanskii-Bob. (224); Slov. Russ. (III, 159); Slovar' (IX, 153–4); Plekhov (199); Smirnitskii (497).
Derivation: *paradnyi* (= formal, ceremonial)

parol' = password, oath, fr. Pol. *parol*/Germ. *Parole*. Christ. (20); Smirnov (219, 377); Vasmer (II, 217); Fasmer (III, 208); Kaiser (245); Grib. (63); Chernykh (II, 7); Slovar' (IX, 216); Fadeev (II, 50–1); Plekhov (200); Smirnitskii (498).

patron = cartridge, fr. Germ. *Patron(e)*/Fr. *patron*. Christ. (34); Smirnov (222); Preob. (II, 27); Vasmer (II, 324); Fasmer (III, 218); Bond (42); Barkh-Bog. (XIV, 173 [1699]); Chernykh (II, 13); Slov. Akad. (IV, 735); Slov. Russ. (III, 163); Slovar' (IX, 301–2); Fadeev (II, 57); Plekhov (201); Smirnitskii (500).

patrul' = patrol (also naval), fr. Du./Fr. *patrouille*. Smirnov (222); Vasmer (II, 324); Fasmer (III, 218); Bond (42); Grib. (63 [*patrol'*]); Chernykh (II, 13); Shanskii-Bob. (227); Slov. Russ. (III, 163); Slovar' (IX, 306–7); Fadeev (II, Plekhov (202); Smirnitskii (500).
Derivations: *patrulirovat', patrul'nyi*

piket = picket, fr. Germ. *Pikett*. Smirnov (225); Vasmer (II, 356); Fasmer (III, 260); Bond (42); Chernykh (II, 31); Shanskii-Bob. (233); Slov. Akad. (IV, 802); Slov. Russ. (III, 218); Slovar' (IX, 1177–8); Smirnitskii (524).

pionir/pioner = sapper, pioneer, fr. Germ. *Pion(n)ier*/Eng. *pioneer*. Christ. (33); Smirnov (227); Vasmer (II, 358); Fasmer (III, 264); Birzhak. (122); Bond (58); Chernykh (II, 33–4); Slovar' (IX, 1199–1201); Smirnitskii (525).

pistolet = pistol, fr. Germ./Fr. *pistolet*, replacing earlier *pistol'* fr. Germ. *Pistole* (Barkh-Bog., XV, 55). Christ. (34); Smirnov (226); Preob. (II, 62); Vasmer (II, 361); Fasmer (III, 267); Grib. (64 [*pistolia*]); Chernykh (II, 35–6); Shanskii-Bob. (234); Slov. Akad. (IV, 819); Slov. Russ. (III, 220); Slovar' (IX, 1237–8); Fadeev (II, 69); Plekhov (206); Smirnitskii (525).

pliats/plats = drill/exercise yard, fr. Germ. *Platz/Militärplatz*. Christ. (51); Smirnov (377); Vasmer (II, 367); Fasmer (III, 276); Bond (42); Shanskii-Bob. (236); Slov. Russ. (III, 226); Slovar' (IX, 1347); Plekhov (208); Smirnitskii (528).
Derivations: *plats-parad, plats-paradnyi*

pluton/g = platoon, fr. Germ. *Ploton(g)/Peloton*/Fr. *peloton*. Smirnov (228); Vasmer (II, 377); Fasmer (III, 288); Barkh-Bog. (XV, 111); Grib. (65); Slov. Russ. (III, 232); Slovar' (IX, 1460–61 [obs.]). Term survived into 19th cent., when replaced by corresponding Russ. term *vzvod*.

portupeia = swordbelt, fr. Fr. *porte-épée*. Smirnov (233); Preob. (II, 110); Vasmer (II, 412); Fasmer (III, 335–6); Chernykh (II, 59); Slov. Russ. (III, 375); Slovar' (X, 1409–10); Plekhov (219–20); Smirnitskii (570).

proviant = provisions, fr. Germ. *Proviant*. Christ. (35); Smirnov (243, 376); Preob. (II, 129); Vasmer (II, 438); Fasmer (III, 371); Kaiser (200); Bond (42); Barkh-Bog. (XX, 103); Otten (473–81); Slov. Akad. (IV, 1086); Slovar' (XI, 960); Smirnitskii (615).

profos = provost (also naval), officer in charge of policing and/or prisoners, fr. Germ. *Profos(s)*. Christ. (32); Smirnov (247); Vasmer (II, 448); Fasmer (III, 385 [also *profoss, prokhvost*]); Bond (59); Grib. (74); Slov. Akad. (IV, 1101); Slov. Russ. (III, 567); Slovar' (XI, 1507 [obs.]); Fadeev (II, 141 [18th cent.]).

ravelin = ravelin (fortification), fr. Germ. *Ravelin*/Fr. *ravelin*. Smirnov (251, 377); Vasmer (II, 480); Fasmer (III, 428); Otten (282, 490); Slov. Akad. (V, 12); Slov. Russ. (IV, 2); Slovar' (XII, 33 [obs.]); Smirnitskii (645 [obs.]).

raketa = rocket, fr. Pol. *rakieta*/Germ. *Rakete*. Christ. (50); Vasmer (II, 488); Fasmer (III, 438); Chernykh (II, 97); Barkh-Bog. (XXI, 265); Slov. Russ. (IV, 39); Slovar' (XII, 565–6); Fadeev (II, 163); Plekhov (250–52); Smirnitskii (663).
Derivations: *raketka* (dim.), *raketnyi, raketonosets* (= [helicopter] gunship)

ranets = knapsack, fr. Germ. *Ranzen*. Smirnov (252); Preob. (II, 182–3); Vasmer (II, 491); (Fasmer III, 442); Bond (42); Shanskii-Bob. (267); Slov. Akad. (V, 72); Slov. Russ. (IV, 40); Slovar' (XII, 582–3); Smirnitskii (663).

rapir/rapira = rapier, foil, fr. Pol./Germ. *Rapier*/Fr.*rapière*. Smirnov (252); Preob. (II, 183); Vasmer (II, 492); Fasmer (III, 443); Chernykh (II, 99); Bond (60); Slov. Akad. (V, 73); Slov. Russ. (IV, 40); Slovar' (XII, 590); Smirnitskii (664). Barkh-Bog. (XXI, 274) cites *rapier/rapir* in 17th-cent. dpl. docs.
Derivation: *rapirnyi*

ratseia/ratsion = ration, fr. Pol. *racja*/Germ. *Ration*. Christ. (44); Smirnov (253); Vasmer (II, 497); Fasmer (III, 450); Kaiser (204); Bond (42); Slov. Russ. (IV, 59); Slovar' (XII, 1031); Plekhov (254); Smirnitskii (677).

redut = redoubt, fr. Germ./Fr. *redoute*. Smirnov (256, 377); Vasmer (II, 504); Fasmer (III, 459); Bond (60); Slov. Akad. (V, 112); Slov. Russ. (IV, 61); Slovar' (XII, 1130); Smirnitskii (679).

rezerva/rezerv = reserve(s) (also naval), fr. Pol. *rezerwa*/Germ./Du. *reserve*/Fr. *réserve*. Smirnov (257); Preob. (II, 194); Vasmer (II, 506); Fasmer (III, 462); Chernykh (II, 107);

Shanskii-Bob. (270); Slov. Russ. (IV, 61); Slovar' (XII, 1148–50); Fadeev (II, 174); Plekhov (257); Smirnitskii (680). Term later acquired broader meaning.
Derivations: *rezervirovat', rezervnyi*

396

rekrut = recruit (also naval), fr. Pol./Germ. *Rekrut*. Christ. (36); Smirnov (260, 378); Preob. (II, 195); Vasmer (II, 508); Fasmer (III, 465); Kaiser (204); Bond (60–1); Slov. Akad. (V, 113); Slov. Russ. (IV, 62); Slovar' (XII, 1194); Fadeev (II, 177); Smirnitskii (681).
Derivations: *rekrutirovat', rekrutskii*

remont = remount service (fresh horses), fr. Fr. *remonte*. Smirnov (260); Vasmer (II, 511); Fasmer (III, 469); Chernykh (II, 111); Wade (185); Slov. Russ. (IV, 62); Slovar' (XII, 1213–14); Fadeev (II, 177–8); Plekhov (258); Smirnitskii (681). Word later broadened to mean "repair(s), maintenance, technical service(s)."
Derivations: *remontër* (= officer in charge), *remontirovat', remontirovka, remontnyi*

transheia = trench, fr. Fr. *tranchée*. Smirnov (294); Vasmer (III, 132); Fasmer (IV, 94); Chernykh (II, 258); Shanskii-Bob. (321); Slov. Akad. (VI, 236); Slov. Russ. (IV, 292); Slovar' (XV, 827–8); Fadeev (II, 307); Plekhov (301); Smirnitskii (797).

trofei = trophy, prize, booty, fr. Fr. *trophée*. Smirnov (296); Vasmer (III, 142); Fasmer (IV, 107); Shanskii-Bob. (325); Slov. Akad. (VI, 274–5); Slov. Russ. (IV, 300); Slovar' (XV, 1013–14); Smirnitskii (803). Srez. (III, 1003) cites both *trofea* and *tropheum*, fr. Lat. *tropheum*, in medieval Slav. texts.

fashina = fascine, bundle of branches used in sieges, fr. Pol. *faszyna*/Germ. *Fashine*. Smirnov (305); Vasmer (III, 203); Fasmer (IV, 188); Shanskii-Bob. (340); Slov. Akad. (VI, 482); Slov. Russ. (IV, 385); Slovar' (XVI, 1285); Plekhov (312); Smirnitskii (844).
Derivations: *fashinka* (dim.), *fashinnik* (collection of), *fashinnnyi*

feierverker = bombardier, fr. Germ. *Feuerwerker*. Smirnov (305); Vasmer (III, 204); Fasmer (IV, 188); Bond (62); Slovar' (XVI, 1296); Ox. Russ. (860).

felt-marshal/fel'dmarshal = field-marshal, fr. Germ. *Feldmarschall*. Christ. (32); Smirnov (86, 305, 380); Vasmer (III, 204); Fasmer (IV, 189); Bond (62); Grib. (94 *[fel'tmarshalok]*); Slov. Akad. (VI, 482); Slov. Russ. (IV, 386); Slovar' (XVI, 1298); Smirnitskii (844).

fel'dsher = field surgeon, medical assistant, fr. Germ. *Feldscher/Feldscherer*. Smirnov (306); Vasmer (III, 204); Fasmer (IV, 189); Bond (43); Chernykh (II, 307); Shanskii-Bob. (341); Slov. Russ. (IV, 386); Slovar' (XVI, 1300); Smirnitskii (844).

flank/flanka/flang = flank, wing (also naut.), fr. Germ. *Flanke*/Du. *flank*/Fr. *flanc*. Christ. (37); Smirnov (309); Vasmer (III, 211); Fasmer (IV, 198); Grib. (94); Chernykh (II, 316); Shanskii-Bob. (344); Slov. Russ. (IV, 389); Slovar' (XVI, 1427); Fadeev (II, 354); Plekhov (314); Smirnitskii (846–7).
Derivations: *flangovyi, flankovat', flankirovat'*

fligel'-ad"iutant = aide-de-camp, fr. Germ. *Flügeladjutant*. Smirnov (309); Vasmer (III,

212); Fasmer (IV, 199); Bond (64); Wade (231); Slov. Akad. (VI, 493); Slov. Russ. (IV, 389); Slovar' (XVI, 1441); Smirnitskii (847).

forpost = advanced post, fr. Du. *voorpost*/Germ. *Vorposten.* Smirnov (313); Vasmer (III, 216); Fasmer (IV, 203); Bond (43); Shanskii-Bob. (345); Slov. Russ. (IV, 391); Slovar' (XVI, 1508); Smirnitskii (848).

fortifikatsiia = fortification, fr. Pol. *fortyfikacja*/Germ. *Fortifikation*/Fr. *fortification.* Smirnov (380); Vasmer (III, 216); Fasmer (IV, 204); Slov. Akad. (VI, 495); Slov. Russ. (IV, 391); Slovar' (XVI, 1517); Fadeev (II, 361); Plekhov (316–7); Smirnitskii (849).

frunt/front = front, fr. Germ./Fr. *front,* replacing earlier *fron'te,* fr. older Germ. *Fronte.* Christ. (36); Smirnov (317, 380); Vasmer (III, 219); Fasmer (IV, 208); Gard. (222–3); Bond (43); Chernykh (II, 325); Shanskii-Bob. (346); Slov. Russ. (IV, 393–4); Slovar' (XVI, 1570–3); Fadeev (II, 364); Plekhov (317); Smirnitskii (850).
Derivations: *frontovik* (= front-line soldier), *frontovoi*

furazh = fodder, forage, fr. Germ. *Fur(r)age*/Fr. *fourrage;* also *furazhirovat'* = to supply with forage, fr. Germ. *fur(r)agieren.* Christ. (37); Smirnov (318, 380); Vasmer (III, 221); Fasmer (IV, 210); Kaiser (199); Bond (43); Chernykh (II, 327); Slov. Russ. (IV, 394); Slovar' (XVI, 1595); Smirnitskii (851).

tseigauz/tseikhgauz = military supply depot, arsenal, storeroom, fr. Germ. *Zeughaus.* Smirnov (320, 381); Vasmer (III, 287); Fasmer (IV, 296); H-W. (117); Kaiser (201); Bond (43–4); Slov. Russ. (IV, 394); Slovar' (XVII, 585–6 [obs.]); Smirnitskii (862).

tsitadel' = citadel, fortress, kremlin, later also part of a ship, fr. Germ. *Zitadelle*/Du. *citadel.* Christ. (36); Smirnov (323); Vasmer (III, 292); Fasmer (IV, 303); Birzhak. (121–2); Chernykh (II, 371–2); Slov. Russ. (IV, 420); Slovar' (XVII, 707); Fadeev (II, 378); Smirnitskii (865). Leeming (47) cites *tsetadela/kitadella* (fr. Ital. *cittadella* via Pol. *citadella*?) in dpl. doc. of 1639.
Derivation: *tsitadel'nyi*

shants/shanets = trench/entrenchment, earthworks, fr. Germ. *Schanze*/Pol. *szaniec.* Christ. (35); Smirnov (325, 381); Preob. (suppl., 87); Vasmer (III, 372); Fasmer (IV, 404); Bond (66); Grib. (99); Slov. Akad. (VI, 852–3 *[shantsy]*); Slov. Russ. (IV, 448); Slovar' (XVII, 1262, 1266); Plekhov (322–3); Smirnitskii (879); Ox. Russ. (892). Gard. (232–3) dates to 1611, Shanskii-Bob. (369) to 17th cent.
Derivations: *shantsevyi, shantsovat'*

shompol/shenpol = ramrod, fr. Germ. *Stempel*/Pol. *sztempel.* Christ. (35); Smirnov (332, 381); Vasmer (III, 420); Fasmer (IV, 466); Bond (44); Grib. (100 *[shonpol]*); Chernykh (II, 420); Slov. Akad. (VI, 911 *[shompal]*); Slav. Russ. (IV, 460); Slovar' (XVII, 1506); Plekhov (324); Smirnitskii (885).

shpitsruten = rod for corporal punishment, used in running the gauntlet, fr. Germ. *Spitzruten/Spiessruten* (Russ. adapts Germ. plural to sing., here as elsewhere). Smirnov

(333); Vasmer (III, 426–7); Fasmer (IV, 474); Kaiser (232); Bond (67); Grib. (100); Shanskii-Bob. (377); Slovar' (XVII, 1533–4); Smirnitskii (886).

shpora = spur, fr. Germ. *Spore.* Christ. (34); Preob. (suppl., 106); Vasmer (III, 427); Fasmer (IV, 475); Bond (44); Chernykh (II, 423); Shanskii-Bob. (377); Slov. Russ. (IV, 462); Slovar' (XVII, 1535–6); Smirnitskii (886).

shtap/shtab = staff, headquarters, fr. Germ. *Stab;* also *shtab-ofitser* = field officer, fr. Germ. *Stabsoffizier.* Smirnov (334, 381); Preob. (suppl., 107); Vasmer (III, 428); Fasmer (IV, 476); Kaiser (148); Bond (44); Grib. (100); Chernykh (II, 424); Slov. Akad. (VI, 916); Slov. Russ. (IV, 463); Slovar' (XVII, 1545); Plekhov (67, 325); Smirnitskii (886). Term *shtab* gradually extended to civil government.
Derivations: *shtabist, shtabnik, shtabnoi, shtabskii*

shturm = storm, assault, fr. Germ. *Sturm*/Pol. *szturm.* Smirnov (338, 381); Preob. (suppl., 108–9); Vasmer (III, 432); Fasmer (IV, 481); H-W. (120); Bond (44); Shanskii-Bob. (379); Slav. Russ. (IV, 464); Slovar' (XVII, 1587–9); Plekhov (326); Smirnitskii (887).
Derivations: *shturmovat'* (cf. Pol. *szturmovać*), *shturmovka, shturmovoi*

shtyk = bayonet, fr. Pol. *sztyk*/Germ. *Stich*/Swed. *stick.* Smirnov (338); Preob. (suppl., 109); Vasmer (III, 432); Fasmer (IV, 481–2); Bond (45); Chernykh (II, 427); Shanskii-Bob. (379); Slov. Akad. (VI, 921); Slov. Russ. (IV, 464); Slovar' (XVII, 1596–7); Plekhov (327); Smirnitskii (887).

eksertsiia/ekzertsitsiia = exercise/s, training (also naval), fr. Germ. *Exerziert/en*/Fr. *exercice/ s.* Slov. Akad. (VI, 1005); Slov. Russ. (IV, 472); Slovar' (XVII, 1742–3 [obs.]); Fadeev (II, 406 [obs.]).

NAUTICAL TERMS

abordazh = boarding, fr. Fr. *abordage.* Vasmer (I, 2); Fasmer (I, 56); Slov. Russ. (I, 1); Slovar' (I, 15–16); Fadeev (I, 9–10); Smirnitskii (31); Ox. Russ. (1).
Derivations: *abordazhnyi, abordirovat'*

admiral/vitse-admiral = admiral/vice-admiral, fr. Du. *admiraal/vice-/vies-/vijs-admiraal*/ Eng. *admiral/vice-admiral.* Smirnov (30–1, 363, 366); Preob. (I, 2); Vasmer (I, 6); Fasmer (I, 62); Shanskii (I, 48–9); Kaiser (193); Barkh. (I, 26); Otten (19, 206–12); Slov. Akad. (I, 10); Slov. Russ. (I, 3, 19); Slovar' (I, 55–6); Fadeev (I, 22, 122); Smirnitskii (34, 95). Title *admiral* known earlier in Russ. (H-W., 55; Barkh-Bog., I, 22; Leeming, 31) but not conferred (Russified) until Peter I.
Derivation: *admiral'skii*

admiral(i)teits/admiralteistvo = civil admiral/admiralty, naval dockyards, fr. Du. *admiraliteit*/Germ. *Admiralität.* Preob. (I, 2); Fasmer (I, 62); Shanskii (I, 49); Kaiser (193); Grib. (5); Barkh. (I, 26–7); Otten (20–22); Slov. Akad. (I, 10); Slov. Russ. (I, 3); Slovar' (I, 56); Fadeev (I, 23); Smirnitskii (34).

amplitud/amplituda = amplitude (nav.), fr. Eng. *amplitude*. Ryan (91–2); Slovar' (I, 120); Fadeev (I, 29); Smirnitskii (37).
Derivation: *amplitudnyi*

ankar/anker = anchor, fr. Du./Germ. *Anker*/Eng. *anchor*/Ital. *ankora*. Smirnov (38); Vasmer I (I, 18); Fasmer (I, 79); Barkh. (I, 70–1); Avery (79); Slov. Russ. (I, 10 [also ankerok]); Slovar' (I, 143–4); Fadeev (I, 31 [obs.]); Smirnitskii (38); Ox. Russ. (8). Term initially used interchangeably with older Russ. *iakor'*, but gradually lost nautical sense and came to mean anchor bolt or post, iron clamp, crutch or brace.

arirgard/ariergarda/ar'ergard = rearguard (also mil.), fr. Fr. *arrière-garde*. Christ. (37); Smirnov (44); Vasmer (I, 19); Fasmer (I, 92); Slov. Russ. (I, 12); Slovar' (I, 302); Fadeev (I, 38); Plekhov (18); Smirnitskii (42).

akhtershteven' = sternpost, fr. Du. *achtersteven*. Christ. (39); Smirnov (57); Vasmer (I, 33); Fasmer (I, 98); Rozen (89); Whittall (18); Slov. Russ. (I, 16); Fadeev (I, 44); Smirnitskii (43).

bak/bakan/baken = beacon, buoy, fr. Du. *bak/baken*. Vasmer (I, 42); Fasmer (I, 109); Shanskii (II, 14); Barkh. (I, 129); Slov. Akad. (I, 85); Slov. Rus. (I, 18); Slovar' (I, 247); Fadeev (I, 51); Smirnitskii (45). Russ. *bui* = buoy, from Du. *boei*/Eng. *buoy*/Fr. *bouée*, also used from Petrine period: Christ. (39); Vasmer (I, 138); Shanskii (II, 216); Barkh. (II, 158); Slov. Akad. (I, 375); Slovar' (I, 247); Fadeev (I, 94); Plekhov (21); Smirnitskii (73).
Derivation: *bakenshchik*

balast/ballast = *ballast*, fr. Du./Eng. *ballast*. Christ. (40); Smirnov (54); Vasmer (I, 48); Fasmer (I, 117); Shanskii (II, 25); Whittall (19); Chernykh (I, 69); Slov. Akad. (I, 88); Slov. Russ. (I, 19); Slovar' (I, 257); Fadeev (I, 54); Smirnitskii (45).

banka/bank = thwart, bank, fr. Eng./Germ./Du. *bank*. Vasmer (I, 51); Fasmer (I, 120); Whittall (20); Barkh. (I, 137); Slov. Russ. (I, 21); Slovar' (I, 268); Fadeev (I, 55); Plekhov (22); Smirnitskii (46).

bar = (sand)bank, shoal, fr. Eng. *bar*/Du. *baar*/Fr. *barre*. Vasmer (I, 52); Fasmer (I, 122); Whittall (20); Slov. Russ. (I, 23); Slovar' (I, 271); Fadeev (I, 56); Smirnitskii (46).

barzha = barge, fr. Fr./Eng. *barge*/Ital. *bargia*. Smirnov (56); Vasmer (I, 56); Fasmer (I, 126); Shanskii (II, 43–4); Barkh. (I, 142); Whittall (21–2); Chernykh (I, 74); Slov. Akad. (I, 102); Slov. Russ. (I, 22); Slovar' (I, 277–8); Fadeev (I, 57); Plekhov (22); Smirnitskii (47). Barkh-Bog. (I, 74) cites precedent from 1665.

barka/bark = bark, small boat of galley type, lighter, fr. Ital. *barca*/Eng./Du. *bark*/Fr. *barque*. Christ. (40); Preob. (I, 17); Vasmer (I, 56); Fasmer (I, 127); Gard. (57–8); Shanskii (II, 45); Barkh. (I, 142); Chernykh (I, 75); Whittall (22); Slov. Akad. (I, 102); Slov. Russ. (I, 22); Slovar' (I, 282); Fadeev (I, 59 [both terms]); Smirnitskii (47). Barkh-Bog. (I, 74) cites precedent from 1675; term known much earlier in Novgorod.

beidevind = by the wind, close-hauled, fr. Du. *bij de wind*/Eng. *by the wind*. Barkh. (I, 191); Whittall (23–4); Slov. Russ. (I, 43); Fadeev (I, 64); Smirnitskii (53); Ox. Russ. (23).

bizan' = mizzen, mizzensail, fr. Du. *bezaan*/Germ. *Besan*. Smirnov (58); Preob. (I, 25); Vasmer (I, 85); Fasmer (I, 164); Barkh. (II, 22); Slov. Russ. (I, 46); Slovar' (I, 451); Fadeev (I, 70); Smirnitskii (59).

bims = beam, fr. Eng. *beam/s*. Vasmer (I, 86); Fasmer (I, 166); Shanskii (II, 119–20); Barkh. (II, 23); Whittall (25–6); Slov. Russ. (I, 46); Slovar' (I, 454); Fadeev (I, 70); Plekhov (25); Ox. Russ. (29). Vasmer/Fasmer also lists *bimets*.
Derivation: *bimsovyi*

blok = block, pulley, fr. Germ./Eng. *block*/Du. *blok*. Smirnov (61, 365); Preob. (I, 30); Vasmer (I, 94); Fasmer (I, 176); Barkh. (II, 68); Whittall (26–7); Otten (30–2, 248–9); Chernykh (I, 95); Slov. Akad. (I, 229); Slov. Russ. (I, 62); Slovar' (I, 516);. Fadeev (I, 72); Smirnitskii (63).
Derivations: *blokovyi, blochnyi*

bort = side (of ship), fr. Du. *boord*/Germ. *Bord*. Christ. (40); Smirnov (63); Preob. (I, 38); Vasmer (I, 110); Fasmer (I, 198); Shanskii (II, 173); Barkh.-Bog. (I, 299); Barkh. (II, 13–4); Otten (38–40); Slov. Akad. (I, 288); Slov. Russ. (I, 77); Slovar' (I, 581–3); Fadeev (I, 83); Plekhov (37); Smirnitskii (67).
Derivations: *bortovoi, bortovyi*

bot/botik = boat, fr. Eng. *boat*/Du./Germ. *Boot*. Christ. (38); Smirnov (64); Preob. (I, 39); Vasmer (I, 112); Fasmer (I, 199–200); Rozen (83); Shanskii (I, 177); Gard. (65–6); Grib. (13); Whittall (28–9); Slov. Akad. (I, 302); Slov. Russ. (I, 78); Slovar' (I, 591); Fadeev (I, 84 [both terms, latter obs.]); Plekhov (37); Smirnitskii (68). Barkh-Bog. (I, 302) cites *bot* in 1564 dpl. report from Denmark but not again until 1692.

botsmon/botsman = boatswain, fr. Germ./Du. *bootsman*. Christ. (40); Smirnov (64); Vasmer (I, 113); Fasmer (I, 202); Shanskii (II, 179); Barkh-Bog. (I, 304 [1696]); Barkh. (II, 117); Whittall (29); Chernykh (I, 105–6); Slov. Russ. (I, 78); Slovar' (I, 593); Fadeev (I, 85); Plekhov (38); Smirnitskii (68).

brandar/brander = fire-ship, incendiary vessel, fr. Germ. *Brander*/Du. *brander*. Christ. (40); Smirnov (65); Vasmer (I, 117); Fasmer (I, 207); Bond (126); Barkh-Bog. (I, 315 [1698]); Barkh. (II, 124); Otten (249–52); Slov. Russ. (I, 80); Slovar' (I, 604); Fadeev (I, 86); Smirnitskii (69).

bregantin/brigantina = brigantine, small sailboat, fr. Fr. *brigantine*. Smirnov (66); Vasmer (I, 123); Fasmer (I, 214); Shanskii (II, 196); Barkh-Bog. (I, 329); Barkh. (II, 140 [1697]); Slov. Russ. (I, 82); Slovar' (I, 629); Fadeev (I, 88); Ox. Russ. (42).

brig/brik = brig, fr. Eng. *brig*/Du. *brik*. Preob. (I, 45); Vasmer (I,122); Fasmer (I, 213); Shanskii (II, 195–6); Barkh. (II, 139); Whittall (31); Slov. Russ. (I, 83); Slovar' (I, 628); Fadeev (I, 88); Smirnitskii (31).

buer = small sailboat, single-masted, later ice-boat, sailboat on skis, fr. Du. *boeier*. Smirnov (67); Vasmer (I, 136); Fasmer (I, 231); Shanskii (II, 213); Grib. (14); Barkh. (II, 156);

Chernykh (I, 118); Slov. Akad. (I, 369); Slov. Russ. (I, 87); Slovar' (I, 671); Fadeev (I, 93); Smirnitskii (73).

buksir = tug, tugboat, fr. Du. *boegseer* (?)/Germ. *Buksierer.* Smirnov (67); Vasmer (I, 141); Fasmer (I, 237); Shanskii (II, 221); Barkh. (II, 162); Chernykh (I, 121); Slov. Russ. (I, 88); Slovar' (I, 680); Fadeev (I, 95); Plekhov (40); Smirnitskii (73).

Derivations: *buksirovat'* (cf. Du. *boegseeren*/Germ. *bugsieren*), *buksirnyi, buksirovka*

bulin' = bowline, fr. Du. *boelijn*/Fr. *bouline*/Eng. *bowline.* Smirnov (68); Vasmer (I, 142); Fasmer (I, 239); Whittall (31–2); Slov. Russ. (I, 88); Fadeev (I, 97); Smirnitskii (74); Ox. Russ. (46).

bukht/bukhta = (small) bay, bight, fr. Du. *bogt/bocht*/Swed. *bukt*/Germ. *Bucht.* Preob. (I, 56); Vasmer (I, 156); Fasmer (I, 256); Shanskii (II, 241–2); Kutina I (165); Barkh. (II, 175); Chernykh (I, 128); Slov. Akad. (I, 395); Slov. Russ. (I, 91); Slovar' (I, 712); Fadeev (I, 98); Smirnitskii (75).

bushprit/bousprit = bowsprit, fr. Du. *boegspriet*/Eng. *bowsprit.* Whittall (32); Slov. Russ. (I, 91); Slovar' (I, 714); Fadeev (I, 98–9); Smirnitskii (75).

vatarliniia/vaterlineia/vaterliniia = water-line, fr. Eng. *water-line*/Du. *Waterlinie/waterlijn.* Rozen (86); Shanskii (III, 24); Barkh. (II, 221); Whittall (33–4); Slov. Russ. (I, 101); Slovar' (II, 61–2); Fadeev (I, 103); Plekhov (41); Smirnitskii (80).

vereika/vereia = wherry, fr. Eng. *wherry,* a light sailing boat. Smirnov (72); Preob. (I, 74); Vasmer (I, 186); Fasmer (I, 296); Barkh. (III, 39); Whittall (36–7); Slov. Russ. (I, 111); Slovar' (II, 175); Fadeev (I, 108); Ox. Russ. (52).

Derivations: *vereechka, vereinyi*

verf' = wharf, shipyard, fr. Du. *werf*/Germ. *Werft.* Christ. (39); Smirnov (73); Vasmer (I, 190); Fasmer (I, 301); Shanskii (III, 67–8); Barkh. (III, 54–5); Chernykh (I, 144); Slov. Russ. (I, 113); Slovar' (II, 199–200); Fadeev (I, 111); Smirnitskii (86).

vest = west, west wind, fr. Du. *west.* Smirnov (73); Vasmer (I, 192); Fasmer (I, 304); Shanskii (III, 74); Kutina I (126); Barkh. (III, 69); Slov. Russ. (I, 113); Slovar' (II, 223–4); Fadeev (I, 113); Smirnitskii (87).

vympel = pendant, pennant, fr. Du. *wimpel.* Christ. (38); Smirnov (76); Preob. (I, 103–4); Vasmer (I, 240); Fasmer (I, 368); Shanskii (III, 227); Barkh. (IV, 243); Otten (397–9); Chernykh (I, 173); Slov. Akad. (I, 944–5); Slov. Russ. (I, 213); Slovar' (II, 1114–5); Fadeev (I, 150); Plekhov (63); Smirnitskii (133).

Derivation: *vympel'nyi*

gavan' = harbor, fr. Du. *haven*/Germ. *Hafen.* Christ. (39); Smirnov (77, 368); Preob. (I, 113); Vasmer (I, 248); Fasmer (I, 379); Shanskii (IV, 4); Kutina I (165); Barkh. (V, 78); Otten (280–6); Wade (37); Slov. Akad. (II, 1); Slov. Russ. (I, 252); Slovar' (III, 7); Fadeev (I, 157); Plekhov (65); Smirnitskii (146).

402

galera = galley, fr. Germ. *Galeere*/Pol. *galera*/Ital. *galera,* replacing earlier *galeia* (Srez., I, 509; Barkh.-Bog., IV, 9; Leeming, 55; Avan., II, 316). Smirnov (79, 366); Preob. (I, 117); Vasmer (I, 253); Fasmer (I, 386 [1665]); Shanskii (IV, 14); Gard. (81–2); Kaiser (234); Grib. (20); Leeming (55 [1620]); Barkh. (V, 84); Otten (403); Slov. Akad. (II, 17); Slov. Russ. (I, 254 [obs.]); Slovar' (III, 22); Fadeev (I, 160); Smirnitskii (147). Fasmer (I, 386) and Leeming (55) cite 17th-cent. precedent.

gardemarin = naval cadet, fr. Du. *guardemarine*/Fr. *garde-marine.* Smirnov (81); Vasmer (I, 259); Fasmer (I, 393); Shanskii (IV, 28); Barkh. (V, 89); Slov. Russ. (I, 255); Slovar' (III, 35–6); Fadeev (I, 162); Smirnitskii (147).

gol = hull, fr. Eng. *hull*/Du. *hol.* Vasmer (I, 284); Fasmer (I, 427); Rozen (86); Barkh. (V, 152); Whittall (43); Fadeev (I, 177 [obs.]). Attested as late as 1795, term later replaced by *korpus* (see above, Military Terms) while *gol* became "goal" as in sport, fr. Eng. *goal* (Slovar', III, 208; Smirnitskii, 157).

grot-masht/*grot-machta* = mainmast, fr. Du. *groote mast.* Smirnov (96); Barkh. (V, 245); Otten (67–9); Slov. Russ. (I, 295); Slovar' (III, 423); Fadeev (I, 186); Smirnitskii (167).

dek = deck, fr. Eng. *deck*/Du. *dek.* Christ. (39); Smirnov (100); Vasmer (I, 336); Fasmer (I, 495); Barkh. (VI, 79); Whittall (45–6); Fadeev (I, 203). Attested into early 19th cent., when generally replaced by Russ. *paluba* (Chernykh, I, 618; Slovar', III, 656; Smirnitskii, 495).

dok = dock, fr. Du. *dok*/Eng. *dock.* Christ. (38); Smirnov (109); Vasmer (I, 358); Fasmer (I, 523); Shanskii (V, 156); Barkh. (VI, 184); Whittall (47); Chernykh (I, 260); Slov. Russ. (I, 316); Slovar' (III, 903); Fadeev (I, 217); Smirnitskii (194).

drek = grapnel, small anchor, fr. Du. *dreg(ge)*/Germ. *Dregge.* Slov. Russ. (I, 372); Fadeev (I, 222); Smirnitskii (203); Ox. Russ. (175).

driif/*dreif* = drift, leeway, fr. Eng. *drift*/Du. *drift.* Smirnov (111); Vasmer (I, 369); Fasmer (I, 537); Shanskii (V, 189); Barkh. (VII, 6); Whittall (48); Chernykh (I, 268); Slov. Russ. (I, 372); Slovar' (III, 1107–8); Fadeev (I, 221); Plekhov (95); Smirnitskii (203).
Derivation: *dreifovat'* (= to drift or fall to leeward; cf. Du. *drijven*)

ziuid = south, south wind, fr. Du. *zuid;* also *ziuid-vest* = southwest (wind), fr. Du. *zuidwest,* and ziuid-ost = southeast (wind), fr. Du *zuidoost.* Smirnov (117); Vasmer (I, 465); Fasmer (II, 110); Shanskii (VI, 115); Kutina I (126); Barkh. (VIII, 237–8); Slov. Russ. (II, 98); Slovar' (IV, 1361); Fadeev (I, 255); Smirnitskii (262).
Derivations: *ziuidovyi, ziuid-vestovyi, ziuid-ostovyi*

kabel' = cable, fr. Germ./Du. *kabel*/Eng. *cable.* Vasmer (I, 496); Fasmer (II, 150); Shanskii (VIII, 6); Slov. Russ. (II, 150); Slovar' (V, 622–3); Fadeev (I, 270); Smirnitskii (282).

kambus/*kambuz* = cook room, galley, fr. Du. *kombuis*/Germ. *Kombüse*/*Kämbüse.* Smirnov (127); Vasmer (I, 513); Fasmer (II, 173); Shanskii (VIII, 34–5); Barkh. (IX, 217); Whittall (59–60); Slov. Russ. (II, 155); Slovar' (V, 720); Fadeev (I, 274); Plekhov (123); Smirnitskii (286).

kapor/kaper = small warship, privateer, fr. Du. *kaaper*/Germ. *Kaper*/Fr. *capre*. Smirnov (132); Vasmer (I, 521); Fasmer (II, 184); Kaiser (195); Barkh-Bog. (VII, 62 [1697]); Barkh. (IX, 242); Slov. Akad. (III, 432); Slov. Russ. (II, 160–1); Slovar' (V, 771); Fadeev (I, 277–8); Smirnitskii (287).

kat = cat, a three-masted merchant ship, fr. Du. *kat*/Eng. *cat*. Smirnov (137); Vasmer (I, 539); Fasmer (II, 208); Whittall (50); Barkh. (X, 7); Slov. Russ. (II, 166); Slovar' (V, 859); Fadeev (I, 285); Smirnitskii (290).

kater = cutter, fr. Eng. *cutter*/Du. *kotter*. Preob. (I, 301); Vasmer (I, 540); Fasmer (II, 210); Shanskii (VIII, 95–6); Whittall (51); Barkh. (X, 10); Chernykh (I, 387); Slov. Russ. (II, 166); Slovar' (V, 870); Fadeev (I, 286); Plekhov (125); Smirnitskii (291).

kaiut/kaiuta = cabin, room, fr. Germ. *Kajüte*/Du. *kajuit*. Christ. (40); Smirnov (138); Preob. (I, 303); Vasmer (I, 545); Fasmer (II, 216); Shanskii (VIII, 107); Bond (126); Whittall (44); Otten (77–82); Barkh. (X, 21); Chernykh (I, 390); Slov. Akad. (III, 490); Slov. Russ. (II, 168); Slovar' (V, 898); Fadeev (I, 288); Plekhov (126); Smirnitskii (292).
Derivations: *kaiutka* (dim.), *kaiutnyi*

kvarterdek = quarterdeck, fr. Eng. *quarterdeck*. Smirnov (139); Rozen (89); Whittall (52); Barkh. (X, 25); Otten (538–40); Slov. Russ. (II, 168); Fadeev (I, 289).

kepston/kapston/kabestan = capstan, fr. Eng. *capstan*/Fr. *cabestan*. Vasmer (I, 496); Fasmer (II, 151); Whittall (53); Barkh. (IX, 183); Slov. Russ. (II, 150); Slovar' (V, 624); Smirnitskii (283).

kil' = keel, fr. Germ./Du. *kiel*/Eng. *keel*. Christ. (39); Smirnov (142); Vasmer (I, 557); Fasmer (II, 233); Shanskii (VIII, 129); Whittall (54); Barkh. (X, 35); Otten (215–9); Slov. Akad. (III, 529); Slov. Russ. (II, 172); Slovar' (V, 942–3); Fadeev (I, 292); Plekhov (127); Smirnitskii (293).

kliuver/kliver = jib, fr. Du. *kluiver*/Germ. *Klüver*. Smirnov (144); Vasmer (I, 569–70); Fasmer (II, 250); Shanskii (VIII, 155); Barkh. (X, 56); Slov. Russ. (II, 177); Slovar' (V, 1025); Fadeev (I, 298); Smirnitskii (296).

knis/knisa/kni = knee, gusset, fr. Du. *knie/knies* (dim. *knitje*)/Eng. *knee/knees*. Smirnov (84, 144); Vasmer (I, 580); Fasmer (II, 264); Rozen (130); Whittall (55); Barkh. (X, 70); Otten (550–2); Slov. Russ. (II, 182); Slovar' (V, 1074); Fadeev (I, 301); Smirnitskii (298).

koika = berth, bunk, later also cot, hammock, (hospital) bed, fr. Du. *kooi*. Preob. (I, 330); Vasmer (I, 592); Fasmer (II, 280); Shanskii (VIII, 189–90); Barkh. (X, 85); Wade (90); Slov. Russ. (II, 187); Slovar' (V, 1126); Fadeev (I, 302–3); Smirnitskii (299).

kompas = (magnetic or sea) compass, fr. Pol./Du. *kompas*/Germ. *Kompass*. Smirnov (150, 371); Preob. (I, 342–3); Vasmer (I, 610); Fasmer (II, 305–6); Shanskii (VIII, 239–40); Gard. (133); Bond (126); Barkh-Bog. (VII, 268 [1696]); Barkh. (X, 124–5); Otten (119–12); Ryan (92); Wade (92); Slov. Akad. (III, 764–5); Slov. Russ. (II, 195); Slovar' (V, 1255–6); Fadeev (I, 308); Plekhov (134); Smirnitskii (304). Leeming (69) lists *kompaz*, 1678.

konvoi = convoy (naval, etc.), fr. Du. *konvooi*/Fr. *convoi;* also *konvoir* = escort, convoy, fr. Du. *konvooier.* Christ. (36, 38); Smirnov (152); Vasmer (I, 612); Fasmer (II, 308); Shanskii (VIII, 250–1); Kaiser (189); Barkh-Bog. (VII, 270 [1698]); Grib. (41); Barkh. (X, 130); Chernykh (I, 421); Slov. Akad. (III, 766); Slov. Russ. (II, 196); Slovar' (V, 1276); Fadeev (I, 312); Plekhov (135); Smirnitskii (305).
Derivations: *konvoinyi, konvoevat', konvoirovat'* (cf. Fr. *convoyer*)

korser/kurser/korsar = corsair, pirate, fr. Germ. *Korsar/Kursar*/Ital. *corsaro.* Smirnov (164); H-W (80); Shanskii (VIII, 336); Barkh. (XI, 188); Slov. Russ. (II, 207); Slovar' (V, 1477); Fadeev (I, 324); Smirnitskii (312).

kriuis/kreis/kruiz = cruise, fr. Eng. *cruise*/Germ. *Kreuz;* also *kriuiser/kruiser/kreiser* = cruiser, fr. Du. *kruiser*/Eng. *cruiser.* Christ. (39); Smirnov (372); Vasmer (I, 658); Fasmer (II, 369–70); Shanskii (VIII, 379); Whittall (59); Otten (490); Barkh. (XI, 56); Chernykh (I, 441); Slov. Russ. (II, 218, 231); Slovar' (V, 1612); Fadeev (I, 332–3); Smirnitskii (317); Ox. Russ. (305, 308).
Derivations: *kreiserskii, kreiserstvo* (= cruise), *kreisirovat'*

kuk/kokh/kok = (ship's) cook, fr. Du. kuk/*kok*/Germ. *Koch*/Eng. *cook.* Smirnov (164); Fasmer (II, 281); Shanskii (VIII, 190); Bond (90); Barkh. (X, 85); Slovar' (V, 1127); Fadeev (I, 303); Smirnitskii (299).

kurs = course, ship's course, fr. Du. *koers*/Eng. *course.* Barkh. (XI, 87–8); Slov. Russ. (II, 238); Fadeev (I, 342–3); Plekhov (144); Smirnitskii (325–6); Ox. Russ. (314). Term later added academic and other senses.
Derivations: *kursovoi, kursirovat'* (= to course, ply between)

lavir/lavirovat' = to tack (about), fr. Du. *laveeren*/Germ. *lavieren*/Pol. *lawirować.* Smirnov (172); Preob. (I, 426); Vasmer (II, 3); Fasmer (II, 444–5); Bond (126); Barkh. (XI, 100–01); Chernykh (I, 462); Shanskii-Bob. (162); Slov. Russ. (II, 241); Slovar' (VI, 13); Fadeev (I, 345); Smirnitskii (327).
Derivation: *lavirovanie* (= tacking)

lag/log = log, device for gauging speed of a ship, fr. Du./Eng. *log.* Smirnov (180); Vasmer (II, 3); Fasmer (II, 445); Whittall (60); Barkh. (XI, 103); Slov. Russ. (II, 242); Slovar' (VI, 19); Fadeev (I, 345); Plekhov (145); Smirnitskii (327).

lotsman = pilot, fr. Du. *loodsman*/Germ *Lotse(mann).* Christ. (38); Smirnov (182); Vasmer (II, 63); Fasmer (II, 525); Kaiser (194); Whittall (61–2); Barkh. (XI, 234–5); Slov. Russ. (II, 265); Slovar' (VI, 379); Fadeev (I, 363); Plekhov (150); Smirnitskii (339).
Derivation: *lotsmanskii, lotsmanstvo*

liuger/luger = lugger, a three-masted sailing vessel, fr. Eng. *lugger*/Ger. *Lugger.* Vasmer (II, 78); Fasmer (II, 545); Whittall (62); Slov. Russ. (II, 277); Fadeev (I, 365); Smirnitskii (341).

matroz/matros = seaman, sailor, fr. Germ. *Matrose*/Du. *matroos.* Christ. (39); Smirnov (190, 374); Preob. (I, 515); Vasmer (II, 106); Fasmer (II, 583); Bond (126); Barkh-Bog. (IX, 47

[1697]); Chernykh (I, 515); Wade (117–8); Slov. Akad. (IV, 62); Slov. Russ. (II, 291); Slovar' (VI, 711); Fadeev (I, 379); Plekhov (154–5); Smirnitskii (349).

masht/mashta/macht/machta = mast, fr. Du./Germ. *Mast*/Pol. *maszt.* Christ. (40); Smirnov (191); Preob. (I, 517); Vasmer (II, 108); Fasmer (II, 586); Kaiser (233); Bond (126); Barkh-Bog. (IX, 50 [1696]); Otten (122–33, 324–7); Chernykh (I, 517); Slov. Akad. (IV, 63); Slov. Russ. (II, 292); Slovar' (VI, 727); Fadeev (I, 379); Plekhov (155); Smirnitskii (349).

michman = midshipman, warrant officer, fr. Du. *mitsman*/Eng. *midshipman.* Smirnov (197); Preob. (I, 540); Vasmer (II, 140); Fasmer (II, 630); Whittall (66); Chernykh (I, 535); Slov. Akad. (IV, 157); Slovar' (VI, 1066); Fadeev (I, 399); Smirnitskii (360).
Derivation: *michmanskii.*

navigator = navigator, seafarer, fr. Du./Germ./Eng. *navigator*/Fr. *navigateur.* Smirnov (201); Vasmer (II, 191); Fasmer (III, 34); Ryan (93); Slovar' (VII, 71); Fadeev (I, 413 [obs.]); Smirnitskii (376).

navigatsiia = navigation, sailing, fr. Pol. *nawigacja*/Du. *navigatie*/Germ./Eng./Fr. *navigation.* Smirnov (202); Vasmer (II, 191); Fasmer (III, 34); Ryan (93); Chernykh (I, 555); Shanskii-Bob. (196); Slov. Russ. (II, 352); Slovar' (VII, 72); Fadeev (I, 415); Plekhov (170); Smirnitskii (376).

nord = north, north wind, fr. Du. *noord;* also *nord-vest* = northwest (wind), fr. Du. *nordwest,* and *nord-ost* = northeast (wind), fr. Du. *nordoost.* Smirnov (205); Vasmer (II, 227); Fasmer (III, 83); Kutina I (126); Bond (75); Slov. Russ. (II, 465); Slovar' (VII, 1397); Fadeev (I, 430); Smirnitskii (430).
Derivations: *nordovyi, nord-vestovyi, nord-ostovyi*

ost = east, east wind, fr. Du. *oost.* Smirnov (214); Vasmer (II, 286); Fasmer (III, 164); Kutina I (126); Slov. Russ. (III, 91); Slovar' (VIII, 1159); Fadeev (II, 32); Smirnitskii (471).

paketbot = packetboat, fr. Eng. *packetboat*/Du. *pakketboot*/Germ. *Paketboot.* Christ. (38); Smirnov (216); Vasmer (II, 303); Fasmer (III, 188); Kaiser (153); Whittall (69–70); Slov. Russ. (III, 155); Slovar' (IX, 38); Fadeev (II, 43).

perlin' = hawser, cable, fr. Du. *paarllijn/paardelijn.* Smironov (224); Vasmer (II, 342); Fasmer (III, 242); Grib. (64); Slov. Russ. (III, 214); Slovar' (IX, 1039); Fadeev (II, 66); Smirnitskii (521); Ox. Russ. (513).

pirat = pirate, fr. Germ. *Pirat*/Fr. *pirate.* Smirnov (226); Vasmer (II, 359); Fasmer (III, 265); Kaiser (195); Bond (126–7); Chernykh (II, 34); Shanskii-Bob. (234); Slov. Russ. (III, 219); Slovar' (IX, 1208); Fadeev (II, 68); Smirnitskii (525).

port = port, gun-port, port-hole; also port, seaport, fr. Germ./Eng. *port.* Smirnov (233); Vasmer (II, 411); Fasmer (III, 334); Rozen (86); H-W. (98); Kutina I (165); Whittall (72–3); Slov. Akad. (IV, 1002); Slov. Russ. (III, 375); Slovar' (X, 1398); Fadeev (II, 106); Smirnitskii (570). Leeming (90) cites two possible precedents.

reil'/rel's = rail, fr. Eng. *rail*. Vasmer (II, 510); Fasmer (III, 467); Whittall (75); Chernykh (II, 110); Slovar' (XII, 1202–3); Smirnitskii (681). Term later more broadly applied, to include rails in a railroad (cf. Shanskii-Bob, 271).
Derivation: *rel'sovyi*

rumb = rhumb, compass line/point, fr. Eng. *rhumb*/Fr. *rumb*. Smirnov (267); Preob. (II, 223); Vasmer (II, 546); Fasmer (III, 516); Whittall (76–7); Ryan (93); Shanskii-Bob. (277); Slov. Russ. (III, 78); Slovar' (XII, 1565); Fadeev (II, 187–8); Plekhov (261); Smirnitskii (690).

rur/rul' = rudder, helm, later also steering wheel, fr. Du. *roer*/Fr. *roue/rouler*. Smirnov (267); Preob. (II, 223); Vasmer (II, 546); Fasmer (III, 516); Birzhak. (123–4); Grib. (78); Chernykh (II, 127–8); Shanskii-Bob. (277); Wade (188); Slov. Akad. (V, 221); Slov. Russ. (IV, 78); Slovar' (XII, 1564–5); Fadeev (II, 185–7); Plekhov (261); Smirnitskii (690).

signal = signal (naut.), fr. Du. *signaal*/Germ./Eng./Fr. *signal*. Smirnov (276); Preob. (II, 284); Vasmer (II, 622); Fasmer (III, 618); Bond (42–3); Grib. (81); Chernykh (II, 161); Shanskii-Bob. (288); Slov. Russ. (IV, 123); Slovar' (XIII, 766–7); Fadeev (II, 208); Plekhov (267); Smirnitskii (712). Term gradually acquired broader meaning.
Derivations: *signalizirovat'* (cf. Germ. *signalisieren*), *signal'nyi*

storm/shturm/shtorm = strong gale, fr. Eng./Du. *storm*/Germ. *Sturm*. Christ. (40); Smirnov (337); Preob. (suppl., 108); Vasmer (III, 430); Fasmer (IV, 479); Kutina I (192); Otten (182–4); Chernykh (II, 425–6); Shanskii-Bob. (378); Slov. Akad. (VI, 920); Slov. Russ. (IV, 463–4); Slovar' (XVII, 1569–70); Fadeev (II, 400); Plekhov (326); Smirnitskii (887).
Derivations: *shtormovoi, shtormovat'* (= to ride out/weather a storm)

takalazh/takelazh = rigging, fr. Du. *takelage*. Smirnov (287); Vasmer (III, 70); Fasmer (IV, 12); Otten (194–8); Shanskii-Bob. (312); Slov. Russ. (IV, 268); Slovar' (XV, 52); Fadeev (II, 280); Plekhov (289); Smirnitskii (775).
Derivations: *takelazhit', takelazhnyi*

trap = ship's ladder, fr. Du. *trap*. Smirnov (294); Vasmer (III, 132); Fasmer (IV, 94); Chernykh (II, 258); Shanskii-Bob. (321); Slov. Russ. (IV, 293); Slovar' (XV, 828); Fadeev (II, 307); Plekhov (301); Smirnitskii (797).

fal'shbort = false board, i.e. bulwark, rails, fr. Germ. *Falschbord*. Vasmer (III, 200); Fasmer (IV, 184); Bond (127); Slov. Russ. (IV, 384 *[fal'sh"-borty]*); Slovar' (XVI, 1228); Fadeev (II, 347); Smirnitskii (842); Ox. Russ. (858).

fal'shkil' = false keel (attached to bottom of true keel), fr. Eng. *false keel*/Germ. *Falschkiel*. Bond (127); Whittall (90); Slovar' (XVI, 1231); Fadeev (II, 347); Smirnitskii (843).

farvater = fairway, channel (nav.), fr. Du. *vaarwater*/Germ. *Fahrwater*. Christ. (39); Smirnov (304); Vasmer (III, 202); Fasmer (IV, 185); Chernykh (II, 303); Shanskii-Bob. (340); Slov. Russ. (IV, 385); Slovar' (XVI, 1259–60); Fadeev (II, 348); Plekhov (312); Smirnitskii (843).

flag = ensign, later flag more generally, fr. Du. *vlag*/Eng. *flag*/Germ. *Flagge*. Christ. (39);

Smirnov (308); Vasmer (III, 211); Fasmer (IV, 197); Chernykh (II, 316); Shanskii-Bob. (344); Slov. Akad. (VI, 492); Slov. Russ. (IV, 388); Slovar' (XVI, 1420–1); Fadeev (II, 351–3); Plekhov (313–4); Smirnitskii (846).

flagman = squadron commander, flag officer, admiral, fr. Du. *vlagman.* Smirnov (308); Vasmer (III, 210); Fasmer (IV, 197); Slov. Russ. (IV, 388); Slovar' (XVI, 1422–3); Fadeev (II, 353); Plekhov (314); (Smirnitskii (846).
Derivation: *flagmanskii*

flagshtok = flagstaff, fr. Du. *vlagsto(c)k.* Smirnov (308); Vasmer (III, 211); Fasmer (IV, 198); Slov. Russ. (IV, 388); Slovar' (XVI, 1424); Smirnitskii (846).

flortimbers = floor timbers, fr. Eng. *floor timbers.* Smirnov (310); Vasmer (II, 212–3); Fasmer (IV, 199); Rozen (87); Whittall (91); Slov. Russ. (IV, 389 *[flortimbersy]*); Fadeev (II, 355 [obs.]).

flot = fleet, navy, fr. Du. *vloot*/Germ./Fr. *flotte*/Pol. *flota.* Christ. (38); Smirnov (310, 380); Vasmer (III, 213); Fasmer (IV, 199); Birzhak. (125–6); Otten (571–2); Chernykh (II, 317); Shanskii-Bob. (344); Wade (232); Slov. Akad. (VI, 493–4); Slov. Russ. (IV, 389); Slovar' (XVI, 1445–6); Fadeev (II, 355); Plekhov (314–5); Smirnitskii (847).
Derivations: *flotskii, flotovodets* (= fleet commander)

fliugel'/fliuger = weather-vane, also pennant, fr. Germ. *Flügel*/Du. *vleugel.* Smirnov (310); Vasmer (III, 213); Fasmer (IV, 200); Bond (127); Grib. (95); Otten (267–8); Chernykh (II, 317–18); Shanskii-Bob. (344); Slov. Akad. (VI, 494); Slov. Russ. (IV, 389); Slovar' (XVI, 1451); Fadeev (II, 356); Smirnitskii (847).

fok-zeil'/fok = foresail, fr. Dutch *fok(zeil).* Smirnov (311); Vasmer (III, 213); Fasmer (IV, 200); Slov. Russ. (IV, 390); Slovar' (XVI, 1456); Fadeev (II, 356); Smirnitskii (847)

fok-rei = fore-yard, fr. Du. *fokkera/fokkeree.* Vasmer (II, 213); Fasmer (IV, 200); Otten (54); Slov. Russ. (IV, 390); Slovar' (XVI, 1457); Smirnitskii (847).

fok"-masht/fok-machta = foremast, fr. Du. *fokkemast.* Smirnov (311); Vasmer (III, 213); Fasmer (IV, 200); Otten (53–4); Slovar' (XVI, 1457); Fadeev (II, 357); Smirnitskii (847).

forshteven = stem, fr. Du. *voorsteven.* Smirnov (315); Vasmer (III, 217); Fasmer (IV, 205); Otten (269–71); Slovar' (XVI, 1521); Fadeev (II, 361–2); Smirnitskii (849).

fregat = frigate, fr. Du. *fregat*/Eng. *frigate.* Christ. (38); Smirnov (316); Vasmer (III, 218); Fasmer (IV, 207); Slov. Akad. (VI, 495–6); Slov. Russ. (IV, 393); Slovar' (XVI, 1559–60); Fadeev (II, 363–4); Plekhov (317); Smirnitskii (850).
Derivations: *fregatnyi, fregatovyi*

shvabra = mop, swab, fr. Du. *s/zwabber*/Germ. *Schwabber.* Smirnov (327); Preob. (suppl., 92); Vasmer (III, 382); Fasmer (IV, 417); Chernykh (II, 407); Slov. Akad. (VI, 863–4); Slov. Russ. (IV, 451); Slovar' (XVII, 1311–2); Fadeev (II, 386); Smirnitskii (880).

shiper/shkiper = skipper, also storekeeper, fr. Du. *schipper*/Eng. *skipper.* Smirnov (329, 382);

407

Vasmer (III, 407); Fasmer (IV, 449); Grib. (100); Otten (367–8); Shanskii-Bob. (374–5); Slov. Akad. (VI, 892–3); Slov. Russ. (IV, 458); Slovar' (XVII, 1445); Fadeev (II, 393); Plekhov (324); Smirnitskii (884). Gard. (241–2) cites 16th-cent. precedents in Russ. ref. foreigners; suggests term reborrowed directly from Du. or Eng. in Petrine period.
Derivation: *shkiperskii*

shkvadra/eskadra = squadron, fr. Fr. *escadre*/Ital. *squadra*/Du. *esquader*/Eng. *squadron*, perhaps via Pol. *szwadron*. Christ. (33); Smirnov (350, 381); Preob. (suppl., 126); Vasmer (III, 463); Fasmer (IV, 521); Rozen (146); Leeming (101); Otten (189–91); Slov. Russ. (IV, 474); Slovar' (XVII, 1914); Fadeev (II, 415); Plekhov (330); Smirnitskii (895).

shkval = squall, fr. Eng. *squall*. Vasmer (III, 406); Fasmer (IV, 447); Whittall (94–5); Chernykh (II, 415); Slov. Russ. (IV, 458); Slovar' (XVII, 1442–3); Fadeev (II, 392–3); Smirnitskii (884).

shkyna/shkhuna = schooner, fr. Du. *schooner*. Vasmer (III, 408); Fasmer (IV, 451); Rozen (87); Whittall (95–6); Slov. Russ. (IV, 458); Slovar' (XVII, 1636); Fadeev (II, 402); Plekhov (327); Smirnitskii (888).

shliup/shliupka = sloop/small boat, ship's boat, fr. Du. *sloep*. Christ. (40); Smirnov (330); Vasmer (III, 412); Fasmer (IV, 455–6); Chernykh (II, 418); Slov. Akad. (VI, 909–10); Slov. Russ. (IV, 459); Slovar' (XVII, 1479–80); Fadeev (II, 394–5); Plekhov (324); Smirnitskii (885).
Derivation: *shliupochnyi*

shpil' = capstan, later also spire, fr. Du. *spijl*/Germ. *Spill(e)*. Smirnov (333); Vasmer (III, 425–6); Fasmer (IV, 473); Wade (254); Slov. Russ. (IV, 461); Slovar' (XVII, 1528); Fadeev (II, 397); Plekhov (325); Smirnitskii (886).

shteven' = stem-, stern-post, fr. Germ./Du. *steven*. Christ. (39); Smirnov (335–6); Vasmer (III, 429); Fasmer (IV, 478); Otten (383–7); Slov. Russ. (IV, 463); Slovar' (XVII, 1560); Fadeev (II, 399); Smirnitskii (887); Ox. Russ. (899).

shtil' = calm (wind), fr. Du. *stil*/Germ. *Stille*. Vasmer (III, 430); Fasmer (IV, 479); Bond (127); Shanskii-Bob. (378); Slov. Russ. (IV, 463); Slovar' (XVII, 1564); Fadeev (II, 399); Plekhov (325); Smirnitskii (887).

shtiurman/shturman = helmsman, navigator, fr. Du. *stuurman*/Germ. *Steuermann*. Christ. (39); Smirnov (339); Preob. (suppl., 109); Vasmer (III, 432); Fasmer (IV, 481); Bond (127); Otten (237–41); Chernykh (II, 427); Shanskii-Bob. (379); Slov. Akad. (VI, 920); Slov. Russ. (IV, 464); Slovar' (XVII, 1589); Fadeev (II, 401); Plekhov (326); Smirnitskii (887).

ekipazh = crew, ship's officers and men, also staff/personal staff more generally, fr. Du. *equipage*/Fr. *équipage*. Christ. (43); Smirnov (345); Preob. (suppl., 126); Vasmer (III, 458); Fasmer (IV, 515); Chernykh (II, 440); Slov. Russ. (IV, 472–3); Slovar' (XVII, 1747); Fadeev (II, 406–7); Plekhov (328); Smirnitskii (891).

iunga = cabin boy, ship's boy, fr. Germ. *(Schiffs)junge*/Du. *jongen*. Vasmer (III, 470);

Fasmer (IV, 530); Bond (127); Chernykh (II, 459); Shanskii-Bob. (385); Slov. Russ. (IV, 476); Slovar' (XVII, 1986); Fadeev (II, 419); Plekhov (331); Smirnitskii (897).

iakhta = yacht; in Peter's time, usually small heavily armed warship used in patrolling, fr. Germ. *Jacht*/Du. *jagt*/Eng. *yacht.* Christ. (40); Smirnov (353); Preob. (suppl., 141); Vasmer (III, 500); Fasmer (IV, 570); Gard. (257–9); Bond (127); Slov. Akad. (VI, 1060); Slov. Russ. (IV, 486); Slovar' (XVII, 2117); Fadeev (II, 425); Smirnitskii (901).

409

Note: A large number of highly specialized nautical terms, e.g. those naming the many parts of an eighteenth-century sailing ship (a standard English dictionary lists over 250 such terms: see *Webster's Third New International Dictionary,* 1966, pp. 2001, 2097), were imported under Peter into Russian primarily from Dutch and English; most of these, now quite obsolete, are not listed here. Nor are most of the naval ranks imported under Peter, or many navigational terms. Further examples of such words can be found in Avery, Ryan, Whittall, pp. 18 ff., and Otten, pp. 521–554 and passim.

OFFICIAL TERMS
(INCLUDING LEGAL, ADMINISTRATIVE, ECCLESIASTICAL, DIPLOMATIC, AND COURT)

advokat = lawyer, fr. Germ. *Advokat.* Smirnov (30); Vasmer (I, 6); Fasmer (I, 62); H-W. (55); Shanskii (I, 46); Kaiser (219); Bond (116); Barkh. (I, 25); Slov. Russ. (I, 3); Slovar' (I, 52–3); Smirnitskii (34).
Derivations: *advokatskii, advokatstvo, advokatura* (cf. Germ. *Advokatur*)

administratsiia = administration. Fr. Pol. *administracja*/Lat. *administratio*/Germ./Fr. *administration.* Smirnov (30); Vasmer (I, 6); Fasmer (I, 62); Shanskii (I, 48); Kaiser (175); Chernykh (I, 29); Slov. Russ. (I, 3); Slovar' (I, 54–5); Smirnitskii (34).
Derivations: *administrativnyi, administrator*

akkreditovat' = to accredit (dpl.), fr. Pol. *akredytować*/Fr. *accréditer.* Smirnov (32); Vasmer (I, 9); Fasmer (I, 66); Shanskii (I, 62); Barkh. (I, 38); Slov. Russ. (I, 5 *[akreditovat']*); Slovar' (I, 75); Smirnitskii (35).
Derivations: *akkreditiv* (= letter of accreditation, credential; cf. Fr. *lettre accréditive*), *akkreditivnyi*

akord/akkord = accord, agreement (dpl.), fr. Pol. *akord*/Germ. *Akkord*/Fr./Eng. *accord.* Smirnov (32); Vasmer (I, 8–9); Fasmer (I, 66); Shanskii (I, 61); Kaiser (87); Grib. (5); Barkh. (I, 37); Chernykh (I, 33); Slovar' (I, 74–5).

akt = act, document, fr. Pol./Germ. *Akt*/Fr. *acte.* Christ. (26); Smirnov (32); Vasmer (I, 9); Fasmer (I, 66); Kaiser (172); Barkh. (I, 39–40); Chernykh (I, 34); Slov. Russ. (I, 5); Slovar' (I, 80–1); Smirnitskii (35). Term known earlier, fr. Pol. *akt*/Lat. *actus,* in theatrical and other meanings (cf. H-W., 56; Leeming, 33).
Derivation: *aktovyi*

aktuarius/aktuarii = actuary, fr. Germ. *Aktuarius.* Smirnov (32); Vasmer (I, 9); Fasmer (I, 67); Kaiser (172); Grib. (6); Barkh. (I, 40); Slov. Akad. (I, 18); Slov. Russ. (I, 5); Slovar' (I, 81).

aktsiza/aktsiz = excise tax, fr. Germ. *Akzise*/Fr. *accise.* Vasmer (I, 10); Fasmer (I, 67); Kaiser (187); Slov. Akad. (I, 18); Slov. Russ. (I, 5); Slovar' (I, 89); Ox. Russ. (5).
Derivation: *aktsiznyi*

410

amnistiia = amnesty, fr. Pol. *amnistja*/Lat. *amnestia*/Fr. *amnistie*, etc. perhaps via Ukr. *amnistiia.* Christ. (25); Vasmer (I, 11); Fasmer (I, 76); Shanskii (I, 93); Kaiser (240); Birzhak. (139); Barkh. (I, 60–1); Chernykh (I, 41–2); Slov. Russ. (I, 8); Slovar' (I, 118); Smirnitskii (37).

apelliatsiia = appeal (judicial), fr. Pol. *apelacja*/Lat. *appelatio*/Germ. *Appellation.* Christ. (25); Smirnov (41); Vasmer (I, 20); Fasmer (I, 81); H-W. (58); Shanskii (I, 124–5); Kaiser (222); Barkh. (I, 78); Slov. Russ. (I, 10); Slovar' (I, 162–3); Smirnitskii (39).
Derivations: *apellirovat', apelliant, apelliatsionnyi*

arbitr = arbiter, arbitrator, fr. Ukr. *arbitr*/Pol./Lat. *arbiter.* Shanskii (I, 135–6); Barkh. (I, 86); Chernykh (I, 50); Slovar' (I, 177); Smirnitskii (40).

arenda = lease, rent, fr. Pol. *arenda*/Germ. *Arrende*/Swed. *arenda.* Smirnov (43); Preob. (I, 8); Vasmer (I, 23); Fasmer (I, 85); Shanskii (I, 138); Kaiser (242); Barkh. (I, 87); Slov. Akad. (I, 44); Slov. Russ. (I, 11); Slovar' (I, 179–80); Smirnitskii (40–1). Vasmer/Fasmer dates to 17th cent.
Derivations: *arendovat'* (cf. Pol. *arendować*), *arendator, arendnyi, arendovanie*

aresht/arest = arrest, fr. Pol. *arest/areszt*/Germ. *Arrest*/Du. *arrest.* Christ. (25); Smirnov (43–4, 364); Vasmer (I, 23); Fasmer (I, 85); Shanskii (I, 139–40); Kaiser (233); Bond (116); Koch. II (34–5); Barkh. (II, 88–9); Otten (577–8); Chernykh (I, 51); Slov. Akad. (I, 45); Slov. Russ. (I, 12); Slovar' (I, 180–1); Smirnitskii (41).
Derivations: *arestant* (cf. Germ. *Arrestant*), *arestantskii, arestovat'* (cf. Pol. *arestować*)

artikul = article, clause (of a decree), fr. Germ. *Artikel,* perhaps via Ukr. *artykul*/Pol. *artykuł,* replacing (or reviving) earlier *artykul* (D'iachenko, II, 880; Leeming, 38; also Srez., I, 28, fr. Lat. *articulus*). Christ. (25); Preob. (I, 8); Vasmer (I, 26); Fasmer (I, 89); H-W. (60); Shanskii (I, 148); Kaiser (177); Koch. II (102); Barkh-Bog. (I, 49 [1697]); Barkh. (I, 96–7); Otten (22–3); Slov. Akad. (I, 49); Slov. Russ. (I, 13); Slovar' (I, 192); Ox. Russ. (11).

arkhiv = archive/s, fr. Germ. *Archiv.* Smirnov (47); Vasmer (I, 27); Fasmer (I, 90); Shanskii (I, 153–4); Kaiser (173); Bond (96); Barkh. (I, 99); Chernykh (I, 55); Slov. Akad. (I, 51); Slov. Russ. (I, 13); Slovar' (I, 197–99); Smirnitskii (42). D'iachenko (II, 881) lists as Slav. fr. Lat. *archivum,* no date.
Derivation: *arkhivnyi*

arkhivarius = archivist, keeper of archives, fr. Germ. *Archivarius*/Lat. *archivarius.* Smirnov (47); Vasmer (I, 27); Fasmer (I, 90); Shanskii (I, 155); Kaiser (p. 172); Bond (101); Barkh. (I,

99); Slov. Russ. (I, 13); Slovar' (I, 198 [obs.]); Smirnitskii (42). D'iachenko (II, 881) lists as Slav., no date.

assessor/asessor = assessor, fr. Pol. *asesor*/Lat. *assessor*/Germ. *Assessor*. Christ. (27); Smirnov (48); Preob. (I, 9); Vasmer (I, 30); Fasmer (I, 93); Shanskii (I, 157–8); Kaiser (119); Barkh. (I, 106); Slov. Akad. (I, 57); Slov. Russ. (I, 114); Slovar' (I, 202–3 [obs.]); Ox. Russ. (11 [obs.]).

assistent = assistant, fr. Pol. *assystent*/Germ. *Assistent*. Smirnov (49); Vasmer (I, 30); Fasmer (I, 94); Shanskii (I, 163); Bond (69); Barkh. (I, 107); Chernykh (I, 56); Slovar' (I, 208); Smirnitskii (42).
Derivation: *assistirovat'* (cf. Germ. *assistieren*)

attestatsiia/attestat = certification/certificate, testimonial, fr. Pol. *atestacyja*/Lat. *attestatio*/Germ. *Attestat*. Smirnov (50); Shanskii (I, 173–4); Kaiser (184); Barkh-Bog. (I, 58 [1698]); Barkh. (I, 113); Chernykh (I, 59); Slov. Akad. (I, 61); Slov. Russ. (II, 15); Slovar' (I, 219–20); Plekhov (19); Smirnitskii (43). Leeming (38) cites precedent of 1666.
Derivations: *attestovat'* (cf. Pol. *atestować*), *attestovanie*

audientsiia = audience, reception, fr. Pol. *audyjencyja*/Germ. *Audienz*/Lat. *audientia*. Christ. (30); Smirnov (50, 364); H-W. (61); Shanskii (I, 174–5); Kaiser (185); Bond (96); Barkh. (I, 114–5); Slov. Akad. (I, 62); Slovar' (I, 221–2); Smirnitskii (43). Leeming (38) cites precedent of 1612, Segeev II (65–6) of 1673.

bal = ball, dance, fr. Pol./Fr. *bal*/Germ. *Ball*. Christ. (48); Smirnov (54); Vasmer (I, 44); Fasmer (I, 111); Shanskii (II, 17–18); Barkh. (I, 130); Chernykh (I, 66); Slov. Akad. (I, 91); Slov. Russ. (I, 20); Slovar' (I, 250); Smirnitskii (45).
Derivation: *bal'nyi*

ballotirovat' = to ballot, vote for, fr. Germ. *ballotieren*/Du. *balloteren*. Smirnov (54); Vasmer (I, 48); Fasmer (I, 117); H-W. (61); Shanskii (II, 26–7); Kaiser (238); Barkh. (I, 133); Wade (20); Chernykh (I, 69); Slov. Russ. (I, 20 [*balotirovat'*]); Slovar' (I, 258); Smirnitskii (45).
Derivations: *ballotirovaniie, ballotirovka* (= vote, voting)

bandit = bandit, robber, fr. Pol. *bandyt*/Germ. *Bandit*. Vasmer (I, 351); Fasmer (I, 120); Shanskii (II, 32–3); Leeming (40); Barkh. (I, 136); Chernykh (I, 70 [*banda*]); Slovar' (I, 264–5 [*banda*]); Smirnitskii (46).
Derivations: *banditizm, banditskii*

baron = baron, fr. Pol./Germ./Fr. *baron*. Smirnov (57); Preob. (I, 17); Vasmer (I, 57); Fasmer (I, 128); H-W. (62); Shanskii (II, 47); Kaiser (212); Leeming (40); Bond (138); Barkh-Bog. (I, 74 [1663]); Barkh. (I, 143); Slov. Akad. (I, 104); Slov. Russ. (I, 23); Slovar' (I, 284); Smirnitskii (47). See note at *graf* below.
Derivations: *baronskii, baronstvo, baronsha* (= wife of)

vivat = viva, hurrah (interj.), fr. Germ./Lat. *vivat*. Smirnov (73); Vasmer (I, 198); Fasmer (I, 311); H-W. (64); Shanskii (III, 42); Otten (517–18); Slovar' (II, 345–6).

vizita/vizit = visit (official), fr. Fr. *visite,* perhaps via Pol. *wizyta.* Christ. (48); Smirnov (74, 366); Vasmer (I, 199); Fasmer (I, 313); Shanskii (III, 95); Sergeev II (72–5); Barkh-Bog. (II, 177); Barkh. (III, 160); Otten (518–20); Chernykh (I, 150); Slov. Russ. (I, 125); Slovar' (II, 368–9); Plekhov (47); Smirnitskii (93). Term gradually applied more broadly.
Derivation: *vizitnyi*

vikarii = vicar (eccl.), fr. Pol. *wikary*/Lat. *vicarius.* Smirnov (74, 366); Preob. (I, 83); Vasmer (I, 199); Fasmer (I, 314); H-W. (64); Kaiser (186); Barkh. (III, 161); Slov. Russ. (I, 125); Slovar' (II, 370); Ox. Russ. (68). D'iachenko (I, 76) lists as Slav. fr. Lat., no date.

vitse- = vice-, in various titles, e.g. *vitse-kantsler,* fr. Germ. *Vize-kanzler; vitse-prezident,* fr.Germ. *Vizepräsident.* Vasmer (I, 208); Fasmer (I, 326); Sergeev I (182–5); Barkh. (III, 180); Otten (391–4); Slov. Russ. (I, 129); Slovar' (II, 403–4); Smirnitskii (95).

garantiia = guarantee (dpl.), fr. Pol. *gwarancyja*/Ger./Fr. *garantie;* also *garantirovat'* fr. Pol. *gwarantować*/Germ. *garantieren*/Fr. *garantir.* Christ. (25); Smirnov (81); Vasmer (I, 258); Fasmer (I, 392); Shanskii (IV, 27–8); Kaiser (92); Sergeev II (37–9); Barkh. (V, 89); Slovar' (III, 34–5); Smirnitskii (147).

geral'd/gerol'd = herald, fr. Germ. *Herold;* also *gerol'dmeister* = master herald, fr. Germ. *Heroldmeister.* Smirnov (88); Vasmer (I, 266); Fasmer (I, 403 [1659]); Shanskii (IV, 57); Kaiser (213); Bond (96, 102); Slov. Russ. (I, 260); Slovar' (III, 84); Smirnitskii (150, 149).
Derivations: *geral'dika* (= heraldry), *geral'dicheskii, gerol'dskii*

gofmeister = court official in charge of staff, fr. Germ. *Hofmeister;* also *ober-gofmeister* = chief steward, fr. Germ. *Oberhofmeister.* Smirnov (207); Vasmer (I, 301; II, 238); Fasmer (I, 449; III, 99); Gard. (93); Kaiser (160); Bond (121, 124); Barkh. (V, 204); Slov. Akad. (II, 288); Slov. Russ. (I, 285; III, 10); Slovar' (III, 347); Ox. Russ. (139).

graf = count, fr. Germ. *Graf.* Smirnov (94, 367); Preob. (I, 155–6); Vasmer (I, 304); Fasmer (I, 453); Kaiser (211); Bond (138); Barkh. (V, 223); Slov. Akad. (II, 323); Slov. Russ. (I, 289); Slovar' (III, 373–4); Smirnitskii (165). Like *baron,* term known from 16th cent. in Russ. as foreign title (Gard., 59, 95; H-W., 67; Shanskii, IV, 162; Barkh-Bog., IV, 125; Kot., 456) but not granted by Russ. ruler (Russified) until Peter I.
Derivations: *grafinia* (= countess), *grafskii, grafstvo, grafchik* (dim.)

gubernator = governor, fr. Pol./Germ./Lat. *gubernator.* Smirnov (97, 368); Vasmer (I, 317); Fasmer (I, 469); Shanskii (IV, 191); Kaiser (126); Barkh. (VI, 6); Chernykh (I, 225); Slov. Akad. (II, 417); Slov. Russ. (I, 300); Slovar' (III, 465–6); Smirnitskii (170). Leeming (59) cites term in 1638 dipl. report fr. Poland; Kot. (457, 387) uses ref. Poland only.

guberniia = province, fr. Pol. *gubernja.* Smirnov (97, 368); Vasmer (I, 317 [fr. Russ. *gubernator*]); Fasmer (I, 469); Kaiser (125–6); Leeming (59); Slov. Akad. (II, 417); Slov. Russ. (I, 300); Slovar' (III, 464–6); Smirnitskii (170).
Derivation: *gubernskii*

dama = lady (of the court), fr. Pol. *dama*/Germ./Fr. *dame.* Christ. (48); Smirnov (99);

Preob. (I, 174); Vasmer (I, 328); Fasmer (I, 483); Shanskii (V, 11); Kaiser (161, 215); Barkh. (VI, 31–2); Chernykh (I, 231); Slov. Russ. (I, 307); Slovar' (III, 551–3); Smirnitskii (173). Derivations: *damskii, damochka* (dim.)

deviz = device, motto (in heraldry), fr. Germ./Fr. *devise.* Vasmer (I, 334); Fasmer (I, 492); H-W. (68); Shanskii (V, 37–8); Barkh. (VI, 64–5); Slov. Russ. (I, 315); Slovar' (III, 632); Smirnitskii (177).

413

degradatsiia = degradation (in rank), fr. Pol. *degradacja*/Lat. *degradatio.* Smirnov (99); Shanskii (V, 42–3); Kaiser (204); Barkh. (VI, 69); Slovar' (III, 642–3); Smirnitskii (178). Term later acquired more general meaning.
Derivation: *degradirovat'*

dezhur = on duty, fr. Germ. *Dejour*/Fr. *(être) de jour.* Smirnov (99); Vasmer (I, 336); Fasmer (I, 494); Shanskii (V, 46); Birzhak. (116–7); Barkh. (VI, 70–1); Wade (46–7); Slov. Russ. (I, 316); Slovar' (III, 646–7); Plekhov (81–2); Smirnitskii (178–9). Term itself soon obsolete but survived in derivations.
Derivations: *dezhurit'* (= to be on duty), *dezhurnyi, dezhurstvo.*

deklaratsiia = declaration (dpl.), fr. Pol. *delkaracja*/Lat. *declaration*/Germ. *Deklaration*/Fr. *déclaration.* Vasmer (I, 337); Fasmer (I, 495); Shanskii (V, 55–6); Kaiser (181); Grib. (25 *[deklaras'on]*); Barkh. (VI, 79–80); Slov. Russ. (I, 316); Slovar' (III, 661–2); Smirnitskii (180). Derivation: *deklarirovat'*

dekret = decree, fr. Pol./Germ. *dekret*/Lat. *decretum.* Smirnov (100, 368); Vasmer (I, 337); Fasmer (I, 495); Kaiser (178); Shanskii (V, 58–9); Bond (96); Barkh. (VI, 81); Chernykh (I, 238); Slovar' (III, 665–6); Smirnitskii (180). Vasmer/Fasmer cites possible precedent of 1635, Barkh-Bog. (IV, 203) of 1652, Leeming (48) of 1665; D'iachenko (II, 142) lists as Slav. fr. Lat., no date.
Derivations: *dekretirovat'* (cf. Germ. *dekretieren*), *dekretnyi*

departament = department, fr. Pol. *departament*/Fr. *département.* Vasmer (I, 340); Fasmer (I, 499); Shanskii (V, 73); Kaiser (185); Barkh. (VI, 98); Slov. Russ. (I, 318); Slovar' (III, 705–6); Smirnitskii (182).

deputat/deputatsiia = deputy/deputation, fr. Pol. *deputat/deputacja*/Lat. *deputatus/deputatio.* Christ. (26); Smirnov (102); Vasmer (I, 340); Fasmer (I, 499); Shanskii (V, 75); Kaiser (97); Barkh. (VI, 99); Chernykh (I, 242); Slov. Akad. (II, 590); Slov. Russ. (I, 318); Slovar' (III, 707–8); Smirnitskii (183). Barkh-Bog. (IV, 219) and Leeming (49) cite *deputiat* in earlier 17th-cent. refs. Poland; Vasmer/Fasmer dates *deputat* to 1618.

dinastiia = dynasty, fr. Germ./Fr. *dynastie*/Lat. *dynastia.* Vasmer (I, 352); Fasmer (I, 515); Shanskii (V, 123); Barkh. (VI, 133); Slov. Russ. (I, 323); Slovar' (III, 794); Smirnitskii (187).

diplom = diploma, fr. Pol. *dyplom(a)*/Lat. *diploma*/Germ. *Diplom*/Fr. *diplôme.* Smirnov (106); Vasmer (I, 352); Fasmer (I, 515); Shanskii (V, 124–5); Kaiser (108); Barkh. (VI, 134); Chernykh (I, 254); Wade (49); Slov. Akad. (II, 672); Slov. Russ. (I, 323); Slovar' (III, 795–6);

Smirnitskii (187). Vasmer/Fasmer dates *diplom/diploma* to 17th cent. Term later acquired academic significance.

diplomata/diplomat = diplomat, fr. Pol. *dyplomata*/Germ. *Diplomat*/Fr. *diplomate*. Smirnov (106); Vasmer (I, 352); Fasmer (I, 515); Barkh. (VI, 134); Chernykh (I, 254); Slov. Russ. (I, 323); Slovar' (III, 796); Smirnitskii (187).
Derivations: *diplomaticheskii, diplomatiia*

direktor = director, fr. Pol. *dyrektor*/Lat. *director*/Germ. *Direktor;* also *direktsiia* = board, management, fr. Pol. *dyrekcya*/Lat. *directio,* and *direktorat* = board, directorate, fr Germ. *Direktorat.* Smirnov (106); Vasmer (I, 352–3); Fasmer (I, 515); Shanskii (V, 127); Kaiser (168); Bond (96); Barkh. (VI, 135–6); Slov. Akad. (II, 672); Slov. Russ. (I, 323); Slovar' (III, 799–800); Smirnitskii (187).

dokument = document, fr. Pol./Germ. *Dokument.* Smirnov (109); Vasmer (I, 358); Fasmer (I, 523); Shanskii (V, 159–60); Kaiser (220); Bond (96–7); Leeming (50); Barkh. (VI, 190); Slov. Russ. (I, 345); Slovar' (III, 921–2); Plekhov (92); Smirnitskii (194).
Derivations: *dokumental'nyi, dokumentatsiia, dokumentirovat'*

dublikat = duplicate, fr. Pol. *duplikat*/Germ. *Duplicat*/Lat. *duplicatus.* Smirnov (112); Shanskii (V, 202); Kaiser (183); Barkh. (VII, 23); Slovar' (III, 1147–8); Smirnitskii (205).

zhandarm = gendarme, fr. Germ. *Gendarm*/Fr. *gendarme.* Vasmer (I, 410); Fasmer (II, 34); Shanskii (V, 276); Barkh. (VII, 95); Chernykh (I, 291); Slov. Russ. (I, 399); Slovar' (IV, 27); Smirnitskii (212).

imperator = emperor, fr. Lat. *imperator,* perhaps via Pol. *imperator.* Smirnov (117); Vasmer (I, 480); Fasmer (II, 129); H-W. (73); Kaiser (103); Barkh. (IX, 85); Otten (287–8); Slov. Akad. (III, 296–7); Slov. Russ. (II, 131); Slovar' (V, 306); Smirnitskii (272). Shanskii (VII, 57–8) offers dubious 16th-cent. precedent; Barkh-Bog. (VI, 231) cites term in 17th-cent. ms. *alfavit,* Leeming (59) in a *Kozmografiia* of 1670. Title formally adopted by Peter I in 1721 and remained official title of Russian ruler to 1917.
Derivation: *imperatorskii* (= imperial; cf. Pol. *imperatorski*)

imperatritsa = empress, possibly fr. Fr. *impératrice;* but cf. Russ. *tsar'/tsaritsa.* Vasmer (I, 480); Fasmer (II, 129); Shanskii (VII, 85–6); H-W. (73); Kaiser (104); Barkh. (IX, 85); Slov. Akad. (III, 296); Slov. Russ. (II, 131); Slovar' (V, 307); Smirnitskii (272). Title formally conferred on Catherine, wife of Peter I, in 1724; thereafter official title of female rulers or consorts to 1917.

imperiia = empire, fr. Lat. *imperium,* perhaps via Pol. *imperja.* Smirnov (118); Vasmer (I, 480); Fasmer (II, 129); H-W. (73); Kaiser (104); Barkh. (IX, 86); Chernykh (I, 344–5); Slov. Akad. (III, 296); Slov. Russ. (II, 131); Slovar' (V, 309); Smirnitskii (272). Shanskii (VII, 59), Barkh-Bog. (VI, 231), and Leeming (59) offer same dubious 16th-cent. precedent. Official name of Russian state from 1721 to 1917.

inkvizitor = inquisitor, fr. Pol. *inkwizytor*/Lat./Germ. *Inquisitor;* also *inkvizitsiia* = inquisition, fr. Pol. *inkwizycyja*/Lat. *inquisitio.* Smirnov (120); Vasmer (I, 483); Fasmer (II, 133); Shanskii (VII, 78–9); Kaiser (207–8); Barkh. (IX, 95); Slov. Russ. (II, 132); Slovar' (V, 354–5); Smirnitskii (273). Leeming (59) cites term in 1667 trans. from Span.

inkognito = incognito, fr. Pol./Ital. *incognito.* Christ. (53); Shanskii (VII, 79); Barkh. (IX, 96); Chernykh (I, 348); Slov. Russ. (II, 132); Slovar' (V, 356–7); Smirnitskii (273).

415

inspektor = inspector, fr. Pol./Germ. *Inspektor;* also *inspektsiia* = inspection, fr. Pol. *inspekcja*/Lat. *inspectio.* Smirnov (120, 369); Vasmer (I, 484); Fasmer (II, 135); Shanskii (VII, 85–6); Kaiser (169); Barkh-Bog. (VI, 245–6 [1680]); Barkh. (IX, 100–01); Chernykh (I, 349); Slov. Akad. (III, 306); Slov. Russ. (II, 133); Slovar' (V, 371–2); Smirnitskii (274).
Derivations: *inspektirovat', inspektorskii, inspektorsha* (= wife of)

instantsiia = instance (jud.), fr. Pol. *instancja*/Germ. *Instantia/Instanz.* Smirnov (120); Vasmer (I, 484), Fasmer (II, 135); Shanskii (VII, 87); Kaiser (221); Grib. (35); Barkh. (IX, 101); Chernykh (I, 349); Slov. Russ. (II, 133); Slovar' (V, 374); Smirnitskii (274).

institutsiia/institut = institution, esp. (later) educational, fr. Pol. *instytucja*/Germ. *Institut.* Smirnov (121); Vasmer (I, 485); Fasmer (II, 135); Shanskii (VII, 87); Kaiser (178); Barkh. (IX, 101); Chernykh (I, 349–50); Slov. Russ. (II, 133); Slovar (V, 376–7); Plekhov (116–7); Smirnitskii (274). Vasmer/Fasmer notes term initially also taken to mean "information."

instruktsiia = instruction/s, direction/s, fr. Pol. *instrukcja*/Du. *instructie*/Lat. *instructio.* Christ. (30); Smirnov (121, 370); Vasmer (I, 485); Fasmer (II, 135); Kaiser (178); Bond (102); Leeming (59–60 [1660]); Barkh. (IX, 102); Chernykh (I, 350); Slov. Russ. (II, 133); Slov. Akad. (III, 306); Slovar' (V, 379); Fadeev (I, 267); Plekhov (117 [*instruktazh,* mil.]); Smirnitskii (274). Barkh-Bog. (VI, 246) and Leeming (59–60) cite precedents of 1656, 1660; Shanskii (VII, 89), questionably, of 1633.

interes = interest (esp. of the state or sovereign), fr. Pol. *interes*/Germ. *Interesse.* Smirnov (122, 370); Vasmer (I, 385); Fasmer (II, 136); H-W. (73); Kaiser (101); Grib. (35); Chernykh (I, 352); Slov. Russ. (II, 134); Slovar' (V, 394–6); Smirnitskii (274). Term later acquired more general meaning.
Derivations: *interesovat'* (cf. Pol. *interesować*), *interesnyi*

intriga = intrigue, fr. Pol. *intryga*/Germ. *Intrige*/Fr. *intrigue.* Smirnov (123); Vasmer (I, 485); Fasmer (II, 136); Shanskii (VII, 104); Barkh. (IX, 106); Chernykh (I, 354); Slov. Russ. (II, 134); Slovar' (V, 409–10); Smirnitskii (275). Term later acquired theatrical and romantic connotations.
Derivation: *intrigovat'*

kabinet = cabinet, council, also consulting room, study, file box, fr. Germ. *Kabinett*/Fr. *cabinet,* replacing earlier *gabinet* fr. Pol. *gabinet.* Christ. (47); Smirnov (77, 125); Vasmer (I, 496); Fasmer (II, 151); Shanskii (VIII, 6); Kaiser (122); Bond (97); Barkh. (IX, 183–4); Chernykh (I, 364); Wade (77); Slov. Akad. (III, 350–1); Slov. Russ. (II, 150); Slovar' (V, 624–6); Smirnitskii (283).

kavaler = knight, member of knightly order, cavalier; later also romantic admirer, escort, dance partner, fr. Pol. *kawaler*/Germ. *Kavalier.* Christ. (27); Smirnov (125, 370); Vasmer (I, 497); Fasmer (II, 152); H-W. (74); Shanskii (VIII, 18–19); Kaiser (214); Bond (52); Barkh. (IX, 185–6); Chernykh (I, 365); Slov. Akad. (III, 352); Slov. Russ. (II, 150); Slovar' (V, 631); Smirnitskii (283). Koch. I (114), Barkh-Bog. (VII, 10), and Leeming (66–7) cite various Pol. precedents. The first Russ. knightly order (*orden,* below), members thus named, founded by Peter I.

kamerger = chamberlain, fr. Germ. *Kammerherr.* Christ. (28); Smirnov (127); Vasmer (I, 514); Fasmer (II, 174); H-W. (75); Shanskii (VIII, 37); Kaiser (160); Bond (122); Slov. Akad. (III, 408); Slov. Russ. (II, 157); Slovar' (V, 729); Smirnitskii (286).
Derivation: *kamergerskii*

kamer"iunker = gentleman of the bedchamber (court), fr. Germ. *Kammerjunker.* Smirnov (124); Shanskii (VIII, 38); Kaiser (161); Barkh. (IX, 226); Slov. Akad. (III, 409); Slov. Russ. (II, 157); Slovar' (V, 731–2 [obs.]).

kandidat = candidate, fr. Pol./Germ. *Kandidat*/Du. *kandidaat.* Smirnov (130); Vasmer (I, 517); Fasmer (II, 179); H-W. (75); Shanskii (VIII, 42–3); Kaiser (166); Bond (97); Barkh-Bog. (VII, 53–4 [1674]); Chernykh (I, 373–4); Wade (80); Slov. Akad. (III, 425); Slov. Russ. (II, 159); Slovar' (V, 749–50); Smirnitskii (287).
Derivation: *kandidatskii*

kantseliariia = chancellery, office, fr. Pol. *kancelarja*/Lat. *cancellaria.* Christ. (27); Smirnov (370); Preob. (I, 293); Vasmer (I, 520); Fasmer (II, 182); Shanskii (VIII, 49); Kaiser (136); Barkh. (IX, 237–8); Chernykh (I, 275); Wade (81); Slov. Akad. (III, 429–30); Slov. Russ. (II, 160); Slovar' (V, 763–4); Smirnitskii (287). Though term known in Russ. from 17th cent. (Barkh-Bog., VII, 60; Leeming, 62; Sergeev I, 192–4; Sergeev II, 137–41), offices so-called first established in Rus. under Peter I.
Derivations: *kantseliarist* (= clerk), *kantseliarskii*

kantsler = chancellor, fr. Pol. *kanclerz*/Germ. *Kanzler.* Christ. (28); Smirnov (131); Vasmer (I, 520); Fasmer (II, 182); Shanskii (VIII, 50); Kaiser (123); Barkh. (IX, 239); Slov. Akad. (III, 430); Slov. Russ. (II, 160); Slovar' (V, 765); Smirnitskii (287). Term appeared in Russ. docs. as early as 16th cent., usually ref. Poland (Barkh-Bog., VII, 60; Leeming, 62–3; Sergeev I, 177–82); office established in Rus. by Peter I.
Derivation: *kantslerskii*

kapel'meister = conductor, bandmaster, fr. Germ. *Kapellmeister.* Smirnov (132); Vasmer (I, 521); Fasmer (II, 184); Shanskii (VIII, 52); Bond (120); Barkh. (IX, 241); Slov. Russ. (II, 160); Slovar' (V, 770); Smirnitskii (287).
Derivation: *kapel'meisterskii.*

kapituliatsiia = capitulation, surrender, fr. Pol. *kapitulacja*/Lat. *capitulatio*/Ger. *Capitulation/Capitulatio.* Christ. (26); Smirnov (133); Vasmer (I, 522); Fasmer (II, 185); Shanskii

(VIII, 55); Kaiser (88); Slov. Russ. (II, 162); Slovar' (V, 780–1); Plekhov (123–4); Smirnitskii (288).

Derivations: *kapitulirovat'* (cf. Pol. *kapitulować*/Germ. *kapitulieren*), *kapituliant, kapituliantskii*

kittel'/kitel' = (uniform) jacket, tunic, fr. Germ. *Kittel.* Vasmer (I, 563); Fasmer (II, 241); Shanskii (VIII, 139); Bond (72, 130); Barkh. (X, 43); Slov. Russ. (II, 174); Slovar' (V, 978); Plekhov (127); Smirnitskii (294); Ox. Russ. (280).

417

kodeks = code (law), also codex (litt.), fr. Germ. *Kodex*/Lat. *codex.* Smirnov (144); Vasmer (I, 588); Fasmer (II, 275); H- W. (78); Shanskii (VIII, 185); Kaiser (178); Bond (118); Barkh. (X, 78); Slovar' (V, 1105); Smirnitskii (299). Barkh-Bog. (VII, 217) cites somewhat earlier use ref. foreign law code.

kollegium/kollegiia = council, board, fr. Pol. *kolegium/kolegja*/Germ. *Kollegium*/Lat. *collegium.* Smirnov (145, 370); Vasmer (I, 600); Fasmer (II, 292); Shanskii (VIII, 202–3); Kaiser (114); Bond (103); Barkh. (X, 96–7); Slov. Akad. (III, 709); Slov. Russ. (II, 189); Slovar' (V, 1162–3); Smirnitskii (301). Barkh-Bog. (VII, 242) cites *kolegia* in dpl. report of 1621. Derivations: *kollegial'nyi, kollegial'no, kollezhskii*

koloniia = colony, fr. Pol. *kolonja*/Germ. *Kolonie*/Lat. *colonia.* Smirnov (146); Vasmer (I, 602); Fasmer (II, 295); Shanskii (VIII, 211); Barkh-Bog. (VII, 250–1 [1693]); Barkh. (X, 103); Leeming (68 [undated ms.]); Slov. Russ. (II, 190); Slovar' (V, 1181–2); Smirnitskii (301).

komissiia = commission, committee, fr. Pol. *komisja*/Germ. *Kommission.* Smirnov (149); Vasmer (I, 608); Fasmer (II, 303); Kaiser (140); Barkh. (X, 119); Slov. Akad. (III, 762–3); Slov. Russ. (II, 195); Slovar' (V, 1236–7); Smirnitskii (304). Shanskii (VIII, 231), Barkh-Bog. (VII, 263), and Leeming (68–9) cite 17th-cent. dpl. precedents, usually ref. Poland.

kommissar/komissar = commissar, fr. Pol. *komisarz*/Germ. *Kommissar;* also *kommissariat/komissariat* = *commissariat,* fr. Germ. *Kommissariat.* Christ. (26); Smirnov (148); Vasmer (I, 608); Fasmer (II, 302); Shanskii (VIII, 231); Kaiser (138); Bond (97); Otten (242); Barkh. (X, 118); Chernykh (I, 417–8); Slov. Akad. (III, 763); Slov. Russ. (II, 195); Slovar' (V, 1234); Smirnitskii (303). Terms appear in various forms in 17th-cent. docs., usually ref. Poland (Barkh-Bog., VII, 262–3; Leeming, 68).

kommissioner/komissioner = commissioner, agent, fr. Germ. *Kommissionär*/Fr. *commissionaire.* Smirnov (148); Vasmer (I, 608); Fasmer (II, 302); Shanskii (VIII, 231); Kaiser (141); Bond (97); Barkh. (X, 118–19); Slov. Russ. (II, 195); Slovar' (V, 1235–6); Smirnitskii (303).

komplement/kompliment = compliment, fr. Germ. *Kompliment*/Du./Eng./Fr. *compliment.* Christ. (18); Smirnov (151); Vasmer (I, 611); Fasmer (II, 306); Shanskii (VIII, 243); Grib. (41); Sergeev II (75–9); Barkh. (X, 126); Chernykh (I, 420); Slov. Russ. (II, 195); Slovar' (V, 1262); Smirnitskii (305).

konventsiia = convention, agreement, treaty, fr. Pol. *konwencja*/Lat. *conventio*. Smirnov (152); Vasmer (I, 612); Fasmer (II, 308); Shanskii (VIII, 249); Kaiser (88); Barkh. (X, 129); Slov. Russ. (II, 196); Slovar' (V, 1274); Smirnitskii (305).

kongress = congress, fr. Pol. *kongres*/Germ. *Kongreß*. Christ. (31); Smirnov (261); Vasmer (I, 612); Fasmer (II, 308); Shanskii (VIII, 252–3); Kaiser (87); Bond (97); Barkh. (X, 130); Slov. Akad. (III, 766); Slov. Russ. (II, 196); Slovar' (V, 1278); Smirnitskii (305).

418

konstitutsiia = constitution, fr. Pol. *konstitucja*/Lat. *constitutsio*/Germ. *Konstitution*. Christ. (30); Smirnov (155, 371); Vasmer (I, 616); Fasmer (II, 313); Shanskii (VIII, 268–9); Kaiser (179); Barkh. (X, 142); Chernykh (I, 423); Slov. Russ. (II, 198); Slovar' (V, 1317–8); Smirnitskii (307). Barkh-Bog. (VII, 282) cites term in dpl. doc. of 1658.
Derivation: *konstitutsionnyi*

konsul = consul (dpl.), fr. Pol./Germ. *Konsul*/Lat. *consul*. Christ. (28); Smirnov (156, 371); Vasmer (I, 616); Fasmer (II, 313); Shanskii (VIII, 270); Kaiser (97); Barkh. (X, 142); Otten (107); Chernykh (I, 423); Slov. Akad. (III, 779); Slov. Russ. (II, 198); Slovar' (V, 1321); Smirnitskii (307). Barkh-Bog. (VII, 282) and Leeming (70–1) cite term in three 17th-cent. mss.; but "judging by its few appearances in Russ. dpl. docs., the word was not active in Russ. in 17th cent." (Sergeev I, 165).
Derivations: *konsul'skii, konsul'stvo*

kontora = office, bureau, fr. Du. *kantoor*/Germ. *Kontor,* perhaps via Pol. *kantor*. Smirnov (156); Preob. (I, 346–7); Vasmer (I, 616); Fasmer (II, 313); Shanskii (VIII, 275); Kaiser (135); Chernykh (I, 424); Slov. Akad. (III, 780); Slov. Russ. (II, 198); Slovar' (V, 1327); Smirnitskii (307).
Derivations: *kontorka, kontorskii, kontorshchik*

kontrabanda = contraband, smuggling, fr. Fr. *contrebande*. Smirnov (156); Vasmer (I, 616); Fasmer (II, 313); Shanskii (VIII, 276); Kaiser (229); Barkh. (X, 145); Slov. Russ. (II, 198); Slovar' (V, 1329); Fadeev (I, 315); Plekhov (136); Smirnitskii (307).

kontrakt = contract, fr. Pol./Germ. *Kontrakt*/Lat. *contractus*. Christ. (25); Smirnov (157); Vasmer (I, 616); Fasmer (II, 314); Shanskii (VIII, 278); Kaiser (242); Bond (97); Barkh. (X, 146); Slov. Akad. (III, 780); Slov. Russ. (II, 198); Slovar' (V, 1331); Smirnitskii (307). Vasmer/ Fasmer cites precedent of 1638.
Derivation: *kontraktovat'*

kontributsiia = contribution (imposed), war indemnity, fr. Germ. *Contribution*/Pol. *kontribucja*/Lat. *contributio*. Christ. (37); Smirnov (158); Vasmer (I, 616); Fasmer (II, 314); Kaiser (186); Barkh. (X, 148); Slov. Russ. (II, 198); Slovar' (V, 1339); Smirnitskii (307).

kontrolor/kontroler/kontrolër = controller, inspector, fr. Germ. *Kontrolleur*/Fr. *contrôleur*. Smirnov (158); Vasmer (I, 616); Fasmer (II, 314); Shanskii (VIII, 280–1); Kaiser (144); Barkh. (X, 149); Chernykh (I, 424); Slov. Russ. (II, 199); Slovar' (V, 1340–1); Smirnitskii (307–8).
Derivations: *kontrolerovat'/kontrolirovat'* (= to control, check; cf. Fr. *controler*)

konfederatsiia = confederation, alliance, fr. Pol. *konfederacja*/Lat. *confoederatio*. Smirnov (158); Vasmer (I, 617); Fasmer (II, 315); Kaiser (91); Barkh. (X, 150); Slovar' (V, 1349); Smirnitskii (308). Barkh-Bog. (VII, 283) cites term in 1665 *kuranty,* Leeming (70 *[kanfadaratseia]*), in dpl. report from Poland; Kot. (518 *[konfederatsstvo]*, 388–9) uses term to mean conspiracy.

419

konferentsiia = conference, fr. Pol. *konferencja*/Lat. *conferentia*/Germ. *Conferenz.* Christ. (29); Smirnov (159); Vasmer (I, 617); Fasmer (II, 315 [1679]); Shanskii (VIII, 287); Kaiser (177); Barkh. (X, 151); Slov. Akad. (III, 781); Slov. Russ. (II, 199); Slovar' (V, 1350); Smirnitskii (308).

konfirmatsiia = confirmation, ratification, fr. Pol. *konfirmacja*/Germ. *Konfirmation* Smirnov (160); Vasmer (I, 617); Fasmer (II, 315); Kaiser (223); Barkh. (X, 152–3); Slov. Akad. (III, 781); Slov. Russ. (II, 199); Slovar' (V, 1353–4 [obs.]); Smirnitskii (308 [obs.]).
Derivation: *konfirmovat'*

konfiskatsiia = confiscation, fr. Pol. *konfikacja*/Germ. *Confiskation.* Smirnov (160); Vasmer (I, 617); Fasmer (II, 315); Kaiser (237); Barkh. (X, 153); Slov. Russ. (II, 199); Slovar' (V, 1354); Smirnitskii (308).
Derivations: *konfiskovat', konfiskovanie*

kontsert = concert (dpl.), fr. Du. *concert*/Germ. *Konzert.* Smirnov (161); Vasmer (I, 618); Fasmer (II, 316); Kaiser (92); Bond (97); Barkh. (X, 155[4]); Chernykh (I, 425). Term obsolete in this sense by 20th cent.

korrespondent = correspondent, fr. Du. *correspondent*/Ger. *Korrespondent;* also *korrespondentsiia* = correspondence, fr. Du. *correspondentie*/Germ. *Korrespondenz.* Christ. (41, 43); Smirnov (163, 371); Vasmer (I, 634); Fasmer (II, 337); Shanskii (VIII, 334); Kaiser (97); Bond (142); Barkh. (X, 188–9); Chernykh (I, 432); Slov. Russ. (II, 207); Slovar' (V, 1473–4); Smirnitskii (312).

kredit = credit (dpl.), faith, trust, later also credit in financial sense, fr. Germ. *Kredit;* also *kreditor* = creditor, fr. Germ. *Kreditor.* Christ. (20, 41); Smirnov (166, 371); Preob. (I, 380); Vasmer (I, 658); Fasmer (II, 369); H-W. (81); Shanskii (VIII, 378–9); Kaiser (254); Bond (110–11); Barkh. (X, 248); Chernykh (I, 441); Slov. Russ. (II, 218); Slovar' (V, 1609–10); Smirnitskii (317). Cf. *akkreditovat'* above.
Derivations: *kreditnyi, kreditovat'*

kriminal/kriminalist = criminal case, criminalist, crime detector, fr. Pol. *kryminal/ kryminalista*/Germ. *Kriminalist.* Smirnov (167); Vasmer (I, 664); Fasmer (II, 377); Shanskii (VIII, 393); Kaiser (224); Bond (116); Barkh. (XI, 17); Slovar' (V, 1658); Smirnitskii (319).
Derivations: *kriminalistika* (= criminal law), *kriminal'nyi*

kurator = curator, fr. Germ. *Kurator*/Lat. *curator.* Smirnov (170); Vasmer (I, 698); Fasmer (II, 423); Shanskii (VIII, 451); Kaiser (159); Bond (116); Barkh. (XI, 82); Slov. Russ. (II, 237); Slovar' (V, 1857); Ox. Russ. (313).
Derivations: *kuratorskii, kuratorstvo*

kurier/kur'er = messenger, courier, fr. Pol. *kurjer*/Germ. *Kurier*. Christ. (42); Smirnov (171, 372); Preob. (I, 419); Vasmer (I, 703); Fasmer (II, 430); Shanskii (VIII, 459); Kaiser (152); Sergeev I (173–76); Bond (73); Barkh. (XI, 89); Slov. Russ. (II, 239); Slovar' (V, 1885); Smirnitskii (326).
Derivation: *kurierskii*

kurtizan/kurtizanka = courtesan , fr. Fr.*courtisan/courtisane*. Smirnov (171, 372); Vasmer (I, 702); Fasmer (II, 429); H-W. (82); Barkh. (XI, 88); Slovar' (V, 1879); Smirnitskii (326).

lakai/lakei = lackey, footman, manservant, fr. Germ. *Lakai*/Fr. *laquais*. Smirnov (173); Preob. (I, 430–1); Vasmer (II, 9); Fasmer (II, 452); Kaiser (164); Barkh-Bog (VIII, 165–6 [1706]); Barkh. (XI, 110); Chernykh (I, 464); Shanskii-Bob. (163); Slov. Russ. (II, 243); Slovar' (VI, 39); Smirnitskii (328).

leib-medikus/leib-medik = court physician, fr. Germ. *Leibmedikus*. Christ. (27); Vasmer (II, 27); Fasmer (II, 477); Kaiser (163); Bond (123); Barkh. (XI, 146); Slov. Russ. (II, 250); Slovar' (VI, 141); Smirnitskii (331).

livreia = livery, fr. Ital. *livrea*/Germ./Fr. *livrée*. Smirnov (178); Preob. (I, 451–2); Vasmer (II, 40); Fasmer (II, 494); Barkh. (XI, 173–4); Chernykh (I, 480); Slov. Russ. (II, 253); Slovar' (VI, 213–14); Smirnitskii (334).

litsenziia = license, fr. Pol. *licencja*/Lat. *licentia*. Smirnov (180); H-W. (83); Barkh. (XI, 200); Slovar' (VI, 287); Fadeev (I, 359–60); Smirnitskii (336).

magistrat = magistrate, magistracy, town council, fr. Pol./Germ. *Magistrat*. Smirnov (184); Kaiser (133); Grib. (47); Slov. Akad. (IV, 2); Slov. Russ. (II, 279); Slovar' (VI, 471–2); Ox. Russ. (332). Barkh-Bog. (IX, 6) cites precedent of 1669.
Derivation: *magistratskii*

mandat = mandate, fr. Germ./Fr. *mandat*. Smirnov (186); Kaiser (179); Slovar' (VI, 590); Smirnitskii (345). Barkh-Bog. (IX, 26) and Sergeev II (171–2) cite term in 16th-cent. dpl. reports from Poland; D'iachenko (II, 1042) lists as Slav. fr. Pol., no date.

manifest = manifesto, fr. Germ. *Manifest*/Fr. *manifeste*. Christ. (30); Smirnov (186, 374); Vasmer (II, 96); Fasmer (II, 569 [1658]); Kaiser (179); Chernykh (I, 508); Slov. Russ. (II, 285); Slovar' (VI, 605–6); Smirnitskii (346).

marka = stamp, mark, sign, later postage stamp, fr. Germ. *Marke*. Vasmer (II, 99); Fasmer (II, 579); Bond (111); Chernykh (I, 511); Shanskii-Bob. (179–80); Slov. Russ. (II, 287); Slovar' (VI, 630–2); Smirnitskii (346).

maska/maskarad = mask/masquerade, fr. Germ. *Maske/Maskerade*/Fr. *masque/mascarade*. Smirnov (190); Preob. (I, 512); Vasmer (II, 101–2); Fasmer (II, 577, 578); H-W. (86); Chernykh (I, 512); Shanskii-Bob. (180); Slov. Akad. (IV, 49); Slov. Russ. (II, 288); Slovar' (VI, 657); Smirnitskii (347).
Derivations: *maskaradnyi, maskirovat', maskirovka*

medal' = medal, fr. Germ./Fr. *médaille*, replacing earlier *medalia*. Smirnov (191); Preob. (I, 519); Vasmer (II, 110); Fasmer (II, 589); H-W. (86); Kaiser (215); Chernykh (I, 519); Shanskii-Bob. (182); Slov. Akad. (IV, 73); Slov. Russ. (II, 293); Slovar' (VI, 750); Plekhov (155); Smirnitskii (350).
Derivations: *medal'nyi, medal'shchik*

ministr = minister (in var. capacities), fr. Fr. *ministre*/Germ. *Minister*. Smirnov (197); Vasmer (II, 136); Fasmer (II, 624); Kaiser (123); Grib. (50); Sergeev I (169–73); Chernykh (I, 533); Shanskii-Bob. (187); Slov. Akad. (IV, 139–40); Slov. Russ. (II, 305); Slovar' (VI, 1019); Smirnitskii (358).
Derivations: *ministerskii, ministerstvo*

monarkh = monarch, autocrat, fr. Germ. *Monarch*/Lat. *monarcha*, perhaps via Pol. *monarcha;* also *monarkhiia* = monarchy, autocracy (cf. Pol./Lat. *monarchia*). Vasmer (II, 154); Fasmer (II, 649); Kaiser (101); H-W. (89); Bond (97); Otten (327–31); Slov. Akad. (IV, 249); Slov. Russ. (II, 321); Slovar' (VI, 1217); Sminitskii (365). Shanskii-Bob. (189–90) and Leeming (80) cite earlier 17th-cent. precedents; D'iachenko (I, 316) lists *monarkh/ monarsheski* as Slav. fr. Gr., no date. Barkh-Bog. (IX, 257–8) cites first application to Russ. ruler in 1695; thereafter both terms frequent in Russ. docs.
Derivation: *monarkhicheskii*

moneta = money, coin, fr. Pol./Ukr. *moneta*/Lat. *moneta*. Smirnov (199, 374); Preob. (I, 554); Vasmer (II, 154); Fasmer (II, 650); H-W. (89); Kaiser (155); Barkh-Bog. (IX, 260 [1698]); Grib. (51); Chernykh (I, 541–2); Shanskii-Bob. (190); Wade (125); Slov. Akad. (IV, 251); Slov. Russ. (II, 322); Slovar' (VI, 1226–7); Smirnitskii (365). D'iachenko (II, 1047) lists as Slav. from Petrine period.
Derivations: *monetka* (dim.), *monetnyi, monetchik* (= mint worker).

neutral'nyi/neitral'nyi = neutral, fr. Pol. *neutralny*/Germ. *neutral*. Smirnov (204); Vasmer (II, 209); Fasmer (III, 59); Kaiser (90); Chernykh (I, 567); Slov. Russ. (II, 438, 455); Slovar' (VII, 932–3); Smirnitskii (409).
Derivations: *neitralitet* (cf. Germ. *Neutralität*), *neitral'nost'*

notarii/notarius = notary, fr. Lat. *notarius*. Smirnov (206); Preob. (I, 613–4); Vasmer (II, 228); Fasmer (III, 85); H-W. (92); Kaiser (170); Chernykh (I, 578–9); Shanskii-Bob. (204); Slov. Russ. (II, 467); Slovar' (VII, 1423); Smirnitskii (431). Barkh-Bog. (XI, 430) cites term in various spellings, to mean scribe or secretary, in much earlier texts; D'iachenko (I, 357) lists as Slav. fr. Lat., no date, also in earlier (Byzantine) sense.

orden = order, decoration, fr. Germ. *Orden*. Christ. (27); Smirnov (212); Vasmer (II, 275); Fasmer (III, 150); Kaiser (213); Bond (41); Chernykh (I, 603); Shanskii-Bob. (215); Slov. Akad. (IV, 639); Slov. Russ. (III, 77); Slovar' (VIII, 1012–3); Plekhov (189); Smirnitskii (466).
Derivations: *ordenskii, ordenonosnyi* (= decorated [with]), *ordenonosets* (= order-bearer)

pazh = page, fr. Pol. *paü.*/Germ./Fr. *page*. Smirnov (216); Vasmer (II, 300); Fasmer (III,

184); Kaiser (161); Shanskii-Bob. (221); Slov. Akad. (IV, 692–3); Slov. Russ. (III, 154); Slovar' (IX, 31–2); Smirnitskii (494).

pakt = pact, fr. Germ. *Pakt.* Christ. (25); Smirnov (216); Kaiser (88); Bond (98, 41); Shanskii-Bob. (221); Slovar' (IX, 42); Smirnitskii (494).

partizant/partisan/partizan = partisan, member of a party, fr. Germ./Fr. *partisan.* Smirnov (219); Vasmer (II, 318); Fasmer (III, 209); Kaiser (90); Birzhak. (107); Chernykh (II, 8); Shanskii-Bob. (225); Slov. Russ. (III, 161); Slovar' (IX, 225–6); Smirnitskii (499); Ox. Russ. (491). Term later added meaning of guerilla fighter, irregular soldier.
Derivations: *partizanskii, partizanstvo*

partiia = party, group, detachment (mil.), later also batch, lot, etc., fr. Pol. *partja*/Germ./Fr. *partie.* Vasmer (II, 318); Fasmer (III, 209–10); Kaiser (90); Birzhak. (105–6); Shanskii-Bob. (225); Slov. Russ. (III, 161); Slovar' (IX, 233–9); Ox. Russ. (491).
Derivation: *partiinyi*

pas/paz/pashport/pasport = pass, passport, fr. Swed./Germ. *pass/Passport*/Du. *pas/paspoort*/Fr. *passe/passeport.* Christ. (28); Smirnov (221); Preob. (II, 21); Vasmer (II, 321); Fasmer (III, 213); Kaiser (150); Bond (105); Otten (166–9); Chernykh (II, 10); Slov. Akad. (IV, 723); Slov. Russ. (III, 162); Slovar' (IX, 260–1); Smirnitskii (499, 500). Vasmer/Fasmer, Gard. (165–6), Barkh-Bog. (XIV, 158), and Sergeev II (183–8) cite various 17th-cent. precedents, all ref. foreign practice.

patent = patent, fr. Germ. *Patent*/Fr. *patente.* Christ.(30); Smirnov (222, 375); Preob. (II, 26); Vasmer (II, 323); Fasmer (III, 216); Kaiser (166); Bond (98); Grib. (63); Chernykh (II, 12); Shanskii-Bob. (226); Slov. Akad. (IV, 734); Slov. Russ. (III, 163); Slovar' (IX, 282–3); Smirnitskii (500).

patriot = patriot, fr. Germ. *Patriot*/Fr. *patriote.* Christ. (23); Smirnov (222); Preob. (II, 27); Vasmer (II, 324); Fasmer (III, 217); Birzhak. (133); Bond (143); Shanskii-Bob. (226); Slov. Russ. (III, 163); Slovar' (IX, 296–7); Smirnitskii (500).
Derivations: *patriotizm* (cf. Fr. *patriotisme*), *patrioticheskii*

patron = patron, protector, fr. Germ./Fr. *patron.* Smirnov (222); Preob. (II, 27); Vasmer (II, 324); Fasmer (III, 217); Kaiser (247); Barkh-Bog. (XIV, 173); Chernykh (II, 13); Shanskii-Bob. (226–7); Slov. Russ. (III, 163); Slovar' (IX, 300–1); Smirnitskii (500).

plakat = placard, public notice, fr. Du. *plakkaat*/Germ. *Plakat.* Christ. (30); Smirnov (227); Vasmer (II, 364); Fasmer (III, 272); Kaiser (182); Chernykh (II, 37); Shanskii-Bob. (235); Slovar' (IX, 1292); Smirnitskii (527).

politika = policy, politics, art or science of, fr. Pol. *polityka*/Lat. *politica*/Germ. *Politik*/Du. *politiek*/Fr. *politique.* Christ. (17); Smirnov (231); Preob. (II, 93); Vasmer (II, 393); Fasmer (III, 310); Kaiser (86); Bond (98); Chernykh (II, 52); Shanskii-Bob. (243); Slov. Akad. (IV, 965–6); Slov. Russ. (III, 314); Slovar' (X, 997–8); Smirnitskii (558). Kot. (616, 392) uses term in sense of customs, manners; Grib. (67) cites it in sense of politeness, *politesse.*
Derivations: *politik, politikan, politicheskii, politichnyi*

politsiia = police, fr. Pol. *polizja*/Germ. *Polizei;* also *politseimeister/ober-politseimeister* = chief of police/senior police chief, fr. Germ. *Polizeimeister/Oberpolizeimeister.* Christ. (25); Smirnov (231); Preob. (II, 93); Vasmer (II, 393); Fasmer (III, 310); Kaiser (149); Birzhak. (138–9); Bond (116, 119); Grib. (67 *[politsa]*); Chernykh (II, 52–3); Shanskii-Bob. (243); Slov. Akad. (IV, 966–7); Slov. Russ. (III, 314 *[politsmeister]*, 11); Slovar' (X, 1006, 1008–9); Smirnitskii (558).

Derivations: *politseiskii, politseimeisterskii*

post = post, official place, station, fr. Germ. *Post(en)*/Du. *post*/Fr. *poste.* Christ. (36); Smirnov (234, 376); Vasmer (II, 416); Fasmer (III, 341); Otten (407); Chernykh (II, 60); Slov. Russ. (III, 396); Slovar' (X, 1520–22); Fadeev (II, 109–10); Plekhov (221); Smirnitskii (574).

pochtamt = (head) post office, fr. Pol. *posztamt*/Germ. *Postamt.* Vasmer (II, 421); Fasmer (III, 349); Kaiser (151); Bond (111); Chernykh (II, 63); Shanskii-Bob. (250); Slov. Russ. (III, 413); Slovar' (X, 1731); Smirnitskii (580). Basic word *pochta* (= post, mail, fr. Pol. *poszta/poczta*) known from 16th cent. (Gard., 170; Leeming, 89; Shanskii-Bob., 250; Wade, 169; also Christ., 42, Vasmer, II, 421, Fasmer, III, 348–9, Chernykh, II, 63, and Slovar', X, 1728–30) but ref. Poland (cf. Barkh-Bog., XVIII, 79); latter dates first ref. to post in Rus. to 1697; so also Slov. Akad. (IV, 1021–2).

Derivation: *pochtamtskii*

prezident = president, fr. Pol. *prezydent*/Germ. *Präsident.* Smirnov (236, 376); Vasmer (II, 428); Kaiser (167); Bond (98); Shanskii-Bob. (252); Slov. Akad. (IV, 1078); Slov. Russ. (III, 439); Slovar' (XI, 206–7); Smirnitskii (589). Fasmer (III, 358), Barkh-Bog. (XVIII, 231), and Leeming (91) cite precedents in 17th-cent. dpl. docs.; offices thereof (and of *vitse-prezident*) created in Rus. by Peter I.

Derivations: *prezidentskii, prezidentstvo*

prerogativ/a = prerogative, fr. Germ. *Prärogative*/Pol. *prerogatywa*/Fr. *prérogative.* Smirnov (385); Vasmer (II, 429); Fasmer (III, 360); Kaiser (107); Slovar' (XI, 272); Smirnitskii (592).

pretendent = pretender, claimant, aspirant, fr. Germ. *Prätendent;* also *pretenziia* = claim, pretension, fr. Pol. *pretenzja*/Germ. *Prätention.* Christ. (21); Smirnov (238–9, 376); Vasmer (II, 430); Fasmer (III, 361); Kaiser (86); Bond (98); Sergeev II (141–4); Chernykh (II, 66); Slovar' (XI, 301); Smirnitskii (593).

privilegiia = privilege, fr. Germ. *Privilegie.* Christ. (24); Smirnov (240); Preob. (II, 125); Vasmer (II, 431); Fasmer (III, 363); Kaiser (108); Bond (99); Slov. Russ. (II, 456); Slovar' (XI, 377); Smirnitskii (595). Kot. (638, 393) uses *privilie* ref. Ukr. cossacks and townsmen.

Derivation: *privilegirovannyi*

provintsiia = province (administrative unit created by Peter I), fr. Pol. *prowincja*/Lat. *provincia*/Germ. *Provinz;* also *provintsial* = provincial, fr. Pol. *prowincjaÄ*/Germ. *Provinzial.* Christ. (29); Smirnov (243, 376); Vasmer (II, 438); Fasmer (III, 371); Kaiser (127); Bond (146); Barkh-Bog. (XX, 103 [1698]); Leeming (93 [1681]); Shanskii-Bob. (256); Slov. Russ. (III, 518); Slovar' (XI, 964–5); Smirnitskii (615).

Derivation: *provintsial'nyi*

423

provokatsiia = provocation, fr. Pol. *prowokacja*/Lat. *provocatio*/Germ. *Provokation*. Smirnov (243–4); Vasmer (II, 438); Fasmer (III, 372); Kaiser (222); Chernykh (II, 69); Slovar' (XI, 980–1); Plekhov (228); Smirnitskii (616). D'iachenko (I, 507) lists as Slav. legal term fr. Lat., citing Petrine doc.

424

proklamatsiia = proclamation, leaflet, fr. Pol. *proklamacja*/Lat. *proclamatio*/Germ. *Proklamation*. Smirnov (244); Vasmer (II, 440); Fasmer (III, 374); Kaiser (181); Barkh-Bog. (XX, 151 [1682]); Chernykh (II, 70); Shanskii-Bob. (257); Slovar' (XI, 1150); Smirnitskii (622).

prokuror/ober-prokuror = procurator/chief procurator, i.e. public prosecutor/investigating magistrate, fr. Germ. *Prokuror/Oberprokuror*, replacing earlier *prokurator* fr. Pol./Lat. *procurator* (Srez., II, 1539; Barkh-Bog., XX, 157; Leeming, 92). Smirnov (245); Vasmer (II, 440); Fasmer (III, 374); Kaiser (143); H-W. (100); Bond (119); Chernykh (II, 70–1); Shanskii-Bob. (257); Slov. Akad. (IV, 1087); Slov. Russ. (III, 516, 11); Slovar' (XI, 1170); Smirnitskii (623); Ox. Russ. (633).
Derivations: *prokurorskii, prokurorstvo, prokurorsha* (= wife of)

protektsiia = protection, patronage, influence, fr. Pol. *protekcja*/Lat. *protectio*/Germ. *Protektion*. Christ. (20); Smirnov (246); Vasmer (II, 446); Fasmer (III, 382); Kaiser (93); Chernykh (II, 73); Shanskii-Bob. (258); Slovar' (XI, 1441); Smirnitskii (631).
Derivation: *protektsionnyi*

protest = protest, remonstrance, fr. Pol./Germ./Du. *protest,* replacing earlier *protes* (Barkh-Bog., XX, 248). Christ. (25); Smirnov (246); Vasmer (II, 446); Fasmer (III, 382); Kaiser (86); Chernykh (II, 73); Shanskii-Bob. (258); Slov. Russ. (III, 561); Slovar' (XI, 1443–4); Smirnitskii (631).
Derivations: *protestovat'* (cf. Pol. *protestować*), *protestovannyi*

protokol = protocol, record of proceedings, report, fr. Du. *protocol*/Germ. *Protokoll*/Fr. *potocole*. Christ. (31); Smirnov (247); Preob. (II, 136); Vasmer (II, 447); Fasmer (III, 383–4); Kaiser (171); Bond (99); Chernykh (II, 74); Shanskii-Bob. (259); Slov. Akad. (IV, 1100); Slovar' (XI, 1475); Smirnitskii (633).
Derivations: *protokolirovat'* (cf. Germ. *protokollieren*), *protokol'nyi*

protses/protsess = process, legal action/procedure, trial, fr. Germ. *Prozess*. Christ. (25); Smirnov (248); Vasmer (II, 448); Fasmer (III, 386); Kaiser (220); Bond (99); Slov. Russ. (III, 568); Slovar' (XI, 1533); Smirnitskii (635).

publika = public, audience, fr. Pol. *publika*/Germ. *Publikum*/Lat. *publicum*. Smirnov (248); Preob. (II, 147); Vasmer (II, 458); Fasmer (III, 398); Kaiser (181); Chernykh (II, 80); Shanskii-Bob. (260); Slov. Russ. (III, 576); Slovar' (XI, 1646); Smirnitskii (638).
Derivations: *publikovat', publichno, publichnyi*

punkt = point, item, clause, later also specific place, fr. Germ. *Punkt*/Lat. *punctum*. Christ. (29); Smirnov (249); Vasmer (II, 464); Fasmer (III, 406); H-W. (101); Gard. (177); Kaiser (89); Bond (99); Otten (482–4); Chernykh (II, 83); Shanskii-Bob. (261); Slov. Akad. (IV,

1178); Slov. Russ. (III, 578); Slovar' (XI, 1682–4); Fadeev (II, 144); Plekhov (237); Smirnitskii (639). Gard. (177), Barkh-Bog. (XXI, 45), and Leeming (93) cite 17th-cent. precedents.

rang = rank (also mil.), class, rating (naval), fr. Du./Germ./Fr. *rang*. Christ. (22); Smirnov (251, 377); Vasmer (II, 491); Fasmer (III, 442); Preob. (II, 182); Kaiser (165); Bond (42); Otten (485–8); Chernykh (II, 99); Slov. Akad. (V, 72); Slov. Russ. (IV, 40); Slovar' (XII, 579); Fadeev (II, 165); Plekhov (252); Smirnitskii (663).

Derivation: *rangovyi*

ratifikatsiia = ratification (dpl.), fr. Pol. *ratifikacja*/Lat. *ratificatio*. Smirnov (252); Vasmer (II, 459); Fasmer (III, 447); Kaiser (90); Shanskii-Bob. (268); Slov. Russ. (IV, 58); Slovar' (XII, 1020); Smirnitskii (677).

Derivations: *ratifikatsionnyi, ratifikovat'* (cf. Pol. *ratyfikować*), *ratifikovanie* (cf. Pol. *ratyfikowanie*), *ratifitsirovat'* (cf. Ger. *ratifizieren*)

reviziia = revision, inspection, fr. Pol. *rewizja*/Lat. *revisio*/Germ. *Revision*. Smirnov (254); Preob. (II, 191); Vasmer (II, 501); Fasmer (III, 455); Kaiser (222); Chernykh (II, 103–4); Shanskii-Bob. (269); Slov. Russ. (IV, 60); Slovar' (XII, 1082–3); Smirnitskii (678).

Derivations: *revizionnyi, revizovat', revizor* (= inspector; cf. Pol. *rewizor*/Germ. *Revisor*)

revoliutsiia = revolution, fr. Pol. *rewolucja*/Germ. *Revolution*/Fr. *révolution*. Smirnov (254); Preob. (II, 191); Vasmer (II, 501); Fasmer (III, 456); Preob. (II, 191); Kaiser (225); Chernykh (II, 104–5); Shanskii-Bob. (269); Slov. Russ. (IV, 60); Slovar' (XII, 1097–8); Smirnitskii (678).

Derivations: *revoliutsioner, revoliutsionnyi*

regaliia/regalii = regalia, fr. Pol. *regalja*/Germ. *Regalie/Regalia*/Lat. *regalia*. Smirnov (254); Vasmer (II, 502); Fasmer (III, 456); Kaiser (105); Shanskii-Bob. (269); Slov. Russ. (IV, 60); Slovar' (XII, 1099–1100); Plekhov (256); Smirnitskii (678).

registrator = registrar, fr. Germ. *Registrator*. Smirnov (255); Preob. (II, 193); Vasmer (II, 502); Fasmer (III, 457); Kaiser (171); Bond (106); Grib. (77); Chernykh (II, 105); Slov. Russ. (IV, 60); Slovar' (XII, 1104–5); Smirnitskii (679).

Derivation: *registratorskii*

reglament = regulation/s, statute, fr. Pol. *reglament*/Germ. *Reglement*/Fr. *règlement*. Christ. (31); Smirnov (255); Preob. (II, 193); Vasmer (II, 502); Fasmer (III, 457); Kaiser (179); Chernykh (II, 105); Shanskii-Bob. (269–70); Slov. Russ. (IV, 60); Slovar' (XII, 1007–8); Smirnitskii (679).

Derivation: *reglamentnyi*

rezident = resident (dpl.), fr. Pol. *rezydent*/Germ. *Resident*/Fr. *résident*. Smirnov (257, 378); Vasmer (II, 506); Fasmer (III, 462); Kaiser (96); Bond (99); Shanskii-Bob. (270); Slov. Akad. (V, 112); Slov. Russ. (IV, 61); Slovar' (XII, 1153–4); Smirnitskii (680). Though attested in 17th-cent. dpl. docs. (Christ., 26; Gard., 181–2; Barkh-Bog., XXII, 137; Leeming, 94–5; Sergeev I, 159–65), this term, like closely related *rezidentsiia*, fixed in Russ. with dpl. service estab. Peter I.

425

rezidentsiia = residence (official), fr. Germ. *Rezidenz,* perhaps via Pol. *rezydencyja*/Lat. *residentsia.* Smirnov (257); Vasmer (II, 56); Fasmer (III, 462); Kaiser (96); Barkh-Bog. (XXII, 137); Leeming (94); Shanskii-Bob. (270); Slov. Russ. (IV, 61); Slovar' (XII, 1154); Smirnitskii (680). Sergeev II (110) cites precedent of 1674.

426 *rezoliutsiia* = resolution, fr. Pol. *rezolucja*/Lat. *resolutio*/Germ. *Resolution*/Fr. *résolution.* Christ. (21); Smirnov (258, 377); Vasmer (II, 506); Fasmer (III, 462); Kaiser (180); Otten (484–5); Chernykh (II, 107–8); Shanskii-Bob. (270); Slovar' (XII, 1162–3); Smirnitskii (680).

rekomendovat' = to recommend, fr. Pol. *rekomendować;* also *rekomendatsiia* = recommendation, fr. Pol. *rekomendacja*/Fr. *recommandation.* Christ. (30); Smirnov (259); Vasmer (II, 508); Fasmer (III, 465); Chernykh (II, 108–9); Slov. Russ. (IV, 61); Slovar' (XII, 486–9); Smirnitskii (681).

renegat = renegade, fr. Germ. *Renegat*/Fr. *renégat.* Smirnov (260); Vasmer (II, 512); Fasmer (III, 469–70); Shanskii-Bob. (271); Slovar' (XII, 1216); Smirnitskii (681).
Derivations: *renegatstvo* (= desertion, apostasy), *renegatskii, renegatstvovat'*

report/raport = report, fr. Pol. *raport*/Germ./Du. *rapport*/Eng. *report.* Smirnov (252); Preob. (II, 183); Vasmer (II, 492); Fasmer (III, 443); Kaiser (176); Chernykh (II, 99); Shanskii-Bob. (267); Slov. Russ. (IV, 41); Slovar' (XII, 590–1); Fadeev (II, 165); Plekhov (253); Smirnitskii (664).
Derivation: *raportovat'* (cf. Pol. *raportować*)

repressaliia/repressalii = reprisal, repressive measures, fr. Pol. *repressalja.* Smirnov (261); Kaiser (87); Slovar' (XII, 1235–6); Fadeev (II, 178); Smirnitskii (682).

respublika = republic, fr. Lat. *res publica,* replacing earlier *republik/republika,* fr. Germ. *Republik*/Pol. *republica* (cf. Barkh-Bog., XXII, 146). Christ. (10); Smirnov (262–3); Vasmer (II, 515); Fasmer (III, 474); Kaiser (106); Birzhak. (128); Chernykh (II, 113); Shanskii-Bob. (272); Slov. Akad. (V, 117–8); Slov. Russ. (IV, 63); Slovar' (XII, 1245–6); Smirnitskii (682).
Derivations: *respublikanskii, respublikanets*

saliut = salute, as in artillery salute, fr. Du. *saluut*/Germ. *Salut*/Eng. *salute.* Smirnov (270); Vasmer (II, 573); Fasmer (III, 551); Chernykh (II, 137); Shanskii-Bob. (280); Slov. Russ. (IV, 88); Slovar' (XIII, 72–3); Fadeev (II, 192); Plekhov (262); Smirnitskii (694).
Derivation: *saliutovat'*

svita = suite, retinue, fr. Germ./Fr. *suite.* Smirnov (271); Preob. (II, 262); Vasmer (II, 595); Fasmer (III, 581); Chernykh (II, 148); Shanskii-Bob. (283); Slov. Russ. (IV, 100); Slovar' (XIII, 388–9); Smirnitskii (702).

sekvestr = sequestration, fr. Pol. *seqwestr*/Ger. *Sequester.* Smirnov (272); Vasmer (II, 603); Fasmer (III, 592); Kaiser (95); Slov. Russ. (IV, 116); Slovar' (XIII, 579); Smirnitskii (707).
Derivation: *sekvestrovat'* (cf. Pol. *sekwestrować*).

sekta = sect, fr. Pol. *sekta.* Smirnov (273); Preob. (II, 271); Vasmer (II, 603); Fasmer (III,

593); Leeming (97); Shanskii-Bob. (285); Slov. Russ. (IV, 116); Slovar' (XIII, 589); Smirnitskii (708).

Derivations: *sektant, sektantskii, sektantstvo*

senat = senate, fr. Pol./Germ. *Senat.* Smirnov (274, 378); Preob. (II, 275); Vasmer (II, 609); Fasmer (III, 601); H-W. (105); Kaiser (111); Bond (100); Shanskii-Bob. (286); Slov. Akad. (V, 419–20); Slov. Russ. (IV, 119); Slovar' (XIII, 642–3); Smirnitskii (709). Like *senator*, term known mainly ref. Poland (cf. Leeming, 98) until Peter I founded Russ. *Senat* (1711).

Derivation: *senatskii*

sessiia = session, sitting, fr. Pol. *sesja*/Lat. *sessio*/Du. *sessie*/Germ./Fr. *session.* Smirnov (275); Vasmer (II, 617); Fasmer (III, 612); Kaiser (120); Chernykh (II, 158–9); Shanskii-Bob. (287); Slovar' (XIII, 721); Smirnitskii (711). Vasmer/Fasmer cites precedent of 1634, Leeming (98) of 1661.

sinod = synod (eccl.), fr. Pol. *synod*/Germ. *Synode*/Lat. *synodus.* Smirnov (276); Preob. (II, 288); Vasmer (I, 627); Fasmer (III, 625); Kaiser (207); Slov. Akad. (V, 454); Slov. Russ. (IV, 128); Slovar' (XIII, 833–4); Smirnitskii (714). D'iachenko (II, 600) lists as Slav. fr. Gr., citing "our Holy Synod" estab. Peter I.

Derivations: *sinodskii, sinodal'nyi* (cf. Pol. *synodalny*)

stat/shtat = staff, administration, service, official doc. specifying same, fr. Germ. *Staat.* Smirnov (335); Preob. (suppl., 107); Vasmer (III, 429); Fasmer (IV, 477); Kaiser (148); Bond (100); Shanskii-Bob. (378); Slov. Akad. (VI, 710–11); Slov. Russ. (IV, 463); Slovar' (XVII, 1556–7); Plekhov (325); Smirnitskii (886). In ref. a sovereign political entity (a state) term remained foreign in Russ.

Derivations: *statskii, shtatnyi, shtatskii* (cf. Germ. *staats-*)

statut = statute, fr. Germ. *Statut.* Smirnov (281, 378); Vasmer (III, 5); Fasmer (III, 747); Kaiser (180); Bond (107); Slov. Russ. (IV, 222); Slovar' (XIV, 790–1); Smirnitskii (757). Leeming (100) cites possible precedent of 1655.

subordinatsiia = subordination, fr. Pol. *subordinacja*/Germ. *Subordination.* Smirnov (283); Vasmer (III, 38); Fasmer (III, 792); Kaiser (165); Slovar' (XIV, 1133); Plekhov (286); Smirnitskii (767).

subsidiia = subsidy, bounty, fr. Germ./Lat. *subsidium.* Christ. (20); Smirnov (284); Vasmer (III, 38); Fasmer (III, 793); Chernykh (II, 215); Shanskii-Bob. (307); Slovar' (XIV, 1134); Smirnitskii (767).

Derivations: *subsidirovat', subsidirovanie*

suvren/suveren = sovereign, fr. Fr. *souverain*/Germ. *Souverän.* Smirnov (284); Kaiser (101); Birzhak. (131–2); Slovar' (XVI, 1141); Smirnitskii (767).

Derivations: *suverenitet* (cf. Germ. *Souveränität*), *suverennyi*

titul = title (various), fr. Pol. *tytuł*/Germ./Lat. *titulus,* replacing earlier *tit'la/tit'l* (cf. Srez., III, 960). Vasmer (III, 108); Fasmer (IV, 62); Kaiser (209); Slov. Russ. (IV, 281); Slovar' (XV,

427

477–8); Smirnitskii (786); Ox. Russ. (804). Leeming (103) cites possible 17th-cent. precedents.

Derivations: *titulovat'* (= to style, to designate by rank or calling), *titul'nyi*

traktat = treaty, treatise, fr. Pol./Germ. *Traktat*/Lat. *tractatus*. Christ. (24); Smirnov (293, 379); Vasmer (III, 131); Fasmer (IV, 93); Kaiser (89); Bond (100); Shanskii-Bob. (321); Slov. Akad. (VI, 236); Slov. Russ. (IV, 292); Slovar' (XV, 796 [obs.]); Smirnitskii (796); Ox. Russ. (813). Leeming (104) cites two 17th-cent. trans. fr. Pol. to mean tract, pamphlet; Kot. (714, 395) uses term twice, probably as Polonism, to mean formal treaty on foreign model.
Derivation: *traktovat'* (= to treat of, discuss, interpret; cf. Pol. *traktować*)

tribunal = tribunal (civil or military), fr. Germ. *Tribunal*/Lat. *tribunal*. Christ. (25); Vasmer (III, 138); Fasmer (IV, 102); Kaiser (219); Bond (116); Grib. (90); Slovar' (XV, 957); Plekhov (302); Smirnitskii (801). D'iachenko (II, 1113) lists as Slav., no date.

ul'timatum = ultimatum, fr. Germ./Lat. *ultimatum*. Smirnov (298); Vasmer (III, 183); Fasmer (IV, 161); Kaiser (94); Bond (99); Chernykh (II, 289); Shanskii-Bob. (334); Slovar' (XVI, 563); Fadeev (II, 336); Plekhov (307); Smirnitskii (824).

fiskal = fiscal, finance inspector (office estab. Peter I), spy; later also sneak, snitch, tattletale, fr. Pol. *fiskał*/Germ. *Fiskal*. Smirnov (308); Vasmer (III, 210); Fasmer (IV, 197); Kaiser (141); Grib. (94); Shanskii-Bob. (343); Slov. Russ. (IV, 388); Slovar' (XVI, 1411–2); Smirnitskii (846).
Derivations: *fiskal'nyi, fiskal'stvo*

formuliar = official form, service record, fr. Germ. *Formular*. Smirnov (313); Vasmer (III, 216); Fasmer (IV, 203); Kaiser (184); Bond (100); Shanskii-Bob. (345); Slov. Russ. (IV, 391); Slovar' (XVI, 1507–8); Fadeev (II, 360); Smirnitskii (848).
Derivation: *formuliarnyi*

freilina = maid of honor, lady in waiting, fr. Germ. (Hof)fräulein, probably via Pol. *frejlina*. Smirnov (316); Vasmer (III, 219); Fasmer (IV, 207); Bond (125); Shanskii-Bob. (346); Slov. Russ. (IV, 393); Slovar' (XVI, 1562); Smirnitskii (850).

tseremoniia = ceremony, fr. Pol. *ceremonija*/Germ. *Zeremonie*/Lat. *caerimonia*. Christ. (18); Smirnov (321); Vasmer (III, 290); Fasmer (IV, 300); Leeming (45); Sergeev II (70–2); Chernykh (II, 367); Shanskii-Bob. (357); Slov. Akad. (VI, 663–4); Slov. Russ. (IV, 419); Slovar' (XVII, 661–6); Smirnitskii (864). D'iachenko (II, 802) lists as Slav. fr. Gr., no date.
Derivations: *tseremonial/tseremonial'nyi* (cf. Pol. *ceremoniał*/Germ. *Zeremoniell*), *tseremonnyi, tseremonnost'*

tsekh = guild, corporation (of artisans, traders), later shop, department, fr. Pol. *cech*/Germ. *Zeche*. Vasmer (III, 291); Fasmer (IV, 301); Chernykh (II, 368); Shanskii-Bob. (357); Slov. Akad. (VI, 626); Slov. Russ. (IV, 419); Slovar' (XVII, 673–4); Smirnitskii (864).
Derivation: *tsekhovyi*

shef = chief (mil.), head, patron, fr. Fr. *chef*. Smirnov (328); Preob. (suppl., 97); Vasmer (III,

395); Fasmer (IV, 434); Chernykh (II, 410–11); Shanskii-Bob. (373); Slov. Russ. (IV, 455); Slovar' (XVII, 1382–3); Smirnitskii (882).
Derivations: *shefstvo, shefstvovat'*

shpion = spy, fr. Germ./Du. *spion*. Christ. (36); Smirnov (333–4); Preob. (suppl., 105–6); Vasmer (III, 426); Fasmer (IV, 474); Kaiser (225); Birzhak. (114); Bond (85); Chernykh (II, 423); Shanskii-Bob. (377); Slov. Russ. (IV, 462); Slovar' (XVII, 1531); Smirnitskii (886).
Derivations: *shpionskii, shpionstvo, shpionchik* (dim.), *shpionit'*

shtandart/standart = official flag, standard, banner, fr. Du. *standaard*/Germ. *Standarte*. Smirnov (335, 381); Preob. (suppl., 107); Vasmer (III, 429); Fasmer (IV, 477); Chernykh (II, 198); Slov. Russ. (IV, 463); Slovar' (XVII, 1554); Fadeev (II, 398–9); Smirnitskii (756, 886).

shtraf = fine, penalty, fr. Germ. *Strafe*. Christ. (25); Smirnov (337); Preob. (suppl., 108); Vasmer (III, 431); Fasmer (IV, 480); H-W. (120); Kaiser (236); Bond (116–7); Chernykh (II, 426); Slov. Akad. (VI, 918–19); Slov. Russ. (IV, 464); Slovar' (XVII, 1573–4); Smirnitskii (887).
Derivations: *shtrafnoi, shtrafovat'*

iurisdiktsiia = jurisdiction, fr. Pol. *jurysdykcja*/Germ. *Jurisdiktion*. Smirnov (352); Vasmer (III, 472); Fasmer (IV, 533); Kaiser (215); Slovar' (XVII, 1999); Smirnitskii (897).

iurisprudentsiia = jurisprudence, fr. Pol. *jurysprudencja*/Ger. *Jurisprudenz*. Vasmer (III, 472); Fasmer (IV, 533); Kaiser (84); Slovar' (XVII, 2000); Smirnitskii (897).

iurist = jurist, lawyer, fr. Germ. *Jurist*. Christ. (25); Smirnov (352); Vasmer (III, 472); Fasmer (IV, 533); Kaiser (84); Bond (117, 119); Shanskii-Bob. (385); Slov. Russ. (IV, 477); Slovar' (XVII, 2000); Smirnitskii (897).

iurnal/zhurnal = official record, journal, later also periodical, magazine, fr. Germ./Fr. *journal*/Du. *journaal*. Christ. (30); Smirnov (114–5, 382); Vasmer (I, 434); Fasmer (II, 68); Shanskii (V, 299–300); Kaiser (172); Birzhak. (167–8); Barkh. (VII, 148); Otten (472); Chernykh (II, 309); Wade (60); Slov. Akad. (II, 1198); Slov. Russ. (I, 415); Slovar' (IV, 191–2); Fadeev (I, 229–30); Plekhov (98); Smirnitskii (218).
Derivations: *zhurnalist* (cf. Fr. *journaliste*), *zhurnalistika* (= journalism)

iustitsiia = justice (office), fr. Germ. *Justiz/Justicia*/Du. *justitie*/Lat. *iustitia*. Smirnov (352, 382); Vasmer (III, 474); Fasmer (IV, 535); Kaiser (215); Bond (120); Grib. (102); Chernykh (II, 462); Shanskii-Bob. (385); Slov. Russ. (IV, 477); Slovar' (XVII, 2008–9); Smirnitskii (897).

Note: As indicated elsewhere in this volume, a large number of generic European and especially Germanic political and administrative terms–typically, names for officials and their offices, terms of judicial or diplomatic protocol–were adopted by the Petrine regime. Many of these neologisms more or less rapidly became obsolete and/or remained foreign in Russian (e.g., *al(l)ians/al(l)iantsia, ambasada/ambasador, konket/konketa* = conquest) and so are not listed here. Further examples of such terms include, with exceptions entered above, official titles with the German prefixes *leib-* (e.g., *leib-dragun, leib-eger', leib-regiment, leib-shkvadron,* etc.) and *ober-* (*ober-komissar, ober-vakhmeister, ober-gauptman, ober-kvartirmeister, ober-leitenant,* etc.); another series of offices and titles involving German *kammer-* or *land-* (e.g., *kamer-kollegium* fr. Germ. *Kammer-Collegium, kamer-shreiber* fr.Germ. *Kammerschreiber, land-komissar* fr. Germ. *Landkommissar; land-sekretar'* fr. Germ. *Landsekretär; landrikhter* fr. Germ. *Landrichter*); still others using German *rat* = council, e.g. *landrat, geimrat* (fr. Germ. *Geheimrat*), *ratsger* (= alderman, fr. Germ. *Ratsherr*) or *ratsshtub* (= town hall, fr. Germ. *Ratsstube*); and such ephemeral titles as *rentmeister* (= treasury official, fr. Germ. *Rentmeister*) or *shreiber* (= clerk, fr. Germ. *Schreiber*). Another such class of ephemera related to the Imperial court established by Peter I, where German borrowings again predominated (e.g., *gof-doktor* fr. Germ. *Hofdoktor, kamer-frau* fr. Germ. *Kammerfrau,* etc.). The numerous Germanic place-names officially adopted by the Petrine regime, some of which have endured including, most famously, *Sanktpeter(s)burkh* (Petrine spelling) later *Sankt-Peterburg,* fr. Germ. *Sankt Petersburg; Petergof* (Germ. *Peterhof*); *Ekaterinburg* (Germ. *Katharinenburg*), also are not listed here. Additional examples of mostly Germanic ephemera may be found in Smirnov, passim; in Kaiser and Otten, passim; and/or in Bond, pp. 56–57, 101–107, 117–125, 149–152.

OTHER TECHNICAL TERMS
(SCIENTIFIC, TECHNOLOGICAL, MEDICAL, MATHEMATICAL, MUSICAL, ACADEMIC, LITERARY, PHILOSOPHICAL, ART-ARCHITECTURAL, ABSTRACT)

abris = plan, drawing; later contour, outline, fr. Germ. *Abriss*/Pol. *abrys.* Christ. (45); Smirnov (27); Vasmer (I, 2); Fasmer (I, 57); Shanskii (I, 18); Bond (68); Barkh. (I, 10); Slovar' (I, 17); Fadeev (I, 10); Smirnitskii (31).

absoliut/absoliutnyi = absolute (political power), fr. Germ. *absolut*/Pol. *absolutny.* Smirnov (27); Vasmer (I, 2); Fasmer (I, 57); Kaiser (103); Barkh. (I, 11); Chernykh (I, 22); Slovar' (I, 18); Smirnitskii (31).
Derivations: *absoliutizm, absoliutist, absoliutistskii*

avtor = author, fr. Ukr. *avtor*/Lat. *auctor(em).* Smirnov (29); Vasmer (I, 4); Fasmer (I, 60); Shanskii (I, 35–6); Barkh. (I, 19); Chernykh (I, 26); Slov. Russ. (I, 2); Slovar' (I, 36–7); Smirnitskii (33). Leeming (39) cites earlier appearance of *autor,* fr. Pol. *autor.*
Derivations: *avtorskii, avtorstvo*

avtorizovat' = to authorize, fr. Pol. *autoryzować.* Smirnov (29); Vasmer (I, 4); Fasmer (I, 60); Kaiser (98); Slovar' (I, 37); Smirnitskii (33).

avtoritet = authority, fr. Germ. *Autorität.* Christ. (23); Smirnov (29); Vasmer (I, 4); Fasmer (I, 60); H-W. (55); Kaiser (98); Bond (133); Barkh. (I, 19–20); Chernykh (I, 27); Slov. Russ. (I, 2); Slovar' (I, 37–8); Smirnitskii (33).
Derivation: *avtoritetnyi*

adres = address, fr. Pol. *adres*/Germ./Fr. *adresse;* also *adresovat'* = to address, fr. Pol. *adresować*. Smirnov (31); Vasmer (I, 6); Fasmer (I, 62); Shanskii (I, 49–50); Kaiser (153); Barkh. (I, 27–8); Chernykh (I, 29); Slov. Russ. (I, 3); Slovar' (I, 56–8); Smirnitskii (34).
Derivations: *adresant, adresat, adresnyi, adresovat'*

akuratnyi/akkuratnyi = accurate, punctual, orderly, careful, fr. Pol. *akuratny*/Germ. *akkurat*/Lat. *accuratus*. Christ. (54); Smirnov (32); Vasmer (I, 9); Fasmer (I, 66); Shanskii (I, 63–4); Barkh. (I, 38); Chernykh (I, 33); Slov. Russ. (I, 5); Slovar' (I, 76–7); Smirnitskii (35).
Derivations: *akkuratno, akkuratnost'*

aksioma = axiom, fr. Lat. *axioma,* perhaps via Germ. *Axiom*. Smirnov (32); Vasmer (I, 9); Fasmer (I, 66); Kutina I (74–5); Barkh. (I, 39); Chernykh (I, 34); Slov. Akad. (I, 17); Slov. Russ. (I, 5); Slovar' (I, 80); Smirnitskii (35).

akter/aktër = actor, fr. Germ. *Aktor*/Fr. *acteur*/Lat. *actor*. Vasmer (I, 9); Fasmer (I, 67); Shanskii (I, 68); Barkh. (I, 40); Chernykh (I, 34); Slov. Russ. (I, 5); Slovar' (I, 81–3); Smirnitskii (35).
Derivations: *akterskii/aktërskii, aktërstvo*

aktsent = accent, stress, fr. Du./Fr. *accent*/Germ. *Akzent*/Lat. *accentus*. Barkh. (I, 41); Chernykh (I, 35); Slovar' (I, 87–8); Smirnitskii (36).
Derivation: *aktsentirovat'* (cf. Du. *accentueren*/Germ. *akzentuieren*)

aktsiia = action, initially in military sense, soon more generally, fr. Pol. *akcja*/Lat. *actio*/Du. *aktie*/Germ. *Aktie*. Smirnov (33); Vasmer (I, 10); Fasmer (I, 67); Chernykh (I, 36); Shanskii (I, 72); Barkh. (I, 42–3); Slovar' (I, 90); Smirnitskii (36).

algebra = algebra, fr. Pol./Du./Germ./Lat. *algebra*. Smirnov (34); Vasmer (I, 2); H-W. (56); Fasmer (I, 70); Shanskii (I, 73); Bond (68); Koch. II (31–2); Barkh. (I, 44); Chernykh (I, 36); Slov. Akad. (I, 19); Slov. Russ. (I, 6); Slovar' (I, 90–1); Smirnitskii (36).
Derivation: *algebraicheskii* (cf. Germ. *algebraisch*)

alebastr = alabaster, fr. Pol./Germ. *alabaster,* superceding older *alavastr* (Srez., I, 14; Barkh-Bog., I, 28; Leeming, 33; Avan., I, 81). Preob. (I, 5); Vasmer (I, 12); Fasmer (I, 70); Koch. II (31); Barkh. (I, 44–5); Slov. Akad. (I, 18, 19 [listing both]); Slov. Russ. (I, 5–6 [both]); Slovar' (I, 91–2); Smirnitskii (36).

alleia = alley, lane, avenue, path, fr. Pol. *aleja*/Germ. *Allee*/Fr. *allée*. Smirnov (34); Vasmer (I, 13); Fasmer (I, 71); Shanskii (I, 78); Barkh. (I, 49); Chernykh (I, 37); Slov. Russ. (I, 6); Slovar' (I, 96); Smirnitskii (36).

Amerika = America, fr. Germ. *Amerika*/Lat. *America*. H-W. (57); Barkh. (I, 59); Slovar' (I, 115–6); Smirnitskii (37).
Derivations: *amerikanskii, amerikanets*

amfiteatr = amphitheater, fr. Germ. *Amphitheater*/Fr. *amphitéâtre*. Vasmer (I, 17); Fasmer (I, 77); Birzhak. (147); Barkh. (I, 62–3); Slov. Akad. (VI, 1065–6); Slov. Russ. (I, 8); Slovar' (I, 123); Smirnitskii (37).

analizis/analiz = analysis, fr. Lat. *analysis*/Germ./Fr. *analyse*. Smirnov (37); Vasmer (I, 17); Fasmer (I, 77); Barkh. (I, 64–5); Chernykh (I, 42); Slov. Russ. (I, 8); Slovar' (I, 126–8); Smirnitskii (37).
Derivations: *analizirovat', analist/analitik, analiticheskii*

anatomiia = anatomy, fr. Du./Germ *Anatomie*/Pol./Lat. *anatomia;* also *anatom* = anatomist, fr. Du. *anatoom*/Germ. *Anatom*. Smirnov (37); Vasmer (I, 17); Fasmer (I, 77); H-W. (58); Shanskii (I, 104); Leeming (34); Grib.(7); Barkh. (I, 66–7); Chernykh (I, 43); Slov. Akad. (I, 32); Slov. Russ. (I, 9); Slovar' (I, 133–4); Smirnitskii (38).
Derivations: *anatomicheskii, anatomirovat'* (= to dissect)

annotatsiia = annotation, fr. Du. *annotatie*/Lat. *annotatio*. Smirnov (38–9); Barkh. (I, 71); Chernykh (I, 44–5); Slovar' (I, 145); Smirnitskii (38).
Derivation: *annotirovat'* (cf. Du. *annoteren*/Germ. *annotieren*)

Antarktikus/Antarktik/Antarktika = the Antarctic, fr. Lat. *Antarcticus*/Eng. *Antarctic*. Barkh. (I, 72); Slov. Russ. (I, 10); Slovar' (I, 148–9); Fadeev (I, 31); Smirnitskii (39).
Derivation: *antarkticheskii*

antik = antique (Greek and Roman), ancient monument, fr. Fr. *antique*/Lat. *antiquus*. Smirnov (39); H-W. (58); Grib. (7); Slov. Russ. (I, 10); Slovar' (I, 154–5); Ox. Russ. (8).

antipody = antipodes, fr. Lat. *antipodes*. H-W. (58); Shanskii (I, 116); Barkh. (I, 74); Slov. Akad. (I, 37); Slov. Russ. (I, 10); Slovar' (I, 151–2); Fadeev (I, 33); Smirnitskii (39).

apogei = apogee (astron.), climax, acme, fr. Fr. *apogée*. Vasmer (I, 20); Fasmer (I, 81); Shanskii (I, 126); Kutina I (144); Barkh. (I, 79); Chernykh (I, 48); Slov. Russ. (I, 10); Slovar' (I, 164–5); Fadeev (I, 34); Smirnitskii (40).

approbatsiia/aprobatsiia = approbation, approval, confirmation, fr. Pol. *aprobacja*/Lat. *approbatio*/Germ. *Approbation*. Smirnov (42, 363); Vasmer (I, 21); Fasmer (I, 82); Shanskii (I, 132); Kaiser (222); Barkh. (I, 83); Slov. Russ. (I, 11); Slovar' (I, 172); Fadeev (I, 34 [obs.]); Smirnitskii (40).
Derivation: *aprobirovat'*

argument = argument, fr. Pol./Germ./Fr. *argument*. Christ. (23); Smirnov (43); Vasmer (I, 23); Fasmer (I, 84); Shanskii (I, 137); Bond (135); Leeming (37); Barkh. (I, 86); Chernykh (I, 51); Slovar' (I, 178); Smirnitskii (40).
Derivations: *argumentatsiia, argumentovat'* (cf. Pol. *argumentować*), *argumentirovat'* (cf. Germ. *argumentieren*)

ariia = aria (mus.), fr. Ital. *aria*. Smirnov (44); Vasmer (I, 24); Fasmer (I, 86); Barkh. (I, 91); Chernykh (I, 52); Slov. Russ. (I, 12); Slovar' (I, 184); Smirnitskii (41).

aristokratiia = aristocracy, fr. Germ. *Aristokratie,* perhaps via Pol. *aristokracja*. Smirnov (44); Vasmer (I, 24); Fasmer (I, 86); H-W. (59); Bond (137); Slov. Akad. (I, 45); Slov. Russ. (I, 12); Slovar' (I, 182–3); Smirnitskii (41).
Derivation: *aristokraticheskii*

arifmetika = arithmetic, fr. Germ. *Arithmetik*/Lat. *arithmetica,* perhaps via Pol. *arithmetica*/Ukr. *arifmetika.* Smirnov (44); Vasmer (I, 24); Fasmer (I, 86); H-W. (59); Shanskii (I, 142); Kutina I (13–14); Leeming (37); Barkh. (I, 90–1); Chernykh (I, 51–2); Slov. Akad. (I, 45–6); Slov. Russ. (I, 12); Slovar' (I, 183–4); Smirnitskii (41). Barkh-Bog. (I, 47) cites term in 17th-cent. Ukr. docs.
Derivation: *arifmeticheskii*

ark/arko/arkus/arka = arch , fr. Ital. *arco*/Fr. *arc*/Lat. *arcus.* Shanskii (I, 143); Barkh. (I, 91); Chernykh (I, 52); Slov. Russ. (I, 12); Slovar' (I, 184–5); Smirnitskii (41). D'iachenko (II, 879) lists as Slav. fr. Lat. *arcus,* no date.

Arktik/arktika/ar(k)ticheskii (krug) = the Arctic, arctic (circle), fr. Eng. *Arctic, arctic (circle)*/Fr. *arctique.* Shanksii (I, 149); Barkh. (I, 92); Ryan (92); Slov. Russ. (I, 12); Slovar' (I, 186); Fadeev (I, 35); Smirnitskii (41).

arteriia = artery, fr. Pol. *arterya*/Germ. *Arterie*/Lat. *arteria.* Smirnov (46); Vasmer (I, 26); Fasmer (I, 89); Shanskii (I, 147–8); Barkh. (I, 96); Chernykh (I, 54); Slov. Akad. (I, 49); Slovar' (I, 191–2); Smirnitskii (41). Srez. (III, suppl., 6) and Barkh-Bog. (I, 49) cite term in medieval sources.
Derivation: *arterial'nyi*

arkhitekt/arkhitektor = architect, fr. Germ. *Architekt*/Lat. *architector,* replacing sometime *arkhitekton* (Srez., I, 31; Barkh-Bog., I, 53); also *arkhitektura* = architecture, fr. Pol. *architektura*/Lat. *architechtura.* Christ. (45); Smirnov (47, 364); Vasmer (I, 28); Fasmer (I, 91); H-W. (60); Shanskii (I, 155–6); Leeming (36); Bond (68); Koch. II (34); Barkh-Bog. (I, 53 [1697]); Barkh. (I, 101–2); Slov. Akad. (I, 52); Slov. Russ. (I, 14); Slovar' (I, 200); Smirnitskii (42).
Derivations: *arkhitektorskii, arkhitekturnyi*

arkhitrav = architrave (arch.), fr. Ital./Fr. *architrave.* Smirnov (47); Vasmer (I, 28); Fasmer (I, 91); Slov. Akad. (I, 52–3); Slov. Russ. (I, 14); Slovar' (I, 200); Ox.Russ. (11).
Derivation: *arkhitravnyi*

assambleia = assembly, fr. Fr. *assemblée.* Christ. (48); Smirnov (48); Preob. (I, 9); Vasmer (I, 30); Fasmer (I, 93); Shanskii (I, 161); Barkh. (I, 104–5); Slovar' (I, 206); Smirnitskii (42).

astroliabium/astroliabiia = astrolabe, fr. Germ. *Astrolabium.* Vasmer (I, 30); Fasmer (I, 94); H-W. (60); Barkh. (I, 108); Otten (23); Slov. Akad. (I, 58); Slov. Russ. (I, 15); Slovar' (I, 211); Fadeev (I, 39); Smirnitskii (42).

astronom = astronomer, fr. Germ. *Astronom*/Fr. *astronome;* also *astronomiia,* fr. Germ/Fr. *astronomie.* Smirnov (49); Vasmer (I, 31); Fasmer (I, 94); H-W. (60); Bond (69); Barkh. (I, 108–9); Slov. Akad. (I, 58); Slov. Russ. (I, 15); Slovar' (I, 211–12); Smirnitskii (42). Kutina I (90) cites *astronom* in 17th-cent. Ukr. doc. *Astronomiia* known earlier in Russ.-Slav. docs. (Srez., I, 32 *[ostronomeia]*; D'iachenko, I, 27; Avan., I, 98; Barkh-Bog., I, 56–7; Leeming, 38 [fr. Pol. *astronomija*]) but only in ancient-medieval sense.
Derivation: *astronomicheskii*

ateista/ateist = athiest, fr. Pol. *ateista*/Germ. *Atheist.* Smirnov (50); Vasmer (I, 31); Fasmer (I, 95); H-W. (60); Grib. (9 *[afeist]*); Barkh. (I, 110); Chernykh (I, 57); Slov. Russ. (I, 15); Slovar' (I, 215); Smirnitskii (43).
Derivations: *ateizm, ateistskii, ateisticheskii*

atlas = atlas (maps), fr. Du./Germ. *Atlas,* perhaps via Pol. *atlas.* Vasmer (I, 31); Fasmer (I, 96); Shanskii (I, 171); Bond (69); Barkh. (I, 111); Chernykh (I, 58); Wade (18); Slov. Akad. (I, 60); Slov. Russ. (I, 15); Slovar' (I, 216); Smirnitskii (43).

atmosfera = atmosphere, fr. Lat. *atmosphaera.* Kutina I (149–50); Kutina II (164–6); Barkh. (I, 11–12); Slov. Akad. (I, 60–1); Slov. Russ. (I, 15); Slovar' (I, 217–8); Fadeev (I, 40–1); Smirnitskii (43).
Derivations: *atmosfericheskii, atmosfernyi*

atom = atom, fr. Germ. *Atom*/Fr. *atome*/Lat. *atomus.* H-W. (60–61); Shanskii (I, 172); Kutina II (104–7); Birzhak. (156–7); Barkh. (I, 112); Chernykh (I, 58); Slov. Akad. (I, 61); Slovar' (I, 218); Smirnitskii (43).
Derivations: *atomicheskii, atomnyi*

aforizm = aphorism, fr. Ukr. *aforizm*/Lat. *aphorismus.* Barkh. (I, 117); Chernykh (I, 60); Slov. Akad. (I, 63); Slov. Russ. (I, 16); Slovar' (I, 225); Smirnitskii (43).
Derivation: *aforisticheskii*

Afrika = Africa, fr. Germ. *Afrika*/Lat. *Africa.* Vasmer (I, 32); Fasmer (I, 97); Barkh. (I, 117); Slovar' (I, 225); Smirnitskii (43).
Derivations: *afrikanets, afrikanskii*

afront = affront, insult, fr. Pol. *afront*/Germ. *Affront.* Christ. (22); Smirnov (51); Vasmer (I, 51); Fasmer (I, 97); Kaiser (227); Grib. (9); Slovar' (I, 225); Ox. Russ. (13).

baz/bazis/baza = base, basis, fr. Germ./Fr. *base*/Lat./Eng. *basis.* Smirnov (52); Vasmer (I, 39); Fasmer (I, 105); Shanskii (II, 9–10, 11); Barkh-Bog. (I, 65 [1686]); Barkh. (I, 127); Chernykh (I, 64); Slov. Russ. (I, 18); Slovar' (I, 241–2); Fadeev (I, 49–50); Plekhov (20–1); Smirnitskii (44).
Derivations: *bazovyi, bazirovat'sia*

balans = balance, fr. Fr. *balance*/Du. *balans.* Christ. (23); Smirnov (53); Vasmer (I, 45–6); Fasmer (I, 113); Shanskii (II, 21); Barkh. (I, 131); Chernykh (I, 67); Slov. Russ. (I, 19); Slovar' (I, 253–4); Smirnitskii (45).
Derivation: *balansovyi*

baldakhin = canopy, baldachin, fr. Pol./Germ. *Baldachin.* Smirnov (54); Preob. (I, 14); Vasmer (I, 46); Shanskii (II, 23); Barkh. (I, 132); Slov. Akad. (I, 88–9); Slov. Russ. (I, 19); Slovar' (I, 255); Smirnitskii (45). Fasmer (I, 114–5) cites precedent of 1657.

balet = ballet, fr. Germ. *balet/Ballett.* Vasmer (I, 47); Fasmer (I, 115); Shanskii (II, 23–4);

Birzhak. (163–4); Barkh. (I, 132); Chernykh (I, 68); Slov. Russ. (I, 20); Slovar' (I, 255); Smirnitskii (45).
Derivations: *baletmeister* (cf. Germ. *Ballettmeister*), *baletnyi*

balkon = balcony, fr. Germ. *Balkon*/Fr. *balcon*/Ital. *balcone*. Smirnov (54); Vasmer (I, 48); Fasmer (I, 116); Shanskii (II, 24–5); Barkh. (I, 132); Slov. Akad. (I, 89); Slov. Russ. (I, 20); Slovar' (I, 256); Smirnitskii (45).

435

baliustrada = balustrade, fr. Ital. *balaustrata*, perhaps via Germ./Fr. *balustrade*. Vasmer (I, 50); Fasmer (I, 119); H-W. (62); Shanskii (II, 29); Barkh. (I, 135); Slov. Russ. (I, 20); Slovar' (I, 262); Smirnitskii (46).

bandazh = corset (med.), support, truss, fr. Germ./Fr. *bandage*. Vasmer (I, 51); Fasmer (I, 120); Shanskii (II, 31–2); Barkh. (I, 136); Slov. Russ. (I, 21); Slovar' (I, 265); Smirnitskii (46).
Derivations: *bandazhnyi, bandazhnik* (dim.), *bandazhist* (= bandage-maker)

barelief/barel'ef = bas-relief, fr. Fr. *bas-relief*. Vasmer (I, 56); Fasmer (I, 126); H-W. (62); Shanskii (II, 43); Barkh. (I, 142); Chernykh (I, 74); Slov. Russ. (I, 22); Slovar' (I, 277); Smirnitskii (47).

barometr = barometer, fr. Lat./Germ. *Barometer*/Fr. *baromètre*. Smirnov (56); Vasmer (I, 57); Fasmer (I, 128); Shanskii (II, 46); Kutina II (240–1); Barkh. (I, 143); Chernykh (I, 75); Slov. Akad. (I, 104); Slov. Russ. (I, 23); Slovar' (I, 283–4); Fadeev (I, 60); Smirnitskii (47).
Derivation: *barometricheskii* (cf. Pol. *barometryczny*)

bas = bass (mus.), fr. Pol. *bas*/Germ. *Bass*/Fr. *basse*. Vasmer (I, 58); Fasmer (I, 129); H-W. (62); Shanskii (II, 51); Leeming (41); Barkh. (I, 146); Slov. Akad. (I, 108–9); Slov. Russ. (I, 24); Slovar' (I, 289–90); Smirnitskii (47).

bassein = pool, basin, fr. Du./Germ./Fr. *bassin*. Christ. (57); Vasmer (I, 60); Fasmer (I, 132); Shanskii (II, 53); Barkh. (I, 148); Chernykh (I, 77); Slov. Russ. (I, 24); Slovar' (I, 292–3); Fadeev (I, 61); Smirnitskii (47).

bibliotekar' = librarian, fr. Pol. *bibljotekarz*/Germ. *Bibliothekar*. Smirnov (60); Vasmer (I, 84); Fasmer (I, 164); Shanskii (II, 115); Kaiser (173); Barkh. (II, 21); Chernykh (I, 88); Slov. Russ. (I, 46); Slovar' (I, 449); Smirnitskii (59). Term *biblioteka* = library, fr. Pol. *bibljoteka*/ Gr.-Lat. *bibliotheca*, borrowed earlier (Srez., III, suppl., 14; Barkh-Bog., I, 184; Leeming, 43).
Derivation: *bibliotekarskii*

bilet = ticket, slip of paper, fr. Pol. *bilet*/Germ. *Billet*. Smirnov (60); Preob. (I, 25); Vasmer (I, 85); Fasmer (I, 165); H-W. (62); Shanskii (II, 118); Kaiser (183); Barkh. (II, 22–3); Slov. Russ. (I, 46); Slovar' (I, 451–2); Smirnitskii (59).

billion = billion, a thousand million, milliard, fr. Germ./Fr./Eng. *billion*. Vasmer (I, 85); Fasmer (I, 165); Shanskii (I, 118); Kutina I (17–18); Barkh. (II, 23); Chernykh (I,89); Slov. Russ. (I, 46); Slovar' (I, 453); Smirnitskii (59).

botanika/botanik = botany/botanist, fr. Germ. *Botanik*/Lat. *botanica*. Smirnov (63); Vasmer

(I, 112); Fasmer (I, 200); H-W. (63); Shanskii (II, 177); Barkh. (II, 116); Slov. Russ. (I, 78); Slovar' (I, 591); Smirnitskii (68).
Derivations: *botanicheskii, botanizirovat'*

brandspoit = fire-pump, nozzle, fr. Du. *brandspuit*. Vasmer (I, 118); Fasmer (I, 207); Otten (213–5); Slov. Russ. (I, 80); Slovar' (I, 605); Fadeev (I, 87); Smirnitskii (69); Ox. Russ. (40).

brilliant/briliant/bril'iant = diamond, brilliant, fr. Germ./Fr. *brillant*. Preob. (I, 45); Vasmer (I, 123); Fasmer (I, 214); Shanskii (II, 197); Barkh. (II, 140); Chernykh (I, 11–12); Slov. Russ. (I, 83); Slovar' (I, 630); Smirnitskii (70).
Derivation: *brilliantovyi*

bronz/bronza = bronze, fr. Germ. *Bronze*/Fr. *bronze*. Preob. (I, 46); Vasmer (I, 125); Fasmer (I, 217); H-W. (63); Shanskii (II, 200); Barkh. (II, 143); Chernykh (I, 112); Slov. Russ. (I, 83); Slovar' (I, 637–8); Fadeev (I, 91); Smirnitskii (71).

bussol' = (surveying) compass, compass dial, fr. Germ. *Bussole*/Fr. *boussole*. Smirnov (68); Vasmer (I, 152); Fasmer (I, 251); Barkh. (II, 172); Otten (253–4); Slovar' (I, 705); Fadeev (I, 98); Plekhov (40–1); Smirnitskii (75).

biust = bust, fr. Germ. *Büste*/Fr. *buste*. Vasmer (I, 160); Fasmer (I, 261); H-W. (64); Shanskii (II, 248); Barkh. (II, 189); Chernykh (I, 130); Slov. Russ. (I, 97); Slovar' (I, 735–6); Smirnitskii (77).
Derivation: *biustovyi*

vakantsiia/vakansiia = vacancy, fr. Pol. *wakancya*/Germ. *Vakanz(ie)*/Du. *vacantie*. Smirnov (69); Preob. (I, 63); Vasmer (I, 165); Fasmer (I, 267); Shanskii (III, 6); Kaiser (166); Barkh. (II, 202); Chernykh (I, 131–2); Slov. Russ. (I, 98); Slovar' (II, 26–7); Smirnitskii (78); Ox. Russ. (50).
Derivation: *vakantnyi*

vakuum = vacuum, fr. Lat. *vacuum*. Shanskii (III, 7); Barkh. (II, 203); Slovar' (II, 28); Fadeev (I, 100); Smirnitskii (78).

valdgorna/valtorna = French (hunting) horn, fr. Germ. *Waldhorn*. Smirnov (70); Vasmer (I, 167); Fasmer (I, 270); Shanskii (III, 12–13); Bond (69–70); Barkh. (II, 209–10); Slov. Akad. (I, 464); Slov. Russ. (I, 98); Slovar' (II, 39); Smirnitskii (79).
Derivations: *valtornist, valtornyi*

vena = vein, fr. Germ. *Vene*/Lat./Ital. *vena*. Vasmer (I, 182); Shanskii (III, 47); Barkh. (III, 27); Slovar' (II, 154); Smirnitskii (84).
Derivation: *venoznyi*

vertikal/vertikal'/vertikal'nyi = vertical (line, circle, etc.), fr. Lat. *verticalis*. Shanskii (III, 66); Kutina I (51); Slov. Russ. (I, 112); Slovar' (II, 196–7); Fadeev (I, 109–10); Smirnitskii (86).
Derivations: *vertikal'no, vertikal'nost'*

vismut, bismuth, fr. Germ. *Wismuth*. Vasmer (I, 204); Fasmer (I, 320); Shanskii (III, 106); Bond (70); Barkh. (III, 174); Slov. Akad. (I, 713); Slov. Russ. (I, 127); Slovar' (II, 393); Smirnitskii (94).

vokabul/vokabula = vocable, word, fr. Pol. *wokabul(a)*/Germ. *Vocabel*/Lat. *vocabulum*. Smirnov (75); Vasmer (I, 216); Fasmer (I, 335); Birzhak. (163); Grib. (18); Barkh. (IV, 36); Slovar' (II, 603 [*vokabuly,* obs.]); Smirnitskii (106); Ox. Russ. (80 [*vokabuly,* obs. = foreign words, as object of study]).

vol'fram = tungsten, wolfram, fr. Germ. *Wolfram*. Shanskii (III, 156–7); Bond (70); Barkh. (IV, 48); Slov. Russ. (I, 157); Slovar' (II, 641); Smirnitskii (108).

vulkan = volcano, fr. Pol. *wulkan*/Germ. *Vulcan*/Lat. *Vulcanus*. Shanskii (III, 213); Birzhak. (158); Leeming (106); Barkh. (IV, 181–2); Slov. Russ. (I, 188); Slovar' (II, 921–2); Smirnitskii (123).
Derivation: *vulkanicheskii*

gazeta = newspaper, fr. Pol. *gazeta*/Ital. *gazzeta*/Fr. *gazette*. Smirnov (78); Preob. (I, 115); Vasmer (I, 250); Fasmer (I, 382); Shanskii (IV, 9); Barkh. (V, 81); Wade (37); Chernykh (I, 177); Slov. Russ. (I, 253); Slovar' (III, 15–16); Smirnitskii (146).
Derivation: *gazetnyi*

gazon = lawn, grass, fr. Fr. *gazon*. Vasmer (I, 251); Fasmer (I, 382); Shanskii (IV, 10); Barkh. (V, 82); Chernykh (I, 177); Slovar' (III, 17–18); Smirnitskii (146).

galereia = gallery, fr. Ital. *galleria,* perhaps via Pol. *galerya*. Christ. (45); Smirnov (79, 366); Vasmer (I, 253); Fasmer (I, 386); H- W. (65); Shanskii (IV, 15); Grib. (20 [*galeriia]*); Barkh. (V, 84); Chernykh (I, 178); Slov. Akad. (II, 18–19 [*galleria]*); Slov. Russ. (I, 254); Slovar' (III, 22–3); Smirnitskii (147). Leeming (56) lists *galleriia,* 1678.

garmoniia = harmony, fr. Pol./Lat. *harmonia*/Germ. *Harmonie*. Smirnov (81); Vasmer (I, 259); Fasmer (I, 394); H-W. (65); Shanskii (IV, 31); Leeming (56 [*germoniia,* 1681]); Barkh. (V, 90–1); Slov. Russ. (I, 256); Slovar' (III, 39–41); Smirnitskii (148). Leeming (56) lists *germoniia,* 1681.
Derivations: *garmonirovat', garmonist, garmonicheskii*

general'nyi = general, universal, fr. Pol. *generalny*/Lat. *generalis*. Christ. (52); Smirnov (87); Vasmer (I, 265); Fasmer (I, 401); Barkh-Bog. (IV, 18 [1696]); Slov. Akad. (II, 32); Slov. Russ. (I, 259); Slovar' (III, 67–8); Smirnitskii (149).

genius/genii = genius, good spirit, fr. Pol. *geniusz*/Germ./Lat. *genius*/Fr. *génie*. Smirnov (87); Vasmer (I, 265); Fasmer (I, 402); Shanskii (IV, 52); Barkh. (V, 104); Chernykh (I, 185); Slov. Russ. (I, 259); Slovar' (III, 69–70); Smirnitskii (149).
Derivations: *genial'no, genial'nyi, genial'nost'*

geografiia = geography, fr. Lat. *geographia*/Germ. *Geographie;* also *geograf* = geographer, fr. Germ. *Geograph*/Lat. *geographus*. Vasmer (I, 265); Fasmer (I, 402); H-W. (65); Shanskii (IV,

53); Barkh. (V, 104–5); Slov. Akad. (II, 32); Slov. Russ. (I, 259); Slovar' (III, 71–2); Smirnitskii (149). Leeming (57) cites possible precedents of 1661, 1670.
Derivation: *geograficheskii*

438

geodeziia = geodesy, surveying, fr. Germ. *Geodäsie*/Fr. *géodésie.* Smirnov (88); H-W. (66); Shanskii (IV, 54); Barkh. (V, 105); Slov. Akad. (II, 32); Slov. Russ. (I, 259); Slovar' (III, 72); Smirnitskii (149).

geometriia = geometry, fr. Germ. *Geometrie*/Lat. *geometria,* perhaps via Pol. *geometrya.* Smirnov (88); Vasmer (I, 265); Fasmer (I, 402); H-W. (66); Kutina I (29–31); Otten (437–9); Slov. Akad. (II, 33); Slov. Russ. (I, 259); Slovar' (III, 73–4); Smirnitskii (149). Barkh-Bog. (IV, 18) cites various other forms of term in 16th- or 17th-cent. docs.; Avan. (II, 317) lists *geometriiskyi* (ref. land measure) in 14th-cent. source; Leeming (57) cites two precedents, probably fr. Pol. *geometryja;* D'iachenko (I, 121) lists as Slav. fr. Gr., no date.
Derivation: *geometricheskii*

geroi = hero, fr. Germ. *Heroe*/Lat. *heros*/Fr. *héros.* Vasmer (I, 266); Fasmer (I, 403); Shanskii (IV, 62); Barkh. (V, 108); Chernykh (I, 186); Slov. Akad. (II, 34–5); Slov. Russ. (I, 289); Slovar' (III, 80–4); Smirnitskii (150). D'iachenko (II, 944) lists as Slav. fr. Gr. *iros*/Old-Russ. *iroi,* no date.
Derivations: *geroicheskii* (cf. Fr. *héroique*/Germ. *heroisch*), *geroistvo*

gidrografiia = hydrography, fr. Lat. *hydrographia,* perhaps via Germ./Fr. *hydrographie.* Leeming (57, citing undated ms.); Barkh. (V, 113); Slov. Russ. (I, 260); Slovar' (III, 95–6); Fadeev (I, 168); Smirnitskii (150).

gimnaziia = high/middle school, fr. Pol. *gymnazyjum*/Lat./Germ. *Gymnasium,* perhaps via Ukr. *gimnaziia.* Smirnov (89); Vasmer (I, 269); Fasmer (I, 407); H-W. (66); Shanskii (IV, 74); Kaiser (159); Leeming (57); Barkh. (V, 114); Chernykh (I, 187); Slov. Akad. (II, 41); Slov. Russ. (I, 261); Slovar' (III, 102); Smirnitskii (151).

gipoteza = hypothesis, fr. Pol. *hipoteza*/Germ. *Hypothese.* Smirnov (89); Vasmer (I, 269); Fasmer (I, 407); Shanskii (IV, 80–1); Kutina II (64–6); Barkh. (V, 115–6); Slov. Russ. (I, 261); Slovar' (III, 107); Smirnitskii (151).
Derivation: *gipoteticheskii* (cf. Germ. *hypothetische*)

gipotenuza = hypotenuse (math.), fr. Lat. *hypotenusa*/Fr. *hypoténuse.* Shanskii (IV, 80); Kutina I (59); Barkh. (V, 116); Slov. Russ. (I, 261); Slovar' (III, 107); Smirnitskii (151).

globus = globe, fr. Germ./Lat. *globus.* Smirnov (90, 367); Vasmer (I, 274); Fasmer (I, 414); Shanskii (IV, 95); Kutina I (47–9); Grib. (22 *[glob]*); Barkh. (V, 128–9); Ryan (92); Wade (40); Slov. Akad. (II, 85); Slov. Russ. (I, 265); Slovar' (III, 137); Fadeev (I, 175); Smirnitskii (153).

gneis = gneiss (mineral), fr. Germ. *Gneiss.* Bond (71); Slov. Russ. (I, 268); Slovar' (III, 176); Smirnitskii (155); Ox. Russ. (131).

gobelen = tapestry, gobelin, fr. Germ. *Gobelin*/Fr. *Gobelins* (tapestry factory). Vasmer (I, 281); Fasmer (I, 423); H-W. (66); Barkh. (V, 7); Slovar' (III, 189); Smirnitskii (155).

goboi/goboist = oboe/oboist, fr. Germ. *Hoboe/Hoboist*. Smirnov (91); Vasmer (I, 282); Fasmer (I, 423); Barkh-Bog. (IV, 50 [1704]); Barkh. (V, 147); Slov. Russ. (I, 270); Slovar' (III, 189–90); Smirnitskii (156).

439

gonoreia = gonorrhea, fr. Lat. *gonorhoea*. Barkh. (V, 164); Slov. Russ. (I, 276); Slovar' (III, 255); Smirnitskii (159).

gorizont = horizon, flood-mark, fr. Du./Germ. *Horizont*, perhaps via Pol. *horyzont*. Smirnov (92); Vasmer (I, 295); Fasmer (I, 441); Shanskii (IV, 134); Kutina I (51, 124–5); Barkh. (V, 172); Chernykh (I, 205); Slov. Akad. (II, 242); Slov. Russ. (I, 278); Slovar' (III, 290–2); Fadeev (I, 180); Smirnitskii (160).
Derivations: *gorizontal'/nyi* (cf. Du. *horizontaal*/Germ. *horizontal*/Pol. *horizontalny*), *gorizontal'nost'*

goshpital'/gospital' = hospital, fr. Germ. *Hospital*/Du. *hospitaal*, replacing earlier *shpital* fr. Pol. *szpital*/Germ. *Spital* (cf. Leeming, 101). Christ. (47); Smirnov (92); Vasmer (I, 299); Fasmer (I, 445); H-W. (67); Shanskii (IV, 146); Kaiser (157); Barkh. (V, 189); Chernykh (I, 208–9); Slov. Akad. (II, 272); Slov. Russ. (I, 283); Slovar' (III, 327–8); Plekhov (76); Smirnitskii (162).
Derivations: *gospital'nyi, gospitalizatsiia*

graver/gravër = engraver, fr. Pol. *grawer*/Germ./Fr. *graveur;* also *graviura* = engraving, print, fr. Pol. *grawiura*/Fr. *gravure*. Vasmer (I, 302); Fasmer (I, 450); Slov. Russ. (I, 286); Slovar' (III, 352); Smirnitskii (164).
Derivations: *gravërnyi, gravirovat'* (cf. Pol. *grawerować*), *graviurka* (dim.)

gradus = degree, fr. Pol./Lat. *gradus*. Smirnov (93, 367); Vasmer (I, 303); Fasmer (I, 451); Shanskii (IV, 156); Kutina I (70–3, 135); Kutina II (176–7); Kaiser (166); Leeming (58); Grib. (23); Barkh. (V, 211–12); Otten (65–7); Chernykh (I, 211); Wade (42–3); Slov. Russ. (I, 287); Slov. Akad. (II, 295); Slovar' (III, 355); Fadeev (I, 182); Smirnitskii (164).
Derivations: *gradusnyi, gradusnik* (= thermometer)

grifel' = slate pencil, fr. Germ. *Griffel*. Smirnov (94); Vasmer (I, 309); Fasmer (I, 459); Shanskii (IV, 174); Bond (71); Barkh. (V, 236); Chernykh (I, 218); Slov. Akad. (II, 349); Slov. Russ. (I, 292); Slovar' (III, 404–5); Smirnitskii (166).
Derivation: *grifel'nyi* (= slate, adj.)

grot = grotto, fr. Du. *grot*/Germ. *Grotte*/Fr. *grotte*/Ital. *grotta*. Vasmer (I, 311); Fasmer (I, 461); H-W. (67); Shanskii (IV, 178–9); Barkh. (V, 245); Slov. Akad. (II, 368); Slov. Russ. (I, 294); Slovar' (III, 423); Smirnitskii (167).

dam/damba = dam, dike, fr. Du./Eng. *dam*/Germ. *Damm*. Smirnov (99); Vasmer (I, 328); Fasmer (I, 484); Shanskii (V, 9–10); Barkh. (VI, 31); Chernykh (I, 231); Slov. Russ. (I, 307); Slovar' (III, 554); Fadeev (I, 196); Smirnitskii (173).

deduktsiia = deduction, fr. Fr. *déduction*/Lat. *deductio*. Barkh. (VI, 70); Slovar' (III, 645); Smirnitskii (178).

dekan = dean (acad.), fr. Germ. *Dekan*/Lat. *decanus*. Vasmer (I, 336); Fasmer (I, 495); Shanskii (V, 54); Barkh. (VI, 79); Chernykh (I, 238); Slov. Russ. (I, 316); Slovar' (III, 659); Smirnitskii (179).

deklinatsiia = declination (astron.), fr. Germ. *Declination*/Lat. *declinatio*. H-W. (68); Barkh. (VI, 80); Otten (45–6); Ryan (94). Term later replaced by calque *sklonenie* (Shanskii-Bob., 291; Slov. Russ., IV, 133; Slovar', III, 662; Smirnitskii, 717).

del'ta = delta, fr. Pol./Germ./Lat. *delta*. Shanskii (V, 62); Leeming (49); Barkh. (VI, 92); Chernykh (I, 239); Slovar' (III, 685); Fadeev (I, 203); Smirnitskii (181).

demokratiia = democracy, fr. Pol. *demokracja*/Germ. *Demokratie*/Lat. *democratia*. Smirnov (101); Vasmer (I, 339); Fasmer (I, 498); H-W. (69); Shanskii (V, 67); Kaiser (106); Barkh. (VI, 93); Chernykh (I, 240); Wade (47); Slov. Russ. (I, 317); Slovar' (III, 690–2); Smirnitskii (182). Barkh-Bog. (IV, 212) cites *dimokratiia* in 17th-cent. ms. *alfavit* (cf. Srez., II, 671). Derivations: *demokraticheskii* (cf. Germ. *demokratisch*), *demokratizirovat'*

demonstratsiia = demonstration, fr. Pol. *demonstracja*/Lat. *demonstratio*/Germ. *Demonstration*. Smirnov (101); Vasmer (I, 339); Fasmer (I, 498); Shanskii (V, 68); Barkh. (VI, 94); Chernykh (I, 240–1); Slovar' (III, 693–5); Fadeev (I, 204); Smirnitskii (182). Derivations: *demonstrirovat'* (cf. Germ. *demonstrieren*), *demonstratsionnyi*, *demonstrativno*

definitsiia = definition, fr. Pol. *definicya*/Lat. *definitio*. H-W. (69); Shanskii (V, 95); Barkh. (VI, 120); Slovar' (III, 756); Smirnitskii (185).

diagonal'/nyi = diagonal (line), fr. Germ./Fr. *diagonale*/Eng. *diagonal*/Lat. *diagonalis*. Vasmer (I, 350); Fasmer (I, 512); Shanskii (V, 106); Kutina I (61); Barkh. (VI, 123); Chernykh (I, 250); Slovar' (III, 769); Smirnitskii (186).

dialekt = dialect, fr. Pol. *dyalekt*//Germ. *Dialekt*/Fr. *dialecte*/Lat. *dialectus*. Vasmer (I, 350); Fasmer (I, 512); Shanskii (V, 108); Barkh. (VI, 124); Chernykh (I, 250); Slov. Akad. (II, 680); Slovar' (III, 770–1); Smirnitskii (186). Barkh-Bog. (IV, 242) and Leeming (49) cite several 17th-cent. precedents.
Derivation: *dialektal'nyi* (cf. Pol. *dialektalny*/Fr. *dialectal*)

diametr = diameter, fr. Pol. *dyametr*/Fr. *diamètre*. Smirnov (120); Vasmer (I, 350); Fasmer (I, 512); H-W. (69); Shanskii (V, 110); Kutina I (61, 63–4); Barkh. (VI, 125); Slov. Akad. (II, 681); Slovar' (III, 773–4); Smirnitskii (186). Barkh-Bog. (IV, 243) lists *diametra* (1607).

diktator = dictator, fr. Pol. *dyktator*/Lat. *dictator*. Smirnov (105); H-W. (70); Shanskii (V, 119); Kaiser (102); Barkh. (VI, 132); Slovar' (III, 787–8); Smirnitskii (187). Barkh-Bog. (IV, 246) and Anan. (II, 468) cite 14th-, 16th-, 17th-cent. ms. precedents.

disputa/disputatsiia/disput = dispute, disputation, public debate, fr. Pol. *disput(a)*/Germ.

disput/Lat. *disputatio.* Smirnov (107); Vasmer (I, 353); Fasmer (I, 516); Shanskii (V, 133–4); Kaiser (120); Barkh. (VI, 138–9); Chernykh (I, 255); Slovar' (III, 808–9); Smirnitskii (188). Derivation: *disputirovat'*

distantsiia = distance, range (mil.), fr. Pol. *distancya*/Lat. *distantia.* Christ. (22); Smirnov (107); Vasmer (I, 353); Fasmer (I, 516); Shanskii (V, 135); Barkh. (VI, 139–40); Otten (46–7); Slov. Russ. (I, 324); Slovar' (III, 810–11); Plekhov (89); Smirnitskii (188).

441

distsiplina = discipline, also branch of learning, fr. Pol. *dyscyplina*/Germ. *Disciplin(e)*/Lat. *disciplina.* Christ. (20); Smirnov (108, 368); Vasmer (I, 353); Fasmer (I, 516); Shanskii (V, 137); Barkh. (VI, 141); Chernykh (I, 255–6); Slov. Russ. (I, 322); Slovar' (III, 813); Plekhov (89–90); Smirnitskii (188).
Derivation: *distsiplinarnyi*

drama = drama, fr. Ukr./Germ./Lat. *drama.* Vasmer (I, 367); Fasmer (I, 535); Shanskii (V, 183–4); Barkh. (VI, 251); Chernykh (I, 266); Slov. Akad. (II, 743–4); Slov. Russ. (I, 370); Slovar' (III, 1087–90); Smirnitskii (202).
Derivation: *dramaticheskii* (cf. Fr. *dramatique*)

Evropa = Europe, fr. Pol./Germ. *Europa.* Vasmer (I, 389–90); Fasmer (II, 6); Shanskii (V, 244); Barkh. (VII, 58); Slovar' (III, 1223–5); Smirnitskii (208).
Derivations: *evropeets, evropeizatsiia, evropeizirovat'* (cf. Germ. *europäisierung, europäisieren*), *evropeiskii*

zon/zona = zone, fr. Germ./Fr. *zone*/Lat. *zona.* Vasmer (I, 461); Fasmer (II, 104); Shanskii (VI, 107); Kutina I (131–2); Barkh. (VIII, 226); Chernykh (I, 328); Slov. Russ. (II, 96); Slovar' (IV, 1327–8); Fadeev (I, 253–4); Plekhov (109–10); Smirnitskii (260). Leeming (107) cites precedent of 1670.
Derivations: *zonal'nyi, zonal'nost'*

ideia = idea, fr. Pol. *idea/ideja*/Lat. *idea.* Smirnov (117); Preob. (I, 265); Vasmer (I, 471); Fasmer (II, 117); Shanskii (VII, 12); Birzhak. (154–5); Barkh. (VIII, 250); Chernykh (I, 336); Slov. Akad. (III, 203); Slov. Russ. (II, 101); Slovar' (V, 48–50); Smirnitskii (263).
Derivation: *ideinyi*

idilliia = idyll, fr. Pol. *idylla*/Germ./Fr. *idylle*/Lat. *idyllium.* Preob. (I, 265); Vasmer (I, 471); Fasmer (II, 117); Shanskii (VII, 13); Barkh. (VIII, 251); Chernykh (I, 336); Slov. Russ. (II, 101); Slovar' (V, 50–1); Smirnitskii (263).

izdanie = publication, edition, calque of Germ. *Herausgabe/Ausgabe*/Fr. *édition;* also *izdavat'* = to publish, calque of Germ. *herausgeben.* Shanskii (VII, 28–9); Barkh-Bog. (VI, 146 [1686]); Barkh. (IX, 31–2); Slov. Russ. (II, 112); Slovar' (V, 150–1); Smirnitskii (266). Anan. (III, 501–2) lists earlier *izdanie* = expense, outlay, *izdati* = to give, give out (cf. Barkh-Bog., VI, 146–8; Grib., 34).
Derivations: *izdatel'* (cf. Germ. *Herausgeber*/Fr. *éditeur*), *izdatel'stvo*

illiuminatsiia = illumination (fireworks), lights, fr. Germ./Fr. *illumination,* perhaps via Pol.

iluminacja/Lat. *iluminatio*. Smirnov (117); Vasmer (I, 478); Fasmer (II, 127); H-W. (73); Shanskii (VII, 50–1); Barkh. (IX, 78); Slov. Russ. (II, 130); Slovar' (V, 286); Smirnitskii (271). Derivations: *illiuminatsionnyi, illiuminirovat'*

indigo = indigo, fr. Germ./Fr./Span. *indigo*. Vasmer (I, 482); Fasmer (II, 131); Shanskii (VII, 71); Barkh-Bog. (VI, 235 [1723]); Barkh. (IX, 93); Slov. Russ. (II, 132); Slovar' (V, 337–8); Smirnitskii (273).

inzhener = engineer, fr. Pol. *inżenier/indzienier*/Du./Germ. *Ingenieur*/Fr. *ingénieur*. Smirnov (119); Vasmer (I, 483); Fasmer (II, 133); Barkh. (IX, 94–5); Chernykh (I, 347); Slov. Russ. (II, 132); Slovar' (V, 349–50); Fadeev (I, 262); Smirnitskii (273). Known somewhat earlier in Russ., in 18th cent. term usually restricted to milit. (cf. Gard., 108–9; Shanskii, VII, 76; Barkh-Bog., VI, 236; Leeming, 60; Slov. Akad., III, 305–6).
Derivations: *inzhenernyi, inzhenerskii*

instruktor = instructor, fr. Pol./Ukr. *instruktor*/Lat. *instructor*. Shanskii (VII, 88–9); Barkh-Bog. (VI, 245–6 [1680]); Barkh. (IX, 102); Slovar' (V, 378–9); Fadeev (I, 263); Plekhov (117); Smirnitskii (274).

instrument = instrument, tool, fr. Ukr./Pol./Germ./Du. *instrument*. Christ. (29); Smirnov (121, 370); Vasmer (I, 485); Fasmer (II, 135); H-W. (73); Shanskii (VII, 89); Kaiser (88); Bond (72); Barkh-Bog. (VI, 246 [1679]); Barkh. (IX, 102); Otten (70–5); Ryan (92); Chernykh (I, 350–1); Slov. Russ. (II, 133); Slov. Akad. (III, 306); Slovar' (V, 379–80); Smirnitskii (274).
Derivations: *instrumental'nyi, instrumental'shchik* (= toolmaker).

interval = interval (arch.), fr. Germ. *Intervall*. Smirnov (121); Vasmer (I, 485); Fasmer (II, 135); Bond (133); Shanskii (VII, 96); Barkh. (IX, 108); Chernykh (I, 352); Slov. Russ. (II, 133); Slovar' (V, 392); Fadeev (I, 263); Plekhov (117); Smirnitskii (274). Term gradually acquired broader meaning of space/time between things.

informatsiia = information, fr. Pol. *informacja*/Lat. *informatio*. Smirnov (123); Vasmer (I, 485); Fasmer (II, 136); Shanskii (VII, 108–9); Barkh. (IX, 108); Chernykh (I, 355); Slovar' (V, 418); Fadeev (I, 294); Plekhov (118); Smirnitskii (275).
Derivations: *informatsionnyi, informirovat'*

ipokhondriia = hypochondria, fr. Pol. *hipochondrija*/Germ. *Hypochondrie*/Lat. *hypochondria*. Smirnov (90, 124); Vasmer (I, 486); Fasmer (II, 137); H-W. (74); Shanskii (VII, 112); Barkh. (IX, 111); Slov. Akad. (III, 311); Slov. Russ. (II, 134); Slovar' (V, 424); Smirnitskii (275).

ispolnitel' = executor, performer (theater), calque of Fr. *exécutant*/Russ. *ispolnit'* = to perform (cf. Kot., 505). Shanskii (VII, 126); Barkh-Bog. (VI, 280 [1680]); Barkh. (IX, 133–4); Slov. Russ. (II, 140); Slovar' (V, 494); Smirnitskii (278).
Derivation: *ispolnitel'nyi*

istoriia = history, fr. Pol. *historyja*/Germ. *Historie*/Lat. *historia*, replacing earlier *gistoriia*; also *istorik* = historian (cf. Pol. *historyk*/Germ. *Historiker*), replacing earlier *gistorik* (Barkh-Bog., IV, 21; Leeming, 57). Smirnov (124, 370); Vasmer (I, 490); Fasmer (II, 143); H-

W. (74); Shanskii (VII, 133–4); Barkh. (IX, 158–60); Chernykh (I, 360); Slov. Akad. (III, 317–9); Slov. Russ. (II, 145); Slovar' (V, 551–4); Smirnitskii (280). Srez. (I, 1151; also suppl., 133) cites early use of both terms in sense of story, storyteller (cf. Barkh-Bog., VI, 330–1).
Derivation: *istoricheskii*

kazamet/kazemat = casement, fr. Fr. *casemate*/Pol. *kazamata*/Ital. *casamatta*. Smirnov (126); Preob. (I, 282–3); Vasmer (I, 503); Fasmer (II, 159–60); Shanskii (VIII, 18); Barkh. (IX, 195); Slov. Russ. (II, 152); Slovar' (V, 664–5); Fadeev (I, 273); Plekhov (122); Smirnitskii (284).

443

kalendar' = calendar, fr. Pol. *kalendarz*/Du./Germ. *Kalender*/Eng. *calendar*. Vasmer (I, 508); Fasmer (II, 166); H-W. (74); Otten (439–40); Barkh. (IX, 212); Chernykh (I, 370); Wade (78–9); Slov. Akad. (III, 398–9); Slov. Russ. (II, 153); Slovar' (V, 704–5); Fadeev (I, 273); Smirnitskii (285). Shanskii (VIII, 20), Barkh-Bog. (VII, 34), and Leeming (62) cite several 17th-cent., usually dpl., precedents; D'iachenko (I, 241) lists as Slav. fr. Old-Slav. *kolendar'*/Lat. *calendarium*.
Derivation: *kalendarnoi/kalendarnyi*

kamer/kamara/kamera = special chamber, room, fr. Germ. *Kammer*/Du. *kamer*/Lat. *camera*, replacing earlier *komora* (Srez., I, 1266). Smirnov (127); Preob. (I, 289); Vasmer (I, 514); Fasmer (II, 174); Shanskii (VIII, 36–7); Kaiser (116); Bond (52–3); Barkh. (IX, 223–4); Otten (289–92); Chernykh (I, 372); Wade (79); Slov. Akad. (III, 408); Slov. Russ. (II, 157); Slovar' (V, 728); Fadeev (I, 275); Smirnitskii (286).
Derivation: *kamernyi*

kamerdiner = valet, fr. Germ. *Kammerdiener*. Smirnov (127); Vasmer (I, 514); Fasmer (II, 174); Shanskii (VIII, 37); Kaiser (164); Barkh. (IX, 224–5); Slov. Akad. (III, 409); Slov. Russ. (II, 157); Slovar' (V, 729); Smirnitskii (286).

kanal = canal, fr. Germ. *Kanal*/Du. *kanaal*/Fr. *canal*/Eng. *canal*, perhaps via Pol. *kanał*. Smirnov (130, 372); Vasmer (I, 516); Fasmer (II, 177); Shanskii (VIII, 41); Kutina I (181); Leeming (62); Otten (87- 90); Slov. Akad. (III, 423–4); Slov. Russ. (II, 158); Slovar' (V, 743); Fadeev (I, 276); Smirnitskii (286).

kanikula/y = holiday(s), vacation, fr. Pol. *kanikuła*/Lat. *canicula* (dim. of *canis* = dog): astron. term referring to the Dog Star (Sirius) of the constellation Canis Major and period of its conjunction with the sun, in Julian calendar = July 22-Aug. 23 and hottest time of year or "dog days," hence academic or other (summer) vacation and usually pl. in Russ. from Petrine times (e.g. *PiB*, X, 627). Vasmer (I, 518); Fasmer (II, 180); H-W. (75); Shanskii (VIII, 44); Leeming (63); Barkh. (IX, 232); Chernykh (I, 374); Slov. Akad. (III, 426 ["Lat. So-called time fr. 12 July to 12 August, when it's very hot."]); Slov. Russ. (II, 159); Slovar' (V, 751); Smirnitskii (287).

kant = edge, edging, piping, fr. Pol. *kant*/Germ. *Kante*. Vasmer (I, 519); Fasmer (II, 181); Shanskii (VIII, 48); Bond (72); Slov. Russ. (II, 160); Slovar' (V, 757–8); Plekhov (123); Smirnitskii (287).

kapella = choir, chapel, fr. Germ. *Kapelle*/Ital. *cappella*/Lat. *capella*. Christ. (45); Smirnov

(132); Vasmer (I, 521); Fasmer (II, 184); Shanskii, VIII, 52); Bond (142); Barkh. (IX, 240); Slovar' (V, 768); Smirnitskii (287).

kapital/kapitel' = capital (arch.), fr. Fr. *capitale*/Germ. *Kapitell*/Ital. *capitello.* Smirnov (133)); Vasmer (I, 522); Fasmer (II, 185); Shanskii (VIII, 54–5); Barkh-Bog. (VII, 63 [1689]); Barkh. (IX, 243, 244–5); Slov. Akad. (III, 433); Slov. Russ. (II, 161); Slovar' (V, 779); Smirnitskii (288).

karantin = quarantine, fr. Ital. *quarantena*/Fr. *quarantaine,* perhaps via Ukr. *karantin.* Vasmer (I, 527); Fasmer (II, 192); Shanskii (VIII, 65); Barkh. (IX, 253); Chernykh (I, 379); Wade (82); Slov. Akad. (III, 443–4); Slov. Russ. (II, 162); Slovar' (V, 803); Fadeev (I, 280); Plekhov (124); Smirnitskii (288).

karat = carat, fr. Germ. *Karat*/Ital. *carato.* Vasmer (I, 528); Fasmer (II, 194); Shanskii (VIII, 66); Barkh-Bog. (VII, 73–4 [1703]); Barkh. (IX, 253–4); Slov. Russ. (II, 162); Slovar' (V, 805); Smirnitskii (288).

karbunkul = carbuncle (med.), fr. Pol. *karbunkuł*/Germ. *Karbunkel*/Lat. *carbunculus.* Vasmer (I, 530); Fasmer (II, 195); Shanskii (VIII, 68); Slov. Akad. (III, 445); Slov. Russ. (II, 163); Slovar' (V, 812); Smirnitskii (289). Barkh-Bog. (VII, 77) and Leeming (65) cite precedent of 1670.

karkas = frame, framework, fr. Du./Pol. *karkas*/Germ./Fr. *carcasse.* Vasmer (I, 533); Fasmer (II, 200); Shanskii (VIII, 71); Barkh. (IX, 258–9); Slov. Akad. (III, 447); Slov. Russ. (II, 163); Slovar' (V, 819); Fadeev (I, 281); Smirnitskii (289).

karnival/karnaval = carnival, fr. Pol. *karnawal*/Germ. *Karneval*/Fr. *carnaval*/Ital. *carnevale.* Vasmer (I, 534); Fasmer (II, 202); Shanskii (VIII, 73); Barkh. (IX, 260); Wade (83–4); Slov. Russ. (II, 163); Slovar' (V, 825); Smirnitskii (289).

karniz = cornice, ledge (arch.), fr. Germ. *Karni(e)s.* Smirnov (163); Preob. (I, 300); Vasmer (I, 534); Fasmer (II, 202); Shanskii (VIII, 73); Barkh-Bog. (VII, 82 [1689]); Barkh. (IX, 261); Slov. Akad. (III, 450); Slov. Russ. (II, 164); Slovar' (V, 825–6); Smirnitskii (289).

karta = map, chart, fr. Pol. *karta*/Germ. *Karte*/Du. *kaart*/Lat. *charta.* Smirnov (135, 370); Preob. (I, 300); Vasmer (I, 535); Fasmer (II, 203); H-W. (76); Shanskii (VIII, 74–5); Bond (72); Barkh-Bog. (VII, 83, 2. [1697]); Barkh. (IX, 262); Chernykh (I, 382); Wade (84); Slov. Akad. (III, 451–3); Slov. Russ. (II, 164); Slovar' (V, 827–9); Fadeev (I, 282); Plekhov (124); Smirnitskii (289).

kartina = picture (painting), initially also map, fr. Ital. *cartina* and/or Russ. dim. of *karta* (see above). Smirnov (136); Preob. (I, 300); Vasmer (I, 536); Fasmer (II, 204); Shanskii (VIII, 77); Barkh-Bog. (VII, 84 [1700/1704]); Barkh. (IX, 265); Slov. Akad. (III, 453); Slov. Russ. (II, 164); Slovar' (V, 833–5); Smirnitskii (289).
Derivations: *kartinka* (dim.= a print), *kartinnyi*

karton = pasteboard, cardboard, fr. Germ./Du. *karton*/Fr. *carton.* Vasmer (I, 536); Fasmer

(II, 204); Shanskii (VIII, 78); Barkh. (IX, 266); Chernykh (I, 383); Wade (84); Slov. Russ. (II, 164); Slovar' (V, 838); Smirnitskii (289).

kartush = cartouche (arch.), fr. Fr. *cartouche*/It. *cartoccio.* Smirnov (136); Vasmer (I, 536); Fasmer (II, 205); Shanskii (VIII, 80–1); Barkh. (IX, 267); Slovar' (V, 844).

kaskad = cascade, fr. Fr. *cascade.* Smirnov (136); Vasmer (I, 537); Fasmer (II, 206); Shanskii (VIII, 84); Barkh. (IX, 269); Slov. Russ. (II, 165); Slovar' (V, 852); Smirnitskii (290).
Derivation: *kaskadnyi*

445

kastrat = castrato (mus.), eunuch, fr. Ital. *castrato.* Smirnov (137); Vasmer (I, 539); Fasmer (II, 208); Shanskii (VIII, 87–8); Barkh. (X, 6); Slov. Russ. (II, 165); Slovar' (V, 857–8); Smirnitskii (290).
Derivations: *kastratsiia, kastrirovat'* (cf. Germ. *Kastration, kastrieren*)

kvadrant = quadrant, fr. Germ. *Quadrant*/Eng. *quadrant.* Smirnov (138); Vasmer (I, 545); Fasmer (II, 216); Shanskii (VIII, 108); Barkh-Bog. (VII, 102–2., 3. [1688, 1700]); Barkh. (X, 21–2); Otten (113–16); Ryan (92); Slov. Akad. (III, 494); Slov. Russ. (II, 168); Slovar' (V, 900); Fadeev (I, 289); Smirnitskii (292).

kvarts = quartz, fr. Germ. *Quarz.* Vasmer (I, 546); Fasmer (II, 218); Shanskii (VIII, 113); Barkh. (X, 27); Chernykh (I, 391); Slov. Akad. (III, 494); Slov. Russ. (II, 169); Slovar' (V, 911); Smirnitskii (292).
Derivation: *kvartsevyi*

kizel'gur = chalky type of stone, fr. Germ. *Kieselgur.* Bond (72); Slovar' (V, 937–8).

klavesin = harpsichord, fr. Fr. *clavecin;* also *klavikort/klavikordy* = clavichord, fr. Germ. *Klavikord/Klavichord.* Smirnov (142); Vasmer (I, 564); Fasmer (II, 243); H-W. (78); Shanskii (VIII, 141–2); Barkh. (X, 45); Slov. Akad. (III, 551 *[klavisin],* 552 *[klavikord]*); Slov. Russ. (II, 175 *[klavikordy]*); Slovar' (V, 983); Smirnitskii (295).

klapon/klapan = valve, fr. Germ. *Klappe/Klappen.* Preob. (I, 311); Vasmer (I, 565); Fasmer (II, 244); Shanskii (VIII, 144–5); Bond (72); Barkh. (X, 47); Chernykh (I, 399); Slov. Russ. (II, 175); Slovar' (V, 990–1); Fadeev (I, 296); Smirnitskii (295).

klass = class, fr. Germ. *Klasse*/Fr. *classe.* Christ. (23); Smirnov (144); Vasmer (I, 566); Fasmer (II, 244); H-W. (78); Shanskii (VIII, 145–6); Barkh. (X, 48); Chernykh (I, 399); Wade (88); Slov. Akad. (III, 590–1); Slov. Russ. (II, 175); Slovar' (V, 992–4); Smirnitskii (295).
Derivations: *klassnyi, klassicheskii*

klemma = clamp, later terminal (electrical), Germ. *Klemme.* Bond (73); Slovar' (V, 1014); Smirnitskii (296).

klima/klimat = climate, fr. Lat. *clima*/Germ. *Klima*/Fr. *climat.* Preob. (I, 315–6); Vasmer (I, 570); Fasmer (II, 250); Shanskii (VIII, 158); Kutina I (132–3); Barkh. (X, 57–8); Chernykh (I,

401); Slov. Akad. (III, 611); Slov. Russ. (II, 178); Slovar' (V, 1030); Fadeev (I, 298); Smirnitskii (296). Barkh-Bog. (VII, 171–2) and Leeming (67) cite possible 17th-cent. precedents.
Derivation: *klimaticheskii*

kobal't = cobalt, fr. Germ. *Kobalt*/Lat. *cobaltum*. Shanskii (VIII, 175–6); Bond (73); Barkh. (X, 73); Slov. Russ. (II, 183); Slovar' (V, 1082); Smirnitskii (298).
Derivation: *kobal'tovyi*

kolika/i = colic, fr. Du. *kolika*/Germ. *Kolik*/Lat. *colica*. Preob. (I, 335); Vasmer (I, 599); Fasmer (II, 291); Shanskii (VIII, 200–1); Barkh. (X, 93); Chernykh (I, 412); Slov. Russ. (II, 189); Slovar' (V, 1158); Smirnitskii (301). Barkh-Bog. (VII, 240) cites possible 17th-cent. precedent.

kolonna = column (arch.), later also in mil. and other senses, fr. Ital. *colonna*/Germ. *Kolonne*. Smirnov (146); Vasmer (I, 602); Fasmer (II, 295); Shanskii (VIII, 211–12); Barkh. (X, 103); Chernykh (I, 413); Slov. Akad. (III, 721); Slov. Russ. (II, 191); Slovar' (V, 1183–4); Fadeev (I, 304); Smirnitskii (301). Barkh-Bog. (VII, 251) cites precedents (fr. Gr.) of 1653, 1686.

kommunikatsiia = communication, fr. Pol. *komunikacja*/Lat. *communicatio*. Smirnov (149); Vasmer (I, 609); Fasmer (II, 303); Shanskii (VIII, 235–6); Grib. (41); Barkh. (X, 122); Slov. Russ. (II, 195); Slovar' (V, 1246); Fadeev (I, 308); Plekhov (133); Smirnitskii (304).
Derivation: *kommunikatsionnyi*

kompanii/kampanii/kumpaniia/kompaniia = company (in various, later mainly commercial senses), fr. Eng. *company*/Pol. *kompanja*/Germ. *Kompanie*/Fr. *compagnie*. Smirnov (149–50, 372); Vasmer (I, 610); Fasmer (II, 305); Shanskii (VIII, 238–9); Kaiser (258–9); Otten (102–9); Barkh. (X, 123); Chernykh (I, 419); Slov. Akad. (III, 764); Slov. Russ. (II, 195); Slovar' (V, 1253–4); Smirnitskii (304). Gard. (132–3), Barkh-Bog. (VII, 267), and Leeming (69) cite 17th-cent. precedents, usually ref. foreign groups.

kompleksiia/komplektsiia = build, constitution (human body), fr. Pol. *kompleksja*/Lat. *complexio*. Christ. (21); Smirnov (150); Vasmer (I, 611); Fasmer (II, 306); Shanskii (VIII, 243); Barkh. (X, 126); Slovar' (V, 1261); Smirnitskii (305).

komplet/komplekt = complete set, complement, specified number, fr. Germ. *Komplet/Komplekt;* also *komplektovat'* = to complete, replenish, recruit, fr. Germ. *komplettieren/komplektieren.* Smirnov (150–1); Preob. (I, 343); Vasmer (I, 610); Fasmer (II, 306); Shanskii (VIII, 242–3); Barkh. (X, 125); Slov. Akad. (III, 765); Slovar' (V, 1260); Fadeev (I, 311); Plekhov (134); Smirnitskii (304).
Derivations: *komplektnyi* (= complete), *komplektovanie* (= acquisition, staffing, recruitment/recruiting)

kompozitsiia = composition, fr. Pol. *kompozycja*/Lat. *compositio*. Smirnov (153); Vasmer (I, 611); Fasmer (II, 306); Shanskii (VIII, 244); Barkh. (X, 127); Slov. Russ. (II, 195); Slovar' (V, 1263–4); Smirnitskii (305).

konditsion/konditsiia = condition, fr. Germ. *Kondition*/Pol. *kondycja*/Lat. *condicio.* Christ. (20); Smirnov (153); Vasmer (I, 613); Fasmer (II, 309); Kaiser (241); Shanskii (VIII, 254); Bond (135); Barkh. (X, 131); Slov. Russ. (II, 196); Slovar' (V, 1281–2); Ox. Russ. (292).

konspiratsiia = conspiracy, fr. Pol. *konspiracja*/Lat. *conspiratio*/Germ. *Konspiration*/Fr. *conspiration.* Shanskii (VIII, 266); Barkh. (X, 141); Slovar' (V, 1314–5); Smirnitskii (307). 447
Derivations: *konspirativnyi* (= secret), *konspirator, konspirirovat'* (cf. Germ. *konspieren*)

kontinent = continent, mainland, fr. Germ. *Kontinent*/Fr. *continent*/Lat. *continentis (terrae).* Kutina I (200); Shanskii (VIII, 274–5); Barkh. (X, 144); Slovar' (V, 1326); Fadeev (I, 315); Smirnitskii (307).
Derivation: *kontinental'nyi*

kontroversiia/kontroverziia/kontroverza = controversy, fr. Lat. *controversia.* H-W. (79); Barkh. (X, 149); Slovar' (V, 1340); Ox. Russ. (295).

konus = cone, fr. Lat. *conus*/Germ. *Konus.* Vasmer (I, 617); Fasmer (II, 314); Shanskii (VIII, 257); Kutina I (50); Barkh. (X, 150, 135 *[konicheskii]*); Slov. Akad. (III, 781); Slov. Russ. (II, 199, 197 *[konicheskii]*); Slovar' (V, 1291); Smirnitskii (308, 306 *[konicheskii]*).
Derivation: *konicheskii*

konfuziia/konfuz = confusion, discomfiture, fr. Pol. *konfuzja*/Lat. *confusio*/Fr. *confus/e/* Germ. *Konfus.* Smirnov (160); Vasmer (I, 617); Fasmer (II, 315); Shanskii (VIII, 290–1); Grib. (41); Barkh. (X, 154); Chernykh (I, 425); Slovar' (V, 1356–7); Smirnitskii (308).
Derivations: *konfuzit'* (= to disconcert), *konfuzno, konfuznyi* (= awkward)

kontsept/kontseptsiia = concept, fr. Pol. *concept*/Germ. *Konzept*/Lat.*conceptus.* Smirnov (160); Shanskii (VIII, 304–5); Bond (133); Barkh. (X, 155); Slovar' (V, 1362); Smirnitskii (308).

kontsert = concert (mus.), fr. Pol. *koncert*/Germ. *Konzert.* Shanskii (VIII, 294–5); Barkh-Bog. (VII, 283 [1688]); Barkh. (X, 155); Chernykh (I, 425); Slov. Akad. (III, 781); Slov. Russ. (II, 199); Slovar' (V, 1362–3); Smirnitskii (308). Leeming (70) cites precedents of 1664, 1679.
Derivations: *kontsertant* (cf. Pol. *koncertant* = performer), *kontsertirovat'*

kon"iunktura = juncture, conjuncture, situation, fr. Po. *koniunktura*/Lat. *coniunctura.* Smirnov (161); Shanskii (298–9); Barkh. (X, 158); Slovar' (V, 1371); Smirnitskii (309); Ox. Russ. (296).

kopiia = copy, fr. Pol. *kopija/kopia*/Lat. *copia*/Du./Germ. *Kopie.* Christ. (30); Smirnov (161); Vasmer (I, 620); Fasmer (II, 318); H-W. (79); Kaiser (183); Barkh. (X, 162); Chernykh (I, 427); Slov. Russ. (II, 201); Slovar' (V, 1392–3); Smirnitskii (309–10). Barkh-Bog. (VII, 297) cites two 17th-cent. precedents.

korpuskul'/korpuskula = corpuscle, fr. Lat. *corpusculum.* Shanskii (VIII, 331); Barkh. (X, 187); Slovar' (V, 1469); Smirnitskii (312).
Derivation: *korpuskuliarnyi*

kran = tap, faucet, also crane, fr. Du. *kraan*/Germ. *Krahn/Kran*. Smirnov (127); Preob. (I, 377); Vasmer (I, 655); Fasmer (II, 366); Shanskii (VIII, 370); Barkh. (X, 226); Chernykh (I, 439); Slov. Akad. (III, 900); Slov. Russ. (II, 215); Slovar' (V, 1575); Fadeev (I, 330); Smirnitskii (315–6).

448

kristall = crystal, glass, fr. Germ. *Kristall,* supplementing earlier *khrustal'*. Vasmer (I, 664); Fasmer (II, 378); H-W. (81); Bond (73); Barkh-Bog. (VIII, 58, 1. [1686]); Grib. (43); Barkh. (XI, 181); Chernykh (I, 443); Slov. Akad. (III, 955–6); Slov. Russ. (II, 223); Slovar' (V, 1660–1); Smirnitskii (319).
Derivations: *kristal'nyi, kristallizirovat'*

kron/krona = crown (of tree, etc.), fr. Germ. *Krone*. Smirnov (168); Vasmer (I, 667); Fasmer (II, 381); Shanskii (VIII, 406); Bond (142); Barkh. (XI, 33); Slov. Russ. (II, 225); Slovar' (V, 1698); Smirnitskii (320).

kubus/kub = cube, fr. Lat. *cubus*/Germ. *Kubus*/Fr. *cube*. Vasmer (I, 677); Fasmer (II, 394); Shanskii (VIII, 427); Kutina I (50); Barkh. (XI, 61–2); Chernykh (I, 450); Slov. Akad. (III, 1051–2); Slov. Russ. (II, 232); Slovar' (V, 1777); Smirnitskii (323).
Derivation: *kubicheskii*

kuvert/konvert = cover (including tablecloth), envelope, fr. Germ. *Kuvert*/Fr. *couvert*. Smirnov (152); Vasmer (I, 612); Fasmer (II, 308); Kaiser (153); Shanskii (VIII, 250); Grib. (44); Barkh. (X, 129); Chernykh (I, 421); Wade (93); Slovar' (V, 1275); Smirnitskii (305).

kunshtkamor/kunstkamera = cabinet of curiosities, museum founded by Peter I, fr. Germ. *Kunstkammer*. Smirnov (169); Vasmer (I, 694); Fasmer (II, 418); Shanskii (VIII, 445); Kaiser (159); Bond (90); Grib. (44); Barkh. (XI, 74–5); Slov. Russ. (II, 255); Slovar' (V, 1840); Ox. Russ. (312).

kurioznyi/kur'ëznyi = curious, amusing, fr. Germ. *kurios*/Lat. *curiosus*. Christ. (54); Smirnov (171); Vasmer (I, 703); Fasmer (II, 430); Barkh. (XI, 84); Chernykh (I, 458); Slovar' (V, 1884); Smirnitskii (326).

laboratoriia = laboratory, fr. Germ. *Laboratorium*/Lat. pl. *laboratoria*. Smirnov (172); Vasmer (II, 2); Fasmer (II, 443); Bond (73–4); Barkh. (XI, 99–100); Chernykh (I, 461); Shanskii-Bob. (162); Slov. Akad. (III, 1125); Slov. Russ. (II, 241); Slovar' (VI, 9–10); Smirnitskii (327).

lazaret = hospital, infirmary, field hospital (mil.), sick-bay (naut.), fr. Du. *lazaret*/Germ. *Lazarett*. Smirnov (172); Preob. (I, 429); Vasmer (II, 6); Fasmer (II, 449); Kaiser (158); Bond (39); Barkh. (XI, 107–8); Chernykh (I, 463); Shanskii-Bob. (162–3); Slov. Akad. (III, 1133); Slov. Russ. (II, 243); Slovar' (VI, 31–2); Fadeev (I, 346); Plekhov (145); Smirnitskii (327).
Derivation: *lazaretnyi*

landshaft = landscape (painting), fr. Germ. *Landschaft,* replacing somewhat earlier *lenchaft/lenshaft*. Christ. (45); Vasmer (II, 12); Fasmer (II, 457); H-W. (82); Bond (142);

Barkh. (XI, 115); Chernykh (I, 465); Shanskii-Bob. (163); Slov. Russ. (II, 244); Slovar' (VI, 54–5); Smirnitskii (328).
Derivation: *landshaftnyi*

lantseta/lantset = lancet (med.), fr. Germ. *Lanzette*/Fr. *lancette*/Eng. *lancet*. Smirnov (175); Vasmer (II, 13); Fasmer (II, 458); Barkh. (XI, 116); Chernykh (I, 466); Shanskii-Bob. (164); Slov. Akad. (III, 1138); Slov. Russ. (II, 244); Slovar' (VI, 57–8); Smirnitskii (328).

449

latun' = brass, fr. Germ. *Latun*. Preob. (I, 437–8); Vasmer (II, 18); Fasmer (II, 465); Bond (74); Barkh. (XI, 127); Slov. Russ. (II, 246); Slovar' (VI, 82); Fadeev (I, 347); Smirnitskii (329). Barkh-Bog. (VIII, 180) cites precedent of 1672.
Derivation: *latunnyi*

lektsion/lektsiia = lecture, reading, fr. Germ. *Lection*/Pol. *lekcja*/Lat. *lectio*. Smirnov (177); Vasmer (II, 28); Fasmer (II, 478); H-W. (83); Barkh. (XI, 148); Slov. Russ. (II, 250); Slovar' (VI, 149); Smirnitskii (331).

linei/liniia = line, as in line of battle, also street (SPb.), later also in other senses, fr. Du./Germ. *Linie*/Lat. *linea*, perhaps via Pol. *linia;* also *lineika* = line, ruler. Smirnov (147, 373); Preob. (I, 454); Vasmer (II, 43); Fasmer (II, 428); H-W. (83); Kutina I (35–7); Kaiser (250); Otten (118–22, 117); Barkh. (XI, 180–1); Chernykh (I, 482–3); Shanskii-Bob. (168); Wade (109); Slov. Akad. (III, 1212–13); Slov. Russ. (II, 254); Slovar' (VI, 233–6); Fadeev (I, 357–8); Plekhov (148); Smirnitskii (334). Barkh-Bog. (VIII, 235–6) and Leeming (76) cite precedents of 1680s.

literatura = literature, fr. Pol. *literatura*/Lat. *litteratura*. Smirnov (179); Vasmer (II, 46); Fasmer (II, 502); H-W. (83); Barkh. (XI, 190); Chernykh (I, 485); Shanskii-Bob. (169); Slov. Russ. (II, 256); Slovar' (VI, 262–3); Smirnitskii (335).
Derivations: *literaturnyi, literator* (= writer), *literatorskii*

logarifm = logarithm, fr. Fr. *logarithme*/Germ./Lat. *logarithmus*. Smirnov (180); Vasmer (II, 51); Fasmer (II, 509); Kutina I (77); Barkh. (XI, 214); Ryan (92); Chernykh (I, 488); Shanskii-Bob. (170); Slov. Akad. (III, 1257); Slov. Russ. (II, 261); Slovar' (VI, 317); Smirnitskii (337).
Derivation: *logarifmicheskii*

lotereia = lottery, raffle, fr. Germ. *Lotterie*/Du. *loterij*/Fr. *loterie*/Ital. *loteria*. Smirnov (181); Preob. (I, 471); Vasmer (II, 61); Fasmer (II, 522); Kaiser (244); Barkh. (XI, 233); Chernykh (I, 492); Shanskii-Bob. (172); Slov. Russ. (II, 265); Slovar' (VI, 372); Smirnitskii (339).
Derivation: *lotereinyi*

malevat' = to paint, daub, fr. Pol. *malovać*/Germ. *malen;* also *maliar* = painter, decorator, fr. Ukr. *mal'ar*/Pol. *malarz*/Germ. *Maler*. Preob. (I, 505); Vasmer (II, 91–2); Fasmer (II, 562); H-W. (85); Koch. I (120); Barkh-Bog. (IX, 243 [1690]); Otten (317–8); Shanskii-Bob. (177); Wade (115); Slov. Russ. (II, 281); Slovar' (VI, 524); Smirnitskii (343, 345).

manir/manira/maner/manera = manner, style, method, fr. Germ. *Manier*/Pol. *maniera*/Fr.

manière. Christ. (19–20); Smirnov (186, 373); Preob. (I, 508); Vasmer (II, 95); Fasmer (II, 568); Bond (136); Grib. (48); Shanskii-Bob. (178); Slov. Russ. (II, 285); Slovar' (VI, 597–8); Smirnitskii (346).

marganets = manganese, fr. Germ. *Mangan(erz)*. Preob. (I, 510); Vasmer (II, 98); Fasmer (II, 572); Bond (74); Chernykh (I, 510); Shanskii-Bob. (179); Slov. Akad. (IV, 44–5); Slov. Russ. (II, 286); Slovar' (VI, 623–4); Smirnitskii (346).
Derivations: *margantsevyi, margantsovistyi*

masshtab = scale, fr. Germ. *Massstab*. Christ. (49); Smirnov (191); Vasmer (II, 103); Fasmer (II, 579); Bond (74); Chernykh (I, 514); Shanskii-Bob. (181); Slov. Akad. (IV, 64 [*mashtab*]); Slov. Russ. (II, 290, 292 [*masshtab, mashtab*]); Slovar' (VI, 687–8); Fadeev (I, 377–8); Plekhov (154); Smirnitskii (348).

matematika = mathematics, fr. Pol. *matematyka*/Lat. *mathematica*/Germ. *Mathematik*. Vasmer (II, 104); Fasmer (II, 580); H-W. (86); Otten (134–6); Chernykh (I, 514); Shanskii-Bob. (181); Slov. Akad. (IV, 56); Slov. Russ. (II, 290); Slovar' (VI, 690–1); Smirnitskii (348). Barkh-Bog. (IX, 41) and Leeming (78) cite precedents of 1664, 1672.
Derivation: *matematicheskii*

materiia = matter, material, content, fr. Germ. *Materie*/Pol./Lat. *materia*. Christ. (49); Smirnov (190, 374); Preob. (I, 514); Vasmer (II, 104); Fasmer (II, 581); H-W. (86); Kutina II (34–5, 38–41); Bond (74); Barkh-Bog. (IX, 42 [1691]); Grib. (49); Otten (221–8); Shanskii-Bob. (181); Slov. Akad. (IV, 56–7); Slov. Russ. (II, 290); Slovar' (VI, 700–1); Smirnitskii (349). Leeming (78) cites two possible (undated) precedents.

matritsa = matrix, also die, mold, fr. Germ. *Matrize*/Du. *matrijs*/Fr. *matrice*/Lat. *matrix*. Vasmer (II, 105); Fasmer (III, 583); Slov. Russ. (II, 291); Slovar' (VI, 710–11); Smirnitskii (349); Ox. Russ. (339).
Derivations: *matritsirovanie, matritsirovat', matrichnyi*

makhina/mashina = machine, fr. Lat. *machina*/Germ. *Maschine*/Fr. *machine*. Smirnov (191); Preob. (I, 517); Vasmer (II, 108); Fasmer (II, 584, 586); Kutina II (234–6); Bond (74); Grib. (49); Chernykh (I, 517); Shanskii-Bob. (182); Slov. Akad. (IV, 62–3); Slov. Russ. (II, 292); Slovar' (VI, 728–31); Plekhov (154); Smiritskii (349).

medik = medical person, fr. Germ. *Medik(us)*, perhaps via Pol. *medyk*. Christ. (46); Smirnov (192, 374); Preob. (I, 519); Vasmer (II, 111); Fasmer (II, 590); Koch. II (85); Barkh-Bog. (IX, 59 [1705]); Otten (230, 422); Shanskii-Bob. (182); Slov. Russ. (II, 294); Slovar' (VI, 761); Smirnitskii (350). Leeming (78–9) lists *medikus*, 1680.

medikament = medicine, fr. Germ. *Medikament*. Smirnov (192); Vasmer (II,111); Fasmer (II, 590); Bond (74); Barkh-Bog. (IX, 59 [1706]); Otten (228–31); Slov. Russ. (II, 294); Slovar' (VI, 761–2); Smirnitskii (350).

meditsina = medicine (science of), fr. Germ. *Medizin*/Lat. *medicina*, perhaps via Pol. *medycyna*. Smirnov (192, 374); Vasmer (II, 111); Fasmer (II, 590); Koch. II (85); Kaiser (157);

450

Barkh-Bog. (IX, 59 [1695]); Leeming (78 [1676]); Otten (568); Chernykh (I, 519–20); Slov. Akad. (IV, 76–7); Slov. Russ. (II, 294); Slovar' (VI, 763); Smirnitskii (350).
Derivation: *meditsinskii*

mezanin/mezonin = mezzanine (floor), later also attic, fr. Fr. *mezzanine*. Preob. (I, 522); Vasmer (II, 113); Fasmer (II, 594); Chernykh (I, 521); Slov. Russ. (II, 296); Slovar' (VI, 796); Smirnitskii (351).
Derivations: *mezoninnyi, mezoninchik* (dim.)

451

melodiia = melody, fr. Pol./Ital./Lat. *melodia*. Vasmer (II, 115); Fasmer (II, 596); Barkh-Bog. (IX, 81 [1681]); Chernykh (I, 522); Slov. Russ. (II, 297); Slovar' (VI, 817); Smirnitskii (352). Barkh-Bog. (IX, 81) cites precedent of 1681; Leeming (79) lists *meliudieia* from undated ms.
Derivations: *melodicheskii, melodichnost', melodichnyi*

meridian = meridian, fr. Germ./Eng. *meridian*/Du. *meridiaan*/Fr. *méridian*/Lat. *meridianus*. Kutina I (126–7); Barkh-Bog. (IX, 98 [1703]); Ryan (92); Chernykh (I, 524); Shanskii-Bob. (184); Slov. Akad. (IV, 94); Slov. Russ. (II, 298); Slovar' (VI, 853–4); Fadeev (I, 385); Plekhov (157); Smirnitskii (353).

metal/metall = metal, fr. Germ. *Metall*/Du. *metaal*/Lat. *metallum*, perhaps via Pol. *metal*. Christ. (23); Smirnov (194, 374); Preob. (I, 531); Vasmer (II, 125); Fasmer (II, 609); Kutina I (184–5); Bond (75); Chernykh (I, 526–7); Shanskii-Bob. (185); Slov. Akad. (IV, 95–6); Slov. Russ. (II, 300); Slovar' (VI, 896–7); Smirnitskii (355). Barkh-Bog. (IX, 122) and Leeming (79) cite possible 17th-cent. precedents.
Derivations: *metallist, metallicheskii*

metamorfozis/metamorfoza = metamorphosis, fr. Germ. *Metamorphosis*/Lat. *metamorphosis*. Smirnov (194); H-W. (87); Bond (136); Shanskii-Bob. (184); Slovar' (VI, 902–3); Smirnitskii (355).

metafizika = metaphysics, fr. Pol. *metafizyka*/Lat. *metaphysica*/Germ. *Metaphysik*. Smirnov (195); Vasmer (II, 125); Fasmer (II, 609); H-W. (87); Slov. Akad. (IV, 96); Slov. Russ. (II, 300); Slovar' (VI, 909); Smirnitskii (355).
Derivation: *metafizicheskii*

meteor = meteor, fr. Fr. *météore*/Germ. *Meteor*. Smirnov (195); Vasmer (II, 126); Fasmer (II, 610); Kutina I (102–3); Chernykh (I, 527); Shanskii-Bob. (185); Slov. Russ. (II, 300); Slovar' (VI, 914); Smirnitskii (355).
Derivation: *meteoricheskii*

mekhanika = mechanics, fr. Germ. *Mechanik*; also *mekhanik* = mechanic, fr. Germ. *Mechaniker/Mechanikus*, perhaps via Pol. *mechanic*. Smirnov (195); Vasmer (II, 127–8); Fasmer (II, 612); H-W. (88); Kutina II (200–3); Barkh-Bog. (IX, 131 [1709]); Slov. Akad. (IV, 103); Slov. Russ. (II, 301); Slovar' (VI, 936–7); Smirnitskii (356).
Derivation: *mekhanicheskii*

mikrometr = micrometer, Germ. *Mikrometer*. Smirnov (195); Bond (75); Slov. Russ. (II, 308); Slovar' (VI, 974); Fadeev (I, 392); Smirnitskii (357).

mikroskop = microscope, fr. Germ. *Mikroskop*/Fr. *microscope.* Smirnov (196); Vasmer (II, 134); Fasmer (II, 621); Kutina II (196); Bond (75); Chernykh (I, 530); Shanskii-Bob. (186); Slov. Akad. (IV, 130); Slov. Russ. (II, 303); Slovar' (VI, 976); Smirnitskii (357).
Derivations: *mikroskopicheskii, mikroskopiia*

452

mikstura = (liquid) medicine, mixture, fr. Pol. *mikstura*/Lat. *mixtura*/Du. *mixtuur*/Fr. *mixture.* Smirnov (196); Vasmer (II, 134); Fasmer (II, 621); Chernykh (I, 530–1); Shanskii-Bob. (186); Slov. Russ. (II, 303); Slovar' (VI, 980); Smirnitskii (357).

million = million, thousand thousand, fr. Germ./Fr. *million,* perhaps via Pol. *mil(l)ion.* Smirnov (196); Vasmer (II, 134); Fasmer (II, 621); H-W. (88); Kutina I (17–18); Chernykh (I, 531); Shanskii-Bob. (187); Slov. Akad. (IV, 130–1); Slov. Russ, (II, 303); Slovar' (VI, 987–8); Smirnitskii (357). Barkh-Bog. (IX, 150) and Leeming (79) cite precedents in dpl. docs.

mineral = mineral, fr. Germ. *Mineral*/Fr. *minéral.* Smirnov (196); Vasmer (II, 136); Fasmer (II, 623–4); Kutina I (184–5); Bond (75); Grib. (50); Chernykh (I, 532–3); Slov. Akad. (IV, 139); Slov. Russ. (II, 305); Slovar' (VI, 1010); Smirnitskii (358).
Derivation: *mineral'nyi*

minuta = minute, fr. Pol./Lat. *minuta*/Germ./Fr. *minute.* Christ. (44); Smirnov (197, 374); Preob. (I, 538); Vasmer (II, 137); Fasmer (II, 625); H-W. (88); Kutina I (70–2); Ryan (93 [*polminuta* = half-minute]); Otten (141–2); Chernykh (I, 534); Shanskii-Bob. (187); Wade (122); Slov. Akad. (IV, 140–1); Slov. Russ. (II, 305); Slovar' (VI, 1027–9); Fadeev (I, 397); Smirnitskii (359). Fasmer also cites *miniuta* in 17th-cent. doc.
Derivations: *minutka* (dim.), *minutnyi*

moda = mode, manner, fashion, pattern, fr. Germ./Fr. *mode.* Smirnov (198, 374); Vasmer (II, 145); Fasmer (II, 636); H-W. (89); Barkh-Bog. (IX, 232 [1699]); Grib. (51); Chernykh (I, 537); Shanskii-Bob. (188); Slov. Russ. (II, 316); Slovar' (VI, 1128–30); Smirnitskii (363).
Derivations: *modnyi, modno*

model' = model, fr. Pol. *model*/Germ. *Modell*/Fr. *modèle.* Christ. (51); Smirnov (198, 374); Preob. (I, 544); Vasmer (II, 145); Fasmer (II, 636); Barkh-Bog. (IX, 232 [1703]); Shanskii-Bob. (188); Slov. Russ. (II, 316); Slovar' (VI, 1131–2); Fadeev (I, 400); Smirnitskii (363).
Derivations: *model'ka* (dim.), *model'nyi*

moment = moment, instant; feature, element, fr. Germ. *Moment.* Christ. (44); Smirnov (198); Preob. (I, 554); Vasmer (II, 154); Fasmer (II, 649); H-W. (89); Bond (133); Chernykh (I, 541); Shanskii-Bob. (189); Slov. Russ. (II, 321); Slovar' (VI, 1215–6); Smirnitskii (365).
Derivation: *momental'nyi*

muzeum/muzei = museum, fr. Fr. *muséum/musée*/Germ./Du. *museum.* Preob. (I, 566); Vasmer (II, 170); Fasmer (III, 5); Chernykh (I, 548); Shanskii-Bob. (192); Slov. Russ. (II, 330); Slovar' (VI, 1350–1); Smirnitskii (369).
Derivation: *muzeinyi*

muzika/musika/muzyka = music, fr. Pol. *muzyka*/Lat./Ital. *musica*/Germ. *Musik.* Smirnov

(200, 374); Preob. (I, 566); Vasmer (II, 170–1); Fasmer (III, 6–7); Bond (75); Chernykh (I, 548); Shanskii-Bob. (193); Wade (127); Slov. Akad. (IV, 325–6); Slov. Russ. (II, 330); Slovar' (VI, 1352–4); Smirnitskii (369). Barkh-Bog. (IX, 311) and Leeming (82) cite several possible precedents, latter also noting earlier Pol. meaning "orchestra" and Russ. borrowings thereof; D'iachenko (I, 320) lists Slav. *musikia/musikii* (= singer)/*musikiisk* (adj.), no date.; Kot. (545, 390) uses term to mean type of foreign music.

453

Derivations: *muzykal'nost', muzykal'nyi, muzykal'no, muzykant* (cf. Germ. *Musikant* = musician), *muzykantskii*

muskul = muscle, fr. Lat. *musculus.* Vasmer (II, 178); Fasmer (III, 16); Chernykh (I, 549); Shanskii-Bob. (193); Slov. Russ. (II, 332); Slovar' (VI, 1379); Smirnitskii (369).
Derivation: *muskul'nyi*

mufta = sleeve joint, coupling, fr. Du. *mouwtje*/Germ. *Muffe.* Preob. (I, 572); Vasmer (II, 180); Fasmer (III, 18); Bond (75); Shanskii-Bob. (193); Slov. Russ. (II, 333); Slovar' (VI, 1392); Fadeev (I, 409); Smirnitskii (370).
Derivations: *muftishka/muftochka* (dims.), *muftochnyi*

nabliudenie = observation, later also supervision, surveillance, reconnaissance, calque of Lat. *observatio.* Kutina I (93–4); Kutina II (45–6); Slov. Russ. (II, 347); Slovar' (VII, 38–9); Fadeev (I, 412); Plekhov (168); Smirnitskii (374).
Derivations: *nabliudatel', nabliudatel'nyi, nabliudat'*

natural'nyi = natural, fr. Pol. *naturalny*/Lat. *naturalis;* also *naturalizovat',* fr. Pol. *naturalizować.* Smirnov (203); Vasmer (II, 201); Fasmer (III, 49); Kaiser (107); Kutina II (21); Barkh-Bog. (X, 289 [1680]); Chernykh (I, 561–2); Slov. Russ. (II, 415–6); Slovar' (VII, 597–8); Smirnitskii (396). *Natura* = nature, probably also fr. Pol./Lat., entered Russ. somewhat earlier (Preob., I, 595; Barkh-Bog., X, 289; Kot., 556, 390; Shanskii-Bob., 199).

natsiia = nation (people), fr. Pol. *nacja*/Lat. *natio*/Germ./Fr. *nation.* Smirnov (203, 375); Vasmer (II, 203); Fasmer (III, 51); H-W. (91); Kaiser (101); Birzhak. (132–3); Chernykh (I, 562); Shanskii-Bob. (199); Slovar' (VII, 646–7); Smirnitskii (397).
Derivations: *natsional'nyi* (cf. Fr. *national*), *natsional'nost'*

nul'/nol' = nought, zero, fr. Du. *nul*Germ./Eng. *null*/Lat. *nullus.* Smirnov (206); Preob. (I, 611); Vasmer (II, 226); Fasmer (III, 81–2); Kutina I (20–1); Birzhak. (159); Bond (76); Barkh-Bog. (XI, 448 [1688]); Otten (151–4); Chernykh (I, 577); Shanskii-Bob. (204); Wade (134–5); Slov. Russ. (II, 468–9, 465); Slovar' (VII, 1387–9); Smirnitskii (429, 433).

numeratsiia = numeration, numbering, fr. Pol. *numeracja*/Lat. *numeratio.* Vasmer (II, 231); Fasmer (III, 89); Otten (154- 6); Slov. Russ. (II, 469); Slovar' (VII, 1450); Smirnitskii (433).
Derivations: *numeratsionnyi, numerovat'* (cf. Pol. *numerować*)

obelisk = obelisk, fr. Pol./Du./Germ./Eng. *obelisk*/Fr. *obélisque*/Lat. *obeliscus.* Smirnov (207); Vasmer (II, 238); Fasmer (III, 98); Chernykh (I, 584); Shanskii-Bob. (206); Slov. Russ. (III, 9); Slovar' (VIII, 92); Smirnitskii (437).

obligatsiia = obligation, commitment, also debt, promissory note; later bond, debenture, fr. Pol. *obligacja*/Lat. *obligatio*/Germ. *Obligation*. Smirnov (208); Vasmer (II, 241); Fasmer (III, 103); Kaiser (244); Chernykh (I, 587); Slov. Russ. (III, 17); Slovar' (VII, 210); Smirnitskii (440); Ox. Russ. (422).

observatoriia = observatory, fr. Du./Germ./Lat. *observatorium*/Fr. *observatoire*. Smirnov (208); Vasmer (II, 245); Fasmer (III, 109); Kutina I (95); Bond (76); Chernykh (I, 589); Slov. Russ. (III, 33); Slovar' (VIII, 436); Fadeev (II, 11); Smirnitskii (446).

ob"ekt = object, fr. Lat. *objectus*. H-W. (92); Kutina II (194); Slovar' (VIII, 559–60); Smirnitskii (450). Shanskii-Bob. (209, 251) dates term's appearance in Russ., fr. Pol. *objekt*, to 16th cent.; also suggests arrival of Lat. *objectus* in 18th cent. produced calque *predmet*.

oval = oval, fr. Germ. *Oval*/Fr. *ovale*. Vasmer (II, 248); Fasmer (III, 112); Birzhak. (159); Slov. Akad. (IV, 607); Slov. Russ. (III, 42); Slovar' (VIII, 590–1); Smirnitskii (452).
Derivations: *oval'no, oval'nost', oval'nyi*

ovatsiia = ovation, fr. Germ./Fr. *ovation*/Lat. *ovatio*. Vasmer (II, 248); Fasmer (III, 113); Chernykh (I, 590); Shanskii-Bob. (209); Slovar' (VIII, 591); Smirnitskii (452).

okaziia = occasion, occurrence, opportunity, unexpected event, fr. Pol. *okazya*/Lat. *occasio*/Germ. *Okasion*. Christ. (18); Smirnov (210); Preob. (I, 642); Vasmer (II, 259); Fasmer (III, 127); H-W. (92); Barkh-Bog. (XII, 316 [1683]); Grib. (58); Chernykh (I, 593); Shanskii-Bob. (211); Slovar' (VIII, 766); Smirnitskii (457).

okulist = oculist, fr. Germ. *Okulist*/Fr. *oculiste*. Vasmer (II, 262); Fasmer (III, 131); H-W. (92); Otten (232); Shanskii -Bob. (212); Slov. Russ. (III, 62); Slovar' (VIII, 831); Smirnitskii (460). Barkh-Bog. (XII, 352) cites precedent of 1645.

opera = opera, fr. Ital. *opera*/Germ. *Oper/Opera*. Smirnov (211); Preob. (I, 653); Vasmer (II, 271); Fasmer (III, 144); Bond (76); Grib. (59); Chernykh (I, 599); Shanskii-Bob. (213); Wade (142); Slov. Russ. (III, 68); Slovar' (VIII, 889–90); Smirnitskii (462).
Derivation: *opernyi*

operatsiia = operation (mil. and med., later also in other senses), fr. Lat. *operatio*/Du. *operatie*/Pol. *operacja*/Germ. *Operation*. Smirnov (211); Preob. (I, 653); Vasmer (II, 271); Fasmer (III, 144); Chernykh (I, 600); Shanskii-Bob. (213); Slov. Russ. (III, 68); Slovar' (VIII, 892–3); Fadeev (II, 23); Plekhov (186–7); Smirnitskii (462).
Derivation: *operatsionnyi*

optika = optics, fr. Germ. *Optik(a)*/Lat. *optica*. Smirnov (212, 375); Vasmer (II, 273); Fasmer (III, 147); H-W. (93); Kutina II (196); Shanskii-Bob. (214); Slov. Akad. (IV, 637); Slov. Russ. (III, 75); Slovar' (VIII, 971–2); Plekhov (188); Smirnitskii (465).

oranzhereia = orangerie, greenhouse, conservatory, fr. Germ./Fr. *orangerie*. Smirnov (212); Preob. (I, 655); Vasmer (II, 274); Fasmer (III, 148); Chernykh (I, 602); Shanskii-Bob. (215); Slov. Russ. (III, 76); Slovar' (VIII, 995); Smirnitskii (466).
Derivations: *oranzhereika* (dim.), *oranzhereinyi*

orator = orator, fr. Pol./Germ./Lat. *orator*. Smirnov (212); Preob. (I, 655); Vasmer (II, 274); Fasmer (III, 148); Chernykh (I, 602); Shanskii-Bob. (215); Slov. Akad. (IV, 638); Slov. Russ. (III, 77); Slovar' (VIII, 995–6); Smirnitskii (466). Barkh-Bog. (XIII, 62) cites term in two 17th-cent. mss.
Derivations: *oratorskii, oratorstvovat'*

oratoriia = oratorio (mus.), fr. Ital. *oratorio*. H-W. (93); Slov. Russ. (III, 77); Slovar' (VIII, 996); Smirnitskii (466).

original = original, fr. Pol. *oryginał*/Lat. *originalis*/Germ. *Original*. Smirnov (213); Vasmer (II, 277); Fasmer (III, 152); Chernykh (I, 604); Shanskii-Bob. (216); Slovar' (VIII, 1022–3); Smirnitskii (467); Ox. Russ. (454).
Derivations: *original'no, original'nost', original'nyi*

oriental'nyi = oriental, eastern, fr. Pol. *orientalny*/Fr. *oriental*. Christ. (54); Vasmer (II, 277); Fasmer (III, 152); Chernykh (I, 604–5); Slovar' (VIII, 1025); Smirnitskii (467).
Derivation: *orientalist* (cf. Fr. *orientaliste*)

ornament = ornament, fr. Pol./Germ. *Ornament*/Fr. *ornement*/Lat. *ornamentum*. Smirnov (214); Vasmer (II, 278); Fasmer (III, 153); Bond (76); Chernykh (I, 605); Shanskii-Bob. (216); Slovar' (VIII, 1034); Smirnitskii (467).
Derivations: *ornamental'nyi* (cf. Pol. *ornamentalny*/Germ. *ornamental*/Fr. *ornemental*), *ornamentirovat'* (cf. Germ. *ornamentieren*)

paliastr/piliastra/piliastr = pilaster (arch.), fr. Pol. *pilaster*/Ukr. *piliastra*/Ital. *pilastro*/Fr. *pilastre*. Vasmer (II, 357); Fasmer (III, 262); Slav. Russ. (III, 219); Slovar' (IX, 1195); Smirnitskii (524); OxRuss. (517).

panel' = panel, pavement, fr. Germ. *Panel*/Du. *paneel*/Fr. *pannel*/Eng. *panel*. Preob. (II, 11); Vasmer (II, 309); Fasmer (III, 197); Bond (76–7); Shanskii-Bob. (223 [19th cent.!]); Slov. Akad. (IV, 710–11 *[paneli]*); Slov. Russ. (III, 158); Slovar' (IX, 103–4); Smirnitskii (496).
Derivation: *panel'nyi*

paragraf = paragraph, fr. Germ. *Paragraph*/Fr. *paragraphe*. Smirnov (217, 375); Vasmer (II, 313); Fasmer (III, 203); Kaiser (179); Bond (98); Chernykh (II, 4); Shanskii-Bob. (224); Slov. Akad. (IV, 713); Slov. Russ. (I, 159); Slovar' (IX, 152–3); Smirnitskii (496).

paralizh/paralich = paralysis, palsy, fr. Pol. *paraliż*/Germ. *Paralis/Paralyse*. Smirnov (217); Preob. (II, 16); Vasmer (II, 314); Fasmer (III, 204); Barkh-Bog. (XIV, 151 [1679]); Chernykh (II, 5); Shanskii-Bob. (224); Slov. Akad. (IV, 714); Slov. Russ. (III, 159); Slovar' (IX, 168–9); Smirnitskii (497). Vasmer/Fasmer cites precedent of 1659.
Derivations: *paralizovat', paralichnyi*

parallel/parallel' = parallel, fr. Eng. *parallel*/Germ. *Parallele*/Fr. *parallèle*. Smirnov (218, 375); Vasmer (II, 314); Fasmer (III, 204); Kutina I (54); Ryan (93); Chernykh (II, 5); Shanskii-Bob. (224); Slov. Akad. (IV, 714); Slov. Russ. (III, 159); Slovar' (IX, 171–2); Fadeev (II, 48); Plekhov (199); Smirnitskii (497).
Derivation: *parallel'no, parallel'nyi, parallel'nost'*

parallelogramm = parallelogram, fr. Germ. *Parallelogramm*/Eng. *parallelogram*. Smirnov (218); Vasmer (II, 314); Fasmer (III, 204); Kutina I (44); Bond (77); Ryan (93); Slovar' (IX, 170–1); Smirnitskii (497).

park = park, large formal garden, also artillery park, later also yard, fr. Fr. *parc*/Germ. *Park*, replacing earlier *parka/perka* (Barkh-Bog., XIV, 154, 307–8). Preob. (II, 18); Vasmer (II, 317); Fasmer (III, 207); Chernykh (II, 6); Shanskii-Bob. (224); Slov. Russ. (III, 160); Slovar' (IX, 195–7); Plekhov (200); Smirnistkii (498).
Derivation: *parkovyi*

partikuliarnyi = private, unofficial, civil, fr. Pol. *partykularny*/Germ. *partikular*. Christ. (52); Vasmer (III, 318); Fasmer (III, 209); Grib. (63); Slovar' (IX, 231); Ox. Russ. (491 [obs.])

pashkvil'/paskvil' = lampoon, libel, pasquinade, fr. Pol. *paszkwil*/Germ. *Pasquill*. Smirnov (220); Vasmer (II, 320); Fasmer (III, 211–12); Kaiser (227); Chernykh (II, 9–10); Slov. Russ. (III, 161); Slovar' (IX, 254–5); Smirnitskii (499).
Derivations: *paskviliant* (= lampoonist), *paskvil'nyi*

pedestal/p'edestal = pedestal, fr. Germ. *Piedestal*/Fr. *piédestal*. Smirnov (250); Vasmer (II, 476); Fasmer (III, 422); Birzhak. (148); Chernykh (II, 89); Slov. Russ. (III, 584); Slovar' (XI, 1807); Smirnitskii (642).

pension/pensiia = pension, fr. Germ./Fr. *pension;* also *pansioner/pensioner* = pensioner, holder of pension (academic grant, stipend, etc.), fr. Germ. *Pensionär*/Fr. *pensionnaire*. Smirnov (223); Vasmer (II, 310, 334); Fasmer (III, 232); H-W. (94); Kaiser (244); Bond (146); Chernykh (II, 19); Shanskii-Bob. (229); Slov. Akad. (IV, 760); Slov. Russ. (III, 166); Slovar' (IX, 379–80); Smirnitskii (502).

pergament = parchment, fr. Germ. *Pergament,* replacing earlier *pargamin* fr. Pol. *pargamen* (cf. Leeming, 87–8). Christ. (51); Smirnov (223); Preob. (II, 39); Vasmer (II, 337); Fasmer (III, 235); Bond (143); Otten (470–1); Chernykh (I, 20); Shanskii-Bob. (229); Slov. Russ. (III, 169); Slovar' (IX, 415–6); Smirnitskii (503). D'iachenko (I, 415) lists as Slav., no date.

periferiia = periphery, fr. Germ./Fr. *périphérie*/Eng. *periphery*/Pol. *periferja*/Lat. *peripheria*. Vasmer (II, 342); Fasmer (III, 241); Kutina I (66); Chernykh (II, 22); Shanskii-Bob. (230); Slov. Russ. (III, 213); Slovar' (IX, 1035); Smirnitskii (521).
Derivations: *periferiinyi, pericheskii*

perpendikuliar = perpendicular, fr. Germ./Eng. *perpendicular*/Lat. *perpendicularis*. Smirnov (224, 376); Vasmer (II, 343); Fasmer (III, 243); Kutina I (52–3); Ryan (93); Chernykh (II, 23–4); Shanskii-Bob. (231); Slov. Akad. (IV, 773); Slov. Russ. (III, 214); Slovar' (IX, 1047); Smirnitskii (521).
Derivations: *perpendikuliarno, perpendikuliarnost', perpendikuliarnyi*

personal'nyi = personal, fr. Pol. *personalny*. Smirnov (224); Vasmer (II, 343); Fasmer (III, 244); Kaiser (85); Barkh-Bog. (XIV, 311 [1699]); Slovar' (IX, 1054–5); Smirnitskii (522). *Persona* (various spellings) = person, fr. Pol./Lat. *persona*, had entered Russ. earlier (Fasmer,

III, 244; Barkh-Bog., XIV, 310; Leeming, 88), though often to mean "portrait"; latter term fixed in Petrine period (see *portret* below).

piramid/piramida = pyramid, fr. Eng. *pyramid*/Germ./Fr. *pyramide*. Preob. (II, 60); Vasmer (II, 359); Fasmer (III, 264–5); Kutina I (43, 44); Chernykh (II, 34); Shanskii-Bob. (234); Slov. Akad. (IV, 816); Slov. Russ. (III, 219); Slovar' (IX, 1204–7); Smirnitskii (525). Barkh-Bog.(XV, 47) and Leeming (89) cite possible precedents.

Derivations: *piramidal'nyi* (cf. Eng. *piramidal*/Fr. *pyramidal*), *piramidka* (dim.)

457

plan = plan (arch.), later in various other senses, fr. Germ./Du./Fr./Eng. *plan*. Christ. (45); Smirnov (227); Preob. (II, 67); Vasmer (II, 365); Fasmer (III, 273); Shanskii-Bob. (235); Slov. Akad. (IV, 862); Slov. Russ. (III, 224–5); Slovar' (IX, 1303–7); Fadeev (II, 72); Plekhov (207); Smirnitskii (527).

Derivations: *planër, planirovat', planovyi*

plintus = plinth (arch.), fr. Lat. *plinthus*. Vasmer (II, 372); Fasmer (III, 282); Slov. Akad. (IV, 895–6); Slov. Russ. (III, 228); Slovar' (IX, 1403); Smirnitskii (530).

Derivations: *plintusnyi, plintusovyi*

polirovat' = to polish, fr. Germ. *polie(e)ren*/Lat. *polire*/Fr. *polir*. Smirnov (230); Preob. (II, 93); Vasmer (II, 393); Fasmer (III, 309); Birzhak. (144–5); Bond (77); Chernykh (II, 52); Shanskii-Bob. (243); Slov. Russ. (III, 313); Slovar' (X, 993); Smirnitskii (557).

Derivations: *poliroval'nyi, polirovka, polirovshchik*

poluostrov = peninsula, calque of Germ. *Halbinsel*. Kutina I (157); Slov. Russ. (III, 321); Slovar' (X, 1104); Fadeev (II, 99); Smirnitskii (561).

pomp/pumpa/pompa = pump, fr. Du. *pomp*/Eng. *pump*/Germ./Fr. *pompe,* perhaps via Pol. *pompa*. Christ. (22); Smirnov (232); Vasmer (II, 403); Fasmer (III, 323); H-W. (98); Grib. (75); Leeming (90); Whittall (72–3); Otten (350–55); Shanskii-Bob. (246); Slov. Akad. (IV, 1178); Slov. Russ. (III, 329); Slovar' (X, 1207); Fadeev (II, 102–3); Smirnitskii (564).

ponton = pontoon, fr. Germ./Du./Fr. *ponton*. Smirnov (232); Preob. (II, 104); Vasmer (II, 405); Fasmer (III, 325–6); Chernykh (II, 56); Slov. Akad. (IV, 995); Slov. Russ. (III, 340); Slovar' (X, 1249); Fadeev (II, 103); Plekhov (219); Smirnitskii (566).

Derivations: *pontonër, pontonnyi*

portret = portrait, fr. Du./Germ. *Porträt*. Christ. (45); Smirnov (233); Preob. (II, 110); Vasmer (II, 412); Fasmer (III, 335); Chernykh (II, 59); Shanskii-Bob. (247); Slov. Akad. (IV, 1001); Slov. Russ. (III, 375); Slovar' (X, 1406–7); Smirnitskii (570).

Derivations: *portretist* (cf. Fr. *portraitiste*), *portretnyi*

poeta/poet = poet, fr. Lat. *poeta*/Fr. *poète*/Germ. *Poet*. Preob. (II, 119); Vasmer (II, 422); Fasmer (III, 350); Grib. (66); Leeming (90 [1679]); Chernykh (II, 64); Slov. Akad. (IV, 1023); Slov. Russ. (III, 417); Slovar' (X, 1765); Smirnitskii (581).

printsip = principle, fr. Germ. *Prinzip*/Fr. *principe,* perhaps via Pol. *pryncyp*. Smirnov (241);

Vasmer (II, 433); Fasmer (III, 365); Bond (133); Otten (176–9); Chernykh (II, 67); Shanskii-Bob. (254); Slovar' (XI, 638–9); Smirnitskii (605).

458

proba = test, trial, sample, experiment, later also standard, hallmark, fr. Pol. *proba*/Germ. *Probe*/Lat. *proba*. Christ. (41); Smirnov (376); Preob. (II, 128); Vasmer (II, 437); Fasmer (III, 370); H-W. (99); Kaiser (156); Kutina II (56); Bond (77); Barkh-Bog. (XX, 94 [1700]); Grib. (73); Chernykh (II, 68); Shanskii-Bob. (256); Wade (174); Slov. Akad. (IV, 1085); Slov. Russ. (III, 513–4); Slovar' (XI, 908–9); Smirnitskii (614); Ox. Russ. (622).
Derivations: *probirka* (= test tube), *probirovat'* (cf. Germ. *probieren*), *probirnyi*

problema = problem, fr. Germ. *Problem(a)*/Pol./Lat. *problema*. Smirnov (242, 377); Vasmer (II, 437); Fasmer (III, 371); Kutina I (76); Ryan (93); Chernykh (II, 68); Slov. Akad. (IV, 1086 [*problemma*]); Slov. Russ. (III, 515); Slovar' (XI, 929); Smirnitskii (614).
Derivation: *problematicheskii, problemnyi*

progres/progress = progress, fr. Pol. *progres*/Germ. *Progress*. Christ. (23); Smirnov (244); Vasmer (II, 438); Fasmer (III, 372); Bond (134); Chernykh (II, 69); Shanskii-Bob. (256); Slovar' (XI, 1010–11); Smirnitskii (617).

proekt = project, design, scheme, draft, fr. Germ. *Projekt*. Christ. (20); Smirnov (244); Preob. (II, 129); Vasmer (II, 439); Fasmer (III, 373); Kaiser (179); Bond (134); Chernykh (II, 70); Shanskii-Bob. (256); Slov. Russ. (III, 526); Slovar' (XI, 1065); Smirnitskii (619).
Derivations: *proektnyi, proektirovat'*

proportsiia = proportion, fr. Pol. *proporcja*/Lat. *proportio*/Germ. *Proportion*/Eng. *proportion*. Christ. (18); Smirnov (245); Vasmer (II, 441–2); Fasmer (III, 376); Kaiser (259); Kutina I (25–6); Barkh-Bog. (XX, 198 [1699]); Ryan (93); Slov. Akad. (IV, 1089); Slov. Russ. (III, 547–8); Slovar' (XI, 1293–4); Smirnitskii (626). Barkh-Bog. (XIX, 27) also cites *preportsiia* in doc. of 1681.
Derivations: *proportsional'no, proportsional'nyi, proportsional'nost'*

professor = professor, fr. Du./Germ. *Professor*/Lat. *professor*. Smirnov (247); Preob. (II, 136); Vasmer (II, 447); Fasmer (III, 384); Kaiser (159); H-W. (100); Bond (78); Barkh-Bog. (XX, 273 [1699]); Chernykh (II, 75); Shanskii-Bob. (259); Slov. Akad. (IV, 1100–01); Slov. Russ. (III, 566); Slovar' (XI, 1501–2); Smirnitskii (634).
Derivations: *professorskii, professorstvo, professorsha* (= wife of)

profil' = profile, fr. Du. *profiel*/Germ./Fr. *profil*. Smirnov (247); Vasmer (II, 447–8); Fasmer (III, 384); Birzhak. (160); Bond (78); Chernykh (II, 75); Slov. Akad. (IV, 1101); Slov. Russ. (III, 566); Slovar' (XI, 1505); Plekhov (235); Smirnitskii (634).
Derivation: *profil'nyi*

pul's = pulse, fr. Germ. *Puls*/Fr. *pouls*. Vasmer (II, 463); Fasmer (III, 405); Chernykh (II, 82); Shanskii-Bob. (261); Slov. Akad. (IV, 1178); Slov. Russ. (III, 577); Slovar' (XI, 1677); Smirnitskii (639).
Derivations: *pul'sirovat', pul'sometr*

punsovyi/puntsovyi = crimson, bright red, fr. Pol. *ponsowy*/Fr. *ponceau.* Smirnov (749); Preob. (II, 152); Vasmer (II, 464); Fasmer (III, 406); Chernykh (II, 83); Shanskii-Bob. (261); Slov. Akad. (IV, 1178); Slov. Russ. (III, 578); Slovar' (XI, 1687–8); Smirnitskii (639).

p'esa = play (theater), piece (mus.), fr. Germ. *Piece*/Fr. *pièce.* Vasmer (II, 476); Fasmer (III, 422); H-W. (101); Chernykh (II, 89); Slovar' (XI, 1808); Smirnitskii (643).

459

radius = radius, fr. Germ./Du./Lat. *radius.* Smirnov (251); Preob. (II, 172); Vasmer (II, 482); Fasmer (III, 430); Kutina I (64); Kutina II (181); Bond (78); Ryan (93); Chernykh (II, 94–5); Shanskii-Bob. (264); Slov. Russ. (IV, 4); Slovar' (XII, 74–5); Plekhov (246); Smirnitskii (647).

raketa = rocket, fr. Germ. *Rakete*/Du. *raket.* Christ. (50); Preob. (II, 178); Vasmer (II, 488); Fasmer (III, 438); Otten (233–5); Shanskii-Bob. (266); Slov. Akad. (V, 67); Slov. Russ. (IV, 39); Slovar' (XII, 565–6); Fadeev (II, 163); Plekhov (250); Smirnitskii (663). Barkh-Bog. (XXI, 265) and Chernykh (II, 97) cite precedents of 1673, 1680.
Derivations: *raketka* (dim.), *raketnyi*

reguliar/reguliarnyi = regular, fr. Germ. *regulär*/Pol. *regularny*/Lat. *regularis.* Christ. (53); Smirnov (256); Vasmer (II, 503); Fasmer (III, 458); Chernykh (II, 106); Shanskii-Bob. (270); Slov. Russ. (IV, 61); Slovar' (XII, 1113–14); Smirnitskii (679).
Derivations: *reguliarno, reguliarnost'* (cf. Pol. *regularność*)

reestr = list, register, index, roll, fr. Pol. *rejestr.* Christ. (28); Smirnov (257); Vasmer (II, 504); Fasmer (III, 460); Slov. Akad. (V, 112); Slov. Russ. (IV, 61); Slovar' (XII, 1132); Smirnitskii (679).

rezon = reason, cause, fr. Fr. *raison.* Smirnov (258); Vasmer (II, 506); Fasmer (III, 463); H-W. (101); Grib. (77); Slovar' (XII, 1163–4); Smirnitskii (680).
Derivation: *rezonnyi, rezonër* (= reasoner, arguer, philosophizer, moralizer), *rezonërstvovat'* (= to argue, reason, philosophize, moralize)

religiia = religion, fr. Pol. *religija*/Lat. *religio*/Germ. *Religion.* Christ. (17); Preob. (II, 195); Vasmer (II, 509); Fasmer (III, 466); Birzhak. (166–7); Chernykh (II, 109); Shanskii-Bob. (271); Slov. Russ. (IV, 62); Slovar' (XII, 1199); Smirnitskii (681). Leeming (94) cites precedent of 1666; D'iachenko (I, 547) lists as Slav. fr. Lat. *religio,* no date.
Derivations: *religioznyi, religiozno, religioznost'*

reputatsiia = reputation, fr. Pol. *reputacja*/Lat. *reputatio*/Du. *reputatie*/Germ. *Reputation*/Fr. *réputation.* Smirnov (262); Vasmer (II, 514); Fasmer (III, 473); Chernykh (II, 112); Slovar' (XII, 1240–1); Smirnitskii (682).

retsept = prescription (med.), fr. Germ. *Rezept*/Pol. *recepta*/Lat. *receptum.* Smirnov (265); Preob. (II, 199); Vasmer (II, 518); Fasmer (III, 477); Barkh-Bog. (XXII, 150 [1691]); Otten (355); Shanskii-Bob. (272); Slov. Akad. (V, 118); Slov. Russ. (IV, 63); Slovar' (XII, 1272–3); Smirnitskii (683). Chernykh (II, 114) cites precedent of 1672; Leeming (94) lists *retsepta,* 1677.

retsidiv = relapse, fr. Germ. *Rezidiv*/Lat. *recidivus*. Smirnov (265); Vasmer (II, 518); Fasmer (III, 478); Bond (134); Shanskii-Bob. (272); Slov. Russ. (IV, 65); Slovar' (XII, 1274–5); Smirnitskii (683).
Derivations: *retsidivizm, retsidivist*

460

risunok/risovat' = drawing/to draw, f. Pol. *rysunek/rysować*. Christ. (45); Smirnov (265); Preob. (II, 204); Vasmer (II, 524); Fasmer (III, 486); Chernykh (II, 116); Wade (185); Slov. Akad. (V, 145–7); Slov. Russ. (IV, 65); Slovar' (XII, 1325–8, 1331–33); Smirnitskii (684).

rombus/romb = rhomb(us) (math.), fr. Germ./Lat. *rhombus*/Fr. *rhombe*/Eng. *rhomb*. Smirnov (266); Vasmer (II, 534); Fasmer (III, 500); Kutina I (44); Bond (79); Shanskii-Bob. (275); Slov. Akad. (V, 159); Slov. Russ. (IV, 71); Slovar' (XII, 1454–5); Smirnitskii (687).

salamandra = salamander, fr. Lat. *salamandra*/Fr. *salamandre*. Smirnov (268); Preob. (II, 246); Vasmer (II, 571); Fasmer (III, 549); Chernykh (II, 136); Slov. Russ. (IV, 37); Slovar' (XIII, 60–1); Smirnitskii (694). Barkh-Bog. (XXIII, 23) lists precedent of 1670.

sekans = secant (math.), fr. Lat. *secans*. Slov. Russ. (IV, 116); Slovar' (XIII, 578); Smirnitskii (707).

sektor = sector (math.), fr. Lat. *sector*/Germ. *Sektor*/Eng. *sector*. Vasmer (II, 604); Fasmer (III, 593); Slov. Russ. (IV, 116); Slovar' (XIII, 590–1); Smirnitskii (708). Term gradually acquired broader meaning.

sekunda = second, fr. Pol. *sekunda*/Germ. *Sekunde*/Lat. *secunda/us*. Preob. (II, 271); Vasmer (II, 604); Fasmer (III, 593); Kutina I (70–2); Chernykh (II, 151); Shanskii-Bob. (285); Slov. Russ. (IV, 116); Slovar' (XIII, 592–3); Fadeev (II, 205); Smirnitskii (708). Cf. *minuta* above.

sekundant = second (as in a duel), fr. Germ. *Sekundant*. Smirnov (273); Vasmer (II, 604); Fasmer (III, 594); H-W. (105); Kaiser (228); Bond (143); Shanskii-Bog. (285); Slov. Russ. (IV, 116); Slovar' (XIII, 593–4); Smirnitskii (708).

seminarist = seminarist, fr. Germ. *Seminarist*/Pol. *seminarysta;* also *seminarium/seminariia* = seminary, fr. Germ. *Seminarium*/Pol. *seminarjum*. Smirnov (274); Preob. (II, 274); Vasmer (II, 608); Fasmer (III, 599); Kaiser (159); Bond (79); Shanskii-Bob. (285); Slov. Russ. (IV, 118); Slovar' (XIII, 629); Smirnitskii (709).

sinus = sine (math.), fr. Lat./Germ. *sinus*. Smirnov (276); Vasmer (II, 627); Fasmer (III, 625); Ryan (93); Shanskii-Bob. (289); Slov. Russ. (IV, 126); Slovar' (XIII, 839); Smirnitskii (714).

sistema = system, fr. Germ. *System*/Fr. *système*/Lat. *systema*. Smirnov (276); Vasmer (II, 629); Fasmer (III, 628); H-W. (106); Bond (134); Shanskii-Bob. (289); Slov. Russ. (IV, 127); Slovar' (XIII, 854–5); Fadeev (II, 214–20); Plekhov (268–70); Smirnitskii (715).
Derivations: *sistematicheskii, sistemnyi,*

situatsiia = situation, fr. Pol. *sytuacja*/Lat. *situatio*/Fr. *situation*. Christ. (23); Smirnov (277);

Vasmer (II, 629); Fasmer (III, 629); Chernykh (II, 165); Shanskii-Bob. (289); Slov. Russ. (IV, 127); Slovar' (XIII, 862); Smirnitskii (715).
Derivations: *situativnyi, situatsionnyi*

skul'ptor = sculptor, fr. Pol. *skulptor*/Lat. *sculptor;* also *skul'ptura* = sculpture, fr. Pol. *skulptora*/Lat. *sculptura.* Slov. Russ. (IV, 142); Slovar' (XIII, 1090–2); Smirnitskii (720).
Derivations: *skul'ptorskii, skul'pturnyi, skul'ptorsha* (= wife of)

461

slesar' = fitter, metal worker, fr. Germ. *Schlosser,* perhaps via Pol. *ślosarz/ślusarz.* Smirnov (278); Preob. (II, 321); Vasmer (II, 660); Fasmer (III, 670); Bond (79); Chernykh (II, 175); Wade (201); Shanskii-Bob. (293); Slov. Akad. (V, 528); Slov. Russ. (IV, 146); Slovar' (XIII, 1203); Smirnitskii (723).
Derivations: *slesarskii, slesarstvo*

sliuz/shliuz = sluice, lock, fr. Du *sluis*/Germ. *Schleuse.* Smirnov (330); Vasmer (II, 668; III, 412?); Fasmer (III, 681; IV, 455); Otten (492–6); Chernykh (II, 417–18); Slov. Akad. (V, 586–7); Slov. Russ. (IV, 459); Slovar' (XVII, 1477–8); Fadeev (II, 394); Plekhov (324); Smirnitskii (885).
Derivations: *shliuzovanie, shliuzovat', shliuzovoi*

spirt = spirits, alcohol, fr. Eng. *spirit*/Lat. *spiritus.* Smirnov (281); Preob. (II, 365); Vasmer (II, 708); Fasmer (III, 735); Otten (361–3); Shanskii-Bob. (300); Slov. Russ. (IV, 200); Slovar' (XIV, 520); Smirnitskii (749). Chernykh (II, 194) cites precedent of 1663.
Derivation: *spirtovyi*

stal' = steel, fr. Pol./*stal*/Du. *staal*/Germ. *Stahl.* Smirnov (281); Preob. (II, 371); Vasmer (III, 2); Fasmer (III, 744); Chernykh (II, 197–8); Shanskii-Bob. (302); Wade (208); Slov. Akad. (V, 700); Slov. Russ. (IV, 218); Slovar' (XIV, 713–4); Smirnitskii (756).
Derivation: *stal'noi*

statuia = statue, fr. Pol./Lat./Ital. *statua.* Christ. (46); Preob. (II, 374); Vasmer (III, 5); Fasmer (III, 747–8); Bond (80); Chernykh (II, 199); Slov. Akad. (V, 710); Slov. Russ. (IV, 222); Slovar' (XIV, 791–2); Smirnitskii (757).

student = student, fr. Pol./Germ. *Student.* Smirnov (283); Vasmer (III, 34); Fasmer (III, 787); H-F. (108); Shanskii (306); Kaiser (159); Bond (80); Chernykh (II, 213–14); Slov. Russ. (IV, 241); Slovar' (XIV, 1095–6); Smirnitskii (766). Before 18th cent. ref. only foreign (Polish) students: cf. Kot. (394), Chernykh (II, 213).
Derivations: *studentka* (= female), *studentskii/studencheskii, studentstvo/studenchestvo*

summa = sum (math.), fr. Germ. *Summe*/Du./Lat. *summa.* Vasmer (III, 45); Fasmer (III, 802); Kaiser (253); Kutina I (22–3); Ryan (94); Chernykh (II, 218); Slov. Akad. (V, 966–7); Slov. Russ. (IV, 249); Slovar' (XIV, 1194–5); Smirnitskii (769).

sfera = sphere, fr. Pol. *sfera*/Germ. *Sphära*/Lat. *sphaera.* Vasmer (III, 54); Fasmer (III, 802); Kutina I (47, 92); Chernykh (II, 220); Slov. Akad. (V, 1001); Slov. Russ. (IV, 253); Slovar' (XIV, 1257–9); Fadeev (II, 274); Smirnitskii (770).
Derivation: *sfericheskii*

sferoid = spheroid (math.), fr. Eng. *spheroid*/Germ. *Sphäroid*. Slov. Russ. (IV, 253); Slovar' (XIV, 1259); Smirnitskii (770)
Derivation: *sferoidal'nyi* (cf. Eng. *spheroidal*)

462

tabel'/tablitsa = table, list, fr. Lat. *tab(u)la*/Du. *tabel*/Pol. *tabela/tablica*/Ukr. *tablitsa*. Christ. (50); Smirnov (286–7, 389); Vasmer (III, 65); Fasmer (IV, 6); H-W. (109); Kaiser (184); Leeming (102); Otten (500–02); Shanskii-Bob. (311); Slov. Akad. (VI, 3–4); Slov. Russ. (IV, 266); Slovar' (XV, 11–14); Plekhov (287–8); Smirnitskii (774).
Derivations: *tablichka* (dim.), *tabel'nyi, tablichnyi*

tangens = tangent (math.), fr. Lat. *tangens*. Slov. Russ. (IV, 270); Slovar' (XV, 95); Smirnitskii (777).
Derivation: *tangentsial'nyi*

tants/tanets = dance, fr. Germ. *Tanz*/Pol. *taniec*. Christ. (50); Vasmer (III, 75); Fasmer (IV, 18–19); Chernykh (II, 227–8); Slov. Akad. (VI, 25); Slov. Russ. (IV, 270); Slovar' (XV, 96–7); Smirnitskii (777). Before Peter term used only ref. foreign dancing (cf. Kot., 390).
Derivation: *tantsevat'* (cf. Pol. *tańcować*)

tantsmeister = dancing master, fr. Germ. *Tanzmeister*. Smirnov (287); Vasmer (III, 76); Fasmer (IV, 19); Bond (80); Slov. Akad. (VI, 25); Slov. Russ. (IV, 270); Slovar' (XV, 105); Smirnitskii (777).

teatr = theater, fr. Fr. *théâtre*/Germ. *Theater*. Smirnov (288); Vasmer (III, 87); Fasmer (IV, 34); Grib. (88); Chernykh (II, 231–2); Shanskii-Bob. (314); Slov. Akad. (VI, 73, 1065); Slov. Russ. (IV, 274); Slovar' (XV, 180–2); Smirnitskii (779).
Derivations: *teatral'nyi* (cf. Fr. *théâtral*/Germ. *theatralisch*)

tema = subject, topic, theme, fr. Germ./Lat. *thema*. Smirnov (288); Vasmer (III, 91); Bond (134); Chernykh (II, 234); Shanskii-Bob. (315); Slov. Russ. (IV, 275); Slovar' (XV, 237–9); Smirnitskii (780).

tenor = tenor (mus.), a tenor, fr. Pol./Germ./Du./Fr./Eng. *tenor*/Ital. *tenore*. Smirnov (289); Vasmer (III, 93); Fasmer (IV, 42); Chernykh (II, 235–6); Shanskii-Bob. (315); Slov. Russ. (IV, 276); Slovar' (XV, 278); Smirnitskii (781).
Derivations: *tenornyi, tenorovyi*

teoriia = theory, fr. Germ./Du. *theorie*/Pol. *teorja*/Lat. *theoria*. Smirnov (289); Vasmer (III, 94); Fasmer (IV, 43); H-W. (110); Kutina II (66–9); Bond (134–5); Chernykh (II, 236); Shanskii-Bob. (315); Slov. Russ. (IV, 276); Slovar' (XV, 294–6); Smirnitskii (782).
Derivation: *teoreticheskii* (cf. Germ. *theoretisch*).

tipografiia = printing house/press, fr. Pol./Lat. *typographia*. Smirnov (290); Vasmer (III, 106); Fasmer (IV, 60); H-W. (111); Bond (80); Leeming (103); Chernykh (II, 244); Slov. Akad. (VI, 121); Slov. Russ. (IV, 280–1); Slovar' (XV, 452); Smirnitskii (786).
Derivations: *tipograficheskii, tipografskii*

tiran = tyrant, fr. Pol. *tyran*/Germ. *Tyrann*. Vasmer (III, 107); Fasmer (IV, 60); Kaiser (102);

Slov. Akad. (VI, 122 *[tirann]*); Slov. Russ. (IV, 281); Slovar' (XV, 458–9); Smirnitskii (786). Leeming (103) cites precedent of 1670.
Derivations: *tiranit', tiranskii, tiranicheskii*

ton = tone, fr. Pol./Germ./Fr. *ton*. Smirnov (291); Vasmer (III, 119); Fasmer (IV, 76); Bond (143); Leeming (104 [1679]); Shanskii-Bob. (319); Slov. Russ. (IV, 287); Slovar' (XV, 602–7); Smirnitskii (790).

463

torf = peat, fr. Du. *turf*/Germ. *Torf*. Christ. (50); Smirnov (292); Vasmer (III, 127); Fasmer (IV, 87); Bond (80); Chernykh (II, 253); Shanskii-Bob. (320); Slov. Akad. (VI, 211); Slov. Russ. (IV, 290); Slovar' (XV, 697); Smirnitskii (793).

tragediia = tragedy, fr. Pol. *tragedja*/Lat. *tragoedia*/Germ. *Tragödie*. Vasmer (III, 121); Fasmer (IV, 92); Chernykh (II, 256); Slov. Akad. (VI, 235–6); Slov. Russ. (IV, 292); Slovar' (XV, 785–7); Smirnitskii (795). Leeming (104) lists doubtful 16th-cent. precedent.
Derivations: *tragicheskii, tragichno*

trakt = high road, highway, fr. Pol./Germ. *Trakt*. Christ. (43); Smirnov (294); Vasmer (III, 131); Fasmer (IV, 93); Chernykh (II, 256); Shanskii-Bob. (321); Slov. Russ. (IV, 292); Slovar' (XV, 794–5); Smirnitskii (796).

transport = transport, fr. Germ./Du./Eng./Fr. *transport*. Smirnov (294, 379); Vasmer (III, 132); Fasmer (IV, 94); Otten (503–7); Chernykh (II, 257); Shanskii-Bob. (321); Slov. Russ. (IV, 292–3); Slovar' (XV, 816–8); Fadeev (II, 306); Plekhov (301); Smirnitskii (796–7).
Derivations: *transportirovat', transportirovka, transportnyi*

traur = mourning (dress), fr. Germ. *Trauer*. Smirnov (294); Vasmer (III, 133); Fasmer (IV, 95); Birzhak. (149–50); Bond (135); Chernykh (II, 259); Slov. Akad. (VI, 238); Slov. Russ. (IV, 293); Slovar' (XV, 840–1); Smirnitskii (797).
Derivation: *traurnyi*

trigonometriia = trigonometry, fr. Germ. *Trigonometrie*/Lat. *trigonometria*. H-W. (112); Otten (507–8); Shanskii-Bob. (323); Slov. Akad. (VI, 267); Slov. Russ. (IV, 298); Slovar' (XV, 959); Smirnitskii (801).
Derivation: *trigonometricheskii*

tropikus/tropik = tropic, fr. Lat. *tropicus*/Eng. *tropic*. Vasmer (III, 141); Fasmer (IV, 105); Kutina (129–30); Chernykh (II, 264); Shanskii-Bob. (324–5); Slov. Akad. (VI, 272–3); Slov. Russ. (IV, 300); Slovar' (XV, 1005); Fadeev (II, 309); Smirnitskii (802).
Derivation: *tropicheskii*

tul'pan/tiul'pan = tulip, fr. Du. *tulband*/Germ./Fr. *tulipan*. Vasmer (III, 164); Fasmer (IV, 136); Chernykh (II, 277); Shanskii-Bob. (329); Slov. Akad. (VI, 322); Slov. Russ. (IV, 309–10); Slovar' (XV, 1216); Smirnitskii (808).
Derivations: *tiul'pannyi, tiul'panchik* (dim.)

universal'nyi = universal, fr. Pol. *uniwersalny*/Lat. *unversalis*. Smirnov (299); Vasmer (III,

184); Fasmer (IV, 162); Kaiser (180–1); Chernykh (II, 290); Shanskii-Bob. (334); Slovar' (XVI, 653–4); Smirnitskii (826).
Derivation: *universal'no, universal'nost'*

464

universitet = university, fr. Germ. *Universität*. Smirnov (299); Vasmer (III, 184); Fasmer (IV, 162); Kaiser (158); Bond (80); Chernykh (II, 290); Shanskii-Bob. (334); Slov. Akad. (VI, 446–7); Slov. Russ. (IV, 348); Slovar' (XVI, 654–5); Smirnitskii (826).
Derivation: *universitetskii*

fabula = fable, story, plot, fr. Lat. *fabula*. Smirnov (301); Vasmer (III, 199); Fasmer (IV, 182); Slovar' (XVI, 1199–1200); Smirnitskii (842).

fakul'tet = faculty, fr. Du. *faculteit*/Germ. *Fakultät*. Christ. (52); Smirnov (302); Vasmer (III, 200); Fasmer (IV, 183); Kaiser (158); Bond (81); Chernykh (II, 301); Shanskii-Bob. (339); Slov. Akad. (VI, 481); Slov. Russ. (IV, 384); Slovar' (XVI, 1219–20); Smirnitskii (842).
Derivation: *fakul'tetskii*

fal'ts = rabbet, groove, fold, fr. Germ. *Falz*. Vasmer (III, 200); Fasmer (IV, 184); Bond (81); Slov. Russ. (IV, 384); Slovar' (XVI, 1226); Smirnitskii (842).
Derivations: *faltseval'nyi, fal'tsevat', fal'tsovka* (= a folding)

fantasia/fantaziia = fantasy, fancy, fr. Pol. *fantazyja*/Gr./Lat. *phantasia*. Smirnov (304); Vasmer (III, 201); Fasmer (IV, 185); Leeming (52–3); Chernykh (II, 302); Shanskii-Bob. (340); Slov. Russ. (IV, 384); Slovar' (XVI, 1245–8); Smirnitskii (843).

fasad = façade, fr. Germ. *Fassade*/Fr. *façade*. Vasmer (III, 203); Fasmer (IV, 187); H-W. (114); Chernykh (II, 304); Shanskii-Bob. (340); Slov. Russ. (IV, 385); Slovar' (XVI, 1271); Smirnitskii (843).
Derivations: *fasadik/fasadishko* (dims.), *fasadnyi*

feierverk = fireworks, fr. Germ. *Feuerwerk*. Christ. (50); Smirnov (305, 380); Vasmer (III, 204); Fasmer (IV, 188); Bond (81); Grib. (94 *[feiverk]*); Otten (262–5); Chernykh (II, 306); Shanskii-Bob. (341); Slov. Akad. (VI, 482); Slov. Russ. (IV, 386); Slovar' (XVI, 1294–5); Smirnitskii (844).

fenomen = phenomenon, fr. Lat. *phaenomenon*. Kutina II (46–9); Birzhak. (152); Slovar' (XVI, 1308–9); Smirnitskii (844).

fekhtmeister = fencing instructor, fr. Germ. *Fechtmeister*. Smirnov (307); Vasmer (III, 206); Fasmer (IV, 191); Bond (81); Slov. Russ. (IV, 386–7); Slovar' (XVII, 1329 [obs.]); Smirnitskii (844).
Derivations: *fekhtoval'nyi, fekhtoval'shchik, fekhtovanie, fekhtovat'* (cf. Pol. *fechtować*)

fisika/fizika = physics, fr. Pol. *fizyka*/Lat. *physica*. Smirnov (307–8); Vasmer (III, 207); Fasmer (IV, 193); Kutina II (20–9); Chernykh (II, 310); Shanskii-Bob. (342); Slov. Akad. (VI, 485–6); Slov. Russ. (IV, 387); Slovar' (XVI, 1352–3); Smirnitskii (845).
Derivations: *fizik* (cf. Pol. *fizyk* = physicist), *fizicheskii*

fleit/fleita = flute (music), fr. Germ. *Flöte*/Du. *fluit*. Christ.(46); Vasmer (III, 212); Fasmer

(IV, 199); H-W. (115); Gard. (65); Otten (51–2); Chernykh (II, 316); Slov. Akad. (VI, 492–3); Slov. Russ. (IV, 389); Slovar' (XVI, 1436); Smirnitskii (847).

fligel' = wing (of building), fr. Germ. *Flügel*/Du. *vleugel*. Vasmer (III, 212); Fasmer (IV, 199); Bond (81); Chernykh (II, 317); Shanskii-Bob. (344); Slov. Akad. (VI, 493); Slov. Russ. (IV, 389); Slovar' (XVI, 1441); Smirnitskii (847).

465

flius = dental abcess, gumboil, flux, fr. Germ. *Fluss*. Christ. (46); Vasmer (III, 213); Fasmer (IV, 200); Bond (82); Chernykh (II, 318); Shanskii-Bob. (344); Slov. Russ. (IV, 389); Slovar' (XVI, 1453); Smirnitskii (847); Ox. Russ. (863).

fokus = focus, fr. Germ. *Fokus*/Lat. *focus*. Smirnov (311); Vasmer (III, 214); Fasmer (IV, 201); Kutina II (195–6); Chernykh (II, 319); Shanskii-Bob. (344); Slov. Russ. (IV, 390); Slovar' (XVI, 1458–9); Smirnitskii (847).
Derivation: *fokusnyi*

fol'ga = foil, fr. Pol. *folga*/Germ. *Folie*/Lat. *folia*. Vasmer (III, 214); Fasmer (IV, 201); Chernykh (II, 319); Shanskii-Bob. (344–5); Slov. Akad. (VI, 494); Slov. Russ. (IV, 390); Slovar' (XVI, 1464–5); Smirnitskii (847).
Derivations: *fol'govshchik* (= maker of), *fol'govyi*

fontana/fontan = fountain, fr. Ital. *fontana*/Germ. *Fontäne*, perhaps via Pol. *fontana*. Smirnov (311); Vasmer (III, 215); Fasmer (IV, 202); Leeming (54); Grib. (95); Chernykh (II, 321); Shanskii-Bob. (345); Slov. Akad. (VI, 495); Slov. Russ. (IV, 390); Slovar' (XVI, 1474–5); Smirnitskii (848).
Derivations: *fontannyi, fontanirovat'* (= to gush, spring forth), *fontanchik* (dim.), *fontanshchik* (= maker or keeper of)

forma = form, model, also mold, later also uniform (dress), fr. Pol./Lat. *forma*. Smirnov (312); Vasmer (III, 215); Fasmer (IV, 203); Kaiser (220); Kutina II (77–80); Chernykh (II, 321–2); Shanskii-Bob. (345); Slov. Akad. (VI, 495); Slov. Russ. (IV, 391); Slovar' (XVI, 1480–9); Fadeev (II, 359–60); Plekhov (314); Smirnitskii (848).
Derivations: *formennyi, formirovat', formovat'* (cf. Pol. *formovać*)

fronton = pediment (arch.), fr. Fr. *fronton*/Ital. *frontone*. Vasmer (III, 219); Fasmer (IV, 208); H-W. (116); Slov. Russ. (IV, 394); Slovar' (XVI, 1576–7); Smirnitskii (850).
Derivations: *frontonnyi, frontonchik* (dim.)

fundament = foundation, fr. Ukr./Pol./Germ. *Fundament*. Christ. (21); Smirnov (317); Vasmer (III, 220); Fasmer (IV, 210); H-W. (116); Chernykh (II, 326); Shanskii-Bob. (347); Slov. Akad. (VI, 496); Slov. Russ. (IV, 394); Slovar' (XVI, 1588–9); Smirnitskii (851). Leeming (55) cites precedent of 1679.

fundamental'nyi = fundamental, fr. Pol. *fundamentalny*/Lat. *fundamentalis*. Christ. (52); Smirnov (317); Vasmer (III, 221); Fasmer (IV, 210); Otten (56–7); Slov. Russ. (IV, 394); Slovar' (XVI, 1589); Smirnitskii (851).
Derivation: *fundamental'nost'* (= fundamentality, solidity)

kharakter = character (various, including rank or status, honor), fr. Pol./Germ. *Charakter*/

Lat. *character.* Smirnov (319, 386); Vasmer (III, 230); Fasmer (IV, 223); Kaiser (166); Chernykh (II, 333); Shanskii (349); Slov. Russ. (IV, 396); Slovar' (XVII, 35–40); Fadeev (II, 367–8); Smirnitskii (852). Leeming (46) cites precedent of 1670.

khimiia = chemistry, fr. Pol. *chimja*/Germ. *Chymie/Chemie;* also *khimik* = chemist, fr. Pol. *chimik.* Smirnov (319); Vasmer (III, 241); Fasmer (IV, 237); H-W. (117); Chernykh (II, 339); Shanskii-Bob. (350); Slov. Akad. (VI, 532–3); Slov. Russ. (IV, 400); Slovar' (XVII, 132–4); Smirnitskii (853).
Derivation: *khimicheskii*

khirurg = surgeon, fr. Germ. *Chirurg*/Lat. *chirurgus;* also *khirurgiia* = surgery, fr. Germ. *Chirurgie*/Lat. *chirurgia,* replacing earlier *khirogra* fr. Pol. *chiragra/chirogra* (Leeming, 46). H-W. (117); Chernykh (II, 340); Shanskii-Bob. (350); Slov. Akad. (VI, 534); Slov. Russ. (IV, 400); Slovar' (XVII, 138); Smirnitskii (853).
Derivation: *khirurgicheskii*

khronologiia = chronology, fr. Pol./Lat. *chronologia*/Germ. *Chronologie.* Vasmer (III, 273); Fasmer (IV, 278); H-W. (117); Slov. Akad. (VI, 596); Slov. Russ. (IV, 413); Slovar' (XVII, 490); Smirnitskii (860).
Derivation: *khronologicheskii*

tsement = cement, fr. Du. *cement*/Germ. *Zement.* Smirnov (321); Vasmer (III, 288); Fasmer (IV, 298); Chernykh (II, 365); Shanskii-Bob. (357); Slov. Russ. (IV, 418); Slovar' (XVII, 616–7); Fadeev (II, 373); Smirnitskii (863).
Derivations: *tsementirovat', tsementnyi*

tsilinder/tsilindr = cylinder, fr. Germ. *Zylinder.* Smirnov (322); Vasmer (III, 292); Fasmer (IV, 302); Kutina I (44, 50); Bond (82); Ryan (94); Shanskii-Bob. (358); Slov. Akad. (VI, 627); Slov. Russ. (IV, 419); Slovar' (XVII, 690); Fadeev (II, 376); Smirnitskii (865).
Derivation: *tsilindricheskii*

tsimbaly = cymbals, fr. Pol. *cymbały*/Germ. *Zymbal.* Smirnov (322); Koch. I (104); Leeming (47 *[tsinbal]*); Bond (93); Shanskii-Bob. (358); Slov. Russ. (IV, 421 *[tsymbaly]*); Slovar' (XVII, 691–2); Smirnitskii (865).

tsink = zink, fr. Germ. *Zink.* Preob. (suppl., 47–8); Vasmer (III, 292); Fasmer (IV, 302); Bond (82); Slov. Akad. (VI, 627); Slov. Russ. (IV, 420); Slovar' (XVII, 695); Smirnitskii (865).
Derivation: *tsinkovyi*

tsokol' = socle (arch.), fr. Germ. *Sockel.* Smirnov (323); Preob. (suppl., 48); Vasmer (III, 292); Fasmer (IV, 304); Slov. Akad. (VI, 628); Slov. Russ. (IV, 420); Slovar' (XVII, 717–18); Smirnitskii (865).

tsyrkul'/tsirkul' = (drawing) compass/es, pair of, fr. Pol. *cyrkiel*/Germ. *Zirkel.* Smirnov (322, 381); Preob. (suppl., 48); Vasmer (III, 292); Fasmer (IV, 302); Gard. (226–7); Kutina I (43–6); Koch. II (49); Otten (43–5); Ryan (94); Chernykh (II, 371); Shanskii-Bob. (359);

Wade (241); Slov. Akad. (VI, 628); Slov. Russ. (IV, 420); Slovar' (XVII, 700–1); Fadeev (II, 377); Smirnitskii (865).

tsyfir'/tsifir'/tsifra = figure/s, numeral/s (Arabic), cipher, counting, fr. Du. *cijfer*/Germ. *Ziffer*/Pol. *cyfra*/Lat./Ital. *cifra*. Vasmer (III, 296); Fasmer (IV, 303); Kutina I (14, 18–21); Gard. (228–31); Leeming (47); Bond (82–3); Otten (418–21); Chernykh (II, 272); Shanskii-Bob. (359); Slov. Akad. (VI, 632); Slov. Russ. (IV, 421); Slovar' (XVII, 713–4); Smirnitskii (865).
Derivations: *tsifirnyi, tsifrovoi, tsifrovat'*

shakhta = mine, mine shaft, pit, fr. Pol. *szacht(a)*/Germ. *Schacht*. Smirnov (326); Preob. (suppl., 92); Vasmer (III, 381); Fasmer (IV, 416); Bond (83); Chernykh (II, 406); Shanskii-Bob. (371); Slov. Russ. (IV, 450); Slovar' (XVII, 1306–7); Smirnitskii (880).
Derivations: *shakhtër* (= miner), *shakhtnyi*

shifer = slate, fr. Germ. *Schiefer*. Vasmer (III, 462); Fasmer (IV, 444); Bond (83); Shanskii-Bob. (374); Slov. Akad. (VI, 890); Slov. Russ. (IV, 457); Slovar' (XVII, 1427); Smirnitskii (883).
Derivation: *shifernyi*.

shikhta = layer, bed (of ore), charge (furnace), fr. Germ. *Schicht*. Bond (83); Slov. Russ. (IV, 457); Slovar' (XVII, 1431); Smirnitskii (884).

shlagbaum = turnpike, barrier, fr. Germ. *Schlagbaum*. Smirnov (331); Vasmer (III, 409); Fasmer (IV, 452); Kaiser (192); Bond (83–4); Shanskii-Bob. (375); Slov. Russ. (IV, 458); Slovar' (XVII, 1461); Smirnitskii (884).

shlak = slag, dross, fr. Germ. *Schlacke*. Smirnov (330); Vasmer (III, 409); Fasmer (IV, 452); Bond (84); Chernykh (II, 417); Shanskii-Bob. (375); Slov. Akad. (VI, 894); Slov. Russ. (IV, 459); Slovar' (XVII, 1461–2); Smirnitskii (884).
Derivation: *shlakovat'*

shlikh = ore sludge, fr. Germ. *Schlich*. Vasmer (III, 411); Fasmer (IV, 455); Bond (84); Slov. Russ. (IV, 459); Slovar' (XVII, 1475–6).
Derivation: *shlikhovyi*

shlikhta = size, type of glue, fr. Germ. *Schlichte*. Vasmer (III, 411); Fasmer (IV, 455); Bond (84); Slov. Russ. (IV, 459); Slovar' (XVII, 1476); Smirnitskii (885).
Derivation: *shlikhtovat'*

shpaler/shpalera = tapestry, also/later espalier, trellis, fr. Germ. *Spalier*/Ital. *spaliera*, probably via Pol. *szpaler/szpalera*. Christ. (47); Smirnov (332, 381); Preob. (suppl., 104); Vasmer (III, 423); Fasmer (IV, 470); H-W. (119); Gard. (247–8); Otten (373–5); Slov. Akad. (VI, 669–70 [*shpalery*]); Slov. Russ. (IV, 461 [*shpalery*]); Slovar' (XVII, 1518–9); Smirnitskii (885–6).
Derivation: *shpalernyi*

shpits = point, peak, spire, steeple, fr. Du. *spits*/Germ. *Spitze*. Smirnov (333); Vasmer (III,

426); Fasmer (IV, 474); Bond (85); Chernykh (II, 423); Slov. Akad. (VI, 915); Slov. Russ. (IV, 462); Slovar' (XVII, 1533, obs.); Smirnitskii (886); Ox. Russ. (899 [obs.]).

shprits = syringe, fr. Germ. *Spritze*. Smirnov (334); Preob. (suppl., 106); Vasmer (III, 427); Fasmer (IV, 475); Bond (85); Slov. Russ. (IV, 462); Slovar' (XVII, 1537–8); Smirnitskii (886).
Derivations: *shpritseval'nyi, shpritsevanie, shpritsevat'*

468

shpunt = groove, tongue, rabbet, fr. Pol. *szpunt*/Germ. *Spund*. Preob. (suppl., 106); Vasmer (III, 427); Fasmer (IV, 475); Bond (85); Slov. Russ. (IV, 462); Slovar' (XVII, 1539); Fadeev (II, 398); Smirnitskii (886).
Derivations: *shpuntovat'* (cf. Pol. *szpuntować*), *shpuntoval'nyi*

shpur = bore-hole, blast-hole, fr. Germ. *Spur (Bohrspur)*. Bond (85); Slov. Russ. (IV, 462); Slovar' (XVII, 1541); Smirnitskii (886).
Derivation: *shpurovyi*

shrift = print, type, typeface, script, fr. Germ. *Schrift*. Vasmer (III, 428); Fasmer (IV, 476); Bond (85); Shanskii-Bob. (377); Slov. Russ. (IV, 462); Slovar' (XVII, 1543–4); Smirnitskii (887).

shtanga = (metal) bar, rod, beam, fr. Germ. *Stange*. Vasmer (III, 429); Fasmer (IV, 477); Bond (86); Shanskii-Bob. (378); Slov. Russ. (IV, 463); Slovar' (XVII, 1553); Smirnitskii (886).

shtempel' = stamp, fr. Germ. *Stempel*. Smirnov (336, 382); Vasmer (III, 430); Fasmer (IV, 478); Kaiser (156); Bond (86, 100); Shanskii-Bob. (378); Slov. Akad. (VI, 916); Slov. Russ. (IV, 463); Slovar' (XVII, 1561–2); Smirnitskii (887).
Derivations: *shtempelit', shtempel'nyi, shtempelevat'*

shtil'/stil' = style, fr. Germ. *Stil*/Fr. *style*. Christ. (22, 44); Smirnov (282); Preob. (II, 386); Vasmer (III, 15); Fasmer (IV, 478); Bond (134); Grib. (100); Slov. Akad. (VI, 916–17); Slov. Russ. (IV, 225); Slovar' (XIV, 876–9); Smirnitskii (760).

shtok = stock, stick, rod, shoot, fr. Germ. *Stock*. Smirnov (337); Bond (86); Slov. Russ. (IV, 463); Slovar' (XVII, 1565); Fadeev (II, 399); Smirnitskii (887).

shtrikh = stroke, dash, line, later also touch, trait, fr. Du. *streek/strijk*/Germ. *Strich*. Smirnov (338); Vasmer (III, 431); Fasmer (IV, 480); Bond (86); Slov. Russ. (IV, 464); Slovar' (XVII, 1577); Smirnitskii (887).
Derivations: *shtrikhovat'* (= to shade, hatch), *shtrikhovka* (= shading, hatching), *shtrikhovoi*

shtukaturit' = to plaster, stucco, fr. Germ. *Stukkatur* (= stucco). Preob. (suppl., 108); Birzhak. (148–9); Chernykh (II, 426); Slov. Akad. (VI, 919–20); Slov. Russ. (IV, 464); Slovar' (XVII, 1583); Smirnitskii (887).
Derivations: *shtukatur* (= plasterer), *shtukatur(k)a* (= plastering), *shtukaturnyi*

shtuf = piece of ore, fr. Germ. *Stufe*. Vasmer (III, 432); Fasmer (IV, 481); Bond (87); Slov. Akad. (VI, 920–1); Slov. Russ. (IV, 464); Slovar' (XVII, 1593); Smirnitskii (887).

shurf = excavation, digging, fr. Germ. *Schurf.* Vasmer (III, 439); Fasmer (IV, 490); Bond (87); Slov. Russ. (IV, 465); Slovar' (XVII, 1617); Smirnitskii (888).
Derivations: *shurfovanie, shurfovat'*

ekvator = equator, fr. Germ. *Äquator*/Lat. *aequator*/Eng. *equator.* Vasmer (III, 458); Fasmer (IV, 515); H-W. (120); Kutina I (119–22); Ryan (92); Chernykh (II, 439); Slov. Russ. (IV, 472); Slovar' (XVII, 1732); Fadeev (II, 404–5); Plekhov (328); Smirnitskii (890).

469

ekzempliar = specimen, copy, fr. Germ./Lat. *exemplar,* perhaps via Pol. *egzemplarz.* Smirnov (344); Vasmer (III, 458); Fasmer (IV, 515); H-W. (120); Kaiser (183); Bond (144); Chernykh (II, 440); Slov. Russ. (IV, 472); Slovar' (XVII, 1741–2). Smirnitskii (891).

eksamen/ekzamen = examination, fr. Pol. *egzamen*/Germ./Lat. *examen.* Smirnov (343); Preob. (suppl., 126); Vasmer (III, 458); Fasmer (IV, 515); Chernykh (II, 349); Slov. Russ. (IV, 472); Slovar' (XVII, 1736–7); Smirnitskii (890–1).
Derivations: *ekzamenator, ekzamenatsionnyi, ekzamenovat'* (cf. Pol. *egzaminować*)

ekspeditsiia = expedition, later also section, department, also dispatch/forwarding, dispatch office, fr. Pol. *ekspedycja*/Du. *expeditie*/Germ. *Expedition.* Smirnov (346); Vasmer (III, 458); Fasmer (IV, 516); Kaiser (182); Chernykh (II, 442); Slov. Russ. (IV, 473); Slovar' (XVII, 1773–5); Smirnitskii (892); Ox. Russ. (904).
Derivation: *ekspeditsionnyi*

eksperiment = experiment, fr. Du./Germ. *Experiment*/Lat. *experimentum,* perhaps via Pol. *eksperyment.* Smirnov (346); Kutina II (51–2); Vasmer (III, 459); Fasmer (IV, 516); Bond (87); Chernykh (II, 442); Slov. Russ. (IV, 473); Slovar' (XVII, 1775); Smirnitskii (892).
Derivations: *eksperimental'nyi* (cf. Pol. *eksperymentalny*/Germ. *experimentall*), *eksperimentirovat'* (cf. Germ. *experimentieren*)

ekstrakt = extract, fr. Pol. *extract*/Du./Germ. *Extrakt.* Christ. (30); Smirnov (347); Vasmer (III, 459); Fasmer (IV, 516); Kaiser (177); Bond (100–1); Grib. (101); Chernykh (II, 444); Slov. Russ. (IV, 473); Slovar' (XVII, 1796–7); Smirnitskii (892). Leeming (60) cites two earlier versions of term.

element = element (physics), fr. Du./Germ. *Element.* Smirnov (349); Vasmer (III, 459–60); Fasmer (IV, 517); Kutina II (108–12); Grib. (101); Chernykh (II, 446); Slov. Russ. (II, 473); Slovar' (XVII, 1836–8); Fadeev (II, 412–3); Smirnitskii (893).
Derivation: *elementnyi*

ellipsis/ellips = ellipsis (math.), fr. Germ./Fr. *ellipse*/Eng. *ellipsis.* Vasmer (III, 460); Fasmer (IV, 517); Kutina I (44, 50); Chernykh (II, 446); Slov. Russ. (IV, 474); Slovar' (XVII, 1844); Smirnitskii (894).
Derivation: *ellipticheskii*

emblema = emblem, fr. Lat. *emblema*/Du. *embleem*/Fr. *emblème.* Smirnov (349); Vasmer

(III, 460); Fasmer (IV, 518); H-W. (121); Chernykh (II, 447); Slov. Russ. (IV, 474); Slovar' (XVII, 1853–4); Plekhov (329–30); Smirnitskii (894).

epokha = epoch, fr. Germ. *Epocha/Epoche*/Lat. *epocha*. Vasmer (III, 462); Fasmer (IV, 520); H-W. (122); Birzhak. (160); Slov. Russ. (IV, 474); Slovar' (XVII, 1904–5); Smirnitskii (895).

470

essentsiia = essence, fr. Lat. *essentia*, perhaps via Pol. *essencyja*/Germ. *Essencia*. Christ. (46); Smirnov (350); Vasmer (III, 463); Fasmer (IV, 521); Leeming (61); Chernykh (II, 452); Slov. Russ. (IV, 474); Slovar' (XVII, 1921–2); Smirnitskii (895). Barkh-Bog. (V, 60) cites doubtful precedent of 1673.

estamp = print, engraving, plate, fr. Fr. *estampe*. Vasmer (III, 463); Fasmer (IV, 522); H-W. (122); Slov. Russ. (IV, 474); Slovar' (XVII, 1922); Smirnitskii (895).

effekt = effect, fr. Germ. *Effekt*. Christ. (23); Vasmer (III, 465); Fasmer (IV, 524); Chernykh (II, 456); Slov. Russ. (IV, 475); Slovar' (XVII, 1959–61); Smirnitskii (896).
Derivations: *effektnyi, effektno*

ekho = echo, fr. Germ. *Echo*. Smirnov (351); Vasmer (III, 465); Fasmer (IV, 524); H-W. (123); Grib. (102); Slov. Russ. (IV, 475); Slovar' (XVII, 1965); Smirnitskii (896).

iubilei = jubilee, anniversary, fr. Germ. *Jubiläum*. Smirnov (351); Preob. (suppl., 127); Vasmer (III, 466); Fasmer (IV, 525); Bond (135); Chernykh (II, 457); Slov. Russ. (IV, 475); Slovar' (XVII, 1969); Smirnitskii (897).
Derivation: *iubileinyi*

Note: A large number of technical terms borrowed during the Petrine era particularly from German were never fully assimilated in Russian: for example, numerous words related to mining and metallurgy, beginning with *bergauer* = miner, fr. Germ. *Berghauer*; *bergverk* = mine, fr. Germ. *Bergwerk*, etc.; or numerous mathematical and scientific terms, starting with the slightly Russified Latin names for the basic arithmetical operations–*additsio, substraktsiia, multiplikatsiia, diviziia*–for which Russian equivalents, however unstable, already existed (cf. Kutina I, 17). Another set of terms incorporated Germ. *Meister* together with various prefixes to produce e.g. *bergmeister* (= mining official: still found in Slov. Akad., I, 122), *bruken-meister* (= master bridge builder), *mintsmeister* (= mint master), etc. Numerous examples of such more or less rapidly obsolete technical loanwords can be found in Smirnov, passim, Kutina I and Kutina II, passim, Otten, passim, and Bond, pp. 87–95. Other Petrine neologisms, more abstract in meaning and Latin or Greek (or Greek via Latin) in origin (but borrowed usually from German–to judge by spelling/pronunciaton–or perhaps German via Polish), persisted in specialized Russian usage long thereafter, and are recognizable even today, though usually as foreign or obsolete terms: e.g., *applikatsiia* = application (cf. Lat. *applicatio*/Fr. *application*); *dedikatsiia* = (book) dedication (Pol. *dedykacya*/Lat. *dedicatio*); *diskurs* = discourse (Germ. *Diskurs*); *irreguliarnyi* = irregular (Germ. *irregulär/irregularisch*/Lat. *irregularis*); *konverzatsiia* (Germ. *Konversation*, Fr./Eng. *conversation*); *observatsiia* = observation (Lat. *observatio*; *pretekst* =

pretext (Germ. *Prätekst*/Lat. *praetextum*); *respekt* = respect (Germ. *Respekt*/Pol. *respekt*/ Lat. *respectus*); *satisfaktsiia* = satisfaction, compensation (Pol. *satisfakcja*); etc.

COMMERCIAL TERMS
(INCLUDING FINANCIAL, INDUSTRIAL, AND RELATED)

aktsion/aktsiia = share, stock, fr. Fr. *action*/Germ./Du. *actie;* also action, esp. mil., fr. Ukr. *aktsiia*/Pol. *akcja*/Lat. *actio.* Smirnov (33); Vasmer (I, 10); Fasmer (I, 67); Shanskii (I, 72); Birzhak. 140–41; Barkh. (I, 42–3); Chernykh (I, 36); Slov. Russ. (I, 5); Slovar' (I, 89–90); Smirnitskii (36).
Derivations: *aktsioner* (= shareholder), *akstionernyi, aktsionnyi*

bank = bank, fr. Germ. *Bank*/Fr. *banque.* Christ. (41); Smirnov (203); Vasmer (II, 207); Fasmer (I, 120); Kaiser (252); Shanskii (II, 33); Barkh. (I, 137); Chernykh (I, 70); Wade (20); Slov. Akad. (I, 94); Slov. Russ. (I, 21); Slovar' (I, 265–7); Smirnitskii (46). Barkh-Bog. (I, 69) cites precedent of 1660.
Derivations: *bankovskii, bankovyi*

banker/bankir = banker, fr. Du./Germ. *Bank(i)er*/Fr. *banquier.* Christ. (41); Smirnov (55); Vasmer (I, 52); Fasmer (I, 121); Kaiser (252); Shanskii (II, 34–5); Barkh. (I, 138); Slov. Akad. (I, 94); Slov. Russ. (I, 21); Slovar' (I, 266); Smirnitskii (46).
Derivations: *bankirskii, bankirstvo*

bankrut/bankrot = bankrupt, fr. Du. *bankroet*/Fr. *banqueroute*/Germ. *bank(e)rott.* Smirnov (55); Vasmer (I, 52); Fasmer (I, 121); H-W. (62); Kaiser (255); Shanskii (II, 35); Barkh. (I, 138); Chernykh (I, 71); Slov. Akad. (I, 95); Slov. Russ. (I, 21); Slovar' (I, 268–9); Smirnitskii (46).
Derivations: *bankrutstvo, bankrotstvo, bankrotit'sia/obankrotit'sia*

birzh/birzha = bourse, (stock) exchange, fr. Du. *beurs*/Pol. *birüá*/Germ. *Börse*/Fr. *bourse.* Christ. (41); Smirnov (60); Preob. (I, 26); Vasmer (I, 86); Fasmer (I, 166); Kaiser (256); Shanskii (II, 122); Barkh. (II, 24); Chernykh (I, 90); Slov. Akad. (I, 169–70); Slov. Russ. (I, 47); Slovar' (I, 457–8); Smirnitskii (59).
Derivations: *birzhevik, birzhevoi*

brak = spoilage, waste, fr. Germ. *Brak/Brack.* Christ. (41); Smirnov (65); Preob. (I, 42); Vasmer (I, 117); Fasmer (I, 206); Kaiser (256); Bond (109–10); Chernykh (I, 108); Wade (25–6); Slov. Akad. (I, 318); Slov. Russ. (I, 79); Slovar' (I, 602–3); Smirnitskii (68).
Derivations: *brakovat', brakovka*

bukhgalter = book-keeper, accountant, fr. Germ. *Buchhalter.* Smirnov (68); Vasmer (I, 156); Fasmer (I, 255); Shanskii (II, 241); Kaiser (146); Bond (96); Barkh. (II, 175); Chernykh (I, 128); Slov. Akad. (I, 394–5); Slov. Russ. (I, 91); Slovar' (I, 711–2); Smirnitskii (75).
Derivations: *bukhgalteriia* (= book-keeping; cf. Germ. *Buchhalterei*), *bukhgalterskii*

valets/val'tsy = roller/roller press, fr. Germ. *Walze.* Bond (70); Slov. Russ. (I, 98); Slovar' (II, 41); Smirnitskii (79).
Derivations: *val'tsovyi, val'tsevat', val'tsovka, val'tsovshchik*

veksel' = bill of exchange, fr. Germ. *Wechsel.* Christ. (40); Smirnov (72, 366); Vasmer (I, 179); Fasmer (I, 287); Shanskii (III, 40); Kaiser (257); Bond (110); Barkh. (III, 8); Otten (508–12); Chernykh (I, 139); Slov. Akad. (I, 583); Slov. Russ. (I, 107); Slovar' (II, 132–3); Smirnitskii (83).
Derivation: *veksel'nyi*

verstat'/verstak = workbench, Germ. *Werkstatt,* perhaps via Pol. *warsztat.* Preob. (I, 76); Vasmer (I, 189); Fasmer (I, 300); Bond (70); Barkh-Bog. (II, 94 [1677]); Chernykh (I, 143–4); Slov. Russ. (I, 112); Slovar' (II, 188–9); Smirnitskii (85); Ox. Russ. (59).

galantereia = fancy goods, haberdashery, toiletries, fr. Du./Germ./Fr. *galanterie.* Christ. (41); Smirnov (78); Preob. (I, 116); Vasmer (I, 252); Fasmer (I, 385); Shanskii (IV, 13); Bond (110); Barkh. (V, 83); Chernykh (I, 177–8); Slov. Russ. (I, 254); Slovar' (III, 21); Smirnitskii (147).
Derivation: *galantereinyi*

gildiia/gil'diia = guild, (mercantile) class, order, fr. Germ. *Gilde,* perhaps via Pol. *giełda.* Smirnov (89); Preob. (I, 123); Vasmer (I, 268); Fasmer (I, 406); Shanskii (IV, 72); Kaiser (135); Bond (112); Grib. (22); Barkh. (V, 113–4); Slov. Akad. (II, 41); Slov. Russ. (I, 261); Slovar' (III, 100); Smirnitskii (151).

debet = debt, debit, fr. Pol./Germ./Lat. *debet.* Shanskii (V, 33–4); Kaiser (253); Barkh. (VI, 63); Slovar' (III, 625); Smirnitskii (177).

domkrat = jack, fr. Du. *dommekracht/dommekragt.* Smirnov (112); Vasmer (I, 362); Fasmer (I, 527); Shanskii (V, 167); Barkh. (VI, 205); Slov. Russ. (I, 349 [also *damkrat*]); Slovar' (III, 965); Fadeev (I, 219); Smirnitskii (196).

inventarium/inventar' = inventory, stock, equipment, fr. Germ. *Inventarium/Inventar.* Smirnov (118); Vasmer (I, 481); Fasmer (II, 130); Shanskii (VII, 67); Bond (112); Chernykh (I, 345–6); Slov. Russ. (II, 132); Slovar' (V, 327); Fadeev (I, 260); Smirnitskii (272).
Derivations: *inventarizatsiia, inventarizirovat', inventarnyi*

kapital = capital, fr. Germ. *Kapital*/Fr. *capital.* Smirnov (132); Vasmer (I, 521–2); Fasmer (II, 185); Kaiser (259); Shanskii (VIII, 53–4); Barkh. (IX, 242–3); Chernykh (I, 375–6); Wade (81); Slov. Akad. (III, 432); Slov. Russ. (II, 160–1); Slovar' (V, 773–4); Smirnitskii (287).
Derivation: *kapital'nyi*

kassa = cashbox, till, later also booking-office/ticket-window, fr. Pol. *kassa*/Germ. *Kasse*/Ital. *cassa.* Smirnov (136); Vasmer (I, 538); Fasmer (II, 207); Shanskii (VIII, 85); Kaiser (173); Barkh. (IX, 269); Chernykh (I, 384–5); Slov. Russ. (II, 165); Slovar' (V, 853); Smirnitskii (290).
Derivation: *kassovyi*

kassirer/kassir = cashier, fr. Germ. *Kassierer/Kassier.* Smirnov (136); Vasmer (I, 538); Fasmer (II, 207); Shanskii (VIII, 86); Kaiser (173); Bond (110); Barkh. (IX, 269–70); Slov. Russ. (II, 165); Slovar' (V, 854); Smirnitskii (290).

Derivations: *kassirovat'* (= to cash in, also to annul, quash), *kassirskii, kassirsha* (= female cashier)

473

kvitantsiia = receipt, fr. Du. *kvitantie.* Smirnov (140); Vasmer (I, 547); Fasmer (II, 219); Shanskii (VIII, 115–6); Kaiser (183); Barkh. (X, 30); Chernykh (I, 392); Wade (86); Slov. Russ. (II, 170); Slovar' (V, 918); Smirnitskii (293).

kommerts/kommertsiia = commerce, fr. Germ. *Kommerz*/Lat. *commercium.* Christ. (42); Smirnov (149); Vasmer (I, 609); Fasmer (II, 303); Shanskii (VIII, 233); Kaiser (251); Barkh. (X, 121); Chernykh (I, 418); Slov. Akad. (III, 762); Slov. Russ. (II, 195); Slovar' (V, 1242); Smirnitskii (304).
Derivation: *kommercheskii*

konosoment/konosament = consignment, bill of lading, fr. Germ. *Konossement.* Smirnov (154); Bond (110); Barkh. (X, 139); Slov. Russ. (II, 198); Slovar' (V, 1305); Fadeev (I, 314); Smirnitskii (306).

kreditiv = letter of credit, fr. Germ. *Kreditiv.* Smirnov (166); Kaiser (98); Grib. (43); Barkh. (X, 248); Slov. Russ. (II, 218); Slovar' (V, 1610).
Derivation: *kreditivnyi*

likvidatsiia = liquidation, fr. Pol. *likwidacja*/Lat. *liquidatio*/Germ. *Liquidation.* Smirnov (178); Vasmer (II, 42); Fasmer (II, 496); Kaiser (253); Barkh. (XI, 176); Slov. Russ. (II, 253); Slovar (VI, 220); Smirnitskii (334).
Derivations: *likvidirovat', likvidnyi*

makler = broker, fr. Germ. *Makler.* Smirnov (185); Preob. (I, 380); Vasmer (II, 90); Fasmer (II, 561); Kaiser (252); Bond (113); Chernykh (I, 504); Shanskii-Bob. (177); Slov. Akad. (IV, 16–17); Slov. Russ. (II, 281); Slovar' (VI, 512); Smirnitskii (343).
Derivations: *maklerskii, maklerstvo*

manufaktura = manufactory, fr. Du./Fr. *manufacture*/Germ. *Manufaktur* and/or Pol. *manufaktura*/Lat. *manufactura.* Smirnov (187, 373); Vasmer (II, 97); Fasmer (II, 570); Kaiser (251); Chernykh (I, 509–10); Shanskii-Bob. (179); Slov. Akad. (IV, 30); Slov. Russ. (II, 286); Slovar' (VI, 614); Smirnitskii (346).

monopoliia = monopoly, fr. Pol. *monopolja*/Germ. *Monopolia.* Vasmer (II, 155); Fasmer (II, 650); Kaiser (255); Shanskii-Bob. (190); Slov. Russ. (II, 322); Slovar' (VI, 1236–7); Smirnitskii (365–6).
Derivations: *monopolizirovat', monopolist, monopolisticheskii*

negotsiant = merchant, fr. Germ. *Negoziant.* Smirnov (203); Vasmer (II, 207); Fasmer (III, 57); Bond (111); Slov. Russ. (II, 430); Slovar' (VII, 787); Ox. Russ. (391 [obs.]).

pakgauz = storehouse, warehouse, fr. Germ. *Packhaus.* Smirnov (216); Vasmer (II, 303);

Fasmer (III, 188); Bond (111); Shanskii-Bob. (221); Slov. Russ. (III, 155); Slovar' (IX, 36–7); Smirnitskii (494).

preiskurant = price list, fr. Du. *prijscourant*/Germ. *Preiskurant*/Fr. *prix courant*. Smirnov (237); Vasmer (II, 428); Fasmer (III, 358); Bond (111–12); Chernykh (II, 65); Slovar' (XI, 216); Smirnitskii (590).

produkt = product, fr. Germ. *Produkt*. Smirnov (244); Vasmer (II, 439); Fasmer (III, 373); Bond (77); Slov. Russ. (III, 526); Slovar' (XI, 1051–2); Smirnitskii (619).

protsent = percentage, rate, fr. Du. *procent*/Germ. *Prozent*. Christ. (42); Smirnov (248); Preob. (II, 137); Vasmer (II, 448); Fasmer (III, 386); Kaiser (253); Bond (112); Chernykh (II, 75); Slov. Akad. (IV, 1101); Slov. Russ. (III, 568); Slovar' (XI, 1531–2); Smirnitskii (635).
Derivation: *protsentnyi*

rynok = market(-place), fr. Ukr. *rynok*/Pol. *rynek*/Germ. *Ring*. Preob. (II, 230); Vasmer (II, 557); Fasmer (III, 530); Chernykh (II, 130); Shanskii-Bob. (278); Wade (189); Slov. Akad. (V, 237); Slov. Russ. (IV, 81); Slovar' (XII, 1626); Smirnitskii (691). Barkh-Bog. (XXII, 276) cites *rinok* in 17th-cent. ms. *alfavit;* and elsewhere (XXII, 164) cites *rinka* in two 16th-cent. docs.
Derivation: *rynochnyi*

taksa = statutory price, tariff, fr. Germ. *Taxe*. Smirnov (287); Vasmer (III, 71); Fasmer (IV, 13); Kaiser (191); Bond (112); Chernykh (II, 225–6); Shanskii-Bob. (312); Slov. Russ. (IV, 269); Slovar' (XV, 64); Smirnitskii (776).
Derivations: *taksatsia, taksatsionnyi, taksirovat'* (= to fix price of; cf. Germ. *taxieren*)

tarif = tariff, fr. Germ./Fr. *tarif*. Smirnov (228); Vasmer (III, 79); Fasmer (IV, 24); Kaiser (191); Slov. Akad. (VI, 28); Slov. Russ. (IV, 271); Slovar' (XV, 125–6); Smirnitskii (777).
Derivation: *tarifnyi*

traktir = tavern, fr. Pol. *traktyer*. Smirnov (293); Vasmer (III, 131); Fasmer (IV, 93); Chernykh (II, 256); Shanskii-Bob. (321); Slov. Akad. (VI, 236); Slov. Russ. (IV, 292); Slovar' (XV, 796); Smirnitskii (796).
Derivations: *traktirnyi, traktirchik* (dim.), *traktirshchik* (= tavern-keeper)

fabrika = factory, mill, fr. Pol. *fabryka*/Ital. *fabricca*/Lat. *fabrica*. Christ. (45); Smirnov (301); Vasmer (III, 199); Fasmer (IV, 181); Kaiser (253); Leeming (52); Chernykh (II, 298–9); Shanskii-Bob. (339); Wade (231); Slov. Akad. (VI, 479); Slov. Russ. (IV, 383); Slovar' (XVI, 1192–3); Smirnitskii (841).
Derivations: *fabrikovat'* (cf. Pol. *fabrykować*), *fabrichnyi*

fabrikant = factory owner, manufacturer, fr. Germ. *Fabrikant*/Fr. *fabricant*. Smirnov (301); Vasmer (III, 199); Fasmer (IV, 181); Kaiser (253); Birzhak. (143–4); Bond (80); Slov. Akad. (VI, 479); Slov. Russ. (IV, 383); Slovar' (XVI, 1193–4); Smirnitskii (841).
Derivation: *fabrikantskii*

faktor = factor, agent, trader, fr. Pol./Germ. *Faktor*. Smirnov (301); Vasmer (III, 199); Fasmer (IV, 183); Kaiser (253); Leeming (52 [1667; cf Kot., 727, 387]); Chernykh (II, 301);

Shanskii-Bob. (339); Slov. Russ. (IV, 384); Slovar' (XVI, 1216 [obs.]). Leeming (52) cites use of term by Kotoshikhin, 1667 (cf. Kot., 727, 387).

faktura = invoice, bill, fr. Germ. *Faktur/a.* Smirnov (301); Vasmer (III, 199–200); Fasmer (IV, 183); Kaiser (253); Bond (80–1); Slov. Russ. (IV, 384); Slovar' (XVI, 1218); Fadeev (II, 347); Smirnitskii (842).

475

frakht = freight, fr. Du. *vracht*/Germ. *Fracht.* Smirnov (316); Vasmer (III, 218); Fasmer (IV, 206); Kaiser (255); Slov. Russ. (IV, 393); Slovar' (XVI, 1557–8); Fadeev (II, 363); Smirnitskii (850).
Derivation: *frakhtovat'*

shteiger = mine foreman, fr. Germ. *Steiger.* Smirnov (336); Vasmer (III, 429); Fasmer (IV, 478); Bond (86); Slov. Russ. (IV, 463); Slovar' (XVII, 1560–1 [obs.]); Smirnitskii (887); Ox. Russ. (899).

OTHER TERMS
(GASTRONOMICAL, CULINARY, SARTORIAL, DOMESTIC,
PERSONAL, QUOTIDIAN)

abrikos = apricot, fr. Du. *abrikoos.* Preob. (I, 2); Vasmer (I, 2); Fasmer (I, 57); Shanskii (I, 18); Barkh. (I, 10); Chernykh (I, 22); Wade (15); Slov. Akad. (I, 41 *[aprikos]*); Slov. Russ. (I, 1–2); Slovar' (I, 17); Smirnitskii (25).
Derivations: *abrikosnyi, abrikosovyi*

azart = chance, excitement, ardor, fervor, fr. Du. *hazard*/Germ./Fr. *hasard.* Christ. (23); Smirnov (78, 366 *[gazard]*); Preob. (I, 3); Vasmer (I, 6); Fasmer (I, 63); H-W. (55); Shanskii (I, 53); Barkh. (I, 33–30–1); Chernykh (I, 30); Slov. Russ. (I, 4); Slovar' (I, 62–3); Smirnitskii (34–5).
Derivation: *azartnyi* (= fortuitous, reckless, excitable, venturesome)

ambitsiia = ambition, fr. Pol. *ambicja*/Lat. *ambitio.* Christ. (23); Smirnov (36); Vasmer (I, 16); Fasmer (I, 75); H-W. (57); Shanskii (I, 90); Barkh. (I, 58); Chernykh (I, 41); Slovar' (I, 113); Smirnitskii (37).
Derivation: *ambitsioznyi*

ambrosiia/ambroziia = ambrosia, fr. Germ. *Ambrosia*/Lat. *ambrosia.* H-W. (57); Shanskii (I, 90); Grib. (7 *[amvroziia]*); Barkh. (I, 58); Slov. Russ. (I, 8); Slovar' (I, 114); Smirnitskii (37). D'iachenko (I, 14; II, 873) lists Slav. *amvrosia* fr. Gr., no date.

antipatiia = antipathy, aversion, fr. Pol. *antipatja*/Germ. *Antipathie.* Christ. (18); Vasmer (I, 19); Fasmer (I, 79); Shanskii (I, 115–6); Barkh. (I, 74); Slov. Akad. (I, 37); Slov. Russ. (I, 10); Slovar' (I, 151); Smirnitskii (39).

anchoves/anchous = anchovy, fr. Du. *ansjovis*/Germ. *Anschovis.* Smirnov (40); Preob. (I, 7);

Vasmer (I, 20); Fasmer (I, 80); H-W. (58); Barkh. (I, 76–7); Slov. Akad. (I, 38); Slov. Russ. (I, 10); Slovar' (I, 160); Smirnitskii (39).

apartament = apartment, fr. Pol. *apartament*/Germ. *Appartement*/Fr. *apartement*. Christ. (47); Shanskii (I, 123); Barkh. (I, 77); Slovar' (I, 161); Smirnitskii (39).

apel'sin = orange, orange tree, fr. Du. *appelsien*. Preob. (I, 7); Vasmer (I, 20); Fasmer (I, 80); Shanskii (I, 125); Barkh. (I, 78); Chernykh (I, 47–8); Wade (16–17); Slov. Akad. (I, 38); Slov. Russ. (I, 10); Slovar' (I, 163); Smirnitskii (39).
Derivation: *apel'sinovyi*

apetit/appetit = appetite, fr. Pol. *apetyt*/Germ. *Appetit*/Fr. *appétit*. Christ. (22); Smirnov (41); Vasmer (I, 20); Fasmer (I, 81); Shanskii (I, 131); Barkh. (I, 82); Chernykh (I, 49); Slov. Russ. (I, 10); Slovar' (I, 170); Smirnitskii (40).
Derivation: *ap(p)etitno, ap(p)etitnyi*

artishok = artichoke, fr. Du. *artisjok*/Germ. *Artischoke*/Eng. *artichoke*. Vasmer (I, 26); Fasmer (I, 89); Shanskii (I, 150); Barkh. (I, 98); Slov. Akad. (I, 50); Slov. Russ. (I, 13); Slovar' (I, 195); Smirnitskii (42).

bagazh = luggage, baggage, fr. Germ./Du./Fr. *bagage*. Christ. (43); Smirnov (52, 365); Vasmer (I, 36); Fasmer (I, 101); Shanskii (II, 6); Barkh. (I, 124–5); Chernykh (I, 63); Slov. Russ. (I, 17); Slovar' (I, 236–7); Fadeev (I, 49); Smirnitskii (44).
Derivation: *bagazhnyi*

bant = ribbon, band, bow, fr. Pol. *bant*/Germ. *Band*. Christ. (49); Smirnov (55); Vasmer (I, 52); Fasmer (I, 121); Bond (129); Wade (20); Slov. Akad. (I, 95); Slov. Russ. (I, 21); Slovar' (I, 269); Smirnitskii (46).
Derivation: *bantik* (dim.)

bariera/bar'er = barrier, bar, hurdle, fr. Pol. *barjera*/Fr. *barrière*/Germ. *Barriere*. Smirnov (56); Vasmer (I, 58); Fasmer (I, 129); Shanskii (II, 50–51); Slov. Russ. (I, 23); Slovar' (I, 289); Smirnitskii (47).

baul = portmanteau, trunk, fr. Ital. *baule*. Smirnov (58); Preob. (I, 20); Vasmer (I, 63); Fasmer (I, 135–6); Shanskii (II, 59); Barkh. (I, 152); Chernykh (I, 79); Slov. Akad. (I, 111); Slov. Russ. (I, 25); Slovar' (I, 298); Smirnitskii (48).
Derivations: *baulnik* (= maker of), *baulnyi*

biliard/bil'iard = billiards, fr. Germ./Fr. *billiard*, perhaps via Pol. *biljard*. Smirnov (60); Vasmer (I, 86); Fasmer (I, 165); Shanskii (II, 119); Grib. (12 *[biliary]*); Barkh. (II, 23); Chernykh (I, 89–90); Slov. Akad. (I, 169); Slov. Russ. (I, 46, 47); Slovar' (I, 452–3); Smirnitskii (59).
Derivation: *bil'iardnyi*

biskvit = biscuit, sponge-cake, fr. Germ. *Biskuit*/Fr. *biscuit*. Vasmer (I, 88); Fasmer (I, 168);

Shanskii (II, 124–5); Barkh. (II, 25); Chernykh (I, 91); Slov. Russ. (I, 47); Slovar' (I, 460–1); Smirnitskii (60).

Derivation: *biskvitnyi*

bulion/bul'on = broth, clear soup, fr. Fr. *bouillon.* Smirnov (68); Vasmer (I, 143); Fasmer (I, 240); Shanskii (II, 225); Barkh. (II, 163–4); Chernykh (I, 123); Slov. Russ. (I, 88); Slovar' (I, 686); Smirnitskii (74).

477

butylka/butyl' = bottle/large bottle, fr. Pol. *butełka/butel/*Germ. *Buttel.* Christ. (47); Smirnov (68); Vasmer (I, 155); Fasmer (I, 254); Shanskii (II, 238–9); Barkh. (II, 173–4); Wade (28); Slov. Akad. (I, 393–4); Slov. Russ. (I, 91); Slovar' (I, 707–8); Smirnitskii (75).

Derivations: *butylochka* (dim.), *butylochnyi, butyl'nyi*

vafel'/vaflia = wafer, fr. Du. *waf(f)el.* Vasmer (I, 174); Fasmer (I, 280); Shanskii (III, 27); Barkh. (II, 221–2); Chernykh (I, 135); Slov. Russ. (I, 101); Slovar' (II, 63); Smirnitskii (80).

veer = fan, fr. Du. *waaier/*Germ. *Fächer.* Smirnov (77); Vasmer (I, 178); Fasmer (I, 285); Shanskii (III, 36); Barkh. (II, 245); Chernykh (I, 137–8); Wade (31); Slovar' (II, 119–20); Smirnitskii (83).

galstuk/galstukh = (neck)tie, cravat, fr. Du. *halsdoek/*Germ. *Halstuch.* Christ. (49); Smirnov (79, 367); Vasmer (I, 256); Fasmer (I, 389); H-W. (65); Shanskii (IV, 20); Bond (129–30); Barkh-Bog. (IV, 9 [1676]); Barkh. (V, 86); Chernykh (I, 180); Wade (37–8); Slov. Akad. (II, 19); Slov. Russ. (I, 255); Slovar' (III, 27); Smirnitskii (147).

garderob = cloakroom, wardrobe, fr. Germ. *Garderobe/*Fr. *garde-robe.* Vasmer (I, 259); Fasmer (I, 393); Shanskii (IV, 28–9); Barkh. (V, 89); Chernykh (I, 181); Wade (38); Slov. Russ. (I, 255); Slovar' (III, 36–7); Smirnitskii (148).

glazur' = glaze, syrup, fr. Germ. *Glasur.* Christ. (58); Vasmer (I, 272); Fasmer (I, 410); Shanskii (IV, 89–90); Barkh. (V, 125); Slov. Russ. (I, 263); Slovar' (III, 130); Smirnitskii (152).

goroskop = horoscope, fr. Lat. *horoscopus.* Shanskii (IV, 141); Barkh. (V, 179); Slov. Russ. (I, 281); Slovar' (III, 308); Smirnitskii (161).

debosh = debauchery, uproar, riot, fr. Fr. *débauche.* Smirnov (99); Vasmer (I, 333); Fasmer (I, 490); Shanskii (VI, 34–5); Barkh. (VI, 63); Chernykh (I, 234); Slovar' (III, 626); Smirnitskii (177).

Derivations: *deboshir* (= rowdy person, rake; cf. Fr. *débauchée*), *deboshirit'*

delikatnyi = delicate, fr. Pol. *delikatny/*Germ. *delikat/*Fr. *délicat.* Smirnov (101); Vasmer (I, 337); Fasmer (I, 496); Shanskii (V, 60); Barkh. (VI, 85); Chernykh (I, 239); Slovar' (III, 671–2); Smirnitskii (180).

Derivation: *delikatnost'*

defekt = defect, fr. Pol./Germ. *Defekt/*Eng. *defect.* Smirnov (103); Vasmer (I, 348); Fasmer (I, 509); Shanskii (V, 94); Barkh. (VI, 119); Slov. Russ. (I, 322); Slovar' (III, 755); Fadeev (I, 206); Smirnitskii (185).

Derivation: *defektnyi*

duel' = duel, fr. Fr. *duel*/Germ. *Duell*. Vasmer (I, 384); Fasmer (I, 557); H-W. (35, 71); Shanskii (V, 220); Barkh. (VII, 49); Chernykh (I, 276); Slovar' (III, 1196); Smirnitskii (207). Derivation: *duelist* (cf. Fr. *duelliste*)

zal/zala = hall, reception room, fr. Germ. *Saal*/Fr. *salle*/Pol. *sala*. Christ. (48); Smirnov (115); Preob. (I, 241); Vasmer (I, 440); Fasmer (II, 76); Shanskii (VI, 42); Bond (142); Barkh. (VII, 262); Chernykh (I, 315); Slov. Russ. (II, 33, 31); Slovar' (VI, 597–8); Smirnitskii (236).

zont/zontik = umbrella, fr. Du. *zondek/zonnedek*. Smirnov (117); Preob. (I, 256); Vasmer (I, 461); Fasmer (II, 104); Shanskii (VI, 108); Barkh. (VIII, 226–7); Chernykh (I, 329); Slov. Russ. (II, 96); Slovar' (IV, 1329–30); Smirnitskii (260).
Derivations: *zontichek* (dim.), *zontichnyi*

indifferentnyi = indifferent, fr. Pol. *indyferentny*/Fr. *indifférent*. Shanskii (VII, 72); Barkh. (IX, 93); Slovar' (V, 340–1); Smirnitskii (273).
Derivation: *indifferentnost'*

kamzol = camisole, fr. Germ. *Kamisol*/Fr. *camisole*. Christ. (48); Smirnov (129); Preob. (I, 289); Vasmer (I, 514); Fasmer (II, 174); Shanskii (VIII, 38); Grib. (37); Barkh. (IX, 226); Slov. Akad. (III, 419–20); Slov. Russ. (II, 157); Slovar' (V, 733); Ox. Russ. (271).
Derivations: *kamzolets/kamzolik/kamzol'chik* (dims.), *kamzolnyi*

kamin = chimney, flue, fireplace, fr. Germ. *Kamin*. Smirnov (129); Preob. (I, 290); Vasmer (I, 514); Fasmer (II, 174); Shanskii (VIII, 38–9); Bond (72); Slov. Akad. (III, 420); Slov. Russ. (II, 157); Slovar' (V, 733); Smirnitskii (286).

kanareika = canary (bird), fr. Pol. *kanarek*/Lat. *canarica*. Smirnov (130); Preob. (I, 291); Vasmer (I, 516); Fasmer (II, 177–8); Shanskii (VIII, 42); Chernykh (I, 373); Wade (80); Slov. Akad. (III, 424); Slov. Russ. (II, 158); Slovar' (V, 745); Smirnitskii (287).
Derivation: *kanareechnyi*

kapar/kapor = hood, fr. Du. *kaper*. Preob. (I, 294); Vasmer (I, 521); Fasmer (II, 184); Shanskii (VIII, 56–7); Barkh. (IX, 248); Chernykh (I, 376); Slov. Akad. (III, 431); Slov. Russ. (II, 160–1); Slovar' (V, 785–6); Smirnitskii (288). Barkh-Bog. (VII, 66) cites precedent of 1676.

kapriz = whim, caprice, fr. Fr. *caprice*. Vasmer (I, 523); Fasmer (II, 187); Shanskii (VIII, 57–8); Barkh. (IX, 248–9); Chernykh (I, 377); Slov. Russ. (II, 161); Slovar' (V, 788); Smirnitskii (288); Ox. Russ. (273).
Derivations: *kapriznichat'*, *kaprizno*, *kapriznyi*

karp = carp (fish), fr. Pol. *karp*/Fr. *carpe*/Lat. *carpa*. Preob. (I, 300); Vasmer (I, 535); Fasmer (II, 202); Shanskii (VIII, 73–4); Barkh-Bog. (VII, 82); Barkh. (IX, 261); Slov. Akad. (III, 450–1); Slov. Russ. (II, 164); Slovar' (V, 826); Smirnitskii (289).

kastriulia = pan, saucepan, fr. Du. *castrool*/Pol./Germ. *Kastrol*/Fr. *casserole*. Smirnov (137); Vasmer (I, 539); Fasmer (II, 208); Shanskii (VIII, 88); Barkh. (X, 6–7); Chernykh (I, 385); Wade (84); Slov. Akad. (III, 458); Slov. Russ. (II, 165); Slovar' (V, 858–9); Smirnitskii (290).
Derivations: *kastriul'ka* (dim.), *kastriul'nyi*

keglia/i = skittle/s, fr. Germ./Du. *kegel.* Vasmer (I, 548); Fasmer (II, 220); Shanskii (VIII, 117); Barkh. (X, 30); Chernykh (I, 392); Slov. Akad. (III, 503); Slov. (II, 170); Slovar' (V, 919); Smirnitskii (293); Ox. Russ. (278).

konfekta/konfeta/y = candy, sweets, confectionery, fr. Germ. *Konfekte*/Ital. *confetto.* Smirnov (159); Preob. (I, 347); Vasmer (I, 617); Fasmer (II, 315); H-W. (79); Shanskii (VIII, 287–8); Barkh. (X, 150); Chernykh (I, 425); Slov. Russ. (II, 199); Slovar' (V, 1350–1); Smirnitskii (308).

korridor/koridor = corridor, fr. Germ. *Korridor*/Fr. *corridor.* Smirnov (162); Preob. (I, 354); Vasmer (I, 627); Fasmer (II, 328); Shanskii (VIII, 315); Barkh. (X, 172); Slov. Russ. (II, 207); Slovar' (V, 1425–6); Smirnitskii (311).

kotleta/y = cutlet/s, chop/s, fr. Germ. *Kotelette*/Fr. *côtelette.* Vasmer (I, 645); Fasmer (II, 352); Shanskii (VIII, 359); Barkh. (X, 208); Chernykh (I, 435–6); Wade (98); Slov. Russ. (II, 212); Slovar' (V, 1537–8); Smirnitskii (314).
Derivations: *kotletka/kotletochka* (dims.), *kotletnyi*

kofii/kofei/kofe = coffee, fr. Du. *koffie*/Eng. *coffee*/Germ. *Kaffee.* Smirnov (164); Preob. (I, 372); Vasmer (I, 647); Fasmer (II, 355); H-W. (80); Barkh. (X, 210–11); Chernykh (I, 436); Wade (98); Slov. Akad. (III, 282–3); Slov. Russ. (II, 212–3); Slovar' (V, 1543–4); Smirnitskii (314). Shanskii (VIII, 361) and Barkh-Bog. (VII, 387) cite precedent of 1653.

krendel' = knot-shaped biscuit, pretzel, fr. Germ. *Kringel/Krengel,* perhaps via Pol. *kręgiel.* Smirnov (167); Preob. (I, 381); Vasmer (I, 659); Fasmer (II, 371); Shanskii (VIII, 382–3); Bond (139); Barkh. (X, 250); Slov. Akad. (III, 930); Slov. Russ. (II, 219); Slovar' (V, 1617); Smirnitskii (317).
Derivations: *krendelek* (dim.), *krendel'nyi*

krep = crêpe, crape, fr. Germ. *Krepp*/Fr. *crêpe.* Smirnov (167); Vasmer (I, 660); Fasmer (II, 372); Shanskii (VIII, 383); Barkh. (X, 250); Slov. Akad. (III, 930); Slov. Russ. (II, 219); Slovar' (V, 1619); Smirnitskii (317); Ox. Russ. (305).

krochmal/krakhmal = starch, fr. Pol. *krochmal*/Germ. *Kraftmehl.* Smirnov (168); Preob. (I, 380); Vasmer (I, 657–8); Fasmer (II, 369); H-W. (81); Shanskii (VIII, 377); Bond (139–40); Barkh. (X, 246); Chernykh (I, 441); Wade (99); Slov. Akad. (III, 927–9); Slov. Russ. (II, 218); Slovar' (V, 1606); Smirnitskii (317).
Derivations: *krakhmalnyi, krakhmalit'*

kucher = coachman, driver, fr. Germ. *Kutscher.* Smirnov (172); Preob. (I, 424); Vasmer (I, 709); Fasmer (II, 438); Shanskii (VIII, 463); Barkh. (XI, 95); Chernykh (I, 460); Slov. Akad. (III, 1101); Slov. Russ. (II, 240); Slovar' (V, 1910–11); Smirnitskii (326). Barkh-Bog. (VIII, 151) cites term in two 17th-cent. dpl. reports fr. Vienna.
Derivation: *kucherskoi*

laberdan/labardan = a kind of codfish, fr. Du. *labberdaan.* Smirnov (172); Preob. (I, 425); Vasmer (II, 2); Fasmer (II, 443); Barkh. (XI, 98); Chernykh (I, 461); Slov. Russ. (II, 241); Slovar' (VI, 6).

479

lampa = (oil) lamp, fr. Pol. *lampa*/Germ. *Lampe*. Smirnov (173); Preob. (I, 432); Vasmer (II, 11); Fasmer (II, 455); H-W. (82); Barkh. (XI, 112); Chernykh (I, 465); Shanskii-Bob. (163); Wade (104); Slov. Akad. (III, 1137); Slov. Russ. (II, 244); Slovar' (VI, 49); Smirnitskii (328).

latskan = lapel, fr. Germ. *Latz*/*Lätzchen*. Smirnov (175); Vasmer (II, 20); Fasmer (II, 468); Bond (130); Barkh. (XI, 128); Chernykh (I, 470); Shanskii-Bob. (164); Slov. Russ. (II, 246); Slovar' (VI, 84); Smirnitskii (329).

lenta = ribbon, band, tape, fr. Du. *lint*/Germ. *Linte*. Preob. (I, 446–7); Vasmer (II, 31); Fasmer (II, 482); Barkh. (XI, 151); Chernykh (I, 475); Wade (107); Slov. Russ. (II, 250); Slovar' (VI, 157); Smirnitskii (331).
Derivations: *lentochka* (dim.), *lentochnyi*

liker/likër = liqueur, fr. Germ. *Likör*/Fr. *liqueur*. Vasmer (II, 42); Fasmer (II, 496); Barkh. (X, 176); Chernykh (I, 481); Shanskii-Bob. (168); Slov. Russ. (II, 253); Slovar' (VI, 221); Smirnitskii (334).
Derivations: *likërnyi, likërchik* (dim.)

limonad = lemonade, fr. Germ./Du./Fr. *limonade*. Smirnov (179); Vasmer (II, 43); Fasmer (II, 498); Barkh-Bog. (VIII, 235 [1694]); Barkh. (XI, 178); Otten (116–7); Slov. Akad. (III, 1212); Slov. Russ. (II, 254); Slovar' (VI, 226–7); Smirnitskii (334).

lokon = lock, curl, ringlet (of hair), fr. Germ. *Locke/n*. Smirnov (181); Preob. (I, 466); Vasmer (II, 55); Fasmer (II, 514); Bond (130); Barkh. (XI, 222); Chernykh (I, 489); Shanskii-Bob. (170); Wade (111); Slov. Russ. (II, 262); Slovar' (VI, 338); Smirnitskii (338).

manzheta = cuff, fr. Germ. *Manschette*/Fr. *manchette*. Christ. (49); Preob. (I, 508); Vasmer (II, 95); Fasmer (II, 568); H-W. (85); Chernykh (I, 508); Shanskii-Bob. (178); Slov. Akad. (IV, 29); Slov. Russ. (II, 285); Slovar' (VI, 600); Smirnitskii (346).
Derivations: *manzhetka* (dim.), *manzhetnyi*

mebel' = furniture, fr. Pol. *mebel*/Germ. *Möbel*/Fr. *meuble(s)*. Smirnov (191); Preob. (I, 518–9); Vasmer (II, 109); Fasmer (II, 588); Chernykh (I, 518); Shanskii-Bob. (182); Wade (118); Slov. Russ. (II, 293); Slovar' (VI, 744–5); Smirnitskii (350).
Derivations: *mebel'nyi, mebel'shchik* (= furniture maker, dealer)

melankholiia = melancholy, fr. Pol. *melankolia*/Germ. *Melancholie*/Fr. *mélancolie*. H-W. (86); Chernykh (I, 521); Slov. Russ. (II, 296); Slovar' (VI, 800–02); Smirnitskii (351). Barkh-Bog. (IX, 77) cites possible 16th-, 17th-cent. precedents; D'iachenko (I, 301) lists Slav. *melakholik* fr. Gr., citing Petrine doc. of 1721.
Derivations: *melankholik, melankholicheskii/ichnyi* (cf. Germ. *Melancholiker, melancholisch*)

meniu = menu, fr. Fr. *menu*. Chernykh (I, 523); Slovar' (VI, 841); Smirnitskii (353).

monstrum/monstr = monster, fr. Germ./Lat. *monstrum*/Fr. *monstre*. Smirnov (199, 374); Vasmer (II, 155); Fasmer (II, 651); H-W. (90); Slovar' (VI, 1241–2); Smirnitskii (366). Barkh-Bog. (IX, 260) cites *monstrum* in 17th-cent. ms. *alfavit*.

opshlag/obshlag = cuff, fr. Du. *opslag*. Christ. (48); Smirnov (209); Preob. (I, 632); Vasmer (II, 246); Fasmer (III, 110); Chernykh (I, 589); Slov. Russ. (III, 38); Slovar' (VIII, 514–5); Smirnitskii (449).

ordinarnyi = ordinary, usual, fr. Pol. *ordynarny*/Germ. *ordinär/ordinari*/Lat. *ordinarius.* Christ. (53); Smirnov (213); Vasmer (II, 275–6); Fasmer (III, 150); H-W. (93); Barkh-Bog. (XIII, 65 [*ordinariinyi,* 1697]); Otten (341–2); Shanskii-Bob. (215); Slov. Russ. (III, 77); Slovar' (VIII, 1015); Smirnitskii (466).

481

paket = packet, parcel, fr. Du. *pakket*/Germ. *Paket.* Christ. (43); Smirnov (156, 375); Vasmer (II, 303); Fasmer (III, 188); Kaiser (153); Bond (143); Barkh-Bog. (XIV, 125 [1697]); Otten (465–9); Chernykh (I, 615); Slov. Akad. (IV, 696); Slov. Russ. (III, 155); Slovar' (IX, 37–8); Smirnitskii (494).

paruk/peruk/parik = wig, fr. Du. *paruik*/Germ. *Parucke/Perücke*/Fr. *perruque.* Christ. (48); Smirnov (219); Preob. (II, 18); Vasmer (II, 316); Fasmer (III, 206–7); Bond (130); Chernykh (II, 6); Shanskii-Bob. (22); Slov. Akad. (IV, 715); Slov. Russ. (III, 160); Slovar' (IX, 188); Smirnitskii (498).

parukmacher/perukmakher/parikmakher = wig-maker, barber, hairdresser, fr. Du. *p(a)riukmaker*/Germ. *Paruckenmacher/Perückenmacher.* Smirnov (220, 365); Preob. (II, 18); Vasmer (II, 316); Fasmer (III, 207); H-W. (95); Bond (130–1); Chernykh (II, 6); Shanskii-Bob. (224); Slov. Russ. (III, 160); Slovar' (IX, 188); Smirnitskii (498).
Derivations: *parikmakherskii, parikmakherskaia* (= barber's shop)

persik = peach, peach tree, fr. Du. *persik/perzik,* replacing earlier *persika/pr"sika* (Barkh-Bog., XIV, 310). Preob. (II, 46); Vasmer (II, 343); Fasmer (III, 243); Chernykh (II, 24); Shanskii-Bob. (231); Slov. Akad. (IV, 773); Slov. Russ. (III, 214); Slovar' (IX, 1050); Smirnitskii (521).

pozument = galoon, braid, lace (trim), fr. Germ. *Posament.* Christ. (49); Smirnov (230); Preob. (II, 89); Vasmer (II, 388); Fasmer (III, 303–4); Grib. (66); Slov. Russ. (III, 299); Slovar' (X, 797); Smirnitskii (553).
Derivations: *pozumentik* (dim.), *pozumentnyi*

pokal/bokal = glass, goblet, fr. Germ. *Pokal*/Fr. *bocal.* Smirnov (230); Preob. (I, 34); Vasmer (I, 101); Fasmer (I, 185); Bond (141–2); Grib. (66); Slov. Russ. (III, 304; I, 73); Slovar' (I, 546–7); Smirnitskii (65).

portion/portsiia = portion, fr. Pol. *porcja*/Lat. *portio*/Germ./Fr. *portion.* Smirnov (233); Preob. (II, 111); Vasmer (II, 413); Fasmer (III, 337); Chernykh (II, 60); Shanskii-Bob. (248); Slov. Russ. (III, 377); Slovar' (X, 1427–8); Smirnitskii (571).
Derivation: *portsionnyi*

posazhir/pasazhera/passazhir = passenger, fr. Germ./Du. *passagier*/Fr. *passager.* Christ. (43); Smirnov (221); Preob. (II, 21–2); Vasmer (II, 321); Fasmer (III, 213); Chernykh (II, 10);

Shanskii-Bob. (225); Wade (151); Fadeev (II, 55–6); Slov. Russ. (III, 162); Slovar' (IX, 264); Smirnitskii (500).
Derivation: *passazhirskii*

prob/probka = cork, stopper, fr. Du. *prop/propke*. Smirnov (242); Preob. (II, 128); Vasmer (II, 437); Fasmer (III, 370–1); Chernykh (II, 68); Wade (174–5); Slov. Akad. (IV, 1086); Slov. Russ. (III, 515); Slovar' (XI, 927–8); Smirnitskii (614).

provizion/proviziia = provisions, victuals, fr. Germ. *Provision*/Pol. *prowizja*/Du. *provisie*. Smirnov (242); Preob. (II, 129); Vasmer (II, 438); Fasmer (III, 371); Kaiser (252); Chernykh (II, 68–9); Shanskii-Bob. (256); Slov. Russ. (III, 518); Slovar' (XI, 962); Smirnitskii (615).

puder/pudra = powder, fr. Germ. *Puder*/Fr. *poudre*. Smirnov (249); Preob. (III, 150); Vasmer (II, 461); Fasmer (III, 402); Chernykh (II, 81); Shanskii-Bob. (261); Slov. Akad. (IV, 1173); Slov. Russ. (III, 577); Slovar' (XI, 1661); Smirnitskii (639).

ragu = ragout, fr. Fr. *ragoût*. Vasmer (II, 481); Fasmer (III, 429); Chernykh (II, 92); Slovar' (XII, 50); Smirnitskii (646).

revanzh/revansh = revenge, repayment, fr. Pol. *rewanż*/Fr. *revanche*. Smirnov (253); Vasmer (II, 500); Fasmer (III, 454); Chernykh (II, 103); Slovar' (XII, 1076–7); Smirnitskii (678).

salfetka = (table) napkin, serviette, fr. Germ. *Salvette*/Ital. *salvietta*. Smirnov (269); Preob. (II, 247); Vasmer (II, 572); Fasmer (III, 551); Chernykh (II, 137); Wade (190); Slov. Akad. (V, 333); Slov. Russ. (IV, 87); Slovar' (XIII, 69); Smirnitskii (694).
Derivations: *salfetochka* (dim.), *salfetochnyi*

sarzha = serge (cloth), fr. Germ. *Sarsche*/Fr. *sarge*/It. *sargia*. Smirnov (271); Preob. (II, 253); Vasmer (II, 581); Fasmer (III, 562); Bond (131–2); Barkh-Bog. (XXII, 65 [1674]); Shanskii-Bob. (281); Slov. Russ. (IV, 93); Slovar' (XIII, 188); Smirnitskii (697).
Derivation: *sarzhevyi*

sekret = secret, fr. Pol. *sekret*/Fr. *secret*. Christ. (19); Smirnov (273, 378); Preob. (II, 271); Vasmer (II, 603); Fasmer (III, 593); Leeming (97); Otten (419); Chernykh (II, 150); Shanskii-Bob. (284–5); Slov. Russ. (IV, 116); Slovar' (XIII, 580–2); Smirnitskii (707).
Derivations: *sekretno, sekretnyi, sekretnichat'*

sel'derei = celery, fr. Du. *selderij*. Preob. (II, 274); Vasmer (II, 606); Fasmer (III, 597); Chernykh (II, 152); Slov. Akad. (V, 407–8); Slov. Russ. (IV, 117); Slovar' (XIII, 604–5); Smirnitskii (708).

servis/serviz = service, set of dishes, fr. Germ./Fr. *service*. Smirnov (275); Chernykh (II, 156); Slov. Russ. (IV, 119); Slovar' (XIII, 668); Smirnitskii (710).
Derivation: *serviznyi*

serenada = serenade, fr. Pol. *serenada*/Germ. *Serenade*/Ital. *serenata*. Vasmer (II, 615);

Fasmer (III, 608); Chernykh (II, 157); Shanskii-Bob. (287); Slovar' (XIII, 701); Smirnitskii (711).

sort = sort, kind, quality, fr. Du. *soort*/Germ./Fr. *sorte*/Eng. *sort*. Christ. (23); Smirnov (279); Preob. (II, 359); Vasmer (II, 700); Fasmer (III, 725); Kaiser (155); Birzhak. (141–2); Chernykh (II, 189); Slov. Russ. (IV 189); Slovar' (XIV, 335–6); Smirnitskii (743).
Derivations: *sortirovat', sortirovka, sortnost', sortnyi, sortovoi*

483

sous = sauce, fr. Germ./Eng./Fr. *sauce*. Preob. (II, 362); Vasmer (II, 703); Fasmer (III, 728); Chernykh (II, 190); Shanskii-Bob. (300); Slov. Akad. (V, 664); Slov. Russ. (IV, 195); Slovar' (XIV, 413); Smirnitskii (745).
Derivations: *sousnik* (= sauce-/gravy-boat), *sousnyi*

subtel'nyi/subtil'nyi = subtle, delicate, slender, later also tenuous, frail, fr. Pol. *subtelny*/Lat. *subtilis*/Germ./Fr. *subtil*/Du. *subtiel*. Smirnov (284); Vasmer (III, 38); Fasmer (III, 793); Grib. (86); Chernykh (II, 216); Shanskii-Bob. (307); Slovar' (XIV, 1137); Smirnitskii (767); Ox. Russ. (786).
Derivation: *subtil'nost'*

usters/ustersa/ustritsa = oyster, fr. Du. *oester*/Germ. *Auster*/Eng. *oyster*. Smirnov (300); Vasmer (III, 192); Fasmer (IV, 173); Grib. (93); Chernykh (II, 293); Shanskii-Bob. (336); Slov. Akad. (VI, 451); Slov. Russ. (IV, 566); Slovar' (XVI, 990–1); Smirnitskii (835).
Derivation: *ustrichnyi*

familiia = family, family name, fr. Pol. *familja*/Lat. *familia*/Germ. *Familie*. Christ. (47); Smirnov (303, 381); Vasmer (III, 201); Fasmer (IV, 184); H-W. (111); Kaiser (248); Birzhak. (130); Bond (143–4); Grib. (93); Chernykh (II, 301–2); Shanskii-Bob. (339); Slov. Russ. (IV, 384); Slovar' (XVI, 1233–4); Smirnitskii (843).

fartuk = apron, fr. Pol. *fartuch*/Germ. *vortuoch*/*Vortuch*. Vasmer (III, 202); Fasmer (IV, 186); Chernykh (II, 303); Shanskii-Bob. (340); Wade (231); Slov. Akad. (VI, 481); Slov. Russ. (IV, 385); Slovar' (XVI, 1268); Smirnitskii (843).
Derivations: *fartuchek* (dim.), *fartuchnyi*

farfor = china, porcelain, fr. Ukr. *farfor*/Pol. *farfura*. Smirnov (304); Vasmer (III, 202); Fasmer (IV, 186–7); Chernykh (II, 304); Shanskii-Bob. (340); Slov. Akad. (VI, 481); Slov. Russ. (IV, 385); Slovar' (XVI, 1268–9); Smirnitskii (843).
Derivation: *farforovyi*

figa = fig, fig tree, fr. Fr. *figue*/Germ. *Feige*. Vasmer (III, 207); Fasmer (IV, 192); Chernykh (II, 309); Shanskii-Bob. (342); Slov. Akad. (VI, 484); Slovar' (XVI, 1337–8); Smirnitskii (845).

fler/flër = crape, crêpe, fr. Germ. *Flor*. Smirnov (309); Vasmer (III, 212); Fasmer (IV, 199); H-W. (115); Bond (132); Slov. Akad. (VI, 493); Slov. Russ. (IV, 389); Slovar' (XVI, 1439); Smirnitskii (847); Ox. Russ. (863).

frukt = fruit, fr. Pol. *frukt*/Germ. *Frucht*/Du. *vrucht*. Christ. (51); Smirnov (317); Vasmer

(III, 219); Fasmer (IV, 208); H-W. (116); Chernykh (II, 325); Shanskii-Bob. (347); Wade (233); Slov. Russ. (IV, 394); Slovar' (XVI, 1577); Smirnitskii (850).
Derivation: *fruktovyi*

futliar = (carrying) case, container, fr. Germ. *Futteral*. Smirnov (319); Vasmer (III, 222); Fasmer (IV, 212); Bond (143); Shanskii-Bob. (347); Slov. Akad. (VI, 497); Slov. Russ. (IV, 395); Slovar' (XVI, 1602–3); Fadeev (II, 366); Smirnitskii (851).
Derivations: *futliarnyi, futliarchik* (dim.)

tsukat/y = candied fruit, fr. Germ. *S/Zukkade*. Smirnov (324); Vasmer (III, 294); Fasmer (IV, 304); Chernykh (II, 372); Shanskii-Bob. (359); Slov. Russ. (IV, 420); Slovar' (XVII, 721–2); Smirnitskii (865).

shampanskoe (vino) = champagne (wine), fr. Germ. *Champagner(Wein)*/Fr. *Champagne (vin de)*. Smirnov (325); Vasmer (III, 371); Fasmer (IV, 403); H-W. (119); Shanskii-Bob. (369); Wade (249); Slovar' (XVII, 1261); Smirnitskii (879).

shaf/shkaf = cupboard, dresser, fr. Germ. *Shaf/Schaff*. Smirnov (329); Vasmer (III, 405); Fasmer (IV, 447); Chernykh (II, 415); Shanskii-Bob. (374); Wade (252); Slov. Akad. (VI, 892); Slov. Russ. (IV, 458 [also *shkap*]); Slovar' (XVII, 1440–1); Smirnitskii (884).

shel'ma = rogue, swindler, fr. Du./Germ. *Schelm*/Pol. *szelma*. Smirnov (327); Vasmer (III, 389); Fasmer (IV, 426); Chernykh (II, 409); Shanskii-Bob. (372); Slov. Russ. (IV, 453); Slovar' (XVII, 1343); Smirnitskii (881).
Derivations: *shel'movanie* (= public dishonor, defamation), *shel'movat'* (= to expose to same)

shink/shinok = tavern, fr. Germ. *Schenk/e*, perhaps via Pol. *szynk*/Ukr. *shink, shinok*. Christ. (50); Smirnov (328); Vasmer (III, 399); Fasmer (IV, 439); Gard. (239–40); Otten (366); Shanskii-Bob. (373); Slov. Akad. (VI, 886); Slov. Russ. (IV, 56); Slovar' (XVII, 1401); Smirnitskii (883).
Derivation: *shinochek* (dim.), *shinochnyi*

shlafrok = housecoat, dressing gown, fr. Pol. *szlafrok*/Germ. *Schlafrock*. Christ. (49); Smirnov (330); Vasmer (III, 409); Fasmer (IV, 452); Bond (132); Slov. Akad. (VI, 894 *[shlaforok]*); Slov. Russ. (IV, 459); Slovar' (XVII, 1464 [obs.]); Ox. Russ. (897 [obs.]).

shleif = train (of dress), fr. Germ. *Schleif*. Vasmer (III, 409); Fasmer (IV, 452); Bond (131); Chernykh (II, 417); Shanskii-Bob. (375); Slov. Russ. (IV, 459); Slovar' (XVII, 1465); Smirnitskii (884).

shokolad = chocolate, fr. Germ. *Schokolade*/Ital. *cioccolata*. Smirnov (332); Vasmer (III, 419); Fasmer (IV, 465); H-W. (119); Chernykh (II, 420); Wade (253–4); Slov. Akad. (VI, 866–7 *[shekolad/shokolod]*); Slov. Russ. (IV, 452, 460); Slovar' (XVII, 1504–5); Smirnitskii (885).
Derivation: *shokoladnyi*

shram = scratch, scar, fr. Pol. *szram*/Germ. *Schram(me)*. Preob. (suppl., 107); Vasmer (III,

428); Fasmer (IV, 476); Bond (85); Chernykh (II, 424); Shanskii-Bob. (377); Wade (254); Slov. Russ. (IV, 462); Slovar' (XVII, 1542); Smirnitskii (886).

Derivations: *shramik* (dim.), *shramnyi*

shtivlety/shtiblety = (lace-up) boots, gaiters, fr. Germ. *Stiefelette/n.* Smirnov (336); Preob. (suppl., 107); Vasmer (III, 430); Fasmer (IV, 478); Bond (132); Chernykh (II, 425); Slov. Akad. (VI, 916); Slov. Russ. (IV, 463); Slovar' (XVII, 1563); Smirnitskii (887); Ox. Russ. (900).

shtof = cloth (damask, brocade), fr. Germ. *Stoff.* Christ. (49); Smirnov (337); Preob. (suppl., 108); Vasmer (III, 430–1); Fasmer (IV, 479); Bond (131); Slov. Akad. (VI, 918); Slov. Russ. (IV, 464); Slovar' (XVII, 1572); Smirnitskii (887); Ox. Russ. (900).

ekipazh = carriage, fr. Germ. *Equipage*/Fr. *équipage.* Smirnov (345); Chernykh (II, 440); Shanskii-Bob. (383); Slov. Russ. (IV, 472–3); Slovar' (XVII, 1746–7); Smirnitskii (891).

Derivations: *ekipazhnik* (dim.), *ekipazhnyi*

NOTES

The full titles and other publishing details of works cited in the notes in short-title form will be found in the Bibliography. (Repeat citations of other works are sometimes also printed in short-title form, usually to distinguish among works by the same author or authors.)

1. INTRODUCTION

1. See especially N. V. Riasanovsky, *The Image of Peter the Great in Russian History and Thought* (New York, 1985); and Kh. Bagger, *Reformy Petra Velikogo: Obzor issledovanii*, trans. (from Danish) V. E. Vozgrin, ed. V. I. Buganov (M., 1985): original ed. H. Bagger, *Peter den Stores reformer: En forskningsoversigt* (Copenhagen, 1979).

2. Cf. E. Schuyler, *Peter the Great, Emperor of Russia: A Study of Historical Biography*, 2 vols. (New York, 1884; republished in photocopy, Ann Arbor, MI, 1965; facsimile reprint, New York, 1967), which is based on original sources and major works in Russian and German; R. K. Massie, *Peter the Great: His Life and World* (New York, 1980), which draws heavily on Schuyler and is more popular than scholarly; and L. Hughes, *Russia in the Age of Peter the Great* (New Haven, CT, and London, 1998), which is based on extensive reading in original sources and the secondary literature in Russian, English, and other languages and is far the most valuable of the three. In German, R. Wittram, *Peter I, Czar und Kaiser: Zur Geschichte Peters des Grossen in seiner Zeit*, 2 vols. (Göttingen, 1964), is a similarly large-scale, extensively researched work whose treatment of war and diplomacy remains unsurpassed. Nothing comparable to these works has been published in other languages (other than Russian).

3. Riasanovsky, pp. 153–65 (p. 154 for the phrase quoted). Reference is to S. M. Solov'ev, *Istoriia Rossii s drevneishikh vremen*, 29 vols. (SPb., 1851–1879; republished M., 1962–1966, 29 vols. in 15, ed. L. V. Cherepnin: vols. 7–9 of this edition, comprising the original vols. 13–18, span the Petrine period: citations hereafter to this edition). Solov'ev's *Istoriia* was published again in the first 15 vols. of *S. M. Solov'ev: Sochineniia*, ed. I. D. Koval'chenko et al. (M., 1988–1996), 20 vols.

4. Solov'ev, *Istoriia*, vol. 9 (1963), pp. 541–53 (p. 548 for the passage quoted); also, vol. 7 (1962), p. 440, for "our revolution *[nasha revoliutsiia]*."

5. E. C. Thaden, *The Rise of Historicism in Russia* (New York, 1999), pp. 193–94; see also pp. 118, 124–27, 143–55, 174–89, 190–97, 235–70 for an exposition of Solov'ev's "organic historicism."

6. Cf. A. A. Chernobaev, "S. M. Solov'ev," in Chernobaev, ed., *Istoriki Rossii XVIII–XX vekov*, 2 vols. (M., 1995), 1, pp. 126–36; essays by N. I. Pavlenko and V. I. Volkova, in S. M. Solov'ev, *Obshchedostupnye chteniia o russkoi istorii*, ed. Volkova (M., 1992), pp. 5–22, 23–186 (pp. 78–107 on the "central place of the Petrine era in Solov'ëv's work"); and the introduction by I. D. Koval'chenko and S. S. Dmitriev to the newest edition of Solov'ev's *Istoriia*, in *Solov'ev: Sochineniia*, ed. Koval'chenko, vol. 1, pp. 6–48. Parts of Solov'ev's history of Peter's reign have been translated into English: see Sergei M. Solov'ev, *Peter the Great: A Reign Begins, 1689–1703*, ed. and trans. L. A. J. Hughes (Gulf Breeze, FL, 1994); and Solov'ev, *Peter the Great: The Great Reforms Begin*, ed. and trans. K. Papmehl (Gulf Breeze, FL, 1981).

7. On Kliuchevskii, see Riasanovsky, pp. 166–76; R. A. Kireeva, "Vasilii Osipovich Kliuchevskii," in Chernobaev, pp. 147–58; M. V. Nechkina, *Vasili Osipovich Kliuchevskii: Istoriia zhizni i tvorchestva* (M., 1974); *Canadian-American Slavic Studies* 20, nos. 3–4 (Fall–Winter 1986), ed. M. Raeff, a special issue of eighteen articles on Kliuchevskii by as many historians, with a bibliography of his works; and R. F. Byrnes, *V. O. Kliuchevskii, Historian of Russia* (Bloomington, IN, 1995), with extensive bibliography.

8. V. Kliuchevskii, *Kurs russkoi istorii*, pt. 4 (M., 1910); reference here and subsequently to the edition of same published as vol. 4 of V. O. Kliuchevskii, *Sochineniia v vos'mi tomakh*, 8 vols. (M., 1956–1959), ed. V. A. Aleksandrov and A. A. Zimin. Kliuchevskii's *Course* has not been adequately translated into English: cf. V. O. Kluchevsky *[sic]*, *A History of Russia*, trans. C. J. Hogarth, 5 vols. (New York, 1911–1931; reprinted New York, 1960), which is frequently erroneous and nearly unreadable. The edition of Part 4 of the *Course* published as Vasili *[sic]* Klyuchevsky, *Peter the Great*, trans. L. Archibald (London, 1958; frequently reprinted), while easy to read, is incomplete as well as seriously inaccurate at times and often misleading; the edition of Part 3 published as V. O. Kliuchevsky, *A Course in Russian History: The Seventeenth Century*, trans. N. Duddington, intro. A. J. Reiber (Chicago, 1968; reprinted Armonk, NY, 1994), is both competent and readable.

9. Kliuchevskii, *Kurs*, vol. 4 (1958), pp. 28–48.

10. Ibid., pp. 62–63, 64, 27, 28, 207.

11. Ibid., pp. 200–201.

12. Miliukov, *Gosudarstvennoe khoziaistvo Rossii v pervoi chetverti XVIII stoletiia i reforma Petra Velikago*, 2nd ed. (SPb., 1905), a thesis submitted at Moscow University and first published in 1892. See further Riasanovsky, pp. 176–78; for this work's influence on Kliuchevskii as he revised his lectures on Peter, see Nechkina, p. 535.

13. Kliuchevskii, *Kurs*, vol. 4 (1958), pp. 224, 220–22.

14. M. K. Stockdale, *Paul Miliukov and the Quest for a Liberal Russia, 1880–1918* (Ithaca, NY, 1996); see chap. 3 for Miliukov the historian.

15. Miliukov, *Gosudarstvennoe khoziaistvo,* p. 546.
16. Particularly E. V. Anisimov, *Podatnaia reforma Petra I* (n. 36 below). In fact, if Miliukov's estimate of population decline was correct Russia had undergone in Peter's time a demographic catastrophe proportionate to that suffered in World War II!
17. P. Miliukov, *Ocherki po istorii russkoi kul'tury,* vol. 1, pt. 1 (Paris, 1937); vol. 2, pts. 1, 2 (Paris, 1931); vol. 3 (Paris, 1930); vol. 1, pt. 2 published posthumously (The Hague, 1964).
18. Ibid., vol. 2, pt. 1, pp. 177–81 (Peter's church reform), pp. 297–301 (literature); vol. 2, pt. 2, pp. 478–82 (architecture), 514–15 (painting and engraving), 611 (music), 732–42 (education).
19. Ibid., vol. 3, pp. 157–217.
20. P. Miliukov et al., *Histoire de Russie,* 3 vols. (Paris, 1932), 1: 267–427; see further Riasanovsky, pp. 179–84.
21. Riasanovsky, pp. 184–91; also M. M. Bogoslovskii, *Istoriografiia, memuaristika, epistoliariia (nauchnoe nasledia),* ed. A. I. Klibanov, comp. L. A. Chernaia (M., 1987), pp. 3–12 (intro. by Chernaia).
22. M. M. Bogoslovskii, *Oblastnaia reforma Petra Velikago: Provintsiia 1719–27 gg.* (M., 1902), especially chap. 1 and pp. 506–21.
23. Riasanovsky, p. 187, paraphrasing Bogoslovskii, *Oblastnaia reforma,* p. 521.
24. Bogoslovskii, *Oblastnaia reforma,* p. 24.
25. Bogoslovskii, *Petr I: Materialy dlia biografii,* ed. V. I. Lebedev, 5 vols. (M., 1940–1948; facsimile reprint, The Hague, 1969).
26. Ibid., vol. 1, p. 10.
27. Bogoslovskii to A. S. Lappo-Danilevskii, May 3, 1918, in Bogoslovskii, *Istoriografiia,* pp. 141–42.
28. Cf. Riasanovsky, chap. 3.
29. Ibid., chap. 4; also C. E. Black, "The Reforms of Peter the Great," in Black, ed., *Rewriting Russian History: Soviet Interpretations of Russia's Past,* 2nd ed. (New York, 1962), pp. 233–59.
30. B. B. Kafengauz and N. I. Pavlenko, eds., *Ocherki istorii SSSR, Period feodalizma: Rossiia v pervoi chetverti XVIII v.: Preobrazovaniia Petra I* (M., 1954), chap. 5, "Russkaia kul'tura" (pp. 629–765).
31. Ibid., p. 765.
32. Ibid., pp. 766–74.
33. Risanovsky, pp. 299–302; also, pp. 235–36, 286, 289–90. A notable example of such specialized work is Pavlenko's biographical study, "Petr I (K izucheniiu sotsial'no-politicheskikh vzgliadov)," in Pavlenko et al., eds., *Rossiia v period reform Petra I* (M., 1973), pp. 40–102.
34. N. I. Pavlenko, *Petr Velikii* (M., 1994): cf. Pavlenko's earlier, far more compact, and abstractly Marxist *Petr Pervyi* (M., 1975); and A. Brikner (Brückner), *Istoriia Petra Velikago* (SPb., 1882), which is a Russian translation (by Brückner himself) of his *Peter der Grosse* (Berlin, 1879).
35. Pavlenko, *Petr Velikii,* especially, regarding culture, pp. 64–81, 93, 108–114, 376–80, 514–48.

489

490

36. E. V. Anisimov, *Podatnaia reforma Petra I: Vvedenie podushnoi podati v Rossii 1719–1728 gg.* (L., 1982).

37. Ibid., p. 290.

38. E. V. Anisimov, *Vremia petrovskikh reform* (L., 1989); condensed English ed., trans. J. T. Alexander, *The Reforms of Peter the Great: Progress through Coercion in Russia* (Armonk, NY, 1993). See also Anisimov's introductory essay, "Tsar'-reformator," in L. Nikolaeva, ed., *Petr Velikii: Vospominaniia, dnevnikovye zapisi, anekdoty* (M., 1993), pp. 5–50.

39. Anisimov, *Vremia petrovskikh reform*, pp. 7–14 and passim.

40. Cf. J. Cracraft, *The Petrine Revolution in Russian Imagery* (Chicago, 1997), pp. 34–35, 312–13.

41. S. Fitzpatrick, ed., *Cultural Revolution in Russia, 1928–1931* (Bloomington, IN, 1978, 1984): see especially editor's introduction (pp. 1–7) and the following essay, "Cultural Revolution as Class War" (pp. 8–40). Fitzpatrick's application of the term is incorporated in D. R. Weiner, *Models of Nature: Ecology, Conservation, and Cultural Revolution in Soviet Russia* (Bloomington, IN, 1988), to label the effects of early Stalinist policies on conservation and ecology (see pp. 4–5, chap. 8).

42. M. David-Fox, "What Is Cultural Revolution?" *The Russian Review* 58 (April 1999): 181–201, which with regard to the central concept announced in its title is remarkably unreflective—undertheorized (unhelpful).

43. Cf. A. Appadurai, *Modernity at Large: Cultural Dimensions of Globalism* (Minneapolis, 1996), pp. 1–11.

44. L. A. Scaff, *Fleeing the Iron Cage: Culture, Politics, and Modernity in the Thought of Max Weber* (Berkeley and Los Angeles, 1989), pp. 8, 189 ff.

45. Handy summary with bibliography in J. Turner, ed., *The [Grove] Dictionary of Art,* vol. 21 (New York, 1996), pp. 775–83 (entries by T. Smith and J. Musgrove); see further M. Levensen, ed., *The Cambridge Companion to Modernism* (Cambridge, 1999).

46. W. E. Everdell, *The First Moderns: Profiles in the Origins of Twentieth-Century Thought* (Chicago, 1997).

47. Appadurai, p. 11.

48. D. Lerner, "Modernization: Social Aspects," in D. L. Sills, ed., *International Encyclopedia of the Social Sciences,* vol. 10 (New York, 1968), pp. 386–87. Cf. J. Brode, ed., *The Process of Modernization: An Annotated Bibliography on the Sociocultural Aspects of Development* (Cambridge, MA, 1969), which lists some 12,000 (!) social-scientific studies mainly of the socioeconomic changes wrought in rural communities by industrialization.

49. J. Tomlinson, *Cultural Imperialism: A Critical Introduction* (London, 1991), with numerous references; M. E. Latham, *Modernization as Ideology: American Social Science and "Nation Building" in the Kennedy Era* (Chapel Hill, NC, 2000); Appadurai, p. 9.

50. J. C. Alexander and P. Sztompka, eds., *Rethinking Progress: Movements, Forces, and Ideas at the End of the 20th Century* (Boston, 1990); also, L. Marx and B. Mazlish, eds., *Progress: Fact or Illusion?* (Ann Arbor, 1996).

51. M. B. Jansen, ed., *Changing Japanese Attitudes toward Modernization* (Princeton, 1965), pp. 20–23.

52. Cracraft, *Revolution in Imagery*, chaps. 4, 5, 6 passim.

53. Ibid., especially pp. 190–220.

54. On Peter's social policies and their effects, see especially Anisimov, *Vremia petrovskikh reform*, pp. 300 ff.; also Anisimov, "Izmeniia v sotsial'noi strukture russkogo obshchestva v kontse XVII-nachale XVIII veka," *Istoriia SSSR* 1979, no. 5 (May): 35–51; and for more detail, with special attention to women, Hughes (n. 2 above), chap. 6.

55. Jansen, pp. 22–23.

56. A. Kahan, "Continuity in Economic Activity and Policy during the Post-Petrine Period in Russia," *Journal of Economic History* 25 (March 1965): 61–85; and further, Kahan, *The Plow, the Hammer, and the Knout: An Economic History of Eighteenth-Century Russia*, ed. R. Hellie (Chicago, 1985), pp. 1–6 and passim, with abundant detail. See also, following Kahan, W. Daniel, "Entrepreneurship and the Russian Textile Industry from Peter the Great to Catherine the Great," *Russian Review* 54, no. 1 (January 1995): 1–25.

57. Cf. T. McDaniel, *Autocracy, Modernization, and Revolution in Russia and Iran* (Princeton, 1991).

58. See J. M. Price, "Economic Activity," in J. S. Bromley, ed., *The New Cambridge Modern History*, vol. 6: *The Rise of Great Britain and Russia, 1688–1725* (Cambridge, 1971), p. 835; and suggestive remarks in M. Mann, *The Sources of Social Power*, vol. 1: *A History of Power from the Beginning to A.D. 1760* (Cambridge, 1986), pp. 473–75. See further E. Heckscher, *Mercantilism*, 2 vols. (London, 1955); and E. Rich and C. H. Wilson, eds., *The Cambridge Economic History of Europe*, vol. 4: *The Economy of Expanding Europe in the Sixteenth and Seventeenth Centuries* (Cambridge, 1967), chap. 8 (by C. H. Wilson).

59. A. Gerschenkron, *Europe in the Russian Mirror: Four Lectures in Economic History* (Cambridge, 1970), pp. 69–76. Elsewhere Gerschenkron argues a much more problematic relationship between serfdom and the later industrialization of Russia: see his "Russia: Agrarian Policies and Industrialization, 1861–1917," in Gerschenkron, *Continuity in History and Other Essays* (Cambridge, MA, 1968), pp. 140–248.

60. W. L. Blackwell, *The Industrialization of Russia: An Historical Perspective*, 3rd ed. (Arlington Heights, IL, 1994), p. 7. Kahan, Gerschenkron, and Blackwell, in the works just cited, struggle to rescue Petrine economic history from the distortions of Russian historians, both pre-Soviet and Soviet–the former owed to a preoccupation with Russian "backwardness" and/or distinctiveness vis-à-vis "the West," the latter to Marxist bias. On this point see further review essays by Gerschenkron collected in his *Continuity in History*, pp. 409 ff.

61. Cf. U. Hannerz, *Transnational Connections: Culture, People, Places* (London and New York, 1996), especially chap. 4, "The Global Ecumene as a Landscape of Modernity," conjoining the concepts of globalization and modernization. Prospectuses of the new global period in human history are offered in P. Pomper et al., eds., *World History: Ideologies, Structures, and Identities* (Malden, MA, and Oxford, 1998) and in, less coherently, F. Jameson and M. Miyoshi, eds., *The Cultures of Globalization* (Durham, NC, and London, 1998).

62. Indeed, one Russian student suggests that "Peter's reform movement represents an

492

important new departure in modern world history: it pioneered the process of modernization that was later to develop on a worldwide scale" (A. Chubanov, *Russia's Bitter Path to Modernity: A History of the Soviet and Post-Soviet Eras* [New York, 2001], p. 6). See further E. P. Hoffmann and R. F. Laird, *The Politics of Economic Modernization in the Soviet Union* (Ithaca, NY, 1982); B. Kerblay, *Modern Soviet Society*, trans. (from French) R. Sawyer (New York, 1983); V. A. Krasil'shchikov et al., *Modernizatsiia: zarubezhnyi opyt i Rossiia* (M., 1994); S. Ia. Matveeva, ed., *Modernizatsiia v Rossii i konflikt tsennostei* (M., 1994); V. M. Mezhiev, ed., *Modernizatsiia i natsional'naia kul'tura* (M., 1995); D. A. Alisov et al., *Kul'tura i intelligentsiia Rossii v epokhu modernizatsii*, 2 vols. (Omsk, 1995); J. R. Blasi, M. Kroumova, and D. Kruse, *Kremlin Capitalism: Privatizing the Russian Economy* (Ithaca, NY, 1997). Cf. D. L. Hoffman and Y. Kotsonis, eds., *Russian Modernity: Politics, Knowledge, Practices* (London and New York, 2000), which attempts to apply modernization theory to twentieth-century Russian developments in more neutral, historically sensitive ways.

63. C. E. Black, *The Dynamics of Modernization: A Study in Comparative History* (New York, 1966). For the older historiography, see especially J. H. Randall, *The Making of the Modern Mind*, 50th anniversary ed. (New York, 1976), introduction by J. Barzun.

64. Black, pp. 4–13, 24–26. A good standard account of the Scientific Revolution is in R. R. Palmer and J. Colton, *A History of the Modern World*, 3rd ed. (New York, 1965), chap. 7, with current bibliography (pp. 950–52). For a critical survey of the standard account together with a revisionist synthesis and "up-to-date interpretation" of the same Scientific Revolution (still there, still capitalized), see S. Shapin, *The Scientific Revolution* (Chicago, 1996). Another synthetic account, focusing on technology, is R. M. Adams, *Paths of Fire: An Anthropologist's Inquiry into Western Technology* (Princeton, 1996), pp. 53 ff.

65. R. Porter, "The Scientific Revolution," in Porter and M. Teich, eds., *Revolution in History* (Cambridge, 1986), pp. 290–91.

66. Bernard le Bovier de Fontenelle (1657–1757), *Éloge du Czar Pierre Ier . . . Prononcé à l'Assemblée Publique de l'Académie des Sciences, le 14 Novemb. 1725* (Paris, 1727), p. 5.

67. Cf. T. J. McDonald, ed., *The Historic Turn in the Human Sciences* (Ann Arbor, MI, 1996); also V. E. Bonnell and L. Hunt, eds., *Beyond the Cultural Turn: New Directions in the Study of Society and Culture* (Berkeley and Los Angeles, 1999), especially chap. 1, "The Concept(s) of Culture," by W. H. Sewell, Jr.

68. A. S. Karmin, *Osnovy kul'turologii: morfologiia kul'tury* (SPb., 1997), pp. 10–11, citing, for the original list of 70, M. S. Kagan, *Filosofiia kul'tury* (SPb., 1996), pp. 13–18. On the science of culturology as currently practiced in Russia, see further S. S. Mints, *Rozhdenie kul'turologii* (SPb., 1999).

69. D. Mitchell, *Cultural Geography: A Critical Introduction* (Oxford, 2000), p. 14; M. S. Archer, *Culture and Agency: The Place of Culture in Social Theory* (Cambridge, 1988), pp. 1, 104.

70. A. Grafton, ed., *The Transmission of Culture in Early Modern Europe* (Philadelphia, 1990), editor's introduction, pp. 1–7, reporting on discussions held between 1986 and 1988 at the Davis Center, Princeton University.

71. Recent helpful contributions include P. Burke, "Reflections on the Origins of Cultural History," in J. H. Pittock and A. Wear, eds., *Interpretation and Cultural History* (New York, 1991), pp. 5–24, and Burke, *Varieties of Cultural History* (Ithaca, NY, 1997); D. R. Kelley, "The Old Cultural History," *History of the Human Sciences* 9, no. 3 (Aug. 1996): 101–26; A. Swingewood, *Cultural Theory and the Problem of Modernity* (New York, 1998); and B. C. Sax, "Truth and Meaning in Cultural History," introduction to Sax and P. S. Gold, eds., *Cultural Visions: Essays in the History of Culture* (Amsterdam, 2000).

72. The formula belongs of course to the anthropologist Clifford Geertz, much cited by historians: "Believing, with Max Weber, that man is an animal suspended in webs of significance he himself has spun, I take culture to be those webs, and the analysis of it to be therefore not an experimental science in search of law but an interpretive one in search of meaning"; Geertz, *The Interpretation of Cultures: Selected Essays* (New York, 1973), p. 5. The succeeding qualifier is from a critique of Geertz advanced by N. B. Dirks, an anthropologist-historian, in McDonald (n. 67 above), pp. 17 ff.

73. F. de Saussure, *Course in General Linguistics,* ed. C. Bally et al., trans. (from French) R. Harris (London, 1983; first published 1916); and further, P. J. Thibault, *Re-reading Saussure: The Dynamics of Signs in Social Life* (New York, 1997). A stimulating recent statement of the methods and goals of *historical* linguistics is R. Lass, *Historical Linguistics and Language Change* (Cambridge, 1997): "Language change happens in the spatio-temporal world; historical linguistics is the craft we exercise on its apparent results, in order to tell coherent stories about it" (p. xiv); "Historical linguistics is historiography, the discipline that makes stories and/or interpretations out of what happened to languages over time" (p. 17); indeed, "the appropriate stance for the linguist ought to be external or 'God's-eye,' rather than internal or 'speaker's-head.' Historians in any case have always typically adopted such a position, because it enables us to look at a language as one might look at any other historically evolved object, and ask not only how it came to be what it is, but what scars its history has left, how that history helps us to understand the scars, and how they in turn help us to understand history" (p. 12).

74. Cf. C. Poynton, "Linguistics and Discourse Analysis," in Poynton and A. Lee, eds., *Culture and Text: Discourse and Methodology in Social Research and Cultural Studies* (Lanham, MD, 2000), pp. 19–39.

75. M. A. K. Halliday, *Language, Context and Text: Aspects of Language in a Social-Semiotic Perspective* (Oxford, 1989).

76. Cf. D. C. Greetham, *Theories of the Text* (Oxford, 1999).

77. Phrase lifted from A. D. H. Hayes, introduction to Hayes, ed., *Text in Context: Essays by Members of the Society for Old Testament Study* (Oxford, 2000), p. xvi, where it signals an effort to preserve some order in this venerable branch of learning: "The wide diversity of concerns and approaches which now characterize Old Testament study may in large part be directly traced to the plurality which now characterizes the academic community. A framework of coherence is required, in a way that was not necessary for earlier volumes in this series, if that diversity is not to become confusion."

78. Cracraft, *Revolution in Imagery*, p. 28; the phrase "language of power" derives from B. Anderson, *Imagined Communities: Reflections on the Origin and Spread of Nationalism* (London, 1983).

79. Worth, "Language," p. 26. Note: full citation of works cited in short-title form, as here, and not previously cited in this chapter, will be found in the Bibliography.

80. Schenker, *Dawn of Slavic,* pp. xvi, 71, and passim.

81. Ibid., pp. 194 ff. The sheer volume of scholarship evoked by the *Igor Tale* is on display in L. A. Dmitriev et al., eds., *Entsiklopediia "Slova o polku Igoreve,"* 5 vols. (SPB., 1995).

82. Worth, "Language," pp. 29–30.

83. Birnbaum, "Church Slavonic Literature," pp. 33, 34.

84. See Schenker, *Dawn of Slavic,* pp. 165 ff., with a chart of the Glagolitic and Cyrillic alphabets and appended writing samples; also, in greater detail, Nandriș and Auty, *Old Church Slavonic* and, concentrating on the origins of the two alphabets, Istrin, *1100 let.*

85. Shitsgal, *Russkii tipograficheskii shrift* (1974), chap. 1.

86. Cf. R. Mathiesen, "The Church Slavonic Language Question: An Overview," in Picchio, *Slavic Language Question,* vol. 1, pp. 61–64; and more broadly, employing somewhat different terminology, Uspenskii, *Istoriia russkogo iazyka,* pp. 181 ff. Uspenskii also emphasizes the development from the fourteenth century of two distinct eastern Slavic "redactions" of Church Slavonic, namely a southwestern or Lithuanian (or Ruthenian) variant and a Muscovite one, an emphasis tied to his overall aim of tracing the origins of modern literary Russian and perhaps overstated accordingly.

87. J. Cracraft, *The Petrine Revolution in Russian Architecture* (Chicago, 1988), pp. 88 ff. and passim (hereinafter cited as Cracraft, *Revolution in Architecture*); Cracraft *Revolution in Imagery,* pp. 5 ff., 22–6, 48 ff., 82 ff., etc.

88. This is the overall theme of the two volumes edited by Picchio and others, *Slavic Language Question;* see Picchio's introductory essay, vol. 1, pp. 1–42.

89. As quoted in C. Grayson, *A Renaissance Controversy: Latin or Italian?* (Oxford, 1959), p. 6.

90. Ibid., pp. 18–19. For further details of this "march toward normalization," see G. Devoto, *The Language of Italy,* trans. V. L. Katainen (Chicago, 1978), pp. 235 ff.

91. Cracraft, *Revolution in Imagery,* pp. 22 ff.

92. Devoto, p. 253.

93. R. Posner, *Linguistic Change in French* (Oxford, 1997), p. 18.

94. Ibid., pp. 27, 41–3, 49, 83–4, 171; also P. Rickard, *A History of the French Language,* 2nd ed. (London, 1989), pp. 81–99, 104–5; and, for a concise and somewhat revisionist survey, W. Ayres-Bennet, "Elaboration and Codification: Standardization and Attitudes towards the French Language in the Sixteenth and Seventeenth Centuries," in M. M. Parry et al., eds., *The Changing Voices of Europe: Social and Political Changes and Their Linguistic Repercussions* (Cardiff, UK, 1994), pp. 53–73.

95. R. Penny, *A History of the Spanish Language* (Cambridge, 1991). The history of the standardization of English is more problematic: see L. Wright, ed., *The Development*

of Standard English 1300–1800: Theories, Descriptions, Conflicts (Cambridge, 2000). "Still, there is broad agreement, linked to certain large-scale linguistic features, and dates of a sort: by around 1500 we are out of Middle and into Early Modern; by around 1700 we are into Modern English, i.e., 'our own language'—if in a rather different form from any now written or spoken" (R. Lass, "Introduction," *The Cambridge History of the English Language,* vol. 3: *1476–1776,* ed. R. Lass [Cambridge, 1999], p. 9).

96. Mathiesen (n. 86 above), p. 52.

97. B. Strumin'skyj, "The Language Question in the Ukrainian Lands before the Nineteenth Century," in Picchio, *Slavic Language Question,* vol. 1, p. 15; also Stankiewicz, *Grammars and Dictionaries,* pp. 147–48, whose entries are corrected with respect to Belorussian transliteration by H. Leeming, in a note in *Slavonic and East European Review* 67, no. 2 (April 1989): 258. Smotryc'kij, in particular, is "usually identified as ethnically Ukrainian or Belarusian depending on the nationality of the writer in question: in the present study his language and ethnic identity are described as Ruthenian, in reference to the common linguistic-ethnic identity out of which both modern Ukrainian and Belarusian entities arose" (S. M. Pugh, "Morphological Competition in Ruthenian: A Panchronic Perspective," in Press, *Festschrift for Drage,* p. 91, n. 2); I follow this practice here.

98. Worth, "Language," p. 35.

99. N. B. Mechkovskaia, "Grammatiki, bukvari i ritoriki v velikorusskoi iazykovoi situatsii vtoroi poloviny XVII veka," in Sjöberg, Ďurovič, and Birgegård, eds., *Dolomonosovskii period iazyka,* pp. 11–19.

100. Schenker, *Dawn of Slavic,* p. 190; Schenker later (pp. 193–4) quotes the Russian Slavicist D. S. Likhachev to the same effect. Cf. Nandriş and Auty, *Old Church Slavonic,* vol. 1, p. 2: "[Church Slavonic] became the language of culture for the Orthodox peoples of eastern Europe . . . and played [there] a role similar to that of Latin in the West."

101. F. Svejkovský, "The Conception of the 'Vernacular' in Czech Literature and Culture of the Fifteenth Century," and M. R. Mayenowa, "Aspects of the Language Question in Poland from the Middle of the Fifteenth Century to the Third Decade of the Nineteenth Century," in Picchio, *Slavic Language Question,* vol. 1, pp. 321–36 and 337–69. On Polish, see also S. Urbańczyk, "The Origins of the Polish Literary Language," in G. Stone and D. Worth, eds., *The Formation of the Slavonic Literary Languages* (Columbus, OH, 1985), pp. 105–13, with further references; and K. Croxen, "Thematic and Generic Medievalism in the Polish Neo-Latin Drama of the Renaissance and Baroque," *Slavic and East European Journal* 43, no. 2 (1999): 265–98.

102. Cf. Picchio, "Models and Patterns," pp. 439–67; also Birnbaum: "Generally speaking, the Slavic Greek Orthodox variety of medieval culture, including the Church Slavonic literary tradition, continued at least until the end of the 17th century and perhaps even into the early decades of the 18th century" (Birnbaum, "Church Slavonic Literature," p. 21).

103. Worth, "Language," p. 27.

104. Nandriş and Auty, *Old Church Slavonic,* p. 14 (emphasis added).

105. Cf. Kortava, *Moskovskii prikaznyi iazyk,* pp. 16–19.

106. Worth, "Literary Language?" p. 7.

107. W. J. Ong, *Orality and Literacy: The Technologizing of the Word* (New York, 1986), chap. 3: "The law itself in oral cultures is enshrined in formulaic sayings, proverbs, which are not mere jurisprudential decorations, but themselves constitute the law" (p. 35), and so forth.

108. Worth, "Language," pp. 31–2, 35–6.

109. See especially Kotkov et al., *Moskovskaia pismennost' XVII veka,* a collection of some 250 documents; Kotkov et al., *Gramotki XVII-nachala XVIII veka,* another 528 letters and notes from the later seventeenth and, in a few instances, the first decade of the eighteenth century; and Kotkov, *Moskovskaia rech'* (p. 282 for the words quoted), with a supplementary appendix of 17 texts of similar date, type, and provenance. See also, arguing similarly, Volkov, *Leksika chelobitnykh,* and Larin et al., *Nachal'nyi etap.*

110. As posited, e.g., by Unbegaun, "Le russe littéraire?", pp. 149–58; reprinted in Unbegaun, *Selected Papers on Russian and Slavonic Philology* (Oxford, 1969), pp. 299–311.

111. Kortava, *Moskovskii prikaznyi iazyk;* also Remneva, *Istoriia iazyka,* chap. 3. Cf. A. E. Pennington's detailed commentary on a major late Muscovite chancery document (= Kot., Appendix II, Works Cited), particularly her conclusion: "The *prikaznyj jazyk* is not a standard language in any acceptable sense of the term: its functions are by definition too limited. . . . However, [it] did apparently achieve considerable stability, almost approaching a supra-dialectical norm, in orthography, morphology, phraseology, and syntax, which was to a considerable extent independent of the Ch.[urch] Sl.[avonic] norm" (p. 400).

112. Mechkovskaia (n. 99 above), pp. 19–24; and for the loanwords, Alekseev, *Slovari inostrannykh iazykov v azbukovnike.*

113. Ong, pp. 37 ff.

114. V. A. Chernov, as cited by Kortava, *Moskovskii prikaznyi iazyk,* p. 24.

115. See the extended discussion in Uspenskii, *Istoriia russkogo iazyka,* pp. 244 ff.; also Uspenskii, "Language Situation in Muscovite Rus," pp. 365–85. Uspenskii's notion of diglossia in Muscovy has frequently been challenged: see Collins, "On Diglossia," pp. 79–94. V. M. Zhivov, a former collaborator of Uspenskii, now rejects "diglossia" in favor of various "registers of written Russian" in Muscovy: Zhivov, *Iazyk i kul'tura,* preface (p. 1) and chap. 1; see also the review of this work by A. Zoltán in *Russian Linguistics* 23, no. 2 (May 1999): 181–85.

116. The subject of a large scholarly literature: for an introduction in English, see Brown, *Seventeenth-Century Russian Literature,* especially pp. 97–156, with bibliography (pp. 165–74).

117. Ibid., pp. 10–93, with further references; Brown describes the language of a prominent tale of the period as "awkward and unliterary, a curious hodgepodge of the colloquial and the bookish" (p. 70). See further Kortava, *Moskovskii prikaznyi iazyk,* pp. 28–9, 86–96, and Zhivov, *Iazyk i kul'tura,* pp. 52–59. Several works on sacred imag-

ery written in later seventeenth-century Muscovy and exhibiting a "hybrid-Slavonic" character are discussed at length in Cracraft, *Revolution in Imagery*, pp. 82–92.

118. See again collections edited by Kotkov, as cited above (n. 109). Uspenskii notes that in the *Ulozhenie* (law code) of 1649, compiled in Moscow mainly in chancery Russian, whole passages—those dealing with such "sacred matters" as oath taking—are in Church Slavonic (Uspenskii, *Istoriia russkogo iazyka*, pp. 318–19; excerpt reproduced in our Appendix I, no. 4). Similarly the frequently cited report on Muscovite affairs written about 1666 in Stockholm by the renegade Muscovite official G. Kotoshikhin (= Kot., Appendix II, Works Cited), who moves from a chancery Russian laced with Latin and other neologisms to Church Slavonic when discussing icon veneration (Uspenskii, pp. 61–62). At the same time Uspenskii (pp. 61, 319), among other specialists, finds it difficult to classify linguistically the even better known *Life (Zhitie)* dating to 1672–1676 of the dissident Archpriest Avvakum: "an entirely idiosyncratic mélange of the conventional Russo-Slavonic . . . with the most earthy, plebian vernacular," says Brown, *Seventeenth-Century Russian Literature* (p. 70).

119. See R. I. Avanesov and S. V. Bromlei, eds., *Dialektologicheskii atlas russkogo iazyka*, 2 atlases plus 3 vols. of commentary (M., 1986–1996), and historical observations by Avanesov, vol. 1, commentary, pp. 26–28. A handy introduction is Gorshkova, *Istoricheskaia dialektologiia*; in English, R. Auty, "The Russian Language," in Auty, Obolensky, and Kingsford, eds., *An Introduction*, pp. 32–35, or, in much greater detail, Vlasto, *Linguistic History of Russia*, chap. 6. Uspenskii stresses that until the eighteenth century "the Russian language," in contrast to the codified Church Slavonic, was "essentially an amalgam [*sovokupnost'*: aggregate] of various East Slavic dialects" (Uspenskii, *Istoriia russkogo iazyka*, p. 50).

120. Worth, "Language," p. 36.

121. Ludolf's *Grammatica Russica* has been published in a facsimile edition by Oxford University (Clarendon) Press (Oxford, 1959), ed. B. O. Unbegaun; a Russian edition, *G. V. Ludol'f, Russkaia grammatika*, ed. B. A. Larin, was published, with a partial translation of the original Latin and editorial notes and commentary, at Leningrad, 1937: cf. *Opis. II*, appendix 3, no. 1 (pp. 311–13) for a description of the Ludolf based on two copies preserved in Russian libraries whose inscriptions indicate, incidentally, that they were originally owned by foreign scholars. Details of Ludolf's career in J. S. G. Simmons, "H. W. Ludolf and the Printing of His *Grammatica Russica* at Oxford in 1696," *Oxford Slavonic Papers* 1 (1950): 104–29; and in J. Tetzner, *H. W. Rudolf und Russland* (Berlin, 1955).

122. Simmons, pp. 106–7; and further, Tetzner, pp. 23–31.

123. Simmons, pp. 107 ff.; also Tetzner, on Ludolf's "ideology," pp. 16–22.

124. Simmons, p. 111.

125. Ibid., p. 112.

126. Ludolf, *Grammatica Russica,* facs. edn., editor's introduction, p. x; a facsimile reproduction of the special dedication is appended here to the last page (97) of the *Grammatica*.

127. Simmons, pp. 117–8.

128. Quoted in ibid., p. 128 (n. **U**).

129. Cracraft, *Revolution in Imagery*, pp. 88–90.

130. Ludolf, *Grammatica Russica*, facs. edn., editor's introduction, pp. viii–x.

131. As printed in Tetzner, pp. 114, 124–6, 135–7, 142–3; and in R. D. Shepeleva, "Pis'ma G.-V. Ludol'fa 1698 g.," in Dem'ianov, *Istochniki russkogo iazyka*, pp. 196–99.

132. Ludolf, *Grammatica Russica*, facs. edn., editor's introduction, pp. xi, viii.

133. Unbegaun, "Russian Grammars," p. 105. Ludolf's grammar was also known to the Anglican chaplain serving in St. Petersburg in the 1720s, who proposed to publish an improved edition of it—a proposal that never came to fruition: see J. Cracraft, ed., introduction to *For God and Peter the Great: The Works of Thomas Consett, 1723–1729* (New York, 1982), pp. 29–30.

134. Details in B. A. Uspenskii, "Dolomonovskie grammatiki russkogo iazyka (itogi i perspektivy)," in Sjöberg, Ďurovič, and Birgegård, eds., *Dolomonovskii period iazyka*, pp. 106–18. Since Uspenskii wrote the Ridley ms., mentioned by him, has also been published: G. Stone, ed., *A Dictionarie of the Vulgar Russe Tongue, Attributed to Mark Ridley* (Cologne, 1996); see pp. 43–52 for the grammar.

2. THE NAUTICAL TURN

1. Cf. Avery (Appendix II, Works Cited), which lists (pp. 77–82) 138 such galley terms plus a few derivations; Avery also adduces evidence that by the end of the eighteenth century almost all these "terms of Italian origin had completely fallen out of general use in the professional language of the Russian sailor" (pp. 90–91).

2. U.S. Admiral Alfred Mahan, *The Influence of Sea Power upon History, 1660–1783* (Boston, 1890), is doubtless the primary text, as acknowledged most recently by R. Harding, *Seapower and Naval Warfare, 1650–1830* (London and Annapolis, MD, 1999), pp. xix and passim; the conceptualization of J. P. LeDonne, *The Russian Empire and the World, 1700–1917: The Geopolitics of Expansion and Containment* (Oxford, 1997), is explicitly indebted to it and other works by Mahan (pp. xii, 336, 371–78 passim, 379). For the Russian navy's strategic role from Peter's time to 1917, see further LeDonne, pp. 8–20, 23–26, 113–15, 144–46, 150–51, 212–15, 292–93, 297–300, 304–07, 339–45; essays by H. Ragsdale, E. V. Anisimov, and H. Bagger in Ragsdale and V. N. Ponomarev, eds., *Imperial Russian Foreign Policy* (Cambridge, 1993); and, in the large Western literature devoted to Soviet foreign policy, B. Dismukes and J. M. McConnell, eds., *Soviet Naval Diplomacy* (New York, 1979). Perhaps the best known Russian work combining naval history and grand strategy is Admiral S. G. Gorshkov, *Morskaia moshch' gosudarstva* (M., 1976), written when the Russian (Soviet) navy was experiencing its greatest strength and prestige to date.

3. 2. P. N. Miliukov has been perhaps the most vociferous critic in the historical literature; his harsh judgement is recapitulated in L. Hughes, *Russia in the Age of Peter the Great* (New Haven, CT, and London), pp. 88–9. E. V. Anisimov, while also critical, equates Peter's costly naval program with the much later and also very costly Soviet space program and thus finds it acceptable, apparently, in scientific as well as political

terms (Anisimov, *Vremia petrovskikh reform* [L., 1989], p. 115). Admiral Gorshkov's study of history, however, convinced him that "without a powerful navy Russia could not be one of the great powers" and that this was "well understood by Peter I, who is rightly considered the founder of the Russian navy. Precisely with the help of this navy was the long hard struggle of the Russian people for return of outlets to the Baltic Sea [earlier] taken from them brought to an end" (Gorshkov, p. 115).

4. The classic work is F. F. Veselago, *Ocherk russkoi morskoi istorii*, vol. 1 (SPb., 1875), 652 pp., which draws extensively, for the early phase of Peter's naval program, on S. I. Elagin, *Istoriia russkago flota: Period Azovskii* (SPb., 1864), which is supplemented by two large volumes of documents: Elagin, comp., *Istoriia russkago flota: Period Azovskii, Prilozhenie*, 2 vols. (SPb., 1864); see also the relevant parts of Veselago, *Kratkaia istoriia russkago flota*, 2 vols. (SPb., 1893–95; reprinted in one volume, M./L., 1939). Extensive documentation is printed in vols. 1–4 of *Materialy dlia istorii russkago flota*, 17 vols. (SPb., 1865–1904), and in vols. 1–3 of *Opisanie del Arkhiva Morskago Ministerstva za vremia s poloviny XVII do nachala XIX stoletiia*, 10 vols. (SPb., 1877–1906). More or less detailed histories of Peter's navy are in F. N. Gromov and I. V. Kasatronov, eds., *Tri veka rossiiskogo flota, 1696–1996*, 3 vols. (SPb., 1996), 1, pp. 22–63; V. D. Dotsenko, *Admiraly Rossiiskogo flota: Rossiia podnimaet parusa* (SPb., 1995), pp. 6–140; V. A. Zolotarev and I. A. Kozlov, *Flotovodtsy Rossii* (M., 1998), chaps. 1 (Peter I) and 2 (F. M. Apraksin); D. W. Mitchell, *A History of Russian and Soviet Sea Power* (New York, 1974), pp. 16–41; Anisimov, pp. 115–20; R. Wittram, *Peter I, Czar und Kaiser: Zur Geschichte Peters des Grossen in seiner Zeit* (Göttingen, 1964), vol. 2, pp. 17–27; Hughes, pp. 80–89; and I. Grey, "Peter the Great and the Creation of the Russian Navy," *History Today* 11, no. 9 (Sept. 1961): 625–31. Monographic studies include E. V. Tarle, *Russkii flot i vneshniaia politika Petra I* (SPb., 1994; first publ. 1949); P. A. Krotov, *Gangutskaia bataliia 1714 goda* (SPb., 1996); E. J. Phillips, *The Founding of Russia's Navy: Peter the Great and the Azov Fleet, 1688–1714* (Westport, CT, 1995); and more specialized works cited below.

5. M. Mollat du Jourdin, *Europe and the Seas*, trans. (from French) T. L. Fagan (Cambridge, MA, 1993), pp. 153 ff. for the words quoted and p. 174 for the estimate of Europe's maritime population ca. 1700. On the diffusion of shipbuilding and navigational techniques in Europe from late medieval times into the seventeenth century, see essays by R. W. Unger in J. B. Hattendorf, ed., *Maritime History*, vol. 1: *The Age of Discovery* (Malabar, FL, 1996), pp. 21–49; for the North Sea–Baltic world in particular, D. Kirby and M.-L. Hinkkanen, *The Baltic and the North Seas* (London and New York, 2000).

6. D. Loades, *The Tudor Navy: An Administrative, Political, and Military History* (Aldershot, UK, 1992), pp. 5, 8–9. A portolan (from Italian *portolano/portolani* = sailing direction/s) was usually a simple chart illustrating details of a coastline, including ports, anchorages, rocks, and shoals, as well as indicating the distance between ports and the direction from one to the next. From the thirteenth century, "rhumb" lines providing compass bearings were added to portolan charts; but such charts could give no guidance on the open seas. Declination: the angular distance of a celestial

body north or south of the equator as measured from the earth's center. Backstaff: a navigational instrument for measuring the altitude of the sun, so-called because the navigator had the sun behind him when using it.

7. J. Glete, *Navies and Nations: Warships, Navies and State Building in Europe and America, 1500–1860*, 2 vols. continuously paginated (= vol. 48, pts. 1 and 2, of Acta Universitatis Stockholmiensis / Stockholm Studies in History, Stockholm, 1993), pp. 102 ff.: for the English navy ca. 1500–1650, see pp. 129–35.

8. B. Capp, *Cromwell's Navy: The Fleet and the English Revolution* (Oxford, 1989), pp. 4, 6, 396; also Glete, pp. 173–87.

9. Figures from J. H. Owen, *War at Sea under Queen Anne* (Cambridge, 1938), pp. 15, 26 and appendixes A, B, C, D (pp. 271–80); N. A. M. Rodger, *The Wooden World: An Anatomy of the Georgian Navy* (London, 1986), appendix I (pp. 348–49); J. S. Bromley and A. N. Ryan, "Navies," in Bromley, ed., *The Rise of Great Britain and Russia, 1688–1725* (= vol. 6 of *The New Cambridge Modern History* [Cambridge, 1971]), pp. 790–93.

10. Bromley and Ryan, p. 791; J. Black and P. Woodfine, *The British Navy and the Use of Naval Power in the Eighteenth Century* (Atlantic Highlands, NJ, 1989), pp. 37, 39, 47; and, for the whole period ca. 1650–1713, Glete, pp. 173 ff., and Harding (n. 2 above), chaps. 4–6.

11. G. J. Marcus, *A Naval History of England,* vol. 1: *The Formative Centuries* (London, 1961), pp. 2–3.

12. T. J. Willan, "Trade between England and Russia in the Second Half of the Sixteenth Century," *Economic History Review* 63 (1948): 307–21; Willan, *The Early History of the Russia Company* (Manchester, UK, 1956).

13. Claims to preeminence in shipbuilding and ship design advanced in this period and later by historians, obviously colored by nationalist bias, have yet to be sustained by systematic comparative research, as Harding (n. 2 above), pp. 129–34, clearly points out. Harding himself suggests that by 1700 or so, English and Dutch shipwrights were equally well regarded and "in great demand across Europe" (p. 132); that "French warship design [was] considered the best in Europe during the first half of the eighteenth century" (idem.); but that, as places to build ships, British yards "had a number of advantages over European rivals" (p. 134). All three points came to be understood, remarkably, by Tsar Peter.

14. A. Cross, *By the Banks of the Neva: Chapters from the Lives and Careers of the British in Eighteenth-Century Russia* (Cambridge, 1997), pp. 44 ff., with further references, to which should be added H. Kaplan, *Russian Overseas Commerce with Great Britain during the Reign of Catherine II* (= vol. 218 of *Memoirs of the American Philosophical Society,* Philadelphia, 1996). For the Dutch dominance of the Baltic trade from about 1600 on into the eighteenth century, see J. I. Israel, *Dutch Primacy in World Trade, 1585–1740* (Oxford, 1989), pp. 43–48, 152–56, and passim. The commercial considerations dominating, from the English side, Peter's visit to England of 1698 are stressed, with new evidence, by W. F. Ryan, "Peter the Great's English Yacht: Admiral Lord Carmarthen and the Russian Tobacco Monopoly," *The Mariner's Mirror* 69, no. 1 (Feb. 1983): 65–87.

15. Cf. G. V. Scammell, *The First Imperial Age: European Overseas Expansion, 1400–1715* (Boston, 1989), and C. M. Cipolla, *Guns, Sails and Empires: Technological Innovation and the Early Phases of European Expansion, 1400–1700* (New York, 1965, 1996); also J. H. Parry, *The Age of Reconaissance* (London, 1963), and Israel (n. 14 above).

16. On Chancellor and the early Muscovy (later Russia) Company, see further L. Berry and R. O. Crummey, *Rude and Barbarous Kingdom: Russia in the Accounts of Six-teenth-Century English Voyagers* (Madison, WI, 1968), pp. ix–xvii, 3–41; and for more on Cabot and his English pupils, D. W. Waters, *The Art of Navigation in England in Elizabethan and Early Stuart Times* (London, 1958), pp. 78 ff.

17. Cross (n. 14), pp. 174–5; Ryan (Appendix II, Works Cited), pp. 77 ff.; and A. I. Andreev, "Petr I v Anglii v 1698 g.," in Andreev, ed., *Petr Velikii: sbornik statei* (M./L., 1947), pp. 63–103.

18. The draft is printed in N. G. Ustrialov, *Istoriia tsarstvovaniia Petra Velikago*, vol. 1 (SPb., 1858), pp. 397–401, from the original in Peter's hand (except as noted presently) now at TsGADA: Kabinet Petra I, otd. 1, kn. 38.

19. Veselago, *Kratkaia istoriia* (1939), pp. 10–11; A. V. Viskovatov, *Kratkii istoricheskii obzor morskikh pokhodov russkikh i morekhodstva ikh voobshche do iskhoda XVII stoletiia*, ed. K. V. Bazilevich (SPb., 1994; first published SPb., 1864), pp. 87–113; Iu. P. Tushin, *Russkoe moreplavanie na Azovskom, Kaspiiskom i Chernom moriakh (XVII vek)* (M., 1978), pp. 44–50; also Phillips (n. 4 above), pp. 18–27.

20. Cf. *PiB*, vol. 1, no. 8 (p. 127) and note, p. 488.

21. Notebooks printed in ibid., nos. 1–3 (pp. 1–10): see especially no. 2 (p. 9); letters to mother in ibid., nos. 4–9 (pp. 10–12): see especially no. 6 (p. 11).

22. Details in M. M. Bogoslovskii, *Petr I: Materialy dlia biografii*, 5 vols. (M., 1940–1948), 1, pp. 66–74, 103–4, 119–21, 138–46.

23. *PiB*, vol. 1, nos. 14–18 (pp. 15–17), p. 490.

24. Ibid., nos. 33–36 (pp. 26–28), no. 84 (p. 61).

25. Ibid., no. 22 (p. 20).

26. Ibid., no. 29 (p. 24). Details of Peter's "campaigns" to Archangel in 1693 and 1694 in Bogoslovskii (n. 22 above), vol. 1, pp. 149–68, 176–93.

27. *PiB*, vol. 1, nos. 19 ff. (pp. 18 ff.), nos. 33–34 (pp. 26–27), no. 38 (p. 30), no. 84 (p. 61), etc.

28. See Cracraft, *Revolution in Architecture*, pp. 114–21 and figs. 57–62.

29. *PiB*, vol. 1, no. 128 (pp. 116–17).

30. V. P. Zagorovskii, *Petr Velikii na voronezhskoi zemle: istoricheskii ocherk* (Voronezh, 1996), p. 7. Detailed accounts of shipbuilding at Voronezh and the buildup of the Azov fleet in 1695–1698 and thereafter are in Bogoslovskii, vol. 1, pp. 360–65, and vol. 2, pp. 127–75; Iu. M. Lavrikov, "Robotniki voronezhskikh verfei 1696–1711," in V. P. Zagorovskii et al., eds., *Voronezhskii krai na iuzhnykh rubezhakh Rossii: XVII–XVIII vv.* (Voronezh, 1981), pp. 77–89; A. M. Abbasov, ed., *Voronezh, kolybel' flota russkogo: petrovskii sbornik* (Voronezh, 1995); Veselago, *Ocherk*, chaps. 3 and 4; and Phillips, pp. 38–44, 59–112.

31. Cracraft, *Revolution in Architecture*, pp. 119–20.

32. See Cracraft, *Revolution in Imagery,* pp. 130–40, with further references.

33. See Cruys's new biography, by R. L. Ose, in T. Titlestad, ed., *Kornelius Kriuis, Admiral Petra Velikogo* (Stavanger, Norway, 1998), especially pp. 42–51.

34. *PiB,* vol. 1, no. 140 (pp. 135–37).

35. Peter's actual certificate, in Dutch, is reproduced in Ustrialov (n. 18 above), vol. 3, appendix 4 (p. 468). See further J. Driessen, *Tsaar Peter de Grote en zijn Amsterdamse vrienden* (Utrecht, 1996), for a full account of Peter in Amsterdam, which he visited again in 1716–17.

36. Jan Tessing, a printer and bookseller who fulfilled important commissions from Peter (see Chapter 6).

37. Details in A. G. Cross, *By the Banks of the Thames: Russians in Eighteenth-Century Britain* (Newtonville, MA, 1980), chap. 6; Cross, *Banks of the Neva* (n. 14 above), chap. 5; and Cross, *Peter the Great through British Eyes: Perceptions and Representations of the Tsar since 1698* (Cambridge, 2000), chap. 2.

38. See, incrementally, Cross, *Banks of the Thames,* p. 146, Cross, *Banks of the Neva,* p. 160, and Cross, *British Eyes,* pp. 26–28; and for details of the *Royal Transport,* which duly sailed to Russia but later perished at sea, Ryan (n. 14 above), pp. 67–68. The documents transmitting and receiving the royal yacht, from British and Russian archives, are printed in S. Dixon et al., eds. and trans., *Britain and Russia in the Age of Peter the Great: Historical Documents* (London, 1998), nos. 10 (pp. 7–8), 12 (p. 10).

39. J. Perry, *The State of Russia under the Present Czar* (London, 1716), pp. 164, 165; Filippo Balatri, in the journal-memoir of his years (1699–1701) in Russia, as quoted in D. L. Schlafly, "Filippo Balatri in Peter the Great's Russia," *JGO* 45, no. 2 (1997): 187.

40. *SIRIO* 39, p. 115 (Whitworth); L. N. Maikov, ed., *Rasskazy Nartova o Petre Velikom* (SPb., 1891), p. 10.

41. See Cracraft, *Revolution in Imagery,* pp. 131–36, with a full-length reproduction of the portrait (fig. 21). For the three-masted, fully rigged, fifty-two–gun warship that Peter built at Voronezh in 1700—he called it the *Predestination (Predestinatsiia)*—and a contemporary etching thereof, see ibid., p. 169 and fig. 41 (p. 170).

42. Cross, *Banks of the Neva,* pp. 161–67, 172–74; Cross, *British Eyes,* p. 37. Cross's depiction of the primacy of British shipbuilders in Petrine Russia is fully supported by I. A. Bykhovskii, *Petrovskie korabely* (L., 1982), pp. 88–96. According to an official Russian report of July 25, 1698, some 110 British naval personnel had arrived at Archangel for service in Russia (Dixon, no. 21 [pp. 18–19]). A memo in Peter's hand dated Voronezh March 11, 1705, indicates how highly he and his men valued the English shipwrights (ibid., no. 58 [p. 49]); indeed, his personal papers abound in such evidence, e.g., at TsGADA, F. 396, op. 2, d. 1081, ll. 1–22: see note of Aug. 6, 1715, dispensing a sum of money to "ship master Brown *[brounu]*" for distribution among the "English officers *[afitseram]* and under-officers." In July 1719 the British envoy in Russia reported that it would be difficult to recall the British shipwrights working in Russia since they received "considerable sallaries . . . besides presents upon occasion and other advantages . . . in short the Czar omits nothing that can endear himself to them or that may engage them to continue in his service for life" (ibid., no. 227 [pp. 204–05]).

43. Schlafly, p. 182; Ose (n. 33 above), p. 49.
44. Harding (n. 2), pp. 135, 144.
45. Cross, *Banks of the Thames,* pp. 148–49.
46. Cross, *Banks of the Neva,* pp. 45 ff.; A. Kahan, *The Plow, the Hammer, and the Knout: An Economic History of Eighteenth-Century Russia,* ed. R. Hellie (Chicago, 1985), pp. 163–266 (p. 247 for the phrase quoted).
47. Cracraft, *Revolution in Architecture,* p. 121. Anisimov offers a total of "not fewer than 1,104 ships and other vessels" (*Reformy,* p. 118), while a total of 1,051 ships (480 sail, 571 oar-powered) is given in Gromov and Kasatronov, eds., *Tri veka* (n. 4 above), vol. 1, p. 58. For the ship construction in connection with the Persian campaign, see V. P. Zagorovskii, "Korablestroenia v Tavrove v poslednie gody tsarstvovaniia Petra I," in Zagorovskii (n. 30 above), pp. 90–98.
48. Krotov (n. 4 above); Iu. N. Bespiatykh, *Istoriia znamenitogo srazheniia: shvedskaia ekspeditsiia na Arkhangel'sk v 1701 godu* (Archangel, 1990); and documents in Iu. N. Bespiatyk et al., comps., *Trevozhnye gody Arkhangel'ska, 1700–1721: dokumenty po istorii Belomor'ia v epokhu Petra Velikogo* (Archangel, 1993).
49. Veselago, *Ocherk,* p. 411.
50. Cross, *Banks of the Neva,* p. 167; also Harding, pp. 189, 221. Gromov and Kasatronov, eds., (n. 4 above) indicate (vol. 1, p. 53) that by 1721 Sweden was down to eleven ships of the line and three frigates (from thirty-eight and ten in 1700, at the beginning of the Northern War, when Russia had none of either type). Glete (n. 7) in several tables and diagrams provides more extensive figures for comparison: these indicate Russian naval predominance in 1720 over both Sweden and Denmark in total number of battleships, but much closer matches when all warships (frigates, bomb vessels) are counted and strength is calculated in total displacement in tons (Glete, Table 22:24 [p. 235] and Diagram 22:5 [p. 236]).
51. C. A. G. Bridge, ed., *History of the Russian Fleet during the Reign of Peter the Great, by a Contemporary Englishman (1724)* (London, 1899 = vol. 15 of Publications of the Navy Records Society), p. 114 (author has since been identified as Captain John Deane [1680?–1761], not to be confused with John Deane the shipwright); for Capt. Deane's list of the ships in the Baltic fleet as of 1724, see pp. 130–32. Apparently counting all ships, seaworthy or not, Anisimov says that by late 1724 the Baltic fleet consisted of 34 ships of the line and 15 frigates armed with a total of 2,226 cannon (Anisimov [n. 3 above], pp. 119–20, citing 1961 archival work by G. A. Nekrasov and an article by P. A. Krotov, "Sozdanie lineinogo flota na Baltike pri Petre I," *Istoricheskie zapiski* 116 [1988]: 313–31); similarly Hughes, who offers a total of "36 ships of the line, 16 frigates, 70 galleys, and 280 other vessels" (Hughes [n. 3 above], p. 82, citing N. Iu. Berezovskii et al., *Rossiiskii imperatorskii flot, 1696–1917: Voenno-istoricheskii spravochnik* [M., 1993], p. 36); and Gromov and Kasatronov, eds. (n. 4 above), which lists (vol. 1, p. 53) 36 ships of the line in the Baltic fleet in 1722, 9 frigates, 85 other sail, and 396 brigantines and galleys for a grand total of 526 vessels. If all major warships listed by Capt. Deane were counted, the total would be 40 (11 by his reckoning "old" or "very old, unfit for sea," etc.; he lists another 31 as "broke up" or "cast away"). These numerical

503

discrepancies prove the importance of using contemporary lists of warships, like any other primary source, critically: cf. warnings in Glete, especially pp. 96–100, and Harding, pp. 289–93.

52. Phillips (n. 4), p. 127.

53. Russian *morskoi* (adj.), in a fine example of semantic expansion, is variously translated in this volume as "sea," "nautical," "marine," "maritime," or "naval," depending on context.

54. Veselago, *Ocherk*, pp. 537–38, 63.

55. Ibid., p. 538; the articles are printed in Elagin, *Prilozhenie* (n. 4 above), vol. 1, appendix 1, no. 33 (pp. 58–60).

56. Elagin, *Istoriia flota* (n. 4 above), p. 99.

57. *PSZ*, vol. 4, no. 2267 (pp. 485–92).

58. Veselago, *Ocherk*, pp. 539–41.

59. Hughes (n. 3 above), p. 85.

60. *PiB*, vol. 6, no. 1955 (pp. 85–86): "Piter" to K. N. Zotov in London, Sept. 10, 1707, responding to Zotov's letter to his father seeking permission to go to sea, as reproduced in ibid., p. 339.

61. *ZAP*, no. 19 (p. 42): extract from Zotov's journal recording Peter's order.

62. Ibid., nos. 20 (p. 43), 76, 77 (pp. 75–77).

63. *Opis. I*, no. 171 (pp. 181–83); copy also at LC–Law Library (Rare Books Reserve).

64. *Opis. I*, nos. 75 (pp. 145–46), 79 (pp. 146–47), 880 (pp. 479–80); nos. 160 (pp. 179–80), 196 pp. 189–90), 307 (pp. 239–40). A copy of the 1718 Russian edition of the Danish statute, *Instruktsiia o morskikh Artikulakh . . . ,* is also at LC–Law Library (Rare Books Reserve).

65. *ZAP*, no. 22 (p. 43): original in Peter's hand.

66. Ibid., no. 24 (p. 44): original in Peter's hand, dated May 19, 1715.

67. R. H. Warner, "Peter the Great's Combat Admiral George Paddon, Captain, R.N.," *The Mariner's Mirror* 75, no. 1 (Feb. 1989): 11–13; contract printed in *Materialy flota* (n. 4 above), vol. 3, no. 193 (pp. 144–45).

68. In fact, one of Peter's attendants in England in 1698 recorded that he talked much with local officials precisely about "admiralty regulations *[admiralteiskie reglamenty]*": Andreev, "Petr I v Anglii" (n. 17 above), p. 87.

69. Warner, p. 16.

70. Veselago, *Ocherk*, p. 541.

71. *Opisanie Arkhiva* (n. 4 above), vol. 2, no. 453 (pp. 284–85).

72. *ZAP*, no. 45 (p. 57): original in Peter's hand. That the procedure outlined here by Peter was actually followed in the preparation of the *Naval Statute* has been demonstrated by Claes Peterson, "Der Morskoj Ustav Peters des Grossen: Ein Beitrag zu seiner Entstehungsgeschichte," *JGO* 24, no. 3 (1976): 345–56.

73. E.g., *Opisanie Arkhiva*, vol. 1, no. 21 (p. 50), and vol. 3, no. 649 (p. 272); and *ZAP*, no. 46 (pp. 57–58); also Peterson, passim.

74. *ZAP*, no. 75 (pp. 74–75): original in Peter's hand.

75. *Opis. I*, no. 444 (pp. 284–87); *Opis. II*, Appendix VI, no. 444 (p. 349); *Opis. III*, no. 102 (p. 38); copy also at HU–Law School Library (Special Collections—Rare Russian).

76. *Opis. I*, no. 674 (pp. 368–70).

77. *ZAP*, no. 79 (p. 78): original in Peter's hand.

78. *Opis. I*, nos. 465 (p. 293), 500 (p. 302); 508 (p. 304); *Opis. III*, nos. 106 (p. 38), 118 (p. 40).

79. *Opis. I*, nos. 508, 509 (pp. 375–76); *Opis. III*, no. 120 (p. 40). Description based on copy of the *Extract from the Naval Statute/Vypiska iz Morskago ustava* (SPb., 1728) at LC–Rare Books.

80. Opis. *I*, nos. 684 (pp. 375–76), 760 (pp. 420–21), 792 (pp. 440–41); *Opis. III*, nos. 175 (p. 49), 229 (p. 61), 257 (p. 66); *Svodnyi katalog*, vol. 3, nos. 2967–2974 (pp. 43–44).

81. Veselago, *Ocherk*, p. 546; N. G. Sergeeva, *Rossiiskii flot (1720–1917): Bibliograficheskii spravochnik izdanii morskogo vedomstva* (SPb., 1995), pp. 13–14 (nos. 1, 3, 4, 5 ff.).

82. *PSZ*, vol. 6, no. 3485, dated (erroneously) April 13, 1720.

83. *Kniga ustav morskoi, Sanktpeterburg 1763*, facsimile ed., L. M. Kuznetsov et al., eds. (M., 1993).

84. Cracraft, *Revolution in Imagery*, pp. 170–77.

85. *Opis. I*, p. 285.

86. Quotations from *Kniga ustav morskoi*, 1763 facs. ed., Preface, pp. 2–3.

87. Ibid., pp. 4–10.

88. Ibid., p. 10.

89. *Opis. II*, no. 131 (pp. 219–20), indicating that the sermon was printed in traditional or church Cyrillic type at the Alexander-Nevskii monastery press on Oct. 14, 1720. Copies of this pamphlet are reprinted, in now standard Russian types and spellings, in Eremin, ed., *Prokopovich: sochineniia*, pp. 102–12 (editor's notes, pp. 468–69), and in Grebeniuk and Derzhavina, eds., *Panegiricheskaia literatura*, pp. 234–41 (editors' comments, pp. 115–20).

90. Eremin, ed., *Prokopovich: sochineniia*, pp. 103–12 (p. 104 for the reference to the preface to the *Naval Statute*).

91. *Kniga ustav morskoi*, part 1, section 1, p. 13.

92. Ibid., pp. 13–14; book 1, chap. 1, pp. 1 ff.

93. Veselago, *Ocherk*, pp. 543–47; Gromov and Kasatronov, eds. (n. 4 above), pp. 61–63.

94. Cf. Avery (Appendix II, Works Cited), p. 82.

95. Ibid., p. 80.

96. Cf. Bond (Appendix II, Works Cited), p. 147.

97. Ibid., p. 128.

98. Cf. Whittall (Appendix II, Works Cited), p. 45.

99. Ibid., p. 63.

100. Avery, p. 81.

101. Ibid., p. 80.

102. *Kniga ustav morskoi*, bk. 3, chap. 1, art. 90 (p. 60).

103. Ibid., bk. 5, chaps. 1–20 (pp. 113 ff.).

104. Ibid., bk. 1, chap. 1, art. 2 (p. 33).

105. Ibid., bk. 1, chap. 1, p. 3.

106. Ibid., bk. 3, chap. 1, pp. 39–40.

107. Ibid., bk. 5, chap. 1, p. 113.

505

506

108. An outline of K. N. Zotov's career is in F. Veselago, ed., *Obshchii morskoi spisok* (SPb., 1885), pp. 156–58. See further *Rbs,* vol. 7, pp. 474–76; and Pekarskii, *Nauka i literatura,* vol. 1, pp. 157–62 (reproducing Zotov's reports from Paris—for which see further unpublished items at TsGADA, F. 396, op. 2, d. 1082, ll. 144–45; F. 9, otd. I, kn. 53, l. 94: latter addressed from Moscow to "Monseur Sotoff gentilhomes de Sa Majiste Czarienne a Paris").

109. *Opis. I,* no. 828 (pp. 456–57); details from copy at GBL.

110. George Paddon, rear admiral of the Baltic fleet in 1717–1719, was distressed to discover that among "the sons of great men which his majesty [Peter] has ordered to sea, not one in twenty will ever come to make officers" (quoted in Warner, "Paddon" [n. 67 above], p. 13).

111. Cf. Dutch *kabelaaring,* a thick chain or rope around the capstan for raising the anchor: Barkh. (Appendix II, Works Cited), IX, p. 183.

112. *Vinbom(en)/vymbom/vindbom* = lever for rotating the capstan, from Dutch *windboom(en)* (Barkh., III, 164).

113. From English *stopper* = device for securing a cable (*OED,* X, 1032).

114. Cf. Dutch *beating/Swedish beting/Danish beding,* etc.= English *bitt,* usually plural and meaning strong posts firmly fastened in pairs to the deck of a ship for fastening cables, belaying ropes, etc. (*OED,* I, 884–85; Barkh., II, 25–26).

115. *Sarving/sarven'* = service, from English (obs.) *sarving/*Dutch *serving,* here the binding, braiding, or wrapping of a rope, rod, and so forth, with a small cord or the like to protect or strengthen it (*OED,* IX, 514; Whittall [Appendix II, Works Cited], pp. 77–78; Vasmer [Appendix II, Works Cited], II, 580).

116. Cf. Dutch *bakboord, bras.*

117. Cf. Dutch *geytouw/gytouw, fok, voormarszeil.*

118. Cf. Dutch *stuurboord.*

119. Cf. Dutch *magerman* (Vasmer, II, 86).

120. Cf. Dutch *grotemars.*

121. Cf. Dutch *grootzeil.*

122. *Gordin/gorden'* = rope with pulley for raising something aloft, from Dutch *gording* (cf. Barkh., V, 168); also cf. Dutch *groot reil(ing).*

123. Apparently English *fo'c'sle* (= forecastle) plus *galion,* an old term for the fore part of a ship (*OED,* IV, 430, 19).

124. Cf. Dutch *blindezeil.*

125. Cf. Dutch *boven.*

126. Cf. Dutch *voor, groot bramzeil.*

127. Cf. Dutch *kluiffok.*

128. *Opis. I,* nos. 3, 35, 88, 95, 98, 136, 149, 150, 183, 184, 188, 189, 193, 194, 363, 364, 371, 406, 441, 447, 452, 524, 757.

129. Ibid., nos. 210, 332, 383, 405, 654.

130. Ibid., nos. 197, 201, 220, 408, 666, 695, 733; also *Opis. II,* nos. 25, 27.

131. *Opis. I,* nos. 102, 159, 230, 367, 370, 569.

132. Ibid., nos. 583–585, 735, 742, 788, 816–818, 830, 864.

133. Ibid., nos. 38–40, 80, 110, 508, 674, 675, 684, 760, 794, 849.

134. Ibid., appendix 1, no. 15 (pp. 290–92), and no. 23 (p. 83).

135. Ibid., pp. 292, 318 ff.

136. Ibid., no. 576 (p. 327); *Opis. II*, appendix 4, no. 576 (pp. 349–50); *Opis. III*, no. 135 (p. 42); *Svodnyi katalog*, vol. 2, no. 4324 (p. 258): details from the St. Petersburg 1739 edition at BAN.

137. *Svodnyi katalog*, vol. 2, no. 4344 (p. 262): comments based on copy at GBL.

138. On Mordvinov's career, see Veselago, *Spisok*, pp. 254–59; Dotsenko, *Admiraly* (n. 4 above), pp. 148 ff. For his letters and papers, see S. A. Mordvinov, *Zapiski Admirala Semena Ivanovicha Mordvinova, pisannyia sobstvennoiu ego rushkoiu*, ed. S. Elagin (SPb., 1868); and V. A. Bil'basov, ed., *Arkhiv grafov Mordvinovykh*, 10 vols. (SPb., 1901–1903), vol. 1.

139. BL, Additional MS. 28092, f. 53.

140. Ryan (n. 14 above), pp. 80–81.

141. Ibid.; also N. Hans, "The Moscow School of Mathematics and Navigation (1701)," *Slavonic and East European Review* 29 (1950–51): 532–33; and especially Ryan (Appendix II, Works Cited), pp. 76 ff.

142. Petition and official follow-up at TsGADA, F. 196, op. 3, no. 2297, ll. 1–90b.

143. TsGADA, F. 396, kn. 1684, l. 44.

144. Zagorovskii (n. 30 above), pp. 101–02. The basic history of the Moscow School is still F. Veselago, *Ocherk istorii Morskago kadetskago korpusa* (SPb., 1885), chap. 1, which has been mined and sometimes supplemented by later students, including notably V. V. Romanov et al., *Kolybel' flota: Navigatskaia shkola-Morskoi korpus k 250-ti letiiu so dnia osnovaniia Shkoly matematicheskikh i navigatskikh nauk, 1701–1951 g.* (Paris, 1951), pp. 15–24; Hans (n. 141 above), pp. 532–36; Ryan (Appendix II, Works Cited), pp. 75–81; and M. J. Okenfuss, "Russian Students in Europe in the Age of Peter the Great," in J. G. Garrard, ed., *The Eighteenth Century in Russia* (Oxford, 1973), pp. 136–39.

145. Full description in *Opis. II*, no. 25 (pp. 83–86); copy also at NYPL.

146. A. Vucinich, *Science in Russian Culture: A History to 1860* (Stanford, 1963), p. 54.

147. Ryan (Appendix II, Works Cited), pp. 83–84 and n. 71 (p. 102).

148. Luppov, *Kniga v Rossii*, pp. 12, 15.

149. The basic history of the Naval Academy is, again, Veselago, *Ocherk Morskago korpusa*, chaps. 2, 3; see also Romanov (n. 144 above), pp. 24–28. The key documents registering Peter's decision in September 1715 to found the Naval Academy are itemized in *Opisanie Arkhiva* (n. 4 above), vol. 3, nos. 647, 649 (pp. 267, 274). Veselago's data on the social-occupational background of the academy's student body are confirmed proportionately by a list of 61 students dated March 1705, at TsGADA, F. 35, op. 1, no. 300, ll. 1–4: 20 of these were themselves—or were sons of—government clerks; 12, minor clergy or church officials; 11, nobility; 6, townsmen; 4, soldiers; and 8, "volunteers," i.e., free peasants.

150. *Opisanie Arkhiva*, vol. 2, nos. 412 (pp. 177–78, 212), 440 (p. 247).

151. F. C. Weber, *The Present State of Russia*, vol. 1 (London, 1723; facsimile reprint, New York, 1968), p. 180. For Weber, see Cracraft, *Revolution in Architecture*, especially pp. 196 ff.

152. Cracraft, *Revolution in Imagery*, especially pp. 145–47, with portrait (fig. 26).

507

508

153. *Opis. I*, no. 666 (pp. 362–63).

154. Perry (n. 39 above), pp. 211–12.

155. Cracraft, *Revolution in Imagery*, p. 276.

156. Ryan (Appendix II, Works Cited), p. 99 (n. 45); *Opis. II*, no. 27 (pp. 89–90); *Opis. I*, no. 220 (pp. 200–01).

157. *Opis. I*, no. 408 (p. 272); *Svodnyi katalog*, vol. 3, no. 8542 (p. 421): copy of this (1739) ed. also at LC-Rare. A supplement to the latter, perhaps also by Farquharson, was published by the Naval Academy Press in 1745 under the title *Arkhimedovyi teoremy*: see *Svodnyi katalog*, vol. 1, no. 327 (p. 63).

158. *Opis. I*, no. 733 (pp. 407–08).

159. *Svodnyi katalog*, vol. 3, no. 7676 (p. 284).

160. Ibid., supplement, no. 196 (p. 38).

161. Ibid., vol. 2, no. 4024 (p. 213); on Malygin's career, Veselago, *Obshchii spisok* (n. 108 above), pp. 237–39.

162. *Svodnyi katalog*, vol. 3, no. 6664 (p. 145).

163. BL, MS. Sloane 3227; see further Ryan (Appendix II, Works Cited), pp. 81–90.

164. Ryan (Appendix II, Works Cited), p. 80; Vucinich (n. 146 above), pp. 52–54.

165. *Rbs*, vol. 21, "Farvarson, Andre Danilovich" (pp. 22–3).

166. Quoted in Cross, *Banks of the Neva* (n. 14 above), pp. 175–76.

167. Ibid., p. 176.

168. Romanov (n. 144 above), pp. 59 ff.; Veselago, *Ocherk Morskago korpusa* (n. 144), chaps. 4 ff.

169. Cross, *Banks of the Thames* (n. 37 above), pp. 54–55.

170. A contemporary English naval source notes that the title derived from the Dutch *admiraliteitsheer* and corresponded "in some measure to . . . 'Lord of the Admiralty'": Bridge (n. 51 above), p. 5. Accordingly, the title is usually translated "civil admiral."

171. *PiB*, vol. 1, no. 128 (pp. 116–17).

172. Elagin, *Prilozhenie* (n. 4 above), vol. 2, appendix 5, no. 13 (p. 212).

173. *Materialy flota* (n. 4 above), vol. 3, pt. 2, p. 355.

174. O. Iu. Mikhalev, "Ocherk istorii Voronezhskogo admiralteistva," in A. N. Akin'shin et al., eds., *"Morskim sudam byt'!" Rossiiskomu voenno-morskomu flotu-300 let: Mezhvusovskii sbornik nauchnykh trudov* (Voronezh, 1996), pp. 126–45; D. R. Jones, ed., *The Military-Naval Encyclopedia of Russia and the Soviet Union*, vol. 3 (Gulf Breeze, FL, 1981), pp. 29–31 ("Admiralteits"), 69–70 ("Admiralty Court"), 139–44 ("Admiralty Office"); Phillips (n. 4 above), pp. 59–85.

175. Kahan (n. 46 above), pp. 86–88 and passim; Veselago, *Ocherk morskoi istorii* (n. 4 above), pp. 439–54, 499–536; Jones, pp. 74–119 ("Admiralty, Main"); Phillips, pp. 85–124; Cracraft, *Revolution in Architecture*, pp. 174 ff., 193 ff.

176. *ZAP*, no. 265 (pp. 219–20): Peter to the Senate, Dec. 15, 1717, naming the new colleges and their presidents and vice presidents.

177. *Opis. I*, no. 674 (pp. 368–70).

178. Veselago, *Ocherk morskoi istorii*, pp. 454–98; Jones, pp. 42 ff.; J. LeDonne, *Absolutism and Ruling Class: The Formation of the Russian Political Order, 1700–1825* (Oxford, 1991), pp. 106 ff.

179. Hughes (n. 3 above), p. 81.

180. Eremin, ed., *Prokopovich: sochineniia*, p. 106.

181. Bogoslovskii (n. 22 above), vol. 1, p. 65 (fig. 21); Grebeniuk and Derzhavina, eds., *Panegiricheskaia liteatura*, pp. 118, 237 (fig.). For Ivan Zubov, see Cracraft, *Revolution in Imagery*, pp. 173, 178, 184–88.

182. *SIRIO* 49, no. 65 (pp. 345–47): Campredon to the king, St. Petersburg, June 13 (new style), 1723. The occasion is also mentioned in Peter's *Pokhodnyi zhurnal 1723 goda* (SPb., 1865), p. 15; and is described in his detailed diary of Petrine court life in 1721–1725 by F. W. von Bergholtz, attendant of Duke Karl Friedrich of Holstein: *Dnevnik Kammer-iunkera Berkhgol'tsa*, trans. I. Ammon, pt. 3 (M., 1860), pp. 109–10.

183. Bergholtz, pp. 176–78.

184. Cracraft, *Revolution in Architecture*, p. 218 and fig. 105A (p. 219).

185. Hughes, pp. 277–78; *PSZ*, vol. 7, no. 4562 (p. 345): Peter's decree of Sept. 2, 1724.

186. M. Sarantola-Weiss, "Peter the Great's First Boat: A Symbol of Petrine Influence in Imperial Russia," in M. DiSalvo and L. Hughes, eds., *A Window on Russia: Papers from the V International Conference of the Study Group on Eighteenth-Century Russia* (Rome, 1996), pp. 40–41.

187. O. (P.) Beliaev, *Kabinet Petra Velikago* (SPb., 1793), pt. 2, pp. 117–21.

188. I. Pushkarev, *Istoricheskii ukazatel' dostopamiatnostei Sanktpeterburga* (SPb., 1846), p. 219. Foreign tourists found the *botik* highlighted in Baedeker's famous guidebook, last published in 1914: see *Baedeker's Russia 1914* (reprinted London, 1971), p. 174.

189. Sarantola-Weiss, pp. 37–38, 41.

190. M. A. Orlov et al., eds., *Leningrad: putevoditel'*, 2 vols. (M./L., 1933).

191. Cf. S. M. Serpokryl, comp., *Leningrad: putevoditel'* (L., 1972), pp. 107, 126; L. I. Bastareva and V. I. Sidorova, *Petropavlovskaia krepost': illiustrirovannyi putevoditel'*, 2nd ed. (L., 1972), pp. 79–80.

192. D. Martin, "Ship of State, State of Mind," *New York Times*, Feb. 14, 1997, p. A19.

193. As witness the various commemorative works cited above, e.g., Gromov and Kasatronov, eds. (n. 4 above) and Sergeeva (n. 81). See similarly M. Iu. Gordenev, *Morskie obychai, traditsii i torzhesvennye tseremonii Russkogo imperatorskogo flota* (M., 1992), which also deals briefly with language.

194. Hughes (n. 3 above), p. 88.

195. R. Harding, "Naval Warfare 1453–1815," in J. Black, ed., *European Warfare 1453–1815* (New York, 1999), p. 115. Glete (n. 7 above) provides the fullest account: see pp. 6–15 and 477–89 for analytic summaries of the author's complex, abundantly detailed presentation.

196. Harding, "Naval Warfare," p. 107. For the Baltic in particular, see also K. J. V. Jespersen, "Warfare and Society in the Baltic, 1500–1800," also in Black, pp. 180–200 and fig. 7.1 (p. 193), graphing the Danish-Swedish-Russian naval race in the region from 1600 to 1810.

197. M. S. Anderson, *War and Society in Europe of the Old Regime, 1618–1789* (New York, 1988), p. 94.

198. See Glete, pp. 31–65.

199. Ibid., p. 135.

509

200. Anderson, pp. 99, 96.

201. Harding, "Naval Warfare," p. 111; and further, Harding, *Seapower* (n. 2 above), pp. 18–19, 221–23. See also Jespersen, pp. 198–200, and P. Padfield, *Tide of Empires: Decisive Naval Campaigns in the Rise of the West*, 2 vols. (London and Boston, 1979, 1982), 2, pp. 184–88.

202. Glete, pp. 196–97. See also J. Glete, "Warfare at Sea 1450–1815," in J. Black, ed., *War in the Early Modern World, 1450–1815* (London, 1999), pp. 44–46, stressing Peter's "realistic and cautious attitude" in building and deploying his Baltic fleet.

203. For the origin, in 1739, and early significance of this famous phrase, see Cracraft, *Revolution in Architecture*, pp. 228 ff.

204. Renewed appreciation of St. Petersburg's importance in Russian history and culture is attested by M. S. Kagan, *Grad Petrov v istorii russkoi kul'tury* (SPb., 1996); O. G. Ageeva, *Grad Sviatogo Petra: Peterburg v russkom obshchestvennom soznanii nachala XVIII veka* (SPb., 1999); and N. V. Kaliazina and E. A. Kaliazin, *Okno v Evropu* (SPb./M., 1999). An outpouring of such sentiment occurred in 2003, the tercentenary of the city's founding: see D. Iu. Sherikh, *Peterburg: 300 let den' za dnem* (M., 2003), among the many other commemorations published in Russia.

205. Description with photo in *New York Times,* Jan. 25, 1997, p. A12.

3. MILITARY MODERNIZATION

1. The concept of a military revolution in early modern Europe was launched by M. Roberts in a lecture given in 1955: see the somewhat revised edition thereof published in Roberts, *Essays in Swedish History* (London, 1967), chap. 5 ("The Military Revolution, 1560–1660"). Roberts's lecture-essay has prompted extensive discussion, reconsideration, and revision: see G. Parker, *The Military Revolution: Military Innovation and the Rise of the West* (Cambridge, 1988); J. Black, *A Military Revolution? Military Change and European Society, 1550–1800* (London and Atlantic Highlands, NJ, 1991); Black, *European Warfare, 1660–1815* (London, 1994), especially pp. 3–37; D. Eltis, *The Military Revolution in Sixteenth-Century Europe* (New York, 1995); and J. Bérenger, ed., *La Révolution militaire en Europe (XVe–XVIIIe siècles)* (Paris, 1998). Other major works of interest here are F. Tallett, *War and Society in Early-Modern Europe, 1495–1715* (New York, 1992) and, more broadly, W. H. McNeill, *The Pursuit of Power: Technology, Armed Force, and Society since A.D. 1000* (Chicago, 1982).

2. Cracraft, *Revolution in Architecture*, pp. 11–25, 56–66, and passim.

3. Maj. Gen. B. P. Hughes, *Firepower: Weapons Effectiveness on the Battlefield, 1630–1850* (London, 1974), pp. 8 ff.; also McNeill, chap. 4. Gen. Hughes notes, on the second point, that "there were changes, it is true, in their [the weapons mentioned] rates of fire, their mobility and, to a lesser extent, their accuracy; but the period can be regarded as that in which smooth-bore [as opposed to rifled] armament reached the peak of its performance" (ibid., p. 8). He also notes that the flint-lock musket supplanted the slower, heavier match-lock musket in the later seventeenth century (p. 10).

4. Tallett, pp. 4–9 with Tables 1, 2. More figures, somewhat variant, in McNeill, pp. 110–

11; M. S. Anderson, *War and Society in Europe of the Old Regime, 1618–1789* (New York, 1988), pp. 82–94; and P. Wilson, "Warfare in the Old Regime, 1648–1789," in J. Black, ed., *European Warfare, 1453–1815* (New York, 1999), pp. 78–85 with Table 3.1 (p. 80). Elsewhere it's been calculated that at least one million men were under arms in 1710, when European armies reached their early modern numerical peak: see H. M. Scott, "Europe Turns East: Political Developments in the Eighteenth Century," in E. Cameron, ed., *Early Modern Europe* (Oxford, 1999), p. 307.

511

5. In addition to works cited in Cracraft, *Revolution in Architecture*, p. 346, n. 2, see C. Duffy, *Fire and Stone: The Science of Fortress Warfare, 1660–1860*, 2nd ed. (London, 1996).

6. Tallett, p. 13.

7. On this neglected point, see remarks by J. Black, "Introduction," in Black, pp. 1–4; also Tallett, pp. 232–45.

8. Tallett, pp. 19–20; similarly J. Black, in his "Introduction" to Black, ed., *The Origins of War in Early Modern Europe* (Edinburgh, 1987), where he highlights "religion and dynasticism" as the main causes of early modern European warfare, especially the latter: "The crucial role of the monarch in most European societies . . . and the dynastic perspective of monarchical ambitions ensured a basic continuity in the conduct of international relations" throughout the period (p. 8). See also J. R. Hale, *War and Society in Renaissance Europe, 1450–1620* (New York, 1985), pp. 22–45, who stresses among the causes of war in this period "the tenacity with which the monarch-tycoons of early modern Europe pursued their [territorial] ambitions," territory "expressed in the idiom of inheritance" (p. 23); and essays by S. Gunn and J. Black on the roles first of religion and then of absolutism in European warfare between 1500 and 1715, in Cameron (n. 4 above), pp. 102–33, 206–30.

9. R. M. Hatton, *Charles XII of Sweden* (New York, 1968), pp. xiv, 511–27.

10. See, e.g., M. Roberts, *The Swedish Imperial Experience, 1560–1718* (Cambridge, 1979); K. J. V. Jespersen, "Warfare and Society in the Baltic, 1500–1800," in Black, *European Warfare*, pp. 180–200.

11. A. F. Upton, *Charles XI and Swedish Absolutism* (Cambridge, 1998), pp. 7, 211–12, 260.

12. Cracraft, *Revolution in Imagery*, pp. 68–69 (with fig. 9), 190–92, 216.

13. Cf. J. Cracraft, "Empire versus Nation: Russian Political Theory under Peter I," *Harvard Ukrainian Studies* 10, no. 3/4 (December 1986): 524–41 passim.

14. The principal works in English on pre-Petrine military modernization in Russia are R. Hellie, *Enserfment and Military Change in Muscovy* (Chicago, 1971), chaps. 9–13, and J. L. H. Keep, *Soldiers of the Tsar: Army and Society in Russia, 1462–1874* (Oxford, 1985), chaps. 1–4, both with extensive references; but see more recently, and with quite different emphases, W. C. Fuller, *Strategy and Power in Russia, 1600–1914* (New York, 1992), chap. 1. The fullest account of Peter's youthful war games is in M. M. Bogoslovskii, *Petr I: Materialy dlia biografii*, 5 vols. (M., 1940–1948), 1, especially pp. 30–37, 117–49, 168–71, 192–209; but see also R. H. Warner, "The Kožuchovo Campaign of 1694, or the Conquest of Moscow by Preobraženskoe," *JGO* 13, no. 4 (1965): 487–96; and Cracraft, *Revolution in Architecture*, pp. 114–15 (with fig. 57).

15. Hellie, pp. 230, 156, 184, 196, 226, 222, 201.

16. Ibid., pp. 230–31.

17. Fuller, p. 34.

18. Keep, pp. 91–2.

19. Fuller, chap. 2.

20. In addition to works by Glete and others cited there (Chap. 2), see more generally essays by C. Tilly and S. E. Finer in C. Tilly, ed., *The Formation of National States in Western Europe* (Princeton, 1975), pp. 3–163; M. Mann, *The Sources of Social Power*, vol. 1: *A History of Power from the beginning to* A.D. *1760* (Cambridge, 1986), chaps. 14, 15; and Tallett (n. 1 above), especially pp. 188 ff.—all in essence arguing that in early modern Europe, in Tilly's summation, "War made the state, and the state made war" (Tilly, p. 42).

21. A. Kahan, *The Plow, the Hammer, and the Knout: An Economic History of Eighteenth-Century Russia* (Chicago, 1985), chap. 3.

22. Cf. G. Ágoston, "Ottoman Warfare in Europe, 1453–1826," in Black, *European Warfare*, pp. 118–44, which notes that by 1732 Ottoman reformists regarded Peter's military and naval program in Russia "as an example worthy of imitation" (p. 143). See further R. Murphey, *Ottoman Warfare, 1500–1700* (New Brunswick, NJ, 1999), which, while maintaining that the Ottoman Empire remained an up-to-date and "universally acknowledged European 'superpower'" until 1700 or so, concedes that thereafter vis-à-vis Russia and the other powers its armed forces suffered from increasingly serious fiscal and technical shortfalls.

23. *SIRIO* 49, no. 57 (pp. 309–23; p. 310 for passages quoted): Campredon to the king, March 13, 1723.

24. On the Petrine military revolution in Russia, see, in addition to Fuller (n. 14 above), chap. 2, the more or less detailed studies by Keep (n. 14), chaps. 5, 6; R. Hellie, "The Petrine Army: Continuity, Change, and Impact," *Canadian-American Slavic Studies* 8, no. 2 (Summer 1974): 237–53; C. Duffy, *Russia's Military Way to the West: Origins and Nature of Russian Military Power, 1700–1800* (London, 1981), chap. 2; and L. Hughes, *Russia in the Age of Peter the Great* (New Haven, CT, and London), chap. 3; also R. Wittram, *Peter I, Czar und Kaiser: Zur Geschichte Peters des Grossen in seiner Zeit*, 2 vols. (Göttingen, 1964), 2, pp. 5–56. More general studies include D. B. Ralston, *Importing the European Army: The Introduction of European Military Techniques and Institutions into the Extra-European World, 1600–1914* (Chicago, 1990), chap. 2: "Military Reform under Peter the Great, His Predecessors, and His Successors"; and B. L. Davies, "The Development of Russian Military Power, 1453–1815," in Black, *European Warfare*, pp. 145–79. In Russian the main work is by L. B. Beskrovnyi: see especially his *Russkaia armiia i flot v XVIII veke: ocherki* (M., 1958), chaps. 1–4; also, on the infantry, O. Leonov and I. Ul'ianov, *Reguliarnaia pekhota 1698–1801* (M., 1995), chap. 1; and, at a more popular level, A. L. Borodulin and Iu. E. Kashtanov, *Armiia Petra I* (M., 1994), which is well illustrated. M. D. Rabinovich, "Formirovanie reguliarnoi russkoi armii nakanune Severnoi voiny," in V. I. Shunkov et al., eds., *Voprosy voennoi istorii Rossii XVIII i pervaia polovina XIX vekov* (M., 1969), studies Peter's initial military reforms, while the same author's "Sotsial'noe proiskhozhdenie i imushchestvennoe

polozhenie ofitserov reguliarnoi russkoi armii v kontse Severnoi voiny," in N. I. Pavlenko et al., eds., *Rossiia v period reform Petra I* (M., 1973), pp. 133–71, is a detailed investigation, as its title indicates, of the social background of regular Russian army officers around 1721. War and military reform are constant themes of E. V. Anisimov, *Vremia petrovskikh reform* (L., 1989), and N. I. Pavlenko, *Petr Velikii* (M., 1994), currently the leading general histories of Peter's reign in Russian (see Chap. 1).

513

25. *Kniga ustav voinskii . . .* (SPb., 1719), p. [1]; copy at HU–Law School Library (Rare Unclassed).

26. Copy at NYPL. Cf. Hellie, *Enserfment* (n. 14 above), pp. 187–88; Cracraft, *Revolution in Imagery*, p. 155 (in reference to the illustrations).

27. L. G. Beskrovnyi, ed., *Khrestomatiia po russkoi voennoi istorii* (M., 1947), p. 117, followed by excerpts, reprinted in modern orthography, from the *Uchen'e* (pp. 117–23).

28. Hellie, *Enserfment*, pp. 167–68; excerpts printed in Beskrovnyi, *Khrestomatiia*, pp. 84–92.

29. Cf. L. Fronsperger, *Kreigsbuch, ander Theyl: Von Wagenburgh vmb die Feldleger* (Frankfurt, 1573; facs. reprint, Stuttgart, 1968).

30. See V. D. Nazarov, "O datirovke 'Ustava ratnykh i pushechnykh del'," in Shunkov et al., eds. (n. 24 above), pp. 216–21.

31. *Uchen'e i khitrost'* (NYPL copy), passim. Cf. Vasmer, II, p. 689, and Chernykh, II, pp. 185–86 *(soldat)*; Vasmer, I, p. 522, Chernykh, I, p. 376, Shanskii, VIII, p. 54, Barkh-Bog., VII, p. 63, and Gard., pp. 114–15 *(kapitan)*; Vasmer, II, p. 615, Chernykh, II, p. 157, and Gard., p. 192 *(serzhant)*; Barkh-Bog., IX, p. 325 (*mushket,* etc.); Vasmer, II, p. 502, Barkh-Bog., XXII, pp. 130–31, and Gard., pp. 179–81 *(regiment/polk)*; Vasmer, II, p. 507, Barkh-Bog., XXII, p. 139, and Gard., pp. 182–83 *(reitar)*; Vasmer, I, p. 366, Shanskii, V, p. 181, and Barkh-Bog., IV, 349 *(dragun)*; Vasmer, II, p. 539, and Chernykh, II, p. 124 *(rota)*; Vasmer, III, p. 392, and Slovar', XVII, cols. 1353–54 *(sherenga)*; and Chernykh, II, p. 28, and Barkh-Bog., XV, p. 31 *(pekhota).* Readers are reminded that the full titles of the etymological and historical dictionaries cited here and hereafter in abbreviated form (Vasmer, Chernykh, Slovar', etc.) are found in Appendix II under "Works Cited."

32. P. P. Epifanov, "Voinskii ustav Petra Velikogo," in A. I. Andreev, *Petr Velikii: sbornik statei* (M./L., 1947), pp. 167–213 (pp. 171–74 for the *Ustav Veide*); and L. G. Beskrovnyi, *Ocherki po istochnikovedeniiu voennoi istorii Rossii* (M., 1957), pp. 109–10. The *Ustav Veide* was printed at St. Petersburg in 1841 in a small edition and is now, as Epifanov notes (p. 173, n. 3), a bibliographical rarity: my quotations from it are taken from his and Beskrovnyi's summaries. G. P. Meshcheriakov, "Iz istorii voenno-teoreticheskoi mysli v Rossii v pervoi chetverti XVIII v.," in Shunkov et al. (n. 24 above), pp. 97–109, found that while the *Ustav Veide* was never printed in Peter's time it circulated in manuscript, from which extracts were copied by officers into their journals (p. 98).

33. Cf. Beskrovnyi, *Ocherki*, p. 109.

34. For *fuzeia,* from Polish *fuzyja/fuzja,* French *fusil,* which came and went with the flintlock in Russian, see Vasmer, III, p. 220, and Slov. Akad., VI, col. 496; also Slovar', XVI, col. 1583. For *baginet,* from German *Bagonet/Bajonett,* French *baïonnette,* which had

514

an even more transitory existence in Russian, being replaced, even in Petrine times, by *shtyk;* see Barkh., I, p. 125.

35. Hellie, *Enserfment,* pp. 181 ff.; Hellie, "Petrine Army," pp. 239–40.

36. *Opis. II,* nos. 9 (pp. 61–2), 12 (p. 66), 13 (p. 66), 17 (p. 72–4), 33 (p. 100). See further Epifanov (n. 32 above), pp. 175–79; also Beskrovnyi, *Ocherki,* pp. 110–11, and Meshcheriakov (n. 32), pp. 98–99.

37. *PiB,* vol. 1, no. 304 (pp. 347–53).

38. *SIRIO* 39, no. 12 (pp. 52–65; pp. 55, 56 for the passages quoted): Whitworth to Secretary Harley, March 14/25, 1705. Cf. Epifanov, pp. 179–80.

39. *PiB,* vol. 2, no. 408 (pp. 7–13); *PiB,* vol. 3, no. 765 (pp. 227–61); *PiB,* vol. 4, no. 2062 (pp. 150–54).

40. *PiB,* vol. 3, no. 662 (pp. 77–79).

41. Epifanov, pp. 184–85.

42. *PiB,* vol. 5, no. 1531 (p. 40).

43. Ibid. (pp. 39–41): decree to A. I. Repnin, Jan. 24, 1707.

44. Meshcheriakov (n. 32 above), p. 100; the document is printed in *PiB,* vol. 4, pt. 1, no. 1138 (pp. 141–42).

45. *PiB,* vol. 4, pt. 2, p. 687.

46. Cf. Polish *fendrych*/German *Fähndrich* = lieutenant, a now obsolete word in Russian that sometime after Peter became a jocular term of disrespect in the Imperial army: see Slovar' (Appendix II, Works Cited), XVI, col.1306.

47. Barkh-Bog. (Appendix II, Works Cited) notes (XV, p. 111) that at its inception, in the *Ustav Veide* of 1698, the term *plutong* (platoon) referred to a small military detachment formed for sequential firing; also, that on one occasion in 1700 Peter ordered a *sherenga* (row of soldiers) divided into eight platoons.

48. *PiB,* vol. 7, pt. 1, no. 2304 (pp. 99–104, 461–2).

49. Epifanov, p. 178.

50. Quoting Duffy (n. 24 above), p. 22: the document is printed in *PiB,* vol. 8, pt. 1, pp. 6–13; see also Meshcheriakov, p. 103.

51. *PiB,* vol. 8, pt. 1, pp. 8–9; cf. Beskrovnyi, *Ocherki,* pp. 113–14. See further, for additional pre-1716 military directives to be found in manuscript in official Russian archives, Epifanov, pp. 80–95.

52. *PiB,* vol. 12, pt. 1, no. 5024 (pp. 17–25, 279–91).

53. Ibid., no. 5234 (pp. 182–91, 470–73).

54. *PiB,* vol. 13, nos. 5830–32 (pp. 37–41, 227–28).

55. *Opis. I,* nos. 130 (pp. 165–66), 170 (pp. 181–82), 151 (pp. 175–76), 60 (pp. 130–31). On Crompein/Krompen, see further C. Peterson, *Peter the Great's Administrative and Judicial Reforms: Swedish Antecedents and the Process of Reception,* trans. M. Metcalf (Stockholm, 1979), pp. 316, 337–38.

56. *Opis. I,* nos. 10 (16, 34), 11 (15), 12, 13, 14 (17, 33), 19, 22 (42), 24 (44), 36, 43, 48, 49, 51, 68, 145, 152 (subsequent editions in parentheses).

57. Ibid., no. 152 (pp. 176–77).

58. Beskrovnyi, *Ocherki,* p. 115.

59. *Opis. I,* nos. 207 (pp. 192–93), 234 (pp. 208, 193), 253 (pp. 217–18; copy also at LC-Rare), 301 (p. 235), 388 (pp. 267–68; copy also at LC-Rare), 592 (p. 331).

60. *Svodnyi katalog,* vol. 1, nos. 2964–66 (p. 43); P. N. Berkov, ed., *Izdaniia grazhdanskoi pechati vremeni Imp. Elizavety Petrovny, 1741–1761,* vol. 1: *1741–1753* (M./L., 1935), no. 305 (pp. 159–60).

61. Meshcheriakov (n. 32 above), p. 107 (n. 29); Duffy (n. 24), p. 30; *Opis. I,* p. 193.

62. *PSZ,* vol. 5, no. 3006 (pp. 203–453).

63. Copy at HU–Law School Library, as noted above (n. 25); cf. *Opis. I,* no. 388 (pp. 267–68), and Beskrovnyi, *Ocherki,* pp. 115 ff.

64. A. M. Korotkikh, "Voennoe sudoproizvodstvo v Rossii v pervoi chetverti XVIII v.," in A. N. Akin'shin et al., eds., *"Morskim sudam byt'!" Rossiiskomu voenno-morskomu flotu-300 let: mezhvuzovskii sbornik nauchnykh trudov* (Voronezh, 1996), pp. 165–84; Beskrovnyi, *Ocherkii,* pp. 115–21; Duffy, pp. 30–32; Epifanov (n. 32), pp. 195–213.

65. See R. S. Wortman, *The Development of a Russian Legal Consciousness* (Chicago, 1976), pp. 13 ff.

66. Epifanov, pp. 195, 199–200.

67. Upton (n. 11 above), pp. 79–81.

68. P. O. Bobrovskii, *Voenno pravo v Rossii pri Petre Velikom,* vol. 2: *Artikul voinskii,* pt. 1 (SPb., 1882), pp. vi–xvi, 4–18, and passim; pt. 2 (SPb., 1886), pp. 220 ff. Bobrovskii's work is unaccountably dismissed by Epifanov (p. 167).

69. Peter's draft of the preface, written and dated (March 31, 1716) by him, is printed in *ZAP,* no. 37 (pp. 51–52).

70. *Ustav voinskii* (1719 ed.), chap. 5 (p. 9); chap. 7 (p. 10).

71. Ibid., chap. 6 (p. 9).

72. Duffy, p. 30; cf. Beskrovnyi, *Ocherki,* pp. 115–16.

73. *Ustav voinskii,* chap. 10 (p. 15).

74. Duffy, p. 31; Beskrovnyi, *Ocherki,* p. 117.

75. *Ustav voinskii,* chap. 10 (p. 14); Duffy, p. 31. Cf. Meshcheriakov, p. 107.

76. Duffy, p. 31; Beskrovnyi, *Ocherki,* p. 121.

77. Duffy, p. 32; Beskrovnyi, *Ocherki,* pp. 117–18.

78. Meshcheriakov, p. 107.

79. Cf. German *Generalkriegszahlmeister:* Bond (Appendix II, Works Cited), p. 50.

80. Cf. German *Generalwagenmeister* (Bond, p. 49).

81. Cf. German *Gewaltiger/Gewaltherr* and *Rumormeister* (Vasmer, I, p. 264; Bond, pp. 49, 61).

82. Cf. German *kantonieren.*

83. Epifanov, p. 204.

84. Cf. D'iachenko (Appendix II, Works Cited), I, p. 93; Kot. (Appendix II, Works Cited), p. 431.

85. Cf. German *General-Feldzeugmeister* (Bond, p. 50).

86. Cf. French *approche* (Vasmer, I, p. 21); usually plural, as here, and meaning deep, zigzag trenches dug to support a siege, the term soon became obsolete in Russian (Slovar', I, cols. 172–173).

87. Cf. French *en chef*; the term soon became obsolete in Russian (Slovar', I, col. 160).

88. *Ustav voinskii,* chap. 10 (p. 13).

89. Technical terms, common in contemporary Europe, for walls built in the course of a siege.

90. *Ustav voinskii,* chap. 10 (pp. 14–15).

91. Cf. German *Rendezvousplats* (Vasmer, I, p. 491).

92. *Ustav voinskii,* chap. 10 (pp. 15–17).

93. Cf. German *Reveille* (Bond, p. 60); also Dutch *taptoe*/English *taptoo* (Vasmer, III, p. 76), the latter an obsolete form of *tattoo* = last call, or taps (*OED*, XI, p. 88).

94. Cf. German *Runde/Rundwache* (Vasmer, II, p. 547; Bond, p. 61).

95. *Ustav voinskii,* chap. 50 (pp. 58–59).

96. Excerpts from a draft of Peter's Articles of War, showing his many handwritten emendations, are printed in *ZAP*, no. 33 (pp. 48–50).

97. E.g., Keep (n. 14 above), pp. 108 ff., 165 ff.

98. *Karaul,* like other military terms mentioned previously, entered Russian before Peter's time: cf. Barkh-Bog., VII, pp. 74–5; Chernykh, I, p. 380 (suggesting ultimate Mongol origin).

99. Dueling came to Russia in Peter's time, brought by foreign officers in Russian service: see I. Reyfman, "The Emergence of the Duel in Russia: Corporal Punishment and the Honor Code," *Russian Review* 54, no. 1 (Jan. 1995): pp. 26–43.

100. Cf. Tallett (n. 1 above), especially chap. 4 and pp. 232 ff.

101. Keep, pp. 165–68.

102. Cf. Keep, pp. 172–3, 223–24, etc.

103. *Kniga ustav voinskii/Artikuly voinskie* (1719 ed.), chap. 3, art. 20 (pp. 7–8).

104. See Upton (n. 11 above), especially chap. 13.

105. Peterson (n. 55 above), pp. 337–38; Peterson also refers to the work of P. O. Bobrovskii, cited above (n. 68).

106. Translation printed in *ZAP*, no. 235 (pp. 183–92). Oddly, Peterson does not refer to this important document in either its original Swedish or its Russian version. On the *Land Law* in Sweden, see Upton, especially pp. 236 ff.

107. *ZAP*, no. 235, p. 184.

108. Cf. German *Kriegsrecht* = military law, perhaps confused with *Kriegsgericht* = court martial (Bond, p. 118), though the former can also mean military judgment, justice, or court.

109. This term commonly referred at the time to charges or acts of treason: see N. B. Golikova, *Politicheskie protsessy pri Petre I* (M., 1957), p. 26 and passim.

110. Cf. German *Salvus Konduktus* (Bond, p. 61).

111. Peterson, pp. 338–39.

112. Leonov and Ul'ianov (n. 24 above), pp. 14–17, 22–23, and appendix 3 (pp. 263–81) passim; Bogoslovskii (n. 14 above), vol. 4, pp. 175–82; Beskrovnyi, *Russkaia armiia* (n. 24 above), pp. 22 ff; Rabinovich, "Formirovanie regulairnoi armii" (n. 24 above).

113. See Cracraft, *Revolution in Architecture,* pp. 114–19, for the Azov campaigns and

Gordon's account of them, still in manuscript at BL; also Bogoslovskii, vol. 1, pp. 193 ff., and Warner (both at n. 14 above).

114. L. G. Beskrovnyi, "Voennye shkoly v Rossii v pervoi polovine XVIII v.," *Istoricheskie zapiski* 42 (1953): 288, citing archival sources.

115. Ibid., pp. 290–91.

116. J. R. Hale, "Military Education in Early Modern Europe," in Hale, *Renaissance War Studies* (London, 1983), p. 225. See also A. Corvisier, *Armies and Societies in Europe, 1494–1789*, trans. A. T. Siddall (Bloomington, IN, 1979), pp. 105–8.

117. Hale, *War and Society* (n. 8 above), pp. 145–46.

118. *ZAP*, no. 4 (pp. 33–34): secretary's record of Peter's interview with Patriarch Adrian, Oct. 4, 1700.

119. Figures from Beskrovnyi, "Voennye shkoly," pp. 285–86; see also Bogoslovskii, vol. 4, pp. 183–85.

120. *PiB*, vol. 2, no. 421 (pp. 39–50).

121. See Rabinovich, "Sotsial'noe proiskhozhdenie ofitserov" (n. 24 above), Table 1 (pp. 138–39) for data showing that by 1721 only 281 of a total 2,245 officers of the Russian field army (infantry and cavalry), or 12.6%, were still foreigners—although that number still included nearly a third of all regimental commanders (colonels), the highest rank listed; Rabinovich does not provide any data here regarding general officers, who in 1710, for example, at the height of the Swedish War, were predominately foreign: nine of thirteen infantry generals, nine of twelve cavalry, and all the chief engineers (Hughes [n. 24 above], p. 66).

122. Beskrovnyi, "Voennye shkoly," pp. 293–95.

123. Ibid., pp. 298–99.

124. *Opis. I*, nos. 10 (pp. 78–79), 14 (pp. 82–83), 16 (p. 84), 17 (pp. 84–85), 33 (pp. 105–06), 34 (p. 106). For Picart (Pickaerdt, Pickaert, or Pikart), see again Cracraft, *Revolution in Imagery*, pp. 170 ff.

125. Duffy, *Fire and Stone* (n. 5 above), p. 188.

126. Cf. German *Kupferstich/Kupferstecher* = copperplate engraving/engraver.

127. *PiB*, vol. 9, pt. 1, no. 2959 (pp. 12–13; pt. 2, p. 540): Peter I to I. A. Musin-Pushkin, Jan. 4, 1709.

128. Ibid., no. 3015 (pp. 50–51): Peter to Musin-Pushkin, Jan. 25, 1709. For details of the Rimpler editions, see *Opis. I*, nos. 11 (pp. 79–80) and 15 (pp. 83–84).

129. Cracraft, *Revolution in Architecture*, pp. 140, 151–53.

130. As demonstrated by N. D. Bludilina, "I. N. Zotov, Kratkie svedeniia po geografii Evropy: O Frantsii (1705)," in Lebedev and Bludilina, *Rossiia i zapad*, pp. 350–62. Like his brother Konon, Ivan Zotov (1687–1723) had studied in France, where he then served in a subordinate diplomatic capacity.

131. See *Opis. I*, no. 49 (pp. 118–19; copy also at NYPL), and supplementary references in Cracraft, *Revolution in Architecture*, p. 349 (n. 21).

132. *Opis. I*, no. 19 (pp. 86–88); also Cracraft, *Revolution in Imagery*, pp. 177, 180, 183 (Blicklant), 165 ff. (Schoonebeck).

133. *Opis. I*, no. 786 (pp. 436–37); also Cracraft, *Revolution in Architecture*, pp. 111–13, 140.

134. Cf. Cracraft, *Revolution in Imagery*, pp. 165 ff.

135. Leonov and Ul'ianov (n. 24 above), p. 285.

136. C. Duffy, *Siege Warfare: The Fortress in the Early Modern World* (London, 1979), p. 248; also Duffy, *Fire and Stone*, pp. 11–13.

137. *Opis. I*, nos. 24 (pp. 93–94), 44 (pp. 114–15); *Opis. III*, p. 347 (nos. 24, 44). See further references in Cracraft, *Revolution in Architecture*, p. 349, n. 20.

138. At LC-Rare.

139. Definitions here and below from Duffy, *Fire and Stone*, pp. 183–85.

140. Cf. Bond (Appendix II, Works Cited), pp. 50, 54.

141. Ibid., pp. 51–52.

142. Ibid., p. 45.

143. Only *berma*, *kaponir*, and *redan* of the terms just mentioned are among the more than 2,800 entries, both current and obsolete, entered in Shapkin (Appendix II, Works Cited): see pp. 25, 124, 256.

144. Except for *poligon*, in the technical sense just mentioned, none of these other terms appear in Vasmer or the Slovar', our most comprehensive etymological and lexical authorities (Appendix II, Works Cited). Other partial exceptions: the Slovar' lists *fortetsiia*, citing Pushkin (XVI, col. 1516), but as an obsolete term, while Vasmer, listing both it and *fortetsa* (III, 216), suggests earlier Polish or Ukrainian origins; also, most Russian dictionaries list *fut*, but only as an "English" or "foreign" unit of measurement.

145. *Opis. I*, no. 12 (pp. 80–82, with reproduction of sample plate); for the Armory Chamber, the initial site of Peter's graphic revolution, see Cracraft, *Revolution in Imagery*, pp. 107 ff.

146. *Opis. I*, nos. 22 (pp. 90–92), 42 (pp. 112–13).

147. See Cracraft, *Revolution in Imagery*, pp. 159–60.

148. *Opis. I*, no. 36 (p. 107).

149. *Opis. I*, no. 51 (pp. 120–22, with frontispiece reproduced; for the latter see also Cracraft, *Revolution in Imagery*, p. 174, fig. 45).

150. *Opis. II*, appendix VII, no. 22 (p. 347); *Opis. III*, no. 4 (p. 16). For de Witte, see Cracraft, *Revolution in Imagery*, pp. 172–73.

151. *Opis. I*, no. 42 (p. 42).

152. From a copy of the second, 1710 edition at LC-Rare.

153. Cf. German *Schwärmer* = a small rocket (Bond, p. 83). See also Vasmer (III, 283) and Slovar' (XVII, col. 1319), noting that the term is obsolete.

154. *Petarda* = petard, firecracker, here "a bell-like [explosive] device used for blowing in a gate" (Duffy, *Fire and Stone*, p. 185), from German *Petarde*/French *pétard*. *Petardir* = one who makes or fires petards, from German *Petardier* (Bond, p. 58, obs.). Slovar' (IX, cols. 1102–03) lists *petarda* in these senses, but not *petardir*; similarly Vasmer (II, 349), suggesting Polish *petarda* as possible source.

155. Cf. German *Kartaune* = a kind of cannon, now obsolete. Russian *kartaun* but not

German original listed in Barkh. (IX, p. 263), citing the Braun among other Petrine texts.

156. Cf. German *Zentner* (Latin *centenarius*) = a hundredweight (Bond, p. 82). Listed in Vasmer (III, p. 289) as a Petrine neologism, the term is defined in the Slovar' (XVII, col. 634) as "a single measure of weight in the metric system equal to 100 kilograms."

519

4. BUREAUCRATIC REVOLUTION

1. C. Tilly, ed., *The Formation of National States in Western Europe* (Princeton, 1975), including an extensive bibliography; especially valuable here is Tilly's lengthy opening chapter, "Reflections on the History of European State-Making" (pp. 3–83), which draws on his collaborators' more specialized studies. The term "national" in the volume's title is something of a misnomer since, as Tilly promptly points out, its authors concentrate on "the development of states rather than nations" and regard the "national state" as a later and peculiar, rather than necessary or inevitable, outcome of the process (p. 6 and passim). "Western" is also somewhat misleading, since the volume as a whole devotes considerable attention to Scandinavia, Prussia, the Austrian Habsburg dominions, and the rest of Germany as well as France, Britain, Italy, Spain, Switzerland, and the Netherlands. Hence the volume would be more accurately entitled, "State-Making/State-Building in Europe, 1500–1800."

2. Tilly, pp. 27, 34, 70, and passim.

3. Ibid., pp. 42, 73, 74–75. In asserting the crucial linkage between warfare and modern state-building, Tilly draws particularly on the long essay by his collaborator S. E. Finer, "State- and Nation-Building in Europe: The Role of the Military" (ibid., pp. 84–163), whose generalizations are based primarily on intensive study of early modern France, England, and Brandenburg-Prussia. Finer himself later provided a general account of the rise of the modern state in Europe, in Finer, *A History of Government from the Earliest Times*, 3 vols. (Oxford, 1997), 2, pt. 2.

4. See works by Glete, Black (two collections), and Anderson cited in Chap. 2 (nn. 7, 195–97, 202) and by Parker, Black (four works), Eltis, Bérenger, Tallett, McNeill, Scott, Hale (two works), Gunn, Mann, and Corvisier cited in Chap. 3 (nn. 1, 4, 8, 20, 116).

5. F. Tallett, *War and Society in Early-Modern Europe, 1495–1715* (New York, 1992), p. 188.

6. H. M. Scott, "Europe Turns East: Political Developments in the Eighteenth Century," in E. Cameron, ed., *Early Modern Europe* (Oxford, 1999), pp. 321 ff.; Tallett, pp. 198–200, 202, 206. A massive demonstration of this overarching development is J. S. Bromley, ed., *The Rise of Great Britain and Russia, 1688–1715/25* (= vol. 6 of *The New Cambridge Modern History* (Cambridge, 1970). See also D. McKay and H. M. Scott, *The Rise of the Great Powers, 1648–1815* (New York, 1983), and, with respect to the rise of the British "fiscal-military state," J. Brewer, *The Sinews of Power: War, Money and the English State, 1688–1783* (Oxford, 1989).

7. H. H. Gert and C. Wright Mills, eds. and trans., *From Max Weber: Essays in Sociology* (New York, 1946), pp. 196–204 (from Weber, *Wirtschaft und Gesellschaft* [Tübingen,

520

1921–22], pt. 3, chap. 6); also J. LaPalombara, "Bureaucracy and Political Development: Notes, Queries, and Dilemmas," in LaPalombara, ed., *Bureaucracy and Political Development* (Princeton, 1967), pp. 48–50. Weber's definition of ideal, true, or classical bureaucracy has been followed, with elaborations or variations, by most later students of political systems; e.g., in the volume edited by LaPalombara just cited see essays by LaPalombara himself (pp. 39–48) and by S. N. Eisenstadt (pp. 98 ff.), or the essays collected in W. Reinhard, ed., *Power Elites and State Building* (Oxford, 1996). Among students of Russia see similarly M. Raeff, "The Russian Autocracy and Its Officials," in Raeff, *Political Ideas and Institutions in Imperial Russia* (Boulder, CO, 1994), pp. 78 ff. (essay first published 1957); J. P. LeDonne, *Absolutism and Ruling Class: The Formation of the Russian Political Order, 1700–1825* (New York, 1991), p. ix; or W. M. Pintner and D. K. Rowney, eds., *Russian Officialdom: The Bureaucratization of Russian Society from the Seventeenth to the Twentieth Century* (Chapel Hill, NC, 1980), editors' introduction, pp. 10 ff.

8. See again J. Glete, *Navies and Nations: Warships, Navies and State Building in Europe and America, 1500–1860,* 2 vols. continuously paginated (Stockholm, 1993); pp. 6–8 for the sentences quoted.

9. H. Rosenberg, *Bureaucracy, Aristocracy and Autocracy: The Prussian Experience, 1660–1815* (Cambridge, MA, 1958).

10. N. S. Kollmann, *Kinship and Politics: The Making of the Muscovite Political System, 1345–1547* (Stanford, 1987), p. 147; V. A. Kivelson, *Autocracy in the Provinces: The Muscovite Gentry and Political Culture in the Seventeenth Century* (Stanford, 1996), p. 8.

11. See Cracraft, *Revolution in Imagery,* pls. 7, 11, and the related discussion of such imagery, especially pp. 114–15, 190–91.

12. There is no agreement among specialists on the exact number of such offices in seventeenth-century Muscovy; estimates range from 77 to 96, to which total Plavsic "could add another 10 to 20": B. Plavsic, "Seventeenth-Century Chanceries and Their Staffs," in Pintner and Rowney (see n. 7 above), p. 21, n. 3.

13. On Muscovy's urban network in a comparative frame, see Cracraft, *Revolution in Architecture,* p. 65, and *Revolution in Imagery,* pp. 24, 26–27, with further references.

14. The volumes by Kollmann and Kivelson, just cited, provide thorough bibliographical and critical coverage of Muscovite political history. On Muscovite patrimonialism, see also the extended discussion in R. Pipes, *Russia under the Old Regime* (New York, 1974), chaps. 2–4; and on the state's "hypertrophy," R. Hellie, "The Role of the State in Muscovy," paper presented April 27, 1999, to the Russian/Soviet Studies Workshop, University of Chicago, with references to the author's voluminous publications on the subject.

15. I follow again the edition of A. E. Pennington (= Kot., Appendix II, Works Cited), Text, pp. 12 ff. In her introduction (pp. 7–11) Pennington provides details of Kotoshikhin's original Russian manuscript, now in the library of Uppsala University, and of the five contemporary manuscripts in Swedish translation that survive.

16. Following established practice I usually translate Kotoshikhin's *gosudar'* and

gosudarstvo as "sovereign" and "state," but they could equally well be rendered "lord" and "dominion," which would preserve their patrimonial character.

17. Kot., pp. 139–40.
18. P. V. Lukin, *Narodnye predstavleniia o gosudarstvennoi vlasti v Rossii XVII veka* (M., 2000), extensively documented and referenced.
19. L. R. Lewitter, "Introduction," *Ivan Pososhkov: The Book of Poverty and Wealth,* ed. and trans. Lewitter and A. P. Vlasto (Stanford, 1987), p. 17. All references to the *Ulozhenie* follow R. Hellie, ed. and trans., *The Muscovite Law Code (Ulozhenie) of 1649, Part I: Text and Translation* (Irvine, CA, 1988), which is based on the text published in 1830 in the *PSZ,* vol. 1, no. 1 (pp. 1–161), which is based in turn on the version printed in Moscow (three editions, all dated 1649) from the original manuscripts compiled in 1648; Hellie prints both this Russian text and his English translation on facing, identically numbered pages. For details see also Hellie, "Ulozhenie of 1649," in *MERSH* vol. 40 (1985), pp. 192–98, with full bibliography, and his article in *Russian History* 15, nos. 2–4 (1988): 155–80.
20. Cf. D'iachenko (Appendix II, Works Cited), II, pp. 687–88; also Kot. (Appendix II, Works Cited), Index of Forms, pp. 697–99.
21. Lewitter, p. 17.
22. M. Villey, *La Formation de la pensée juridique moderne* (Paris, 1968). Cf. M. Raeff, *The Well-Ordered Police State: Social and Institutional Change through Law in the Germanies and Russia, 1600–1800* (New Haven, 1983), especially pp. 20–22 for general comments and pp. 43 ff. for Germany, with numerous further references.
23. This cumbersome, abuse-prone form of record keeping (a single scroll, lacking index or table of contents, might be several hundred meters long) was abolished by decree of Peter I in 1702 (*ZAP,* no. 236 [p. 195]) in favor of the codex, or single sheets bound in books—an innovation adopted in Europe centuries before.
24. Lewitter, p. 29, citing figures first adduced by V. O. Kliuchevskii and corrected by P. N. Miliukov. On church lands and their inhabitants, see J. Cracraft, *The Church Reform of Peter the Great* (Stanford, 1971), pp. 83 ff.
25. Cf. D'iachenko, I, p. 496; Kot., Index of Forms, pp. 640–41.
26. The subject of Kivelson's work, cited above (n. 10).
27. Seè Kollmann (n. 10 above), who also debunks any notion that the occasional Assemblies of the Land *(Zemskie sobory),* the last of which met in 1653, were "a proto-parliamentary institution. . . . [They] met irregularly . . . and had no fixed membership or statehouse; their members were not elected but selected, were expected to vote unanimously in a mass assembly, and had no right of initiative. [Their] agendas were fixed by court leaders; their members merely rubber-stamped government policies" (pp. 185–86). For Pososhkov and his criticism, see Lewitter, especially pp. 192–245 (text and commentary); for Avraamii and his, M. Ia. Volkov, "Monakh Avraamii i ego 'Poslanie Petru I,'" in N. I. Pavlenko et al., eds., *Rossiia v period reform Petra I* (M., 1973), pp. 311–36. Plavsic also found "plenty of evidence" of extensive venality in seventeenth-century Muscovite administration (Plavsic, in Pintner and Rowney [n. 7

521

above], pp. 32–33, 38); as did M. N. Tikhomirnov, *Rossiiskoe gosudarstvo XV–XVII vekov* (M., 1973), especially pp. 353 ff. On late Muscovite administration, see Lewitter, pp. 34–35; P. B. Brown, "Early Modern Russian Bureaucracy: The Evolution of the Chancellery System from Ivan III to Peter the Great, 1478–1717" (PhD diss., University of Chicago, 1978); and the useful survey based on standard Russian authorities in C. Peterson, *Peter the Great's Administrative and Judicial Reforms: Swedish Antecedents and the Process of Reception,* trans. M. Metcalf (Stockholm, 1979), pp. 33–42.

28. This summary draws principally on E. V. Anisimov's detailed monograph, *Gosudarstvennye preobrazovaniia i samoderzhavie Petra Velikogo v pervoi chetverti XVIII veka* (SPb., 1997); A. A. Preobrazhenskii and T. E. Novitskaia, eds., *Zakonodatel'stvo Petra I* (M., 1997), a comprehensive volume of both documents and commentary; A. N. Medushevskii, *Utverzhdenie absoliutizma v Rossii* (M., 1994), chaps. 4–6; and the older work by B. I. Syromiatnikov, *"Reguliarnoe" gosudarstvo Petra Pervogo i ego ideologiia* (M./L., 1943).

29. Described in Cracraft, *Revolution in Architecture,* pp. 179 ff.

30. Cf. J. S. Coleman, "Modernization: Political Aspects," in D. L. Sills, ed., *International Encyclopedia of the Social Sciences,* vol. 10 (New York, 1968), p. 395; also LaPalombara (n. 7 above), pp. 39 ff. The most thorough treatment of Peter's abolition of the patriarchate and creation of the Holy Synod is still Cracraft, *Church Reform.*

31. Cracraft, *Revolution in Imagery,* especially pp. 257 ff.

32. A. G. Man'kov, "Proekt Ulozheniia Rossiiskogo gosudarstva 1720–1725 gg.," in S. L. Pestich et al., eds., *Problemy feodal'noi Rossii: Sbornik statei* (L., 1971), pp. 157–66, based on the papers of the responsible commission. Additional evidence of Peter's promotion of this project dating from late 1718 is published in *ZAP,* nos. 57, 73, 74, 105, 106, 175 (pp. 64, 73–74, 92, 129); for Senate decrees of August 1720 setting up the commission, see also *ZAP,* nos. 93, 94 (pp. 85–86). These documents make it clear that, apart from Tsar Aleksei's *Ulozhenie* of 1649, Swedish prototypes were prominent in drafting the "new Ulozhenie."

33. As recently reaffirmed, with extensive illustration (uniforms, medals, official insignia, portraits, etc.), by L. E. Shepelev, *Chinovnyi mir Rossii: XVIII–nachalo XX v.* (SPb., 1999). On Petrine ideology see also J. Cracraft, "Empire versus Nation: Russian Political Theory under Peter I," *Harvard Ukrainian Studies* 10, no. 3/4 (Dec. 1986): 524–40; and O. G. Ageeva, "Imperskii status Rossii: K istorii politicheskogo mentaliteta russkogo obshchestva nachala XVIII veka," in A. A. Gorskii, *Tsar' i tsarstvo v russkom obshchestvennom soznanii* (M., 1999), pp. 112–40. On the struggle from Peter's time forward to separate justice from administration, culminating in the Judicial Reform of 1864, see R. S. Wortman, *The Development of a Russian Legal Consciousness* (Chicago, 1976).

34. Cf. Raeff (n. 22 above), pp. 181–221.

35. Lewitter (n. 19 above), pp. 15, 39 ff., 50, 73.

36. Cf. A. F. Upton, *Charles XI and Swedish Absolutism* (Cambridge, 1998), especially Chap. 3, "The Defining of the Absolute Monarchy"; and more discursively, P. K. Monod, *The Power of Kings: Monarchy and Religion in Europe, 1589–1715* (New Haven,

CT, 1999), with numerous further references. See also Scott, in the essay cited earlier (n. 6 above), who observes that Peter's "essentially personal style of monarchy had its counterparts all across [early modern] Europe. A minority of states were either constitutional monarchies . . . or republics. By far the majority were absolute monarchies, whose rulers claimed full sovereignty over their subjects and personally directed the work of government" (p. 314). For Russian work on "absolutism" in Russia from Peter's time, see the collective volume, set in a Marxist framework, edited by N. M. Druzhinin et al., *Absoliutizm v Rossii (XVII–XVIII vv.)* (M., 1964); Medushevskii's monograph and the collaborative volume edited by Preobrazhenskii and Novitskaia, both cited above (n. 28); and Anisimov, also cited there, who prefers to characterize the Petrine and subsequent Imperial Russian state, much too narrowly in my view, as the traditional Muscovite "autocracy" in newly bureaucratized form.

37. *Opis. I,* nos. 431, 432 (pp. 280–82); *Opis. III,* nos. 100 (p. 37), 311 (p. 77: German edition).
38. *Opis. III,* no. 395 (p. 104); *Svodnyi katalog,* vol. 1, nos. 1348–1365 (pp. 214–16); vol. 3, no. 8821 (p. 466).
39. *Opis. I,* nos. 783 (p. 435), 838 (p. 461), 843 (pp. 462–63); *Opis. III,* no. 247 (p. 64).
40. See *Opis. I,* p. 281, for examples of such eighteenth-century inscriptions in copies of the 1720 edition.
41. *ZAP,* no. 254 (p. 213).
42. Or so Dr. Lee would claim: see A. [G.] Cross, *Peter the Great through British Eyes: Perceptions and Representations of the Tsar since 1698* (Cambridge, 2000), p. 36, citing Lee's later published memorandum.
43. N. V. Kalachov, ed., *Doklady i prigovory, sostoiavshiesia v Pravitel'stvuiushchem Senate v tsarstvovanie Petra Velikago,* 4 vols. (SPb., 1880–1891), 1, pp. 122–23; *PiB,* vol. 12, pt. 1, no. 5024 (p. 24).
44. *ZAP,* nos. 25, 27 (pp. 44–45), 32 (p. 47), 34 (p. 50)—all in Peter's own hand.
45. *ZAP,* nos. 255 (p. 213), 258 (p. 215).
46. *ZAP,* nos. 330, 331 (pp. 269–75).
47. See Chapter 5.
48. Cf. Peterson (n. 27 above), p. 59, and further, Raeff (n. 22 above).
49. On Fick's career, see Peterson, pp. 62–84; also A. R. Cederberg, *Heinrich Fick: Ein Beitrag zur russischen Geschichte des XVIII. Jahrhunderts* (Tartu/Dorpat, 1930 = Acta et Commentationes Universitatis Tartuensis [Dorpatensis], B [Humaniora], vol. 17).
50. *PSZ,* vol. 5, nos. 3129 (p. 525), 3133 (pp. 527–28), 3255 (p. 601); *ZAP,* nos. 261, 263, 265, 266 (pp. 216–21).
51. *ZAP,* no. 264 (p. 219), in Peter's own hand.
52. *ZAP,* no. 60 (p. 66), in Peter's hand; *PSZ,* vol. 5, no. 3261 (pp. 603–4).
53. *ZAP,* nos. 49, 51 (pp. 60–61), 267 (p. 221)—all in Peter's hand.
54. *ZAP,* editor's note, pp. 411–12.
55. Ibid. (p. 412).
56. Peterson, pp. 118–19, 121–22.
57. Ibid., pp. 89, 158.

58. The successive drafts of the *General Regulation* are printed in *ZAP*, pp. 413–512: for the text as first printed on February 27, 1720, see pp. 482–512. My further discussion is based on this text compared with that printed at the Moscow Synodal Press (in the civil type) on March 20, 1725 (copy at GBL; see excerpts in Appendix I, no. 35). The 1720 printed edition, its punctuation and orthography variously updated, is reprinted in the *PSZ*, vol. 6, no. 3534 (pp. 111–60), and in Preobrazhenskii and Novitskaia (n. 28 above), pp. 99–124.

59. Peterson, p. 10.

60. Ibid., pp. 109–10.

61. This is a constant theme of Peterson's massive study; so also of A. N. Medushevskii's essay, *Reformy Petra I i sud'by Rossii: nauchno-analiticheskii obzor* (M., 1994), which draws on the detailed research informing his *Utverzhdenie absoliutizma v Rossii* (n. 28 above).

62. Cf. W. J. Ong, *Orality and Literacy: The Technologizing of the Word* (New York, 1986), chaps. 4, 5; although Ong concedes that, whereas the shift from orality to literacy "transformed human consciousness" in various definable ways (pp. 79 ff.), the "effects of print on thought and style have yet to be assessed fully" (p. 123).

63. Peterson, pp. 151 ff.

64. *ZAP*, editor's note, p. [553].

65. *Svodnyi katalog*, vol. 3, nos. 5888–5892 (p. 21).

66. J. P. LeDonne, *Ruling Russia: Politics and Administration in the Age of Absolutism, 1762–1796* (Princeton, 1984), pp. 208, 223, and passim.

67. This discussion of the Revenue College's *Regulation* is based on the original text as printed in *ZAP*, no. 416 (pp. 559–69)—which, like all the documents printed in this incomparable collection, has been updated only in capitalization and punctuation. Cf. updated text in *PSZ*, vol. 5, no. 3466 (pp. 671–76).

68. Peterson, pp. 402–05.

69. J. P. LeDonne, *Absolutism and Ruling Class: The Formation of the Russian Political Order, 1700–1825* (New York, 1991), pp. 42 ff.

70. Peterson, pp. 103 (table) and 135 (table), the latter providing slightly different numbers of foreigners serving in the early Petrine colleges, mostly in senior staff as opposed to voting-member positions. The latter table also indicates two foreigners serving in the Admiralty College in 1720 (only one, Cruys, a voting member) in contrast, at the other extreme, to the seventeen (four voting) who served initially in the Revenue College.

71. *ZAP*, no. 103 (p. 91).

72. *Opis. I*, no. 674 (pp. 368–70; copies also at LC-Rare and HU–Law School Library (Rare Russica, with Dutch text).

73. *Opus I*, nos. 794 (pp. 442–43), 849 (p. 465; copy also at LC-Rare).

74. *Svodnyi katalog*, III, nos. 5871–76 (pp. 19–20), 5899 (p. 22); reprinted again in *PSZ*, vol. 6, no. 3937 (pp. 525–637).

75. A. J. Violette and D. R. Jones, "Admiralty College," in Jones, ed., *The Military-Naval*

Encyclopedia of Russia and the Soviet Union, vol. 3 (Gulf Breeze, FL, 1981), pp. 42–66, with bibliography.

76. F. F. Veselago, *Ocherk russkoi morskoi istorii,* vol. 1 (SPb., 1864), pp. 454 ff.

77. P. V. Verkhovskoi, *Uchrezhdenie Dukhovnoi Kollegii i Dukhovnyi reglament,* 2 vols. (Rostov-on-Don, 1916; facs. reprint, Westmead, UK, 1972); see vol. 2: *Materialy,* pt. 1, nos. 1–4 (pp. 3–105), for Verkhovskoi's critical edition of the *Dukhovnyi reglament* and contemporaneously published Manifesto, Oath, and Supplement, based on the original manuscripts.

78. *PSZ,* vol. 5, no. 3239 (pp. 594–95); *ZAP,* no. 58 (pp. 64–65); and further, Cracraft, *Church Reform* (n. 24 above), pp. 147 ff.

79. *Opis. I,* no. 606 (pp. 335–38); also *Opis. II,* nos. 141, 142 (p. 227), for two more issues in 1721, and Cracraft, *Church Reform,* pp. 157–62, 165–66.

80. *Opis. II,* no. 149, (pp. 230–33); also *Opis. III,* no. 342 (p. 89).

81. A copy of this June 14, 1722, edition of the *Dukhovnyi reglament* is at LC–Law Library (Rare); excerpts reproduced in Appendix I, no. 30.

82. *Opis. II,* nos. 188, 192 (pp. 254–55, 258–59); *Opis. III,* no. 359 (p. 92).

83. *PSZ,* vol. 6, nos. 3718 (pp. 314–46) and 4022 (pp. 699–715 = the Supplement).

84. *Svodnyi katalog-kir,* nos. 147, 163, 240, 426, 595, 696, 889, 894, 1192, 1349; *Svodnyi katalog,* vol. 2, no. 2069; Verkhovskoi, vol. 1, pp. 206–13.

85. Verkhovskoi, vol. 1, pp. 215–21; also J. Cracraft, "Feofan Prokopovich: A Bibliography of His Works," *Oxford Slavonic Papers,* new series vol. 8 (1975), nos. 79, 101–4, 106–8. Scholarly editions include, apart from Verkhovskoi's, that by C. Tondini, *Règlement Ecclésiastique de Pierre le Grand* (Paris, 1874; based on the Moscow 1861 edition), which also reprints the St. Petersburg 1785 Latin edition, and A. V. Muller, trans. and ed., *The Spiritual Regulation of Peter the Great* (Seattle, 1972; based on the *PSZ* edition). A modernized Russian edition based on a copy of the complete Moscow 1722 edition is printed in Preobrazhenskii and Novitskaia (n. 28 above), pp. 540–603.

86. Verkhovskoi, vol. 2, pt. 1, pp. 6–7 (and nn. 9, 24), 11 (n. 24).

87. Ibid., p. 6.

88. All of Peter's emendations and emphases are clearly indicated by Verkhovskoi in his critical edition of the *Ecclesiastical Regulation* and its Supplement.

89. Verkhovskoi, vol. 2, pt. 1, pp. 84 (and n. 9), 85 (n. 22).

90. Cracraft, *Church Reform,* pp. 233 ff.

91. The Russian church in Peter's time consisted of twenty-six dioceses, each composed of anywhere from fewer than 200 to more than 1,000 parishes and staffed by a total of 61,111 priests, deacons, and cantors; some 800 monasteries were home to 25,207 monks, nuns, and novices; and taxpaying, mainly peasant households living on church lands totaled more than 150,000 (figures from various sources, mostly dating to the early 1720s, in Cracraft, *Church Reform,* p. 220 and n. 1, p. 251 and n. 2, p. 252 and n. 1, p. 87 and n. 1, p. 260 and n. 2, p. 85 and n. 1).

92. Cf. Verkhovskoi, vol. 1, pp. 492–94; and further, for the Swedish "Church Law" of 1686 in its Swedish context, Upton (n. 36 above), pp. 108–11 and passim. A "Königl:

525

Kirchen-Gesetz und Ordnung" dated 1686 was among the documents Heinrich Fick brought back from Sweden in 1716: see Cederberg, "Fick" (n. 49 above), supplement I, p. 58, no. 61.

93. This discussion of the text of the *Ecclesiastical Regulation* is based on Verkhovskoi's critical edition of the original mss. compared with the copy of the first complete Moscow printed edition referenced above (n. 81).

94. Cf. 1 Corinthians 14:33, 40: "For God is not a God of confusion but of peace," and "all things should be done decently and in order."

95. Cf. 1 Peter 5:1–3: "So I exhort the elders. . . . Tend the flock that is your charge, not by constraint but willingly, not for shameful gain but eagerly, not by domineering over those in your charge but by being examples to the flock."

96. Cracraft, *Church Reform,* chap. 2.

97. M. Weber, *The Sociology of Religion,* trans. E. Fischoff (Boston, 1993; first German edition, 1922), p. 9.

98. Cracraft, *Church Reform,* pp. 177–79.

99. *Opis. I,* no. 696 (pp. 381–82); *Opis. II,* no. 179 (pp. 251–53).

100. The extent of Prokopovich's authorship is still unresolved: see J. Cracraft, "Did Feofan Prokopovich Really Write *Pravda voli monarshei?*" *Slavic Review* 40, no. 2 (Summer 1981): 173–93.

101. *ZAP,* no. 144 (pp. 113–14).

102. Pekarskii, *Nauka i literatura,* vol. 2, no. 524 (pp. 571–75).

103. *Opis. III,* nos. 592 (p. 177; copies also at BL, NYPL), 593 (pp. 177–78). For pressruns and copies returned, see figures in Pekarskii, *Nauka i literatura,* vol. 2, p. 665.

104. Cracraft, "Prokopovich Bibliography," no. 105 (p. 24; also no. 91, p. 22); copy also at LC–Law Library (Rare).

105. *Svodnyi katalog,* vol. 3, nos. 7733, 7736 (pp. 293–94).

106. *PSZ,* vol. 7, no. 4870.

107. A. Lentin, ed. and trans., *Peter the Great: His Law on the Imperial Succession in Russia, 1722: The Official Commentary (Pravda voli monarshei)* (Oxford, 1996): Lentin prints (pp. 119–281) a modernized text of the *Pravda* based on the Moscow 1726 edition together with his English translation, on facing pages, and extensive notes and commentary.

108. For the succession law, see *Opis. I,* no. 664 (p. 361–62), and *PSZ,* vol. 6, no. 3893; for a brief account of the post-Petrine succession disputes, see Lentin, pp. 65–69, and further, J. Cracraft, "The Succession Crisis of 1730: A View from the Inside," *Canadian-American Slavic Studies* 12, no. 1 (Spring 1978): 61–85.

109. This discussion of the *Pravda* is based on the Lentin edition compared with the copy of the Moscow 1726 edition at NYPL.

110. Lentin, p. 31; see also pp. 289, 290 for lists of the *Pravda's* biblical and patristic sources.

111. *Pravda,* Lentin edition, p. 152.

112. Ibid., pp. 184, 186.

113. Ibid., pp. 187, 188.

114. Lentin, pp. 2, 32, 45. See more generally P. Hazard, *European Thought in the Eighteenth*

Century, trans. J. L. May (Harmondsworth, UK, 1965; first published Paris, 1946), especially pt. 2, chap. 5 and pt. 3, chap. 4.

115. *Pravda,* Lentin edition, p. 144.

116. Publishing details in *Opis. I,* nos. 259 (pp. 219–20), 380 (p. 265), 719 (pp. 398–99); Pekarskii, *Nauka i literatura,* vol. 2, p. 585; and W. E. Butler, introduction to *A Discourse Concerning the Just Causes of the War between Sweden and Russia: 1700–1721, by P. P. Shafirov* (Dobbs Ferry, NY, 1973), pp. 31–38, which volume contains a facsimile reprint of the first or 1717 St. Petersburg Russian edition followed by a facsimile of the 1723 English translation. Copies of the 1717 and 1719 Russian editions are also at NYPL; a copy of the 1722 Russian edition is also at LC-Rare (with bookplate of Emperor Alexander II).

117. This description and further discussion of the *Razsuzhdenie* is based on the 1973 facsimile reprint compared with the copy of the 1722 edition at LC.

118. *Opis. I,* p. 220.

119. Details of Shafirov's career from E. Likhach, "Shafirov, baron Petr Pavlovich," in *Rbs,* vol. 22, pp. 553–67, with bibliography; see also Shafirov entry, by G. E. Munro, in *MERSH,* vol. 34, pp. 122–26.

120. One of six Petrine politicians so treated in D. O. Serov, *Stroiteli imperii: Ocherk gosudarstvennoi i kriminal'noi deiatel'nosti spodvizhnikov Petra I* (Novosibirsk, 1996).

121. Butler (n. 116 above), p. 7.

122. Ibid., pp. 7–14.

123. *Razsuzhdenie,* p. 5.

124. Ibid., p. 22.

125. Ibid., pp. 25, 66, 77.

126. See Cracraft, *Revolution in Architecture,* especially chap. 8; and Cracraft, *Revolution in Imagery,* pp. 190 ff. and chap. 5.

127. *Opis. I,* nos. 2 (p. 69), 7 (pp. 76–77), 56 (p. 127); *Opis. III,* nos. 9 (p. 17), 429 (pp. 115–16; copy also at LC-Rare).

128. Peter I introduced the secular celebration of the New Year on January 1, along with calculation of the year from the birth of Christ, by a decree in December 1699 (*PSZ,* vol. 3, no. 1736). Previously Russians had counted the year, Byzantine-style, from the creation of the world—by which method 1699 was 7208—and had inaugurated the year on September 1, primarily as a religious observance.

129. Cf. Volkov, *Leksika russkikh chelobitnykh XVII veka,* especially pp. 122–38, and Sergeev II (Appendix II, Works Cited). The hundreds of diplomatic documents printed in successive volumes of the *PiB* offer compelling evidence of this Europeanizing trend under Peter, fully in place by 1712. The centrality of Louis XIV's court in this diffusion of polite behavior is argued by N. Elias, *The Civilizing Process: A History of Manners,* trans. E. Jephcott (New York, 1978); but see also R. Muchembled, *L'Invention de l'Homme Moderne: Sensibilités, moeurs et comportments collectifs sous l'ancien régime* (Paris, 1988).

130. See further Joukovskaia, "Naissance de l'épistolographie en Russie," pp. 657–90.

131. F. C. Weber, *The Present State of Russia,* 2 vols. (London, 1722–1723), 1, p. 148 and au-

thor's preface, p. [iii]. On Weber, his service in Russia, and his book, see further Cracraft, *Revolution in Architecture,* pp. 196 ff.

5. SCIENCE AND LITERATURE

1. See S. L. Chapin, "Science in the Reign of Louis XIV," in P. Sonnino et al., eds., *The Reign of Louis XIV: Essays in Celebration of Andrew Lossky* (Atlantic Highlands, NJ, 1990), p. 183, for the Paris academy, and below, this chapter, for its St. Petersburg counterpart: quotations are from the *Project* of January 1724 establishing the latter, also as cited below.

2. For science, the best survey in English is A. Vucinich, *Science in Russian Culture: A History to 1860* (Stanford, 1963), especially chap. 2; see also L. R. Graham, *Science in Russia and the Soviet Union: A Short History* (New York, 1993), pp. 16–31. For literature, see works cited later in this chapter and in Chapter 6. For both, see also L. Hughes, *Russia in the Age of Peter the Great* (New Haven, CT, and London, 1998), chap. 9, with further references.

3. Vucinich, p. 52.

4. Ryan, "Astronomy," p. 54. Readers are reminded that works cited only in short-title form, as here, normally are listed in full in the Bibliography.

5. V. K. Kuzakov, *Ocherki razvitiia estestvennonauchnykh i tekhnicheskikh predstavlenii na Rusi v X–XVII vv.* (M., 1976).

6. Vucinich, p. 54.

7. *Zemlemerie,* or *zemlemerenie* (= land-measuring): cf. D'iachenko (Appendix II, Works Cited), I, p. 200.

8. *Opis. I,* no. 1 (pp. 67–69).

9. *PiB,* vol. 7, pt. 1, no. 2371 (p. 159), and pt. 2, pp. 731–32; vol. 9, pt. 1, no. 2959 (p. 12), no. 3015 (p. 50), and pt. 2, p. 542.

10. *Opis. I,* nos. 5, 6 (pp. 74–76).

11. *Opis. I,* no. 18 (pp. 85–86; copy also at LC-Rare); Cracraft, *Revolution in Imagery,* pp. 170 ff. and fig. 43 (p. 172).

12. *Opis. III,* no. 411 (p. 110); *Svodnyi katalog,* vol. 1, no. 780 (p. 133; copy also at LC-Rare).

13. Described in Cracraft, *Revolution in Imagery,* pp. 266–68.

14. Ibid., pp. 271 ff. (p. 274).

15. On Bruce as a modern man of science, see V. Boss, *Newton and Russia: The Early Influence, 1698–1796* (Cambridge, MA, 1972), pp. 15–35 and passim; on Bruce the avid collector, N. Polunina and A. Frolov, *Kollektsionery staroi Moskvy* (M., 1997), pp. 69–72, with bibliography; on Bruce the astronomer and collector, A. Cross, *By the Banks of the Neva: Chapters from the Lives and Careers of the British in Eighteenth-Century Russia* (Cambridge, 1997), p. 226, with further references; on Bruce as Peter's companion in England in 1698, A. Cross, *Peter the Great through British Eyes: Perceptions and Representations of the Tsar since 1698* (Cambridge, 2000), p. 31; overall, *Rbs,* 3: 416–19 (by P. N. Maikov), and Hughes (n. 2 above), p. 423 and passim (pp. 238–39 for Peter's

funeral). A selection of Bruce's correspondence with Peter is reproduced in Pekarskii, *Nauka i literatura,* vol. 1, pp. 291–303.

16. Cf. V. L. Chenakal, "Prakticheskaia atronomiia v Rossii dopetrovskogo i petrovskogo vremeni," in M. I. Belov, ed., *Voprosy geografii petrovskogo vremeni* (L., 1975), pp. 41–44 and figs. 5, 6, 7.

17. *Opis. I,* no. 134 (pp. 168–70; copy also at LC-Rare).

18. *Svodnyi katalog,* vol. 1, nos. 182 (p. 49), 451–54 (pp. 84–85); vol. 2, nos. 3283, 3284 (p. 88), 3364 (p. 103), 4423–26 (p. 277); vol. 6, no. 906 (p. 93).

19. *Opis. I,* nos. 241 (pp. 211–12), 793 (441–42; copy also at LC-Rare); Pekarskii, *Nauka i literatura,* vol. 2, nos. 349 (pp. 388–89), 572 (p. 621).

20. See Bruce's letter to Peter of Nov. 2, 1716, in Pekarskii, *Nauka i literatura,* vol. 1, pp. 299–300.

21. Kutina I (Appendix II, Works Cited), pp. 86 ff.; *Svodnyi katalog,* vol. 3, nos. 7862, 7863 (pp. 313–14).

22. Boss (n. 15 above), p. 116.

23. Ibid., pp. 50–67.

24. D. J. B. Shaw, "Geographical Practice and Its Significance in Peter the Great's Russia," *Journal of Historical Geography* 22, no. 2 (April 1996): 160–76; D. M. Lebedev, *Geografiia v Rossii petrovskogo vremeni* (M./L., 1950); M. I. Belov, "Rol' Petra I v rasprostranenii geograficheskikh znanii v Rossii," in Belov, *Voprosy geografii petrovskogo vremeni* (L., 1975), pp. 4–23; and for the Petrine cartographic program, Cracraft, *Revolution in Imagery,* pp. 271–81 and figs. 85–87.

25. Shaw, pp. 163–64.

26. Reference is to the translation into a "learned Church Slavonic" by Epifanii Slavinetskii (resident in Moscow 1649–1675) and associates of Johan Blaeu, *Theatrum orbis Terrarum, sive Atlas Novus* (Amsterdam, 1645): see D. M. Lebedev, *Geografiia v Rossii XVII veka* (M./L., 1949), pp. 211–12; also N. A. Kopanev, "Gollandskie izdateli-knigotorgovtsy i delo Petra Velikogo," in N. Kopaneva et al., eds., *Petr I i Gollandiia* (SPb., 1997), pp. 244–45.

27. *Opis. I,* nos. 37 (pp. 108–10), 158 (pp. 178–79), 204 (p. 192), 214 (p. 196).

28. It has also been suggested that the book was excerpted from the translation of the Blaeu *Atlas* just referred to (n. 26): see D. M. Sharypkin, "Shvedskaia tema v russkoi literature petrovskoi pory," in M. P. Alekseev, ed., *Russkaia kul'tura XVIII veka i zapadno-evropeiskie literatury: sbornik statei* (L., 1980), p. 10.

29. G. S. Tikhomirov, *Bibliograficheskii ocherk istorii geografii v Rossii XVIII veka* (M., 1968), pp. 8–12 ff., 86–88, 99; *Opis. I,* pp. 108–10.

30. For the Varenius, see *Opis. I,* no. 306 (pp. 237–39; copy also at HU-Houghton); for the Hübner, *Opis. I,* no. 366 (pp. 259–60; copy also at LC-Rare).

31. E. V. Lukicheva, "Fedor Polikarpov–perevodchik 'Geografiia general'noi' Bernarda Vareniia," in Makogonenko and Moiseeva, *Problemy literaturnogo razvitiia,* pp. 290–91.

32. Discussion based on the copy at HU-Houghton.

33. Polikarpov's ms. of 1716 is at BAN, Petrovskaia galereia No. 72; cf. Lukicheva, pp. 291 ff.

34. Peter to Musin-Pushkin, the official in overall charge of the Moscow Press, July 2, 1717 as quoted by Lukicheva, p. 292; also Luppov, *Kniga v Rossii,* p. 101.

35. Lukicheva, pp. 293–94; also Zhivov, "Istoricheskaia morfologiia," pp. 287–92.

36. Zhivov suggests that the editing was actually done by Polikarpov's old teacher at the Slavonic-Greek-Latin Academy in Moscow, Sofroniia Likhudii (see Chap. 6), who considered the relation of Slavonic and Russian analogous to that of literary and demotic Greek (Zhivov, *Iazyk i kul'tura,* pp. 94–96, 99–101) and so, presumably, was reluctant to replace the one with the other; equally at fault, Zhivov seems to imply, was the fact that this editor was not a native Russian.

37. See Cracraft, *Revolution in Imagery,* pp. 276–78, for Kirillov and the Geography Department. Tikhomirov (n. 29 above), in tracking the rapid progress of geography in eighteenth-century Russia, only lists—does not cede importance to or even comment on—translated works, a puzzling omission given the otherwise thorough coverage of his work. Lukicheva, on the contrary, observes (p. 296) that the Russian Varenius was one of "those translations of scientific literature which played a major role in the development of a national Russian literary language and in the formation of the terminology of Russian science."

38. This discussion is based on the copy at LC (n. 30 above). Note that *karta* rather than *landkarta* (cf. German *Landkarte*) became standard Russian for "map."

39. Cf. Cracraft, *Revolution in Imagery,* pp. 1–5, 271–81.

40. Pekarskii, *Nauka i literatura,* vol. 1, p. 300.

41. T. S. Maikova, "Petr I i 'Gistoriia Sveiskoi voiny'," in N. I. Pavlenko et al., eds., *Rossiia v period reform Petra I* (M., 1973), pp. 103–32; S. L. Peshtich, *Russkaia istoriografiia XVIII veka,* 3 vols. (L., 1961, 1965, 1971), 1, pp. 154–76. Many of the military and diplomatic "campaign journals" kept by Peter and his lieutenants, the main sources for the projected history of his reign, were subsequently published, viz. M. M. Shcherbatov, ed., *Zhurnal ili podennaia zapiska . . . imp. Petra Velikago s 1698 goda, dazhe do zakliucheniia nishtadtskago mira,* 2 vols. (SPb., 1770, 1772), supplemented by the *Pokhodnye zhurnaly* for the years 1695–1735 published in St. Petersburg, 1853–1855.

42. Maikova, pp. 116, 132, and passim; Peshtich, vol. 1, chaps. 3–8; A. B. Kamenskii, *Arkhivnoe delo v Rossii XVIII veka: Istoriko-kul'turnyi aspekt* (M., 1991).

43. Peshtich, 1, pp. 222–75; E. C. Thaden, *The Rise of Historicism in Russia* (New York, 1999), pp. 15 ff.

44. Thaden, pp. 17–18.

45. *Razsuzhdenie* (see Chap. 4), p. 20.

46. Cf. J. L. Black, *G.-F. Müller and the Imperial Russian Academy* (Kingston, Ontario, 1986), pp. 6–7, 22. The project of translating the Pufendorf into Russian went back at least until 1708: TsGADA, F. 138, d. 1708, l.5.

47. *Opis. I,* nos. 320 (pp. 246–47; copies also at NYPL, HU–Law School [Rare]), 744 (pp. 412–13).

48. J. Cracraft, *The Church Reform of Peter the Great* (Stanford, CA, 1971), pp. 129–30, 169–70.

49. This discussion of the Russian Pufendorf is based on the copy at HU–Law School (n. 47 above).

50. Tally by L. Krieger, *The Politics of Discretion: Pufendorf and the Acceptance of Natural Law* (Chicago, 1965), p. 256.

51. *Svodnyi katalog,* vol. 2, no. 5768 (p. 489).

52. Krieger, p. 182.

53. Ibid., pp. 184–86.

54. *Opis. I,* p. 247; Pekarskii, *Nauka i literatura,* vol. 1, pp. 326. The story of Peter rebuking Buzhinskii for omitting the offending passage and ordering it restored is among the *Original Anecdotes of Peter the Great Collected from the Conversation of Persons of Distinction at Petersburgh and Moscow* published by Jacob Staehlin (von Stählin), member of the St. Petersburg Academy of Sciences from 1735; see this English edition (London, 1788), pp. 217–19.

55. M. J. Okenfuss, *The Rise and Fall of Latin Humanism in Early-Modern Russia* (New York, 1995), pp. 91, 105, 112, 121, 122, 124, 126, 130, 133, 182, 191.

56. Krieger, pp. 22, 256.

57. *ZAP,* no. 202 (p. 148).

58. *Opis. III,* no. 491 (pp. 146–47); *Svodnyi katalog,* vol. 2, no. 5769 (p. 489). Excerpt reproduced in Appendix I, no. 37.

59. Okenfuss, p. 103.

60. Discussion based on copy at GBL.

61. *Opis. I,* nos. 23 (p. 92), 53 (pp. 122–23; copy also at NYPL), 260 (p. 221), 726 (pp. 400–401), 833 (p. 459).

62. Okenfuss, p. 160; see also pp. 67, 106, 122, 124, 126, 130, 133, 183, 192 for its presence in various noble and clerical libraries. In 1765 it was prescribed for students at Moscow University (ibid., p. 167), and a manuscript note in a copy of the 1724 edition at BAN records that "this book was sold by the former *komissar* Mikhail Voinov to the state peasant Gerasim Ivanov." Alexander the Great had long been a favorite subject among Russian readers, to judge from the number of Alexander manuscript tales dating from the fifteenth to the eighteenth century on deposit in the main Russian libraries. For some of the earlier texts see the collection edited by D. S. Likhachev, *Aleksandriia* (M./L., 1965).

63. Cf. Eremin, *Russkaia povest',* and Moiseeva, *Russkie povesti;* the latter includes edited texts of three such tales dating to the late Petrine period, one of which, the "History of the Brave Russian Cavalier Alexander *[Gistoriia o khrabrom rossiiskom kovalere Aleksandre]*" (pp. 211 ff.), Moiseeva posits, was influenced by translated stories of Alexander the Great (pp. 59–60).

64. Okenfuss, p. 64.

65. *Istoria, V nei zhe pishet, o razorenii grada troi . . . :* see *Opis. I,* nos. 20 (pp. 88–89), 59 (p. 130), 231 (pp. 207–08; copy also at NYPL).

66. *Opis. I*, no. 699 (pp. 384–86; copies also at HU-Houghton, LC-Rare, NYPL).

67. Cracraft, *Revolution in Imagery*, pp. 207, 210, 224; Pekarskii, *Nauka i literatura*, vol. 1, pp. 252–55.

68. Pekarskii, *Nauka i literatura*, vol. 1, pp. 253–54: dedication reprinted here from ms. at GPB. For Peter's interest in the work, see *ZAP*, no. 142 (pp. 112–13): letter to Synod of Oct. 18, 1722, ordering that a copy be sent to him in Astrakhan, where he had stopped on his Persian campaign.

69. Cf. B. H. Sumner, *Peter the Great and the Ottoman Empire* (Oxford, 1949).

70. S. Ćirković, "Mauro Orbini: His Life and Work," in Ćirković and P. Rehder, eds., *Mauro Orbini: Il Regno degli Slavi* (facs. ed., Munich, 1985), pp. 7–23.

71. Ibid., pp. 15 ff.

72. Discussion based on the copy at HU-Houghton (n. 66 above), pp. 68–76, from which a page is reproduced in Appendix I, no. 31.

73. Ibid., appended *Rassmotrenie*, separately paginated (pp. 4–11), p. 10.

74. *Opis. I*, nos. 113, 299. The work, attributed to the monk Innokentii Gizel', was first published at the Kiev Monastery of the Caves in 1681 (*Opis. II*, no. 10).

75. Pekarskii, *Nauka i literatura*, vol. 1, p. 254.

76. See Consett's signed inscription on the flyleaf of the copy at HU-Houghton; and for Consett himself, J. Cracraft, ed., introduction to *For God and Peter the Great: The Works of Thomas Consett, 1723–1729* (Boulder, CO, 1982); p. 29 for the reference to the Orbini.

77. Pekarskii, *Nauka i literatura*, vol. 2, p. 576.

78. Peshtich (n. 41 above), vol. 1, p. 103.

79. J. G. Garrard, "The Emergence of Modern Russian Literature and Thought," in Garrard, ed., *The Eighteenth Century in Russia* (Oxford, 1973), p. 7. Debate over the literary significance of the Petrine period has itself produced a subliterature: instructive contributions include P. N. Berkov, "O literature tak nazyvaemogo perekhodnogo perioda," in Robinson, *Russkaia literatura*, pp. 19–32; I. Z. Serman, "Nereshennye voprosy istorii russkoi literatury XVIII veka," *Russkaia literatura*, 1973 (no. 1), pp. 11–28; Iu. V. Stennik, "Problema periodizatsii russkoi literatury XVIII veka," in N. D. Kochetkova et al., eds., *Itogi i problemy izucheniia russkoi literatury XVIII veka* (L., 1989 = vol. 16 of *XVIII vek*); Romodanovskaia, *Russkaia literatura na poroge novogo vremeni;* and Nikolaev, *Literaturnaia kul'tura*, pp. 3–11, 133–35, and passim.

80. Drage, *Russian Literature*, chap. 1. Compact biographies of all writers mentioned are in V. Terras, ed., *Handbook of Russian Literature* (New Haven, CT, 1985).

81. Quoting C. Kelly, "The Origins of the Russian Theatre," in R. Leach and V. Borovsky, *A History of Russian Theatre* (Cambridge, 1999), p. 19; see further Borovsky, "The Organisation of the Russian Theatre, 1645–1763," in ibid., pp. 41–56; S. Karlinsky, *Russian Drama from Its Beginnings to the Age of Pushkin* (Berkeley, 1985), pp. 7–59; and, for new and more precise detail, Starikova, "Dokumental'nye utochneniia," and Starikova, *Teatr v Rossii*. The basic collection of texts is Derzhavina, *Ranniaia russkaia dramaturgiia*, in 5 vols. On the importance of translated literature in the development

of a modern Russian literary culture more generally, see Nikolaev, *Literaturnaia kul'tura*, pp. 11–37, and Levin, *Istoriia perevodnoi literatury:* the initial chapters in each of the latter's two volumes, written by various specialists, detail the translation of European literary works during the Petrine period, much of it done on private rather than official initiative and most of it never published.

82. Segel, introduction to *Literature of Eighteenth-Century Russia,* vol. 1, pp. 34, 59.

83. See Grebeniuk and Derzhavina, *Panegiricheskaia literatura:* six of the ten examples reproduced here (pp. 150 ff.) are by Prokopovich, two others by Gabriel Buzhinskii, one each by Feofilakt Lopatinskii and Joseph Turuboiskii–the last named, like Buzhinskii and Lopatinskii, a sometime teacher at the Moscow Slavonic-Greek-Latin Academy. Eleven of Prokopovich's sermons or speeches are reprinted in Eremin, *Prokopovich: Sochineniia,* pp. 23 ff. with useful editorial notes, pp. 459 ff. For a complete list of Prokopovich's known orations, printed and in manuscript, including translations, see J. Cracraft, "Feofan Prokopovich: A Bibliography of His Works," *Oxford Slavonic Papers* 8 (1975): nos. 9–78 (pp. 12–19).

84. See Panchenko, *Russkaia sillabicheskaia poeziia,* with texts; also Panchenko, *Russkaia stikhotvornaia kul'tura.*

85. Cf. Eleonskaia, *Russkaia oratorskaia proza XVII veka,* with its concluding chapter on "The Fates of Oratorical Prose in the 18th Century."

86. Segel, *Literature of Eighteenth-Century Russia,* vol. 1, pp. 38–39; see also pp. 141–48 for an example of Prokopovich's oratory, the "Sermon on the Interment of . . . Peter the Great" preached in the fortress church of Sts. Peter and Paul in St. Petersburg on March 8, 1725, as translated by Segel from the text reprinted in Eremin, *Prokopovich: Sochineniia,* pp. 126–29. This comparatively short oration, first printed in the civil type at St. Petersburg on March 14, 1725, was perhaps Prokopovich's best-known literary work–to judge from the number of contemporary and subsequent reprintings, manuscript copies to be found in the main Russian libraries, and published translations so far located (see Cracraft, "Prokopovich Bibliography," no. 49 [p. 15]).

87. Cracraft, "Prokopovich Bibliography," no. 5 (p. 11).

88. N. D. Kochetkova, "Oratorskaia proza Feofana Prokopovicha i puti formirovaniia literatury klassitsizma," in Makogonenko and Moiseeva, *Problemy literaturnogo razvitiia,* p. 65.

89. N. [I.] Novikov, *Opyt istoricheskago slovaria o rossiiskikh pisateliakh* (SPb., 1772), pp. 173–85.

90. Kochetkova, p. 80. Nikolaev, *Literaturnaia kul'tura,* suggests that Prokopovich (along with A. Kantemir) played a somewhat analogous role in the development of modern Russian poetry (pp. 98–102, 106–12, 131–32); Karlinsky (n. 81 above), that Prokpovich's play *Vladimir,* in tandem with contemporary school drama more generally, "prepared both the language and the audience for the French-based neoclassical drama [of Trediakovskii et al.] that succeeded it" (pp. 24–33).

91. Cracraft, "Prokopovich Bibliography," nos. 89, 98, 100 (pp. 21–3).

92. Cf. J. Cracraft, "Feofan Prokopovich," in Garrard, ed. (n. 79 above), pp. 75–105, with further references; and V. M. Nichik, *Feofan Prokopovich* (M., 1977), especially chap. 3.

534

93. Eremin, *Prokopovich: Sochineniia,* remains the best edition of Prokopovich's literary works; for a supplementary list of all known works, many of which were written in Latin or Polish, see Cracraft, "Prokopovich Bibliography." Prokopovich's play in verse *Vladimir,* written and performed (or simply recited) at the Kiev Academy in 1705, is discussed together with other works produced while a teacher there (his most productive literary period) in J. Cracraft, "Prokopovyč's Kiev Period Reconsidered," *Harvard Ukrainian Studies* 2, no. 2 (June 1978): 138–57. Virtually all of Prokopovich's writings after 1716, when he settled in Russia–sermons and speeches, legislative acts, polemical discourses, official histories, etc.–were more or less political in content.

94. *Opis. II,* no. 103 (pp. 193–95; copy also at LC-Rare); Cracraft, "Prokopovich Bibliography," no. 62 (p. 17). The sermon is reprinted in now standard Russian types and spellings in Eremin, *Prokopovich: sochineniia,* pp. 48–59 with editorial notes, pp. 463–66; and in Grebeniuk and Derzhavina, *Panegiricheskaia literatura,* pp. 208–19 with editorial commentary, pp. 107–11. Further discussion here based on the copy of the July 1717 edition at LC.

95. The only one of Prokopovich's orations to have been printed in his time in the new civil type as well as the traditional Cyrillic was his speech of March 1725 on Peter's interment (see n. 86 above).

96. Asterisks here and below denote Church-Slavonicisms and variously obsolete or archaic terms and forms as judged by the standards of modern Russian.

97. "Let every person be subject to the governing authorities. For there is no authority except from God, and those that exist have been instituted by God."

98. J. Cracraft, "Theology at the Kiev Academy during Its Golden Age," *Harvard Ukrainian Studies* 8, nos. 1 and 2 (June 1984): 71–80; M. Okenfuss, "The Jesuit Origins of Petrine Education," in Garrard, ed. (n. 79 above), pp. 106–30, both with numerous further references. On Iavorskii (Yavorskii) and his career in Russia, see further Cracraft, *Church Reform* (n. 48 above), pp. 122–24, 162–64, and passim.

99. G. Florovskii (Father Georges Florovsky), *Puti russkago bogosloviia* (Paris, 1937; reprinted Paris, 1983), p. 56.

100. A. Kniazeff, *L'Insitut Saint-Serge: De l'Académie d'autrefois au rayonnement d'aujourd'hui* (Paris, 1974), pp. 13–14.

101. See W. L. Daniel, *Gregorii Teplov: A Statesman at the Court of Catherine the Great* (Newtonville, MA, 1991), chap. 1. Almost all of the surviving philosophical and theological courses taught in Russia in the eighteenth century, along with sundry religious writings of the time, remain in manuscript in the main Russian libraries and archives, awaiting detailed study (e.g., at TsGADA, F. 196, op. 1: the manuscript collection of F. F. Mazurin, in 325 folios; or F. 381, op. 1: a collection of more than 1,500 seventeenth- and eighteenth-century manuscripts belonging to the Moscow Synodal Press). On the various schools established in Russia by Kievans (or their students) pursuant to the *Ecclesiastical Regulation,* see again Okenfuss, "Petrine Education," and Cracraft, *Church Reform,* pp. 261–76.

102. On Paus, see Nikolaev, *Literaturnaia kul'tura,* pp. 26–27 and passim; and Kroneberg, *Studien,* pp. 21–23, 25, with further references, particularly to works by E. Winter.

103. *Opis. I*, nos. 226 (pp. 205–06), 237 (p. 209), 378 (pp. 263–64), 753 (pp. 417–18); Pekarskii, *Nauka i literatura*, vol. 2, no. 339 (pp. 381–83); *Svodnyi katalog*, 2, no. 2343. The first or St. Petersburg July 1717 edition has been reprinted in facsimile (M., 1990); our further discussion is based on it.

104. From Polish *szlachectwo* and the term commonly used under Peter for "nobility," but here interchangeably with Russian *dvorianstvo*, the term that eventually supplanted it.

105. E.g., G. Marker and R. May, eds. and trans., *Days of a Russian Noblewoman: The Memories of Anna Labzina, 1758–1821* (DeKalb, IL, 2001).

106. See Hughes (n. 2 above), pp. 186–202 passim and chap. 8, especially pp. 290 ff.

107. See Cracraft, *Revolution in Imagery*, e.g., figs. 68 and 69 (pp. 212, 220), p. 213 and pl. 21, pl. 20, and the new-style portraits passim.

108. Luppov, *Knigi v Rossii*, pp. 103, 137, 143.

109. Pekarskii, *Nauka i literatura*, vol. 2, p. 382; Hughes, pp. 193, 289.

110. Cf. Hughes, pp. 192–93.

111. Cf. O. Hufton, *The Prospect before Her: A History of Women in Western Europe*, vol. 1: *1500–1800* (London, 1995), chap. 1 and passim; more specifically, S. H. Mendelson, *Women in Early Modern England, 1550–1720* (Oxford, 1998), especially chaps. 2–4.

112. F. C. Weber, *The Present State of Russia*, vol. 1 (London, 1723), pp. 18–19, 148, and author's preface, p. [ii].

113. *Opis. I*, no. 226 (p. 205).

114. *Etiket*, from French *étiquette*, entered Russian sometime later in the eighteenth century: cf. Chernykh (Appendix II, Works Cited), vol. 2, p. 454. Students of the Europeanization of Russian manners and morals, and particularly of the state's propagandization of refined conduct via publication of translated etiquette manuals, all date the process to the Petrine era and particularly to the publication of the *Mirror* in 1717: see especially C. Kelly, *Refining Russia: Advice Literature, Polite Culture, and Gender from Catherine [II] to Yeltsin* (Oxford, 2001), pp. 18 ff., 409 ff.; also A. A. Nikishenkov, *Traditsionnyi etiket narodov Rossii XIX-nachalo XX vv.* (M., 1999), pp. 31 ff., and E. Lavrent'eva, *Svetskii etiket pushkinskoi pory* (M., 1999), pp. 11 ff.

115. N. F. Demidova, ed., "Instruktsiia V. N. Tatishcheva o poriadke prepodavaniia v shkolakh pri Uralskikh kazennykh zavodakh," *Istoricheskii arkhiv* 5 (1950): 170.

116. *Opis. II*, no. 133 (p. 121); for further details of the *Primer*'s publication, see Cracraft, "Prokopovich Bibliography," no. 123 (pp. 26–27). This discussion of its contents is based on a copy of the twelfth impression (St. Petersburg, November 1724) at GBL, as cited in Cracraft, *Church Reform*, pp. 276–87, which also cites the Synod decrees just referred to (p. 287).

117. Cracraft, "Theology at Kiev," p. 78, citing works by Archbishop Makarii of Kazan' (1868) and the Rev. A. Kniazeff of the Institut Saint-Serge, Paris (1974).

118. T. Consett, *The Present State and Regulations of the Church of Russia* (London, 1729), pp. xii–xiii.

119. Ibid., pp. xiii–xiv. For more such foreign criticisms, referring particularly to alleged Russian "icon worship" and Petrine efforts to combat it, see Cracraft, *Revolution in Imagery*, pp. 71–80, 294–305.

120. Cf. Cracraft, *Church Reform*, pp. 21–28, 287–90.

121. N. A. Konstantinov, "Nachal'noe obrazovanie v Rossii pervoi poloviny XVIII veka," in Konstantinov and V. Ia. Struminskii, eds., *Ocherki po istorii nachal'nogo obrazovaniia v Rossii* (M., 1953), pp. 44–46.

122. L. L. Kutina, "Foefan Prokopovich, Slova i rechi: Leksiko-stilisticheskaia kharakteristika," in Sorokin, *Literaturnyi iazyk*, p. 50.

123. Cf. P. V. Verkhovskoi, *Uchrezhdenie Dukhovnoi Kollegii i Dukhovnyi Reglament* (Rostov-on-Don, 1916), vol. 1, pp. 388–89.

124. Boss (n. 15 above), pp. 93–96, with both original Latin and English versions of the communication.

125. *ZAP*, no. 330 (pp. 270–71). For Leibniz's correspondence with Peter I, see V. Ger'e (W. Guerrier), ed., *Sbornik pisem i memorialov Leibnitsa, otnosiashchikhsia k Rossii i Petru Velikomu* (SPb., 1873; German edition, *Leibniz in seinen Beziehungen zu Russland und Peter dem Grossen*, Leipzig, 1873); and more generally, N. P. Kopaneva and S. B. Koreneva, eds., *G. V. Leibnits i Rossiia* (SPb., 1998), with complete bibliography (pp. 57–74).

126. Cf. Cracraft, *Revolution in Imagery*, pp. 2–3, 275–76. The Paris Académie des Sciences was preceded of course by the Academia del Cimento of Florence (1657) and several other, short-lived academies in Italy.

127. The standard history of the St. Petersburg Academy's first century is K. V. Ostrovitianov, ed., *Istoriia Akademii nauk SSSR (1724–1803)* (M./L., 1958): see p. 30 for Peter's note on the Fick memo; also, briefer in compass but more detailed, Iu. Kh. Kopelevich, *Osnovanie Peterburgskoi Akademii nauk* (L., 1977). P. P. Pekarskii, *Istoriia imperatorskoi Akademii Nauk v Peterburge*, 2 vols. (SPb., 1870, 1872), is still valuable, while the best account in English is in Vucinich (n. 2 above): see pp. 65–122 and 139–57 for the academy in the eighteenth century. The basic documentary collection is M. I. Sukhomlinov, ed., *Materialy dlia istorii [to 1750] Imperatorskoi Akademii Nauk*, 10 vols. (SPb., 1885–1900).

128. J. T. Alexander, "Medical Developments in Petrine Russia," *Canadian-American Slavic Studies* 8, no. 2 (1974): 199, quoting W. H. Gantt, *Russian Medicine* (New York, 1937), p. 49.

129. Alexander, "Medical Developments," pp. 199–200, quoting contemporary sources; A. B. Radzium, "Anatomicheskaia kollektsiia Riuisha v Sankt-Peterburge," and A. M. Lëiendeik, "Moralisticheskoe znachenie kollektsii Frederika Riuisha," in Kopaneva et al., eds., (n. 26 above), pp. 90–126.

130. *ZAP*, no. 4 (p. 34).

131. B. Haigh, "Design for a Medical Service: Peter the Great's Admiralty Regulations (1722)," *Medical History* 19 (1975), pp. 129–46. For Dr. Bidloo, his hospital and school, see Alexander, pp. 207–10, with further references.

132. M. V. Unkovskaya, "Learning Foreign Mysteries: Russian Pupils of the Aptekarskii Prikaz, 1650–1700," *Oxford Slavonic Papers* 30 (1997): 1–20; I. Liubimenko, "Vrachebnoe i lekarstvennoe delo v Moskovskom gosudarstve," *Russkii istoricheskii zhurnal* 1, no. 4 (Fall 1998): 42–74.

133. Here again Peter followed an established European pattern: cf. B. Moran, ed., *Patronage and Institutions: Science, Technology, and Medicine at the European Court, 1500–1750* (Rochester, NY, 1991).

134. Ostrovitianov (n. 127 above), pp. 25–26; M. S. Filippov, ed., *Istoriia Biblioteki Akademii nauk SSSR, 1714–1964* (M./L., 1964), p. 13.

135. Alexander (n. 128 above), pp. 198–221. For the apothecary shops chartered by Peter, several of which survived in Moscow into the nineteenth and even the twentieth century, see A. Oreshnikov, "Danil Gurchin, moskovskii aptekar' nachala XVIII stoletiia," in D. N. Anuchin et al., *Sbornik statei v chest' P. S. Uvarovoi* (M., 1916), pp. 47–55. For Erskine, see further M. B. Mirskii, "Doktor Robert Erskin—pervyi rossiiskii arkhiatr," *Otechestvennaia istoriia* 1995, no. 2, pp. 135–45; a copy of his will is at TsGADA, F. 9, otd. I, kn. 53, ll. 147–49. For Schumacher, see Black (n. 42 above), pp. 4, 7, 8–9, and passim; for Blumentrost, ibid., chap. 1 and passim, and Pekarskii, *Istoriia Akademii*, vol. 1, pp. 1–15. Kopelevich (n. 127 above) attempts (pp. 54–55), counterfactually, to minimize Blumentrost's role here.

136. Schumacher's report is printed in Pekarskii, *Nauka i literatura*, vol. 1, pp. 533–58.

137. Ostrovitianov, pp. 30 ff.; Boss (n. 15 above), pp. 103–5; Pekarskii, *Istoriia Akademii*, vol. 1, pp. 4–5; Kopelevich, pp. 32–64. Both the Summer Palace and the Kikin Chambers (*Palaty*) survive in St. Petersburg in much their original (Petrine) form: see Cracraft, *Revolution in Architecture*, pl. 54 (p. 320) and pl. 56 (p. 322).

138. TsGADA, F. 9, otd. I, kn. 53, l. 222; printed in Pekarskii, *Nauka i literatura*, vol. 1, pp. 532–33.

139. The original manuscript of the *Project*, annotated by Peter I, is preserved at TsGIA: F. 1329, op. 1, No. 26, ll. 89–100; it is printed in Ostrovitianov, appendix 1 (pp. 429–35): our subsequent discussion is based on this text, which faithfully reproduces the original. On the institutionalization of science in contemporary Europe, see C. A. Russell, *Science and Social Change in Britain and Europe, 1700–1900* (New York, 1983), especially chap. 5; and H. Dorn, *The Geography of Science* (Baltimore, 1991).

140. Russell, pp. 69 ff.

141. Elizabeth's *Reglament Imperatorskoi Akademii Nauk i Khudozhestv* is reproduced, from the original manuscript in the academy's archives, in Ostrovitianov, appendix 4 (pp. 436–53).

142. Ostrovitianov, p. 32. It might be noted that the prototypical Paris Academy of Sciences went its "uncertain" way for more than thirty years without a royal charter: Russell, pp. 70–71, citing R. Hahn, *The Anatomy of a Scientific Institution: The Paris Academy of Sciences, 1666–1803* (Berkeley and Los Angeles, 1971).

143. See various papers at TsGADA, F. 9, otd. I, kn. 53, ll. 161 ff., 220–22, 564–70, etc.

144. For a recent tribute, with a full bibliography of Bayer's published works, see E. P. Karpeev et al., *Gotlib Zigfrid Baier-akademik Peterburgskoi Akademii nauk* (SPb., 1996).

145. As reported by Jacob von Stählin (Staehlin), member of the Academy of Sciences from 1735 until his death in St. Petersburg in 1785, in his *Original Anecdotes* (n. 54 above), p. 344; written and first published (1785) in German, the *Anecdotes* were pub-

lished in Russian editions at St. Petersburg or Moscow in 1786, 1787, 1788, 1789, and frequently thereafter, in French in 1787, English in 1788, etc.

146. Ostrovitianov, pp. 34–36; Vucinich (n. 2 above), pp. 71–76; also Black (n. 46), pp. 7–13: G. F. Müller, the subject of Black's biography, was a history graduate of Leipzig University and one of the first student-teachers to be appointed to the St. Petersburg Academy of Sciences, where he arrived in November 1725 and remained until his death (in Moscow) in 1783, compiling a distinguished record as a geographer and ethnographer as well as a historian.

147. Kopelevich (n. 127 above), pp. 87–88; Black, pp. 9–10. For a contemporary engraving of the academy's first home in St. Petersburg, which it occupied from 1726 until moving into even grander new premises in the 1780s, see Cracraft, *Revolution in Architecture,* p. [231], fig. 113.

148. Sukhomlinov (n. 127 above), vol. 1, pp. 273–75.

149. Vucinich, p. 77. On Joseph Delisle and his brothers Louis and Guillaume, a cartographer commissioned by Peter I to map Russia, see M. A. Chabin, "La curiosité des savants français pour la Russie dans la première moitié du XVIIIe siècle," *Revue des études slaves* 57, no. 4 (1985): 565–76, which draws on the Delisle family papers.

150. See, successively, Ostrovitianov, pp. 102–7, 127–40; Filippov (n. 134 above), pp. 25 (Table 3), 71 (Table 2); *Opis. III,* no. 571 (p. 168) (for the *Kalendar'*); *Commentarii Academiae Scientiarum Imperialis Petropolitanae,* 14 vols. (SPb., 1728–51); Black, chap. 3; O. Neverov, "'His Majesty's Cabinet' and Peter I's *Kunstkammer,*" in O. Impey and A. MacGregor, eds., *The Origins of Museums: The Cabinet of Curiosities in Sixteenth- and Seventeenth-Century Europe* (Oxford, 1985), pp. 54–61; T. V. Staniukovich, *Kunstkamera Peterburgskoi Akademii nauk* (M./L., 1953); contributions on the buildup of Peter's scientific collections at the Kunstkamera by O. Ia. Neverov and others in Kopaneva et al., eds. (n. 26 above), pp. 9–195; and I. V. Breneva, *Istoriia Instrumental'noi palaty Peterburgskoi Akademii nauk, 1724–1766* (SPb., 1999). We will return to the academy's printing activities in Chapter 6.

151. *Commentarii Academiae,* vol. 1 (SPb., 1728; copy at HU-Widener).

152. Vucinich, p. 78. For the "flowering of the Academy Press" between 1727 and 1755, see Marker, *Publishing, Printing,* pp. 44–50; Marker suggests that a monthly series of notes on historical, genealogical, and geographical matters published by the academy between 1728 and 1742 constituted the first "concession to public interest made by anyone in the history of Russian printing" (ibid., p. 50). Another series, the *Ezhemesiachnyia sochineniia i izvestiia o uchenykh delakh,* 20 vols. in 10, regularly published from 1755 to 1764 and edited by Academician G. F. Müller, was the first of the "thick journals" (serious periodicals addressed to a general readership) to appear in Russian and proved, for its time, to be very popular (cf. Black, chap. 6; copy also at LC). For the broader significance of the academy's "journalistic" publications from 1727, see also the detailed account in Berkov, *Istoriia zhurnalistiki,* pp. 56 ff.

153. E.g., L. Schulze, "The Russification of the St. Petersburg Academy of Sciences and Arts in the Eighteenth Century," *The British Journal for the History of Science* 18, pt. 3 no. 60 (November 1985): 305–35.

154. *Reglament* of 1747, Ostrovitianov ed., pp. 440 (sect. 19), 443 (sect. 37), 445 (sect. 45). As Schulze notes (p. 309, n. 8), the academy's proceedings *(protokoly)* were recorded in Latin until 1734, in German until 1741, in Latin again until 1766, in German again until 1772, and in French until the end of the eighteenth century; but from 1751 they were translated into Russian for presentation to the academy's president, i.e. as the official record: cf. *Protokoly Zasedanii Konferentsii Akademii Nauk s 1725 po 1803 goda,* 4 vols. (SPb., 1897–1911).

155. Pekarskii, *Istoriia Akademii,* vol. 1, pp. 503–16; Baumann, "Adodurovs Bedeutung." Adodurov translated, among other works, the course of study or *Raspolozhenie uchenii* prepared by Academician Bülfinger for the young Emperor Peter II (succeeded Catherine I in 1727, died in 1730), which was published, without a date, by the Academy of Sciences Press; earlier assumed to have appeared in 1728, a directive dated December 20, 1731, has been found ordering that it be printed without delay, indicating a later date of publication: see *Svodnyi katalog,* vol. 1, no. 575 (p. 104; copy also at LC-Rare): following the work's title page Adodurov is identified both as its translator (from German) and as an *ad"iunkt* of the academy. Adodurov also helped prepare a German grammar for Russian students published by the Academy of Sciences Press in 1730: *Svodnyi katalog,* vol. 3, no. 8226 (p. 373).

156. Data from Ostrovitianov, appendix 5 (pp. 453–60); also Schulze, pp. 310–11, 331–32.

157. Indeed recent scholarship dates the real beginnings of the University of St. Petersburg not to its formal foundation as such in 1819, but to Peter's foundation of the academy in 1724: Iu. D. Margolis and G. A. Tishkin, *Otechesvu na pol'zu, a rossiianam na slavy: Iz universitetskogo obrazovaniia v Peterburge v XVIII–nachale XIX veka* (L., 1988).

158. The importance of "Russian academic Latin" particularly in the development of science in eighteenth-century Russia is vigorously argued by Vorob'ev, *Latinskii iazyk,* chap. 3. The first Latin grammar printed in Russia, *Sokrashchenie Grammatiki latinskoi, v pol'zu uchashchagosia latinskomu iazyku Rossiiskago iunoshestva,* was compiled at the academy (by Vasilii Lebedev) and published by its press in 1746 (copy at HU-Houghton).

159. Russell (n. 139 above), p. 89.

160. Vucinich, pp. 181, 182–83; also A. Vucinich, *Empire of Knowledge: The Academy of Sciences of the USSR (1917–1970)* (Berkeley and Los Angeles, 1984), with lengthy introductory chapter on the period 1725–1917. M. D. Gordin, "The Importation of Being Earnest: The Early St. Petersburg Academy of Sciences," *Isis* 91, no. 1 (March 2000): 1–31, also argues, rather laboriously, for the wider social and cultural significance of the academy's foundation.

6. THE LANGUAGE QUESTION

1. E. L. Eisenstein, *The Printing Press as an Agent of Change: Communications and Cultural Transformations in Early-Modern Europe,* 2 vols. (Cambridge, 1979), is the main work (digested in Eisenstein, *The Printing Revolution in Early Modern Europe* [Cambridge, 1984]); but see also R. Chartier, ed., *The Culture of Print: Power and the Uses of*

Print in Early Modern Europe, trans. (from French) by L. G. Cochrane (Princeton, 1989), and L. Febvre and H. J. Martin, *L'Apparition du livre* (Paris, 1958). Various qualifications of Eisenstein's theses, particularly with respect to the relationship between the print and the scientific revolutions in England, are advanced in A. Johns, *The Nature of the Book: Print and Knowledge in the Making* (Chicago, 1998). Figures on incunabula and early presses from C. A. Clair, *A History of European Printing* (New York, 1976), appendixes 1 and 2 (pp. 431–46). For the print revolution and the rise of the modern nation-state, see B. Anderson, *Imagined Communities: Reflections of the Origin and Spread of Nationalism* (London, 1983); and for connections between language and national identity in modern Europe, M. Perkins, *Nation and Word, 1770–1850: Religious and Metaphysical Language in European National Consciousness* (Aldershot, UK, 1999). The roughly contemporaneous revolution in Europe in the production and reproduction of newly naturalistic imagery, whether to illustrate books or broadsides or in suites of prints or single sheets, is discussed in Cracraft, *Revolution in Imagery,* pp. 5–26, with further references.

2. Febvre and Martin, especially pp. 27–46.

3. See Cracraft, *Revolution in Imagery,* pp. 23–24, with further references.

4. Marker, *Publishing, Printing,* p. 19; also P. N. Berkov, "Russkaia kniga kirillovskoi pechati kontsa XVII—pervoi chetverti XVIII veka," in *Opis. II,* pp. 9–11. The first page of the first book printed at Moscow, the *Apostol* (Acts of the Apostles plus Epistles) of 1564, is reproduced in Appendix I (no. 1).

5. Cracraft, *Revolution in Imagery,* p. 150 and n. 1 (p. 336). The total given of pre-Petrine book production in Ukraine and Belorussia does not count the far more numerous titles printed there in Latin and Polish.

6. TsGIAL, F. 1329, op. 1, kn. 24, l. 135. See further Cracraft, *Revolution in Imagery,* pp. 189–90, citing V. Uchastkina, *A History of Rusian Hand Paper-Mills and Their Watermarks,* ed. J. S. G. Simmons (Hilversum, Holland, 1962), pp. 4–6, 15–47.

7. Luppov, *Kniga v Rossii,* p. 61–63.

8. As calculated by Marker, *Publishing, Printing,* p. 25, table 1.1 (derived from data found mainly in *Opis. I* and *Opis. II*).

9. A feat that both Luppov, *Kniga v Rossii,* and Marker, *Publishing, Printing,* nevertheless attempt. The interconnections among urbanization, the print revolution, and rising rates of literacy have long been recognized by scholars: cf. B. Stock, *The Implications of Literacy* (Princeton, 1983) and especially, for our period, R. A. Houston, *Literacy in Early Modern Europe: Culture and Education, 1500–1800* (London, 1988), pp. 31 ff. and passim.

10. *Opis. II,* nos. 2 (pp. 52–54), 107 (pp. 197–98).

11. Ibid., no. 15 (p. 68–72); copy also at HU-Houghton.

12. *PiB,* vol. 1, no. 291 (pp. 328–31).

13. For details of the enterprise, see T. A. Bykova, "Knigoizdatel'skaia deiatel'nost' Il'i Kopievskogo i Iana Tesinga," in *Opis. II,* appendix 4 (pp. 318–41); also N. A. Kopanev, "Gollandskie izdateli-knigotorgovtsy i delo Petra Velikogo," in N. Kopaneva et al., eds., *Petr I i Gollandiia* (SPb., 1997), pp. 246–49. The enterprise appears to have been

run, down to 1708, through the Ambassadorial Office, whose officials perhaps guided the choice of titles to be translated and printed: see TsGADA, F. 138, d. 1708, 7 ll.

14. *Opis. II*, appendix 1, nos. 4, 5, 6, 9, 15, 12, 14, 13, 7, 10, 11 (pp. 278–92).

15. Ibid., nos. 17 (p. 294), 18 (p. 294), 21 (pp. 299–300).

16. Bykova, p. 341.

17. *Opis. I*, nos. 58 (pp. 128–30), 73 (p. 143), 229 (p. 200); ibid., nos. 334 (pp. 251–52), 525 (p. 308); *Svodnyi katalog*, vol. 2, no. 3118 (p. 66). For the *Aesop's Fables*, see further R. B. Tarkovskii, *Starshii russkii perevod basen Ezopa i perepischiki ego teksta* (L., 1975).

18. *Opis. II*, nos. 9 (pp. 61–62), 12 (p. 66), 13 (p. 66), 17 (pp. 72–74), 33 (p. 100).

19. Ibid., no. 25 (pp. 83–86).

20. *PiB*, vol. 1, no. 304 (pp. 347–53).

21. *Opis. II*, no. 27 (pp. 89–90).

22. Ibid., nos. 24 (p. 83), 31 (pp. 94–98). For the earlier *kuranty*, see the successive volumes of *Vesti-kuranty* (M., 1972–1996), ed. S. I. Kotkov et al., covering the years 1600–1660; they have been analyzed, with particular attention to their foreign sources, by R. Schibli, *Die ältesten russischen Zeitungsübersetzungen (Vesti-Kuranty), 1600–1650* (Bern, 1988); also Maier, "Second-Hand Translation," pp. 209–42.

23. Berkov, *Istoriia zhurnalistiki*, pp. 24–52, 56 ff.; V. I. Shcherbakov, "Gazeta 'Vedomosti' (1703–1727)," in Lebedev and Bludilina, eds., *Rossiia i zapad*, pp. 438–45.

24. *Opis. I*, no. 220 (pp. 200–201). For the *Vedomosti* in the civil type, see ibid., nos. 47, 54, 65, 74, 138, 177, 222, 262, 338, 409, 531, 657, 728, 767, 865 (to 1725), and *Opis. III*, appendix 4 (pp. 192–224) (1725 to 1727); also *Svodnyi katalog*, vol. 4, pp. 9–114 (1725 to 1800).

25. Cf. V. Terras, ed., *Handbook of Russian Literature* (New Haven, CT, 1985), pp. 376–77. See further I. A. Shliapkin, *Sv. Dmitrii Rostovskii i ego vremia* (SPb., 1891).

26. *Opis. II*, nos. 1 (pp. 49–52), 3 (pp. 54–58), 11 (pp. 64–66), 47 (pp. 124–26), 89 (pp. 182–83), 95 (pp. 186–87), 100 (pp. 190–91), 120 (p. 208); *Svod. kat.-kirillovskoi*, nos. 578 (pp. 203–4), 603 (p. 212), 666 (p. 233), 771 (pp. 264–65), 1012 (p. 347), 1108 (p. 383), 1227 (pp. 429–30).

27. Berkov, "Russkaia kniga kirillovskoi pechati" (n. 4 above), p. 18.

28. Quoted in ibid., p. 23.

29. Zhivov, *Iazyk i kul'tura*, pp. 79, 77 (n. 5), 75. A volume of letters directed to Polikarpov at the Moscow press is at TsGADA, F. 381, op. 1, d. 423: see l. 23 for Musin-Pushkin's letter of Feb. 24, 1709.

30. Shitsgal, *Graficheskaia osnova*; Shitsgal, *Grazhdanskii shrift*, chaps. 1–4 and documents, pp. 255–65; Shitsgal, *Russkii tipograficheskii shrift*, pt. 2.

31. Shitsgal, *Grazhdanskii shrift*, p. 114.

32. Cf. German *Drucker*/Dutch *drukker* = printer.

33. *PiB*, vol. 4, no. 1281 (p. 301).

34. *PiB*, vol. 5, no. 1545 (pp. 53–54).

35. Ibid., pp. 416–17. The Russian text of the contract is at TsGADA, F. 237, op. 1, No. 2192, ll. 1–5.

36. *PiB*, vol. 5, no. 1803 (p. 310) and pp. 711–13.

37. As cited in T. A. Bykova, "Pervye obraztsy grazhdanskikh shriftov," in *Opis. I*, appendix 6, p. 535.

38. In its publications dating from as early as 1704 the Moscow Printing House *(Pechatnyi dvor)* was styled interchangeably, and from 1710 almost exclusively, the Moscow Press *(Tipografiia)*.

39. *PiB*, vol. 5, no. 1763 (p. 271).

40. *PiB*, vol. 7, pt. 1, no. 2371 (pp. 158–59); ibid., pt. 2, pp. 731–34, 938, 953–54; etc.

41. As cited in Bykova, "Pervye obraztsy," p. 534.

42. *Opis. I*, no. 1 (pp. 68–69).

43. Ibid., no. 18a (p. 86); *PiB*, vol. 9, pt. 1, no. 2957 (pp. 12–13).

44. *PiB*, vol. 9, pt. 2, pp. 542–43.

45. *PiB*, vol. 10, no. 3581 (p. 27); *Opis. I*, no. 32 (pp. 104–5).

46. Shitsgal, *Russkii grazhdanskii shrift*, pp. 46–114; for examples of items printed at Moscow and, from 1711, at St. Petersburg in this second version of the civil type, see also *Opis. I*, figs. 10 (p. 121), 12 (p. 129), 13 and 13a (pp. 132–33), 14 (p. 139), 16 (pp. 160–61), 17 (p. 167), etc.; also Appendix I, nos. 16 ff.

47. Bykova, "Pervye obraztsy," pp. 537–40; and further, on technical aspects of the process, P. N. Berkov, "Russkaia kniga grazhdanskoi pechati pervoi chetverti XVIII veka," in *Opis. I*, pp. 11–39.

48. As argued by Marker, *Publishing, Printing*, while chastising Soviet scholars who downplay or ignore the relevant data (see pp. 31 ff.).

49. Cf. R. J. Tuttle, "Vignola," in J. Turner, ed., *The [Grove] Dictionary of Art*, vol. 32 (London, 1996), pp. 502–8.

50. Cf. Cracraft, *Revolution in Architecture*, especially pp. 151–52.

51. *PiB*, vol. 7, pt. 1, no. 2994 (p. 32); ibid., pt. 2, p. 600; ibid., pt. 1, no. 3412 (pp. 375–77); ibid., pt. 2, p. 1236.

52. Discussion based on a copy of the Moscow 1712 edition at GBL.

53. Cf. Vlasto, *Linguistic History*, p. 251.

54. Ibid., pp. 251–80; also Schenker, *Dawn of Slavic*, pp. 155–64, both with further references and many lexical examples. Surprisingly little attention is paid to lexis in the standard histories of Russian—indeed, as remarked in Chapter 1, in linguistic scholarship generally.

55. Vlasto, *Linguistic History*, pp. 280–83. See further works by Kochman (Koch. I, II) and Leeming (Appendix II, Works Cited); also Leeming, "Medical Terms," pp. 89–109; editor's commentary in Kot. (Appendix II, Works Cited), pp. 382–96; and Dem'ianov, *Inoiazychnaia leksika*.

56. Totals calculated from figures in E. A. Birzhakova et al. (Birzhak., Appendix II, Works Cited), pp. 171–74. Anglophones may be interested to note by comparison that an estimated 1,900 words entered English—average 95 a decade—in the *two centuries* from 1500 to 1700, half of them borrowed mainly from Latin or French (or Latin via French), the other half formed by affixation; and that this total was approximately the same—"almost as great"—as that for the next two centuries: see C. Barber, *Early Modern English* (Edinburgh, 1997), pp. 220–21.

57. Cf. Cracraft, *Revolution in Architecture*, pp. 3, 116–22, 131–41, 147 ff.; Cracraft, *Revolution in Imagery*, pp. 140–46, 167 ff., etc.

58. Leeming, "Medical Terms," especially pp. 105 ff.

59. The term *nauka komertsii* occurs in a draft letter of June 1716 from Peter's personal secretary to a Moscow merchant concerning the necessity of sending merchants' sons to Holland "and other places" for training in business: TsGADA, F. 9, otd. I, kn. 53, l. 56. The most detailed survey in English of economic developments under Peter is A. Kahan, *The Plow, the Hammer, and the Knout: An Economic History of Eighteenth-Century Russia*, ed. R. Hellie (Chicago, 1985), pp. 1–4 and passim.

60. *Opis. II*, no. 135 (pp. 221–23). See further Horbach, *Die vier Ausgaben*.

61. See Babaeva, *Polikarpov*, pp. 14 and nn. 16, 17 (pp. 19–20), citing Horbach, *Die vier Ausgaben*.

62. Babaeva, *Polikarpov*, p. 16; the complete text of the grammar, from a manuscript of 1725 preserved at GPB, is reproduced in fine Cyrillic types on pp. 239–335.

63. Details from ibid., chap. 1; also V. V. Fursenko, "Polikarpov-Orlov, F. P.," in *Rbs* 14 (SPb., 1905), pp. 346–51. On the Likhudy brothers and their introduction of the systematic study of Greek in Moscow (in Russia), see Yalamas, "Significance of Standard Greek," pp. 1–49.

64. Zhivov, *Iazyk i kul'tura*, p. 79. See also O. B. Strakhov, "Attitudes to Greek Language and Culture in Seventeenth-Century Muscovy," *Modern Greek Studies Yearbook* 6 (1990): 123–55, which stresses nevertheless the ambiguity of these attitudes.

65. Babaeva, *Polikarpov*, pp. 9–17, citing Zhivov, *Iazyk i kul'tura*, chap. 2. For the intellectual world of the Grecophile Muscovite traditionalists of the later seventeenth century, to which we have hardly done justice here, see further Fonkich, *Grechesko-russkie kul'turnye sviazi*; also, the fresh research recorded in N. N. Zapol'skaia and O. B. Strakhova, "Zabytoe imia: Petr Postnikov (Iz istorii russkoi kul'tury kontsa XVII-nachala XVIII vekov)," *Paleoslavica* 1 (1993): pp. 111–48, and Strakhova, "Literaturnaia deiatel'nost' Evfimiia Chudovskogo," *Paleoslavica* 3 (1995): 41–161; O. Strakhov, "The Issue of a 'Nonstandard' Translation of the Holy Scriptures in Muscovite Rus'," in M. S. Flier and D. Rowland, eds., *Medieval Russian Culture* (Berkeley and Los Angeles, 1994), pp. 93–106, and Strakhov, "Antiquity and Muscovite Traditionalists in the Seventeenth Century," *Paleoslavica* 7 (1999): 116–35; I. Ševčenko, "A New Greek Source for the Nikon Affair," ibid., pp. 65–83; and essays by B. L. Fonkich and D. A. Alamas, in S. N. Kisterev, ed., *Ocherki feodal'noi Rossii: Sbornik statei* (M., 2000), pp. 237–311, all with close attention to contemporary texts.

66. *Opis. II*, no. 194 (pp. 261–64).

67. Babaeva, *Polikarpov*, pp. 15–16, 17, 20 (n. 21).

68. See Cracraft, *Revolution in Architecture*, chap. 4, and *Revolution in Imagery*, chap. 3, especially pp. 81–92, 107–30.

69. It is the first item reproduced in facsimile in Unbegaun, ed., *Drei russische Grammatiken*; cf. *Opis. II*, no. 21 (pp. 299–300; copy also at BL).

70. Unbegaun, "Russian Grammars," pp. 105–9.

71. Keipert, Uspenskii, and Živov, eds., *Glück: Grammatik*, with further references (pp. 164–73); also Ďurovič, "Ob istochnikakh paradigmatiki," pp. 81–90.

72. B. A. Uspenskii, "Dolomonosovskie grammatiki russkogo iazyka (itogi i perspektivi)," in Sjöberg, Ďurovič, and Birgegård, eds., *Dolomonosovskii period iazyka*, pp. 93–103; the manuscript is at HU-Houghton (Kilgour MS. Russ. 5).

73. *Opis. II*, no. 35 (pp. 103–06; copies also at LC-Rare and NYPL).

74. *Opis. I*, nos. 334 (pp. 251–52), 525 (p. 308). Another edition, now entitled *Latinorossiiskaia i nemetskaia slovesnaia kniga*, was published by the St. Petersburg Academy Press in 1732: *Svodnyi katalog*, vol. 2, no. 3118 (p. 66). See also Vomperskii, *Slovari*, nos. 4 (pp. 8–9), 15 (p. 15), 18 (p. 16), and 33 (p. 24).

75. *Opis. I*, no. 228 (p. 206; copy also at NYLP); Vomperskii, *Slovari*, no. 12 (p. 14). For Peter's instigation of the project, see his letter to Bruce of Nov. 13, 1716, at TsGADA, F. 9, otd. I, kn. 53, l. 61.

76. Cf. Van der Baar, "Russian Dictionary," pp. 19–32, with further references—though not to E. E. Birzhakova, "Iz istorii russko-inoiazychnoi leksikografii XVIII v.: 'Russko-gollandskii leksikon' Iakova Briusa," in Birzhakova and Kutina, eds., *Slovari v Rossii*, pp. 23–37.

77. E.g., the German-Slavonic/Russian dictionary, based partly on the Polikarpov dictionary of 1704, that was compiled in Moscow ca. 1715, a manuscript copy of which—some 600 pages with 12,000 German entries, each followed by one or more Slavonic and/or Russian translations—is now at the Royal Library in Stockholm: see A. Sjöberg and S. Wesslén, "Nemetsko-russkii slovar' 1715 goda," in Sjöberg, Ďurovič, and Birgegård, eds., *Dolomonosovskii period iazyka*, pp. 271–80. See also the manuscript *leksikon* probably compiled in the 1730s by V. N. Tatishchev and consisting of some 16,300 Russian and Slavonic entries that was found at BAN and was probably used in compiling the Slov. Akad. of 1789–94 (Appendix II, Works Cited), all as reported by Aver'ianova, ed., *Rukopisnyi leksikon*.

78. Cf. Horbatsch and Freidhof, eds., *Weismanns Lexikon*, facsimile reprint in 3 vols.; the appended grammar only is reprinted in facsimile in Unbegaun, ed., *Drei Grammatiken*, second item.

79. P. Kosta, "Das Weismannsche 'Petersburger Lexicon'," in Horbatsch and Freidhof, eds., *Weismanns Lexikon*, p. 9.

80. C. D. Buck, "The Russian Language Question in the Imperial Academy of Sciences, 1724–1770," in Picchio, Goldblatt, and Fusso, eds., *Slavic Language Question*, vol. 2, p. 205, citing contemporary testimony of G.-F. Müller; also Kosta, pp. 5 ff.

81. *Svodnyi katalog*, vol. 1, no. 1608 (p. 253); V. P. Vomperskii, "Neizvestnaia grammatika russkogo iazyka I. S. Gorlitskogo 1730 g.," *Voprosy iazykoznaniia*, 1969, no. 3, pp. 125–31; Vomperskii, *Slovari*, no. 28 (p. 21). B. A. Gradova has recently shown that the first Russian-French dictionary was compiled in 1725–26, but never published, by Antiokh Kantemir: Gradova, "A. D. Kantemir—sostavitel' pervogo russko-frantsuzskogo slovaria," in M. Di Salvo and L. Hughes, eds., *A Window on Russia* (Rome, 1996), pp. 155–59.

82. Unbegaun, "Russian Grammars," pp. 109–13 (pp. 110, 111 for the words quoted).

83. Uspenskii, *Pervaia russkaia grammatika*; see pp. 4–5, 6 for the words quoted. Uspenskii's characterization here of Adodurov's grammar as "the first" ever compiled

in Russian had to be modified, as we saw earlier in this chapter, by his subsequent discovery of the Afanas'ev manuscript grammar of 1725 (see n. 72 above). See further, on the Petrine beginnings of the larger "emancipation" of literary Russian from Church Slavonic, Uspenskii, *Iz istorii russkogo iazyka*, pp. 3 ff. Levin, "Petr I i russkii iazyk," pp. 212–27, an essay published to honor the tercentenary of Peter's birth (1972), broaches the subject from a more conventionally linguistic viewpoint.

84. M. V. Lomonosov, *Rossiiskaia grammatika* (SPb., 1755; copies at HU-Houghton and NYPL), pp. 5–6, 51–52.

85. The standard, very detailed biographical study is still A. Morozov, *Mikhail Vasil'evich Lomonosov, 1711–1765,* 2nd ed. (L., 1952); see pp. 389–462 for the "Poet and Philologist." On Lomonosov the literary theorist, see further Moiseeva, *Lomonosov.*

86. *Svodnyi katalog,* vol. 2, nos. 3774–80 (pp. 174–75).

87. Stankiewicz, *Grammars and Dictionaries,* p. 115.

88. *Svodnyi katalog,* vol. 1, nos. 881–83 (pp. 147–48); Vomperskii, *Slovari,* nos. 32 (pp. 23–4), 124 (p. 60), 269 (p. 114); Horbatsch and Freidhof, eds., *Weismanns Lexikon,* vols. 1 and 2.

89. See Slovar' (Appendix II, Works Cited), vol. 1, pp. xl–xlii, listing the Weismann among the "most important dictionaries and encyclopedias" consulted, and subsequent references to the Weismann therein, vols. 1–17 passim.

90. Cf. Reyfman, *Trediakovsky;* Romodanovskaia, *Russkaia literatura;* and Bobrik, "Ot ratsionalizma," pp. 37–55.

91. W. G. Jones, "The Russian Language as a Definer of Nobility [from 1729 on]," in Di Salvio and Hughes, eds. (n. 81 above), pp. 293–98.

92. Cf. Zhivov, *Iazyk i kul'tura,* pp. 105–24; but Zhivov, in emphasizing the new Russian's continuity with hybrid Slavonic, seems unnecessarily to discount the role of chancery Russian, which, he instead suggests, was simply "ousted" by the new language.

93. Hüttl-Folter, *Syntaktische Studien;* Litvina, "K voprosu o sintaksise," p. 123–36; and Speck, *Die morphologische Adaptation,* among other studies, dwell on this more specifically grammatical influence.

94. See Buck (n. 80 above), pp. 187–233 (p. 212 for the instruction of 1734). For annotated lists of grammars and dictionaries compiled in eighteenth-century Russia, see Stankiewicz, *Grammars and Dictionaries,* pp. 113–18, 129–33; for dictionaries, broadly understood, Vomperskii, *Slovari.*

95. I. de Madariaga, *Russia in the Age of Catherine the Great* (New Haven, CT, and London, 1981), p. 330.

96. *Svodnyi katalog,* vol. 4, *Ukazatel' tipografii,* pp. 278–90.

97. Cf. L. A. Newman, "The Unpublished Grammar (1783–88) of A. A. Barsov," *Russian Linguistics* 2 (1975): 283–301—on Barsov and a later, more advanced grammar that he compiled but never published.

98. As persuasively argued at length by Zhivov, *Iazyk i kul'tura,* chaps. 2, 3.

99. See Slov. Akad. (Appendix II, Works Cited), vol. 1, pp. xvii–xviii, for a list of the members of the Russian Academy in 1789.

100. Ibid., *Predislovie* (pp. v–xv).

101. Stankiewicz, *Grammars and Dictionaries,* p. 133.

102. Zhivov argues that Peter's creation of the "Russian civil type" was the key to or "prototype" of his larger "language reform," which larger reform in turn led to the "normalization" of modern literary Russian (Zhivov, *Iazyk i kul'tura,* pp. 73–88). See further, for the longer-term orthographical significance of Peter's typographical reform, Osipov, *Istoriia russkoi orfografii,* pp. 138 ff.

103. J. Cracraft, *The Church Reform of Peter the Great* (Stanford, CA, 1971), pp. 301–2; also Kravetskii and Pletneva, *Istoriia tserkovnoslavianskogo iazyka,* pp. 19–23.

104. Figures based on total entries in *Svod. kat.-kirillovskoi, Opis. I* and *Opis. III,* and *Svodnyi katalog,* vols. 1–3.

105. The academy's huge contribution to the institutionalization of Peter's alphabetic and print revolutions is detailed in Shitsgal, *Russkii grazhdanskii shrift,* pp. 117–36, and in Shitsgal, *Russkii tipograficheskii shrift* (1985), pp. 51–73.

106. The practice of calquing increased considerably as the eighteenth century wore on, in response to the increased volume of European literature that was being translated into Russian as well as to inevitable pressures for linguistic "purity": see Mahota, "Calques and Semantic Loans," pp. 68–70, and further, for a "provisional dictionary" of same, Arapova, *Kal'ki.*

107. Zhivov, *Iazyk i kul'tura,* pp. 88–98, 146–54 (p. 146 for the words quoted).

108. See the pioneering work in this regard by the critic, journalist, and publisher N. I. Novikov, *Opyt istoricheskago slovaria o rossiiskikh pisatleiakh [A Historical Dictionary of Russian Writers]* (SPb., 1772), pp. 173–85. An authoritative history in English of the canonization process, with numerous translated examples, is Segel, ed. and trans., *Literature of Eighteenth-Century Russia;* here too Prokopovich is the first of the writers to be so treated (vol. 1, pp. 38–39, 141–48).

109. Kravetskii and Pleteneva, *Istoriia tserkovnoslavianskogo iazyka,* pp. 13 ff.

7. CONCLUSION

1. Cracraft, *Revolution in Architecture.*

2. Ibid., p. 1.

3. Ibid., pp. 173, 243, 266.

4. Cracraft, *Revolution in Imagery,* pp. 5–21.

5. Ibid., chaps. 3–5; for "cultural revolution," see pp. 34–35. For the Moscow Baroque in late seventeenth-century Muscovite architecture, see Cracraft, *Revolution in Architecture,* chap. 4.

6. Cf. E. Kennedy, *A Cultural History of the French Revolution* (New Haven, CT, 1989), which offers a "cultural history of the French Revolution" or a history of the French Revolution as "a profound cultural event" but confines its notion of cultural revolution to the specific context indicated; similarly specific is the approach to the Protestant Reformation as not merely "a legislative and administrative transaction tidily concluded by a religious settlement in 1559 but a profound cultural revolution" adopted in P. Collinson, *The Religion of Protestants: The Church in English Society, 1559–1625* (Oxford, 1982). C. Jones and D. Wahrman, eds., *The Age of Cultural Revolu-*

tions: Britain and France, 1750–1820 (Berkeley and Los Angeles, 2002), despite its title, defines cultural revolution, and not very helpfully, only in its concluding essay (by Wahrman): "a radical shift in the mental maps people employed to organize the most fundamental components of their worldview" (p. 280).

7. Cf. L. Ryazanova-Clarke and T. Wade, *The Russian Language Today* (London and New York, 1999), especially chap. 1.

8. Cf. A. B. Kamenskii, *Ot Petra I do Pavla I: Reformy v Rossii XVIII veka* (M., 1999), pp. 80–154, where the perception of a more general "structural" or "systemic" crisis, a "crisis of traditionality *[krizis traditsionalizma]*," gripping late seventeenth-century Muscovite society is amplified; Kamenskii lists "overcoming this crisis" as the "first obvious result" of the Petrine reforms (p. 155).

9. See Cracraft, *Revolution in Imagery*, pp. 262–63, with further references.

10. Ibid., pp. 294–305; Cracraft, *Revolution in Architecture*, pp. 39–56, 257 ff.

11. Cracraft, *Revolution in Imagery*, pp. 305–11, with reference particularly to A. Hilton, *Russian Folk Art* (Bloomington, IN, 1995).

12. J. Cracraft, "Opposition to Peter the Great," in E. Mendelsohn and M. S. Shatz, eds., *Imperial Russia, 1700–1917: State, Society, Opposition* (DeKalb, IL, 1988), pp. 22–36.

13. M. Raeff, "Pugachev's Rebellion," in R. Forster and J. P. Greene, eds., *Preconditions of Revolution in Early Modern Europe* (Baltimore, MD, 1970), pp. 161–202; reprinted in Raeff, *Political Ideas and Institutions in Imperial Russia* (Boulder, CO, 1994), pp. 234–67.

14. The persistence of peasant Russia well into the twentieth century has attracted a good deal of attention from scholars, both Russian and foreign: the classic study in English is G. T. Robinson, *Rural Russia under the Old Regime* (New York, 1932). More recent works in English include B. Eklof and S. P. Frank, eds., *The World of the Russian Peasant* (Boston, 1990); C. D. Worobec, *Peasant Russia: Family and Community in the Post-Emancipation Period* (Princeton, NJ, 1991); B. Farnsworth and L. Viola, eds., *Russian Peasant Women* (New York, 1992); several essays in S. P. Frank and M. D. Steinberg, eds., *Cultures in Flux: Lower-Class Values, Practices, and Resistance in Late Imperial Russia* (Princeton, NJ, 1994); D. Moon, *The Russian Peasantry 1600–1930: The World the Peasants Made* (London and New York, 1999); J. Pallot, *Land Reform in Russia, 1906–1917: Peasant Responses to Stolypin's Project of Rural Transformation* (Oxford, 1999); and Y. Kotsonis, *Making Peasants Backward: Agricultural Cooperatives and the Agrarian Question in Russia, 1861–1914* (London, 1999). C. A. Frierson, *Peasant Icons: Representations of Rural People in Late 19th Century Russia* (New York, 1993) is supplemented by Frierson, ed. and trans., *Aleksandr Nikolaevich Engelgardt's Letters from the Country, 1872–1887* (New York, 1993), and by D. L. Ransel, ed. and trans., *Village Life in Late Tsarist Russia: Olga Semyonova Tian-Shanskaia* (Bloomington, IN, 1993).

15. B. Eklof, *Russian Peasant Schools: Officialdom, Village Culture, and Popular Pedagogy, 1861–1914* (Berkeley and Los Angeles, 1986); J. Brooks, *When Russia Learned to Read: Literacy and Popular Literature, 1861–1914* (Princeton, NJ, 1985).

16. Panov, *Istoriia russkogo proiznosheniia;* and review of same, by P. Brang, in *Russian Linguistics* 16 (1992): 137–45, with further references.

17. In addition to the Russian witnesses edited by Frierson and Ransel (n. 14 above), there

548

are the well-known studies, also drawing on extensive personal observation, of August von Haxthausen and Donald Mackenzie Wallace: see Haxthausen, *Studies on the Interior of Russia,* ed. S. F. Starr, trans. (from German) E. L. M. Schmidt (Chicago, 1972; first published 1847–52), and successive editions of Mackenzie Wallace, *Russia* (first published London and New York, 1877).

18. Robinson, *Rural Russia* (1967 ed., Berkeley and Los Angeles); see pp. 126, 258, 244, 2, for the words quoted.

19. An allusion, here as above, to Turgenev's novel of 1859, *Dvorianskoe gnezdo.*

20. Robinson, pp. 1–2, 261–63. See further P. Roosevelt, *Life on the Russian Country Estate: A Social and Cultural History* (New Haven, 1995), well illustrated.

21. See E. V. Anisimov, *Vremia petrovskikh reform* (L., 1989), pp. 9–14 and passim; English ed., Evgenii V. Anisimov, *The Reforms of Peter the Great: Progress through Coercion in Russia,* trans. J. T. Alexander (Armonk, NY, 1993), pp. 3–9, 295–98, and passim. A much more nuanced treatment of the Petrine legacy, still considered enormous in scope but also essentially positive *(postupatel'nyi),* is in Kamenskii (n. 8 above), especially pp. 154–64, 520–26.

BIBLIOGRAPHY

This list includes the full titles and other publishing details of the most important works consulted in preparing this book, with some exceptions. Excluded are the many reference works listed in the Abbreviations preceding Appendix I and in the Works Cited in Appendix II—critical though many of these works obviously were in completing the study. Also excluded are the numerous scholarly works consulted in contextualizing our main documents, all of which are cited in full in the notes. Nor does this list include most of the contemporary sources consulted, whether printed or manuscript, which are also fully cited elsewhere (but useful scholarly editions of important sources *are* listed below). What remains is a select bibliography of scholarship on Russian verbal culture particularly of the period 1650 to 1800, with the emphasis on linguistic studies and the Petrine period.

Alekseev, M. P. *Slovari inostrannykh iazykov v russkom azbukovnike XVII veka. Issledovanie, teksty i kommentarii.* L., 1968.

Arapova, N. S. *Kal'ki v russkom iazyke poslepetrovskogo perioda: Opyt slovaria.* M., 2000.

Auty, R., D. Obolensky, and A. Kingsford, eds. *An Introduction to Russian Language and Literature.* Cambridge, 1977.

Aver'ianova, A. P., ed. *Rukopisnyi leksikon pervoi poloviny XVIII v.* L., 1964.

Babaeva, E. *Fedor Polikarpov, Tekhnologiia. Iskusstvo grammatiki.* SPb., 2000.

Baumann, H. "V. E. Adodurovs Bedeutung für die Entwicklung der russischen Literatursprache." *Zeitschrift für Slawistik* 18, no. 5 (1973).

Berkov, P. N. *Istoriia russkoi zhurnalistiki XVIII veka.* M./L., 1952.

Birnbaum, H. "Toward a Comparative Study of Church Slavonic Literature." In H. Birnbaum, *On Medieval and Renaissance Slavic Writing: Selected Essays.* The Hague, 1974.

Birzhakova, E. E., and L. L. Kutina, eds. *Slovari i slovarnoe delo v Rossii XVIII v.* L., 1980.

Bobrik, M. A. "Ot ratsionalizma k epokhe chuvstitel'nosti: stat'ia A. A. Ryzhevskogo 'O moskovskom narechii' i iazykovye vzgliady XVIII veka." *Russian Linguistics* 17 (1993).

Brown, W. E. *A History of Seventeenth-Century Russian Literature*. Ann Arbor, MI, 1980.

Cocron, F. *La langue russe dans la seconde moitié du XVIIe siècle (Morphologie)*. Paris, 1962.

Collins, D. E. "On Diglossia and the Linguistic Norms of Medieval Russian Writing." In *Studies in Russian Linguistics*. Studies in Slavic and General Linguistics 17. Amsterdam, 1992.

Dem'ianov, V. G. *Fonetiko-morfologicheskaia adaptatsiia inoiazychnoi leksiki v russkom iazyke XVII veka*. M., 1990.

———. *Inoiazychnaia leksika v istorii russkogo iazyka XI–XVII vekov: Problemy morfologicheskoi adaptatsii*. M., 2001.

Dem'ianov, V. G., and N. I Tarabasova, eds. *Istochniki po istorii russkogo iazyka XI–XVII vv*. M., 1991.

Demin, A. S. *Pisatel' i obshchestvo v Rossii v XVI–XVII vekov (Obshchestvennye nastroeniia)*. M., 1985.

———. *Russkaia literatura vtoroi poloviny XVII–nachala XVIII veka. Novye khudozhestvennye predstavleniia o mire, prirode, cheloveke*. M., 1977.

———, ed. *Drevnerusskaia literatura. Izobrazhenie prirody i cheloveka*. M., 1995.

Derzhavina, O. A., ed. *Ranniaia russkaia dramaturgiia (XVII–pervoi poloviny XVIII)*. 5 vols. M., 1972–1976.

Drage, C. L. *Russian Literature in the Eighteenth Century*. London, 1978.

Ďurovič, L. "Ob istochnikakh paradigmatiki sovremennogo russkogo literaturnogo iazyka." *Russian Linguistics* 24, no. 1 (March 2000).

Eleonskaia, A. S. *Russkaia oratorskaia proza v literaturnom protsesse XVII veka*. M., 1990.

Eremin, I. P., ed. *Feofan Prokopovich: sochineniia*. M./L., 1961.

———, ed. *Russkaia povest' XVII veka*. L., 1954.

Fonkich, B. L. *Grechesko-russkie kul'turnye sviazi v XV–XVII vv. (Grecheskie rukopisi v Rossii)*. M., 1977.

Frick, D. A. "Meletij Smotryc'kyj and the Ruthenian Language Question." *Harvard Ukrainian Studies* 9 (1985).

Gorshkov, A. I. *Istoriia russkogo literaturnogo iazyka*. M., 1969.

Gorshkova, K. V. *Istoricheskaia dialektologiia russkogo iazyka*. M., 1972.

Grebeniuk, V. P., and O. A. Derzhavina, eds. *Panegiricheskaia literatura petrovskogo vremeni*. M., 1979.

Horbach (Horbatsch), O. *Die vier Ausgaben der kirchenslavischen Grammatik von M. Smotryckyj*. Wiesbaden, 1964.

Horbatsch, O., and G. Freidhof, eds. *Weismanns Petersburger Lexikon von 1731*. 3 vols. Specimina Philologiae Slavicae 46. Munich, 1982–1983.

Hüttl-Folter, G. *Syntaktische Studien zur neueren russischen Literatursprache: Die frühen Übersetzungen aus dem Französischen*. Vienna, 1996.

Issatschenko, A. *Geschichte der russischen Sprache*. 2 vols. Heidelberg, 1980, 1983.

Istrin, V. A. *1100 let slavianskoi azbuki*. 2nd ed., ed. L. P. Zhukovskaia. M., 1988.

Joukovskäia, Anna. "La naissance de l'épistolographie normative en Russie: Histoire des premiers manuels russes de l'art épistolaire." *Cahiers du monde russe* 40, no. 4 (Oct.– Dec. 1999).

Keipert, H., B. Uspenskii, and V. Živov, eds. *Johann Ernst Glück: Grammatik der russischen Sprache (1704)*. Cologne, 1994.

Kniaz'kova, G. P. *Russkoe prostorechie vtoroi poloviny XVIII v.* L., 1974.

Kolesov, V. V. *Istoricheskaia fonetika russkogo iazyka*. M., 1980.

Kortava, T. V. *Moskovskii prikaznyi iazyk XVII veka kak osobyi tip pis'mennogo iazyka*. M., 1998.

Kotkov, S. I. *Moskovskaia rech' v nachal'nyi period stanovleniia russkogo natsional'nogo iazyka*. M., 1974.

Kotkov, S. I., et al., eds. *Gramotki XVII–nachala XVIII veka*. M., 1969.

———. *Moskovskaia delovaia i bytovaia pismennost' XVII veka*. M., 1968.

Kravetskii, A. G., and A. A. Pletneva. *Istoriia tserkovnoslavianskogo iazyka v Rossii*. M., 2001.

Kroneberg, B. *Studien zur Geschichte der russischen Klassizistischen Elegie*. Wiesbaden, 1972.

Larin, B. A., et al., eds. *Nachal'nyi etap formirovaniia russkogo natsional'nogo iazyka*. L., 1961.

Lebedev, E. N., and N. D. Bludilina, eds. *Rossiia i zapad: gorizonty vzaimopoznaniia. Literaturnye istochniki pervoi chetverti XVIII veka*. M., 2000.

Leeming, H. "Polish and Latin Medical Terms in Pre-Petrine Russian." *Slavonic and East European Review* 42, no. 4 (Dec. 1963).

Levin, Iu. D., ed. *Istoriia russkoi perevodnoi khudozhestvennoi literatury: Drevniaia Rus'. XVIII vek*. 2 vols. SPb., 1995, 1996.

Levin, V. D. "Petr I i russkii iazyk." *Izvestiia Akademii nauk SSSR: seriia literatury i iazyk* 26, no. 3 (May–June 1972).

Likhachev, D. S. *Razvitie russkoi literatury X–XVII vekov*. L., 1973.

Litvina, A. F. "K voprosu o sintaksise tekstov na 'prostom' iazyke nachala XVIII veka." *Russian Linguistics* 23, no. 2 (May 1999).

Lomtev, T. P. *Ocherki po istoricheskomu sintaksisu russkogo iazyka*. M., 1956.

Luppov, S. P. *Kniga v Rossii v pervoi chetverti XVIII veka*. L., 1973.

Mahota, W. "Calques and Semantic Loans in Eighteenth-Century Russian." *Harvard Studies in Slavic Linguistics*, vol. 1. Cambridge, MA, 1990.

Maier, I. "Second-Hand Translation for Tsar Aleksej Mixajlovič: A Glimpse into the 'Newspaper Workshop' at *Posol'skij prikaz* (1648)." *Russian Linguistics* 25, no. 2 (2001).

Makogonenko, G. P., and G. N. Moiseeva, eds. *Problemy literaturnogo razvitiia v Rossii pervoi treti XVIII veka*. VIII vek 9. L., 1974.

Mal'tseva, I. M., A. I. Molotkov, and Z. M. Petrova, *Leksicheskie novoobrazovaniia v russkom iazyke XVIII v.* L., 1975.

Marker, G. *Publishing, Printing, and the Origins of Intellectual Life in Russia, 1700–1800*. Princeton, NJ, 1985.

551

Mileikovskaia, G. *Pol'skie zaimstvovaniia v russkom literaturnom iazyke, XV–XVIII vekov.* Warsaw, 1984.

Moiseeva, G. N. *Drevnerusskaia literatura v khudozhestvennom soznanii i istoricheskoi mysli Rossii XVII veka.* L., 1980.

———. *Lomonosov i drevnerusskaia literatura.* L., 1971.

———, ed. *Russkie povesti pervoi treti XVIII veka.* M./L., 1965.

Moser, M. *Die polnische, ukrainische und weissrussische Interferenzschicht im russischen Satzbau des 16. und 17. Jahrhunderts.* Frankfurt am Main, 1998.

Nandriş, G., and R. Auty. *A Handbook of Old Church Slavonic.* 2 vols. London, 1960.

Nikolaev, S. I. *Literaturnaia kul'tura petrovskoi epokhi.* SPb., 1996.

Osipov, V. I. *Istoriia russkoi orfografii i punktuatsii.* Novosibirsk, 1992.

Panchenko, A. M., ed. *Russkaia sillabicheskaia poeziia XVII–XVIII vv.* L., 1970.

———. *Russkaia stikhotvornaia kul'tura XVII veka.* L., 1973.

Panov, M. V. *Istoriia russkogo literaturnogo proiznosheniia XVIII–XX vv.* M., 1990.

Pekarskii, P. P. *Nauka i literatura pri Petre Velikom.* 2 vols. M., 1862.

Petrova, Z. M., ed. *Razvitie slovarnogo sostava russkogo iazyka XVIII veka.* L., 1990.

Picchio, R. "Models and Patterns in the Literary Tradition of Medieval Orthodox Slavdom." In *American Contributions to the Seventh International Congress of Slavists,* ed. V. Terras. The Hague, 1973.

Picchio, R., H. Goldblatt, and S. Fusso, eds. *Aspects of the Slavic Language Question.* 2 vols. New Haven, CT, 1984.

Press, I., ed. *Festschrift for Professor C. L. Drage.* London, 1995.

Remneva, M. L. *Istoriia russkogo literaturnogo iazyka.* M., 1995.

Reyfman, I. *Vasilii Trediakovsky: The Fool of the "New" Russian Literature.* Stanford, CA, 1990.

Robinson, A. N., ed. *Russkaia literatura na rubezhe dvukh epokh (XVII–nachalo XVIII v.).* M., 1971.

Romanova, N. P. *Slovoobrazovanie i iazykovye sviazi: russko-ukrainsko-pol'skie iazykovye sviazi XVI-XVII vv. i voprosy slovoobrazovaniia.* Kiev, 1985.

Romodanovskaia, E. K. *Russkaia literatura na poroge novogo vremeni. Puti formirovaniia russkoi belletristiki perekhodnogo perioda.* Novosibirsk, 1994.

Ryan, W. F. "Astronomy in Church Slavonic: Linguistic Aspects of Cultural Transmission." In G. Stone and D. Worth, eds., *The Formation of the Slavonic Literary Languages.* Columbus, OH, 1985.

Schenker, A. M. *The Dawn of Slavic: An Introduction to Slavic Philology.* New Haven and London, 1995.

Segel, H. B., ed. and trans. *The Literature of Eighteenth-Century Russia: A History and Anthology.* 2 vols. New York, 1967.

Shitsgal, A. G. *Graficheskaia osnova russkogo grazhdanskogo shrifta.* M./L., 1947.

———. *Grazhdanskii shrift pervoi chetverti XVIII veka (1708–1725): Katalog shriftov i ikh opisanie.* M., 1981.

———. *Russkii grazhdanskii shrift, 1708–1958.* M., 1959.

———. *Russkii tipograficheskii shrift.* M., 1974; rev. ed. M., 1985.

Shvedova, N. Iu., ed. *Russkaia literaturnaia rech' v XVIII veke: frazeologizmy, neologizmy, kalambury.* M., 1968

Sjöberg, A., L. Ďurovič, and U. Birgegård, eds. *Dolomonosovskii period russkogo literaturnogo iazyka. Slavica Suecana* Series B—Studies, vol. 1. Stockholm, 1992.

Sorokin, Iu. S., ed. *Literaturnyi iazyk XVIII veka: Problemy stilistiki.* L., 1982.

Sorokoletov, F. P. *Istoriia voennoi leksiki v russkom iazyke XI–XVII vv.* L., 1970.

Speck, S. *Die morphologische Adaptation der Lehnwörter im Russischen des 18. Jahrhunderts.* Bern, 1978.

Stankiewicz, E. *Grammars and Dictionaries of the Slavic Languages from the Middle Ages Up to 1850.* Berlin and New York, 1984.

Starikova, L. M. "Dokumental'nye utochneniia k istorii teatra v Rossii petrovskogo vremeni." *Pamiatniki kul'tury: Novye otkrytiia 1997.* M., 1998.

———. *Teatr v Rossii XVIII veka: Opyt dokumental'nogo issledovaniia.* M., 1997.

Unbegaun, B. O. "Le russe littéraire est-il d'origine russe?" *Revue des études slaves* 44 (1965). Reprinted in B. O. Unbegaun, *Selected Papers on Russian and Slavonic Philology.* Oxford, 1969.

———. "Russian Grammars before Lomonosov." *Oxford Slavonic Papers* 8 (1958).

———, ed. *Drei russische Grammatiken des 18. Jahrhunderts.* Munich, 1969.

Uspenskii, B. A. *Istoriia russkogo literaturnogo iazyka (XI–XVII vv.).* Munich, 1987.

———. *Iz istorii russkogo literaturnogo iazyka XVIII–nachala XIX veka: Iazykovaia programma Karamzina i ee istoricheskie korni.* M., 1985.

———. "The Language Situation and Linguistic Consciousness in Muscovite Rus'," trans. M. S. Flier. In H. Birnbaum and M. S. Flier, eds., *Medieval Russian Culture.* California Slavic Studies 12. Berkeley and Los Angeles, 1984.

———. *Pervaia russkaia grammatika na rodnom iazyke.* M., 1975.

Van der Baar, A. H. "An Early Eighteenth Century Russian Dictionary." In A. van Holk, ed., *Dutch Contributions to the Seventh International Congress of Slavists.* The Hague, 1973.

Veselitskii, V. V. *Otvlechennaia leksika v russkom literaturnom iazyke XVIII–nachala XIX v.* M., 1972.

Vinogradov, V. V. *Ocherki po istorii russkogo literaturnogo iazyka XVII–XIX vekov.* 3rd ed. M., 1982.

Vlasto, A. P. *A Linguistic History of Russia to the End of the Eighteenth Century.* Oxford, 1986.

Volkov, S. S. *Leksika russkikh chelobitnykh XVII veka. Formuliar, traditsionnye etiketnye i stilevye sredstva.* L., 1974.

———. *Ritoriki v Rossii XVII–XVIII vv.* M., 1988.

Vomperskii, V. P. *Slovari XVIII veka.* M., 1986.

Vorob'ev, Iu. K. *Latinskii iazyk v russkoi kul'ture XVII–XVIII vekov.* Saransk, 1999.

Worth, D. S. "Language." In N. Rzhevsky, ed., *The Cambridge Companion to Modern Russian Culture.* Cambridge, 1998.

———. "Was There a 'Literary Language' in Kievan Rus'?" *The Russian Review* 34, no. 1 (1975).

553

Yalamas, D. A. "The Significance of Standard Greek for the History of the Russian Literary Language and Culture in the Sixteenth–Eighteenth Centuries: The Linguistic Views of the Leikhoudis Brothers." *Modern Greek Studies Yearbook* 9 (1993).

Zhivov, V. M. *Iazyk i kul'tura v Rossii XVIII veka.* M., 1996.

———. "Istoricheskaia morfologiia russkogo literaturnogo iazyka XVIII veka: uzus, normalizatsiia i norma." In M. Di Salvo and L. Hughes, eds., *A Window on Russia.* Rome, 1994.

INDEX

559